American Military History

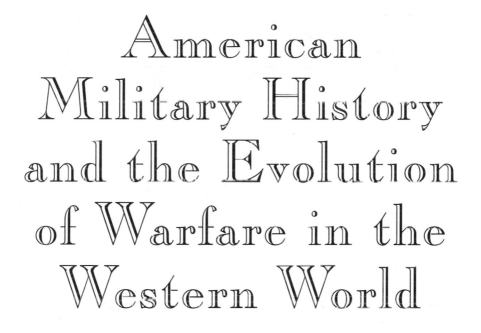

American Military History and the Evolution of Warfare in the Western World

Robert A. Doughty
United States Military Academy

Ira D. Gruber
Rice University

Roy K. Flint
United States Military Academy

Mark Grimsley
The Ohio State University

George C. Herring
University of Kentucky

Donald D. Horward
Florida State University

John A. Lynn
University of Illinois

Williamson Murray
The Ohio State University

D. C. Heath and Company
Lexington, Massachusetts   Toronto

Address editorial correspondence to:

D. C. Heath and Company
125 Spring Street
Lexington, MA 02173

Acquisitions: *James Miller*
Development: *Pat Wakeley*
Editorial Production: *Melissa Ray*
Design: *Alwyn R. Velásquez*
Photo Research: *Picture Research Consultants, Inc./Sandi Rygiel
& Pembroke Herbert*
Art Editing: *Diane Grossman*
Production Coordination: *Richard Tonachel*

The views expressed herein are those of the authors and do not purport to reflect the position of the United States Military Academy, the Department of the Army, or the Department of Defense.

10 9 8 7 6 5 4 3 2 1

PREFACE

American Military History and the Evolution of Warfare in the Western World was first published as part of a larger history, Warfare in the Western World. We wrote that larger history to provide a coherent, readable, and authoritative account of the past four centuries of military operations in the West—to explain, as clearly as possible, how the waging of war has changed from one era to another since the beginning of the seventeenth century. Although we examined the underlying developments in population, agriculture, industry, technology, and politics that affected warfare, we focused on the employment of armed forces. We were most interested in operations, in the conduct of relatively large forces across a specific theater of war. We included warfare at sea and in the air as well as joint operations, but we concentrated on fighting ashore. In short, we set out to write a sound and readable history of military operations in the West since 1600, a history that would appeal to students, general readers, and anyone seeking an authoritative reference on warfare.

To provide the depth and breadth essential to understanding such an extensive and often fragmented subject, we planned a work of two volumes and six parts. The first volume, which begins with Gustavus Adolphus's synthesis of early-seventeenth-century European warfare, analyzes in turn the development of limited warfare in seventeenth- and eighteenth-century Europe the emergence of the citizen soldier and mobile, decisive warfare in the era of the French Revolution and Napoleon; and the shift toward total warfare in the United States Civil War and the application of Prussian organizational skills to European warfare of the mid-nineteenth century. The second volume, which begins with the small wars of the late nineteenth century, considers successively the systematic harnessing of human and material resources for the total warfare of the First World War, the continuation of total warfare in an even more virulent form during the Second World War, and the resort to varieties of limited warfare since 1945, since the creation of atomic and nuclear weapons.

American Military History was, then, first published as part of Warfare in the Western World. Like its parent, it was designed to provide a readable, authoritative history of military operations—in this instance, of operations in the Western world that best convey the American experience of warfare from the seventeenth century to the present. It begins with the crude efforts of British colonists to conquer the Atlantic seaboard of North America and to win their independence from Great Britain; it analyzes the first stirrings of military competence in the new United States (in wars with Britain and Mexico); and it describes the emergence of near total warfare in the Civil War. The volume goes on to consider the flourishing of industrialized warfare in the small wars of the late nineteenth century (including the improvised conduct of the Spanish-American War) and in the far more deadly and static campaigns of World War I (including the American Expeditionary

Force's belated, yet crucial, intervention in the last years of the war). It concludes with an extended account of America's role in the fluid, global operations of World War II, in the more limited warfare that followed the development of atomic and nuclear weapons, and in the frustrating efforts at peacekeeping in the post–Cold War world. It makes clear that American warfare has always been a part of the Western military tradition—sometimes in advance of Europe, sometimes behind, but always within a single, shared tradition.

At least twice during the eighteenth and nineteenth centuries, Americans were in the forefront of fundamental changes in Western warfare. Americans rarely developed highly disciplined forces or skill in complex European tactics, but in the process of winning their independence and preserving their Union, they showed how to mobilize the energies of a people and how to wage near total warfare. In the Revolutionary War they combined militia and regulars, adopted simplified tactics, and relied more on inspiration and understanding than on harsh discipline to create effective fighting forces. And they learned to organize those forces in relatively small operational units so as to draw supplies from the countryside and gain the mobility needed to impose battle on their enemies. Indeed, they anticipated by nearly two decades the methods that French Revolutionaries would use to defeat the standing armies of Europe. Although the French soon taught other Europeans how to make war on an unprecedented scale and with remarkable decisiveness—and rousing fanatical popular resistance in Portugal, Spain, and Russia—they stopped well short of the total warfare that Americans would employ in their Civil War. At the beginning of that war, the United States hoped to preserve the Union without alienating the people of the South, hoped to win the war merely by capturing Richmond and blockading ports. But discovering how costly and difficult it was to defeat large, inspired armies equipped with rifled weapons, the North eventually adopted total war as an instrument of policy. Northern commanders sought not only to wear away Confederate forces in campaigns of attrition but also to exhaust the South by freeing slaves, destroying farms and factories, and breaking the will of the people. With such a strategy, they preserved the United States and carried warfare beyond anything that Europeans had been willing or able to do previously.

For three-quarters of a century after the Civil War, the United States made no substantial contribution to warfare in the Western world. America fell behind Prussia and other European states in preparing systematically for war in the last third of the nineteenth century. Congress and the American people were too preoccupied with domestic affairs and too secure against external threats to heed military reformers. When the 1898 war with Spain revealed how ill prepared the nation was to fight even a second-rate power, Congress supported reforms in the organization, training, and recruiting of the armed forces. But those forces remained strikingly unprepared for the total, industrialized warfare that came to Europe in World War I. Fresh American troops were crucial to sustaining the exhausted allies and to winning the war. Yet they had to use Allied weapons, suffered heavy casualties because they were too aggressive, and contributed little to warfare.

Not until World War II did the United States once again play a significant role in changing warfare. In this most destructive of all wars, the United States was especially innovative in joint operations, in the fluid campaigns that spread around the globe. Its land, sea, and air forces worked effectively together to gain control of the Atlantic and Pacific oceans, to mount successful invasions of North Africa, Sicily, western Europe, and the Philippines, and to contribute substantially to Allied victory. The United States also led in the development of atomic and nuclear weapons that hastened the end of World War II and that have greatly limited warfare since 1945, restricting the size and composition of forces as well as the nature of operations. During this era of limited war, the United States has continued to lead in the invention and application of advanced weapons. The results have not been uniformly successful, but the United States has remained at the forefront of warfare in the Western world.

The telling of this extensive and sometimes fragmented story has been a cooperative effort. Ira Gruber wrote chapters 1 and 2; Mark Grimsley, chapters 3–7; Robert Doughty, chapters 8–12, 19, and 22–23; Williamson Murray, chapters 13–18; Roy Flint, chapter 20; and George Herring, chapter 21. Each of us, of course, has drawn on the work of scores of other scholars; and each has benefitted from the comments of specialists, colleagues, and students who have reviewed portions of this history. We are particularly indebted to Richard Kohn and John Shy, who read carefully an entire draft of the text and drew on their remarkable understanding of military history and sharp critical judgment to suggest ways of improving the whole. We, and our fellow authors, are grateful to all who have had a part in creating this book. We do not imagine that we will have satisfied our critics; we do hope that they and other readers will continue to share their knowledge of warfare with us.

R. A. D. and I. D. G.

CONTENTS IN BRIEF

CONTENTS

MAP SYMBOLS

The symbols shown below are used on the maps in this volume. Most of the symbols suggest the organization of units in particular campaigns or battles. The reader should understand that the organization of military units has changed over time and has varied from army to army or even within armies. For example, the composition and size of Napoleon's corps varied within his own army and differed from those of his opponents; they also differed dramatically from those of armies later in the nineteenth century. The symbols thus indicate the organization of a unit at a particular time and do not indicate its precise composition or size.

Division	X X
Corps	X X X
Army	X X X X
Army Group	X X X X X
Cavalry Screen	• • •
Armor	
Airborne	
Fort	
Mine	
Bridge	
Boundary between Units	—xxxxx—

LIST OF MAPS

1

ANGLO-AMERICAN WARFARE, 1607–1763: THE EMERGENCE OF THE PEOPLE IN ARMS

Anglo-Indian Warfare

The Colonial Wars

The French and Indian War

Just as Europeans of the seventeenth and eighteenth centuries suffered through a succession of wars so too did their colonists in North America. The English, who were far more numerous than other European colonists and more determined to establish permanent settlements, provoked particularly hostile responses from their neighbors in the New World. For more than one-third of their years as colonists (1607–1776), the English were at war. At first—for nearly three-quarters of a century—they fought mainly with American Indians; then, for another seventy-five years, with other European colonists and their Indian allies in wars that were loose extensions of struggles for power in Europe. Finally, in a long, complex war for the conquest of Canada, the French and Indian War (1754–1763), they fought against combinations of European regulars, other colonists, and American Indians.

Except during the last years of the colonial period when British colonists fought with and against regular European forces, warfare in America bore little resemblance to that in Europe. At a time when European states were supporting ever-larger standing armies and waging limited wars, the English colonies in North America were relying on their militia or on expeditionary forces drawn occasionally from the militia to wage nearly unlimited wars of conquest. Colonial forces did use many of the same weapons as regulars, and they sometimes tried to adopt regular methods of marching and firing. Otherwise, colonial forces were raised, trained, and employed very differently than the standing armies of Europe. Neither militia nor provincial expeditionary forces had the organizational permanence of a regular army, and neither had anything like the discipline or training.

1

Their fortifications were primitive; their system of supply was rudimentary; and regular linear tactics, combined-arms warfare, and siegecraft were completely beyond their competence. Indeed, colonial forces were little more than unskilled infantry, equipped with handguns and light artillery and capable of fighting only in loose formations. They tried mainly to exhaust their enemies with small skirmishes and the destruction of their food and shelter. But in their own primitive ways colonial forces fought for far higher stakes than the standing armies of Europe. While Europeans waged limited wars to adjust boundaries and settle dynastic disputes, the English colonists of North America fought to conquer a continent.

Anglo-Indian Warfare

The first English colonists to settle permanently in the New World expected to have to fight to sustain themselves; and they did. During the seventeenth century, they were most often at war with American Indians and only occasionally with themselves or other Europeans. They had hoped to take possession of undeveloped lands in America, to trade with or employ Indians, and to spread the Protestant faith. They were prepared to destroy anyone who opposed them. They soon found that some Indians were hostile at first meeting and that many others became so in time. Indians resented being coerced—being forced to provide food for the English or to accept English laws and religious practices. They also resented being disparaged as a primitive people and becoming economically and culturally dependent on the English. Most of all, they resented the steady increase in the number of English colonists and their expansion into land that had traditionally supported Indian agriculture, hunting, and fishing. These resentments were often expressed in isolated acts of defiance and violence. But when the Indians made concerted efforts to stop English expansion—when they launched widespread attacks in Virginia and Massachusetts—they precipitated unrestrained warfare that involved all colonists and Indians living together on the frontiers of North America. The colonists responded with devastating punitive expeditions in the largest and most destructive of seventeenth-century Anglo-Indian wars: the First and Second Tidewater wars (1622–1632, 1644–1646) and Bacon's Rebellion (1675–1676)—both in Virginia—and King Philip's War (1675–1676) in Massachusetts.

Virginia

Virginians were the first English colonists to wage war with the Indians—the first colonists to create and employ armed forces against their elusive neighbors. To protect themselves against potentially hostile Indians living in their midst, the men who settled at Jamestown in 1607 submitted to a succession of military governors who required all men to drill regularly, maintain fortified communities, and campaign occasionally against the natives. In these earliest campaigns the colonists developed tactics to punish the Indians and push them away from English settlements. Finding it extremely difficult to engage the Indians, the colonists concentrated on destroying their villages, crops, and stores in what were called "feed fights." Feed fights together with strict military rule helped the English survive their first years in Virginia.

Indians were an elusive and frustrating enemy because they sought to wage war without costly battles. Before Europeans arrived, Indians fought one another in relatively bloodless and ritualistic wars. In these wars the aim was to take prisoners who might be enslaved or sacrificed; it was rarely to conquer or destroy an opposing nation. Thus Indians attacked mainly when they had superior numbers and could surprise their enemies, when they could conduct an ambush or raid with a good prospect of taking prisoners. They avoided closing with an enemy of equal strength, preferring to remain at a distance exchanging arrows and protecting themselves with wooden body armor. They also relied on fortifications—ditches and palisades (walls of tree trunks and brush rising twelve feet or more above ground)—to secure their towns. But most Indians, valuing lives above property, were reluctant to assault a fortification or even to defend one when threatened by a larger enemy force. Soon after Europeans arrived, Indians began acquiring metal tips for their arrows and matchlock muskets. By the mid-seventeenth century, Indians of both the Chesapeake and New England would have large numbers of muskets and the skill to repair them, if not to manufacture powder. These weapons would make warfare more lethal; and Indians, responding to European provocations, would seek increasingly to kill the colonists and destroy their property. Even then, Indians remained wary of battle. They continued to raid and ambush their enemies and to retire into swamps and forests rather than risk casualties.

But in 1614, when Indians seemed a relatively passive and poorly equipped enemy, a marriage between an English colonist and an Indian princess brought peace to Virginia and a nearly disastrous relaxation of military preparations. The colonists stopped drilling, neglected their fortifications, and spread out across the Virginia countryside to plant tobacco and turn a profit. This sustained expansion of English settlement alarmed the Indians and left the colonists, now living on private plantations among the natives, vulnerable to attack. In March 1622 the Indians struck, bringing war to the people of Virginia as consuming and destructive as any that would be experienced in Europe during the Thirty Years' War. On that March day the Indians killed 347 colonists and drove the remainder into eight crowded communities along the James River where, during the next winter, another 500 died of malnutrition and disease. Virginia barely survived; by 1624 the English population was only 1,275 (of some 5,000 who had been in or come to the colony since 1618).

After the Massacre of 1622, Virginians embarked on more than two decades of efforts to make their colony secure—to raise and employ the forces needed to drive Indians permanently from English settlements. They began by restoring martial law and raising volunteers for expeditions against the Indians. Those expeditions or feed fights, conducted by infantry

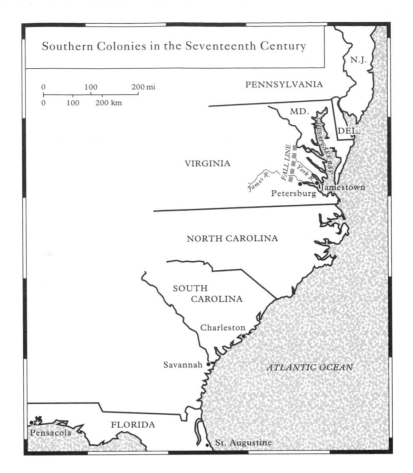

Southern Colonies in the Seventeenth Century

equipped with matchlock muskets, marked the beginning of the First Tide-water War (1622–1632), a war fought to gain the space and time needed to save the colony. For long-term security the leading men of Virginia relied on citizens in arms: they distributed weapons to every colonist, required military service of adult males (1624), and began compensating those on campaign by working their lands. Beginning in 1629, they also made a determined effort to clear all Indians from the peninsula between the James and York rivers, east of Jamestown, and to secure that peninsula by building a six-mile wall linking the rivers near Jamestown. By the end of the First Tidewater War in 1632, Virginians had secured the center of their settlements and were beginning to expand once again.

Over the ensuing fifteen years, Virginians so improved the raising and use of their forces—so contrived to harness the energy of a growing pop-ulation—that they greatly increased their security. In 1634 they organized Virginia into eight counties and made each responsible for maintaining a militia company. The new companies were to protect the counties when attacked, provide men for expeditions against the Indians, and support expe-ditionary forces with food, equipment, and compensatory labor. This system proved its worth in 1644 when Indians rose again, massacring about 500 colonists. In the Second Tidewater War (1644–1646) Virginia drew men from the county militia to launch coordinated offensives against the Indians—traditional feed fights to destroy villages, crops, and stores and force the Indians farther from English settlements. To keep the Indians at bay, the colonists built four forts (blockhouses with protective palisades) from the head of the York River to what would be Petersburg and imposed a peace that excluded Indians—on pain of death—from all of the lands between the James and York rivers, east of the fall line. Virginia, with a population of more than 8,000 Englishmen, was at last firmly and securely established.

For four decades Virginia's defense had depended on the efforts of nearly all adult male colonists—masters, servants, and slaves. After the Second Tidewater War, defense became the responsibility of only a portion of the white adult male population. Virginia's leaders, feeling relatively secure from the Indians and increasingly apprehensive over arming servants and slaves, decided in 1652 to restrict the militia to "freemen or servants of undoubted Fidelity." This more exclusive militia, still organized by counties, was able to provide adequate security against Indians and servants for more than twenty years.

Then, in 1675, Indians from Maryland attacked the north and west frontiers of Virginia, killing 300 colonists and creating turmoil throughout the colony. Sir William Berkeley, the aging royal governor, persisted in relying on forts and mounted militia ranging between forts to protect the frontiers—on a policy that was wholly inadequate. Frontiersmen with exposed estates and other grievances took matters into their own hands. They joined together under a wealthy young landowner, Nathaniel Bacon, defied Governor Berkeley, and attacked any Indians within reach, friend or foe. Thus fighting Indians blended with rebellion in Bacon's Rebellion of 1675–1676. Not until Bacon died and regulars arrived from England was order restored. But after it was, and after the regulars went home, Virginians reverted to their policy of relying on an exclusive militia to control neighboring Indians and rebellious colonists for the remainder of the seventeenth century.

Massachusetts

The purposes and patterns of settlement, in particular the cultivation of tobacco on scattered plantations, had done much to shape Anglo-Indian warfare in seventeenth-century Virginia. By spreading across the land, Virginians had provoked desperate struggles for territory within fifteen years of their arrival at Jamestown; and living as they did on scattered plantations, they had soon come to rely on county militia, expeditionary forces, and feed fights gradually to clear their lands of Indians. In seventeenth-century New England, where purposes and patterns of settlement were different, Anglo-Indian wars were somewhat delayed, although no less desperate when they came. Because many of the first colonists of New England were intensely religious—more interested in achieving salvation than in turning a profit—they settled in small, covenanted communities and pursued subsistence agriculture, trade, and primitive manufacturing. These early New Englanders

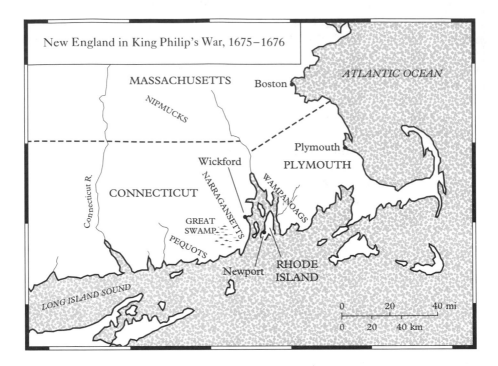

New England in King Philip's War, 1675–1676

also tended to migrate as small communities, coming within fifty years of the first permanent settlement at Plymouth (1620) to live in villages, interspersed among Indian villages, in each of the four English colonies—Massachusetts, Plymouth, Rhode Island, and Connecticut. With few exceptions, New England communities avoided serious trouble with neighboring Indians until 1675; and when serious trouble arose, as with the Pequots of Connecticut in 1636–1637, the colonists were able to rely on their village militia and expeditionary forces to provide security.

But the rapid growth of the English population eventually made the Indians of New England deeply apprehensive and resentful: by 1675 there were more than 35,000 colonists living among 20,000 Indians in Plymouth, Massachusetts, Rhode Island, and Connecticut. When at last the Indians were provoked to fight, the interspersed character of English and Indian settlements made that fighting unusually destructive and widespread. King Philip's War, which started in June 1675 after Plymouth executed three Wampanoag Indians for murdering a Christian Indian, soon engulfed all of New England. The Wampanoags, led by their supreme ruler, King Philip, began attacking English settlements and gathering Indian allies. In late July, Philip escaped to Massachusetts, brought the powerful Nipmucks into the war, and began battering the Connecticut River Valley. That autumn, after Philip had moved back toward Plymouth, the New England colonies launched a preemptive attack on the Narragansetts of Rhode Island.

The campaign against the Narragansetts, larger and more complex than any of the war, illustrated the difficulty that a loose confederation of colonies had in assembling, supplying, and controlling even a small army of unskilled militiamen. Until the autumn of 1675, the colonies had relied mainly on local militia units to defend their towns and on small expeditionary forces to act against Philip. In November, after learning that the powerful Narragansetts of western Rhode Island were sheltering Wampanoags and preparing for war, commissioners from the United Colonies decided to raise an intercolonial force to attack the Narragansetts. By the second week of December some 650 Massachusetts and Plymouth militiamen (volunteers and conscripts armed with matchlocks, flintlocks, and swords) had assembled at Wickford on the western shore of Narragansett Bay, near the center of Narragansett power and only eleven miles by water from Newport. In destroying nearby Indian villages, the English learned that the Narragansetts had retreated to a secret fortified village in the Great Swamp about ten miles southwest of Wickford. Knowing that 300 Connecticut troops were nearby and that their own supplies would soon be exhausted, the Massachusetts and Plymouth troops decided to join their Connecticut allies and proceed at once to attack the Narragansett village.

On December 19 the intercolonial army of nearly 1,000 men pushed through heavy snow to the northern edge of the Great Swamp. There the Connecticut troops who were in the van exchanged fire with a party of Indians. When the Indians withdrew into the frozen swamp, the Connecticut troops followed, eventually reaching the secret village, five or six acres of high ground surrounded by a palisade and containing shelter and supplies for 1,000 Indians. Without waiting for reinforcements or instructions, the Connecticut troops attacked through the one unfinished portion of the palisade. They succeeded in forcing their way into the village but were met there by such heavy musket fire that they had to withdraw. The remainder of the allied army now arrived, and a second attack by the whole of the intercolonial army succeeded in taking the village and burning the Indians' wigwams and stores. Although the undisciplined and intense fighting had taken a heavy toll of the colonists, about 220 killed or wounded (more than 20 percent of their force), the colonists had inflicted even heavier casualties on the Indians and had destroyed their food and shelter. That evening the colonists retired to Wickford. It would be another month before the intercolonial army could assemble men and supplies to continue their offensive. In late January and early February the colonists made a difficult march of about seventy miles from Wickford, through Rhode Island and Massachusetts, to Boston in a futile effort to overtake and destroy what remained of the Narragansetts. On February 5 the army was disbanded.

The war was by no means over; the Indians were still able to punish the colonists. But it was only a matter of time before the colonists' superior numbers, resources, and organization would destroy the Indians of southeast New England. In February and March 1676 the Indians went on the offensive once again, attacking English communities from the Connecticut River Valley to Rhode Island and forcing many colonists to give up their villages and withdraw to towns around Boston. But just when colonists began to despair of defeating or pacifying the Indians and just when they seemed to be suffering most from the loss of their homes and food supplies, the Indians broke off their offensive. Worn by hunger, disease, and losses in battle, the

Indians began to fish, plant, scavenge for food, and surrender. The colonists mounted a final offensive: surprising Indians along the Connecticut River, tracking down others with dogs, and showing little mercy to any they captured. The war ended in the late summer of 1676 with Philip's death and the destruction or deportation of hostile Indians. The colonists had suffered greatly in King Philip's War, losing more than 5 percent of their population and a dozen towns; but they had permanently broken the power of the Indians of southeast New England.

The Colonial Wars

Although fighting between Englishmen and Indians continued through the remainder of the colonial period, that fighting gradually blended with and became subordinate to wars between the English and other European colonists in North America. During the 1680s, disputes over land, trade, and religion produced clashes between South Carolinians and the Spanish in Florida and between New Englanders and the French in Canada. These clashes soon became part of worldwide conflicts among the principal states of Europe. But if European statesmen considered overseas commerce and colonies valuable assets in their struggles to preserve a balance of power, they did little before 1750 to assist their colonists in wars with one another. In King William's War (1689–1697, which was an extension of the War of the League of Augsburg) the settlers of New England and the French of Canada had mainly Indian allies. Similarly in Queen Anne's War (1702–1713, part of the War of the Spanish Succession) and King George's War (1739–1748, part of the War of the Austrian Succession) English and Spanish colonists bore the brunt of fighting on the southern frontiers while English and French colonists, supported by Indians, did the same in the north. Only rarely, in Queen Anne's and King George's wars—brutal and indecisive conflicts—did regular British forces support the colonists.

For more than a century before King William's War, the English had competed with the Spanish, French, and Dutch for the land and wealth of North America. By right of discovery and papal decree the Spanish had first claimed North America in 1494, and they had been able to sustain that claim through most of the sixteenth century—in part because they had a superior fleet and in part because their rivals were preoccupied with European affairs. But as Spain became mired in the Eighty Years' War with the Dutch (1567–1648) and as the Spanish navy and merchant fleet began to decay, the French, Dutch, and English pushed into North America. The French, who had fished off Newfoundland and traded for furs through most of the sixteenth century, established a permanent settlement at Quebec in 1608, made Canada a royal colony in 1663, and claimed the whole Mississippi Valley in 1682. The Dutch, more interested in commerce than in colonies, established a post at New York in 1624 and, by mid-century, a flourishing trade and fishery in the North Atlantic. But neither the French nor the Dutch were as successful as the English in creating permanent settlements in North America; and Englishmen were tenacious in defending their claims to the land and trade of the New World. The English had explored North America in the late fifteenth century, raided Spanish possessions in the West Indies and Central America in the 1560s and 1570s, and after failures along Albemarle Sound in the 1580s, established colonies in the Chesapeake (1607) and New England (1620). While those colonies were taking hold and becoming sources of tobacco, fish, furs, and timber, English merchants and ministers further asserted their interests in America. In the 1620s merchants invested in privateers that attacked French outposts in Nova Scotia and took Quebec (returned in 1632); and during the Anglo-Spanish and Anglo-Dutch wars of the middle of the century, the English government sent squadrons to capture Nova Scotia and New York. Although the English returned Nova Scotia to France in 1667, they also adopted laws (navigation acts of 1651, 1660, 1663, and 1696) to reap the principal benefits of all trade with their American colonies.

In King William's War (1689–1697) the English colonists of North America found the French and Indians together a far more formidable enemy than either had been alone. Although the total English population was nearly twenty times larger than the French, the population of New York and New England was only four or five times that of Canada; and it was far more difficult for the English to coordinate their efforts—divided as they were in separate colonies—than for the French who lived under one centralized administration. After both sides had begun the war with raids across the frontiers of Canada and New York, and after an expedition from Massachusetts had captured the French privateering base at Port Royal in Acadia, New York and New England joined forces in the summer of 1690 for an invasion of Canada. This was an ambitious operation that required two small armies: one proceeding from Albany across Lake George and Lake Champlain to Montreal, the other from Boston by way of the St. Lawrence River to Quebec. Both forces came down with smallpox, and when the one on the lakes turned back, the other was left alone to face the united forces of New France at Quebec. Outnumbered and suffering from cold wet weather as well as illness, the second English force also turned back in October 1690. The war degenerated into savage frontier encounters and maritime commerce raiding. The French lacked the population for sustained offensives. The English lacked the will; their assemblies were ever slow to vote money for defense and to cooperate with one another. Thus the war fell most heavily on frontier settlements, on local militia units, and on Indian allies. The governments of England and France did little more than send warships to the West Indies and return all conquests and prisoners at the Peace of Ryswick.

Queen Anne's War (1702–1713) began much as King William's War had ended—with fighting across frontiers and commerce raiding at sea. South Carolinians and the Spanish colonists in Florida did do more than

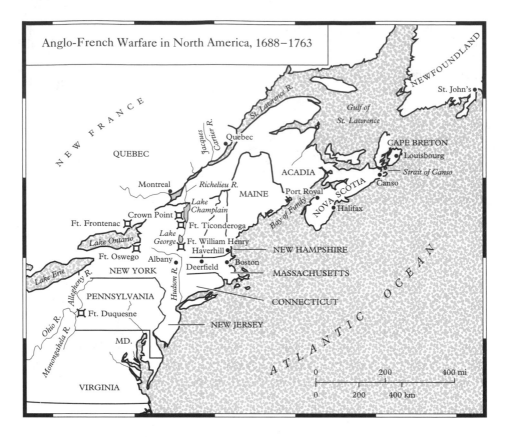

raid frontier settlements: they attacked unsuccessfully St. Augustine, Charleston, and Pensacola in the opening years of the war. But for eight years, New Englanders and French Canadians mainly skirmished in the wilderness and on the high seas. Although the population was growing steadily in the British and French colonies, the French continued to lack the resources for a regular campaign; they hoped that striking at the frontiers of New England would forestall an invasion of Canada or any extension of English settlements. New Englanders began the war without the help of New York and the Iroquois, both of whom preferred to remain neutral. Massachusetts did raise 1,900 men to garrison its frontiers and engage hostile Indians. Yet with money and labor scarce, it was difficult both to garrison frontier posts and to support an invasion of Canada—to raise the volunteers needed for prolonged service away from home. It was also difficult to banish the memory of New England's disastrous expedition to Canada in 1690. Thus until Britain provided direct support in the war, Massachusetts remained mainly on the defensive, absorbing damaging attacks on towns like Deerfield and Haverhill and responding with raids on the coast of what is now Maine and unsuccessful attempts to capture Port Royal.

When Britain did support the colonists, the results were decidedly disappointing. In 1708, New Englanders persuaded the British government to join in conquering Canada. Anticipating the arrival of British forces in 1709, the New Englanders lured New York and the Iroquois from their neutrality and enlisted volunteers for an expedition to Quebec. But the British government, hoping the war would end, delayed sending help until 1710 when a few warships and marines joined the colonists in capturing Port Royal. Only in 1711 did the British provide regular forces enough for an invasion of Canada: 4,300 soldiers, 12 warships, and 40 transports. The colonists responded enthusiastically, if not cooperatively. When in June the British reached Boston, the townspeople raised prices on provisions and obstructed British efforts to recruit seamen and pilots. Thousands of colonists did volunteer to accompany the British to the St. Lawrence and thousands more assembled for a separate colonial expedition across the lakes to Montreal, but the volunteers were not well disciplined or trained. To get the numbers of men required for such operations, the colonists had to recruit many men outside the militia—marginal members of society who saw military service as a chance to improve their fortunes. The British were not pleased with the quality of these provincial volunteers or with Bostonians' efforts in preparing the fleet. And when eight ships went aground on reaching the St. Lawrence, the British promptly canceled the attack on Quebec. The invasion of Canada collapsed amid mutual recriminations.

During King William's and Queen Anne's wars, the British had gradually become superior to the French at sea. Yet they had never vigorously exploited that superiority in North America because they consistently gave priority to war in Europe and because they had considerable difficulty containing a French navy that avoided battle and concentrated on raiding commerce and colonies. Thus during King William's War the French were able not just to batter British merchant shipping in the North Atlantic but also to protect New France while nearly destroying British posts in Newfoundland and Hudson Bay. Until the last years of Queen Anne's War the French continued to have the advantage in North American waters, capturing St. John's, Newfoundland, in 1708, inflicting great damage on British commerce, and holding all of Nova Scotia except Port Royal. Only at the end of Queen Anne's War were the British able to spare ships for expeditions against New France and to surpass the French in commerce raiding. Even then it was not British sea power that won a favorable peace; it was Marlborough and Eugene's success in the Low Countries, the strength of the British economy, and skillful diplomacy that enabled Britain to gain Nova Scotia, Hudson Bay, Newfoundland, and trading privileges in the Spanish Empire at the Peace of Utrecht.

The antagonisms that marred Anglo-American efforts to cooperate in Queen Anne's War reappeared in more virulent form in King George's War (1739–1748). At the beginning of George's war, the colonists were eager to cooperate with British regular forces in attacking neighboring Spanish colonies to make their frontiers permanently secure for settlement and trade. Yet for all their enthusiasm, undisciplined and inexperienced provincials had great trouble working effectively with professional British soldiers and sailors. In 1740 and 1741 Anglo-American expeditions failed to capture Spanish posts at St. Augustine in Florida and at Cartagena on the Spanish Main. Each attempt suffered from disputes between provincials and regulars, and each ended with mutual complaints. Regulars found provincials dirty, ignorant of war, and difficult to manage. Provincials complained of being treated with contempt—of being employed more as laborers than as soldiers, of being pressed into service on British warships, and of being kept under arms well beyond their periods of enlistment.

Even the most successful of Anglo-American operations in George's War created disputes and lingering resentments. In 1744 French forces from Cape Breton Island attacked ports in Nova Scotia and the shipping of New England. Angered by these attacks, the government of Massachusetts organized an expedition against the French base at Louisbourg on Cape Breton—a base established in 1713 on a fine natural harbor and protected by a massive angled-bastion fortress that provided a haven for French warships, privateers, and merchantmen on the eastern approaches to the Gulf of St. Lawrence. Massachusetts raised and funded 2,800 provincial troops. These men, commanded by a prominent colonist, sailed from Boston in March 1745. At Canso in Nova Scotia, they were reinforced by troops from New Hampshire and Connecticut and by British warships from the West Indies. The whole, now under the joint command of a provincial general and a British admiral, proceeded to Cape Breton and took Louisbourg by siege and blockade. The colonists were elated with this victory but dismayed to find their contributions were little appreciated by the British and that they were neither to be fully reimbursed for their expenses nor to be permitted to share in prize money from French ships taken at Louisbourg. The colonists hoped to get British support for an invasion of Canada in 1746 or 1747; instead they were left to garrison Louisbourg and, eventually, to see the British surrender what they had won.

In King George's War, as in their wars against Louis XIV, the British had been superior to the French at sea. But in King George's War their superiority had been so substantial that even while giving priority to the war in Europe—devoting their fleet mainly to protecting their communications with the continent and blockading French and Spanish ports—they were able to gain important advantages over the French in North American waters. The British commitment to America was never very strong. In 1746 they abandoned an attack on Quebec when bad weather and the appearance of a French squadron in the English Channel delayed the sailing of their expedition; and later that year they allowed the same French squadron to reach North America unopposed. (The French might have recaptured Louisbourg had they not lost 8,000 men to illness before the campaign ended.) Even so, the British navy's contribution to the war in America was considerable—in helping capture Louisbourg, in intercepting a convoy bound for Quebec in 1747, and in joining with privateers to gain a clear advantage in commerce raiding in the North Atlantic. At war's end—at the Peace of Aix-la-Chapelle—the British were able to use their successes in North America to offset French gains on the Continent by exchanging

Louisbourg for the territory that Marshal Saxe had taken in the Low Countries. Many colonists were disgusted.

The French and Indian War

In more than a half-century of conflict among English, French, and Spanish colonists of North America, the colonists had been left to do nearly all the fighting. European forces had taken part only fitfully and often ineffectively; and European governments had failed to resolve the disputes over land, trade, and religion that frustrated and alarmed the frontiersmen of each nation. In the final, climactic struggle for the continent—the French and Indian War (1754–1763)—regulars would intervene decisively. British forces and British resources would resolve the long contest for the frontiers of America. But in so doing the British would alienate their colonial allies and awaken a sense of colonial interests and identity that would contribute eventually to the destruction of the British empire in America.

The Beginnings

The British intervened in the French and Indian War primarily to protect their aggressive and uncooperative colonists—not, initially at least, to conquer Canada or Florida. By 1754 the English colonists of North America outnumbered the French 1,042,000 to 55,000 and the Spanish by an even greater margin. But the English were unable to cooperate as effectively as their neighbors, and by 1754 they were everywhere along the frontiers losing contests for land and trade as well as the allegiance of the Indians. In Nova Scotia, French settlements were growing faster than English; in western Pennsylvania the French had defeated the pro-British Miami Indians, built fortresses from Lake Erie to the Allegheny River, and routed all provincial forces that approached them; and on the southern frontiers the French and Spanish were turning the Indians against the English. Delegates from seven English colonies met at Albany in June 1754 to draft a plan of cooperation for defense and Indian affairs. But the Albany Plan was not acceptable to the colonies or to the British government, and the government decided to rely on sending small detachments of regulars to help the colonists secure their frontiers. When the French responded by embarking 3,000 of their own regulars for Canada, the French and Indian War quickly became more than a contest between European colonists and Indian allies. By the summer of 1755, British and French warships had fought off Newfoundland, and Anglo-American forces had both conquered Acadia (deporting most of the French population) and suffered a dramatic defeat along the banks of the Monongahela in western Pennsylvania.

The early appearance of regular British forces in the French and Indian War did not mean that the British government shared the colonists' war aims. By 1755 many leading English colonists had begun to dream of conquering French and Spanish lands in North America. They had learned in more than half a century of conflict to hate their Catholic neighbors and to fear their sudden incursions on frontier settlements. They had also come to see that the French and Spanish and their Indian allies were obstacles to the growing English population—that they restricted access to the rich lands of the Ohio and Mississippi valleys as well as their trade with Indians. To end threats to their frontiers and to open the west to speculators, settlers, and traders, the English colonists needed to do more than haggle with the French and Spanish over existing frontiers; they needed to conquer the French and Spanish colonists and expel them from North America—much as they had conquered and expelled the Indians from the Atlantic seaboard. The British government would be slow to support or even comprehend these war aims. The government would not declare war on France until May 1756 or consider conquering New France until William Pitt became the king's principal minister in December 1756. Until then the British would wage a limited frontier war, while the colonists dreamed of conquest.

Although the colonists had more ambitious war aims than the British government and appealed to the government to help fight their war, they were most uncooperative and ineffective allies. The government did expect the colonists to provide recruits and provisions for British regiments as well as provincial forces to support the regulars. But when in the summer of 1756 British generals arrived to take control of the war, they found the colonists not just unwilling to help recruit men for regular units but also opposed to having provincials serve under regular officers. Colonial assemblies, eager to assert their independence of royal authority, had forbidden provincials to submit to British orders or military justice; and the provincials, having contracted to serve only under their own officers, would have deserted rather than accept British direction. Similarly, the colonists refused to let the British take charge of their systems of supply or to quarter troops at their expense without the approval of the colonial assemblies. To gain the cooperation of the colonists in prosecuting the war, the British commander-in-chief, the Earl of Loudoun, agreed to keep regulars and provincials apart and to let the provincials serve under their own officers who would rank after British majors. Even so, with the exception of New York, the colonies rarely satisfied Loudoun's requests for men, supplies, transportation, and quarters in the campaigns of 1756 and 1757. Those provincials who did come forward were fit mainly for fatigue and garrison duty; they were too poorly trained to be steady under fire and too undisciplined to maintain their health in camp.

Britain Takes Control of the War

In large part because the colonists were such ineffective and difficult allies, Anglo-American forces did not fare well in 1756 or 1757. During the summer and autumn of 1756, while British and colonial officers argued over authority and rank in their combined forces, the French went on the offensive, capturing Fort Oswego and 1,500 provincials on Lake Ontario and ravaging English frontier settlements from New York to the Carolinas. Even after Oswego fell and the French seemed to be preparing to attack Fort William Henry on Lake George, the colonists remained more concerned with establishing the independence of their assemblies than with defending New York. Loudoun concluded that the colonists could not be depended on to win the war and that he would have to rely on regulars, recruited in Britain, to mount the offensives needed to capture Louisbourg and Quebec and end the war in 1757. Yet recruiting an additional 11,000 men in Britain, particularly while the government and its policies were unsettled, took time; and when at last these reinforcements reached Loudoun, it was too late for him to act decisively. By July 1757, the French government had so strengthened its naval forces off Cape Breton as to forestall an attack on Louisbourg or Quebec and to release some troops from Canada for an offensive in New York. On August 9 the French captured Fort William Henry on Lake George and threatened to occupy the upper Hudson. So it was that Anglo-Americans had managed to squander superior resources for two campaigns and to suffer a succession of depressing defeats

Anglo-American failures in the opening campaigns of the French and Indian War should not be attributed entirely to their difficulties in raising an army. The British also had trouble during these first campaigns in taking advantage of the superiority of their navy—gaining and keeping control of the seas off New England and New France. As in earlier colonial wars, the British were more concerned with establishing their superiority in the English Channel than with protecting their possessions overseas; and establishing themselves in the Channel was not easy because the French had rebuilt their fleet since the War of the Austrian Succession and refused to risk that fleet in a major engagement. Thus to defend the British Isles, to contain commerce raiders, and to protect their colonies from roving French squadrons, the British concentrated on blocking French ports. This strategy was not uniformly successful at the beginning of the war. In 1755 two French fleets eluded British squadrons and reached Canada with a reinforcement of 4,000 men; and by June 1757 the French had collected eighteen ships of the line and three frigates at Louisbourg, giving them temporary control of Canadian waters and frustrating Loudoun's plans for a summer offensive toward Quebec.

Ironically, while the British were struggling to exploit their sea power and were learning not to depend on the colonists to win the war, they were coming to accept colonial war aims. William Pitt, who became the king's principal minister in December 1756, was not to be satisfied with sustaining the boundaries of British North America. Believing that Britain's power depended on trade and colonies, Pitt shared the colonists' enthusiasm for conquering Canada and expanding the British Empire into the Ohio and Mississippi valleys. He was therefore prepared to put greater resources into the war in America than his predecessors, and he pressed Loudoun to use those resources decisively—to take Louisbourg and Quebec and conquer Canada in 1757. When Loudoun failed even to attack Louisbourg, Pitt was determined to take control of the war in 1758: to overcome the colonists'

Jeffery, Lord Amherst commanded British forces that conquered Canada in 1759–1760. He was a cautious but very persistent commander who sought victory with few risks.

reluctance to serve by paying for some of the troops they would raise and to encourage his own officers to be more aggressive and obedient by recalling Loudoun and sending two promising young men to commands in America.

Jeffery Amherst was only forty and a colonel when chosen to lead British forces against Louisbourg and Quebec in 1758. Although he had never had an independent command, he had impressed the most influential generals in the British army as an unusually dependable and persistent officer. He had entered the army at fourteen; gone with his regiment to the Low Countries, Germany, and Scotland; won praise for his steadiness under fire at Dettingen and Fontenoy; and served as aide-de-camp to the Duke of Cumberland in the closing campaigns of the War of the Austrian Succession and in the opening campaign of the Seven Years' War. By temperament and experience, Amherst was well equipped to wage the kind of limited war made famous by Marshal Saxe—a war conducted more by sieges, maneuvers, and skirmishes than by general engagements, a war in which commanders sought to minimize casualties even when battle became unavoidable. Amherst was, as his sister described him, "hardly ever in a passion" but "avidly resolute in what he designs." He had the patience, prudence, and persistence not just to prefer, but also to succeed in, a war of sieges and maneuvers. Although he had never commanded, he had had ample opportunity as Cumberland's aide-de-camp during Saxe's conquest of the Austrian Netherlands to study the conduct of armies during the most celebrated campaigns in the history of limited war.

James Wolfe, whom Pitt chose to serve under Amherst at Louisbourg, was also young and without experience in high command; but Wolfe

James Wolfe commanded the British army that captured Quebec in 1759. Far more aggressive than most officers in the age of limited war, he preferred battles to sieges as the best way of deciding a campaign.

was not so composed or patient as Amherst and not so devoted to the conventions of limited war. At thirty-two, Wolfe was one of the youngest and most junior colonels in the army. He had served with his regiment in the Low Countries, Germany, and Scotland—distinguishing himself not only for his courage and control of men in battle but also for his ability to discipline and train men in camp. Like Amherst, he had proved a very knowledgable and effective aide-de-camp during the Scottish Rebellion and the expedition against the French port of Rochefort in 1757. But what set Wolfe apart from Amherst and many of their contemporaries were his extraordinary ambition and his fascination with battle. Wolfe was desperately eager to succeed in his profession—to achieve military fame. He studied incessantly to become worthy of higher command; he put service with his regiment before any personal consideration; and he looked forward to war as the path to preferment. Above all, he regarded battle as the supreme test of his personal courage and professional competence; nothing, he thought, was more rewarding than having the mastery of men under fire—and being recognized for having that mastery. He acknowledged the importance of fortifications and sieges, but he preferred the higher risks and greater potential rewards of battle as the arbiter of wars and reputations.

In choosing Amherst and Wolfe to provide strong leadership, in building up a decided superiority in regular units, and in granting large subsidies to encourage the colonists to serve as provincials, William Pitt believed he was creating Anglo-American forces capable of conquering New France, perhaps in 1758. Amherst and Wolfe would lead the largest and most important of three, coordinated offensives: an amphibious attack on Louisbourg and Quebec carried out by more than 13,000 regulars supported by nearly 40 warships, 15,000 sailors, and 110 transports. James Abercromby would make a secondary attack across Lake Champlain to Montreal with a combined force of more than 20,000 regulars and provincials. And John Forbes would lead about 6,000 men—mostly provincials—against Fort Duquesne. Although Pitt had not selected Abercromby and Forbes to serve in America and although it was not clear how effective they or their provincial allies might be, Anglo-American forces were everywhere expected to be larger and better supported than the French. It was not just that there would be 23,000 regulars, 21,000 provincials, 40 warships, and 15,000 seamen to oppose 6,800 French regulars, 10 warships, and a few thousand Canadians and Indians; it was also that while the British would benefit from an increasingly effective system of supply and transportation, the French would suffer from a succession of bad harvests, the interruption of their overseas trade and supply, and the defection of their Indian allies.

Quebec, 1758–1759

Notwithstanding the very great advantages they possessed, Anglo-American forces did not conquer New France in 1758. They did take the offensive, but the difficulties of campaigning in a vast primitive country, the inexperience and poor judgment of some of their leaders, the chronic weaknesses of provincials, and the competence of their enemies all worked against them. Amherst and Wolfe had the most success. They left Halifax at the end of May and established a beachhead on Cape Breton Island, four miles west of Louisbourg by June 8. Louisbourg was, however, too strongly fortified to invite an assault, and by the time Amherst had brought up his artillery and conducted a prudent siege—overcoming bad weather, smallpox, and persistent defenders to force a surrender—more than six weeks had passed. It was then the end of July, and although Amherst wanted to press on to Quebec, the British had formidable logistical problems to solve before they could sail. They set about at once preparing transports to send nearly 6,000 French prisoners to Europe, replenishing their own ships for the voyage to Quebec, and reembarking their siege train. These preparations had scarcely begun when news arrived that Abercromby had made a rash and disastrous attack on the French fortress of Ticonderoga on Lake Champlain. This news, together with delays in embarking the French prisoners and his own siege guns, forced Amherst to cancel the attack on Quebec. Instead he sent raiding parties to the Gulf of St. Lawrence and the Bay of Fundy and went himself with 4,000 men to relieve Abercromby. It was early October before Amherst reached Abercromby on Lake George—too late for another attempt on Ticonderoga. The British had taken Louisbourg; they had raided Fort Frontenac at the mouth of Lake Ontario; and in November, they would occupy Fort Duquesne. But the conquest of Canada eluded them in 1758.

Pitt was determined to succeed in 1759 in bringing overwhelming force against the beleaguered defenders of New France. Even before the campaign of 1758 ended, he appointed Amherst to replace Abercromby as commander-in-chief of British forces in North America. He also decided to persist in his strategy of having separate armies converge on the center of French population and power in the St. Lawrence Valley. Wolfe would command an amphibious force proceeding up the St. Lawrence to Quebec:

12,000 regulars supported by a fleet of 22 warships and 150 transports. Amherst would lead an even larger army of regulars and provincials across either Lake Champlain or Lake Ontario to Montreal. To complement these principal offensives, a third and smaller force would advance through western Pennsylvania against French outposts in the Ohio Valley. Knowing that the French had suffered heavy losses at Louisbourg and expecting that the British navy would be able to keep reinforcements from reaching Canada, Pitt assumed that his armies would have the numerical superiority needed to crush an enemy that had the distinct advantage of conducting a defense on interior lines.

Although Pitt was unable to raise all the forces he intended, his forces were far superior to the defenders of New France. To encourage British colonists to support the war, Pitt offered not only to furnish provincials with arms, clothing, and provisions but also to reimburse the colonies for recruiting and paying those provincials. Colonial assemblies responded by voting to raise 20,680 of the 21,000 men that Pitt had requested. But ordinary colonists, having suffered through a succession of disappointing and deadly campaigns, were reluctant to enlist. Only 16,835 provincials served in 1759, and few of them were well disciplined or trained. Neither Wolfe nor Amherst had the numbers of skilled men that Pitt expected. Even so, Wolfe with 9,000 regulars and Amherst with 13,000 regulars and provincials had more powerful armies than their opponents. The French government, placing greater emphasis on the war in Europe than on the defense of its North American colonies, sent only 300 men and small quantities of munitions to Canada. Some twenty vessels with provisions did arrive in the spring of 1759 before the British sealed the St. Lawrence, yet the forces of New France suffered through the ensuing campaign from shortages of men, powder, and provisions.

The French made good use of their meager resources. Louis Joseph, Marquis de Montcalm, commander-in-chief in New France, was an experienced and talented regular officer. Montcalm knew that he could not defend Canada as Frederick was defending Prussia. He had neither the men nor the supplies to conduct an aggressive defense on interior lines—to fight the costly battles and sustain the forced marches that such a strategy required. Nor could he risk losing Quebec while shifting his forces to deal separately with the armies converging on Canada. He could try both to hold Quebec and to trade space for time on Lake Champlain and Lake Ontario in hopes that the war would end before all of New France had been conquered. Thus he posted relatively small forces on the lakes to delay the armies advancing on Montreal, to force them to bring up cannon and to build vessels to gain control of those waterways. And thus he deployed the bulk of his troops around Quebec—possibly as many as 14,000 men, mainly militiamen but also several thousand regulars, a thousand provincials, and a few hundred Indians.

Montcalm's disposition of this mixed force in defense of Quebec was particularly skillful. Although Quebec seemed to occupy a position of great natural strength, built upon a headland rising several hundred feet above the St. Lawrence, the town's defenses were far from complete in 1759. The

Louis Joseph, Marquis de Montcalm,
commanded French forces in North America
during the French and Indian War. His
skillful defense of Canada frustrated British
commanders and significantly postponed
French defeat.

eastern and southern faces of the headland were steep enough to discourage an attack from the St. Lawrence, but the northern approach to Quebec across the St. Charles River and the western approaches along the north bank of the St. Lawrence were more gradual and accessible. And the fortifications covering those northern and western approaches were not yet complete. Montcalm knew that his mixed force could not stand against British regulars in open country. He also knew that his fortifications and supplies were not ready to withstand a regular siege of Quebec. He decided, therefore, to spread his forces along the north bank of the St. Lawrence both east and west of Quebec. He would take up positions, some eight to ten miles in length, that were too extensive to be besieged and too well protected by the river, tidal flats, bluffs, and forests to be easily attacked or turned. In these extensive positions, supplied by water from Montreal, he could hope to survive a short Canadian summer. If the British were rash or frustrated enough to attack his lines—as Abercromby had attacked them at Ticonderoga in 1758—even his inferior militiamen might prevail. In late May 1759, Montcalm began entrenching the north bank of the St. Lawrence below, at, and above Quebec; he secured his eastern flank with the Montmorency River, his western with a roving force of 3,000 men.

James Wolfe soon came to appreciate the quality of Montcalm's dispositions. Arriving off Quebec on June 23, Wolfe saw that it would be hazardous to attack and impossible to besiege Montcalm's extensive positions on the north bank of the St. Lawrence. Wolfe was one of the most aggressive

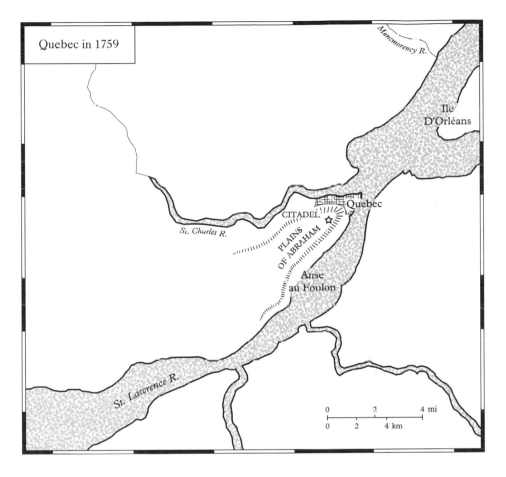

Quebec in 1759

Montmorency R.

Ile D'Orléans

Quebec

CITADEL

St. Charles R.

PLAINS OF ABRAHAM

Anse au Foulon

St. Lawrence R.

| 0 | 2 | 4 mi |
| 0 | 2 | 4 km |

officers of his era, but he was reluctant to waste lives assaulting well-prepared positions. Thus for more than ten weeks after reaching Quebec, he sought ways to bring Montcalm from his lines or to circumvent him. Wolfe continued to hope that Amherst's advance across the lakes would force the French to divert troops from Quebec—to contract their defenses and retire into the town where they might be taken by siege. He also landed troops on the north bank of the St. Lawrence east of the Montmorency River in hopes of being able to launch an offensive across the Montmorency, striking the flank of the French defenders and driving them across the St. Charles into Quebec. And he tried repeatedly to goad Montcalm into abandoning his lines and risking battle by bombarding Quebec, burning more than 1,500 farmhouses in the surrounding countryside, and sending two expeditions up the St. Lawrence to interdict supplies, destroy ships and magazines, and open a communication with Amherst. Only once did Wolfe yield to his frustrations and try to provoke a general engagement by attacking the French in their lines. That attack, launched across the Montmorency on July 31, failed completely: the British, pinned under heavy fire near the river's edge, lost 440 killed and wounded; the French, 60.

The Plains of Abraham

Wolfe's defeat on the Montmorency—indeed, the failure of all his efforts to dislodge the French—eroded his health and confidence. By the end of August he had become desperate enough to seek the advice of his brigadier generals, to ask how best to defeat the French army. His brigadiers, seeing little chance of attacking successfully between the Montmorency and the St. Charles, recommended approaching Quebec from the west along the north bank of the St. Lawrence. Such an approach would, they thought, force the French to risk battle on British terms (to use their militiamen against regulars in open country) or to let the British take Quebec by siege. Wolfe, who had long been inclined toward an attack from the west, accepted but modified his brigadiers' advice. Rather than put his army ashore well to the west of town where the river's bank was low and the landings might have been expected, he decided to risk a landing within two miles of Quebec where the shore rose steeply and where he stood a much better chance of surprising the French and forcing them to accept battle unprepared. In such a battle he could hope to defeat Montcalm and gain Quebec, if not all of Canada, before winter ended another campaign.

In making and carrying out this decision, Wolfe seemed to recover much of his vigor and confidence. After ten weeks of frustration and inactivity, Wolfe looked forward to battle, not merely as a test of his courage and skill but also as a promising solution to a most vexing tactical problem. He moved swiftly, August 31–September 6, removing his army from the east bank of the Montmorency and reassembling some 3,600 troops on board transports in the St. Lawrence, eight miles west of Quebec. By September 9 he had also taken the crucial decision to land within two miles of the town at Anse au Foulon, where a path led up the face of the bluff to the Plains of Abraham, a grassy plateau just outside the walls of the French citadel. Having made this decision, he arranged elaborate demonstrations to divert attention from the landings at the Anse, now scheduled for September 13. Detachments of British warships and transports would draw French forces four miles to the east and eight to the west of Quebec just before Wolfe's troops were to land. Wolfe would demonstrate against Montcalm's flanks while attacking his center.

The attack, carried out with great secrecy, resolution, and speed, succeeded as well as anyone might have hoped. Chance and French assumptions clearly favored the British, as did the superior discipline of their infantry. In the darkness before dawn on September 13, the British were able to dupe those French sentries who challenged their boats; the French were expecting supplies by water and allowed the British to pass without giving a countersign. The British also managed to disperse sentries guarding the path from Anse au Foulon to the Plains of Abraham without provoking a response in force; Montcalm, expecting an attack east of the St. Charles, assumed that the British were making no more than a demonstration. By the time he understood what they were doing and marched his own forces from east of the St. Charles to Quebec, Wolfe had already drawn up 4,800 British soldiers in line of battle, two ranks deep, on the Plains of Abraham.

Seeing that the British were beginning to dig in, and knowing that if allowed to grow stronger they would eventually take Quebec by siege, Montcalm decided to attack. He formed his militiamen and regulars in columns, flanked by skirmishers, and advanced. Wolfe's disciplined regulars remained in their lines even as the French advancing in columns and firing sporadically bore down on them. When the French came within forty yards, the British fired volleys by platoon that thoroughly disrupted the enemy columns. The British then reloaded, stepped forward beyond the smoke of their own muskets, and fired a second, general volley. At that, the French broke, streaming off the Plains of Abraham, back through Quebec, and across the St. Charles. The Battle of Quebec had ended.

Although the British did not immediately exploit their victory, they soon gained possession of Quebec. By the time the French had begun to retreat, Wolfe was dead, his second in command had been wounded, and 658 of his men were casualties (about 13.5 percent of his force). The interruption in British command together with the casualties they had suffered, a rearguard action by Canadian skirmishers, and a brief appearance of the 3,000 French troops who had been posted west of Quebec all discouraged a vigorous pursuit of the retreating French army. A French garrison continued to hold the citadel of Quebec, and survivors of the battle were able to reassemble east of the St. Charles. Yet the French had suffered about the same number and proportion of casualties as the British; Montcalm had been mortally wounded; and, above all, French morale had been broken temporarily. That night the remnants of the French army began to withdraw to the west, leaving the garrison in the citadel to surrender on September 18. By then the French had decided to take up new defensive positions on the Jacques Cartier River, thirty miles west of Quebec. The British had gained Quebec but advanced no farther up the St. Lawrence in 1759.

The Conquest of Canada

The British had again failed to conquer New France. Their efforts fell short not just because Wolfe was delayed in taking Quebec but especially because Amherst was unable to push his forces across Lakes Champlain and Ontario in time to cooperate with Wolfe's army. Amherst had begun the campaign determined to extinguish French power in Canada. But his prudence, along with the inertia of his allies and competence of his enemies, kept him from reaching the St. Lawrence in 1759. By the beginning of May he had begun to assemble forces at Albany capable of mounting parallel offensives toward Montreal: one of 5,000 men to go by way of Lake Ontario and the St. Lawrence; another of more than 8,000, by way of Lake George and Lake Champlain. Provincials were, however, slow to gather; and it was not until the end of May that he could send troops to Lake Ontario or until June 22 that he reached the south end of Lake George. He then expended another month building boats to carry his siege train across Lake George. He was determined to avoid a repetition of Abercromby's disastrous assault on French fortifications. Although Amherst never had to use his siege train—

the French unexpectedly abandoned their works at Ticonderoga (July 26) and Crown Point (July 31)—he did have to devote another eleven weeks to gaining control of Lake Champlain, building vessels and sweeping aside the French sloops that blocked the way to Montreal. When at last the lake was clear, it was mid-October and too late to go on to the St. Lawrence. Amherst knew that Wolfe's army had taken Quebec. He also knew that his forces on Lake Ontario had stopped short of the St. Lawrence, that winter was fast approaching, and that the provincials under his command were chaffing to go home. On October 19 he returned to Crown Point. The campaign was over.

By October 1759 Anglo-American forces had driven the defenders of New France into narrow corridors along the St. Lawrence and Richelieu rivers and cut their communications with France. William Pitt was impatient to complete the conquest of Canada early in 1760 lest negotiations end the war before the British had established their claim to the rest of Canada. But it would take Anglo-American forces another campaign to conquer Canada. Amherst spent the winter of 1759–1760 enlisting the colonists' support for a decisive, converging offensive against Montreal. He would lead 11,000 regulars and provincials from Albany via Lake Ontario and the St. Lawrence to Montreal. Another Anglo-American force of 3,400 would advance north across Lake Champlain and the Richelieu, and yet a third force of 3,800 British regulars would move southwest along the St. Lawrence from Quebec to Montreal. Although Amherst reached Albany in early May, he was unable to set out for Lake Ontario or to send troops to Lake Champlain until late in June. The colonists, anticipating peace, were slow to join his armies; and it took time to build up magazines on Lake Ontario and Lake Champlain. In the interim the French launched a preemptive attack on Quebec that forced Amherst to reinforce the garrison there. Not until early August were all Anglo-American armies advancing on Montreal. But once in motion, they soon brought overwhelming force against New France. On September 6, Amherst reached Montreal; the next day British forces from Quebec and Lake Champlain arrived; and on September 8 the French surrendered.

The conquest of Canada had been achieved at last by an overwhelming concentration of Anglo-American force—primarily regular and provincial land forces commanded by British officers and subsidized by the British government. But the British navy had also since 1758 played an increasingly important part in isolating and destroying New France. New France had never become self-sufficient; its regular forces had always depended on supplies from Europe and on the timely support of French warships off Cape Breton and in the St. Lawrence. Beginning in 1758, the British navy was so superior to the French that it could both blockade the coast of France and control the approaches to New France. Thus in 1758 British warships hastened the surrender of Louisbourg, first by destroying a convoy off Rochefort that was carrying badly needed supplies to the fortress and later by sealing off the fortress itself while Amherst and Wolfe pressed their siege. Similarly in 1759 and 1760 the British navy was able to shut the St. Lawrence to all except insignificant French reinforcements and to give Anglo-American forces the support they needed to take Quebec and Montreal.

The conquest of Canada helped the British win the Seven Years' War, but it considerably complicated their efforts to make a favorable peace. Once Montreal fell, the British were able to divert thousands of regular and provincial troops for service elsewhere against the French and their allies. In the last two years of the war, the British won victories in Europe, the West Indies, the Far East, and North America. Yet even before negotiators met in Paris in the summer of 1762, Anglo-Americans had begun debating the fate of Canada. Many colonists and some Englishmen argued that Britain should retain Canada to provide for the security of the other British colonies in North America by eliminating the French from their borders. Others— primarily Englishmen concerned with the trade and authority of the mother country—urged that Britain retain Guadeloupe (a French West Indies island taken in 1759) and return Canada to France. Keeping Guadeloupe would give Britain a lucrative source of sugar; returning Canada would encourage British colonists in North America to remain dependent on the mother country for their security and would forestall any movement for American independence. In the end the British government decided to keep Canada, provide for the immediate security of the empire, and accept any longer-term risks of rebellion in America.

The conquest of Canada also left American and British veterans with very mixed feelings about each other. There were many colonists who emerged from the war admiring the British for their courage and discipline and celebrating their contributions to victory over New France. There were also British veterans who liked Americans and chose to remain in the colonies after the war. Yet for all the pleasure that Anglo-Americans took in what they had done together, each had enough unpleasant memories of the other to threaten imperial ties. Americans remembered British officers as haughty and merciless—unwilling to consult provincials, careless of their rights and interests, and contemptuous of them as soldiers. Having gone to war expecting to be instructed rather than coerced into their duties and thinking they were part of a Protestant crusade, provincials were repelled by British military justice and godlessness. The British who had made unprece- dented efforts to support the war were deeply offended by the indifference and selfishness of the colonists. It was not just that the colonists made poor soldiers—that they seemed dirty, undisciplined, poorly trained, and cow- ardly—but also that they refused to provide men and supplies, obstructed recruiting, denied quarters for regulars, engaged in profiteering, and traded with the enemy. Such mutual resentments did more than weaken imperial ties; they made each side more likely to underestimate the other and to resort to force as a way of settling future differences.

*   *   *   *

Only fleetingly in the French and Indian War had warfare in the British colonies of North America come to resemble that in Europe. For 150 years before Wolfe faced Montcalm on the Plains of Abraham—while Europeans were surviving the Thirty Years' War, developing ever-larger professional armies, and attempting to limit violence—the British colonies of North America were waging primitive wars of conquest against their neighbors. In these destructive wars, the colonists relied mainly on unskilled militiamen to destroy or displace their enemies, on militiamen who were more effective burning crops, stores, and houses than skirmishing with elusive enemies in the wilderness. Although these wars could fall as heavily on civilians as on soldiers, the British colonists were rarely willing to accept the kind of discipline or to bear the costs required to create forces proficient in regular European warfare. Nor were they often willing to cooperate with other colonists or the British government in large-scale operations against the French and Spanish on their frontiers. Even when British regulars brought European military practices to the French and Indian War—to the siege of Louisbourg, the climactic battle on the Plains of Abraham, and the final offensive against Canada—the British had to alter their warfare to suit American conditions and habits. The British simplified their tactics to accommodate the densely wooded and difficult terrain of North America, eliminating cavalry, reducing their infantry from three ranks to two, and developing light infantry. They also adjusted their war aims, methods of raising men and supplies, and campaign plans to gain the help of colonists who wanted to conquer Canada without bearing the costs of or submitting to the regular military discipline required for so formidable a task. By the middle of the eighteenth century, the British colonists of North America were powerfully committed to their own undisciplined and yet decisive way of war.

SUGGESTED READINGS

Anderson, Fred. *A People's Army: Massachusetts Soldiers and Society in the Seven Years' War* (Chapel Hill: University of North Carolina Press, 1984).

Craven, Wesley Frank. *The Colonies in Transition, 1660–1713* (New York: Harper & Row Publishers, 1968).

―――. *The Southern Colonies in the Seventeenth Century* (Baton Rouge: Louisiana State University Press, 1949).

Ferling, John E. *A Wilderness of Miseries: War and Warriors in Early America* (Westport: Greenwood Press, 1980).

Frégault, Guy. *Canada: the war of the conquest* (Toronto: Oxford University Press, 1969).

Graham, Gerald S. *Empire of the North Atlantic: The Maritime Struggle for North America* (Toronto: University of Toronto Press, 1950).

Leach, Douglas E. *Arms for Empire: A Military History of the British Colonies in North America, 1607–1763* (New York: Macmillan Co., 1973).

―――. *Flintlock and Tomahawk, New England in King Philip's War* (New York: Macmillan Co., 1958).

————. *Roots of Conflict: British Armed Forces and Colonial Americans, 1677–1763* (Chapel Hill: University of North Carolina Press, 1986).

Long, J. C. *Lord Jeffery Amherst* (New York: Macmillan Co., 1933).

Morgan, Edmund S. *American Slavery American Freedom* (New York: W. W. Norton & Co. [1975]).

Pargellis, Stanley M. *Lord Loudoun in North America* (New Haven, Conn.: Yale University Press, 1933).

Richter, Daniel K. *The Ordeal of the Longhouse: The Peoples of the Iroquois League in the Era of European Colonization* (Chapel Hill: University of North Carolina Press, 1992).

Russell, Peter E. "Redcoats in the Wilderness: British Officers and Irregular Warfare in Europe and America, 1740 to 1760," *William and Mary Quarterly* (October 1978), 629–652.

Schutz, John A. *William Shirley: King's Governor of Massachusetts* (Chapel Hill: University of North Carolina Press, 1961).

Shea, William L. *The Virginia Militia in the Seventeenth Century* (Baton Rouge: Louisiana State University Press, 1983).

Shy, John. *A People Numerous and Armed* (New York: Oxford University Press, 1976).

Stacey, C. P. *Quebec 1759: The Siege and the Battle* (New York: Macmillan Co., 1959).

Titus, James. *The Old Dominion at War: Society, Politics, and Warfare in Late Colonial Virginia* (Columbia: University of South Carolina Press, 1991).

Vaughan, Alden T. *American Genesis: Captain John Smith and the Founding of Virginia* (Boston: Little, Brown & Co., 1975).

————. "Pequots and Puritans: The Causes of the War of 1637," *William and Mary Quarterly* (April 1964), 255–269.

Washburn, Wilcomb E. *The Governor and the Rebel: A History of Bacon's Rebellion in Virginia* (Chapel Hill: University of North Carolina Press, 1957).

Waugh, W. T. *James Wolfe: Man and Soldier* (Montreal: L. Carrier & Co., 1928).

Webster, J. Clarence. *The Journal of Jeffery Amherst: 1758 to 1763* (Toronto: Ryerson Press [1931]).

Willson, Beckles. *The Life and Letters of James Wolfe* (London: W. Heinemann, 1909).

2

THE WAR FOR AMERICAN INDEPENDENCE, 1775–1783: THE PEOPLE AT WAR

The Beginnings:
The Militia's War

Strategies for a
Revolutionary War

The Saratoga Campaign:
A Conventional Interlude

A Revolution Within a World
War: Relying on the People
in Arms

The Revolution Preserved:
Unconventional and
Conventional Warfare
in the South, 1780–1783

The War for American Independence was a complex, widespread, and destructive war. It was more than the struggle of thirteen North American colonies for independence from the British Empire, more even than a series of concurrent struggles within those colonies between supporters of the rebellion and of the British government. Once European states intervened on the side of the colonists, the War for American Independence spread throughout the world, from North America to the West Indies and Central America, to the English Channel and the Mediterranean Sea, and to South Africa, India, and the East Indies. In North America, where fighting took place in what would become twenty-seven of the new United States and three Canadian provinces, there were more than 1,500 engagements in eight years. Rebellious colonists, supported at times by their European allies, opposed forces loyal to the British crown—

regular soldiers and seamen, loyal colonists, and Indians—in fighting that claimed the lives of more than 25,000 Americans (0.9 percent of the population in 1780). Indeed, the War for American Independence remains after more than two centuries the second most deadly war per capita in the history of the United States.

Because the War for American Independence was a revolutionary war, it was far different from the limited wars of mid-eighteenth-century Europe. In America both sides understood from the beginning that they were fighting for the allegiance of a people and for the destruction or preservation of one state and the creation of another. Throughout the war, the British argued that they fought to protect loyal colonists from the tyranny of a few ambitious rebels. Thus they tried various strategies: intimidating the rebels with a show of force, combining force and persuasion to break the rebellion without alienating a majority of the colonists, and, eventually, enlisting the support of loyalists in a gradual and cumulative restoration of royal government. The rebels, conversely, had to defeat the British and control the loyalists without losing popular support or destroying the republican principles for which they fought. Hoping to win without having to create the kind of regular army that might deprive them of their liberties, they tried at first to rely on inspired citizen soldiers—unskilled militiamen—to defeat the British and gain a redress of their grievances. But those who had to lead American forces against the British to sustain the revolution and emerging claims to independence, soon saw that unskilled citizen soldiers were rarely a match for regulars. Because the American people remained apprehensive of their own Continental army and unwilling to support it adequately, American commanders had to pursue more evasive and delaying strategies and to rely more on militiamen than they wished—even after the Continental army became a skilled fighting force and France entered the war. Finally, because of their continued dependence on militiamen and partisans, American commanders learned to simplify marching and firing, to command more by persuasion and instruction than by coercion, and to integrate militiamen and regulars—occasionally even riflemen and musketeers—in effective tactical dispositions. By enlisting the support of the people and adopting simplified tactics, both sides in the War for American Independence were departing from the conventions of mid-eighteenth-century European warfare and anticipating changes that would appear more dramatically with the French Revolution.

The Beginnings: The Militia's War

At the beginning of the War for American Independence each side hoped to prevail with minimal force. The British government, assuming that the rebellion in its American colonies was the work of a few ambitious men and that its professional soldiers could easily disperse colonial militiamen, hoped to end the rebellion with little more than a show of force. Leaders of colonial resistance, conversely, believed that inspired patriot militia could successfully resist professional soldiers and persuade the British government to redress American grievances. It was not just that the colonists valued inspiration above discipline but also that they were unwilling to rely on long-serving soldiers to do their fighting, unwilling to create a standing army that might become as destructive of their liberties as any forces of the king. Thus at the beginning of the war, a small army of British regulars stood against American militia and short-term volunteers in circumstances that often favored the unskilled colonists.

From Lexington and Concord to Bunker Hill

In the winter of 1775, after more than a decade of quarreling with its American colonists over taxes and political rights, the British government decided to use force to sustain its authority in Massachusetts, the most disloyal of the colonies. The government ordered its commander-in-chief at Boston, General Thomas Gage, to break the spirit of rebellion by arresting leading colonists, confiscating military stores, and if necessary imposing martial law. Although Gage knew that the colonists had been preparing for months to meet force with force, he decided to assert British authority by sending 800 men to destroy a magazine at Concord, a village seventeen miles west of Boston.

This small force was to achieve far less than Gage had hoped. It marched on the night of April 18–19, exchanged fire early the next morning with seventy militiamen at Lexington, and proceeded to Concord to search for stores and to skirmish with other colonists. About noon the British began their march back to Boston, beset by increasing numbers of militiamen who attacked the flanks of their retiring column. So battered were the regulars by colonists converging on their line of march—by some 3,800 men from more than twenty-four Massachusetts towns—that the British might well have been destroyed had not a relief force of 1,000 men met them near Lexington and escorted them to Boston. Britain's first attempt at intimidating the colonists had clearly failed. Far from demonstrating the overwhelming superiority of British forces, the march to Concord had given the colonists a remarkably favorable opportunity to defeat professional soldiers, to use their inspired but undisciplined and uncoordinated militia with few of the risks that might have been expected in a formal eighteenth-century engagement. At a cost of ninety-five men killed, wounded, and missing (2.5 percent of their total) the colonists had inflicted 286 casualties on the British (16 percent).

Within two months the colonists created a second opportunity to fight on their own terms and to use their militia to their best advantage. News of Lexington and Concord had been received as a call to arms throughout the colonies. By mid-June there were 15,000 New England militia camped around Boston, a loosely organized army under General Artemas Ward of Massachusetts. These New England troops, short on artillery, gunpowder, food, and above all, training, were incapable of storming Boston, now held by about 6,500 regulars. But they were able on the night of June 16 to occupy and fortify positions on Charlestown Neck, which commanded Boston from the north, from across the Charles River. Gage could not ignore what the Americans had done. He had to find a way to force them from Charlestown Neck before they could place artillery there, making Boston untenable. He rejected as too hazardous a plan for trapping the Americans on Charlestown Neck, for putting his troops between the rebels on the Neck and the main body of their forces encamped at Cambridge. He decided instead to land his troops on the easternmost point of the Neck and by advancing to the west drive the rebels back to the mainland. In making this decision, he committed his men to attacking a well-entrenched enemy— to doing precisely what would most likely allow the undisciplined colonists to succeed against his men.

In carrying out Gage's plan, the British did try to avoid a frontal assault on the American works. Major General William Howe, commander of the troops sent to drive the Americans from Charlestown Neck, planned

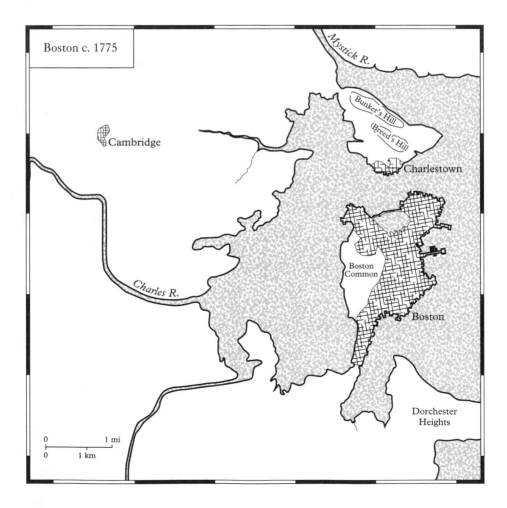

Boston c. 1775

an oblique attack; that is, he planned to land on the east end of the Neck and move against the American lines in echelon, his best troops somewhat advanced on his right flank (along the Mystick River which bounded the Neck on the north) and the remainder, slightly refused, in his center and on his left flank (opposite Breed's Hill, where most of the Americans were dug in). His elite light infantry would attempt to break through the rebel left and take the rest of their forces in flank and rear before the British center and left became heavily engaged. He delayed his attack until mid-afternoon, when he had assembled more than 2,000 men on Charlestown Neck. Then, with his field artillery pushed forward and his infantry in three ranks, he began the attack.

It soon became apparent that Howe's light infantry would be unable to break through the American left on the Mystick shore and that his artillery was ineffective against fieldworks. He might well have reconsidered his plan, but he allowed his attack to continue, to degenerate into a costly frontal assault. His infantry continued to advance across open rising ground toward the center of the American lines. British discipline was no match for the massed fire of the colonists secure in their earthworks. Twice Howe and his men went forward against Breed's Hill; twice they failed. A third bayonet attack succeeded only because Howe had received 400 fresh troops and because the Americans had run out of ammunition and were not properly supported by additional American troops gathered to the west on Bunker's Hill. This engagement, known as the Battle of Bunker Hill, was a nominal British victory. The British did succeed in driving the Americans from Charlestown Neck. Yet they did so at such a cost (the British lost 1,054 killed and wounded or 44 percent of the 2,400 men engaged; the Americans, 441 or 29 percent of their 1,500) as to fail to achieve their strategic purpose. Bunker Hill clearly did not serve to intimidate the rebels, and it left British commanders wary of the costly battles that many would think necessary to end the war quickly and decisively.

Preparing for a Wider War, June 1775 to July 1776

For at least nine months after the Battle of Bunker Hill neither side was able to do more than skirmish with the other. Each knew that it would have to build a larger army and prepare for a more difficult war. However successful the Americans had been relying on untrained militia at Lexington and Concord and Bunker Hill, they realized they would need more and better troops to expel the British from Boston and protect other parts of America. They were not yet ready to consider creating a standing army—one of long-serving professional soldiers who might become as destructive of American liberties as British regulars were seen to be. Americans still wanted to rely on an army of volunteers, serving for six months or a year. Such short-term volunteers would not acquire the discipline and training of regulars. But with simplified tactics and with courage inspired by a religious faith and a sense of America's destiny, they would be able to defeat the British regulars; and they

George Washington commanded the Continental army throughout the War for American Independence. His inspired leadership was essential to preserving the army and winning the independence of the new nation.

would not jeopardize American liberties. The British, for their part, knew that intimidation had failed and that they would need much larger regular forces to destroy the rebel armies, overturn congresses and committees, and restore royal government to North America. They knew as well that the British army had no such forces and that they would have either to expand the army—a costly and lengthy process—or hire foreign troops. They decided to hire foreigners, thereby committing themselves to a measure that would also take time and that would have its own political and military costs.

Even before the Battle of Bunker Hill, the Continental Congress had begun to support and control the militiamen assembled around Boston. As important as any decision that Congress made toward the creation of a Continental army—an army to defend the interests of the thirteen colonies against the British government—was its selection of George Washington as commander-in-chief. Congress saw in Washington—a tall, spare, and impressive man of forty-three—an experienced soldier, a moderate but firm opponent of British taxation, a prominent Virginian who could help bind the

South to New England, and above all, a person whom they could entrust with power. He was, as Congress anticipated, a remarkably good choice. During the Seven Years' War he had commanded militiamen on the frontiers of Virginia, learning not only how to lead his countrymen in battle and to maintain their morale during periods of inactivity but also how to deal with public officials who regularly neglected their soldiers. Although he rose to command Virginia forces and emerged from the war with his reputation intact, Washington failed to satisfy his ambition for military fame and a regular commission in the British army. In the ensuing years of peace he did find increasing contentment as a respected Virginia landowner—as a justice of the peace, vestryman, and member of the House of Burgesses. By 1770 he was also a staunch opponent of British taxation and in 1774–1775 was one of seven Virginia representatives in the Continental Congress. He impressed all who met him in Philadelphia as a man who had the energy, experience, and presence to create an army out of enthusiastic and unruly citizens; the good judgment to preserve that army; and the commitment to republican ideals as well as the control of his own ambitions to keep himself and his army subordinate to the will of Congress.

Washington assumed command of the Continental army at Cambridge, Massachusetts, on July 2, 1775. During the following year he devoted his energies to establishing an effective army, preserving that army against expiring enlistments, and resisting demands that he attack the British before his men were prepared for battle. He began by trying to bring some order and discipline to the 14,000 men camped around Boston: introducing distinctions between officers and men; organizing the army into regiments, brigades, and divisions; and attempting—with little success at first—to provide uniforms for men from different colonies. Although discipline improved, Washington was unable during the summer and fall of 1775 to get enough gunpowder and artillery to attack Boston. Congress, the American people, and even the army became impatient with his refusal to act—to do more than skirmish with the British and cut off their supplies of food and fuel. By December he was struggling to keep even a semblance of an army at Boston. Most enlistments expired on December 31, and Washington found it nearly impossible to persuade men to reenlist while Congress was attempting to create truly continental units (the rank and file did not like serving under officers from other colonies) and while troops at Boston were suffering from shortages of fuel and clothing as well as from inactivity. Not until late February 1776 did Washington have the men, ammunition, and artillery to consider attacking Boston. Even then his officers rejected an assault across the frozen bay, preferring instead to seize Dorchester Heights in hopes of provoking another Bunker Hill. When his troops did succeed in occupying Dorchester Heights, in placing their artillery within range of most of Boston and its harbor, the British decided to give up the town rather than risk a frontal assault on American earthworks. On March 17 the British sailed for Halifax to prepare for a summer offensive against New York. Washington and the Continental army went south to face sterner tests of their military skills.

Strategies for a Revolutionary War

In the campaign of 1776 both sides developed strategies for the unconventional purpose of winning the support of the people. Although the British government was more interested in breaking the rebellion than in cultivating the good will of the colonists, the British commanders-in-chief had different priorities: they shaped their strategies to promote a negotiated settlement and a lasting restoration of the British Empire. Thus they concentrated throughout 1776 on recovering territory so as to minimize casualties, create the impression of British invincibility, and encourage the colonists to accept royal government. Washington too shaped his strategy to gain and keep the support of the American people, to sustain the rebellion even at the risk of losing his army. Thus he defended the middle colonies against greatly superior British forces and used his disintegrating army to attack enemy outposts.

Plans and Preparations for 1776

The British had been forced from Boston sooner than they wished. But they had long intended to begin the restoration of royal government at New York, using it as a base from which to conquer New England and destroy the Continental army. Since news of Bunker Hill reached England in the summer of 1775, the government had intended to shift the war from New England to the middle colonies, from the most disloyal to some of the more loyal of the American colonies. It also agreed to increase its forces significantly and to appoint General William Howe as commander-in-chief. Although Howe received permission in early October to leave Boston, he decided to wait until spring when he would have reinforcements and enough transports to move his army. While he waited—at Boston and then at Halifax—he and the ministry agreed on a plan for ending the rebellion. He would first capture New York City, occupy the Hudson River Valley, take Rhode Island, and send detachments to ravage the coasts from New York to Maine. Then he would push north along the Hudson to join with forces from Canada in completing the encirclement of New England and in attacking the frontiers of Massachusetts. In carrying out these plans, Howe also hoped to lure the Continental army into a decisive battle, which he now thought "the most effectual Means to terminate this expensive War."

Yet before opening the campaign of 1776 at New York, Howe modified his plans. He reached New York from Nova Scotia on June 25, set up his headquarters on Staten Island, and began waiting for the reinforcements needed to attack the rebels entrenched around New York City—on Manhattan, Long Island, and the New Jersey side of the Hudson River. Since it took seven weeks for these reinforcements to straggle in, Howe had many opportunities to reconnoiter American positions and discuss his plans for ending the rebellion with his older brother, Admiral Richard Lord Howe, who arrived on July 12 to command the British navy in American waters. Both

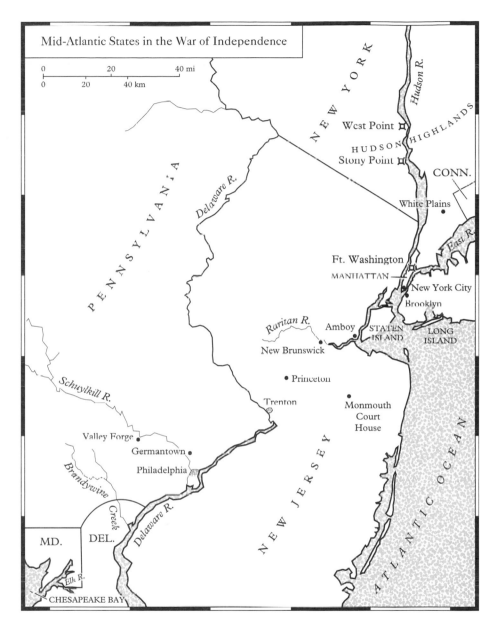

Mid-Atlantic States in the War of Independence

0   20   40 mi
0   20   40 km

NEW YORK

Hudson R.

West Point

HUDSON HIGHLANDS

Stony Point

CONN.

White Plains

PENNSYLVANIA

Delaware R.

East R.

Ft. Washington

MANHATTAN

New York City

Brooklyn

Raritan R.   Amboy   STATEN ISLAND   LONG ISLAND

New Brunswick

Schuylkill R.

Princeton

Trenton

Monmouth Court House

Valley Forge

Germantown

ATLANTIC OCEAN

Philadelphia

NEW JERSEY

Brandywine Creek

Delaware R.

MD.   DEL.

Elk R.

CHESAPEAKE BAY

ATLANTIC

Howes were distinguished officers; both had served in North America during
the Seven Years' War; and both, having strong personal ties with the colonies,
favored a negotiated settlement of Anglo-American differences. Although
they had persuaded the British government to name them peace commissioners as well as commanders-in-chief, they had been unable to get authority to conduct meaningful negotiations, to do more than discuss grievances
after the colonies had surrendered. Even so, Lord Howe was determined to
try to negotiate or, at least, to avoid the kind of fighting that would permanently alienate the colonists. Failing in his initial efforts to open negotiations

(he arrived just after the colonies had declared their independence), he did persuade his brother to modify his strategy. By mid-August General Howe had put aside his hopes of destroying the Continental army in a decisive battle and was concentrating instead on ending the rebellion through a gradual recovery of territory. This new plan promised to create the impression of British invincibility without inflicting heavy casualties on either side—just the use of force that the Howes hoped would encourage the colonists to accept a negotiated settlement and that would spare the British the higher risks and heavier losses of a general engagement.

Like the Howes, George Washington and his generals shaped their strategy to suit political as well as military considerations. Washington felt obligated to defend New York City because Congress and the American people expected him to and because he thought American morale would suffer if he did not. Washington also believed that he should defend New York City to deny the British an ice-free port and to protect American communications along and across the Hudson River, to keep open the main inland routes between the middle colonies and New England. Yet to defend New York City, which occupied the southern tip of Manhattan at the confluence of the Hudson and East rivers, he would have to risk losing his army; he would have to divide his forces among Manhattan, Long Island, and New Jersey in the face of a superior British fleet and army. Thus he worked from mid-April to late August preparing to risk his army defending what many thought indefensible. Assuming the British would strike first on Manhattan, he took particular care in fortifying New York City. He also fortified Brooklyn Heights, which lay across the East River from the city, and the mouths of the Hudson and East rivers. Should the British succeed in taking Brooklyn and placing artillery there, they could make the city untenable; or should they send transports up either the Hudson or East River and land troops on upper Manhattan, they might well capture both the city and its garrison. By August 1776 Washington had over 120 guns and 28,000 men in these separate and vulnerable posts.

Washington's army was remarkably similar in size, composition, organization, and doctrine to the one that was assembling under General Howe. Unlike European armies of the day, both armies at New York in 1776 had been shaped to suit North America and the peculiarities of a revolutionary war. The 28,000 American and 24,000 British troops at New York in August 1776 were primarily infantrymen supported by detachments of light artillery and a few engineers. The basic unit in each army was the infantry regiment (established at 608 men for the Continental army and 477 for the British); and the basic weapons were muskets, bayonets, and light field guns. Because Americans had served with the British in the Seven Years' War and had studied their manuals, books, and histories, both armies intended to fight in much the same way. Americans would use a simplified version of British drill and manual of arms, and both armies would employ what were by European standards relatively simple tactics. Without cavalry to complicate their forces, commanders on both sides would dispense with combined-arms warfare and rely instead on either two or three ranks of infantry supported by light field guns to generate firepower and on columns to gain speed and shock. Neither army had a clear strategic doctrine. Anglo-Americans had no clear preference between the warfare of Saxe and of Frederick the Great—between sieges, skirmishing, and maneuvers on the one hand and decisive engagements on the other. Moreover, commanders in both armies knew that the War for American Independence required strategies that would serve a very unconventional purpose, strategies that would gain the support of the people.

Yet for all the similarities between the opposing forces, the British were much better prepared for war than the Americans. It was not just that the British had the close support of a powerful fleet—30 warships, 400 transports, and thousands of skilled seamen—but especially that the British army was a more experienced, better led, more thoroughly disciplined and trained, and more unified fighting force than the American. British senior officers had seen more of war and had had more opportunities to prove their tactical skills than their American counterparts. Howe knew what his generals had done while commanding regiments in the Seven Years' War; Washington was just beginning to appraise generals imposed on him by Congress and a variety of state governments. Similarly, the British common soldier of 1776 was on average thirty years old with ten years of service in his regiment; the American, twenty years old with less than a year's service. American units varied greatly in quality—from the best disciplined of the Continental and state forces to the rawest militia. Yet even the best of the American troops in 1776 seemed no more than innocent boys by comparison with the regulars of George III.

The Battle of Long Island: Tactics Serving Strategy

By late August 1776 the Howes were at last prepared to use force to end the rebellion. General Howe clearly understood how vulnerable the Americans were at New York, but he rejected a proposal for landing his army on the northern end of Manhattan to trap and destroy the Continental army in New York City. He preferred instead to drive the Americans from the city with as little bloodshed as possible, creating the impression of British invincibility and encouraging the colonists to put down their arms and accept a negotiated settlement. He would shift his army from Staten Island to Long Island, take Brooklyn Heights by siege or intimidation, place his own artillery there, and force Washington to give up New York. He did not seek or expect a general engagement on Long Island. Even after putting 15,000 troops ashore at Gravesend on August 22, and after finding that the Americans were prepared to defend the Heights of Guana which lay across all roads leading from Gravesend to Brooklyn, Howe still hoped to avoid a destructive battle. He ordered another 5,000 men to join him on Long Island and spent five days probing American positions, looking for a way to approach Brooklyn without having to attack the Americans on the densely wooded slopes of the Heights of Guana or at any of the well-defended passes near New York Bay. Finally, he decided to try to turn the extreme left flank of the American army. He would lead 10,000 of his men on a night's march

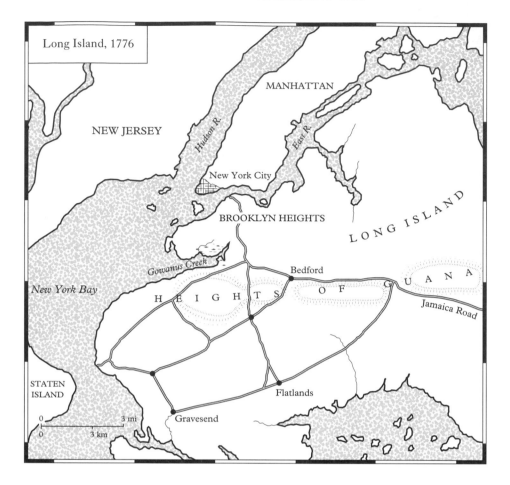

that would take them six miles east of New York Bay, through the Heights of Guana on the Jamaica Road, and into the rear of the American defenders. Thus Howe's efforts to take New York without serious fighting and to avoid a frontal assault on the Heights precipitated the first general engagement of the Revolutionary War.

The British won the ensuing Battle of Long Island because they performed well and because chance, numbers, and, above all, inexperience worked against the Americans. Washington decided to defend the Heights of Guana in hopes of delaying or even defeating the British. He knew he could not hold Brooklyn long against a regular siege; and the Heights, whose overgrown slopes rose from forty to eighty feet above the Long Island plain, offered many strong defensive positions. Yet as the Heights stretched some ten miles to the east of New York Bay, it was naive of Washington to think he could hold such an extensive position with no more than the 3,500 men he deployed there on August 26 (he had another 4,000 at Brooklyn). He was able to put respectable forces at the three passes nearest New York Bay, and he could be fairly confident that Howe would not try to advance through the intervening woods. But he risked the security of his left flank—indeed the safety of all his forces on the Heights of Guana—on five young and inexperienced officers sent to watch the Jamaica Road. Those officers, unwary of Howe's patrols, were captured; and Howe was then able to lead 10,000 men, undetected, through the Jamaica pass at dawn on August 27. Once clear of the pass, Howe rested and fed his men before advancing against the rear of the American units defending the Heights. By 10:00 A.M. his remaining forces had begun diversionary attacks on the front of those same American units. Caught as they were between converging and superior British forces, most Americans surrendered or fled toward Brooklyn. By two in the afternoon the battle had ended. Howe had succeeded in turning the rebels from strong positions without heavy losses (the British suffered 370 casualties, or 1.9 percent of those engaged; the Americans, 1,000, or 28.6 percent). If Howe did not allow his men to exploit their victory—to pursue the Americans into their works at Brooklyn—it was because he was unwilling to risk further losses when he could expect to capture by siege all who remained on Long Island.

That the Battle of Long Island was not more decisive, that it did not destroy more of the Continental army, was in part the result of Howe's intentions; but it was also the result of the nature of the fighting on August 27 and of Washington's subsequent actions and good luck. The north slope of the Heights of Guana with its woods, hedges, small cultivated fields, narrow roads, and rolling terrain clearly favored the Americans, providing cover for men on the defense or in flight and inhibiting those who were attacking or pursuing. Moreover, Howe's insistence that his men use their bayonets to drive the enemy from this difficult country had the effect of tiring and disordering soldiers who had marched all night and who had trouble keeping up with their own units to say nothing of overtaking the fleeing rebels. Finally, because British forces were converging, they had to attack with some caution, taking care not to engage their own men or to mistake Americans for their own; and some Americans did fight well enough to cover the retreat of their comrades. These circumstances as well as Howe's reluctance to press the rebels help to explain why the fighting on August 27 was not more decisive. But it took Howe's continuing interest in conciliation and Washington's considerable leadership and good luck to keep the Americans who remained at Brooklyn on August 28 from becoming prisoners.

Immediately after the battle Howe concentrated on opening a siege of Brooklyn Heights; he took no special measures to prevent the defenders from evacuating their works. Washington at first sent reinforcements to bolster the morale of the garrison at Brooklyn. But seeing that his men were dejected by their defeat and that rain on August 28 and 29 had spoiled their arms and ammunition, he decided to give up Brooklyn to save his army. On the night of August 29–30, he carried out a very skillful and courageous retreat favored by fair winds and a thick morning fog. The British took only three of the nearly 10,000 Americans who had held Brooklyn in the days after the battle.

From Manhattan to Trenton and Princeton: Strategies of Persuasion

Although capturing Long Island did not end the American rebellion, the Howes persisted through the late summer and autumn of 1776 in their strategy of recovering territory to encourage a negotiated peace. Congress did agree after the Battle of Long Island to send representatives to a peace conference with Lord Howe, but when Howe acknowledged that he could offer no concessions until the colonies had surrendered, the conference collapsed. The Howes were disappointed but did not alter their strategy. Rejecting proposals and ignoring opportunities for trapping the Continental army on Manhattan, they executed a series of turning movements, through the East River and Long Island Sound, that forced Washington to abandon New York City and all of Manhattan except Fort Washington at its northern end. In November, after driving the Continental army beyond White Plains, Howe turned south to capture Fort Washington, invade New Jersey, and send an expedition to take Rhode Island. Although he won no decisive battles, his success in limited engagements and in evicting the Americans from New York, New Jersey, and Rhode Island created such an impression of British invincibility, that many Americans considered a reconciliation with the crown. Lord Howe's proclamation of November 30, offering pardon to anyone who within sixty days would swear to obey the king and to remain at peace, attracted some 5,000 subscribers in New York and New Jersey. By mid-December when General Howe sent his troops into winter quarters in villages across New Jersey and at New York City and Newport, the Continental army and the rebellion seemed to be disintegrating. The Howes had missed opportunities for trapping and destroying American forces—the best opportunities that the British would have in the Revolutionary War—yet by mid-December the Howes' strategy of restoring royal government with a minimum of bloodshed and risk seemed close to success.

Washington, thoroughly discouraged by the failure of his army to stand against regulars and by the impending expiration of enlistments for 1776, was considering desperate measures. Congress had tried to help improve the discipline and training of the Continental army, authorizing harsher punishments as well as enlistments for the duration of the war. But these measures, taken in late summer, had as yet done little to make Continentals a match for regulars. By mid-December, defeats and expiring enlistments were threatening to destroy the army and the rebellion. In desperation, Washington decided to act before all his troops had gone home, to attack British outposts in New Jersey. Because the British had scattered their army in small garrisons from the Raritan to the Delaware, Washington hoped he would be able to use surprise and a rapid concentration of force to offset the relative weakness of his troops—to gain a superiority of numbers and firepower that would give his citizen soldiers a chance to defeat Howe's professionals, push them back from the Delaware, and restore American morale.

Although his ensuing attack on the Hessian garrison at Trenton did not go according to plan, Washington was able to create circumstances that clearly favored his men. About dusk on December 25, he led 2,400 men with eighteen cannon across the Delaware some nine miles northwest of Trenton. Two other American detachments were to take part in a complicated attack next morning on the 1,400-man Hessian garrison. Although the weather was so severe that it prevented the other American detachments from crossing the Delaware and kept Washington from reaching Trenton by dawn, he did manage to attack the garrison simultaneously from two sides about 7:45 A.M. The Hessian commander had posted pickets on the roads leading to Trenton, and those pickets did provide a few minutes' warning of the attack. But the Hessians had not taken care to fortify the town or to celebrate Christmas with moderation. By the time they turned out and formed lines of battle across the principal streets, by the time their six field pieces were in action, the town was filled with Americans. The Americans had the advantage of surprise, numbers, and artillery; and when the battle degenerated into a house-to-house struggle, the Americans were able to use initiative and inspiration to overcome their opponents' superior training and discipline. They soon swept the streets and broke Hessian resistance. By 9:00 A.M., Washington's desperate effort had been repaid with a most important victory. At a cost of four men wounded, the Americans had captured 948 Hessians and killed or wounded another 114. A week later Washington again surprised the British, slipping away from 5,500 regulars who threatened to crush his men against the Delaware and defeating the enemy's garrison at Princeton. These victories not only restored Americans' confidence in Washington, the Continental army, and the rebellion but also spoiled the Howes' hopes for a negotiated restoration of royal government. The British now withdrew from all of New Jersey except New Brunswick and Amboy on the Raritan River.

The Saratoga Campaign: A Conventional Interlude

Washington's victories at Trenton and Princeton disrupted British and American planning for 1777 and helped make a conventional campaign along the Hudson River unusually decisive. Howe, stung by defeats in New Jersey, became preoccupied with invading Pennsylvania. That preoccupation and his continued interest in promoting a negotiated peace not only shaped what Washington would do in 1777 but also left another British army to advance south from Canada, virtually unsupported from New York. The second British army under General John Burgoyne would be conducted in a cautiously conventional way. Much as Saxe had sought to recover the Low Countries in the War of the Austrian Succession, Burgoyne sought to extinguish the rebellion: he would advance along the waterways from Canada to New York, relying on a heavy siege train to overcome American fortifications, avoiding destructive battles, and gaining possession of the principal overland routes across the Hudson so as to isolate and conquer New England. Burgoyne's strategy was not designed to conciliate the colonists, merely to end their resistance. But Burgoyne had the misfortune of being unsupported and of eliciting a cautiously conventional strategic response. The Americans blocked his line of advance, cut off his supplies, and waited for shortages to bring a most decisive end to the campaign.

The Effects of Trenton and Princeton

British failures at the end of 1776 blighted their ensuing campaign. General Howe, who felt acutely responsible for the strategy that had led to defeats at Trenton and Princeton, was eager to show that he had been justified in extending his posts to the Delaware, that the people of Pennsylvania were, as he had assumed, loyal to the crown, and that his efforts toward conciliation were not illusory. He planned, therefore, to invade Pennsylvania in 1777. He would concentrate on recovering territory, giving loyalists a chance to assert themselves and encouraging rebels to accept a restoration of royal government. Although he knew that he would be expected to cooperate with British forces advancing south across Lake Champlain from Canada, he refused to do more to support that offensive than provide a detachment on the lower Hudson—possibly to open the Highlands and act in favor of the Canadian army. But if he refused to be diverted from an invasion of Pennsylvania and if he seemed committed to a strategy of recovering territory so as to encourage a negotiated peace, he also talked repeatedly of needing a decisive victory over the Continental army to end the rebellion.

Just as Howe's plans for 1777 were contradictory, so too was his conduct of the campaign. He remained committed to an invasion of Pennsylvania, but he seemed incapable of acting promptly or of deciding clearly whether destroying the Continental army or recovering territory would best complement his hopes for peace. He stayed in winter quarters through much of the spring, giving a variety of reasons for delaying the opening of the campaign and rejecting all criticisms of his plan for going to Pennsylvania by sea. Yet before he embarked, he spent the last half of June trying without success to lure Washington into a decisive battle in New Jersey. He then reverted to a strategy of recovering territory. Although remaining on the Hudson and cooperating with British forces from Canada would have pleased the ministry and might also have forced Washington into a general engagement, Howe embarked for Pennsylvania in late July. His subsequent decision to proceed by way of the Chesapeake Bay, rather than by the Delaware River, seemed to confirm his renewed preference for recovering territory. But once ashore in Pennsylvania—and discovering that the colonists were not as loyal as he had hoped and that Washington would fight for Philadelphia—Howe again sought a decisive battle. He defeated Washington at Brandywine Creek on September 11, but after failing to exploit his victory, he devoted most of the autumn to taking and securing Philadelphia. Only briefly in December did he seek another battle.

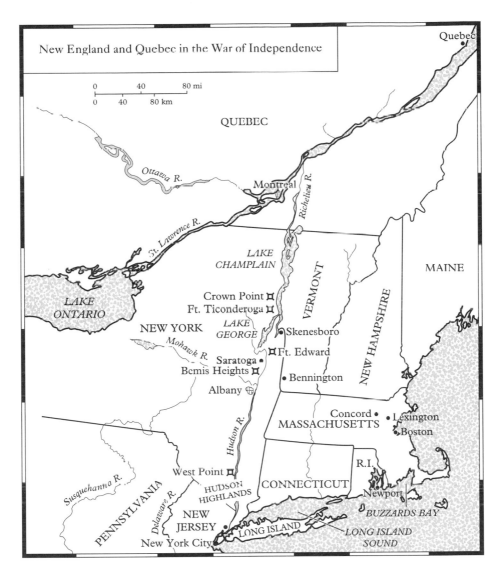

New England and Quebec in the War of Independence

Howe's response to Trenton and Princeton not only blighted his own performance in 1777 but also jeopardized another British army, the army ordered south from Canada under General John Burgoyne. Like Howe, Burgoyne had distinguished himself as a regimental commander in the Seven Years' War and had been sent to Boston in 1775. But when Howe took the army from Boston to New York in 1776, Burgoyne went to Canada to serve as second-in-command to General Guy Carleton. Carleton, who had been expected to proceed across Lake Champlain to join Howe along the Hudson, had been so delayed by shortages and by building boats to clear the lake of rebels that he got no farther than Crown Point in 1776. During the following winter when Burgoyne went to England to discuss plans for

1777, he also managed to blame Carleton for delays in 1776 and to suggest that he, Burgoyne, had the energy needed to force his way across Lake Champlain in time to join Howe for a decisive attack on the frontiers of New England in 1777. King George III and his ministers were persuaded; they ordered Carleton to send Burgoyne with an army of 7,000 regulars supported by Canadians and Indians across Lake Champlain to Albany—to join Howe and to follow his instructions for the remainder of the campaign of 1777. The ministry also told Carleton to send a second force of 675 regulars with Canadians and Indians to join Howe via Lake Ontario, the Mohawk River, and the Hudson. But the ministry, which had already approved Howe's plans for going to Pennsylvania by sea, never did order Howe to cooperate with Burgoyne. It merely sent Howe a copy of its orders to Carleton and told Carleton and Burgoyne to write to Howe for instructions. So it was that the ministry gave Howe the latitude to indulge his preoccupation with Pennsylvania, to destroy any prospect for cooperation between British armies in 1777, and to make Burgoyne's determination to force his way to Albany truly dangerous.

Unlike the British, the Americans clearly benefited from their victories at Trenton and Princeton. But if those victories restored confidence in the Continental army and the revolution, they did not bring Washington the large number of long-term recruits he needed for the campaign of 1777. Immediately after Princeton, Washington was able to use the army and local militia to regain control of New Jersey, to force Americans who had accepted the Howes' offer of pardon to renounce their oaths of allegiance to the king, and to keep the British from drawing food and fodder from the countryside. Whatever their weaknesses in a formal engagement, Continentals and militiamen were quite successful during the winter and spring of 1777 in skirmishing with British foraging parties, inflicting casualties and forcing the British to depend primarily on the British Isles for their supplies. But victories at Trenton and Princeton and success against foragers did not fill the ranks of the Continental army. Americans, knowing that many soldiers had died of illness in 1776 and that bounties for enlistments would probably increase with the demand for men, were reluctant to volunteer. Congress voted to raise an army of 75,760 in 1777; and state and local governments resorted to a variety of measures to fill their quotas: offering bounties in money and land, adopting conscription, and allowing wealthy citizens to hire substitutes. But these measures raised no more than a third of the men Congress wanted, and without large numbers of men serving for three years or for the duration of the war, Washington could not build an effective army. Not until 1778 would he have the substantial training of long-serving men to create a dependable army.

Notwithstanding his difficulties in building an army, Washington's victories at Trenton and Princeton had so raised American expectations of the army as to force him toward a more aggressive strategy than he thought wise. During the winter and spring of 1777, he and his principal aides explained repeatedly to Congress that the Continental army should avoid a general engagement, that it should concentrate instead on controlling loyalists and preventing the British from getting supplies from America. When members of Congress deplored this strategy and encouraged Washington to attack British posts in New Jersey, he replied that he did not have enough disciplined troops to risk an attack; and when in late June 1777 the British tried to draw him into battle, he refused. Not until Howe threatened Philadelphia, the largest city in the United States and an important source of supplies for the Continental army, did he feel compelled to fight to satisfy Congress and preserve American morale. In September he blocked Howe's advance on the city and suffered a nearly disastrous defeat at the Battle of Brandywine. In October, after the city had fallen, he tried to surprise the British camp at Germantown, but his plan was too complicated and the enemy too vigilant for his inexperienced men. Thus Washington was pressed to undertake what he considered imprudent. Those American commanders who opposed the British advancing from Canada were farther from Congress and somewhat freer than Washington to remain on the defensive—to employ the cautious strategy needed to give inexperienced troops a chance to defeat a regular British army.

Toward Saratoga

John Burgoyne reached Quebec on May 6, 1777, to take command of the army that he was to lead from Quebec to Albany. Whatever the Americans might do to resist him on Lake Champlain or along the upper Hudson, Burgoyne knew that he faced a formidable problem in logistics. He proposed to move an army of nearly 9,000 men across more than 350 miles of rivers, lakes, and sparsely settled wilderness. Transporting, feeding, and supplying such a large force in the wilderness and maintaining an ever-lengthening line of communications with Quebec would consume a considerable part of his force. What made his task especially difficult was his insistence on an unusually large artillery and baggage train. The excess baggage was no more than an indulgence to his officers; the 138 guns were an expression of his determination to use firepower rather than men to drive Americans from their entrenchments, for Burgoyne had no intention of repeating the slaughter he had seen at Bunker Hill. Preparing transportation for this heavily equipped force delayed his departure from Quebec for more than a month. He did not embark on Lake Champlain until the third week in June or reach Crown Point (260 miles from Quebec) until July 1. Although he then moved forward rapidly to drive the Americans from Fort Ticonderoga and to reach Skenesboro at the head of Lake Champlain on July 9, he delayed two weeks at Skenesboro while assembling the horses, carts, and artillery he thought necessary to advance the next twenty miles overland to the Hudson. This delay allowed the rebels to regroup and place so many felled trees, broken bridges, and boulders in his way that he did not reach the Hudson at Fort Edward until July 29.

Once on the Hudson, Burgoyne was less than fifty miles from Albany, but he was also more than three hundred from Quebec, his primary source of supply. To go farther, to cross to the west bank of the Hudson and proceed to Albany, would mean giving up communications with Canada. He decided, therefore, to delay his advance until he had gathered the supplies and transportation needed to sustain his march to Albany. That delay would be far longer and more costly than he expected. He not only brought forward food, forage, ammunition, and heavy artillery from Canada by way of Lake Champlain and Lake George but also sent a detachment of 800 men under Lieutenant Colonel Friedrich Baum to collect horses, wagons, cattle, and provisions from a rebel magazine at Bennington, Vermont, some thirty-five miles southeast of Fort Edward. Baum set out on August 11, met resistance and asked for help on August 14, but was overwhelmed two days later at Bennington before help could arrive. Altogether, Baum and the 642 men sent to relieve him lost nearly 1,000 men killed, wounded, and captured in two fierce engagements with 2,000 New Hampshire and Vermont militiamen. (The Americans lost only 70 killed and wounded or 3.5 percent.)

Burgoyne now knew that Howe had embarked for Pennsylvania in late July and could not be expected at Albany. He also knew his army had been reduced to about 5,500 men. He might still have retired safely to Ticonderoga, yet having boasted that he would force his way to Albany and having been ordered to do so by Carleton and Howe, he decided to continue his advance to the south as soon as he had accumulated enough supplies to sustain his army for twenty-five days. On September 13, nearly seven weeks after reaching the Hudson, he left Fort Edward for Albany. Two days later, he crossed to the west bank of the Hudson, giving up his communications with Canada.

Once on the west bank, Burgoyne advanced cautiously. He kept to the main road along the river which gave him access to his supply boats. After three days and only six miles of marching, he learned that an American army was blocking his way to Albany, entrenched across the river road little more than five miles south at a place called Bemis Heights. The American army was at least as numerous as his own and was well dug in on rising ground behind a stream, its right flank on the Hudson and its left extending nearly a mile to the west of the river. Burgoyne was determined to force his way to Albany; he was equally determined to do so without sacrificing his army in a frontal assault on American lines. He decided, therefore, to advance toward the left flank of the American lines to see whether he might turn their position at Bemis Heights or occupy high ground that commanded that position from the west. He organized his army in three divisions: one of 1,100 men under General Riedesel to create a diversion by advancing close along the Hudson, a second of 1,100 under his own command to move against the center and left of the American line, and a third of 2,200 under General Fraser to pass to the west of the enemy works. On September 18 he moved his whole army to within two miles of Bemis Heights. At 10 A.M. the next day his three divisions advanced against the rebels.

The rebels had been preparing their works on Bemis Heights for more than a week before Burgoyne advanced to attack on September 19. They were well aware of his approach that morning, yet they had not agreed on how to meet his attack. Horatio Gates, commander of the northern army, had served as an officer in the British army for twenty-four years before resigning his commission in 1769. He then moved to Virginia, became an ardent patriot, and was appointed a brigadier general in the Continental army in 1775. For all his service in the mid-century wars, Gates was far better at organizing and training soldiers than at leading them in combat. He would have preferred to keep his relatively inexperienced men in their works on Bemis Heights and await Burgoyne's attack. His ambitious and aggressive second, Benedict Arnold, thought those inexperienced men would be more effective if they fought in the woods in front of their works where trees would give them cover and disrupt British linear formations, depriving the British of their advantages in disciplined use of muskets and bayonets. Arnold may also have believed that by advancing he would be able to keep the British from turning the American left flank. If the Americans did fight in front of their fortifications and were defeated, Arnold argued, they might at least fall back on their lines. If they awaited an attack at Bemis Heights and were then defeated, they would probably not be able to keep the British from reaching Albany.

Battles of Freeman's Farm and Bemis Heights,
September 19 and October 7, 1777

Freeman's Farm

Kama Kill

British Lines

Barber Wheatfield

Mill Creek

American Lines

BEMIS HEIGHTS

0   0.5   1 mi

0   0.5   1 km

Hudson R.

The Battles of Freeman's Farm and Bemis Heights

These conflicting ideas shaped the ensuing Battle of Freeman's Farm. Gates, commanding the right wing of his army, remained on Bemis Heights to await the British attack. He allowed his half of the army to be almost completely immobilized by General Riedesel's diversionary advance along the Hudson. Gates authorized his left wing to move forward from its lines to meet the British advance. Thus the Battle of Freeman's Farm began in the woods about a mile north of the American left flank when, shortly after noon on September 19, American riflemen encountered a picket from the right of Burgoyne's army. The Americans routed the picket, became disordered while pursuing, and were in turn routed by another British unit. Arnold, commanding on the left, then brought up regiments of Continentals to support the riflemen and became engaged in heavy fighting with the center of the British army around Freeman's Farm. Throughout the afternoon, the battle swept back and forth across the twenty acres of cleared land south of Freeman's house, the Americans relying on combinations of rifle and musket fire, the British on muskets, light artillery, and bayonets. Although Gates refused to support Arnold with more than a brigade, Arnold might well have destroyed the center of the British army had not Riedesel sent artillery and infantry to attack Arnold's right flank and force him to withdraw. The British held the battlefield. But the Battle of Freeman's Farm was an American victory. At a cost of 319 killed, wounded, and captured, the Americans had inflicted 600 casualties on the British and stopped their march to Albany.

For eighteen days after the Battle of Freeman's Farm the opposing armies remained where they had been when the fighting ended. For a brief time Burgoyne considered renewing his attack. But on the morning of September 21 he received a dispatch from Sir Henry Clinton, commander of British forces at New York City, saying that Clinton would support Burgoyne's offensive by attacking American fortresses in the Highlands of the Hudson on September 22. Encouraged by this news, Burgoyne decided to entrench the ground he held and defer any action until Clinton's thrust up the Hudson had had time to draw American forces from Bemis Heights. Gates, unaware of Clinton, was content to remain on the defensive, improving his lines at Bemis Heights, fortifying the high ground that commanded those lines from the west, and waiting for Burgoyne's army to deteriorate. He knew that the British had provisions for only four weeks and that skirmishing would sap their ammunition and morale, eventually forcing Burgoyne either to attack at a disadvantage or retreat. Moreover, Gates's army was growing stronger. Although most of his reinforcements were unskilled militiamen, by early October he had 11,000 men, well entrenched and supplied, to face fewer than 5,000 regulars. By then Burgoyne was becoming desperate because he had heard nothing to confirm that Clinton was—as he had promised—advancing up the Hudson. Burgoyne had put his own army on short rations, and he knew that if he were to withdraw safely to Canada before winter, he would soon have to retreat. But having committed himself to forcing his way to Albany, he refused to retreat until he had made one last offensive effort. Because his generals rejected a full-scale attack, he decided to make a reconnaissance in force. He would take 1,500 men to probe the American left flank to see whether he might use his whole force to seize high ground that would make Bemis Heights untenable or whether he should retreat at once up the Hudson.

Burgoyne's reconnaissance in force proved to be disastrous for his fragile army. Late in the morning of October 7, he emerged from his lines with 1,500 men and marched southwest toward the ridges commanding Bemis Heights from the west. After advancing about three-quarters of a mile, he stopped to forage in a wheat field. He deployed most of his men in line facing south, presumably to cover the remainder who were foraging. With its flanks resting on woods, Burgoyne's detachment was so vulnerable that it tempted Gates to attack. The ensuing attacks on flanks and center of the British line were not perfectly coordinated, but they were carried out with enough determination to shatter Burgoyne's force. In less than an hour his men were retreating to their fortifications. Benedict Arnold was in this, the Battle of Bemis Heights, again in the middle of the fighting. Although he had no formal authority—he had quarreled with Gates and been relieved of command—he not only helped rout Burgoyne's detachment but also organized a counterattack that carried the extreme right flank of the British lines and made the rest of their works untenable. That night Burgoyne, having failed to recover the right of his line and having suffered 600 casualties (to 150 for the Americans), abandoned the rest of his line and withdrew behind Kroma Kill.

The next night Burgoyne started his retreat up the Hudson. Gates followed two days later, overtaking the British seven miles to the north at Saratoga, surrounding them there on October 12, and impelling Burgoyne to begin negotiations on October 13. Too late did Burgoyne learn that Clinton had broken through the Highlands of the Hudson and was pushing toward Albany. On October 17 his men surrendered their weapons and marched into captivity; soon thereafter other British forces withdrew from Lake Champlain and the Hudson. Howe's preoccupation with Pennsylvania, the ministry's assumption that Howe would cooperate with the Canadian army, Burgoyne's preference for a cautiously conventional strategy, his logistical difficulties, and his determination to reach Albany all had worked together with Gates's strategic caution and Arnold's tactical aggressiveness to give the Americans their greatest victory of the war thus far.

A Revolution Within a World War: Relying on the People in Arms

Burgoyne's surrender in October 1777 had a profound effect on the war and the Revolution: it brought French recognition and support for the rebels, disrupted operations in North America, and forced British and American commanders to rely increasingly on the people to do their fighting. The loss of Burgoyne's army and the prospect of having to divert forces from North America to engage the French in Europe, the West Indies, and India greatly reduced Britain's resources. To continue the war in America with any hope of success, the British had to alter their strategy. They had to rely increasingly on their navy and, above all, on the American people—on those loyal colonists who might now be embodied in militia or more permanent units— to support offensives and consolidate gains. Paradoxical as it might seem, Burgoyne's surrender had much the same effect on the Americans. Because France was now an ally and the Continental army was becoming a nearly professional fighting force, the American people—anticipating victory—so relaxed their support of the war as to force Washington to depend increasingly after 1778 on militiamen and other irregular forces to resist the British and the loyalists. The War for American Independence had always been fought for the allegiance of the people; it was now to be fought by the people as well.

Strategic Consequences of Saratoga

The most important and immediate consequence of Burgoyne's surrender— the surrender of nearly one-fifth of the British army in North America—was to demonstrate the vitality of the Revolution and persuade European states to provide the recognition and support that Americans needed to win their independence. France and Spain had long sought opportunities to weaken Britain, to gain revenge for defeats suffered in the Seven Years' War. In the autumn of 1775, France had sent representatives to the Continental Congress offering goodwill and trade. The following year France and Spain agreed to send arms and ammunition to the rebels and, in 1777, to receive American vessels in their ports. This governmental aid as well as private trade brought the Continental army many essential supplies—indeed, 80 percent of all the powder it would use in the first two-and-one-half years of the war. But until Gates received Burgoyne's surrender and the durability of the Revolution was confirmed, European governments were unwilling to recognize the new United States. Even after news of Saratoga arrived in early December 1777 only France was ready to enter formally into treaties and form an alliance with the United States. These agreements, signed February 6 and announced March 13, 1778, guaranteed American independence and virtually assured that France would enter the war against Britain. By the summer of 1778 France and Britain were at war. Spain joined as France's ally in 1779; and by late 1780 the United Provinces, Denmark, Sweden, Russia—eventually Prussia, Austria, Portugal, and the two Sicilies as well— formed a league of armed neutrality against Britain. So it was that Burgoyne's surrender turned the American Revolution into a war that would be fought around the world and that would contribute substantially to the winning of American independence.

Even before France entered the war on the side of the rebels, the British government knew that Burgoyne's surrender would require sweeping changes in the conduct of the war. The loss of Burgoyne's army substantially reduced the number of troops available for operations against the rebels and substantially increased the risk of foreign intervention. To forestall French or Spanish intervention and to encourage a negotiated settlement of the war, the ministry created a second peace commission and authorized it to make concessions on all issues except American independence. To sustain military pressure on the rebels with a smaller army, the ministry sought a more aggressive commander-in-chief and a strategy better suited to limited resources. The ministry appointed Sir Henry Clinton to replace Sir William Howe and ordered Clinton to rely increasingly on the Royal Navy and loyal colonists to end the rebellion. If Clinton were unable to engage the Continental army in a decisive battle, he was to send expeditionary forces to raid and blockade the ports of New England and to assist loyalists in restoring royal government in Georgia, the Carolinas, and Virginia. Once the South had been recovered, the rebellion in the north would, the ministry hoped, wither under a blockade. Although the rebels had always relied on the people—on militiamen—to do much of their fighting, the British adopted a similar strategy only after Burgoyne's surrender left them short of the regular forces needed to carry on the war. Unwilling to ask Parliament for large reinforcements, and thus jeopardize support for the war among British taxpayers, the ministry took the unconventional step of deliberately attempting to involve the American people in the war, of using loyalist militia to supplement British regulars in putting down the rebellion.

The New Strategy Suspended, Spring and Summer 1778

Before Clinton could carry out this unconventional strategy, France openly declared its support for the rebels; and the British government modified its plans for the American war. When the French announced on March 13 that they had signed treaties and entered into an alliance with the United States, the British assumed that a war with France was inevitable and that ending the American rebellion would temporarily be subordinate not only to launching attacks on the French West Indies but also to defending British possessions on both sides of the Atlantic. On March 21, King George III ordered Clinton to send 5,000 men and eleven warships to capture the French West Indian island of St. Lucia and another 3,000 with a naval escort to defend Florida. Once these forces had been dispatched, Clinton was to give up Philadelphia and possibly even New York City to release troops needed to hold Canada, Rhode Island, Nova Scotia, and Newfoundland; and Lord Howe was to send home twenty warships (nearly one-fourth of his squadron) to help defend the British Isles. Although George III and his ministers had already begun to receive reports that France was preparing a powerful expedition to attack British forces in North America, they did not alter their instructions to Sir Henry Clinton or Lord Howe or even send ships to support them.

Just as the British ministry was slow to reinforce Lord Howe, so too were Howe and Clinton slow to carry out the ministry's strategy for a war against France. The dispatches ordering expeditions to St. Lucia and the Floridas reached Philadelphia on May 8. Because Howe's warships were then scattered from Nova Scotia to Antigua, because it would take weeks to assemble those ships and complete their crews, and because the ministry had warned that a French squadron might be en route to America, Howe and Clinton decided to evacuate Philadelphia and concentrate their forces at New York before sending detachments to St. Lucia and the Floridas. They soon found that even evacuating Philadelphia would be a difficult and time-consuming task. Lacking the transports to embark the army, its baggage, and all the loyalists who wished to remain under British protection, they decided to send only the baggage and loyalists by sea and to march the army through New Jersey to New York City. Howe still had to assemble and prepare the transports, and Clinton had to keep rebel forces at bay while he readied his army for a fighting withdrawal across New Jersey. (Clinton hoped that by going overland to New York he would lure the Continental army into a general engagement in open country, the kind of battle that might decide the war.) Not until June 18 did Howe and Clinton leave Philadelphia for New York City. They did so believing that the French squadron said to have been en route to America had returned to Brest and that only Washington might contest their passage to New York.

Howe and Clinton were right in thinking Washington might be willing to risk battle in New Jersey. His army had emerged from its winter camp at Valley Forge (twenty miles northwest of Philadelphia) larger, healthier, and far better trained than it had been at the end of the previous campaign. The 9,000 men who went to Valley Forge in December 1777 suffered severely during the winter from shortages of food and clothing, from living in dank log huts, and from epidemics of smallpox and typhus. But in March the army had begun to benefit from more food and milder weather and above all, from better training and discipline under the new inspector general, Baron von Steuben, a forty-seven-year-old soldier of fortune who had been a captain in the army of Frederick the Great and who now volunteered his services to the Revolution. Until Steuben arrived, the Continental army was experienced in war and dedicated to the Revolution; but it was not well organized or trained. It owed its success in battle to circumstances in which enthusiasm and courage could offset superior British discipline—as at Bunker Hill, Trenton, or Freeman's Farm. Steuben now undertook to give the army the standardized organization and instruction it needed to engage the British successfully in open country: to deploy from column to line without becoming disordered and to deliver an effective bayonet attack as well as disciplined musket fire. By May 5, when Washington held a grand review to celebrate the Franco-American Alliance, the army was able to march, maneuver, and fire with remarkable skill; and this new skill brought a marked improvement in confidence and morale. The 12,000 Continentals he led out of Valley Forge and across the Delaware were a better army than any that had yet served the United States. Just how much the army had improved became clear when it overtook the British army that was withdrawing through New Jersey. Near Monmouth Court House on June 28, Washington's men did become disordered while attacking the British rear guard. But they were disciplined enough to form a new line of battle under fire, to withstand repeated counterattacks, and to fight veteran, regular troops to a draw. This, the last major engagement of the war in the north, confirmed the effectiveness of Steuben's methods.

Soon after the Battle of Monmouth, a French squadron of twelve ships of the line and four frigates appeared unexpectedly in American waters. This squadron would never justify the fears and hopes that it inspired, but it would thoroughly disrupt the American war for another three months. When the French first arrived at New York on July 11, their ships were more powerful than any that Howe could assemble; and he would have to wait weeks for reinforcements from England. But if Howe and Clinton could do little more than prepare to defend themselves at New York and send troops to Rhode Island, the French soon discovered that their ships were too large—drew too much water—to attack New York safely. They decided, therefore, to accept Washington's proposal for a combined attack on the British garrison at Rhode Island. By August 8 the Americans had landed on Rhode Island and the French were preparing to join them in investing Newport. Although Howe did not have the ships to force his way into Newport, he was able to relieve the British garrison by luring the French to sea where a violent storm dispersed and battered the two squadrons. When on August 20 the French returned to Rhode Island, it was merely to say that they were taking their ships to Boston for repairs. Without French support, the Americans on Rhode Island were vulnerable to attack by the British at New York. The Americans withdrew on August 30 just before Clinton arrived from New York with 5,000 men. Lord Howe, his squadron at last reinforced, went directly to Boston in hopes of engaging the French before they were secure within the harbor. He arrived too late. Except for a British raid in Buzzards Bay the campaign was now over. The first French squadron to reach America had accomplished less than the new allies had hoped or the British feared it would. It had forced a suspension of other operations from late June until late September 1778.

Turning to the People

On October 10 Clinton received instructions to resume the war against the rebellious colonies. After sending expeditions to capture St. Lucia and to reinforce the Floridas, he was to rely once again primarily on the Royal Navy and loyalists to end the rebellion, combining raids and a blockade of New England with a gradual restoration of loyalists to power in the southern colonies. This strategy, set forth on March 8 but suspended after the announcement of the Franco-American alliance, was to be the basic British strategy for the remainder of the American war. Clinton was not optimistic about this strategy, and he knew that it was too late in the year to undertake raids on the coasts of New England. But now that reinforcements had given the British navy control of American waters he decided to give the new strategy a trial. In November after sending 5,000 men to capture St. Lucia, he added 1,000 men to the 2,000–man reinforcement bound for East Florida and ordered the entire force to attack Georgia—to see whether, as the ministry hoped, the loyal colonists would come forward to overthrow the rebels and restore royal government. On December 23, Lieutenant Colonel Archibald Campbell landed near Savannah with 3,000 men and began the reconquest of Georgia.

Campbell was more successful than Clinton expected, but Clinton would not exploit that success for more than a year. By the end of January 1779, Campbell had captured Savannah, gained control of southeast Georgia, and established a post at Augusta. But when he called upon the loyalists of the Georgia backcountry to rise before having crushed the rebels there, he started a civil war that the loyalists could not win. Raw loyalists were no match for veteran rebel militiamen who had controlled Georgia and South Carolina since 1775. Although Campbell remained optimistic that with reinforcements he could recover Georgia and the Carolinas, Clinton refused to be lured from a summer offensive in the middle colonies. Sir Henry hoped to fight a decisive battle with the Continental army or, at least, to restore loyalists to power in parts of New York and New Jersey. As it happened, he raided Virginia and Connecticut and captured two posts on the Hudson River. But Washington refused battle and Clinton did not have the forces to do more. A French fleet kept British troops on St. Lucia from returning to New York for the summer and only 3,300 sickly recruits reached New York from England. Clinton might have gone south in the autumn had not a second French fleet arrived unexpectedly off Savannah. That fleet kept him at New York until December 23. Only then, when he was sure that the French were gone, could he sail with 7,600 men to attack Charleston and begin a full-scale effort to restore loyalists to power in South Carolina and Georgia.

It might seem that the very circumstances that inhibited Clinton throughout 1779 would have encouraged Washington to take the offensive, to hasten an end to the war. They did not—primarily because Washington never had enough men or supplies for a sustained offensive. As the threat of British victory receded, many Americans became preoccupied with their private affairs and were unwilling to take part in or support the war. Without popular support, Congress and the state governments were unable to provide adequately for their forces. Congress, having tried unsuccessfully to pay for the war by issuing paper money, began requisitioning supplies and men from the states. The states were reluctant to impress supplies and often ignored Congress. When the states did adopt conscription, many conscripts evaded service. Thus Washington had to shape his operations to suit scarce resources. During the winter months, he dispersed and even disbanded parts of his army; at other times he pursued a mainly defensive strategy. He avoided general engagements and used small attacks on British outposts (most notably a successful night bayonet attack on Stoney Point, New York, in July 1779) to keep up the morale of revolutionaries through a period of lagging popular support. Indeed, just when his veteran Continentals were gaining in skill and confidence, he had to avoid battle and depend on militiamen supplemented by small detachments of Continentals to oppose the British in the southern states.

The Revolution Preserved: Unconventional and Conventional Warfare in the South, 1780–1783

The War for American Independence was decided at last in the South where each side used combinations of militiamen and regulars in a variety of operations, some unconventional, some remarkably conventional. The British hoped that by capturing Charleston and establishing posts in the interior of South Carolina they would be able to call upon loyalists to restore royal government gradually from south to north. But Americans struck back, using militiamen and partisans to intimidate the loyalists and combinations of militiamen and Continentals to lure the British into destructive battles and debilitating campaigns. The Americans learned to blend unskilled and skilled men, variously armed, in unorthodox but formidable tactical dispositions. They also learned by late 1781 to take their part with the French army in the most orthodox of eighteenth-century military operations—a formal and successful siege. In short, the Americans came to display a remarkable competence in unconventional and conventional warfare.

Charleston to King's Mountain: The British Offensive Arrested

Clinton's invasion of South Carolina began auspiciously. He reached the Carolina coast in February 1780, opened a siege of Charleston on April 1, and captured the town and its garrison on May 12. In capturing the principal American port south of the Delaware with 3,371 men, 300 cannon, and 4 ships of the line, Clinton won one of the most impressive British victories of the war. When he subsequently established posts in the interior of South Carolina, patriot resistance in Georgia collapsed; and South Carolina loyalists came forward in "gratifying numbers" to take oaths of allegiance and enlist in provincial units. Although Clinton's overtures to rebels were unsuccessful, he sailed for New York in June confident that he had broken the rebellion in Georgia and South Carolina and that the regular forces he left behind would be able, with the help of loyalists, to secure North Carolina and advance to the Chesapeake by autumn.

But the rebellion in South Carolina had not been broken, and Clinton's successor, Charles Earl Cornwallis, discovered that organizing loyalists and suppressing rebels was more difficult than either he or Clinton expected. The loss of Charleston had gradually shaken Americans from their complacency, bringing forth a reaffirmation of republican ideals and a greater

The South in the War of Independence

willingness to support the war—at least, to support local militia against loyalists and scattered detachments of regulars. Against such a resurgence of revolutionary feeling, Cornwallis had neither the men nor the supplies to do what was expected of him. His 8,000 regulars were scarcely adequate to garrison Charleston and posts in the interior, keep open lines of supply, and repel rebel forces gathering in North Carolina and Virginia. Moreover, his efforts to augment his regular forces by raising loyalists in the interior of South Carolina failed not just because the people were rallying to the revolution but also because he could not find arms or leaders for the loyalists. And when his supplies of food and fodder ran short and he tried to supplement his dwindling stores with purchases and confiscations, he succeeded mainly in alienating the population. By late July 1780, Cornwallis had clearly failed to restore order to the interior of South Carolina. Attributing his failure to the support that rebels in South Carolina received from North Carolina and Virginia, Cornwallis concluded that he would have to invade North Carolina and destroy rebel forces based there before he could hope to secure South Carolina.

Cornwallis soon destroyed the principal American army in the South and invaded North Carolina, but he was unable to gain control of the South Carolina backcountry, to raise the loyalist support that was now essential to British strategy. On August 9, as he was preparing to march into North Carolina, he learned that General Horatio Gates was advancing on Camden, South Carolina, with an army of 6,000 men. Although Cornwallis had only 2,100 men with him, he decided to attack the Americans rather than retire to Charleston and leave his detachments of regulars and the loyalists of the interior exposed to piecemeal destruction. His army stumbled into Gates's men north of Camden on the night of August 15. Next morning, when the Americans attacked, the British infantry fired a single volley and charged with bayonets fixed, shattering the left and center of the inexperienced rebel forces and winning a "most crushing" victory. At a cost of 324 casualties the British killed, wounded, or captured nearly 1,800 Americans.

To exploit this victory and to secure the interior of South Carolina, Cornwallis decided to proceed with his invasion of North Carolina. On September 8 he marched for Charlotte with the main body of his army, sending a detachment of 1,000 militiamen to sweep west through the mountains of North Carolina and a body of regulars to establish a base on the Cape Fear River. He planned to advance as far as Hillsborough where he would spend the winter raising and training loyalist militia. By early October it was clear that the invasion of North Carolina was not going well. Rebel militia not only succeeded in preventing loyalists from joining Lord Cornwallis but also engaged the British army in a succession of corrosive skirmishes (altogether some thirty-seven small actions in 1780). When on October 7 at King's Mountain the rebels isolated and destroyed the 1,000 loyalist militia who made up the left wing of his army, Cornwallis decided to abandon his invasion of North Carolina. He retired to Winnsboro, South Carolina, to screen the interior of South Carolina and Georgia and await reinforcements.

While Cornwallis struggled to restore royal government in the Carolinas and Georgia, Clinton spent the summer and autumn of 1780 ineffectually at New York. Although he knew that the ministry wanted to emphasize the war in the South, Clinton left only about one-fourth of his troops there. He gathered the remainder at New York—more than 20,000 regulars—to defend New York, seek a decisive battle with Washington, and take advantage of Benedict Arnold's offer to betray the American fortifications guarding the Hudson River at West Point. Clinton had intended to support

British forces in the South by sending a detachment to establish a post in the Chesapeake. But lacking confidence in himself and his plans, he was soon paralyzed by circumstances. When he learned through Arnold that a French fleet and army were bound for Rhode Island (they arrived on July 10), he was unable to persuade the commander of the British squadron at New York to cooperate in occupying Rhode Island or in attacking the French. When a more aggressive British admiral arrived with reinforcements and offered to join in attacking Rhode Island, Clinton lost his enthusiasm for engaging the French. By mid-September he may have been preoccupied with the prospect of recovering West Point or with shortages of provisions for his army. But even after Arnold's conspiracy had been uncovered, Clinton agreed to do no more than send a detachment of 2,500 men to raid the Chesapeake.

　　Despite the resurgence of revolutionary feeling following the loss of Charleston and the British invasion of the Carolina backcountry, Washington never had the forces he needed for offensive operations in 1780. He had preserved his army through the previous winter by disbanding some regiments and impressing supplies for others. Even so, persistent shortages of food and pay drove two Continental regiments to mutiny in May 1780 and limited the size of the army for the rest of the campaign. Washington was able to continue training his men, and when in July a French army of 5,500 men reached Rhode Island, he did propose a combined attack on Clinton's forces at New York. But the French, observing the weakness of the Continental army and the strength of British forces, rejected Washington's proposals. The French commander, Lieutenant General Rochambeau, preferred to talk of plans for 1781. By autumn, shortages of food, clothing, and money forced Washington to disband and disperse his army; and during the winter of 1780–1781, Continentals again mutinied to express their resentment at being neglected by the people of a prosperous country.

Cowpens to Eutaw Springs: The Attrition of British Power

While Washington struggled with shortages and mutinies, Nathanael Greene and Daniel Morgan brought inspired leadership to American forces in the southern states. Greene, who replaced Horatio Gates as commander-in-chief in the Carolinas and Georgia on December 3, 1780, had to organize the defense of a vast, sparsely populated country with few more than 1,000 Continentals and bands of ill-disciplined militia. His militia were able to intimidate loyalists and skirmish successfully with small detachments of regulars, but unless Greene could create unusually favorable circumstances for a battle, even his Continentals could not hope to defeat any substantial concentration of Cornwallis's 10,000 men. To create such circumstances—at least to make the most of his outnumbered and poorly supplied forces—Greene decided to divide and disperse his army. By creating two divisions of roughly 1,000 men and posting those divisions to the northwest and northeast of Cornwallis's camp at Winnsboro, he could better feed his own men,

Nathanael Greene was the most important of the general officers who served under Washington in the Continental army. He led a small army of Continentals, militia, and partisans in a sprawling, mobile offensive that drove the British from most of their posts in the South.

sustain friendly militia, and harass British detachments. Above all, he could tempt Cornwallis to divide the main body of his army, exposing perhaps a part of that army to defeat.

This strategy, carried out in late December 1780 and early January 1781, had just the effect that Greene intended. When in January Cornwallis decided to leave Winnsboro and advance into North Carolina—to sustain loyalists and crush rebel forces—he also decided to divide his army. He would leave 5,000 men to garrison posts in South Carolina, send 1,100 under Banastre Tarleton against the western division of Greene's army, detach another smaller force to establish a supply depot at Wilmington, and advance with the main portion of his army toward Charlotte and the North Carolina piedmont.

Soon after Cornwallis began his march from Winnsboro, Tarleton's detachment became a victim of Green's strategy and Morgan's tactics. In an effort to overtake and destroy the western division of Greene's army, Tarleton had driven his men across the sodden winter terrain of western South Carolina. On the morning of January 17, 1781, after marching eight miles in predawn darkness, he at last came up with Morgan's division at a place called Cowpens, sixty-five miles northwest of Winnsboro. He found the rebels drawn up in a wooded area, clear of underbrush, with their flanks unprotected and their backs to the Broad River. Without taking time to rest his men or reconnoiter the rebel position, he attacked. His haste, together with Morgan's superb management of his 320 Continentals and 720 militiamen, soon destroyed the 1,100 British regulars. Knowing that his militiamen lacked the discipline to stand against regulars, Morgan deployed the militia in two lines, 300 and 150 yards in front of his Continentals, and asked that each line of militia fire twice before retreating behind the Continentals. A small force of 125 cavalry was posted to the rear to cover his exposed flanks. Thus when Tarleton's men attacked, every rebel knew how the battle was to be fought. The militia in the first lines checked the British cavalry and fired two effective volleys into the British infantry before retreating under cover of their own cavalry and the Continentals. The British infantry then rushed forward against the Continentals who received them with volley after volley of disciplined fire. When the British threatened to outflank the American right, the right retired in good order, faced about, and met the British at fifty yards with another volley and fixed bayonets. The British, who had entered the battle tired and who had become disordered in rushing after the retiring militia and Continentals, disintegrated when the Continentals counterattacked. In about an hour and with a loss of twelve killed and sixty wounded (6.2 percent), the Americans killed, wounded, or captured 90 percent of Tarleton's regulars.

Stung by Tarleton's defeat, Cornwallis now became preoccupied with pursuing and destroying Greene's forces—indeed, so preoccupied as to ignore loyalists and to become vulnerable to Greene's strategy of luring the British far from their sources of supply. Cornwallis had begun his march into North Carolina before he learned of Cowpens. He stopped long enough to burn his baggage—to increase the mobility of the 2,200 men under his command—and then plunged after Morgan who was already retiring toward Salisbury. On February 1, Cornwallis forced his way across the Catawba River; two days later he reached Salisbury, in time to capture some of Morgan's baggage but too late to keep him from escaping over the Yadkin toward Guilford Court House. While Cornwallis rested briefly at Salisbury, Greene brought his whole army together at Guilford on February 6. Because his forces remained decidedly inferior to the British, Greene decided to continue his retreat, to continue north across the Dan River and into Virginia where he could hope to gain reinforcements that would be needed for battle. Thus when Cornwallis resumed his pursuit on February 8, he found the rebels an annoying but elusive enemy that crossed the Dan just ahead of his cavalry on February 15. Not having the boats needed to follow Greene into Virginia, Cornwallis turned back to Hillsborough to rest his army and to begin organizing loyalists. In the month since leaving Winnsboro, he had marched more than 225 miles through a wet, cold, and sparsely populated country without achieving the decisive battle he had sought.

Soon after Cornwallis camped at Hillsborough, Greene returned to North Carolina to harass the British, await reinforcements, and seek a favorable opportunity for battle. His light troops, supported by independent units of partisans, were very effective in keeping the British from raising loyalists and foraging successfully. By February 27 they had forced Cornwallis to march from Hillsborough in search of food and a chance to engage the rebels. Greene continued his harassing tactics and avoided battle until he received substantial reinforcements during the second week in March. Then, with a two-to-one advantage—4,400 men to 1,900—he took up a strong defensive position at Guilford Court House and invited attack. Benefiting from Morgan's advice and Cornwallis's desperation, Greene was able to fight at Guilford on March 15 much as Morgan had fought at Cowpens. He placed his 2,600 militia in two lines well in front of his 1,600 Continentals, used his cavalry and light troops to cover his flanks, and persuaded his militia to fire twice before retreating. Although the British shattered his first two lines, they took heavy casualties and were unable to break his

Continentals. Even so, after three hours of destructive fighting, Greene chose to withdraw rather than risk the disintegration of his own forces in an attempt to destroy the British. His army retired in good order having suffered only 5.9 percent casualties while killing or wounding 28 percent of the British. Cornwallis, his army unfit for further action and unable to feed itself in the piedmont of North Carolina, was forced to retreat at once to Wilmington.

Greene lost no time exploiting Cornwallis's retreat; in the next six months he won no battles, but he so punished the British in battles, skirmishes, and sieges as to force them to abandon the Carolinas and Georgia except portions of the coast around Wilmington, Charleston, and Savannah. He began by securing the piedmont of North Carolina; then in early April 1781 he invaded the backcountry of South Carolina, sending a detachment to capture Fort Watson, and leading some 1,300 troops against the principal British post at Camden. Although he was attacked and narrowly defeated at Hobkirk's Hill just north of Camden on April 25, he kept his army together and continued to exert pressure on British outposts. When on May 10 the British abandoned Camden and retired toward Charleston, Greene and various partisan leaders quickly overran other British garrisons in the hinterlands of South Carolina and Georgia. By early June only one British post remained in the interior (at the settlement called Ninety-Six, 150 miles northwest of Charleston), and that post was under siege. The British subsequently relieved and then abandoned Ninety-Six, pulling back all their forces to the coastal plain by mid-July. In September, Greene resumed his offensive, attacking the British army at Eutaw Springs, some fifty-five miles northwest of Charleston. He did not win this battle, but he did inflict such heavy casualties on the British (36 percent) that they retired to Charleston, leaving the rebels in control of all except the seacoasts of the Carolinas and Georgia.

Yorktown: A Conventional End to an Unconventional War

During the spring and summer of 1781, while Greene recovered the interior of the Carolinas and Georgia, the British concentrated their forces in the Chesapeake. Clinton did not intend such a concentration, but Cornwallis, the British government, and circumstances worked together to frustrate Clinton's plans for an offensive in the middle colonies and make Virginia the seat of the war. By the time Cornwallis reached Wilmington from Guilford Court House on April 7, he had decided that he would have to conquer Virginia to end the rebellion in the Carolinas and Georgia. Having made this decision without consulting Clinton, Cornwallis delayed his march to Virginia only long enough to be sure that he could proceed without being attacked en route (to be sure that Greene had gone to South Carolina) and that there would be British troops in Virginia to support him. Clinton had sent those troops to Virginia in two detachments: the first, to satisfy the British government's desire for a naval base in the Chesapeake, to destroy American magazines, and to favor Cornwallis's offensive in the Carolinas;

the second, to protect and assist the first against Franco-American forces assembling in Virginia. Although Clinton decided in early May to send a third detachment to the Chesapeake—to reinforce troops already there—he never intended to make a principal offensive along the James River. He expected many of the 6,200 men he had sent to Virginia between December 1780 and May 1781 to return to New York for a summer campaign against Philadelphia. He was then furious to learn that Cornwallis had reached Petersburg. But Clinton lacked the self-confidence to take firm control over Cornwallis, particularly when he knew that the British government admired Cornwallis's aggressiveness and favored a strategy of recovering the colonies from south to north. Thus while Cornwallis devoted June and July to plundering Virginia, Clinton tried ineffectually to persuade him to release troops for or join in an offensive against Philadelphia. In mid-July when Cornwallis was at last preparing to send 3,000 men to Philadelphia, Clinton abandoned his plans for an offensive in the middle colonies and ordered Cornwallis to keep all troops needed to take and hold a naval base in the Chesapeake. On August 2, Cornwallis began work fortifying Yorktown.

Soon after Cornwallis reached Yorktown, Washington and Rochambeau began to think of going to the Chesapeake to trap and destroy the British forces assembled there. Although the French had been sending warships and troops to America since 1778, those forces had not as yet been able to cooperate effectively with the Continental army. As recently as the winter of 1781, the French had been reluctant to join forces against the British in Virginia; and French ships had failed in both February and March to trap Benedict Arnold's detachment that was raiding along the James River. In early May, after learning that a powerful French fleet under Admiral de Grasse would come to North America during the summer, Washington proposed that all French and American forces be concentrated against the British at New York. Rochambeau, commanding the French troops already at Rhode Island, not only rejected an attack on New York but also proposed that he and Washington march their armies south to join de Grasse against the British in the Chesapeake. Although Washington at first refused to undertake such a long march, Rochambeau secretly urged de Grasse to proceed from the West Indies to the Chesapeake and took his own troops from Rhode Island to the Hudson to join forces with Washington and be closer to Virginia on the overland route. By late July, Washington, having reconnoitered the defenses of Manhattan, agreed that he and Rochambeau lacked the forces to take New York; and when on August 14 he learned that de Grasse was en route to the Chesapeake with twenty-eight of the line and 3,200 men, he decided at once to march south to try to capture Cornwallis. He and Rochambeau left the Hudson on August 21, passed through Philadelphia on September 2, and brought all of their forces safely to Williamsburg on September 26. De Grasse, who had arrived in the Chesapeake on August 31, had already turned away a British fleet from New York and received a reinforcement of eight French ships of the line from Rhode Island (bringing Rochambeau's siege guns and effectively sealing the Chesapeake against any force the British could then gather). On September 28, Washington and Rochambeau marched from Williamsburg to Yorktown.

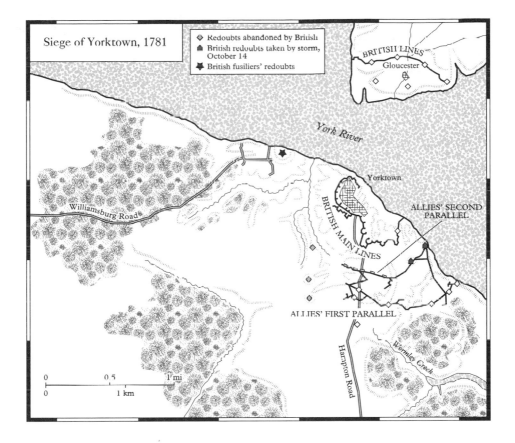

Siege of Yorktown, 1781

◇ Redoubts abandoned by British
♠ British redoubts taken by storm, October 14
♣ British fusiliers' redoubts

BRITISH LINES
Gloucester

York River

Yorktown

ALLIES' SECOND PARALLEL

BRITISH MAIN LINES

Williamsburg Road

ALLIES' FIRST PARALLEL

Hampton Road

Wormley Creek

0   0.5   1 mi

0   1 km

Finding the British too well dug in to invite attack, the allies began a siege that would soon bring them a decisive victory—a victory won by the French navy and by a Franco-American army employing conventional European siegecraft. The siege would be relatively short because the allies had an overwhelming advantage in numbers (16,000 to fewer than 8,000 men) and because the British were isolated in a shallow defensive position against the York River. Cornwallis, lacking the men to hold extensive works, had built a line of entrenchments, redoubts, and batteries close around the village of Yorktown and a similar line across the tip of Gloucester Point just across the York River. He had added another line of works outside the main Yorktown entrenchments but abandoned all except three of those works on September 30 after learning that Clinton intended to sail from New York on October 5 to relieve him.

Once the British withdrew from their outworks, the allies were able to open their first parallel only 600 yards from the main British lines; and once that parallel was completed on October 9, they were able to bring heavy artillery fire against Cornwallis's main line of defense. By October 11, when they began a second parallel 300 yards from the British lines, their guns had silenced nearly all of Cornwallis's artillery and destroyed his ships. Three days later American and French troops took by storm the British redoubts lying along the river east of the town. It was now possible for the allies to extend their second parallel to the river and open a battery that enfiladed the entire British defense. Cornwallis, acknowledging his desperate situation, tried unsuccessfully on October 16 to spike some American guns and to escape across the York. The next day he proposed a meeting to discuss terms of surrender. On October 19, the day Clinton at last sailed from New York, Cornwallis's men put down their arms and marched into captivity. In three weeks and at a cost of 72 killed and 190 wounded (1.6 percent) the allies had won a truly decisive victory.

The siege of Yorktown marked the end of major operations in the War for American Independence. Skirmishing continued for another eighteen months, and Washington had to struggle to keep his army together. But in 1783 peace was at last made and the independence of the new United States was confirmed.

☆   ☆   ☆   ☆

The War for American Independence was far different from the limited wars of mid-eighteenth-century Europe. At a time when most European states relied on highly trained professional armies to settle their differences with the least possible dislocation of civilian life, Anglo-Americans employed combinations of skilled and unskilled soldiers to alter the allegiance of a people. Each side began by trying to gain its political ends with a minimum of force. The British sought to use their small garrison at Boston to intimidate dissidents; the Americans, to use militiamen to resist the garrison and gain a redress of grievances. Each then tried to create and employ more powerful forces without jeopardizing its political goals: the British to end the American rebellion without alienating the people; the Americans, to win their independence without creating a standing army that could deprive them of their liberties. Neither side succeeded. But the Americans fared better than the British, bringing together Continentals and militiamen to capture a British army at Saratoga and gain overt French support. The British, now burdened with a world war as well as a rebellion, turned to loyalists in an effort to continue the war with reduced numbers of regular forces. The Americans, in turn, made the Continental army more professional and used Continentals, militiamen, and partisan bands to keep the British and the loyalists from overrunning the south. By this stage in the war, both sides had become skilled in small-scale, mobile warfare, using simplified methods of fighting suited to citizen-soldiers operating in a vast, sparsely populated, and difficult country. Yet it remained for an army of French regulars, Continentals, and militiamen in cooperation with a French fleet to end the war with a most conventional siege.

Warfare in colonial and revolutionary America was often more modern than that in mid-eighteenth-century Europe; at least, American provincials often came closer than European professionals to anticipating the changes in warfare that would come with the French Revolution. It was not just that Americans waged wars of conquest, that they, like the French revolutionaries, sought to destroy their enemies and permanently alter the boundaries of states; it was also that in North America neither the Indians nor their European allies ever distinguished clearly between soldiers and civilians. War fell on all who lived along the frontiers, and adult freemen were expected to serve in or to support their armed forces. Moreover, because men of every occupation and class served in the militia and provincial forces, and because officers were often appointed by elected governments or elected by their own rank and file, control of American forces depended more on persuasion than on coercion. The citizen-soldiers of British America, like the conscripts of revolutionary France, had to be trained more by instruction and exhortation than by harsh punishment and repetitive training; and they had to be taught relatively simple ways of fighting. Even during the Revolutionary War when Americans tried to create an army capable of standing against British regulars in formal combat—when they tried to give their Continental army professional competence—they were forced to employ persuasion, simplified tactics, and patriotic appeals to turn civilians into soldiers. The Continental army never became truly competent in combined-arms warfare; and all too often Americans had to depend on militiamen and state troops, on the people in arms, to win their independence.

SUGGESTED READINGS

Carp, E. Wayne. *To Starve the Army at Pleasure* (Chapel Hill: University of North Carolina Press, 1984).

Flexner, J. T. *George Washington in the American Revolution (1775–1783)* (Boston: Little, Brown & Co., 1968).

Gross, Robert A. *The Minutemen and Their World* (New York: Hill and Wang, 1976).

Gruber, Ira D. *The Howe Brothers and the American Revolution* (Chapel Hill: University of North Carolina Press, 1974).

Higginbotham, Don. *Reconsiderations on the Revolutionary War* (Westport: Greenwood Press, 1978).

————. *The War of American Independence* (New York: Macmillan Co., 1971).

Mackesy, Piers. *War for America* (Cambridge: Harvard University Press, 1964).

Martin, James Kirby, and Mark Edward Lender. *A Respectable Army: The Military Origins of the Republic, 1763–1789* (Arlington Heights, Ill.: Harlan Davidson, 1982).

Nelson, Paul David. *General Horatio Gates: A Biography* (Baton Rouge: Louisiana State University Press, 1976).

Nickerson, Hoffman. *The Turning Point of the Revolution or Burgoyne in America* (Boston: Houghton Mifflin Co., 1928).

Royster, Charles. *A Revolutionary People at War: The Continental Army and the American Character 1775–1783* (Chapel Hill: University of North Carolina Press, 1979).

Scott, H. M. *British Foreign Policy in the Age of the American Revolution* (Oxford: Clarendon Press, 1990).

Shy, John. *A People Numerous and Armed: Reflections on the Military Struggle for American Independence* (New York: Oxford University Press, 1976).

Smith, Paul H. *Loyalists and Redcoats: A Study in British Revolutionary Policy* (Chapel Hill: University of North Carolina Press, 1964).

Thayer, Theodore. *Nathanael Greene: Strategist of the American Revolution* (New York: Twayne Publishers, 1960).

Wallace, Willard M. *Appeal to Arms: A Military History of the American Revolution* (Chicago: Quadrangle Paperbacks, 1964).

Ward, Christopher. *The War of the Revolution* (New York: Macmillan Co., 1952).

Wickwire, Franklin and Mary. *Cornwallis the American Adventure* (Boston: Houghton Mifflin Co., 1970).

Willcox, William B. *Portrait of a General, Sir Henry Clinton in the War of Independence* (New York: Alfred A. Knopf, 1964).

3

AMERICAN MILITARY POLICY, 1783–1860: THE BEGINNINGS OF PROFESSIONALISM

Arming the New Nation,
1783–1846

The Mexican War

Technological Adaptation
and Strategic Thought

Considering that it was a nation founded in blood, the United States took a notably relaxed attitude toward its military defense during the years between 1783 and 1860. Americans created only a very modest standing army and navy, resented efforts to professionalize the officer corps, and for a long time regarded the permanent armed forces as inimical to sound republican principles. Scornful and suspicious of regular armed forces, they preferred to regard the militia as the chief reliance for defense. Yet in practice, Americans neglected the militia system even more than they did the despised standing army, so that by the mid-nineteenth century the system was practically moribund.

Indeed, in nearly every respect, during its first seventy-five years the United States possessed an uneven military policy and a ramshackle military establishment. Yet during the same period it managed to drive the Native Americans beyond the Mississippi River, hold its own in a second full-scale war with the British, and conquer vast new territories in an amoral but highly successful conflict with Mexico. Judged by results, the new republic turned in a creditable military performance.

Although partly due to circumstance or good fortune, some of America's martial success stemmed from the early emergence of a professional officer corps. Sobered by a brush with disaster during the War of 1812, the army overhauled its bureaucracy, inaugurated an orderly system of officer recruitment, and established professional standards of conduct, particularly through the reform of the U.S. Military Academy. Meanwhile

Congress, despite continuing lip service to the militia, adopted a cadre system that tacitly made the regular army the centerpiece of the nation's land-defense system. Within the new environment, officers increasingly viewed their work as a lifelong calling. Careers grew longer, a distinctive corporate identity emerged, and officers rapidly divorced themselves from partisan politics. By the time of the Civil War, the army officer corps had established an identity, ethos, and outlook that greatly assisted the full flowering of military professionalism in the late nineteenth and early twentieth centuries.

Arming the New Nation, 1783–1846

In its earliest stages, the permanent American military establishment was the product of two factors. First, the political faction known as the Federalists believed the new central government had to develop a significant *national* army and navy. Second, a prolonged period of international upheaval underscored the need for adequate armed forces. Even so, the creation of a permanent military establishment did not occur without significant opposition. Many Americans were unhappy with the idea of creating a standing army. But a significant minority, especially those who had served in the Continental Army, agreed with George Washington, who understood the fear of a standing army but also believed that fear should not be blindly heeded. Unlike European mercenaries who had no stake in the political order, Washington argued, an American army was composed of citizens with common interests—"one people embarked on one cause; acting on the same principle and the same end." Since those interests were the same as that of the larger community, the army logically posed no threat to liberty. Eventually Washington's view triumphed, but it took thirty years, a number of small military incidents, and a major war before that occurred.

The Creation of Permanent Military Forces

After the war with Great Britain ended in 1783, the Confederation turned to the matter of a permanent peacetime military establishment that would be able to police the land and maritime frontier, defend against a full-scale invasion, and help maintain internal order. In 1783 a Congressional committee chaired by Alexander Hamilton asked Washington for his opinion concerning the requirements of such an establishment. Washington responded with "Sentiments on a Peace Establishment," a four-point program that became the basis of the nationalist agenda. First, a small regular army (2,631 officers and men) was required to "overawe" Indians and guard against incursions from Canada and Spanish Florida. Second, a "respectable and well-established Militia" was also needed, preferably under federal as well as state control, with the central government imposing uniformity in training, arms, and organization. It should have two tiers: a volunteer militia to be kept in an advanced state of readiness, and a common militia composed of the remaining male population of military age. Third, the national government must establish arsenals and factories to support the armed forces. And fourth, it must create military academies to foster military science.

The Hamilton Committee greeted Washington's proposals with enthusiasm and modeled its own report along similar lines. But Congress, then predominantly antinationalist in tone, rejected the report. Rather than create a standing army, it elected to disband the Continental Army except for eighty men and a few officers to guard military stores. Instead it created the First American Regiment, composed of 700 militiamen (drawn from four states) to serve one year. This ad hoc arrangement—like the Confederation itself—proved inadequate, and when the Americans scrapped the Articles of Confederation in favor of a new Constitution, they attempted to create a more effective military establishment that would not jeopardize American liberties.

The solution was to divide control of the military establishment. The president would serve as commander-in-chief, but Congress would appropriate money for the armed forces, devise regulations for their government, and hold the authority to declare war. Control of the military establishment was further divided between the national government, which could create a national army and navy, and the states, which maintained control over the militia. A modest system of arsenals and munitions factories also sprang up, and in 1802 Congress authorized creation of a military academy at West Point, New York. (Naval officers continued to be trained aboard warships; Congress would not create the naval academy at Annapolis, Maryland, until 1845.)

Thus by the early years of the nineteenth century the United States possessed a land force roughly corresponding to the model outlined in "Sentiments on a Peace Establishment." The chief departure was the very limited federal control over the militia. Attempts to increase control—for example, to create the sort of volunteer or "federal select" militia favored by Washington—routinely failed. As a result, although in times of emergency the national government could mobilize the militia for a period of ninety days, it had little influence over the peacetime organization, regulation, training and equipment of the militia. Since most state governments were notoriously lax in such matters, the militia—supposedly the nation's chief reliance in wartime—was an uncertain patchwork of units without uniform organization, training, or equipment.

Old World Frictions

These developments occurred against a background of European revolution and war. Less than a year after the American Constitution went into operation, violent political upheaval erupted in France. With their own revolution just recently behind them, Americans watched the unfolding drama in France with more than passing interest. Indeed, as the months rolled on, the

French Revolution exerted an almost tidal pull on American political life. Then, in 1792, the new French republic declared war on Austria, inaugurating twenty-three years of near-continuous war that embroiled not only most of Europe but eventually the United States as well. Moreover, the unfolding French Revolution, as Americans alternately cheered its triumphs and deplored its excesses, deeply influenced the ongoing debate between two emerging factions in American politics: the Federalists, led by Alexander Hamilton, and their Republican opponents, led by Thomas Jefferson.

The Federalists were nationalist in their orientation, comfortable with an active central government, and wary of placing too much power in the hands of the common man. Although at first elated by the events in France, they soon grew to distrust the direction in which the French Revolution was moving. It seemed to have degenerated into radicalism and mob rule. In the burgeoning wars of the French Revolution, therefore, the Federalists usually supported the British, who were fighting against the French. The Republicans, however—more democratic and also suspicious of what seemed the "monarchist" tendencies of the Federalists—were not disillusioned by the excesses of the French Revolution and continued to prefer the French. Officially, the United States was neutral.

The question of whether to back one side or the other had more than academic significance. The wars of the French Revolution were characterized not only by major land battles but also by a long campaign of economic warfare at sea. The British navy blockaded French ports; the French responded by sending out large numbers of privateers and commerce raiders to prowl the world's oceans. Since American merchants traded with both Britain and France, each side freely attacked American vessels bound for enemy ports.

Trouble began first with Great Britain, which routinely seized neutral ships carrying contraband goods to France. The Royal Navy captured 250 American merchant vessels before the Washington administration negotiated a treaty, ratified in 1795, in which the United States essentially accepted the British position on contraband in exchange for a promise that British troops would abandon a number of posts still illegally occupied on American soil. The French, however, interpreted the treaty as an American attempt to aid the British and eventually began seizing American merchant ships on the high seas. In 1798 a two-year undeclared naval war broke out between the United States and France.

These difficulties with Britain and France led to the early growth of the United States Navy. Begun in 1794 with the authorization of six frigates, the new navy at the height of the "Quasi-War" with France boasted fifty-four warships supported by more than a thousand armed merchant vessels. At about the same time Congress created a separate Department of the Navy and authorized construction of the first American ships of the line. American warships not only performed well against the French but also conducted a number of minor but dramatic punitive expeditions against several pirate states in North Africa.

By 1800, however, the Quasi-War had ended. Its main significance was to reinforce the need for adequate American armed forces, so that when the Republican party took power in 1801 with the accession of Thomas Jefferson as president, the Jeffersonians did not dismantle the military establishment created by the Federalists. To be sure, for a time they did reduce the size of the army and navy, mostly in response to a temporary reduction in European tensions. But they basically accepted and, in time, even enhanced the military institutions whose custodianship they inherited. And as a fresh cycle of wars began in 1805, the Jefferson administration found itself sliding into a new and grave crisis with Great Britain.

The War of 1812

Once again the British and French were locked in mortal combat (this time with Napoleon leading France), and once again the navies of both powers seized American and other neutral ships in a bid to throttle each other's commerce. Americans were furious with both nations, but of the two, Britain had the larger navy and thus the greater effect on American shipping. Jefferson and his successor, James Madison, made several efforts to force the British and French to respect American maritime rights, most notably an 1807 Embargo Act that essentially prohibited American exports. Based on the premise that the European powers needed the American trade and could not long do without it, the embargo was intended as an instrument of

Presidents Thomas Jefferson and James Madison tried to use economic coercion to force the British and French to respect U.S. maritime rights, but many Americans resented their policies, as suggested in this contemporary political cartoon. "Ograbme" is "Embargo" spelled backward.

economic coercion. In the short run, however, it hurt American merchants far more than Europeans and generated violent political opposition.

Forced to retreat from outright embargo, the Madison administration struggled to convince Congress to maintain some sort of economic coercion. But increasingly some members of the Republican party demanded that the administration should go farther and declare war on Great Britain. The seizure of American vessels seemed provocation enough, but on top of that the Royal Navy had for years forcibly impressed sailors—some of them U.S. citizens—from American-owned vessels. Further, many Americans living in the South and along the western frontier sought war for other reasons. Many westerners believed the British had been inciting Native American uprisings; they also thought that if war came, it might be possible to grab Canada. Similarly, southerners tended to suspect the British of plotting to seize New Orleans; they also noted that if war broke out they might be able to seize Florida from Spain, whose royal family was then allied with the British.

Madison himself was far from eager for war. But he grew convinced that economic coercion alone would never succeed, because the policy was based on a faulty premise. In earlier years, Britain might have depended on the United States for naval stores crucial to its fleet and seaborne empire. But the growing economic development of Canada gave Britain a viable alternative source and thereby gravely reduced the American bargaining posture. Only a credible threat against Canada could compel the British to respect American maritime rights.

Madison therefore reluctantly asked Congress for a declaration of war. He got one on June 18, 1812, but the margin of the vote was the narrowest for a declaration of war in U.S. history. To a man, the Federalist party rejected the necessity for military action. Deep political divisions persisted throughout the conflict itself, for few on either side tried to create bipartisan support for a struggle against a common foe.

The United States was woefully unprepared in 1812 to take on a major power like Great Britain. Despite recent legislation that authorized an increase to 35,000 men, when war broke out the regular army numbered just 7,000, scattered in various garrisons. A sustained war effort would thus have to be built upon volunteer militia companies backed by the common militia. The naval establishment was no better: just sixteen ships, seven of them frigates, plus swarms of small gunboats. Administrative support had improved little since 1775. Not only was the War Department inadequate to manage a substantial military effort, the federal government had limited ability to finance the war.

Given Canada's importance in Madison's calculations, an invasion of the province was the obvious American strategy. The province was only lightly defended and in theory the Americans should have been able to advance northward in overwhelming strength. Reality proved different. A prompt invasion necessarily depended upon the use of militia forces, yet these were under state control. The best invasion route was north along the Lake Champlain corridor toward Montreal, but the springboard for such an advance—New England—had the least enthusiasm for war of any region in the country.

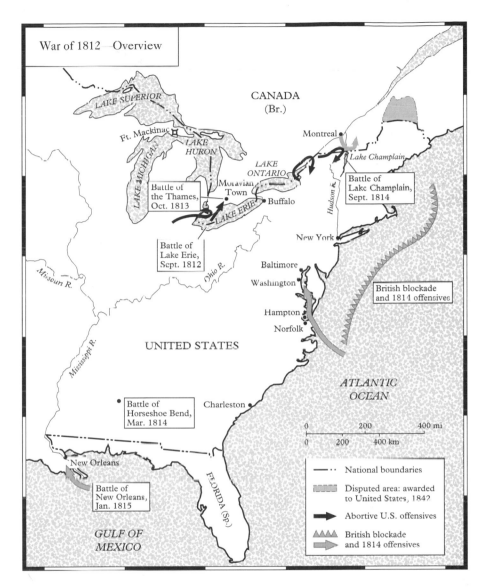

War of 1812—Overview

CANADA (Br.)

Ft. Mackinac

LAKE SUPERIOR

LAKE MICHIGAN

LAKE HURON

Montreal

Lake Champlain

LAKE ONTARIO

Moravian Town

Battle of the Thames, Oct. 1813

Buffalo

Battle of Lake Champlain, Sept. 1814

LAKE ERIE

Hudson R.

New York

Battle of Lake Erie, Sept. 1812

Ohio R.

Baltimore

Washington

British blockade and 1814 offensives

Hampton

Norfolk

Missouri R.

UNITED STATES

Mississippi R.

ATLANTIC OCEAN

Battle of Horseshoe Bend, Mar. 1814

Charleston

0   200   400 mi
0   200   400 km

New Orleans

Battle of New Orleans, Jan. 1815

FLORIDA (Sp.)

— ·· National boundaries

Disputed area: awarded to United States, 1842

Abortive U.S. offensives

British blockade and 1814 offensives

GULF OF MEXICO

Asked by Madison to mobilize their militias, the Federalist New England governors flatly refused, objecting that such forces were intended solely for local defense. A volatile political situation in New York further complicated efforts to mount an offensive into Canada. Instead of a rapid, victorious advance, therefore, practically nothing happened in the key Montreal sector.

By contrast, Americans living in the western frontier region were far more eager for war. There the problem was not so much to raise the necessary volunteers and militia as it was to equip, feed, and manage them. But the modest American government could do none of these things effectively. The initial American thrusts were poorly coordinated, understrength—and disastrous. Numerically inferior but better organized British troops repelled them, seized Detroit, and threatened Michigan Territory and Ohio.

In October 1813, Americans under Major General William Henry Harrison defeated a combined force of British and Indians in the Battle of the Thames, fought on the Lake Erie frontier. Coupled with Andrew Jackson's 1814 win at Horseshoe Bend, Harrison's victory broke the back of Native American resistance east of the Mississippi River.

Fortunately for the United States, Britain was too preoccupied with European matters to mount a major effort in North America. Thus in 1813 the United States had a chance to accomplish what it had failed to do in 1812. But again, poor leadership, inadequate administrative support, and disjointed efforts resulted in scant success. This was particularly true on the Niagara front, where a mixed bag of tactical successes and setbacks resulted in stalemate. Somewhat better results were achieved in the western Lake Erie region. Detroit was recaptured, and Commodore Oliver Hazard Perry destroyed a British squadron near Put-In Bay, Ohio. Major General William Henry Harrison entered Canada, won the Battle of the Thames against a combined British and Native American force, and slew Tecumseh, the great Shawnee chieftain. Yet while these successes secured the western U.S. frontier, they contributed little toward ending the war.

At sea the Royal Navy far outnumbered the diminutive U.S. Navy—even though the British had to concentrate on Napoleon until 1814. Consequently the British were able to blockade the American coast at will. Interestingly, for a long time they chose *not* to blockade New England, since they knew New Englanders generally opposed the war. Indeed the U.S. government even allowed a certain amount of trade with the enemy. American vessels sailed to Spain, for example, and supplied grain to Wellington's army. Even so, by 1814 the blockade had reduced merchant trade to 11 percent of prewar levels.

The blockade was loose enough, however, that U.S. warships had little difficulty getting to sea, and although they could scarcely compete for control of the ocean, American vessels performed very well at commerce-raiding and single-ship duels; sloops and 500 privateers seized over 1,300 British merchantmen. Nevertheless, the British still managed to supply forces in Canada and conduct raids against American coasts. These raids, small at first, expanded dramatically in 1814.

A common nineteenth-century saw declared that "God takes care of fools, drunkards, and the United States." In 1814, America needed providential help. After the defeat of Napoleon in the Saxon campaign of 1813, the British for the first time were able to send large forces across the Atlantic. About 40,000 arrived by year's end. These occupied much of Maine and expanded their raids along the coast. Fortunately for the United States, competent leaders had begun to emerge by this time, especially Jacob Brown, Edmund Gaines, Winfield Scott, and Andrew Jackson.

The United States began the year with two new offensives against Canada—one on the Niagara front and one along the Lake Champlain corridor. Neither came to much, but the Americans handled the Niagara operations much better tactically than the one along Lake Champlain. The British launched three offensives of their own: first, south from Canada via Lake Champlain, a thrust blunted in a naval battle on the lake in September; second, along the Chesapeake Bay, which resulted in the capture and burning of Washington but which failed to seize the privateering base of Baltimore, Maryland; and finally, up the Mississippi River against New Orleans. Forces under Andrew Jackson, in the largest battle of the war, decisively halted this last attack on January 15, 1815. But by then the war was officially over. Six weeks earlier the United States and Great Britain had signed the Treaty of Ghent.

Why did the British, who clearly held the advantage, choose to end the war? For one thing, they could not identify a plausible way to win it. After the Lake Champlain offensive was rebuffed, the Duke of Wellington commented that the United States had no vulnerable center of gravity. "I do not know where you could carry on . . . an operation which would be so injurious to the Americans as to force them to sue for peace." Moreover, with the defeat of Napoleon the reasons for war had largely disappeared. Thus, both sides willingly accepted a peace nominally based on the status quo antebellum.

In some respects the United States achieved significant benefits from the conflict. The war had furnished an opportunity to thrash yet again Native Americans, who were the main losers in the contest. Tecumseh's death at the Battle of the Thames forever ended the most significant threat to white America's settlement of the Old Northwest, while in Alabama, at the 1814 Battle of Horseshoe Bend, Andrew Jackson defeated the Creeks and forced them to cede 23 million acres of land.

But for the most part, the poor American showing in the War of 1812 underscored the essential weakness of its military system. Unreflective nationalists might crow over victories like the battles of Lake Erie and New Orleans, but more reflective observers realized that the country had narrowly

The Battle of New Orleans. This idealized postwar engraving captures the War of 1812 as Americans liked to remember it, with homespun heroes fending off the best Great Britain could send against them. But such triumphs were few, and after the war American policy makers made several needed military reforms.

escaped disaster. The militia had proven unequal to its key role in American defense. The regular army had done better but still suffered from leadership problems, particularly in the war's early stages. The serious administrative deficiencies demonstrated that the War Department required substantial reform, and in the years that followed, American policy makers took significant steps to improve the situation.

Early Attempts to Professionalize

After 1815 the United States entered what one historian has called an "era of free security" in which the country faced little external threat to its existence. He meant that the United States did not need seriously to concern itself with threats from abroad and thus did not have to maintain a sizable army and navy. With minimal risk of foreign invasion, the American armed forces functioned mostly as a "frontier constabulary," a kind of national police force to assist western settlement, intervene in disputes between whites and Native Americans, enforce federal authority, and protect maritime commerce.

Strategically, however, the chief mission of the American army and navy was to defend against foreign invasions. Americans, while continuing to reject creation of a large navy that could challenge an enemy fleet for command of the sea, did permit a modest increase in the number of warships. The navy, then, would function as the first line of defense. The second line was an extensive network of coastal defenses that would hamper an invasion.

Work on such a fortification system began before the War of 1812 but really took off afterward. It consisted of a series of casemate forts guarding not only major harbors but also most navigable inlets. Fifty sites were identified at first; the number eventually ran much higher. The coastal forts were not intended as an absolute defense against attack but rather to ward off sudden raids and force an attacker to come ashore in areas distant from important military objectives. That, in turn, would allow sufficient time to mobilize the militia, which would slow the progress of any invader while a large citizen-based force could be built around the regular army.

Policy makers disagreed about how much reliance to place on the militia, however. Some continued to believe it could function effectively in wartime; others, more skeptical, thought the regular army would have to play the principal role even in a conflict's early stages. The key proponent of the second view was John C. Calhoun, a former "War Hawk" congressman from South Carolina, who became secretary of war in October 1817. Obliged by Congress to reduce the size of the army after the war, he sought to do so without destroying its ability to respond quickly in the event of a crisis. To this end he proposed a cadre system (often called an "expansible army" system) whereby a relatively small peacetime army could be rapidly built up in time of war. He proposed an army that would contain just 6,316 men but would have an officer corps and organization sufficient for an army of 11,558 men. Peacetime units would be kept at about 50 percent strength. In wartime the army could be nearly doubled just by filling out units to wartime strength using federal volunteers; and by adding 288 officers, the army could absorb enough additional privates and noncommissioned officers to raise the total to 19,035 officers and men.

The effect of this cadre proposal was subtle but profound. On the one hand, Congress declined to adopt the plan in its original form—it was too advanced for the time. Republicans had become more comfortable with the army's political reliability, but not enough to acknowledge the regular army unambiguously as the nation's main line of defense. Yet the plan eventually adopted was, in fact, a modified version of the cadre system that tacitly acknowledged Calhoun's central point: that in the event of war, the regular army was the most reliable means of national defense. From that point onward, the regular army officer corps suffered none of the wide-ranging shifts in size that characterized its early years. The frequent deep reductions in force had led many young officers to regard military service as a temporary vocation only. Within the more stable environment created by the Calhoun reforms, young officers could now consider military service a viable, lifelong career. As a result they remained officers longer, took their duties more seriously, and became more competent than their pre–War of 1812 counterparts.

Yet another important postwar development was a major revival at the U.S. Military Academy that marked the real beginning of its traditions. The catalyst was Captain Sylvanus Thayer, appointed West Point superintendent in 1817. Thayer established a four-year curriculum, inaugurated a system that ranked cadets according to merit, and introduced the emphasis on engineering and mathematics that would characterize West Point for several decades. Other indications of a budding professionalism included a more efficient military bureau system and two military schools of practice—one for artillery at Fort Monroe, one for infantry at Leavenworth, Kansas—which flourished briefly until fiscal constraints led to their closure in the late 1830s. Finally, a number of officers began to publish in journals devoted to the study of their craft.

Even so, it would be wrong to mistake these developments for the emergence of a fully mature, professionalized army. True professionalism still lay over a half-century in the future. The Indian pacification duties of this period formed a powerful distraction to the U.S. Army's preparations to wage European-style warfare. A second distraction was the nation's insistence that both the army and navy assist the protean economic expansion that dominated the years after the War of 1812. On land, army engineers deepened harbors and surveyed the routes for turnpikes and—a bit later—railroads as well. At sea, naval officers undertook voyages of exploration, mapped the coastline, and created hydrological charts as aids to navigation. Such duties not only diverted officers from the study of warfare but also shaped their ideas concerning what the military profession was all about. For some, overawing the Indians and surveying the wilderness seemed to have become their primary purpose in life.

Further hampering the professionalizing impetus were two powerful contrary forces: continued suspicions of the regular military establishment and a continuing belief that any man of good character was capable of exercising military leadership. Logically, both developments should have meant a continued commitment to a strong militia. But by the 1830s an odd situation had developed. On the one hand, politicians and citizens still praised the

This whimsical, faintly mocking view of a pre–Civil War militia muster reflects the decline of a venerable American military institution. Though the minuteman tradition remained strong in rhetoric, the actual militia began a steep decline after the War of 1812 and by the time of the Civil War was practically moribund.

militia as a bulwark of liberty. On the other, everyone had long since realized that the militia was, in practice, more or less a joke. Musters became less frequent, militiamen received little or no serious training, and their weapons and equipment were antiquated and poorly maintained.

The federal government could not, and the states would not, reform the militia. Indeed, some states abolished compulsory militia service altogether. Fortunately, volunteer companies took up some of the slack and maintained the tradition of the citizen-soldier. These were units that originally existed independently of the statewide militia systems, although many were later incorporated into them. Often they were the only functional part of the militia. Initially most were run as elite social societies. One had to have a modicum of wealth to join since volunteers bought their own uniforms and drill instructors cost money. Members carefully screened new recruits for good moral fiber and gentlemanly qualities. Over time, clerks, artisans, and laborers formed their own volunteer companies. So did immigrant groups, especially the Irish and Germans. After 1840 some states made the volunteer companies their entire "active militia" force.

The military value of these volunteer units was problematic. Although they provided their own uniforms, they often borrowed their weapons from state armories and rented their horses. They were also usually too small to be of great military significance—many contained about forty to fifty men. And they tended to emphasize martial dash and enthusiasm rather than serious tactical training. Still they provided a substantial reservoir of military experience. A number of future Civil War generals, including some very good ones, served in volunteer units.

Thus, by the mid-1840s, the United States had acquired a basic land-force policy characterized by de facto reliance on a small, peacetime regular army, coupled with the realization that the standing forces would have to be supplemented by a substantial contingent of citizen-soldiers. The available pool of citizen-soldiers varied widely in terms of organization, training, and equipment, but the general standard was low. Americans seldom worried about this, however. The absence of a serious foreign threat and a continued belief in the inherent military prowess of patriotic American males further sustained their confidence.

The Mexican War

Expansion was the hallmark of U.S. foreign policy during this period. Many Americans agreed with the newspaperman John L. O'Sullivan when he declaimed that their nation had a "manifest destiny" to possess all of North America. Examples of this conviction were legion. Already the United States had made two unsuccessful grabs for Canada; had acquired the Louisiana territory from France and Florida from Spain; and had briefly courted armed conflict with Great Britain before agreeing to divide the Oregon Country at the 49th Parallel. Then in 1845 Congress annexed Texas,

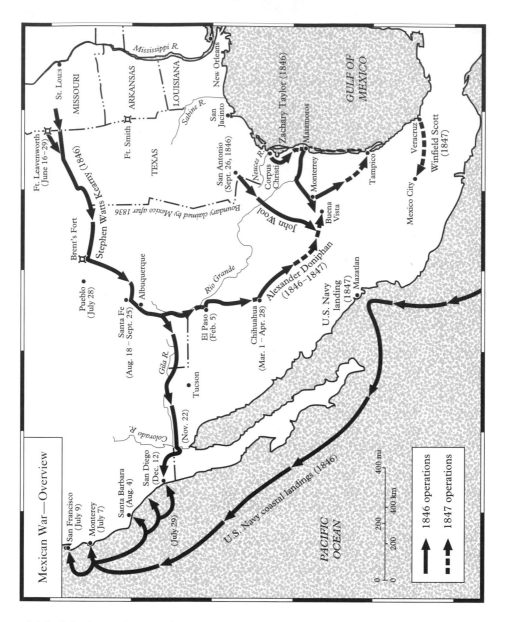

which Mexico still considered a wayward province in revolt, and thereby took a long step toward a major war. The first clashes occurred between U.S. and Mexican forces in 1846; sixteen months later the United States won a resounding triumph and added vast new territories to its already sprawling domain.

Origins and Objectives

Until 1836, Texas had been a province of Mexico. The Mexican government had welcomed American settlement in Texas, only to see a torrent of

Americans flood the province, swamp the ethnic Mexican population, and eventually rise up in an open bid for complete independence. This Texas Revolution culminated in triumph when, after initial setbacks at the Alamo and Goliad, the Texans defeated a Mexican army at the Battle of San Jacinto on April 21, 1836. After ten years as a separate republic, Texas joined the Union in July 1845. Relations between the United States and Mexico rapidly deteriorated, for Mexico had never relinquished its claim to the region.

American ambitions did not end with Texas. A number of Americans were also interested in Upper California and New Mexico, two northern provinces only tenuously under Mexican control. American merchants and politicians especially coveted the magnificent San Francisco harbor, widely regarded as the key to Far Eastern trade. President James K. Polk shared this expansionist vision, and while it is probably not true that he deliberately engineered a military confrontation with Mexico, indisputably he wanted California and New Mexico and was not particular about how he got them. His aggressive policies openly courted war.

Tensions between the United States and Mexico increased when Polk sent an American army into Texas led by Major General Zachary Taylor. After training seven months at Corpus Christi, Taylor's army crossed the Nueces River, the border between Texas and Mexico as the Mexicans understood it, and advanced to the Rio Grande, the border insisted upon by the Texans. For two weeks, Mexican and American forces glared at one another across the disputed boundary. The situation grew more intense, and in April 1846 the Mexicans attacked an American scouting party. "Hostilities," Taylor tersely informed Washington, "may now be considered as commenced."

Like the struggle of 1812–1814, the war was a highly partisan affair for Americans. This time the prowar camp was the Democratic party. Most members of the rival Whig party opposed it on principle, arguing (correctly)

General Zachary Taylor's Mexican War exploits helped make him president, but "Old Rough and Ready," as his soldiers called him, was in many respects a throwback to the amateurism of the War of 1812.

that the United States had no valid claims south of the Nueces. Antislavery Democrats and Whigs also charged that the war's purpose was to spread slavery and thus increase the political power of the southern states. Yet Whig opposition was less united and intransigent than the Federalists had been during the War of 1812. Although Mexico had clearly been provoked, most Whigs believed they could not refuse to support American troops now that they were engaged in combat.

Even so, real enthusiasm for the war tended to be confined politically to the Democratic party and geographically to the South. Because of the conflict's sectional and party overtones, manpower policy was essentially a political question with military implications. Given the soft support for the war, especially in the northeast, the Polk administration decided, by and large, not to use militia. Instead the regular army would double its existing units to 15,000 by filling them up to full strength. Congress also authorized the raising of 50,000 volunteers, most of whom were summoned by Polk from southern states, where support for the war was strongest.

American prewar planning was much better than it had been before the War of 1812. The United States had positioned troops to seize Mexican territory quickly. In addition to Taylor's army along the Texas border, American agents and an "exploring party" under John C. Frémont were in California; there were also naval units off the California shore. Another force under Colonel Stephen Kearny marched against Santa Fe two days after war was declared in May 1846.

American strategists essentially faced two problems. The first was to project U.S. strength into the lands they wanted; this occurred promptly after the declaration of war. The second was to get Mexico to accept an imposed settlement; this proved much trickier. Initially the Polk administration thought it could compel Mexico to the negotiating table by securing California and New Mexico and then holding a few of Mexico's northern provinces as bargaining chips. When that did not work, the Americans finally mounted a remarkable expedition to seize Mexico City itself.

Taylor in Northern Mexico

The Polk administration had entrusted about 4,000 men—most of the regular army—to General Taylor. Dubbed "Old Rough and Ready" by his men, Taylor dressed casually and spoke bluntly. He had as little use for rarefied notions of strategy and tactics as he did for the regulation uniform. In many respects he was a throwback to the amateurish generalship of the War of 1812, but he inspired his troops with confidence. Against a truly capable adversary Taylor might have gotten into serious trouble. As things turned out, however, he compiled a gleaming war record that eventually carried him into the White House.

Although the United States had a larger population than Mexico (17 million as opposed to 7 million) and was far more developed economically, the Mexican government at first believed it held the upper hand. After all, its regular army of 32,000 handily outnumbered the American army of just

In the Battle of Palo Alto, one of the first engagements of the Mexican War, U.S. field artillery proved especially potent at breaking up enemy charges and ensuring an American victory.

8,000. Its foot soldiers were trained in the best Napoleonic tradition and its light cavalry was among the best in the world. Mexican generalship, however, tended to be mediocre and the Mexican supply system was never very good. Fractious political infighting plagued the Mexicans throughout the struggle. And although the American army was usually outnumbered in the field, it was well-equipped and could draw upon a much bigger man-power base. It also possessed superb field artillery, an advantage it drew upon often.

The first major engagements occurred in May 1846, when 4,000 men under General Mariano Arista crossed the Rio Grande near its mouth, intent on thrashing the American upstarts at once. At the Battle of Palo Alto on May 8 he sent his infantry charging into Taylor's lines while his cavalry tried to turn the Americans' flanks. Taylor's artillery, however, crushed these attacks; the American infantry, for the most part, was never seriously engaged. The following day Taylor and Arista clashed again at Resaca de la Palma. Once more the Mexican army was beaten with heavy losses. Mexican casualties in the two battles exceeded 1,600 men; the Americans, by contrast, lost fewer than 200.

Nine days later Taylor crossed the Rio Grande and took possession of Matamoros, where he received substantial reinforcements and awaited instructions from the Polk administration. Eventually it was decided that he should capture Monterrey, the provincial capital of Nuevo León. After restaging his army to Camargo, Taylor began his offensive in August. One month later, having covered the intervening 125 miles, he fought a grueling three-day battle for Monterrey that bled his army heavily. When his opponent offered to yield the town in exchange for an eight-week armistice, Taylor agreed, much to Polk's baffled fury when he learned of the arrangement. The president promptly ordered Taylor to abrogate the truce and resume hostilities. Taylor complied and marched onward to Saltillo, the capital of Coahuila. Meanwhile another American column advanced through the province of Chihuahua. The end of 1846 found the United States firmly in control of much of northern Mexico as well as the coveted regions of California and New Mexico.

The Polk administration had calculated that the Mexican government should sue for peace at this point. It did nothing of the kind. Instead it redoubled its efforts under the charismatic leadership of General Santa Anna, the same man who had conceded Texas independence a decade earlier. Santa Anna was slippery and shrewd. When the war broke out, he had been living in exile in Cuba, a victim of Mexico's near-constant political turmoil. He sent word to Polk that if allowed to return to his homeland he would be willing to negotiate a swift end to the war. Polk therefore instructed the navy to give him safe conduct through its blockade of the Mexican coast. Once ashore, however, Santa Anna trumpeted that he had arrived to save the nation from American imperialism. He soon regained command of Mexico's army and by December 1846 had become president as well.

Early in 1847 it became apparent to Santa Anna that the Americans were planning a new offensive, this one apparently aimed at the coastal port of Veracruz. He also learned that many of Taylor's troops in northern Mexico had been diverted for this new operation. Accordingly, Santa Anna moved north at the head of 20,000 men, hoping to destroy Taylor's force and then swing eastward to defend Veracruz. After a remarkable 200-mile march across desert terrain, Santa Anna confronted the Americans at Buena Vista, just south of Saltillo. Although he had lost a full quarter of his strength in the rapid approach march, he still had 15,000 men to hurl against Taylor's 5,000.

Taylor had assumed the Mexicans could not march an army across such barren country to attack him. But he gamely withdrew a few miles into a naturally strong position near a hacienda called Buena Vista and there awaited the enemy attack. This position—a latticework of hills and ravines—partially nullified the Mexicans' numerical advantage. Even so, Santa Anna hurled his troops forward with great determination. For two days (February 22–23), the battle raged; and on several occasions the American line nearly broke. But Taylor shuttled his troops from one threatened point to another and each time the Americans managed to hold. A particularly crucial ingredient in the American defense was their magnificent field artillery. Without it, one U.S. general remarked, "we could not have maintained our position a single hour." Finally Santa Anna withdrew, having lost 2,000 men killed and wounded. American losses were fewer—about 750—but greater in proportion to the number of troops engaged.

Although Buena Vista sealed "Old Rough and Ready's" reputation and helped vault him into the White House, it was, in many respects, a needless battle. The advanced position held by the Americans was of little strategic value; a better defense could have been made at Monterrey. By electing

General Winfield Scott epitomized the incipient professionalism of the American officer corps in the mid-nineteenth century. His campaign against Mexico City in 1847 was a masterpiece.

to fight at Buena Vista, Taylor risked a disastrous reversal that might have prolonged the war indefinitely.

Scott's 1847 Campaign

While Taylor fought at Buena Vista, a new campaign was beginning along the Mexican coast. Commanded by the U.S. Army's general-in-chief, Winfield Scott, this campaign was aimed at capturing the port of Veracruz on the Gulf of Mexico and then marching inland against Mexico City. With the enemy's capital in American hands, it was believed, Mexican political life would be paralyzed and the Mexicans forced to the conference table.

Thus far, American operations in the war had been characterized by much the same amateurishness as in the War of 1812, notwithstanding their much greater success. Scott's campaign, however, was a masterpiece from beginning to end and displayed considerable thought in planning as well as audacity in execution. A new level of professionalism was on display at Veracruz, where Scott's troops made a well-synchronized landing in surf boats designed expressly for the purpose. Moreover, the fleet of transports had been carefully "combat-loaded," to use a twentieth-century term, so that the items needed first were stored so that they would be the first to be unloaded. The Mexicans chose not to oppose this landing, but even had they done so the Americans would probably still have prevailed, thanks to Scott's meticulous preparations.

Veracruz fell after a brief siege. In April, Scott's army began its advance inland. Ahead of them lay Santa Anna who, with his usual energy, had hustled back from northern Mexico and assembled another army of about 25,000 to confront this new American offensive. Forty miles inland

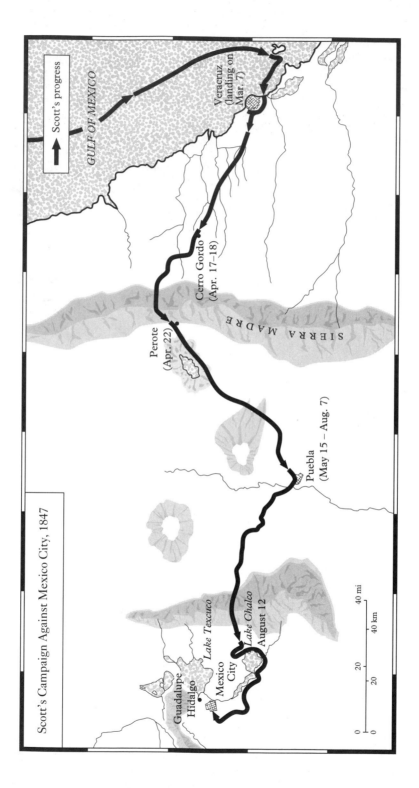

Scott's Campaign Against Mexico City, 1847

GULF OF MEXICO

→ Scott's progress

Veracruz (landing on Mar. 7)

Cerro Gordo (Apr. 17–18)

Perote (Apr. 22)

SIERRA MADRE

Puebla (May 15 – Aug. 7)

Lake Texcuco

Lake Chalco

August 12

Guadalupe Hidalgo

Mexico City

40 mi

40 km

20

20

0

0

the highway from the coast to Mexico City ascended rapidly into the mountains of the Sierra Madre. At a place called Cerro Gordo the Mexican commander elected to make his stand. The position seemed impassable; Scott, however, sent his engineers to locate a path around it and, when one was found, sent an infantry division on a circuitous march around the Mexican left flank and rear, turning the main line of defense. After a sharp little fight, Santa Anna's army fell back in disorder. Scott continued another twelve miles to Jalapa.

At Jalapa the essentially amateur nature of the American military establishment reasserted itself. Seven regiments of Scott's troops were twelve-month volunteers whose enlistments were about to expire. Most flatly refused to reenlist, and Scott had no choice but to let them march back to the coast and board ships back to the United States. At about the same time, realizing that the yellow-fever season would soon grip the lowlands, he withdrew most of the garrisons linking him with Veracruz. Then in August he continued his advance inland. He was now down to just 11,000 troops and had no dependable line of communication. The venerable Duke of Wellington, told of this development, is supposed to have declared flatly, "Scott is lost. . . . He can't take [Mexico] city, and he can't fall back upon his base."

But Scott proved the duke wrong. Husbanding his troops with great care, he masterfully kept up his offensive through a series of adroit maneuvers. His operations generally followed the pattern set at Cerro Gordo. The Mexicans would establish a seemingly impregnable defensive position, but young American officers would reconnoiter tirelessly until they found an unguarded path through or around the Mexican lines. In this fashion, Scott's army advanced within a few miles of the capital.

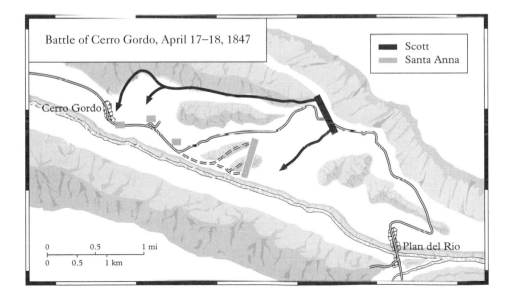

Battle of Cerro Gordo, April 17–18, 1847

Scott
Santa Anna

Cerro Gordo

0   0.5   1 mi
0   0.5   1 km

Plan del Rio

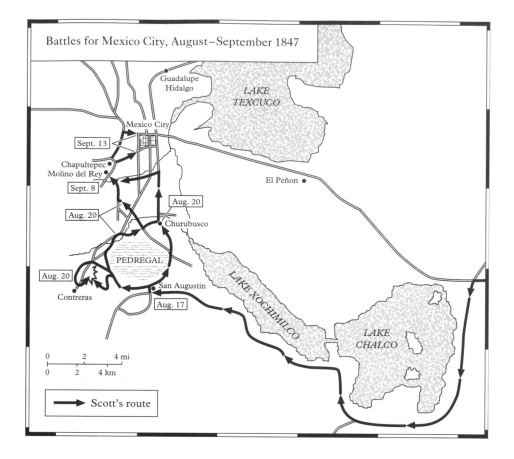

Battles for Mexico City, August–September 1847

The final assaults on Mexico City displayed the American army at its doughty best. Each operation typically began with a careful reconnaissance by engineer officers who probed the enemy lines for weaknesses and generally found them. The terrain was a rough network of hills, marshes, and rock-strewn fields, but Mexican defenders tended to overestimate its difficulty. When told, for example, that American artillery was picking its way through a solidified lava bed called the Pedregal, one Mexican officer laughed. "No! No! You're dreaming, man. The birds couldn't cross that Pedregal." Only when solid shot began to rain on his position did he realize his error.

As the anecdote suggests, American cannoneers often placed their light fieldpieces at the forefront of the fighting. Artillery typically opened an offensive engagement, where its fire helped neutralize enemy cannon, demoralize the defenders, and embolden friendly foot soldiers. When the infantrymen attacked, they tended to work their away around the Mexican flank or exploit gaps in the defenses. Only occasionally did they resort to a frontal attack. When they did, however, severe casualties could result. At the Battle of Molino del Rey, for example, the American division that made the assault lost 25 percent of its strength in a few hours of fighting. But the U.S. troops had formed the habit of winning, so that even when good tactical sense was lacking, their self-confidence and élan prevailed. When the formidable castle of Chapultepec—a key to the defense of Mexico City—fell to the Americans, a stunned Santa Anna remarked, "I believe if we were to plant our batteries in Hell the damned Yankees would take them from us." But although impressive, these American triumphs were ultimately misleading, for they occurred where the enemy possessed smoothbore muskets and artillery. They gave American officers an exaggerated view of the frontal assault's potential. During the Civil War to come, such attacks against rifled muskets and artillery often resulted only in expensive failure.

On September 14, 1847, Scott's army entered the Mexican capital. They had achieved a remarkable success. With fewer than 11,000 troops, the Americans had overcome a force of 30,000, well-entrenched and fighting on the defensive, and killed, wounded, or made prisoner a number of Mexican soldiers equal to Scott's entire army. Nominally the Mexican army remained intact. But just as Scott had predicted, the seizure of the capital so paralyzed Mexican political life that within a few weeks, the Mexicans opened negotiations for peace. The resulting Treaty of Guadalupe-Hidalgo was signed in February 1848. Under its terms, the Americans received Texas (with its boundary stipulated as the Rio Grande) and also gained California and New Mexico. In exchange the United States assumed the claims of American citizens against the Mexican government and also paid Mexico $15 million.

The Americans also gained an unexpected political nightmare. The question of whether the newly acquired territories would be slave or free haunted the nation for the next decade; it eventually exploded into civil war. Ulysses S. Grant, who considered the Mexican War "one of the most unjust ever waged by a stronger against a weaker nation," would see in this a bitter justice. "Nations, like individuals, are punished for their transgressions," he would note in his memoirs. "We got our punishment in the most sanguinary and expensive war of modern times."

The Mexican War was the first successful American attempt to project a major force beyond their own boundaries. The navy played a role similar to that of Great Britain's navy in the American Revolution: it permitted U.S. forces to move at will and to remain, for the most part, in continuous supply. By and large, both American regulars and volunteers performed well. The United States proved able to mobilize and maintain forces over a long period and at considerable distance from American soil.

On the American side, about 30,000 regular officers and men served in the war. Of these, 7,700 died—about 900 in battle, the rest from disease. About 73,000 volunteer officers and men enlisted, but many never left the United States. Of those who did, 607 were killed (most in Taylor's dubious battle at Buena Vista); another 6,400 died of disease.

Most senior American officers turned in the same uneven performance characteristic of previous American wars. The young, West Point–trained officers, however, displayed a consistent military competence rarely seen before. They thus bore testimony to a still-underdevoped but growing military professionalism. Winfield Scott, of course, was the outstanding military strategist of the war—one might say the only real strategist. Yet ironically Taylor, not Scott, became the next president, although Scott made his own bid for the White House in 1852.

The Mexican War is often considered a "dress rehearsal" for the Civil War. It certainly gave many future Civil War commanders experience. But it was really more like a well-fought War of 1812. The armies were still quite limited in size—Scott's entire army, by Civil War standards, would scarcely have made a respectable army corps. Both sides used predominantly smoothbore muskets and cannon with ranges and performance little different from those of the eighteenth century. The objectives of the Mexican War and Civil War were also quite dissimilar. While the Civil War was, in most respects, a total war fought for sheer national survival, the Mexican War was essentially a limited war fought in a manner not terribly different from the dynastic wars of eighteenth-century Europe. Limited in geographic setting, limited in allocation of resources, limited in immediate domestic impact and on the enemy's own political and social system, it bore little resemblance to the cataclysm whose origins it inadvertently sowed.

Technological Adaptation and Strategic Thought

That greater catastrophe, however, lay years in the future. In the meantime the American military congratulated itself on its victory, basked in a brief moment of glory, and then returned to its usual work of policing the now greatly expanded frontier. Discouraged by their colorless peacetime duties, a number of American officers left the service during the 1850s and sought more lucrative employment with the railroads, banks, and mining concerns that grew with the booming economy. Those who remained, however, continued the twin tasks of professionalizing the armed forces and trying to keep pace with the fast-moving technological currents of the day. Their achievements would greatly affect the conduct of the massive conflict now looming, unseen and only dimly felt, just beyond the political horizon.

New Technologies

Arriving in New York harbor in 1861, a visiting Frenchman was charmed by a calliope cheerfully piping away from the fantail of a nearby steamboat. That this novel instrument used steam to make music struck the Frenchman as both charming and appropriate. "The grateful Americans," he wrote, "have introduced that powerful agent of their fortune everywhere and even admit it into the realm of art." It was an apt comment, for no technological force exerted a greater effect on nineteenth-century America than that protean brainchild of James Watt, the steam engine.

This "agent of fortune" had two main incarnations. On water, steamboats freed vessels from the tyranny of wind and currents. On land, smoke-belching railroad trains sent dozens of passengers and tons of freight hurtling along at speeds (25 to 50 miles per hour) that seemed to annihilate distance. Taken together, these two forms of steam transportation battered down the geographical barriers to trade and increasingly brought Americans within the orbit of a single, nationwide market. Their economic value was obvious, their military importance scarcely less so. From the 1820s onward, American soldiers and sailors spent a great deal of time pondering the potentialities of steam power.

The steamboat came first. John Fitch constructed a working steam vessel as early as 1789, and by 1807 Robert Fulton's famous *Clermont* was plying the Hudson River. Seven years later, Fulton built the world's first steam warship to defend New York harbor against British attack. The potential military advantages of such a warship were considerable. It could go anywhere, heedless of adverse wind patterns or periods of calm. It could enter harbors and rivers more easily and thus held special promise for inshore operations against forts. The disadvantages, however, initially seemed daunting. Chief among these were the huge cost of the engines; the reduced cruising radius when using engines; the myriad complications from maintenance problems and coal sources; and the decreased working and living space for the crew, made necessary by the sheer bulk of the steam engines.

The drawbacks did not end there. Steam power was at first quite inefficient, requiring huge quantities of fuel in exchange for comparatively

A splendid example of the U.S. Navy's new generation of steam-powered warships, the USS *Merrimac* was also a fully rigged sailing vessel, partly as an economy measure, partly as insurance in case of mechanical failure. Although scuttled at the outbreak of the Civil War, it was salvaged by the Confederates and converted into the ironclad CSS *Virginia*.

little useful work. The development in 1837 of a high-pressure, reciprocal engine eased this problem a bit, but steam vessels remained energy hogs—particularly in comparison with elegant, inexpensive wind-powered sailing ships. There was also the matter of the huge paddlewheel that propelled the steam vessel through the water. Not only did it dramatically reduce the number of cannon that a warship could mount, the paddlewheel was highly vulnerable to enemy fire. The obvious alternative, the screw propeller, raised technological problems that took time to solve. Not until 1843 did the American navy launch its first propeller-driven warship, the *Princeton*. With its introduction the navy at last had a steam-powered warship that could fully compete with its wind-driven counterpart. But even then the problem of greater expense remained.

A major improvement in naval artillery also occurred during the 1850s. Commander John A. Dahlgren—chief of ordnance at the Washington Navy Yard from 1847 to 1861 (when he became its commandant)—tirelessly sought to develop large but safe shell-firing guns. Eventually he hit upon a durable design—an 11-inch muzzle-loading smoothbore weapon with a distinctive "coke bottle" shape to absorb gunpowder blast. It could fire either solid shot or shell. Shells could splinter the hull of a wooden warship in a way solid shot could not, while solid shot remained useful for duels against shore fortifications. Dahlgren's invention became an important intermediate step between the old-style smoothbore cannon from the days of Nelson and the high-velocity rifled artillery of the future.

The Dahlgren gun also signaled a trend toward mounting fewer but larger guns aboard warships, a trend driven in part by the growing use of steam engines aboard warships. The marriage of steam and ordnance involved a major trade-off as increases in engine size forced reductions in the space available for guns. During this period of transition in naval technology, developing an optimal design for warships proved difficult. The notion of protecting warships with iron plates further complicated the problem. Both Great Britain and France experimented with such "ironclad" vessels, but the United States initially held back. Not until the Civil War would Americans construct armored warships.

On land the army also grappled with the implications of steam and improved ordnance. To be sure, the navy's harnessing of steam power had no exact counterpart in the army. The War Department neither constructed special military trains nor commissioned studies—as did the Prussian general staff—to think systematically about the possible use of railroads in national defense. Nevertheless, inspired by its role in the republic as an important surveyor of potential railroad routes, the War Department did sponsor a number of engineering studies that dealt with such technical matters as track gradients, the design of suspension systems, and so on. Although little was directly related to warfare, such studies gave many engineering officers a close acquaintance with the demands and potentialities of the railroad. When the Civil War came, as a result, most commanders possessed a fairly good understanding of railroads and were quick to exploit this new means of transportation.

By 1860, however, steam warships had not replaced the sailing navy, nor had the railroad eclipsed the army wagon. All steam vessels remained fully equipped with masts, sails, and rigging for purposes of fuel economy or the likely event of engine failure. And where railroad tracks ended, men and supplies still had to be transported by water or, more usually, by teams of horses. Civil War armies typically needed about one draft horse for every two or three soldiers.

Technological innovation also occurred in the realm of army ordnance. Two deceptively simple advances in the realm of small arms contributed heavily to the carnage of the Civil War. The first of these was the percussion cap, the latest advance in the continuing quest to touch off a powder charge with greater reliability. Essentially a small brass fitting with a daub of mercury fulminate painted on the inside, it could be fitted snugly over a nipple at the breach of the weapon; the nipple had a small hole that provided access to the powder charge. When the weapon's hammer fell, it struck the percussion cap with enough force to ignite the mercury fulminate, send a spark into the chamber, and ignite the powder charge. The used cap could then be quickly discarded and a new one emplaced for the next firing. The percussion-cap system dispensed with the need to prime the weapon and achieved a much lower rate of misfire than the flintlock system that had been in use since the seventeenth century. During the Mexican War the American regular army largely eschewed the new-fangled percussion cap, but less hide-bound volunteer units used it widely. By the 1850s the army had adopted this system, and it was in general use during the Civil War.

The other significant advance was the creation of the first truly practical rifled musket. For centuries marksmen had understood that a projectile that spiraled in flight went farther and more accurately than a projectile that did not. The trick, of course, was to put spiral grooves in the barrel that would impart the desired spinning motion. For the grooves to achieve their effect, however, the projectile needed to "grip" the barrel snugly, a requirement that created significant military problems.

Model 1855 Rifled Musket. Civil War rifled muskets employed two new technologies: the percussion cap, which reduced the number of misfires; and the Minié ball, a bullet that enabled rifles to be loaded as rapidly as smoothbores. The result was an unprecedented extension in range and accuracy that transformed the battlefield.

With a smoothbore musket one could simply pour some powder down the barrel and then drop in the bullet, a process that took very little time. With a rifled musket, however, one had to pound the bullet down the barrel with a mallet and a long rod. All that pounding took time. Meanwhile, an enemy armed with a smoothbore musket could hurry forward and shoot first. That was why armies in the eighteenth and early nineteenth centuries mainly used smoothbores. Only special troops used rifles.

In the 1840s, however, a French army captain, Claude E. Minié, invented a way to load a rifled musket as easily as a smoothbore. Called the "Minié ball," it was a cylindro-conoidal bullet that could be dropped right down the barrel. One end of it was hollow. When the rifle was fired, the expanding gas made by the gunpowder widened the sides of this hollow end, and the sides of the hollow end gripped the rifling, creating the spinning effect required for good accuracy. Instead of hitting a target at a maximum of one hundred yards, a good marksman could hit a target with a rifled musket at four times that range or better.

Spurred by the energetic Jefferson Davis, who served as secretary of war in the mid-1850s, the army quickly adopted the rifled musket. It also pondered how to modify its infantry tactics to adapt to this innovation. The fruit of these ruminations, however, amounted to little more than an increase in the regulation marching pace of soldiers on the attack. They must reach the enemy line more rapidly, it was understood, to compensate for the increased range and accuracy of the rifled musket. No one yet guessed what thousands of Minié balls—deadly at ranges of 400 yards and beyond—could really do to troops advancing shoulder-to-shoulder in the old Napoleonic style. As is usual (and quite understandable) in such situations, military men expected that this new development would simply modify the existing tactical environment, not overthrow it.

American Military Thought

Few American officers during the 1850s gave extended attention to the problems of conducting a major war. Most were too busy fighting Indians, angling for promotion, or simply enduring a life of monotonous garrison duty. As future Confederate General Richard S. Ewell remarked, before the Civil War he learned everything there was to know about commanding fifty dragoons and forgot about everything else. Still, some officers did think seriously about strategic matters. And since most of these rose to high rank during the Civil War, their efforts leavened the indifference of their peers and, in fact, gave the conduct of that war a surprising degree of coherence. Like soldiers the world over, these more industrious American officers had to grapple with the legacy of Napoleon. But they also had to consider the military realities of defending a nation with only a small standing army and one that was, after all, separated from any major enemy by 3,000 miles of ocean.

The dean of American strategic thinkers was Dennis Hart Mahan, professor of military science at West Point. A deep admirer of Napoleon, Mahan saw this great captain chiefly through the eyes of the Swiss military theorist Antoine Henri, Baron de Jomini. Jomini emphasized the offensive essence of Napoleonic warfare but gave it an orderly, geometric cast. Similarly, Mahan celebrated the aggressive pursuit of offensive victory but lavished even greater attention upon the problems of defense. Recognizing that, in the event of war, many American soldiers would be half-trained volunteers, Mahan dwelled heavily on using field fortifications to steady new troops and reduce casualties. His ideal was the active defense—to weaken and absorb the enemy's blow, then "when he has been cut up, to assume the offensive, and drive him back at the point of the bayonet."

During his many years at West Point, Mahan drilled his ideas into a generation of cadets and presided over a "Napoleon Club" that studied the emperor's campaigns. His principal disciple, Henry Wager Halleck, translated Jomini's principal works into English and also wrote a somewhat derivative study entitled *Elements of Military Art and Science* (1846). Halleck solemnly extolled not only the virtues of field fortification but also the imperative need to keep one's forces well concentrated and vigilant against surprise attack.

Although never adopted as a West Point text, Halleck's book was probably the strategic treatise most widely read by American officers. But that is not really saying a great deal. Few references to Jomini or formal strategic theory appear in Civil War correspondence, and successful Civil War commanders often regarded their strategy as a matter of applied common sense. As Grant remarked of Napoleon, "[M]y impression is that his first success came because he made war in his own way, and not in imitation of others."

After the Mexican War the U.S. War Department sent a number of officers abroad in an effort to keep abreast of recent European military developments. But the results were not impressive. For example, a trio of officers sent to study the armies of Europe returned to make a bulky but uneven report. From their observations of the Crimean War they commented learnedly on the leggings used by Russian soldiers but failed to say anything about the Russian conscription system. American officers did better when they left the higher realms of military policy and pondered more workaday issues instead. A number of them wrote military manuals or prepared articles on technical aspects of the military profession. Some discussed better ways to train infantry, others offered suggestions on the improvement of cannon, saddles, firearms, and other items of equipment. One historian has argued that in this respect, antebellum officers were at least as professionally active as their late-twentieth-century counterparts.

*   *   *   *

By the eve of the Civil War, the United States had created a modest but reasonably proficient military establishment. Although its regular army numbered just 16,000 men in 1860, the limited standing force was adequate to perform the duties of a "frontier constabulary," and, supplemented by short-term volunteers, it had handily prevailed over a numerically larger opponent during the Mexican War. Moreover, Americans had also created a substantial system of permanent fortifications to guard their coastline.

American forces had also kept abreast of technological improvements. On land, army officers understood the importance of railroads and were well prepared to exploit that new means of transportation during the Civil War. They had also adopted the rifled musket and had attempted, however imperfectly, to anticipate its effect on infantry tactics. At sea, the navy possessed steam warships of advanced design and had also deployed new, state-of-the-art naval guns.

Perhaps most impressively, in the years after the War of 1812 the officer corps took the first significant steps toward true professional status. The U.S. Military Academy, although established in 1802, came into its own with the Thayer reforms of the 1820s. Officers increasingly viewed the military profession as a lifelong career, and a sizable number of them thought seriously about the military art. When the vicissitudes of Congress permitted, they even established schools of practice to train more thoroughly in infantry and artillery tactics.

Yet substantial problems lingered. In the years after the War of 1812 the militia system steadily declined. The presence of some peacetime volunteer companies and the enlistment of additional volunteers in wartime only partially offset the endemic shortage of trained military manpower. A strong amateur tradition also persisted. Most Americans continued to believe that an intelligent man of character, imbued with martial enthusiasm and fired by republican ideals, could make not only a good soldier but also a competent officer. Among its many other effects on American society, the Civil War would mortally challenge this belief.

SUGGESTED READINGS

Bauer, K. Jack. *The Mexican War, 1846–1848* (New York: MacMillan, 1974).

Coffman, Edward M. *The Old Army: A Portrait of the American Army in Peacetime, 1784–1898* (New York and London: Oxford University Press, 1986).

Crackel, Theodore. *Mr. Jefferson's Army: Political and Social Reform of the Military Establishment, 1801–1809* (New York and London: New York University Press, 1987).

Cunliffe, Marcus. *Soldiers and Civilians: The Martial Spirit in America, 1775–1865* (New York: Free Press, 1968).

Hickey, Don. *The War of 1812: A Forgotten Conflict* (Urbana: University of Illinois Press, 1989).

Kohn, Richard H. *Eagle and Sword: The Beginnings of the Military Establishment in America* (New York: Free Press, 1975).

McCaffrey, James M. *Army of Manifest Destiny: The American Soldier in the Mexican War, 1846–1848* (New York and London: New York University Press, 1992).

McKee, Christopher. *A Gentlemanly and Honorable Profession: The Creation of the U.S. Naval Officer Corps* (Annapolis: Naval Institute Press, 1991).

Mahon, John D. *History of the Second Seminole War* (Gainesville: University Presses of Florida, 1968).

Morrison, James L., Jr. *"The Best School in the World": West Point, the Pre–Civil War Years, 1835–1866* (Kent, Ohio: Kent State University Press, 1986).

Prucha, Francis P. *The Sword of the Republic: The United States Army on the Frontier, 1783–1846* (New York: MacMillan, 1969).

Skelton, William B. *An American Profession of Arms: The Army Officer Corps, 1784–1861* (Lawrence: University Press of Kansas, 1992).

Smith, Merritt Roe. *Harper's Ferry and the New Technology* (Ithaca, N.Y.: Cornell University Press, 1977).

Stagg, J. C. A. *Mr. Madison's War: Politics, Diplomacy, and Warfare in the Early American Republic, 1783–1830* (Princeton, N.J.: Princeton University Press, 1983).

Utley, Robert M. *Frontiersmen in Blue: The United States Army and the Indian, 1848–1865* (New York: MacMillan, 1967).

4

THE CIVIL WAR, 1861–1862:
THE LETHAL FACE OF BATTLE

Strategic Overview

War for the Borderland

Cracking the Confederate
Frontier

At 4:30 A.M. on April 12, 1861, a dull boom thudded across the tranquil harbor of Charleston, South Carolina. From the city, observers could clearly see the fuse of a mortar shell as it climbed across the soft moonlit sky, then plunged in a graceful arc toward casemated Fort Sumter near the harbor entrance. A moment later the shell exploded directly above the fort, raining fragments on the federal garrison below. The Civil War—the deadliest conflict in American history and, in many respects, the central episode of that history—had begun.

No one had any idea what to expect. Most Americans supposed the war would be decided by one or two major battles. A few even believed it might end without any serious fighting at all. But nearly everyone agreed that, at most, the struggle would be settled within a year. They also assumed that the fundamental patterns of American society would remain unaltered. Indeed, the preservation of those patterns formed the very object for which Americans on both sides were contending. White Southerners expected to maintain an agrarian, slave-holding society that, in their minds at least, corresponded to the republic established by the Founding Fathers. Northerners sought to restore the unbroken alliance of states toasted by President Andrew Jackson nearly three decades before ("Our Federal Union—it must be preserved!").

But instead of a brief contest, the Civil War raged across the central and southern United States for four long years. And instead of conserving the old America—however defined—it steadily and profoundly reshaped the political, economic, and social contours of the nation. By the time it ended, the original American republic was gone forever.

The Civil War was, as one historian has aptly called it, "the Second

American Revolution." Like the War for Independence, it was a revolutionary conflict, combining the mass politics and passions of the wars of the French Revolution with the technology, productive capacity, and managerial style of an emergent industrial society. Both the Union and the Confederacy fielded armies that dwarfed all military formations previously seen in the New World. They supplied these vast hosts with food, munitions, and equipment shipped by rail and steamship. They connected units hundreds of miles apart with webs of telegraph lines, and motivated soldiers and civilians alike with ceaseless barrages of political propaganda. When necessary they repressed dissent with intimidation and arbitrary arrests. Before the war was half over, both sides abandoned cherished notions of individual liberty and conscripted men to serve in the armies. In their quest to finance the struggle they trampled venerable ideas about limited taxation and fiscal rectitude. And by the war's third year they had begun to accept attacks upon enemy civilians and property as necessary and even virtuous. Both sides mobilized their resources and populations to the utmost limit of their mid-nineteenth-century ability and, when they reached the end of that ability, strove for ways to extend it. The Union and the Confederacy, in short, waged a total war: a war in which both societies pitted their full destructive energies against each other.

Strategic Overview

To understand the course of the war, one must understand its origins, for perceptions concerning the roots of the conflict profoundly shaped the objectives and strategy of both sides. The central issue was slavery, although many Americans did not accept this at the time (and some still do not today). One alternative view suggests that the Civil War was a struggle over "states' rights" versus centralized government—yet most Northerners believed in states' rights as much as most Southerners. Another regards it as a contest between an agrarian South and an industrialized North, neglecting to note that the Northern states were also primarily agricultural—in the case of the midwest, overwhelmingly so. Still another posits a conflict between two allegedly distinct cultures—overlooking the fact that North and South shared a common language, a common history, and a common belief in republican government. Such political, economic, and cultural differences as did exist could be traced, by and large, to a single source: the fact that the South was a slaveholding society and the North was not.

Roots of War

By the mid-nineteenth century, slavery had become the South's bedrock institution. In the 250 years since the first shackled Africans had arrived on American shores (and especially in the decades following the American

Revolution), white Southerners had evolved a complex set of beliefs about their "peculiar institution." Not only did they consider it vital for the cultivation of the region's major cash crops, they also thought it the only acceptable basis on which whites and blacks could coexist. Slaveholders liked to regard their bondsmen essentially as children incapable of self-improvement and therefore in need of their master's lifelong paternal care. Many believed—or affected to believe—that the blacks themselves preferred a life of slavery and benefited from it. Paradoxically most Southerners also possessed a profound if usually unstated fear of a slave revolt. The need to maintain absolute, unquestioned control over their slave population gave Southerners a strong incentive to preserve an ordered, stable society. As a result, social change of any kind occurred in the South more slowly than in the North. And although only one in four Southern families actually owned slaves, most accepted the proslavery philosophy. They either aspired to ownership or, at a minimum, appreciated the advantages of living in a society whose lowest tier remained permanently reserved for blacks.

Northerners, however, increasingly found the "peculiar institution" distasteful. Comparatively little of this distaste reflected humanitarian concern for the slaves. Perhaps 5 percent of the Northern population entertained "abolitionist" sentiments: that is to say, a belief in both immediate, uncompensated emancipation *and* political and social equality for blacks. The vast majority of antislavery Northerners objected to the "peculiar institution" not because of its effect on black people, but because of its effect on whites. It degraded the value of free labor. It encouraged an agrarian society dominated by a comparative handful of wealthy planters who (many believed) monopolized political power in the South. Conversely it discouraged the creation of new industry and economic diversity. And to the extent that slavery was permitted in the western territories, it meant that white families would be forced to live beside blacks, a prospect that many Northern whites considered repugnant.

Until the late 1840s this tension between pro- and antislavery forces remained largely submerged. It surfaced rapidly when the Mexican War broke out. Many Whigs and some Northern Democrats regarded the conflict as nothing but a naked land grab by Southern slaveholders eager to extend slavery into Mexico. In August 1846 antislavery congressman David Wilmot of Pennsylvania introduced a resolution that formally renounced any intention by the United States to introduce slavery into any lands that might be seized from Mexico during the war. This "Wilmot Proviso" failed to pass both houses of Congress, but it succeeded in reinjecting slavery into national political life. For the next fifteen years the question of slavery in the territories constantly dogged American policy makers.

At bottom, the question dividing Americans might be summarized thus: was the United States a slaveholding republic with pockets of freedom in the North, or was it a free republic with pockets of slavery in the South? The answer had profound implications for the very nature of the American experiment and its future. Proslavery Americans sought to extend slavery into the territories because they considered anything less to be an abridgment of their rights and an implicit query against the legitimacy of their way of life. Antislavery Americans wanted to bar the extension of slavery because they believed the system degraded the dignity of free labor and stifled economic diversity. More darkly, they suspected that the slave system sustained a planter aristocracy that controlled political life in the South and was trying to maintain control over national political life as well.

Throughout the 1850s, both sides saw evidence to support their own beliefs. Political compromise grew more difficult. An attempt to permit western settlers to decide for themselves whether a given territory would be slaveholding or free degenerated into violence when the rival factions in Kansas Territory undermined the democratic process through intimidation, fraud, and murder. Then in 1859 the abolitionist terrorist John Brown raided Harpers Ferry, Virginia, hoping to foment a slave insurrection. The operation was a fiasco; Brown was captured and hanged, as were most of his followers who survived the attack itself. But the Harpers Ferry raid shocked the entire white population of the South, especially when they discovered that a few Northern abolitionists had helped finance Brown's attack. The fact that many in the North considered Brown a martyr only increased the Southerners' sense of anger and alienation.

For thirty years some Southerners had discussed the possibility of secession if the national government ever threatened the continued existence of slavery. The election of Republican candidate Abraham Lincoln seemed to bring that threat uncomfortably near. His party openly opposed the extension of slavery in the territories, and although Lincoln renounced any intention to touch slavery where it already existed, as president he would have power to appoint judges and federal marshals in the South. Such officials, indispensable to maintain the system of law and order on which slavery depended, would now be of dubious loyalty to the "peculiar institution." Perhaps most gallingly, Lincoln won election despite the fact that hardly any Southerners had voted for him. In most slaveholding states he had not even been on the ballot.

Many Southerners now sensed that they had lost control of the national government; they could no longer expect that government to preserve slavery. Honor and self-interest dictated that they must leave the Union if they expected to retain control of their own destinies. The secessionist impulse was particularly strong in South Carolina, a state in which slaves outnumbered whites and which had a long tradition of radicalism on the subject of slavery. On December 20, 1860, a convention of South Carolinians unanimously voted to leave the Union. Six other states followed in the next six weeks: Mississippi, Alabama, Louisiana, Georgia, Florida, and Texas. It was the worst crisis the nation had ever faced.

However, eight slave states—North Carolina, Tennessee, Virginia, Arkansas, Maryland, Kentucky, Missouri, and Delaware—remained loyal to the Union. This suggested that many Southerners did not wish to secede, an impression reinforced by the fact that in most of the states that *did* leave the Union, a substantial minority had voted against secession. For these and other reasons, when the Lincoln administration took office in March 1861, it hoped that some means might be found to undermine the secessionist

Perhaps America's greatest war president, Abraham Lincoln combined political skill with dogged determination and at times even ruthlessness.

movement without bloodshed. Perhaps, as Secretary of State William Seward believed, most Southerners would eventually repudiate disunion if given time to reconsider.

In the meantime, however, delegates from the seceded states formed a new nation, the Confederate States of America. Meeting in Montgomery, Alabama, they drafted a new constitution and established a provisional government to be led by Jefferson Davis, a former U.S. senator and secretary of war. One of the new government's first acts was to assume authority over the artillery batteries erected by South Carolina to threaten the tiny Federal garrison of Fort Sumter.

The Confederate government insisted that the Lincoln administration withdraw the garrison: its claim to sovereignty over the seceded South would be meaningless if a "foreign" power continued to occupy one of the Confederacy's principal ports. The symbolism of Fort Sumter was equally important to Lincoln, since to order its evacuation would be a fatal display of weakness. For weeks the standoff persisted. Finally President Davis gave orders that if the fort refused to surrender it must be bombarded. The firing on Fort Sumter on April 12 ended any chance the sectional rift could be repaired without bloodshed. Undermanned, low on food, and cut off from resupply, Fort Sumter surrendered on April 14. The following day Lincoln requested 75,000 three-month volunteers to suppress the rebellion.

Military Resources and Objectives

Lincoln's call for troops triggered a second wave of secession. The upper tier of southern states—Virginia, Arkansas, North Carolina, and Tennessee—all left the Union rather than support the North in a war against the Confederacy. By June the Confederacy consisted of eleven states, sprawling across a territory the size of western Europe and boasting a population of 9 million. Of these, about 5.5 million were whites. Most of the rest were slaves—a huge potential security problem, to be sure, but also a major economic asset.

The Confederacy's aim at the beginning of the war was simple: hold on to the de facto independence already obtained. It did not need to invade the North or dictate a peace treaty on the steps of the White House. All it had to do was to continue the struggle long enough for the North to tire of the war and accept the fact of secession. In many respects this aim was little different from that of the American colonies during the Revolution, a struggle still close enough in time to be almost a living memory. That earlier conflict had been won largely by attrition. The British had captured the colonies' cities almost at will, traversed American territory as they pleased, and dominated the seas that bathed American shores. But they could neither quench the Americans' will to fight nor prevent foreign intervention once the Americans had shown their capacity for sustained resistance.

Conceivably the Confederates might have adopted a similar strategy: pin their forces to the defense of no fixed area or city, draw the invaders in, and wear out the Federals by a protracted war of attrition. Instead Davis and his advisors decided to fight the battle at the frontier. They would repulse incursions and attempt to hold major concentrations of population and resources. A number of considerations made this the obvious strategy. First, the discrepancy in military strength between North and South, although hardly an even match, was far less forbidding than that between Britain and the American colonies. Second, the political pressures within the Confederacy for a conventional defense were also great—every locality clamored for Southern troops to protect it. Third, a conventional defense would give the Confederacy greater legitimacy in the eyes of its own citizens and in those of the world. And finally, the delicate "peculiar institution" needed the stability of law and order to survive. The mere presence of a hostile political party in the White House had threatened that stability enough to spur the cotton states to secession. Given the enormous sensitivity of this issue, the Confederacy could hardly permit Federal armies to plunge deep into Southern territory. Even if formal Federal policy remained one of non-interference with slave labor, an advancing Union army would surely disrupt slave labor, create a flood of runaways, and perhaps even raise the spectre of a race war of slave against master. The Confederacy, then, had many good reasons to defend itself at the border.

The South would not conduct a passive defense, either. Davis preferred what he called the "offensive-defensive." According to his scheme, Confederate forces would permit a Union thrust to develop, gauge its main axis of advance, wait for an advantageous moment, then concentrate and counterattack at a time and place of their own choosing. General Robert E.

Jefferson Davis was highly qualified to be the Confederacy's president, having been a Mexican War hero, Secretary of War in the Franklin Pierce administration, and a senator from Mississippi.

Lee described this operational concept in an 1863 letter: "It is [as] impossible for [the enemy] to have a large operating army at every assailable point in our territory as it is for us to keep one to defend it. We must move our troops from point to point as required, and by close observation and accurate information the true point of attack can generally be ascertained. . . . Partial encroachments of the enemy we must expect, but they can always be recovered, and any defeat of their large army will reinstitute everything."

Confederates worried comparatively little about the larger size and greater resource base of their opponent, partly from overconfidence, but primarily because of a conviction that the war would be brief and comparatively limited—a contest on the scale, say, of the recent Mexican War. But in a longer struggle the North's advantages were substantial. With a population of 20 million, the Northern states obviously possessed a much larger military manpower base, but their industrial capacity was far greater as well. In 1860 the North had over 110,000 manufacturing establishments, the South just 18,000. The North produced 94 percent of the country's iron, 97 percent of its coal and—not incidentally—97 percent of its firearms. It contained 22,000 miles of railroad to the South's 8,500. The North outperformed the South agriculturally as well. Northerners held 75 percent of the country's farm acreage, produced 60 percent of its livestock, 67 percent of its corn, and 81 percent of its wheat. All in all, they held 75 percent of the nation's total wealth.

The North's advantages did not end there. It controlled the resources of a long-established government, including the 16,000 men of its army and the ninety warships of its navy. It had a much better financial structure. The South, by contrast, had no preexisting armed forces, few banks, and relatively little specie. Its wealth lay primarily in land and slaves—assets difficult to convert to liquid capital. Shortly after the war began, the Confederate government made this deficiency even worse by ordering an embargo on the sale of cotton abroad. The decision, intended to pressure textile-producing nations like Great Britain into supporting the Confederacy, only hurt the South's ability to obtain more hard currency.

Even so, most of the North's advantages were potential rather than real. It would take time for the Union to translate its demographic and economic resources into effective strength, and in the interim the Confederacy would create military forces of impressive size. To be sure, the Federals usually held the edge in manpower and heavy weaponry, but only at the margins. And the South possessed considerable advantages of its own. Although the Union possessed more men, it also had the daunting task of projecting large armies across hundreds of miles of territory, much of it difficult to traverse and sparsely populated. Southern forces could rely upon a largely loyal population, whereas Union forces would have to divert large numbers of troops to guard supply lines and garrison key points against guerrilla incursions. Southern forces could fight on the defensive and exploit interior lines to concentrate against separate Union columns. Then too, the fact that Southerners were fighting to defend their homeland made their cause more concrete and thus more potent. Finally, with millions of slaves to keep the Southern economy running, the South could afford to send a larger percentage of its white manpower to war.

Of further benefit to the South was the fact that the Lincoln administration had to contend with an all-but-insoluble political conundrum. It had to maintain as broad a base of domestic support for the war as possible, despite the fact that some Northerners opposed any attempt to coerce the South, while many others believed the attempt must be made without trampling on the constitutional rights of Southerners—including their right to hold slaves. The administration also had to fight the war hard enough to gain victory but not so violently as to foster deep bitterness among the Southern people. The North's objective, after all, was a reunion of the states. If that were to be accomplished it required that the Southern people must eventually choose—grudgingly, perhaps, but essentially voluntarily—to renew their loyalty to the United States government. The dilemma facing the Lincoln administration was thus one of enormous complexity. It had to find a policy vigorous enough to win the war, but not so vigorous as to forfeit domestic support or alienate the South completely.

War for the Borderland

Nowhere was the Union task more delicate than in the borderland, a region consisting of Missouri, Kentucky, Maryland, and the western counties of

Virginia. These were slaveholding areas, each with considerable secessionist sentiment but also with substantial populations loyal to the Federal government. If the Lincoln administration could hold these areas, it stood a fighting chance of containing the rebellion. If, however, the Confederacy gained control of the borderland, it could isolate Washington, D.C., add another million people to its population, and render a Federal victory all but impossible. As both sides mobilized their field armies, they struggled first for control of the border states between them.

Mobilization

Since they shared an identical military heritage, it was scarcely surprising that the Union and Confederacy organized for war in similar ways. Lincoln, of course, had the advantage of preexisting War and Navy departments as well as small, permanent land and naval forces. But the Davis administration quickly created identical departments. In any event the United States prior to 1860 had no experience with a command structure adequate for the unprecedented size and scope of the conflict, and as a result both Davis and Lincoln had to experiment.

The paper organization Davis created was not bad. It combined a secretary of war with an adjutant and inspector general whom Davis expected would perform as a de facto chief of staff. In reality, however, Davis ran much of the war effort himself. The secretary of war position never amounted to much. The job passed from one man to another until the end of the Confederate government's existence. Davis apparently never sought, and certainly never found, a forceful and able secretary of war.

The Union command structure, although similar, had a few important differences. First, Lincoln wisely chose to invest his secretary of war with very wide powers. His initial choice for the position proved corrupt and inefficient, but in January 1862 Lincoln appointed a new man, Edwin M.

As Lincoln's Secretary of War, Edwin M. Stanton presided over a Union army of over one million men and kept it well supplied with arms and equipment.

Stanton of Pennsylvania, who became one of the most energetic and forceful secretaries of war in American history. "Stanton," Lincoln once remarked, "is the rock upon which are beating the waves of this conflict. . . . I do not see how he survives—why he is not crushed and torn to pieces. Without him, I should be destroyed." Lincoln also insisted—except for one brief interlude—on having a general-in-chief. During the course of the conflict he had four of them (Winfield Scott, George B. McClellan, Henry W. Halleck, and Ulysses S. Grant), and his experiences with all but the last were often frustrating. But by maintaining the post he prevented himself from becoming overwhelmed by detail and also, at least in theory, received the benefit of expert military advice.

Both sides spent the first months of the war feverishly generating armies far larger than any the United States had previously fielded. To do so, each mobilized its limited contingents of existing state militia, but these barely began to furnish the necessary manpower. To augment the militia, volunteer troops were enlisted by tens of thousands. In keeping with the traditional American political philosophy, chief responsibility for raising the volunteers reposed not with the central government but rather with the individual states. The Union and Confederate War departments simply asked each state to raise a certain number of regiments. The state governors, in turn, had the task of actually finding, organizing, and equipping the needed men. To do so they often turned to community leaders—men of established standing who could persuade other men to enlist under their command. Thus a prominent local attorney might announce that he was organizing a company of infantry. Other men, familiar with the attorney's reputation and willing to serve with him, would then enroll in the company until its rosters were filled. Afterward they would elect the key company officers and sergeants. The attorney, of course, would invariably be elected captain. The company would then band with other companies into a regiment, and the regiment's colonel would then be selected. Sometimes the governor would appoint him; sometimes he would be elected, if not by the rank and file then by the various company commanders. In this way the states met their quotas. The exact details varied widely but were always in keeping with the loose-jointed, localistic nature of American society.

In their homespun way, Americans were harnessing the same thing that had fired the French Revolution: popular sovereignty, the notion that the people themselves formed the ultimate source of political authority and legitimacy. Nowhere in the nineteenth-century world was this idea more potent than in the United States, and as a result both Northerners and Southerners felt a profound sense of identification with the cause for which their governments were contending. The gulf between the Civil War soldier and his eighteenth-century counterpart could hardly be more absolute. The old European soldier felt little sense of involvement with his sovereign's cause, nor did the peasants and burghers whose taxes paid for the war. By contrast, the Civil War soldier was a member of one of the most intensely politicized societies on earth. His sense of involvement with his cause—whether the cause of Union or the cause of Southern independence—was profound; the communities that sent him to war were equally so. The explosion of martial energy this produced in 1861 was as powerful as that of the French Revolution.

The consequences of popular sovereignty affected the Union and Confederate war efforts in other ways as well. For one thing, the improvised nature of the mobilization gave the state governors an enormous degree of importance and thus considerable influence. Two governors of particular note were Oliver Perry Morton of Indiana and Joseph G. Brown of Georgia. Morton took an almost proprietary interest in his Hoosier regiments and was known to complain vigorously whenever he believed they were being mishandled. He advanced or undercut the careers of several Union commanders. Brown, for his part, became the gadfly of the Davis administration, damned various administration policies, circumvented the operation of military conscription in his state, and often retained supplies and equipment for the use of Georgia troops alone.

Both sides also found it expedient to offer high military rank to important political figures. The Lincoln administration in particular tried to clinch the support of various Northern constituencies by making generals of favorite politicians. Thus Nathaniel P. Banks, former Speaker of the House, received a major general's commission to make sure that New England Democrats backed the Union war effort. Lincoln also made Franz Sigel a major general in order to secure the support of the German-American community. Students of the Civil War have long poured scorn upon these "political generals." But their derision reflects a fundamental misunderstanding of the military ethos that prevailed in mid-nineteenth-century America. A professional officer corps, in the modern sense of the term, hardly existed, and few Americans understood why it should. In the minds of many, the chief attributes of effective command were character and leadership ability, and surely any widely admired political figure possessed these. Such scorn also overlooks the fact that many of these "political generals" performed at least as well as some of their West Point–trained counterparts, while a few of them displayed genuine gifts.

As soon as these newly formed units could gather—erratically uniformed, gawky, ill-disciplined, but filled with ardor—they began to gravitate toward various points along the military frontier. Few of these movements occurred as the result of comprehensive planning on the part of the Union and Confederate high commands. No such planning had occurred; no overarching strategic vision existed on either side. Often a governor or department commander decided what places must be garrisoned or occupied as bases for subsequent advances. At this early stage, the war efforts of both North and South were very much improvised. Like the armies themselves, strategic decision-making was generally an ad hoc affair.

The Border States

Even so, both sides had evident priorities. The Confederacy positioned substantial forces to block the approaches to Richmond; the North, for its part, exerted almost frantic energies to ensure the safety of Washington. The

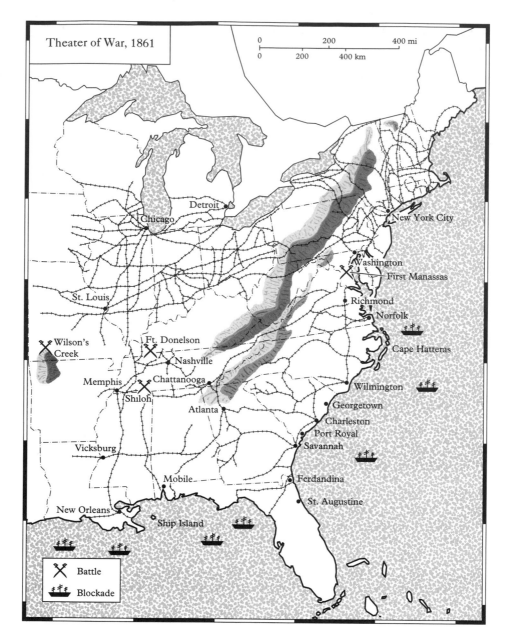

Theater of War, 1861

Federal capital was surrounded by slaveholding territory—Virginia, now part of a hostile power, lay just across the Potomac bridges, while Maryland hemmed in the District of Columbia on its remaining three sides. For a brief but terrifying moment it seemed likely that Maryland might leave the Union as well. Scant days after Fort Sumter, a secessionist mob had pelted Massachusetts troops as they marched through Baltimore en route to Washington; it was also widely rumored that the state legislature would shortly vote to join the Confederacy. The Maryland lawmakers never got the chance, however. Abandoning all concern for constitutional niceties, the

Lincoln administration suspended the writ of habeas corpus, declared martial law, imprisoned suspected persons, and in general clamped on Maryland a military despotism. This development was utterly startling in a nation long-wedded to the concept of limited government. It was also highly effective in keeping Maryland firmly within the Union—whether Marylanders liked it or not.

The Federal government enjoyed similar success in the western counties of Virginia. Economically this mountainous region was more tied to Ohio and Pennsylvania than to tidewater Virginia. It possessed relatively few slaves, a long tradition of resentment toward the more densely populated eastern counties, and considerable Unionist sentiment. In late May, when Federal troops from Ohio first crossed into western Virginia, they were widely received as liberators. The Confederacy had only a few weak units in the region, and those soon departed from the region after a series of minor clashes that nevertheless brought great results. The Federal victories in western Virginia secured Union control over the Baltimore and Ohio Railroad, a strategically invaluable artery between the eastern and western theaters of war. They also paved the way for the creation (in 1863) of the new state of West Virginia.

Kentucky, like western Virginia, was a state settled largely by Southerners but tied geographically and economically to the Ohio River valley. Perhaps not surprisingly, in the sectional squabbles that had preceded the war its citizens had exhibited a strong preference for compromise. The "Great Compromiser" himself, Senator Henry Clay, had been from Kentucky. So was Senator John J. Crittenden, principal proponent of a compromise proposal that had floated briefly during the secession winter. Nowhere was the "war of brothers" image more appropriate than in the Bluegrass State. Sixty percent of white Kentuckians who fought during the conflict wore Union blue; the rest wore gray. And in Kentucky the lines were indeed sometimes drawn within family circles. Crittenden had two sons who became generals on opposite sides.

When war broke out, Kentucky's governor tried in vain to mediate the conflict. When his efforts failed, the legislature voted that the state would maintain "strict neutrality." Lincoln, fearful that a tough policy would push Kentucky into the Confederate fold, gave orders to respect this extralegal neutrality. So did Davis. This anomalous situation lasted only until early September, when Confederate General Leonidas Polk—acting on his own authority—marched into Columbus, Kentucky. The town's position on a high bluff overlooking the Mississippi River gave it strategic value. By seizing Columbus, Polk strengthened the defense of the river, but the political cost was substantial. Although Federal troops (under Major General Ulysses S. Grant) promptly occupied other Kentucky towns at the mouths of the Cumberland and Tennessee rivers, the fact that the Confederacy had violated Kentucky neutrality first made it seem the aggressor. The state legislature embraced the Union; the prosecessionist governor resigned. By the end of the year Federal forces held most of the important points in Kentucky, including Louisville, the largest city, and Frankfort, the capital. The Confederates occupied only a thin strip along the state's southern frontier.

Missouri proved a thornier problem for the Lincoln administration. Although most of its citizens were pro-Union, a substantial minority favored the Confederates, and while Kentuckians adopted a largely neutral stance, the rival factions in Missouri quickly came to blows. Trouble began in mid-May when a mixed force of Union home guards and regulars marched into the camp of prosecessionist state militiamen and disarmed them. The Federal commander, Captain Nathaniel Lyon, had the captured militia herded through the streets of Saint Louis. An angry mob gathered, shouting "Hurrah for Jeff Davis!" and throwing brickbats. Presently someone shot an officer and the Union troops opened fire. At least twenty-eight civilians and two soldiers died in the ensuing melée, and dozens more were wounded.

Although provocative, Lyon's decision to disarm the militia was basically prudent. The prosecessionist militia had already received cannon and ammunition spirited to them from Louisiana; given time they might well have seized control of Saint Louis. Even so, his action and the ensuing riot fueled passions on both sides and promised further violence. To avert the possibility of more internal fighting, Missouri moderates arranged a meeting between Lyon and the prosecessionist governor. But after four hours of negotiation Lyon lost his temper. "Rather than concede to the State of Missouri for one instant the right to dictate to my Government in any matter . . . I would see you . . . and every man, woman, and child in the State, dead and buried. *This means war.*"

In the weeks that followed, Union forces managed to push the secessionist militia—without any major fighting—toward the southwestern part of Missouri. Lyon pursued with about 5,500 men and occupied the town of Springfield. But his forces dangled at the end of a tenuous supply line, he could receive no reinforcements, and soon the 8,000 secessionist militia (led by Major General Sterling Price) were joined by 5,000 Confederate troops under Major General Benjamin McCulloch. Lyon nevertheless refused to retreat and, learning that the Rebels would soon begin an offensive, decided to attack first. On August 10 he struck the enemy at Wilson's Creek, ten miles south of Springfield.

Lyon's attack was an incredible gamble that came amazingly close to success. The rebel troops were poorly trained and equipped, and Lyon managed to achieve surprise with a daring two-pronged attack. A confused, savage battle ensued along the banks of Wilson's Creek. Lyon's men managed to hold their own, despite odds of nearly three-to-one, until Lyon was fatally wounded. With his death the Union forces lost heart. Nearly out of ammunition anyway, they retreated. Eventually they fell back over one hundred miles to Rolla, a railhead town with links to Saint Louis.

Union losses in this battle were 1,300; Southern losses were about the same. The Confederates followed up their victory by marching into the Missouri River valley and capturing the important town of Lexington, Missouri, in mid-September. For a brief period, then, Price's militia controlled half the state. But Price soon discovered he lacked the manpower to hold such a vast region, and in October he withdrew again to the southwest corner of the state. In February 1862 a substantial Union army under Major General Samuel Curtis managed to eject Price from Missouri for good.

Then, in the Battle of Pea Ridge, Arkansas (March 6–8, 1862), Curtis stopped a major Confederate attempt to drive him back.

Almost despite itself, the Union had managed to hold on to Missouri. Its grip was tenuous and remained so. Throughout the war, Missouri was the scene of a continual and vicious guerrilla struggle, particularly in the proslavery Missouri River valley. Still, by early 1862 the Lincoln administration had achieved an important objective—it controlled the borderland.

First Bull Run

From a Union perspective, securing the borderland was a defensive goal. To do so might keep the rebellion within manageable limits, but it did little to defeat the Confederacy. For that the Union needed an offensive plan, and as the spring of 1861 progressed, the Lincoln administration pondered how best to proceed.

Its general-in-chief, the once magnificent but now aging Winfield Scott, proposed a very cautious strategy. Like many Northerners, including Lincoln, Scott believed that popular support for the Confederate regime was shallow; the Southern people, after all, had been until recently loyal citizens of the United States. An adroit approach might detach them from the Davis government and woo their allegiance back to the Union. But how to do this? Scott suggested a three-phase plan. First, blockade the Southern harbors, cutting them off from outside assistance. Second, send a strong column down the Mississippi River to hold that vital artery of commerce and further isolate the Confederate states. Third, wait. If the North did these things, Scott maintained, it "will thus cut off the luxuries to which the people are accustomed; and when they feel the pressure, not having been exasperated by attacks made on them within their respective States, the Union spirit will assert itself; those who are on the fence will descend on the Union side, and I will guarantee that in one year from this time all difficulties will be settled." If, on the other hand, Federal armies invaded the South at any point, "I will guarantee that at the end of a year you will be further from a settlement than you are now." The press, likening the strategy to the coilings of a giant constricting snake, soon dubbed Scott's proposal the "Anaconda Plan."

Some Cabinet members agreed with Scott, but most believed his plan would backfire. The longer the Confederate government functioned, the more legitimacy it would acquire in the minds of the Southern people. For this reason an immediate offensive against Richmond, the capital of that government, seemed imperative. Lincoln concurred with this second view and in late June gave orders that the Union forces assembling around Washington must advance against Richmond. The commander of these troops, Brigadier General Irvin McDowell, objected that his men were as yet too unseasoned for such an operation. Lincoln refused to budge. "You are green, it is true," he said. "But they [the Confederates] are green also. You are all green alike."

On July 16, 1861, McDowell left Washington with about 35,000 men. Twenty-five miles to the southwest lay a smaller Confederate army of

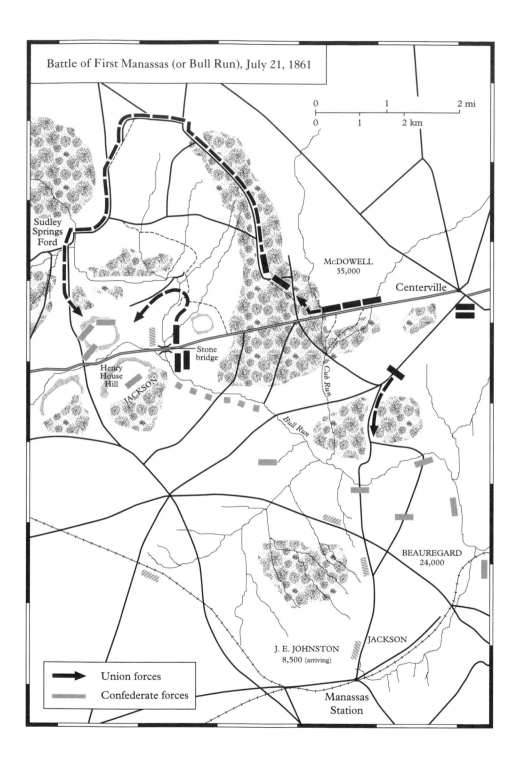

Battle of First Manassas (or Bull Run), July 21, 1861

Sudley
Springs
Ford

McDOWELL
35,000

Centerville

Stone
bridge

Henry
House
Hill

JACKSON

Cub Run

Bull Run

BEAUREGARD
24,000

JACKSON

J. E. JOHNSTON
8,500 (arriving)

Manassas
Station

Union forces

Confederate forces

25,000 men—led by General P. G. T. Beauregard, the victor of Fort Sumter. Beauregard had deployed his brigades along a lengthy stretch of a bramble-choked stream called Bull Run. From this position Beauregard's army held the railroad town of Manassas Junction and blocked the direct overland approach to Richmond.

McDowell outnumbered Beauregard by a considerable margin, and if the Confederates at Manassas had fought unaided he might have won a considerable victory. But fifty miles to the west, 13,000 Rebels under General Joseph E. Johnston guarded the lower Shenandoah Valley. Opposing them was a somewhat larger Union force under an elderly militia general named Robert Patterson. Patterson's mission was to prevent Johnston from reinforcing Beauregard once McDowell advanced; however, he botched the assignment. Leaving a thin screen of cavalry to deceive Patterson, Johnston loaded most of his troops on railcars and sent them rolling down the Manassas Gap Railroad. They reached the Bull Run position on the afternoon of July 21, just as McDowell was pressing home a skillfully prepared attack upon Beauregard's beleaguered men. These reinforcements (coupled with a tenacious defense by Confederate Brigadier General Thomas J. Jackson, who earned the nickname "Stonewall" for his role in the battle) turned the tide against the Federals. Then, just as McDowell had feared, the inexperience of the Union troops transformed a reversal into a rout. The Northerners streamed back toward Washington in a disheveled, uncontrollable mass. It might just as easily have happened to the equally inexperienced Confederates. But it did not, and the Battle of Bull Run became a symbol of Southern prowess and Northern humiliation.

The Union lost about 625 killed in this first major engagement, along with 950 wounded and over 1,200 captured; Confederate casualties numbered 400 killed and about 1,600 wounded. By itself, the battle decided nothing. But in the South it created a sense of dangerous overconfidence, while Northerners regarded it as a stinging summons to greater efforts. From a purely military standpoint its most interesting aspect was the Confederates' use of the railroad to reinforce the threatened Bull Run sector. Without the railroad, Johnston's troops would have reached the battlefield too exhausted for action—if indeed they would have arrived at all.

Cracking the Confederate Frontier

Railroads played a significant role in the struggle for the borderland. The Union thrust into western Virginia was dictated, to a considerable degree, by the need to control the Baltimore & Ohio Railroad, one of the main east-west trunk lines. The Union offensive in Missouri also followed the railroad as far as possible. Meanwhile, along the coast and in the trans-Appalachian west, the Union began to exploit the nineteenth century's other great agent of mechanized power: the steamship. In the months that followed the Bull Run defeat, the Union's edge in sea and riverine power helped it recover from this initial setback. Federal warships began the long, slow process of strangling the South's commerce by blockading its ports, and using Union troops to secure a number of enclaves along the Confederate coast. And in the Mississippi River valley, Union gunboats and transports played a major role in the North's first decisive victories during the winter of 1862.

The Coast, 1861–1862

The seceded states had nearly 3,000 miles of coastline. In part this formed a Confederate asset, because it offered nearly eighty points where Southern blockade runners could find safe harbor. But the long coastline was also a major liability, because it gave Union forces wide opportunity to exploit the North's command of the sea. Defending the long, vulnerable sea frontier diverted many thousands of Confederate troops from duty with the field armies. Even so, Union troops generally had little trouble seizing whatever coastal point they chose. From a Southern perspective, the situation was depressingly like that of the colonists during the American Revolution. The revolutionary general Charles Lee once complained that he felt "like a dog in a dancing school" when confronted by superior British sea mobility. A number of Confederate generals grew familiar with the same sensation.

The first Union beachheads were established primarily as coaling

Union landing at Hatteras Inlet, August 1861. The Union had a formidable edge over the Confederacy in sea power, and troops transported by the U.S. Navy established numerous enclaves along the Southern coast during the course of the Civil War. The enclaves supported the Union blockade and provided springboards for advances inland.

stations for blockaders. In August 1861 a Northern detachment occupied Hatteras Inlet, North Carolina; three months later a larger force seized the magnificent harbor at Port Royal, South Carolina. By March 1862 additional troops had occupied much of eastern North Carolina. Once established, these enclaves provided bases from which Union troops could raid inland. Perhaps as importantly, they acted like magnets for hundreds of slaves who escaped their masters and took refuge within Union lines.

Many of these initial amphibious operations pitted Union warships against the casemated forts that had formed America's principal defensive network since the republic's early years. Conventional wisdom held that in a slugging match between ships and forts, the forts would inevitably prevail, but events challenged this old notion. Armed with the new Columbiad and Dahlgren shell-firing guns, Union warships routinely reduced forts within a few hours. Steam power also made it possible for warships to navigate with greater precision in shallow coastal waters, so that they could perform feats that might have proved fatal for older sailing craft.

The greatest single victory for Union sea power occurred in April 1862, when a Federal fleet engaged the two forts that guarded the Mississippi River below New Orleans. Assisted by a flotilla of mortar boats that rained heavy shells into the forts, the fleet—led by Flag Officer David G. Farragut—managed to steam past the forts and on to nearly defenseless New Orleans. On April 25, Union troops hoisted the Stars and Stripes above the port's customs house. The Confederacy's largest city was gone. Just as bad, Union warships now had access to a long stretch of the lower Mississippi River.

The Emergence of Grant

As the Federal navy prepared to attack New Orleans, a joint force of Northern ground troops and gunboats penetrated the Confederacy's long, vulnerable frontier along the Tennessee-Kentucky border. In the fall of 1861 the rebel general Albert Sidney Johnston—widely considered the South's ablest commander—had constructed a defensive cordon that ran from Columbus, Kentucky, on the Mississippi River to Cumberland Gap in the Appalachian Mountains. Just south of the Tennessee-Kentucky border his troops had also built two major works—Forts Henry and Donelson—to bar Federal navigation on the Tennessee and Cumberland rivers, respectively.

But Johnston had only 43,000 men to hold this 300-mile line. The Federals confronted Johnston with more than twice that many troops, but three factors combined to reduce this numerical edge. First, a significant portion of Union strength had to protect lines of communication once Federal offensive operations began. Second, their massive logistical needs compelled Union armies to move only where railroad or river transportation was available. That, in turn, limited the Federals to just four avenues of approach to the south: down the Mississippi River against Columbus; up the Tennessee River to Fort Henry; up the Cumberland River to Fort Donelson; or along the Louisville & Nashville Railroad to Bowling Green in

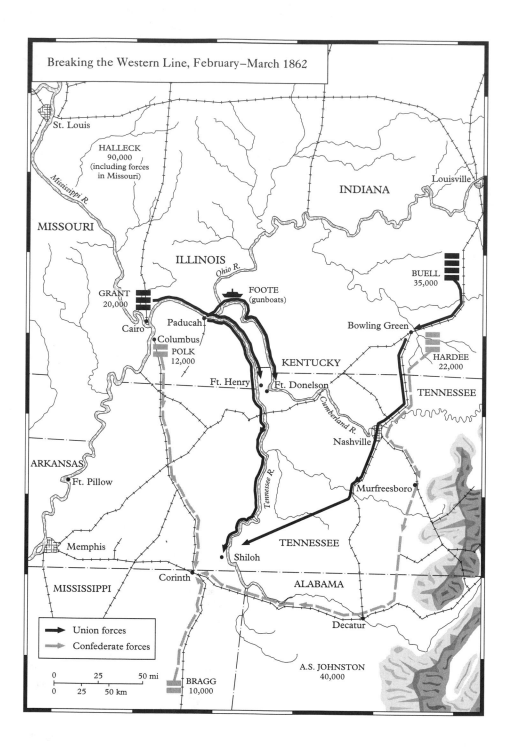

Breaking the Western Line, February–March 1862

south-central Kentucky. Johnston could read a map as well as anyone and had placed most of his forces to block these approaches.

The greatest difficulty affecting the Union high command, however, was of its own making. Whereas Johnston enjoyed complete authority within his theater of operations, the Lincoln administration had divided the same region into two parts: the Department of Missouri, commanded by Major General Henry W. Halleck; and the Department of the Ohio, led by Major General Don Carlos Buell. Their operations could be coordinated only by a third party, Major General George B. McClellan in faraway Washington. Complicating this awkward arrangement were the personalities of the three generals themselves. All were cautious by nature, all displayed great sensitivity about their own administrative domains, and all believed that if the enemy possessed interior lines—an advantage the Confederates actually did possess at the moment   then any attacking force must labor at a forbidding disadvantage. Consequently, this timid, touchy triumvirate dawdled over adopting a plan to crack Johnston's line.

Ultimately this delay was overcome less by any decision on the part of these generals than by the initiative of Brigadier General Ulysses S. Grant, a key Halleck subordinate. The chain of events began early in January 1862, when Grant received orders to take a small force up the Tennessee River and make a diversionary demonstration against Fort Henry. He did so, discovered the fort was much less formidable than previously believed, and urged Halleck to let him attack the fort. As soon as he received Halleck's approval, Grant piled about 15,000 troops aboard transports and

The South's many navigable rivers gave Northern forces excellent access to the Confederate interior, and Union gunboats often cooperated effectively with Union land forces. Sometimes they even accomplished important results on their own, as in their unassisted capture of Fort Henry, Tennessee, in February 1862.

headed up the Tennessee River. A flotilla of gunboats, commanded by Flag Officer Andrew H. Foote, steamed along in support of the expedition. On February 6, Grant landed a few miles below Fort Henry while Foote's gunboats steamed upriver to shell the place. To everyone's surprise, the fort surrendered almost at once. Winter rains had raised the Tennessee to flood stage; most of the fort was under six feet of water. The garrison commander had sent most of his 2,500 men to Fort Donelson, twelve miles east, leaving only a handful of artillerists to confront Foote's naval squadron. After a brief bombardment the Confederates ran up the white flag. The boat crew sent to receive the surrender sailed right through the rebel sally port, and the navy, not Grant, captured Fort Henry.

Things then happened very quickly. With no further fortifications blocking navigation of the Tennessee, Foote's gunboats raided upstream as far south as Muscle Shoals, Alabama. Grant notified Halleck that he planned to attack Fort Donelson at once. Johnston, meanwhile, took the defeat at Fort Henry as a signal that his defensive cordon could not hold much longer. He withdrew part of the garrison at Columbus, abandoned Bowling Green, and sent substantial reinforcements to Fort Donelson.

Reinforcing the fort proved a mistake. On February 13, Grant's army—now increased to about 23,000—invested Donelson. The following day Foote's gunboats attacked and tried to repeat their success at Fort Henry. This time a Confederate fort managed to hold its own. Seriously damaged, the Union flotilla had to retire. Even so, the generals inside Fort Donelson believed Grant would soon surround the place. They elected to break out to the south. The attempt succeeded. But then, incredibly, they ordered everyone to return to the Donelson trenches. After a bizarre council of war in which the two senior commanders abdicated their responsibilities and escaped the fort, the number-three man, Brigadier General Simon Bolivar Buckner, sent a flag of truce to Grant and requested terms of surrender.

Grant's response made him an instantaneous celebrity in the North. "No terms except unconditional and immediate surrender can be accepted. I propose to move immediately upon your works." The terse ultimatum miffed Buckner, who thought it ungenerous, but he had little choice save to accept. The next day approximately 12,500 Confederates lay down their arms. It was the first major Union victory of the war.

With Fort Donelson gone, Federal gunboats could now range up the Cumberland River as well. Nashville, Tennessee's capital city and an important supply center, was abandoned by the Confederates without a fight. Johnston's forces were now in full retreat. Grant's army moved up the Tennessee River to within a few miles of the Mississippi state line. Buell's command, meanwhile, occupied Nashville and advanced cautiously toward a junction with Grant.

Grant's army took up position at a stopping point for Tennessee River steamboats known as Pittsburg Landing. Pittsburg Landing possessed only two significant attributes: it had enough level ground nearby to permit an encampment for 40,000 men; and it was only about twenty miles from the little town of Corinth, Mississippi.

Because of two key railroads intersecting there, Corinth formed the main Federal objective point in the west. North and south ran the Mobile and Ohio line. East and west ran the Memphis and Charleston Railroad—a major trunk line and, in effect, the Confederacy's backbone. Union military and political leaders widely believed that if the Union could occupy two points in the South the rebellion would collapse. One of them was Richmond. Corinth was the other.

General Albert Sidney Johnston also concentrated the Confederate forces that had recently abandoned the Kentucky-Tennessee line in the little Mississippi rail town. In addition, President Jefferson Davis saw to it that Johnston got reinforcements from all over the South, so that by the end of March about 40,000 troops had collected around Corinth. On April 3, Johnston placed the entire force on the road to Pittsburg Landing.

Johnston understood that in numerical terms his army was barely equivalent to Grant's. He knew as well that most of his troops had never been in combat and that many of them were armed only with shotguns and old flintlock muskets. But he also recognized that he had only one chance to redress Confederate fortunes in the west. If he could hit Grant's army at once he might achieve surprise, press it back against the Tennessee River, and destroy it. If he waited more than a few days, Buell's troops would join those of Grant, the numerical odds would become forbidding, and there would be little choice but to concede western and middle Tennessee to the Federals for good.

The roads were bad and the troops unseasoned. It required two full days to negotiate the twenty miles from Corinth to the Union encampment, and along the way the raw Southern troops made so much noise it seemed impossible the Federals could remain unaware of the impending attack. P. G. T. Beauregard, the hero of Manassas and now Johnston's second-in-command, urged that the offensive be abandoned. Johnston would have none of it. "I would fight them if they were a million," he reportedly said, and on the evening of April 5 he deployed his troops for battle.

Shiloh

The terrain around Pittsburg Landing was typical of many Civil War battlefields. The ground was heavily wooded, cut by ravines, and choked with undergrowth. Two sluggish little creeks enveloped the Union encampment and flowed indolently into the Tennessee River. The roads in the area— hardly more than forest tracks—connected a few widely separated farm lots. Bordering the main road from the landing to Corinth was a little wooden church known as Shiloh Meeting House.

Amazingly the Federals had almost no inkling of the impending Confederate attack. A few Union officers suspected something was afoot, but when they approached the senior general in the area—a grizzled redhead named William Tecumseh Sherman—their fears were brusquely dismissed. Convinced the Confederates remained demoralized after their recent defeats, Sherman refused to entertain even the idea that they might launch a counterstroke. "Take your damn regiment back to Ohio," he snarled at one

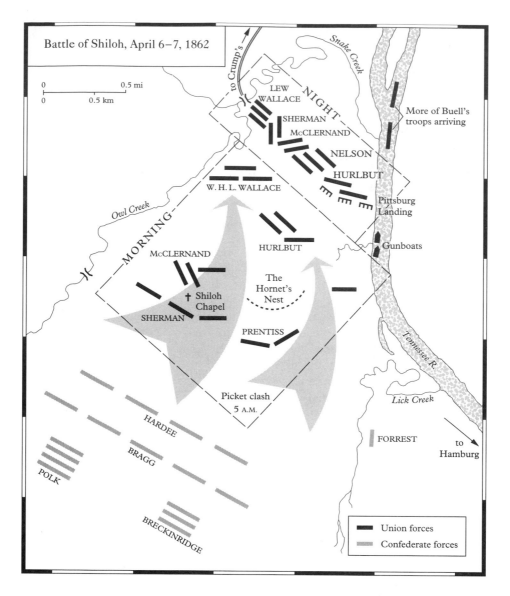

Battle of Shiloh, April 6–7, 1862

nervous colonel. "There is no enemy nearer than Corinth." Grant shared this view of things, and although he visited the encampment on April 5 he felt assured enough to retain his headquarters at Savannah, a town some ten miles downstream. Neither Grant nor Sherman gave orders for the troops to entrench.

Despite some security precautions the Federals were taken largely by surprise on the morning of Sunday, April 6, when Johnston's army came boiling out of the woods. They came in waves, with each of the four Confederate corps piling in one behind the other. Although this unorthodox formation helped the attack get off to a quicker start—it would have required additional hours to deploy the corps in conventional fashion—it soon created severe problems of command and control. The rebel troops crashed through the Federal encampments shortly after dawn, drove the terrified Unionists back toward Pittsburg Landing, and tried to press home their attack. But units from the various corps soon became intermingled, so that by midday the Confederate brigade and division commanders increasingly found themselves trying to lead nothing more than huge armed mobs. Troops who had never seen each other, much less trained together, were forced to carry out Johnston's demanding all-or-nothing offensive.

The Federals were, in some cases, equally disorganized. Thousands—possibly as many as one-fourth of Grant's army—simply ran for the shelter of the steep bluffs that rose from Pittsburg Landing. The rest stayed with their divisions and fought with determination, only to discover time and again that Confederate troops had lapped around their flanks, forcing them to retreat.

Grant reached the battle around 8:30 A.M. The scene that confronted him was ghastly. The thousands of men who had fled the battle now crowded the bluffs at Pittsburg Landing. Beyond them the woodlands around Shiloh Meeting House shook with the concussion of rifle fire and the screams of men. Grant quickly ordered more ammunition brought up and detailed two regiments to round up stragglers. For the rest of the day he rode back and forth along the battle line, pausing now and then to confer with his division commanders. He could see that the battle had degenerated into a huge slugging match, devoid of tactical finesse. For the Federals the important thing seemed just to hold on long enough for reinforcements to arrive.

Near the Union center, Brigadier General Benjamin M. Prentiss's division withdrew to the cover of a narrow road running parallel to the Confederate front. Grant gave Prentiss an emphatic order to hold the position at all costs. The order was obeyed. Prentiss's men drowned every attempt to dislodge them in a hail of gunfire. Before long, with bitter respect, Southerners attacking the position began calling it the "Hornet's Nest."

Meanwhile the remaining Union forces withdrew slowly, grudgingly, against furious but diminishing thrusts by the rebel army. Exactly as instructed, Prentiss held on grimly to the Hornet's Nest. Only at 5:30 P.M., with the position entirely surrounded, did he reluctantly surrender his men. His stand made it possible for Grant's chief artillerist to plant fifty cannon a quarter-mile from the landing and end the threat of the Confederates pushing on to the river. Sundown brought an end to the day's fighting. During the night, while rainstorms lashed the battlefield and surgeons worked feverishly in improvised hospitals, Wallace's and Buell's forces finally arrived. Numbering about 28,000 men, they more than offset Union losses during the day.

Despite the arrival of reinforcements, most of Grant's officers were extremely discouraged. Many of them, including Sherman, believed retreat might be the best course. During the day, Sherman had fought his division with coolness and determination, but he still believed the army had lost this battle and late that night he sought out Grant to tell him so. He found his commander standing beneath a tree in a downpour, rain dripping from his hat, a cigar smoldering between his teeth. Something in Grant's demeanor made Sherman decide not to discuss retreat. Instead he said simply, "Well,

When Ulysses S. Grant won the Union's first major victory at Fort Donelson in February 1862, his capture of 12,000 Confederates made him a hero in the North. But two months later, criticism of his conduct at Shiloh discouraged him so much that he briefly considered resigning.

Grant, we've had the devil's own day, haven't we?" "Yes," Grant agreed, then added: "Lick 'em in the morning, though." Ultimately his stubborn strength made the difference between victory and defeat at Shiloh.

The following day events went as Grant predicted—the Federals "licked" the Confederates. The Southerners, like their Northern counterparts, were utterly exhausted by Sunday's battle. They had gotten badly disorganized and suffered huge numbers of stragglers. They had even lost their commanding general: the previous afternoon a bullet had clipped one of Sidney Johnston's arteries, causing him to bleed to death within minutes. Worst of all, the Confederates had no fresh units to feed into the struggle. Although they fought grimly throughout Monday, April 7, the strongly reinforced Union army ground them down. At sunset, the Rebels began a sullen retreat to Corinth.

The Battle of Shiloh horrified both North and South. In two days' fighting the Confederate army lost 10,699 men killed, wounded, or missing; Union casualties totaled 13,047. The North American continent had never endured anything like it. Shiloh's cost in human lives far exceeded that of any engagement in previous American experience. Losses were five times those of Bull Run. The battle virtually doubled the year-old war's casualty figures. Northerners who considered this shattering toll found it impossible to regard the battle as a Union victory. It seemed more like an unmitigated disaster, and many who had praised Grant a few weeks earlier now clamored for his removal.

Yet Shiloh *was* a Union victory, and a big one, for it confirmed the previous Federal successes at Forts Henry and Donelson. The Confederacy had lost much of western and middle Tennessee, and the Union's victory at Shiloh ensured that the Rebels would not regain this region. Two additional victories soon consolidated the Union's success. On April 7 a force of 30,000 men under Brigadier General John Pope captured Island No. 10, a

Confederate fortress blocking navigation of the Mississippi River near the Kentucky-Tennessee line. And on June 5 a Union flotilla seized Memphis after a brief but savage naval battle.

*   *   *   *

The first year of the Civil War saw the conflict assume very wide dimensions that readily eclipsed any previous war on American soil. Both North and South had created and fielded large armies, led by a combination of professional and amateur officers and manned by enthusiastic though as yet unseasoned volunteers. Both sides were performing at a level much better than American forces during the War of 1812, testimony to the leadership exerted at the top by West Point graduates. The Union side in particular had managed some very creditable feats of army-navy cooperation.

By the end of spring 1862, Federal and Confederate armies had also fought a number of battles that demonstrated that the war would be much bloodier than previous American struggles. Part of this heightened lethality owed to the impact of the rifled musket, but most of it was due to the increased size of the rival armies and the earnestness with which both sides fought. The casualty figures were not exceptional by European standards— Shiloh was no worse than some of the battles fought by Frederick the Great. They seemed worse, perhaps, because the men who were killed and wounded were much more representative of their parent societies than professional European forces were of theirs.

The Northern cause had made excellent progress during the war's first year. Despite a serious early reverse at Bull Run, Union troops had managed to retain control of the crucial border states, to accquire a number of enclaves along the Southern coastline, and to impose a naval blockade of the Confederacy. Most promisingly, they had also broken the Confederate defensive cordon in the western theater. Taken together, these victories suggested that it might well be possible to destroy the rebellion and restore the Union without having to address the politically explosive slavery issue or to destroy large amounts of Southern property.

All eyes now turned to McClellan's great campaign against Richmond. The first six months of 1862 had brought a string of victories: Forts Henry and Donelson, the seizure of the North Carolina coast, the battles of Pea Ridge and Shiloh, the capture of New Orleans, Island No. 10, and Memphis. The Confederacy had been bludgeoned along its entire frontier. Everyone now expected the Army of the Potomac to deliver the death blow.

SUGGESTED READINGS

Catton, Bruce. *The Coming Fury.* (Garden City, N.Y.: Doubleday, 1961).

   . *Terrible Swift Sword.* (Garden City, N.Y.: Doubleday, 1964).

Connelly, Thomas L. *Army of the Heartland: The Army of Tennessee, 1861–1862* (Baton Rouge: Louisiana State University Press, 1967).

Connelly, Thomas L., and Archer Jones. *The Politics of Command: Factions and Ideas in Confederate Strategy* (Baton Rouge: Louisiana State University Press, 1973).

Cooling, Benjamin F. *Forts Henry and Donelson: The Key to the Confederate Heartland* (Knoxville: University of Tennessee Press, 1987).

Davis, William C. *Battle at Bull Run* (Garden City, N.Y.: Doubleday, 1977).

Hattaway, Herman, and Archer Jones. *How the North Won: A Military History of the Civil War* (Urbana: University of Illinois Press, 1983).

Linderman, Gerald F. *Embattled Courage: The Experience of Combat in the American Civil War* (New York: Free Press, 1987).

McDonough, James Lee. *Shiloh: In Hell Before Night* (Knoxville: University of Tennessee Press, 1977).

McPherson, James M. *Battle Cry of Freedom: The Civil War Era* (New York: Oxford University Press, 1988).

Nevins, Allan, *The War for the Union,* 4 vols. (New York: Charles Scribner's Sons, 1959–1971).

Potter, David M. *The Impending Crisis, 1848–1861* (New York: Harper, 1976).

Williams, Kenneth P. *Lincoln Finds a General,* 5 vols. (New York: Macmillan, 1949–1956).

Williams, T. Harry. *Lincoln and His Generals* (New York: Alfred A. Knopf, 1952).

Woodworth, Steven E. *Jefferson Davis and His Generals: The Failure of Confederate Command in the West* (Lawrence: University Press of Kansas, 1990).

5

THE CIVIL WAR, 1862:
ENDING THE LIMITED WAR

"A Single Grand Campaign"
The Failure of Limited War
Confederate Counterstrokes
Autumn Stalemate

By early June 1862 the war seemed all but over. The border states, including western Virginia, were solidly in Union hands. Federal units controlled the lower Mississippi River from the delta to New Orleans and also held the middle reaches of the river as far south as Memphis. Halleck's armies had captured western Tennessee, controlled much of middle Tennessee, and pressed into northern Alabama. Most importantly they had seized the strategic railroad junction at Corinth, Mississippi. This last victory had been virtually bloodless. Halleck's huge force—numbering well over 100,000 men—had crept toward the rail town barely a mile per day. At night it dug extensive entrenchments; Halleck wanted no repetition of the damaging surprise attack at Shiloh. By the end of May, Beauregard, who now commanded Sidney Johnston's army, prudently abandoned Corinth and slipped away to Tupelo, some eighty miles south. Some Northerners regretted the Confederate escape but most simply smiled at this latest Yankee triumph.

Then, abruptly, the Union dream of victory was shattered. McClellan's great offensive against Richmond collapsed. Not only did the rebel capital elude capture, but the Confederate army in the east then began a series of aggressive counterstrokes that carried the war, in a matter of weeks, from the shores of the James River to the banks of the Potomac. In the western theater other Confederate armies carried out similar offensives of their own. With sickening swiftness, many in the North realized that the war would not be short or easy and that its conduct had to change. Until then the Lincoln administration had waged a limited war. Its armies had aimed their blows exclusively against rebel military units and had tried, as far as possible, to preserve the constitutional rights of Southern civilians—including the right to hold slaves. Now many in the North clamored that this "kid glove" warfare, as it was derisively called, must end. The Lincoln administration agreed. The reversals of summer 1862 led directly to the collapse of limited war and the advent of new, more severe measures against the South.

Another development that marked this period was the deployment of the *corps d'armée,* a military organization that had not existed at all in previous American wars. Although nominally begun during the early months of 1862—McClellan adopted the corps system in March 1862 and then Sidney Johnston used a similar arrangement at Shiloh—the corps organization was at first mainly an administrative expedient. Not until midsummer did the corps emerge as an operational unit. From then on, the Union and Confederate armies utilized the corps system not only to control large masses of men more effectively but also to maneuver against one another's flank and rear and, when necessary, to fight independently. Civil War armies began to march and fight in the classic Napoleonic style.

"A Single Grand Campaign"

The greatest hope for an early Union victory reposed in the person of Major General George B. McClellan. Just thirty-four years old when the war broke out, McClellan had quickly risen to high command. Although he had left the army in 1856 to become a railroad executive, his West Point training brought him at once to the attention of Ohio's governor, who placed him in charge of the state's volunteer forces. In the early summer of 1861 he had won a series of minor victories in western Virginia that brought him considerable laurels. Newspapers began calling him "the Napoleon of the present war." When, after the debacle at Bull Run, Lincoln looked about for a commander to replace McDowell, he speedily settled on McClellan.

Arriving in Washington on July 27, McClellan was appalled by the confused condition of McDowell's battered troops. But he quickly rebuilt the force around Washington, which he soon dubbed the Army of the Potomac. In early August, at Lincoln's request, he also sent the president a memorandum detailing his conceptions for winning the war. McClellan wanted most Union strength concentrated for a single, overwhelming thrust against Richmond. To achieve this objective the young general sought to create a juggernaut of 273,000 men and 600 cannon. McClellan's rationale for his plan was largely political. Like many Northerners, he believed the common people of the South were lukewarm in their support for the Confederate government. In McClellan's view, only a display of overwhelming military force, coupled with a lenient policy toward Southern civilians, could create the conditions for a restoration of the Union. Implicit in his plan was the conviction that a lengthy struggle would embitter both North and South and make reunion more difficult.

Called the "Young Napoleon" by an admiring public, George B. McClellan was a talented organizer, a charismatic leader, and a good strategic planner, but he was ultimately hamstrung by frictions with the Lincoln administration and an overcaution verging on timidity.

The vigorous style of McClellan's memorandum promised action, but its substance suggested delay. The young commander did not want to go off half-cocked. He needed time to amass and train the huge army he contemplated, and indeed it is difficult to see how McClellan could have begun this great offensive much before the spring of 1862. Unfortunately, from the outset he never made this clear to either the public or his political superiors. Instead he let them believe that he might commence major offensive actions during the autumn of 1861, and when no sign of this offensive materialized, his near-unanimous bipartisan support began to fade. Democrats and conservative Republicans continued to back McClellan, but the radical wing of the Republican party turned sharply against him.

It did not help that McClellan detested Lincoln, whom he termed "the original Gorilla." Lincoln nevertheless displayed amazing patience with McClellan and in November 1861 even appointed him general-in-chief. But as the months slid by without action, Lincoln's confidence in McClellan declined. Mutual distrust between the president and his chief commander characterized every phase of the great Richmond offensive when it finally began.

Genesis of the Peninsula Campaign

After the Bull Run defeat the strategic situation in Virginia looked like this. McClellan's army held the Union capital and a long stretch of the Potomac River both north and south of the city. The Confederate army, under General Joseph E. Johnston, was concentrated at Centreville, just up the road from the old Bull Run battlefield. The Rebels had also erected batteries that interdicted passage of the lower Potomac River and, in effect, placed Washington under a partial blockade.

By September, McClellan had gathered over 100,000 troops into his Army of the Potomac. Johnston, by contrast, had barely 40,000. Had McClellan been so disposed he might well have advanced directly against the Confederates, but instead he did nothing. McClellan defended his inaction by claiming that Johnston had 150,000 troops, the estimate given to him by Allan Pinkerton, his chief of intelligence. If Johnston really did have 150,000 men, of course, an overland offensive stood little chance of success. Thus McClellan always looked for alternatives. By December he had settled on a scheme to convey most of the Army of the Potomac by sea to Urbanna, a small town on the Rappahannock River about fifty miles northeast of Richmond. This would cut in half the overland distance the army must cover; better yet, it would render the Confederate lines at Centreville untenable, force Johnston's army into precipitate retreat, and possibly create advantageous conditions for a Union attack.

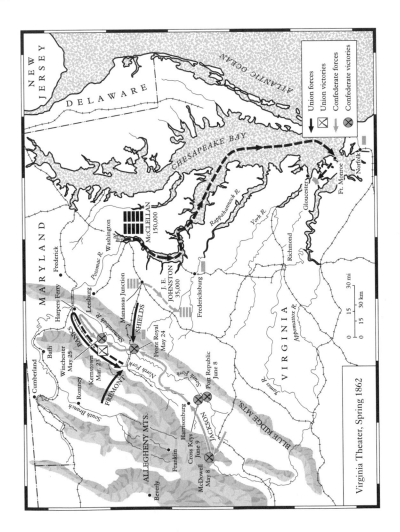

Virginia Theater, Spring 1862

Unfortunately for McClellan, a Confederate redeployment soon rendered his original plan all but impossible. Johnston had long regarded his Centreville position as too exposed. On March 8–9, 1862, the rebel army therefore fell back to a new position behind the Rappahannock in central Virginia. With Johnston's army now much closer to Urbanna and Richmond, the strategic rationale for the Urbanna scheme largely disappeared. Accordingly, McClellan switched to an alternate plan. The Army of the Potomac would still move against Richmond by sea, but instead of landing at Urbanna it would disembark at Fort Monroe. This Union-held outpost lay at the tip of a long peninsula formed by the York and James rivers. It was not so close to Richmond as Urbanna—seventy-five miles as opposed to fifty and the route to the Confederate capital was blocked by a small force stationed at Yorktown, but it still seemed preferable to an overland advance.

Before beginning the great campaign, McClellan took his army on a brief shakedown march to the abandoned Confederate position at Centreville. This served only to exacerbate his already considerable political difficulties, for it soon became obvious that the lines could not possibly have held 150,000 men. Lincoln's doubts about McClellan increased, and on March 12 the president removed him as general-in-chief. Lincoln explained the change by saying that once McClellan took the field he would be fully occupied with command of the Army of the Potomac. The young commander, however, regarded it as an implied rebuke, as it almost certainly was. McClellan began his great campaign under a cloud.

From Yorktown to Seven Pines

The transfer of McClellan's army to Fort Monroe began on March 17. Since the U.S. government possessed nowhere near enough vessels for so great a task, it chartered every available steamer from Maryland to Maine: 113 in all, as well as an additional 276 smaller vessels. Within three weeks 121,500 men, 14,492 animals, 1,224 wagons, and over 200 cannon had reached the tip of the Virginia peninsula. It was—as one astonished British observer remarked—"the stride of a giant" and it showed the extent of the North's advantage in sea power.

The advance inland began on April 4. But just twenty-four hours later it ceased abruptly when Union troops encountered a belt of Confederate fortifications extending across the peninsula from Yorktown to the James River. The existence of this line, while not altogether unexpected, convinced McClellan that a formal siege would be necessary for its reduction. His decision further strained his already poor relationship with the Lincoln administration. Relations became even worse when the administration discovered that McClellan had left nowhere near enough troops to defend Washington during the Army of the Potomac's absence. As a result it withheld McClellan's I Corps—some 40,000 men—and retained it in northern Virginia.

McClellan, furious, now found that he must "crush the rebellion at a single blow" with a significantly reduced force. Nevertheless, although he refused to believe it, he handily outnumbered the Confederates facing him, even after most of Johnston's army abandoned the Rappahannock line and came down to Yorktown. Well aware of his numerical disadvantage, Johnston remarked, "Nobody but McClellan would have hesitated to attack."

For nearly a month, Federal engineers and artillerists sweated to emplace the mammoth siege guns that would blast the Yorktown defenders into oblivion. Johnston, however, did not wait to be blasted. On May 1 he notified Richmond authorities that the Yorktown position was untenable, that he intended to withdraw, and that all possible reinforcements should be concentrated near the Confederate capital. Two nights later his army left Yorktown.

The retreat had severe strategic costs. It opened the York and James rivers to Federal gunboats, led to the abandonment of Norfolk and its navy yard, and forced the scuttling of the daunting Confederate ironclad warship *Virginia*. For a brief time Confederate authorities even contemplated the evacuation of Richmond, but Jefferson Davis's military advisor, General Robert E. Lee, made a passionate plea for the capital's continued defense.

Fortunately for the South, at that point Confederate defenses began to stiffen. On May 15 several artillery batteries at Drewry's Bluff, below Richmond, rebuffed the Federal navy's lunge up the James River. In the Shenandoah Valley, troops under Major General Thomas J. "Stonewall" Jackson, a dour ex-professor of the Virginia Military Institute, won a series of astonishing small victories over much larger Union forces. And although by the end of May McClellan's massive army had come to within seven miles of Richmond, it advanced gingerly. Moreover, it was clear that McClellan, instead of launching an immediate attack, planned to conduct a siege of Richmond.

McClellan had placed his main supply base at White House Landing on the Pamunkey River. A short rail line from Richmond had its terminus there, which offered a reliable way to transport his heavy siege guns to the front. But his choice of base meant that his army had to straddle the Chickahominy River northeast of Richmond. Heavy spring rains rendered the stream almost impassable, thus dividing the Army of the Potomac. On May 31, Johnston took advantage of this and tried to crush the southern wing of McClellan's army in the Battle of Seven Pines. But nothing went right. Johnston's plans were vague and his management of the battle was terrible. The Confederates lost 6,000 troops; the Union, about 5,000. The most important result of the two-day battle was that on June 1 Johnston was severely wounded. To succeed him, Davis appointed Robert E. Lee.

In June 1862, Lee was still comparatively unknown in the South, and what Southerners did know of him they did not like. Although a well-respected figure in the prewar U.S. Army and one of the highest ranking officers to side with the Confederacy, Lee's wartime career to date had been disappointing. In the autumn of 1861 he had conducted a brief, ineffectual campaign in the western Virginia mountains that earned him the derisive nickname "Granny" Lee. In March 1862, President Davis had appointed him his military advisor, a seemingly imposing assignment but one with little formal authority. Small wonder that many Southerners were dismayed to find Lee in charge of Richmond's defense.

Jackson in the Valley

What few knew, however, was that Lee had pronounced ideas about aggressive action. Indeed he had already tried them out. His partner in this venture was "Stonewall" Jackson. The arena in which they tried out their offensive scheme was the Shenandoah Valley. One of the most productive agricultural regions in North America, the Valley also had qualities that arrested the strategist's eye. Its farms produced much of the Confederacy's grain and many of its horses. The Baltimore & Ohio Railroad ran across its northern reaches; thus any Confederate force in full control of the valley also controlled the Union's single most important east-west communications link. And the sheltering mountains on either side made the Valley a natural avenue of invasion into Maryland and Pennsylvania. For these reasons both Federals and Confederates sought to possess the region.

In the fall of 1861 the defense of the Valley became Jackson's responsibility. With only 4,500 men under his command, Jackson's position was precarious from the outset, and in early March 1862, some 38,000 Federals under Major General Nathaniel Banks entered the northern part of the Valley and drove him away from Winchester, the region's largest town. After a short pursuit, Banks left a single division of 9,000 men at Winchester and withdrew the rest back toward Washington. On March 23, hoping to defeat the lone division at Winchester, Jackson attacked.

He failed, but the bold Confederate attack convinced his opponent that Jackson had either received reinforcements or expected them shortly. As a result, Banks returned to the Valley with a second division of 9,000 men. Then Lincoln detached a 10,000-man division from the Army of the Potomac and ordered it to join Major General John C. Frémont's forces in western Virginia, on the theory that if Jackson were strong enough to attack at Winchester he might threaten Frémont as well. Nor was this all. The fact that Banks was no longer available to cover Washington, D.C., during McClellan's germinating peninsula campaign helped spur Lincoln to withdraw McDowell's 40,000-man corps from McClellan's control (as mentioned earlier) and retain it in northern Virginia. Jackson's battlefield defeat thus turned into strategic success; it tied up the movements of nearly 60,000 Federal troops.

It also set the stage for Lee's first major attempt at an offensive-defensive strategy. By mid-April the Confederates in Virginia faced four main threats, of which McClellan was merely the largest. Banks's corps was advancing and had reached Harrisonburg in the central Valley; McDowell's corps in northern Virginia could march south at any time. Frémont's forces in western Virginia also seemed active, and McClellan of course menaced Richmond itself. In every instance the Federals far outnumbered the rebel forces opposing them. A passive defense could never hope to resist so many pressures.

Lee believed the only solution was to combine against one of the Northern forces, eliminate it, and thus dislocate the remaining Union forces. On April 21 he wrote to Jackson suggesting that Jackson should link up with a division led by Major General Richard S. Ewell. He would then hurl his augmented force against Banks's isolated corps. Jackson, however, replied that even with Ewell's help, he would still need 5,000 more troops to attack with any chance of success. When Lee could not furnish the extra 5,000, Jackson proposed a modified plan. Instead of striking Banks, he would unite with 2,800 troops under Confederate Major General Edward Johnson and hit Frémont's advance guard. Then, using both Ewell and Johnson, he would attack Banks. Lee approved the plan and on May 8, Jackson defeated Frémont at the Battle of McDowell, Virginia.

Jackson's victory inaugurated one of the classic campaigns of military history. Reinforced to about 10,000 men after the Battle of McDowell, Jackson united with Ewell—thereby adding another 7,000 troops to his command—and lunged northward toward Banks. Thoroughly misleading the Union commander, Jackson appeared in front of Banks, then suddenly swung around the Union flank, using cavalry to screen his movement. On May 23 he captured a small Union garrison at Front Royal; Banks now frantically withdrew down the Valley before Jackson could cut off his retreat. At

When a series of major defeats shook the Confederacy in early 1862, the exploits of Major General Thomas J. "Stonewall" Jackson helped bolster Southern morale. His campaign in the Shenandoah Valley is still considered a military masterpiece.

Winchester he attempted to make a stand, but in a battle on May 25 the Confederates had little trouble dislodging the Federals and sending them into headlong retreat. Banks did not stop retreating until he crossed the Potomac the next day, having lost 35 percent of his force.

In Washington, Lincoln and his advisors viewed the situation with alarm, mingled with the shrewd awareness that an opportunity now existed to trap Jackson's entire force. A march of forty miles would place Frémont's 15,000 men at Harrisonburg, eighty miles in Jackson's rear. Lincoln instructed Frémont to make this march. Similarly he ordered McDowell at Fredericksburg to detach 20,000 men and seize Front Royal, a move that would imperil Jackson's line of retreat. The main issue was whether the Union forces could move fast enough to close the trap before Jackson could escape. As Lincoln remarked, it was "a question of legs."

The plan failed. For a variety of reasons, Frémont did not advance into the Valley by the most direct route and instead marched northward for a considerable distance, thereby squandering the best chance to trap Jackson. The Confederate commander managed to elude both Frémont and McDowell. Then he chose a position at Port Republic, a small village where two small streams met to form the south branch of the Shenandoah River.

Spring rains had swollen these streams to the point where they could be crossed only at bridges or rare fords; by controlling the crossings at Port Republic, Jackson could concentrate against either Frémont or McDowell while denying his opponents the opportunity to join forces. Then, in two sharp fights on June 8–9, he bested both rivals. A highly religious man, Jackson exulted to Ewell at the close of the second battle, "General, he who does not see the hand of God in this is blind, sir, blind!"

Whether Ewell viewed it that way is open to question, but military analysts have never had trouble discerning in Jackson's Valley campaign the hand of a master campaign strategist. With an army less than half the size of the forces opposed to him, he had managed to defeat the enemy on five major occasions, hold on to the upper third of the Shenandoah Valley, and above all, force the diversion of thousands of Union troops who might otherwise have joined McClellan's army on the peninsula. His success in the Valley played a crucial role in saving Richmond.

The Failure of Limited War

The modest size of his force notwithstanding, Jackson had already advocated an invasion of the North. He insisted that with 40,000 troops he could do it, and although Lee believed such a venture must await the relief of Richmond, he viewed the idea with interest. Lee reinforced Jackson in hopes that Stonewall might crush the remaining Federals in the Valley. But when no Union forces offered themselves for immediate crushing, Lee changed plans and ordered Jackson to bring most of his troops to Richmond. All possible Confederate forces must be concentrated to defend the capital.

In Lee's mind such a defense could not be passive; a passive defense would allow McClellan the maximum benefit of the powerful artillery in his siege train. Therefore, despite numerical inferiority, the Confederates would have to attack. He knew of Napoleon's successful exploits against larger armies and had witnessed Winfield Scott's triumph over a larger Mexican army. Numbers, in Lee's opinion, were important, but not all-important. Initiative, concentration of force at a decisive point, surprise, and determination counted for at least as much. Good intelligence was also vital. Accordingly, on June 11 he summoned to his headquarters Brigadier General Jeb Stuart, the army's twenty-nine-year-old chief of cavalry. Stuart took 1,200 troopers on a two-day reconnaissance completely around McClellan's army. When he returned he told Lee the Federal right wing was "in the air"—that is, it continued several miles north of the Chickahominy River and then simply ended, anchored to no substantial natural obstacle. Also, McClellan's supplies were still being drawn exclusively from White House Landing on the Pamunkey River. No effort had been made to change the Federal base to a forward point on the James River. Armed with this information, Lee decided to concentrate his army on the exposed Union right flank, break it, then pitch into McClellan's rear and cut his supply line. If successful the Federals would be forced to withdraw the way they had come, back down the peninsula.

The Seven Days

McClellan had five corps east of Richmond—arrayed in a north-south line about five miles east of the city—but only one corps north of the Chickahominy. That force, the V Corps under Brigadier General Fitz John Porter, had the dual mission of screening the Federal base at White House Landing and facilitating a juncture with McDowell's corps should it ever be released by Lincoln from its mission of screening Washington. Lee proposed to use the bulk of his 80,000 available troops to crush Porter and leave only 20,000 to hold the Richmond trenches. It was a daring gamble, but Lee expected McClellan to go on the defensive the moment the Confederate attack opened.

On June 23, 1862, Lee met with his key commanders. Stonewall Jackson was there, having left his troops, then en route to Richmond, and ridden fifty miles to attend the meeting. Lee gave him the vital assignment of turning the right flank of the Union V Corps. Jackson promised to be in position by June 26, and Lee shaped his timetable accordingly. But to everyone's astonishment, Jackson failed to carry out his assignment on time and did not report to headquarters news of his situation or whereabouts. Noon came and went on June 26, and nothing happened. Then at 3 P.M. a division commander, Major General A. P. Hill, decided that the offensive could no longer wait for Jackson. Without asking clearance from Lee, he led his troops straight for the packed cannon of the V Corps. Reluctantly, Lee committed his other divisions to support the charge. Without Jackson to turn the flank, however, his carefully planned offensive degenerated into a brutal frontal assault. Thousands of rebel troops fell to Union rifle and artillery fire

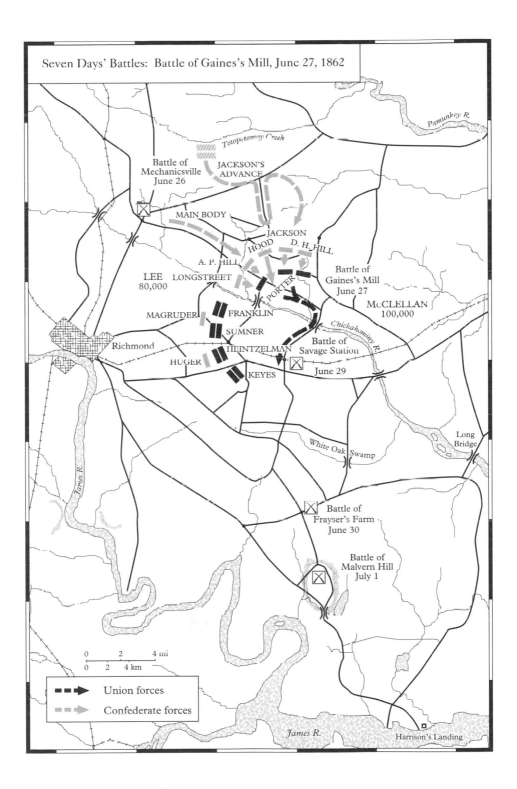

Seven Days' Battles: Battle of Gaines's Mill, June 27, 1862

Pamunkey R.

Totopotomoy Creek

Battle of
Mechanicsville
June 26

JACKSON'S
ADVANCE

MAIN BODY

JACKSON

HOOD   D. H. HILL

A. P. HILL

LEE   LONGSTREET
80,000

PORTER

Battle of
Gaines's Mill
June 27

McCLELLAN
100,000

MAGRUDER   FRANKLIN

SUMNER

Chickahominy R.

Richmond

HUGER

HEINTZELMAN

KEYES

Battle of
Savage Station

June 29

White Oak Swamp

Long
Bridge

James R.

0   2   4 mi
0   2   4 km

Battle of
Frayser's Farm
June 30

Battle of
Malvern Hill
July 1

Union forces

Confederate forces

James R.

Harrison's Landing

without ever piercing the V Corps' formidable positions near Mechanicsville. Worse, the Federals learned of Jackson's belated approach and during the night conducted a skillful withdrawal to even stronger positions at Gaines' Mill, two miles east.

The offensive's second day threatened to be a replay of the first, with much of Lee's force again bludgeoning the Federals in brave but useless charges while Jackson floundered about north of the battlefield. In the afternoon, however, Stonewall finally got his troops into action against the Union right flank, and by dusk the Federals were beaten. Porter successfully withdrew his battered corps south of the Chickahominy. Just as Lee expected, McClellan went over to the defensive. But Lee's own plans never quite worked out. The unfortunate battles at Mechanicsville and Gaines' Mill seemed to set the tone for the entire campaign. Time and again, bad staff work and faulty generalship scuttled spectacular opportunities to maul McClellan's army. Jackson, in strange contrast to his stellar conduct of the Valley campaign, continued to perform poorly—most likely due to the effects of prolonged mental and physical stress.

Still, the victory at Gaines' Mill forced the Federals to abandon their supply base at White House Landing and begin a risky withdrawal south toward a new base along the James River. Lee saw the withdrawal as a chance to demolish McClellan's army completely. But poor intelligence, poor use of artillery, poor tactics and, of course, poor generalship combined to prevent so decisive a result. On June 29 a portion of Lee's army got into a costly but useless fight at Savage Station. The following day saw a botched

The North had good artillery and plenty of it, and when concentrated to deliver massed fire, the results could be devastating. At Malvern Hill on July 1, 1862, Union artillery blasted wave after wave of attacking Confederate infantry. "It was not war," confessed one Southern general, "it was murder."

attempt to envelop the Union army at Frayser's Farm. By July 1, McClellan had nearly made good his withdrawal.

Atop a spacious ridge called Malvern Hill, McClellan deployed much of his field artillery to cover the final stage of his retreat. Swampland on either side of the hill precluded any chance to turn the position, and it appeared much too formidable to be taken by a direct attack. But Lee stubbornly refused to concede McClellan's escape. He ordered a frontal assault. Lines of Confederate soldiers swept forward against the Yankee guns packed along the crest. They were soon shattered as Union artillery tore their ranks to shreds. A Confederate division commander said afterward, "It was not war, it was murder."

But the Seven Days, as the battles between June 26 and July 1 came to be known, resulted in the salvation of Richmond, which was all most Southerners cared about. Lee became a hero. The Army of the Potomac, beaten though not seriously damaged, cowered along the banks of the James at Harrison's Landing. Of the 85,500 Confederates engaged in the battles, 20,141 became casualties, a loss rate of nearly 24 percent. The Federals, by contrast, lost only 15 percent of their own force—15,849 from an army of about 105,000.

A number of historians have since questioned the wisdom of Lee's costly offensive strategy. But the real question is whether he could have saved Richmond in any other way. And the loss of its capital might well have resulted in the Confederacy's political collapse, just as many contemporary observers believed. Even assuming the Confederates were able to relocate their capital and continue the struggle, the loss of Richmond would have opened up the entire eastern Confederacy to further Union attacks. If the South could not successfully defend Virginia, where the gap between sea and mountains was only one hundred miles wide, how could it hope to defend the more open regions farther south?

The End of Conciliation

No sooner did the Army of Northern Virginia dispose of one threat than the Lincoln administration produced another. On June 26, 1862, the Union activated a new "Army of Virginia," composed of three corps under McDowell, Banks, and Frémont, and led by Major General John Pope. Pope came from the war's western theater where he had made a name for himself through the capture of the Mississippi River fortress at Island No. 10. Conceited, pompous, and boastful, he was an easy man to dislike. Soon after assuming command he alienated virtually everyone in his army by issuing a tactless proclamation that seemed a slap in the face to the soldiers who had served in the recent, ill-starred Valley Campaign. The Northern press also derided Pope's broadside.

But Pope soon redeemed himself with a series of draconian orders regarding Virginia civilians. Henceforth, he instructed, the soldiers under his command would live as far as possible off the countryside. They would no longer guard private homes and property. The citizens of occupied territory would be held responsible for guerrilla activity in their midst; the guerrillas themselves would be shot. Persons who refused to take the oath of allegiance would be treated as spies. All in all it seemed clear that Pope intended—as the Northern press put it—to wage war with the kid gloves off.

This sounded a new and increasingly welcome note. Since the beginning of the war most Federal commanders had treated Southern civilians according to the tenets of what was known as the conciliatory policy. This policy assumed that most white Southerners had been hoodwinked into secession by a slaveholding aristocracy, that popular support for the Confederacy was lukewarm at best, and that a program of mild treatment would convince most white Southerners to return to their former allegiance to the United States. As a result, when Union troops first entered Southern territory, they usually promised not to interfere with slavery and to preserve, as far as possible, all constitutional rights. They seldom took food and other supplies from Southern civilians without payment and often furnished guards to protect private homes against intrusion by unruly soldiers.

The Union had no firmer adherent to the conciliatory policy than McClellan. "I am fighting to preserve the Union and uphold its laws," he assured a wealthy Virginia planter, "and for no other purpose." His distaste for the Lincoln administration stemmed, in part, from the conviction that the president was not strong enough to stand up to the pressures for a sterner "war of subjugation" endorsed by the Radical Republicans. When, shortly after the Seven Days' battles, Lincoln came down to Harrison's Landing to visit the Army of the Potomac, McClellan took the occasion to hand the president a letter urging him not to abandon the conciliatory policy. Instead McClellan urged that the government conduct the conflict "upon the highest principles known to Christian Civilization." Private property should be stringently protected and even an "offensive demeanor" by the military toward citizens should receive prompt rebuke. Furthermore, the army should have nothing to do with slavery, "either by supporting or impairing the authority of the master." Lincoln accepted the letter politely. A consummate politician, however, he knew that the time for the limited struggle envisioned by McClellan had run out.

The Drive Toward Emancipation

The war, in any case, had moved beyond conciliation. The major casualty of the shift was slavery. At the war's outset the Lincoln administration had refused to accept any interference with the "peculiar institution," for fear that it would alienate the border states, embitter white Southerners to greater resistance, and alienate many in the North who were willing to support a war for the Union but who rejected fighting to free the slaves. Yet it was clear not only that slavery lay at the root of the struggle but also that the labor of slaves was sustaining the Confederate economy and even being used to construct military fortifications. It was therefore almost impossible for Union troops to battle the Confederacy without disturbing slavery.

Union retreat from Richmond. McClellan's defeat during the Seven Days' battles destroyed the North's hopes for an early victory, scuttled the conciliatory policy, and helped convince Lincoln that the Union could not win the war without attacking slavery.

Indeed, the very presence of Union troops on Southern soil disrupted the stable order on which slavery rested. From the outset, some slaves escaped to Union lines, hoping to gain their freedom. At first—in accordance with orders from Washington—they were returned, but many Northern troops found this policy utterly distasteful. Then, Union Major General Benjamin F. Butler, a former Democratic congressman from Massachusetts, proposed a novel solution to the problem. When a Confederate officer appeared at his headquarters at Fort Monroe, Virginia, demanding the return of several fugitive slaves, Butler rebuffed him. The slaves in question, he said, had been helping to construct Confederate fortifications; as such, he was justified in holding them as "contraband of war." Butler's use of the term was loose, but his argument made excellent practical sense. In early August 1861 the U.S. Congress codified the general principle in its First Confiscation Act, which declared the forfeiture of any slaves used in direct support of the Confederate war effort. The military necessity of such a policy was obvious.

Less obvious was a proclamation issued by Major General John C. Frémont later that month. Then in command of the Department of Missouri and frustrated by the guerrilla warfare in his midst, Frémont decided to free the slaves living in the southern part of the state. Lincoln promptly overruled him. The order was too sweeping, its military purpose unclear. In May 1862, Lincoln overruled Major General David Hunter when Hunter tried the same thing in South Carolina.

Yet by that point Lincoln himself was beginning to move toward a policy of emancipation. In March 1862 he urged Congress to consider a program of compensated emancipation. Six weeks later he signed into law a bill for the compensated emancipation of slaves in the federally regulated District of Columbia. Subsequent legislation ended slavery in the Federal territories—this time without compensation.

Lincoln eagerly waited for the border states to take up his call for compensated emancipation. Their failure to do so profoundly disappointed him. In the meantime, the Peninsula Campaign collapsed and Congress moved toward a harder line, passing a more stringent Second Confiscation Act in July. Lincoln made one final appeal to the congressmen from the border states. When this too failed, Lincoln made his fateful decision to emancipate the slaves by executive order. "We must free the slaves or be ourselves subdued," he told a cabinet member. The slaves were undeniably an element of strength to the Rebels, "and we must decide whether that element should be with us or against us."

On July 22, 1862, Lincoln met with his cabinet and read them a draft of his preliminary Emancipation Proclamation. Most agreed that it was time to issue such a document. The only objection had to do with timing. Secretary of State Seward worried that, given the Union's recent military setbacks, issuing the proclamation immediately would seem like a confession of desperation. Better to wait until a Federal victory. Lincoln saw the logic of this and for the time being put the Emancipation Proclamation aside. In the meantime its existence remained a guarded state secret, while the president waited for a Northern battlefield success.

Confederate Counterstrokes

As it turned out, he had to wait nearly two months. In the meantime McClellan's battered army remained at Harrison's Landing. McClellan asked for 50,000 reinforcements, claiming that with them he could resume

Called "Old Brains," Henry W. Halleck had been a military intellectual in the prewar U.S. Army. As Union general-in-chief from July 1862 to March 1864, he brought greater administrative efficiency to the North's war effort but frustrated Lincoln by his frequent refusal to give field commanders direct orders.

his Richmond offensive. Lincoln considered this pure moonshine. In mid-July he summoned to Washington Major General Henry W. Halleck—his most successful commander to date—and named him general-in-chief. (Since March, when McClellan was relieved of this assignment, the post had been vacant; Lincoln and Stanton had acted, in effect, as the general-in-chief.) Among the first issues Lincoln put to Halleck was what to do with the Army of the Potomac. Although habitually reluctant to make decisions in such matters—he firmly believed that field commanders could best judge their situations—Halleck did little to discourage Lincoln's growing conviction that McClellan's army should be withdrawn. On August 15 the Army of the Potomac began boarding river transports for the return trip. This huge ferrying operation would continue for most of the month.

Meanwhile, in mid-July Pope's new Army of Virginia became active. Pope's mission was threefold: to protect Washington, to ensure Federal control of the Shenandoah Valley, and by operating against the Confederate rail center at Gordonsville, Virginia, to draw Confederate strength from Richmond and thereby divert attention from McClellan. Hindered by the wide dispersion of his forces, his newness to the eastern theater, and his matchless knack for alienating almost everyone, Pope ultimately became the victim of one of Lee's deftest bits of offensive-defensive strategy.

Second Manassas

Lee shaped his planning step by step, constrained by the knowledge that McClellan still lay within striking distance of Richmond. As McClellan's quiescence showed no sign of change, Lee felt assured enough to detach three divisions and send them against Pope's army. These he entrusted to Stonewall Jackson.

On August 9, Jackson fought a preliminary battle against a corps from Pope's army at Cedar Mountain in north-central Virginia. Soon afterward Lee brought most of his army north to join in the struggle against Pope. He knew that McClellan temporarily posed no threat because the Union army had begun its withdrawal from the James River. For nearly two weeks Lee sparred with Pope in the Rappahannock River valley, fruitlessly trying to bring him to bay before McClellan's army reentered the picture.

Lee did not feel strong enough to attack Pope directly, so he elected to maneuver, hoping to cut Pope's communications, threaten Washington, and avoid a general engagement. On August 24 he called Jackson to his headquarters and instructed him to sever the Orange and Alexandria Railroad, Pope's principal line of communications. To accomplish the mission Jackson was given 23,000 troops, leaving Lee with only 32,000 to hold the Rappahannock crossings and fix Pope's attention. Dividing the army violated conventional military wisdom, but Lee saw no alternative. The disparity in numbers between the contending forces rendered the risk unavoidable.

Jackson's execution of the operation gave proof that the military brilliance he displayed in the Shenandoah had not been lost. In a remarkable forced march of fifty-seven miles in two days, Jackson placed his swift

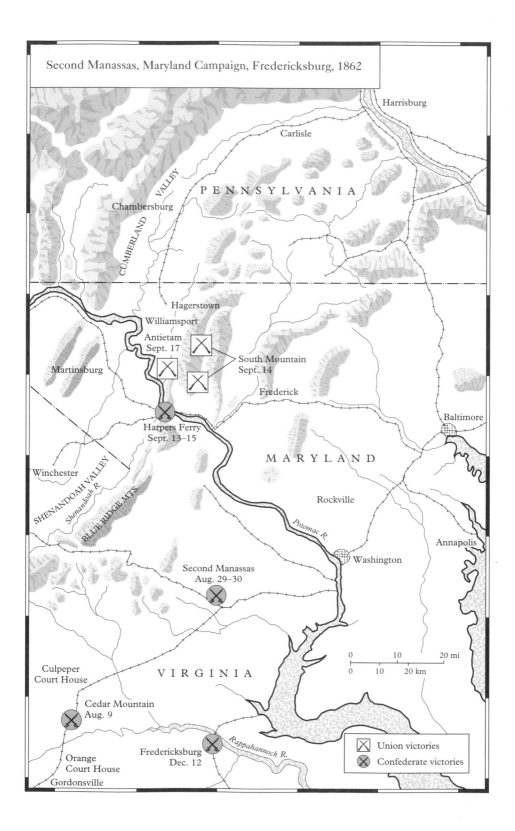

Second Manassas, Maryland Campaign, Fredericksburg, 1862

Harrisburg

Carlisle

P E N N S Y L V A N I A

Chambersburg

CUMBERLAND VALLEY

Hagerstown

Williamsport

Antietam
Sept. 17

Martinsburg

South Mountain
Sept. 14

Frederick

Harpers Ferry
Sept. 13–15

Baltimore

Winchester

M A R Y L A N D

SHENANDOAH VALLEY

Shenandoah R.

BLUE RIDGE MTS.

Rockville

Potomac R.

Annapolis

Second Manassas
Aug. 29–30

Washington

Culpeper
Court House

V I R G I N I A

0   10   20 mi

0   10   20 km

Cedar Mountain
Aug. 9

Orange
Court House

Fredericksburg
Dec. 12

Rappahannock R.

Union victories

Gordonsville

Confederate victories

infantry—jocularly dubbed his "foot cavalry"—squarely upon Pope's line of communications, cut the Orange and Alexandria Railroad, and demolished a gigantic Union supply depot at Manassas Junction. As a finale, he disappeared into a secluded, defensible position a few miles west of Manassas to await developments.

Aware only that Jackson lurked somewhere in his rear, Pope abandoned his defensive line along the upper Rappahannock River and began beating about the countryside in a disorganized attempt to locate Stonewall's forces. Lee, meanwhile, disengaged from the Rappahannock line as well and began a circuitous march aimed at a juncture with Jackson. Around noon on August 29 the Army of Northern Virginia was reunited as Longstreet's divisions assumed positions just southwest of Jackson's line.

Jackson's troops had been in a fierce battle the day before, and Pope assailed them again early on the 29th. But the Federals were unaware that Longstreet was now in the vicinity. On August 30, still blissfully ignorant of Longstreet's presence, Pope struck Jackson yet again. For a time the rebel situation was critical, but then Longstreet's five divisions broke from their cover and smashed the exposed Union left, sending the Federals in wild retreat until their officers could rally them for a stand on the old Bull Run battlefield. There, repeated Confederate attacks failed to dislodge them. It made no difference. Stung by repeated reverses, Pope elected to withdraw his demoralized forces northeast toward Washington. At a cost of 9,500 men, Lee had inflicted 14,500 casualties upon the Federals and cleared northern Virginia of any major Union army. In twelve weeks of campaigning, Lee had reversed the tide of the war in the east.

Antietam

With Pope beaten and McClellan's army withdrawn behind the Washington fortifications, Lee believed it was time to carry the war from Virginia into enemy country. The Union armies were weakened and demoralized, creating the opportunity to seize the initiative. An advance into Union territory might cause Maryland to secede and perhaps even lead Great Britain and France to grant diplomatic recognition to the Confederacy (although Lee doubted either event would ever occur). Most important, entering enemy territory would permit his army to forage in Maryland and give Virginia the chance to harvest its crops unmolested.

An offensive into Maryland would be difficult for even an army of 200,000, much less Lee's ragged, ill-equipped veterans, now reduced to something less than 50,000. But Lee was developing an almost mystical regard for the prowess of his Confederate soldiers. Time and again he asked them for the impossible, and incredibly, they often gave it to him. He grew convinced that there had never been soldiers like them. He also formed a correspondingly dismal picture of the Union forces and, especially, Union leadership. When a subordinate seemed dubious about his offensive plans, for example, Lee blandly explained that McClellan's caution made them quite practical.

Lee's army crossed the Potomac River on September 4–7. The bands played "Maryland, My Maryland" and the ragged soldiers looked in wonderment at the unspoiled countryside around them. From the outset, however, things went badly. To begin with, Lee expected that his thrust northward into Maryland would force the withdrawal of a 12,000-man Union garrison at Harpers Ferry. The garrison blocked the lower Shenandoah Valley, the avenue by which Lee planned to maintain communications with the South. When the garrison stayed in place, Lee had no choice but to reduce it. After a short stay in Frederick, Maryland, he divided his army into four parts. Three of them, under Jackson's overall command, went after Harpers Ferry. The fourth, consisting of Longstreet's corps and a division under General D. H. Hill, proceeded to the town of Boonsboro to await the operation's completion.

At this point additional problems arose. Unfounded reports of Federal units operating around Chambersburg, Pennsylvania, prompted Lee to divide his army further: D. H. Hill remained at Boonsboro while Longstreet shifted northwest to Hagerstown, Maryland. Jackson's forces took longer than anticipated to get into position. Not until September 13—a full day behind schedule—did they surround Harpers Ferry. Although the town's surrender then became a mere matter of time, it turned out that time was something the Confederates did not have.

Lee had miscalculated McClellan's response to the Maryland invasion. The Virginian had believed it would take three or four weeks for McClellan to reorganize the Union armies defeated at Second Manassas. Instead, McClellan did the job in less than seven days. As Jackson's units sewed up Harpers Ferry, the Army of the Potomac arrived at Frederick, Maryland, just one day's hard march from the scattered Confederate army. The situation would become critical if the Union general realized the exposed state of Lee's army. And that is precisely what occurred.

By incredible coincidence, two Federal soldiers found a copy of Lee's plan for the Harpers Ferry operation in a field outside Frederick. This soon-to-be-famous "Lost Order" quickly went to McClellan, who took one look at it and became understandably ecstatic. "Here," he exulted to one of his generals, "is a paper with which if I cannot whip Bobbie Lee, I will be willing to go home." Unfortunately for the Union cause, McClellan lacked the killer instinct required to capitalize on the situation. Instead of an immediate, rapid advance into the center of Lee's widely divided forces, he sent his columns forward at a leisurely pace. He gave Lee just enough time to retrieve the situation.

Lee heard about McClellan's dangerous advance about midnight on September 13. He issued orders for his troops to occupy the passes of South Mountain, a wooded ridge that formed a barrier between the Union army and his own. The next day three Union corps attacked. Lee's forces managed to fend them off for most of the day, but by evening Lee's hopes for a Northern invasion lay in ruins. From then on he was strictly on the defensive.

Lee probably should have withdrawn across the Potomac River as soon as possible. Initially he planned to do so, but word that Harpers Ferry

Union infantrymen charge through a cornfield at Antietam, September 17, 1862, the bloodiest single day of the war. Though McClellan achieved only a drawn-out battle, Lee was nevertheless forced to abandon his invasion of Maryland. Lincoln issued the Emancipation Proclamation five days later.

was about to surrender emboldened him. He chose instead to withdraw about ten miles west of South Mountain and make a stand at Sharpsburg, Maryland, along the banks of Antietam Creek. The wisdom of this decision is questionable—it meant fighting with a wide river directly in his rear—but Lee's conduct of the battle was magnificent. McClellan advanced slowly, cautiously, giving Lee plenty of time to concentrate most of his army. The Union assault did not come until September 17, and then in a piecemeal fashion that allowed Lee to shift his own outnumbered forces from one threatened point to another. The Army of Northern Virginia held its ground, albeit at tremendous cost: 13,700 casualties out of approximately 40,000 engaged. Union losses totaled 12,350 out of about 87,000 present on the field. This Battle of Antietam had the grim distinction of being the bloodiest single day of the Civil War.

It had another significance as well. Although McClellan missed a spectacular chance to destroy Lee's army, the battle looked enough like a Union victory for Lincoln to follow through on the promise he had made in July. On September 22, 1862, he issued the preliminary Emancipation Proclamation. If the South did not abandon the war by January 1, 1863, he warned, the slaves residing in the rebellious areas would become forever free.

The Emancipation Proclamation irretrievably changed the nature of the war. It outraged Southern opinion, the more so since it conjured fears of the race war white Southerners had always feared. Jefferson Davis considered the proclamation "the most execrable measure recorded in the history

Lincoln's decision to issue the Emancipation Proclamation sparked controversy in the North and outraged the South. In this cartoon penned by a Southern sympathizer living in Baltimore, Lincoln is shown writing the proclamation surrounded by demonic images, his foot planted on the U.S. Constitution.

of guilty man" and for a time considered treating captured Federal officers as inciters of servile insurrection. More than ever, the war had become a struggle to the death.

Bragg's Kentucky Raid

Lee's invasion of Maryland was not the only Confederate offensive during this period. At practically the same time as Lee's Maryland campaign, Confederate forces under Major General Earl Van Dorn tried to recapture the important rail center of Corinth, Mississippi, only to be repulsed on October 4. The Confederate offensive that went farthest and lasted longest, however, was the invasion of Kentucky, masterminded by General Braxton Bragg.

Bragg took over the army (soon to be called the Army of Tennessee) at Tupelo, Mississippi, in mid-June, after Beauregard departed abruptly on sick leave. In many respects Bragg was a most capable officer: energetic, determined, aggressive. He possessed a good strategic mind and sound administrative abilities. It would eventually develop, however, that Bragg possessed equally obvious shortcomings. He had an irascible temperament that alienated many around him, including his chief subordinates. And although decisive, even daring at times, during a crisis he often turned cautious, almost as if he no longer grasped the situation. But until these darker qualities manifested themselves, Bragg looked like a remarkable soldier. Indeed, few campaigns of the Civil War were better conceived and—up to a point—better executed, than Bragg's Kentucky raid.

After his bloodless victory at Corinth and before he became general-in-chief, Halleck dispersed his huge army into two main parts. One part—about 31,000 men under Major General Don Carlos Buell—was ordered east toward Chattanooga, Tennessee, another key railroad town and also the gateway into eastern Tennessee, a bastion of Unionist sentiment. The other, consisting of about 67,000 troops, was scattered about in order to consolidate the Federal grip on western Tennessee. Halleck's questionable disposition drained most of the momentum from his western offensive. When, in mid-July, he went east to become general-in-chief, operational control passed to Buell—now in northern Alabama—and Grant, who commanded the dispersed Union troops in western Tennessee.

Grant needed months to reconcentrate sufficient forces to resume offensive operations. In the meantime Buell, advancing toward Chattanooga, ran into a variety of delays from frequent guerrilla incursions, enemy cavalry raids, and the burden of repairing his lines of supply—the railroads leading east from Corinth and south from Nashville.

Grant's immobility and Buell's glacial movements invited some kind of Confederate riposte. Rejecting the option of an advance toward Grant, Bragg decided to shift his army eastward toward Chattanooga, then join forces with Confederate units in eastern Tennessee and embark on an invasion of Kentucky. In so doing he would turn Buell's flank and force him to retreat—perhaps even to abandon middle Tennessee. The move might also encourage Kentucky to join the Confederacy and fill his army's ranks with thousands of Bluegrass volunteers. Leaving a covering force at Tupelo under Major General Earl Van Dorn, Bragg embarked on this new operation in mid-July.

The shift east required over a month to execute. Bragg sent his infantry to Chattanooga via railroad—a long, circuitous journey that carried them as far south as Mobile, Alabama. Meanwhile his slow-moving artillery and wagon trains traveled by road. As Bragg's army completed its concentration, the Confederates in eastern Tennessee, under Lieutenant General Edmund Kirby Smith, began an advance across the Cumberland Plateau into central Kentucky. By the end of August Kirby Smith had reached Lexington. Bragg then rapidly advanced from Chattanooga and within two weeks stood on Kentucky soil.

This gigantic raid terrified the inhabitants of Illinois, Indiana, and Ohio and briefly installed a pro-Confederate governor at Frankfort, the state capital of Kentucky. It also forced Buell's Union army to abandon northern Alabama, relinquish much of central Tennessee except Nashville, and fall back practically to Louisville, Kentucky, before turning east to deal with Bragg's army. By that time it was early October. Bragg then had about 22,500 veteran troops with him, supported by another 10,000 under Kirby

Battle of Munfordville, Kentucky. While Lee advanced into Maryland, a second Confederate army under Braxton Bragg invaded Kentucky. Bragg hoped thousands of Kentucky men would flock to his forces, but few did. "Their hearts are with us," one Confederate general complained, "but their bluegrass and fat cattle are against us."

Smith. Buell had about 60,000 troops, but his imposing numerical advantage was partially offset by the fact that his army contained many unseasoned troops and its organization was largely improvised.

Neither side fully understood the other's dispositions. The Battle of Perryville that ensued began as a meeting engagement when units from both sides stumbled into one another while searching for fresh water in drought-stricken central Kentucky. The main fight commenced at 2 P.M. on October 8 and continued until well into the night. When it was over, the Federals had lost 845 killed, 2,851 wounded, and 515 captured or missing: a total of 4,211. Confederate casualties numbered 510 killed, 2,635 wounded, and 251 captured or missing—3,396 in all. But although the Rebels inflicted greater losses and held most of the battlefield at day's end, Bragg correctly realized he could not capitalize on the victory. Perryville ended his invasion of Kentucky; he withdrew southward to Murfreesboro, Tennessee.

Autumn Stalemate

In many respects the simultaneous Confederate raids into Maryland and Kentucky in the summer and fall of 1862 represented the military high tide of the Southern cause. Never again would a rebel triumph seem so within reach. By the end of August reports from Great Britain had indicated that the British were starved for cotton, impressed by the Confederacy's resilience, and perhaps on the verge of recognizing the Southern nation. A major Confederate victory at that point might have triggered foreign intervention, just as the American triumph at Saratoga had brought about the French alliance during the War for Independence. The population of the South had felt a rising thrill of expectation; Northerners were correspondingly alarmed and depressed. But the moment ended quickly, and autumn brought only a new round of campaigning.

Fredericksburg

After the Battle of Antietam, McClellan, much to the disgust of the Lincoln administration, tamely kept his army in western Maryland until the end of October 1862. Eventually McClellan crossed the Potomac and headed south toward Warrenton, Virginia, but Lincoln had had enough of his excessive caution and on November 7 relieved him of his command.

McClellan's replacement was Major General Ambrose E. Burnside, an amiable, modest soul who had enjoyed success in amphibious operations against the Carolina coast. When offered command of the Army of the Potomac, he tried to decline the job because he felt unequal to the responsibility. Although events would swiftly and amply prove him correct, at the outset he did rather well.

Within a week of assuming command, Burnside started the Union army on a new "On to Richmond" campaign. This one aimed at sliding past Lee's right flank and crossing the Rappahannock River at Fredericksburg, about fifty miles north of the Confederate capital. Lee had to move rapidly to counter the move; initially he even felt he might have to fall back to a position along the North Anna River, about halfway between Fredericksburg and the capital. Burnside, however, soon lost control of the situation and wound up giving Lee the easiest victory of his career.

Burnside's plans required a prompt crossing of the Rappahannock into Fredericksburg before the Confederates could oppose him in force. Unfortunately for him, the necessary pontoon bridges failed to arrive until well into December, giving Lee ample time to concentrate in and around the town. The Army of Northern Virginia took well-nigh impregnable positions on Marye's Heights just west of the city. Burnside foolishly persisted in his now pointless plan of campaign, and on December 11 two Confederate signal guns announced that the Federals were attempting a crossing.

Lee was unfazed. He wanted the Northerners to attack. With his troops posted on Marye's Heights, defeat was out of the question. The only unknown factor was the ultimate size of the Union casualty list. The entire Army of Northern Virginia had the same absolute certainty regarding the battle's outcome. Longstreet asked one of his artillerists about an idle cannon, only to be told that other Confederate guns already covered the ground so well that its use was academic: "A chicken could not live on that field when we open fire on it."

Lee made no serious attempt to keep the Federals from entering Fredericksburg. On December 13, Burnside made six major assaults against

Marye's Heights. All failed. Massed rebel infantry and artillery scythed them down by the hundreds. The Battle of Fredericksburg ended as it was destined to end—in an inexpensive Confederate victory. The Federals lost over 12,500 men; Confederate losses totaled fewer than 5,500. But the constricted battle area offered Lee no scope for a counterattack. He had to content himself with watching the wounded enemy retire to the river's far bank.

Grant's Overland Campaign Against Vicksburg

Meanwhile in Mississippi, Grant had at last gathered enough of an army to inaugurate a late autumn offensive. His objective was Vicksburg, Mississippi. The city stood on high bluffs at a hairpin turn in the Mississippi River, about three hundred miles downstream from Memphis. After the loss of Columbus, Kentucky, and Island No. 10, Vicksburg became the Confederacy's main fortress on the Mississippi; a second bastion was built at Port Hudson, Louisiana, two hundred miles farther south. Between these two points rebel forces still controlled the river. As long as they did, the Confederacy would remain an unbroken nation stretching from Texas to the Virginia capes; as long as they did, midwestern produce could not be shipped down the Mississippi. Capturing Vicksburg thus became a vital Union goal.

In many respects this task was a general's nightmare. The ideal way to attack Vicksburg would have been to move a large army downriver to within striking distance of the city, supply it by river transports, and then maneuver against the city from the northeast. Geography, however, denied Grant so straightforward a solution. Just north of Vicksburg lay the Yazoo River Delta, a vast stretch of woodlands and swamps. The Delta country sprawled along the eastern bank of the Mississippi for about 140 miles; in places it was forty miles across. No army could hope to operate in such a region. There was really only one point north of Vicksburg from which the city could be attacked, albeit with difficulty, and that was at Chickasaw Bluffs immediately above the town. The Chickasaw Bluffs position, however, combined excellent terrain for the defender with scant maneuvering room for the attacker; this unhappy fact, from the Federal point of view, made it an approach of last resort.

South of Vicksburg the ground was less forbidding than the Delta country but almost as inaccessible. The guns of the fortress made it impossible to transport an army there by river, and if Grant tried to march his troops past the city along the west bank, he would find it impossible to keep the army supplied. An attack directly from the west was out of the question: at Vicksburg the Mississippi was a half-mile wide. That left an attack from the east. But in order to get there, Grant would first have to march his army 250 miles; worse, to supply it he would have to depend exclusively on the Mississippi Central Railroad, a conduit that seemed not only inadequate but mortally vulnerable to interdiction by fast-riding Confederate cavalry.

Still, the overland route seemed the least forbidding prospect and in November Grant set forth with his army, now christened the Army of the Tennessee. Initially everything went smoothly. Lieutenant General John C.

Pemberton, the Confederate commander assigned to defend Vicksburg, fell back before Grant's advance and did not stop until he reached Grenada, Mississippi—about one third of the total distance Grant's men would have to cover. Grant got as far as the town of Oxford, after which the roof caved in. Far back in Tennessee, Confederate cavalry raider Nathan Bedford Forrest led a column of horsemen in a lightning stab that wrecked a good portion of the railroad from which Grant received his supplies. Closer to home, a second raid led by Major General Earl Van Dorn struck Grant's advanced supply base at Holly Springs, Mississippi. Grant had no choice but to withdraw his entire force back to Tennessee.

Even so, the loss of Holly Springs afforded Grant an intriguing lesson. With his military foodstuffs destroyed, Grant instructed his troops to live off the countryside. He hoped they could scrounge enough food to keep body and soul together until they could link up with a regular supply line again. Instead the army not only survived but actually *feasted*. It turned out that this part of the country had a huge food surplus; the men found plenty of hams, corn, poultry, and vegetables. Grant was impressed: in the middle of December, a small corner of the state of Mississippi could feed 40,000 extra mouths. It was something he did not forget.

Simultaneously with Grant's abortive drive down the Mississippi Central Railroad, a second force under Sherman embarked at Memphis and steamed down the Mississippi River to Chickasaw Bluffs, just north of Vicksburg itself. The plan called for Grant's army to distract Pemberton's attention while Sherman made a sudden grab for the city. In the wake of Holly Springs the scheme became a fiasco. Grant's precipitous retreat enabled Pemberton to bring one third of his own men back to Vicksburg. They arrived in plenty of time to bolster the lines at Chickasaw Bluffs, and when Sherman attacked on December 29 he received a crisp rebuff. The year ended with Vicksburg looking tougher to crack than ever.

Stone's River

The same might be said of middle Tennessee. After its withdrawal from Kentucky, Bragg's Army of Tennessee took up position at Murfreesboro, astride the railroad that led from Nashville to Chattanooga. Buell's army came south and occupied Nashville. Meanwhile Lincoln, disenchanted with Buell's lack of aggressiveness, replaced him with a new commander, Major General William S. Rosecrans.

Rosecrans had performed capably in previous operations, possessed good administrative abilities, and enjoyed a strong rapport with his troops, who dubbed him "Old Rosy." But like many Union commanders, he did not like to advance until he felt completely ready, and he spent most of November and December gathering tons of supplies at Nashville. Only on December 26 did he move southeast against Bragg's army at Murfreesboro.

The last dawn of 1862 found Rosecrans's army a few miles west of Murfreesboro with the Confederates drawn up in front of them. Rosecrans planned to attack the rebel right flank; Bragg, however, anticipated him and

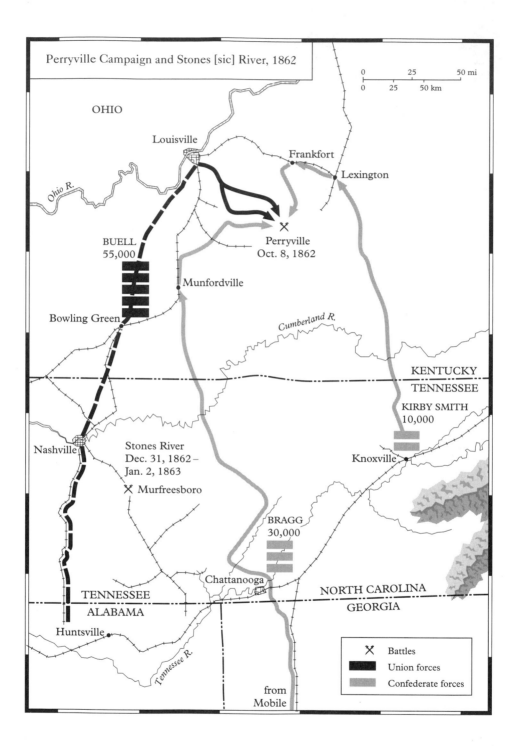

Perryville Campaign and Stones [sic] River, 1862

0   25   50 mi
0   25   50 km

OHIO

Louisville

Frankfort

Lexington

Ohio R.

BUELL
55,000

Perryville
Oct. 8, 1862

Munfordville

Bowling Green

Cumberland R.

KENTUCKY
TENNESSEE

KIRBY SMITH
10,000

Nashville

Stones River
Dec. 31, 1862 –
Jan. 2, 1863

Knoxville

✕ Murfreesboro

BRAGG
30,000

Chattanooga

NORTH CAROLINA

TENNESSEE

GEORGIA

ALABAMA

Huntsville

Tennessee R.

from
Mobile

✕   Battles

      Union forces

      Confederate forces

struck the Union right flank instead. Surprised by the suddenness of the attack and shattered by its weight, the right wing of Rosecrans's army collapsed. By early afternoon the Federal position resembled a jackknife with the blade nearly closed. Only the most desperate fighting saved the Northern army from collapse.

That evening Rosecrans held a council of war and asked his chief subordinates if they thought a retreat in order. His senior corps commander, Major General George H. Thomas, gave the obvious reply: "Hell," he boomed, "this army can't retreat." It was true. The Union situation was so precarious, its sole line of retreat so exposed, that any rearward movement would have quickly dissolved into a rout. Recognizing the logic of this, Rosecrans elected to stand.

New Year's Day of 1863 was quiet as both armies recovered from the previous day's ordeal. Bragg believed he could not press his attack on the Union right flank—his troops in that sector were exhausted and decimated by the vicious fighting there—but neither did he want to give up his hard-won advantage. On January 2, therefore, he ordered his remaining fresh troops to strike the Union left in an attack across Stone's River. This assault, however, delayed until late in the day, was torn apart by Union artillery. With his army now completely worn out, Bragg reluctantly decided to fall back some thirty miles southeast to Tullahoma, Tennessee. The Union army, as shattered by its barren victory as by a major defeat, did not pursue.

$$\star \quad \star \quad \star \quad \star$$

Thus the year 1862, which had begun with the belief that a quick and relatively bloodless victory was still possible, ended in military stalemate. From a Union perspective, the military problem of defeating the Confederacy loomed greater than ever. Geography was one factor. In Virginia, the constricted, river-choked arena made it difficult even for large armies to bring their strength effectively to bear. Fredericksburg had shown that. In the west, great distances meant that the Federals had to supply their forces over long, vulnerable lines of supply—a point rammed home by the cavalry raids of Forrest and Van Dorn.

The respective fighting power of the two opponents was a second factor. Although the Federals usually enjoyed a substantial numerical advantage, the rival armies had shown themselves too evenly matched in strength and resilience. Battles like Stone's River suggested that even the most determined, well-executed assaults wrecked the attacker as much as the defender, and although at Stone's River the attackers were Confederates, the onus of offensive warfare still lay chiefly with the North.

A third factor—and from the Federal point of view the most surprising—was the psychological strength of Southern resistance. At the beginning of 1862 most Northerners subscribed to the belief that popular support for the Confederacy was shallow at best. Lincoln doubted whether secessionists formed a majority anywhere except South Carolina and thought that a large, latent Unionist sentiment lay just below the surface, awaiting only a Federal victory to emerge and throw off the Confederate yoke. Thousands of

Northerners shared this conviction, including Ulysses S. Grant. Looking back on this period of the war years later, Grant wrote that until the spring of 1862, he had supposed the Southern people were not in earnest and that one or two decisive Federal successes would make them quit the war. "[Forts] Donelson and Henry," he continued, "were such victories." But when they led only to the furious Confederate counterattack at Shiloh, "then, indeed, I gave up all idea of saving the Union except by complete conquest."

Most Northerners took a bit longer to reach the same conclusion. The turning point, for most of them, was the defeat of McClellan's peninsula campaign. The failure of this campaign turned many Northerners sharply against a limited war directed solely against Confederate armies. Until then, Union policy makers had fought the war somewhat in the manner of the "cabinet wars" of the eighteenth century. Severe clashes could and did occur, but an important goal was to prevent severe disruptions in the fabric of society. Increasingly, however, the American Civil War became a struggle with no holds barred, more so than even the French Revolution and Napoleonic Wars. A Union soldier aptly expressed the new outlook: "I am like the fellow that got his house burned by the guerillas," he wrote. "[H]e was in for emancipation subjugation extermination and hell and damnation. We are in war and anything to beat the south."

The issuance of the Emancipation Proclamation signaled this major change in the conflict. The struggle was no longer one to quell rebellion. It had become what Lincoln initially feared it would become—a "remorseless, revolutionary struggle" to overthrow the institution on which the South's social and economic structure depended. As a result, measures unthinkable in the war's first year—the seizure or destruction of crops and livestock, the demolition of factories, even the burning of towns and villages—now seemed not only permissible but necessary. The stakes of the conflict, already great, increased still further. The Civil War was becoming a total war.

SUGGESTED READINGS

Cozzens, Peter. *No Better Place to Die: The Battle of Stone's River* (Urbana and Chicago: University of Illinois Press, 1990).

Freeman, Douglas S. *Robert E. Lee,* 4 vols. (New York: Charles Scribner's Sons, 1934–1935).

———. *Lee's Lieutenants: A Study in Command,* 3 vols. (New York: Charles Scribner's Sons, 1942–1944).

Hennessy, John J. *Return to Bull Run: The Campaign of Second Manassas* (New York: Simon and Schuster, 1993).

Jones, Archer. *Confederate Strategy from Shiloh to Vicksburg* (Baton Rouge: Louisiana State University Press, 1961).

McDonough, James Lee. *War in Kentucky: From Shiloh to Perryville* (Knoxville: University of Tennessee Press, 1994).

McWhiney, Grady. *Braxton Bragg and Confederate Defeat,* Vol. 1, *Field Command* (New York: Columbia University Press, 1969).

Sears, Stephen W. *George B. McClellan: The Young Napoleon* (New York: Ticknor & Fields, 1988).

————. *To the Gates of Richmond: The Peninsula Campaign* (New York: Ticknor & Fields, 1992).

————. *Landscape Turned Red: The Battle of Antietam* (New York: Ticknor & Fields, 1983).

Tanner, Robert G. *Stonewall in the Valley* (Garden City, N.Y.: Doubleday, 1974).

Vandiver, Frank. *Mighty Stonewall* (New York: McGraw-Hill, 1957).

6

THE CIVIL WAR, 1863:
MOVING DEMOCRACIES
TOWARD TOTAL WAR

The Austerlitz Chimera

Two Societies at War

Vicksburg and Gettysburg

Struggle for the Gateway

The year 1863 saw the conflict's continued evolution into a total war. The North and South had already fielded large armies composed of volunteers, and the South had adopted a conscription law in April 1862. In March 1863 the Union government followed suit with a conscription law of its own. Both sides continued to mobilize their economic resources to support the war and increasingly saw those resources as legitimate military targets. Northern forces in particular began to confiscate or destroy factories, mills, railroads, and agricultural products that might be used to support Southern armies.

The North moved toward such measures in part because breaking the Confederacy's military strength through combat alone had proven impossible. Although slow to recognize it, both sides possessed armies too large and durable to be destroyed in a single great battle—especially when so strongly supported by the full resources of their societies. In this respect the Union and Confederate forces were perhaps even more resilient than their European predecessors. Frederick the Great had tried to apply all the resources of the state to his defense of Prussia, but he had been unwilling to unleash the passions of his people. During the wars of the French Revolution and Napoleon, the French had roused the people, tapped the resources of the entire nation, and raised mass national armies, but they had not gone to the limits of total war. By 1863 both sides in the Civil War were going farther toward total war than Europeans had been willing or able to go. In such a struggle, the larger population and superior economic muscle of the North promised a Union victory—if the political commitment to continue the struggle could be maintained.

It was a big if. When 1863 began, the Confederate leadership still had reason to hope for ultimate victory. The victories at Fredericksburg, Holly Springs, and Chickasaw Bluffs showed the steadiness of Southern valor, while the bloody standoff at Stone's River at least promised continued stalemate. The North, for its part, seemed to be tiring; the autumn elections had resulted in significant gains for the Democrats, many of whom favored a compromise peace. But 1863 proved to be the military turning point of the Civil War; by year's end the tide ran clearly against the South. The Union success occurred in two thunderclaps: first the almost simultaneous triumphs at Gettysburg and Vicksburg in early July, then—after a harrowing ordeal along the Tennessee-Georgia border—a dramatic autumn victory at Chattanooga.

The Austerlitz Chimera

First, however, the Union had to endure a number of humiliations. In January 1863, Burnside tried to redeem himself with a midwinter offensive northwest of Fredericksburg. Torrential rains drowned the operation; soldiers derisively called it Burnside's "Mud March." Then in April a promising cavalry raid in northern Alabama came to grief when pursuing rebel horsemen under Bedford Forrest bagged the entire Union detachment of 2,000 men. The following month the Army of the Potomac—under yet another commander—suffered a major defeat at Chancellorsville, Virginia.

The Quest for Decisive Battle

Perhaps better than any other, the Chancellorsville battle illustrates the mid-nineteenth-century American fixation with the slashing offensive style of Napoleon. Generals commonly issued Napoleonic addresses to their troops and patterned their operations after famous Napoleonic victories. A perennial favorite was the Battle of Austerlitz, fought on December 2, 1805. The reason for the fixation was simple: the name was synonymous with decisive battle. At Austerlitz, Napoleon had routed the Austrian and Russian armies in a single day and secured an armistice from Austria just two days afterward. Austerlitz thus represented the apogee of military art and displayed, as Dennis Hart Mahan, West Point's strategic guru, expressed it, "those grand features of the art [of war], by which an enemy is broken and utterly dispersed by one and the same blow."

To be sure, not every Civil War commander sought an Austerlitz-like victory. On the Union side, Generals Halleck, Buell, McClellan, and Sherman were more concerned with the occupation of strategic places than the destruction of an enemy army in battle. Among Confederates, Joseph E.

Johnston clearly preferred a defensive strategy—his counterstroke at Seven Pines was practically the only major offensive battle of his career. These, however, were exceptional figures. The majority of commanders cherished the vision of a decisive victory over the enemy.

Almost without exception they met disappointment. The possible explanations for this are legion. To begin with, the increased range and firepower of the rifled musket, especially when combined with field entrenchments (which became an increasingly pronounced feature of Civil War battlefields after 1862), gave defenders a greater edge over their attackers. Then too, Civil War armies typically had a fairly low ratio of cavalry to infantry, and without the combination of speed and power embodied in large formations of heavy cavalry it was almost impossible for a victorious army to catch and destroy a retreating opponent. The heavy woodlands and broken terrain characteristic of Civil War battlefields further limited the utility of cavalry in large engagements. Instead both sides used their horsemen primarily for reconnaissance, screening, and raiding. Thus cavalry charges on a Napoleonic scale occurred only rarely. When they did, however—as at Cedar Creek in 1864—they displayed their traditional ability to overtake retreating infantry, shatter a defeated army, and produce a fairly good approximation of Austerlitz.

Another possible explanation focuses on the organizational limitations of Civil War armies, which were, of course, largely officered by citizen-soldiers. One might also suggest that the failure of Civil War generals to achieve a decisive victory reflected, to a considerable degree, their limited military abilities; after all, it took a Napoleon to win the Battle of Austerlitz.

But perhaps the main reason for the dearth of truly decisive Civil War battles was simply that such battles seldom occurred anywhere, at any time. Although greatly sought-after from the time of Gustavus Adolphus onward, a victory "by which an enemy is broken and utterly dispersed by one and the same blow" occurred, at best, on only a half-dozen occasions each century and required an unusual combination of circumstances to produce. Moreover, even a "decisive" battle was seldom decisive in any ultimate sense. Despite their calamitous defeat at Blenheim, for example, the French fought the War of the Spanish Succession for more than a decade; eventually, indeed, they obtained rather favorable terms for peace. And Austerlitz, of course, was followed ultimately by Leipzig and Waterloo.

Thus to the extent that Civil War commanders quested after decisive battle, they largely pursued a mirage. The Chancellorsville campaign prominently displayed both the seriousness of this quest and its attendant pitfalls and frustrations.

Chancellorsville: Act One

In late January 1863, after his abortive "Mud March," Burnside was replaced as commander of the Army of the Potomac by Major General Joseph Hooker. Although considered an ambitious opportunist, Hooker was also a combative, competent soldier. With astonishing speed and deftness he restored the flagging morale of the Army of the Potomac, largely by improving rations and camp sanitation and by introducing the corps badges that were the prototypes for modern unit patches. Then he prepared for another offensive.

The Army of the Potomac wintered at Falmouth, Virginia, just across the Rappahannock River from Lee's army at Fredericksburg. As the spring of 1863 approached, Hooker formulated an operations plan based largely on the ideas of Montgomery C. Meigs, the Union army's quartermaster general. Meigs had earlier written that "what is needed is a great and overwhelming defeat and destruction of [Lee's] army." His solution was a bold, rapid turning movement around the Confederate left flank—"such a march as Napoleon made at Jena, as Lee made in his campaign against Pope"—with the objective of gaining the Confederate rear. If, Meigs counseled, "you throw your whole army upon his communications, interpose between him and Richmond . . . and he fights, if you are successful, he has no retreat." This was nothing if not the dream of a decisive Napoleonic victory.

Hooker embraced Meigs's plan and also adopted Meigs's additional suggestion to supplement the turning movement by unleashing cavalry against Lee's lines of communication. But he decided to use only a bit more than half his army for the turning movement. The remainder would confront and fix Lee at Fredericksburg. With any luck this second force would distract the Confederates while Hooker made his march. Later, with Union forces established firmly on Lee's flank, Hooker could launch an offensive, and Lee's army could be crushed between the two halves.

Hooker had more than enough troops to do the job: about 110,000 in all. In mid-April a large cavalry force set forth on a major raid against the railroads that linked Lee's army with Richmond. Then on April 28, Hooker placed his great enveloping column in motion. Early next morning Union Major General John Sedgwick, entrusted with the task of fixing Lee, began crossing the Rappahannock River below Fredericksburg under cover of a heavy fog.

Lee's scouts soon brought him word of this latter movement. Word also came from Jeb Stuart of another crossing at Kelly's Ford, some twenty-five miles to the northwest. By evening Lee knew Hooker's main body had forded the Rapidan River and that two large Federal forces threatened him front and rear. Lee had just 59,500 troops with which to oppose an enemy almost twice that size. In effect, Hooker had prepared a gigantic trap for Lee, and conventional wisdom dictated a quick withdrawal before its jaws could spring shut. Lee, however, seldom thought conventionally. He correctly perceived that Sedgwick's thrust was largely a diversion; the situation as a whole was simply his big chance to hit Hooker's army while it was divided.

For the next two days Lee weighed alternatives, finally deciding to concentrate against Hooker's main body. Leaving 10,000 Confederate troops under command of Major General Jubal Early to watch Sedgwick, Lee moved west into the thickets around Chancellorsville, a crossroads eleven miles west of Fredericksburg surrounded by a dense second-growth forest known locally as the Wilderness. Jeb Stuart's cavalry, meanwhile, performed valuable scouting functions and prevented Hooker from finding out much about Lee's forces. By the evening of May 1, Lee knew two important things about the Union army. First, Hooker had stopped advancing. His men were felling trees to reinforce defensive fieldworks, which implied a temporary halt in the Federal offensive. Second, the extreme right of Hooker's army lay "in the air," anchored to no natural obstacle and so inviting attack.

Chancellorsville: Act Two

As a pallid moon rose over the gloomy Wilderness thickets, Lee and Jackson settled down to plot their next move. They conferred for several hours, finally deciding that Jackson would march 28,000 men across Hooker's front and strike that exposed right flank. Lee, meanwhile, would use his 14,000 remaining troops to dupe Hooker into thinking he intended a frontal assault.

As in the Seven Days, if the Union commander realized the true state of affairs, he could turn Lee's gamble into a catastrophe. But in Lee's reckoning Hooker's construction of fieldworks indicated an abdication of the initiative. And whereas Lee had retained his own cavalry to serve as the eyes of the army, Hooker had detached his own to operate against the Confederate supply lines. The Union commander therefore lacked the intelligence-gathering force necessary to grasp sudden changes in the operational picture.

Jackson's flank march did not go off without a hitch. It began three hours late and was not carried off in complete secrecy. Union pickets spotted Jackson's column as early as 9 A.M. By early afternoon scattered musketry betrayed skirmishing between Federals and Confederates along the line of march. Hooker, however, reacted cautiously and Jackson refused to panic. Despite a foray made by a venturesome Union corps against his artillery trains, Jackson continued his advance and by 5:15 P.M. had drawn up his forces astride the Orange Turnpike, west of Chancellorsville, and faced them almost due east. Ahead lay the exposed flank of the Union XI Corps, partially alerted but still largely unprepared.

Jackson gave the order. Suddenly the gnarled thickets filled with the rebel yell and the Confederates went crashing forward in the diminishing light. The XI Corps attempted to make a stand, with units here and there rallying in an attempt to stem the rebel tide, but their tactical situation was hopeless. Jackson pumped additional divisions into the fight as soon as they arrived. Within three hours, the Confederates had driven forward two miles, folding Hooker's lines into a "U" centered upon the large, isolated house called "Chancellorsville," which gave the clearing and battlefield its name. There resistance stiffened, and the Confederate attack lost momentum in the gathering darkness.

Jackson, accompanied by a cavalcade of staff officers, rode forward to reconnoiter. A band of North Carolina troops mistook his party for Union cavalry and opened fire, wounding him dangerously in the left arm. Compounding the mishap, Jackson's senior division commander fell to enemy fire at almost the same moment. Not until midnight did a

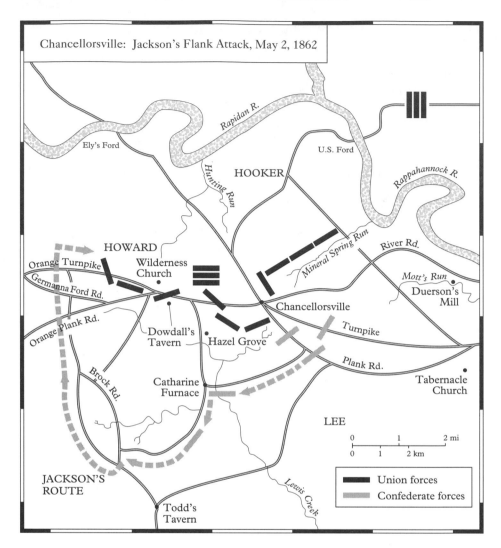

Chancellorsville: Jackson's Flank Attack, May 2, 1862

replacement, Jeb Stuart, assume command of Jackson's corps, and Stuart had almost no idea of Jackson's plans to continue the attack.

Attacks against Hooker's main body continued throughout May 3 without great success. The psychological blow had already been dealt, however. By noon Hooker withdrew his force into an enclave north of Chancellorsville. Meanwhile, Sedgwick's wing at Fredericksburg had shoved aside Early's 10,000 and was moving west at last. But an afternoon counterattack at Salem's Church, about three miles west of Fredericksburg, blunted his advance.

Lee realized he had to turn his full attention to this other threat. Leaving 25,000 troops under Stuart to contain Hooker, the general threw the rest of his army against Sedgwick's two corps. The Confederates, however, could not get into attacking positions until the afternoon of May 4. Sedgwick used the delay to withdraw to safety beyond the Rappahannock.

The Civil War's most famous military partnership was that between Robert E. Lee and Stonewall Jackson. Shown here in a romanticized postwar print, they plan the smashing flank attack that defeated the Union army at Chancellorsville—and cost Jackson his life.

Subsequently, on May 5 Lee again concentrated against Hooker and planned an assault for the following day.

This last decision reflected a tremendous stubborn streak in Lee, for Hooker had plenty of time to prepare his lines against precisely the frontal assault Lee was so determined to make. The implications were stunning: Lee seriously planned to attack an entrenched army numerically superior to his own. He seemed utterly resolved to wreck Hooker's force and blind to the fact that it simply could not be done. Fortunately for the Army of Northern Virginia, the Federals withdrew during the evening. Daybreak found them safely across the Rappahannock. Lee, enraged, vented his wrath against the general who brought the unwelcome news. "Why, General Pender," he said, "That is what you young men always do. You allow those people to get away. I tell you what to do, but you don't do it. Go after them," he added furiously, "and damage them all you can!"

Hooker, however, had long since moved out of reach. It remained only to tally the losses: 13,000 Confederate casualties this time against a total of 17,000 Federals. The Army of Northern Virginia had won again, but had absorbed 20 percent casualties in the process—losses the South could ill-afford. Nor could it replace one loss in particular. On May 10, Stonewall Jackson died of complications following the removal of his wounded arm. For the rest of the war, Lee had to do without the one subordinate who could make his audacious strategies take fire.

At Chancellorsville both commanders had tried—unsuccessfully—to achieve a Napoleonic decisive victory. In the case of Hooker this could be explained simply by a singular failure of nerve. "I just lost confidence in Joe Hooker," the Union general later admitted. The reasons for Lee's failure were obviously more complex. Some historians have maintained that, except for Jackson's tragic wounding, the Confederate counteroffensive would have cut Hooker off from the Rapidan crossings and destroyed that half of the Union army. Such an outcome seems unlikely; it is certainly unprovable. More impressive is the fact that the Federals were able to restore their front fairly rapidly, despite one of the best-executed flank attacks of the war. Rifled muskets and concentrated artillery helped; so did field fortifications. Then too, there was the usual dearth of heavy cavalry: Stuart had plenty of horsemen available for scouting purposes, but nowhere near enough to launch a major attack. The countryside was far too wooded and broken for a mounted charge to succeed anyway. Finally, the Confederate attackers typically suffered heavy casualties and lost cohesion, so that it was difficult to maintain the momentum of attack. In short, despite Hooker's ineptness and Lee's tactical virtuosity, the Confederates failed to achieve anything like an Austerlitz. The Chancellorsville campaign ended with the strategic situation in Virginia virtually unchanged, except that thousands of homes, North and South, had been plunged into mourning.

Two Societies at War

More often than the wars of the French Revolution and Napoleon, the Civil War is called the first total war. In common with the wars from 1792 to 1815, the Civil War encompassed the complete, or near-complete, mobilization of the belligerents' population and resources to fight an enemy. But it went further and also involved the complete, or near-complete, application of violence against that enemy—violence exerted not only against his military force but also against the civilian society that sustained it. Though one could quibble endlessly about whether the North and South mobilized completely, a large percentage of the population and the economy on both sides was bound up in the war effort. And by mid-1863, Federal armies began large-scale operations aimed at the destruction of Southern war resources and, at least to some degree, the demoralization of Southern civilians.

For both sides the problem of mobilization was similar. Each government had to find ways to generate sufficient military manpower, to clothe, equip, and transport its armed forces, and—somehow—to find a way to pay for it all. The magnitude of these tasks was completely unprecedented in American history, but both governments approached them in generally similar ways and, in both cases, with fairly good success.

The Move to Conscription

At first, both the Union and the Confederacy relied upon volunteers to man their armies. This was the traditional American method and politically the only thinkable one in societies that venerated individual liberty and unobtrusive government. Eventually, however, both sides encountered difficulties in securing enough manpower. The South was the first to feel the pinch. By early 1862 volunteering in the Confederacy had fallen off dramatically, while at the same time a string of Federal successes threatened the new nation with early defeat. Spurred by a sense of impending doom, on April 16, 1862, the Confederate Congress passed the first general conscription act in American history (local conscription had been used during the Colonial Wars and the American Revolution). The act made every able-bodied white male between the ages of 18 and 35 liable for military service.

This bill, however, contemplated a very different sort of conscription from the system employed by the French in 1793. Whereas in Europe

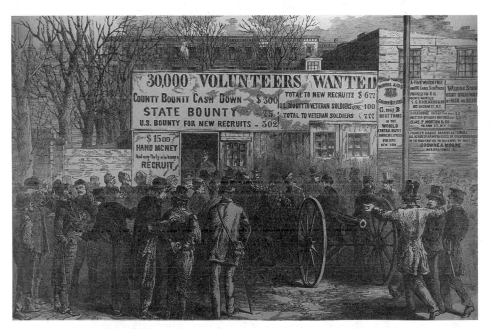

A Northern recruiting office. Like the Confederacy, the Union government secured most of its military manpower through volunteers. But by early 1863 voluntary enlistments had dropped off and many Northern communities offered cash rewards, called "bounties," if men agreed to enlist.

governments used conscription to raise new troops, the Confederate Congress invoked it principally as an incentive for veteran troops to reenlist. Since many of them had signed up for only twelve months, their enlistments were expiring and they might return to civilian life. The Confederate conscription act provided that if the men stayed in the army they could remain in their current units, but if they left they could be drafted and assigned to a new, unfamiliar unit.

As the war continued, however, the Confederate government refined the conscription act so that it became a way to raise new troops as well as encourage veteran soldiers to remain in the ranks. And in February 1864 the Confederate Congress passed a new, more stringent conscription act that declared all white males between 17 and 50 subject to the draft.

The Union government also moved toward conscription, albeit more slowly. In July 1862 the U.S. Congress took the first step when it passed a new Militia Act, authorizing the president to set quotas of troops to be raised by each state and giving him power to enforce the quota through conscription if a given state failed to cough up enough volunteers. But not until March 1863 did the Federal government pass a true draft act, making all able-bodied males between 20 and 45 liable for military service.

In both the North and South, conscription was wildly unpopular, partly because it represented an unprecedented extension of government power into the lives of individuals, but also because of the inequitable way in which it was administered. For example, initially the Confederate Congress permitted a conscript to hire someone to serve in his place. The practice was abolished when the price of a substitute soared beyond $5,000; in the meantime, however, hiring substitutes convinced many ordinary Southerners that the Confederacy's struggle was "a rich man's war and a poor man's fight." Even more upsetting was the so-called "Twenty Negro Law" that exempted one white man for every twenty slaves. This meant that the sons of wealthy plantation owners could be exempted, and even if few men actually took advantage of the law, it contributed to the sense of conscription's unfairness. In the North, the conscription act also permitted the hiring of substitutes; moreover, any man who paid a $300 commutation fee could receive exemption from any given draft call. Ironically the commutation fee, designed to keep the cost of hiring a substitute from soaring out of reach, was intended to help the average man. Instead it only fueled a sense that the draft law was rigged in favor of the wealthy.

In the North, well-to-do communities also frequently raised bounty funds to encourage volunteering, so that their own citizens could elude the draft. Under this system, a man willing to enlist received a cash payment totaling hundreds of dollars. As the war went on and volunteers became harder to find, such bounties increased prodigiously. They soon generated a phenomenon called "bounty-jumping," whereby men went from place to place, enlisted, took their bounties, and then absconded at the first opportunity. One bounty jumper claimed to have done this thirty-two times.

The indirect way in which Civil War conscription operated makes it difficult to assess its effectiveness. It almost certainly encouraged enlistments and, particularly in the South, kept veteran soldiers in the ranks; one

Men of the 107th U.S. Colored Troops. Lincoln's emancipation policy paved the way for the North to begin active recruiting of African-American soldiers.

estimate credits the system with augmenting Union troop levels by 750,000. But the number of men actually drafted was surprisingly small. In the North, barely 46,000 conscripts actually served in the armies. Another 116,000 men hired substitutes, while 87,000 others paid the $300 commutation fee. Between conscripts and substitutes, the Union draft furnished only 6 percent of the North's military manpower. The Confederacy did little better. The available evidence, while incomplete, suggests that roughly 82,000 Southerners entered the army through conscription—about 11 percent of total enlistments.

The political costs of conscription, however, were dramatic. Many Southerners eluded the draft and fought off the enrollment agents who came to conscript them. In some states, especially Georgia and North Carolina, governors who opposed the draft used loopholes in the conscription acts to exempt as many of their citizens as possible. In the North, a number of provost officers lost their lives while attempting to enforce the draft. The worst violence occurred in New York City in July 1863 when angry mobs attacked draft offices, roughed up well-dressed passersby ("There goes a $300 man"), and slaughtered dozens of free blacks, whom they blamed for the war and hence for conscription. All in all, at least 105 people died in the New York City Draft Riot, making it the worst such incident in American history.

Fifty years later, when the United States resorted to the draft in order to fight World War I, officials studied the weaknesses of Union conscription. The result was a much more effective and politically palatable system, since they were able to avoid many pitfalls. In sum, although conscription as practiced in the Civil War filled some of the urgent need on both sides for military manpower, it proved to be an almost textbook case in how not to do it.

The War Economies

Both sides did better at managing their economies, although here again the distended nature of mid-nineteenth-century American society limited what they could accomplish. The Confederate government never achieved a realistic fiscal policy. It passed only a very inadequate income tax, amounting to just one-half of one percent. Instead the Southern leadership financed the war largely through borrowing and by printing fiat money, expedients that eventually spawned a whopping 9,000 percent inflation rate. In April 1863 it also initiated a wildly unpopular "tax-in-kind," by which Confederate agents could seize 10 percent of the goods produced by a given farm or business concern.

Of the two adversaries, the Union tended to perform best, partly because it had a greater population and resource base, and partly because its financial management was much superior to that of the Confederacy. The Lincoln administration's fiscal system was created and managed by Secretary of the Treasury Salmon P. Chase. While it too relied primarily on bonds and paper money, it levied a more extensive income tax, and inflation remained under control in the North. Where the Confederacy generated a mere 5 percent of its revenue through direct taxation, the Federal government managed 21 percent. The South underwrote only about 40 percent of its war expenses through bonds, against 67 percent for the North.

The Lincoln administration managed its war economy principally through alliances with the business community. Cooperation, not coercion, was the preferred mode of operation, and usually it worked very well. For example, although Lincoln quickly secured the legal authority to seize railroads and run them directly in support of the war effort, in practice he relied on Northern railroad men voluntarily to "do the right thing." Only on rare occasions did the Federal government assume overt control of the railroads. Similarly, the Union government constructed no munitions or equipage factories of its own, but rather relied upon a wide array of civilian contractors. And it depended on financiers to make its war-bond program a success.

Ironically, given its commitment to limited government, the Confederate government pursued a much more direct, centralized management of the economy. President Jefferson Davis persuaded Congress to assume control of the telegraph network, to construct new railroads for military purposes, and even to assume direct control of the railroads from private hands. He also urged Congress to encourage and engage in the mining and manufacture of certain essential materials. Congress eventually passed a law that offered inducements to potential manufacturers of such strategically important goods as saltpetre, coal, iron, and firearms. The government set up its own salt works in Louisiana, and the Ordnance Department established a large weapons-building empire. By the end of the war, in fact, the Confederate South had become—in theory at least—one of the most relentlessly centralized nations on earth. World War I would force some European nations to do the same. But the Union example of an alliance between business and government would prove an equally viable—and more effective—means to the same end.

Wartime Resentments

Modern wars often begin with a wave of patriotic outpouring that temporarily drowns dissent. Sooner or later, however, the dissent resurfaces, and a wartime government must master it or perish. For the Union and Confederacy, dissent began early and grew steadily worse as the war progressed. Both governments proved up to the challenge. The Lincoln administration suspended the writ of habeas corpus where necessary, held, at one time or another, an estimated 13,000 political prisoners, and occasionally suspended publication of hostile newspapers. The Confederate government also suspended the writ of habeas corpus and waged an unremitting campaign of repression against the Unionist sympathizers in its midst, most notably in east Tennessee. The imperatives of total war thus impinged not only on the battlefield and the economy, but also on personal liberties.

      In the North, the main opposition came from a faction known as the Peace Democrats—derisively nicknamed "Copperheads" by their opponents. They believed that the Federal government could never achieve reunion through force; they also argued that the horrors of civil war, coupled with the constitutional abuses of the Lincoln administration, were far worse than permitting the South to go its own way. A second group of Democrats, called "Legitimists," supported the war but balked at the Lincoln administration's handling of it, particularly its decision to make emancipation a war aim. Then too, the lower parts of Illinois, Indiana, Ohio, and Maryland contained many persons of Southern ancestry, some of whom were Confederate sympathizers.

      The South had troubles of its own. To begin with, a substantial number of Southerners bitterly despised the Confederate government. The fact that 100,000 white Southerners actually fought for the Union underscores this point. The South also contained a large, restive slave population which might at any moment rise up and attack its masters. Oddly enough, a good many planters also disliked the Confederate experiment, for the war effort required too many sacrifices from them: impressment of livestock, the conscription of slave labor, the confiscation of cotton, and so on.

      Finally, the unexpectedly massive degree to which the Confederate government eventually intervened in the economy alienated many

Southerners. By 1864, three years of war had precipitated what one historian has termed a "revolt of the common people." Ordinary Southerners resented the loss of labor manpower, particularly among nonslaveholders, who had no one to work the land once their able-bodied young men went off to fight. They were also antagonized by the frequent impressments and requisitions of crops, forage, and horseflesh. Class resentment also surfaced. Wealthy families did not suffer privation to the same degree as the poor. The paying of substitutes to avoid conscription was not abolished until 1864.

Thus both the Union and the Confederacy contained large cores of dissent, each with the potential to undermine the war effort. In the North, political success by the Peace Democrats could, at best, impede the vigorous prosecution of the war and, at worst, force a compromise peace. In the South, the "revolt of the common people" threatened to create a condition in which disobedience to the Confederate government could become not only respectable but rampant. If that occurred, a hostile population might encourage deserters, shield them from Confederate authorities, and block efforts to secure the supplies needed to feed and sustain Southern armies. The solution, in each case, was military success. Continued stalemate, especially if punctuated by Confederate victories, benefited the South and kept its dissenters in check. The Lincoln administration, for its part, required tangible evidence of military progress; otherwise the pressures for a compromise peace might prove overwhelming. The harnessing of popular sentiment to the state, made possible by the democratic revolutions, thus proved a two-edged sword for policy makers. It enabled them to tap manpower and economic resources in unprecedented ways. But it also forced them to accommodate popular passions. Thus like many other leaders in the age of mass politics, Lincoln and Davis found themselves riding a tiger.

A Destructive War

As each society mobilized ever more thoroughly to carry on the war, it began to seem necessary to strike not only the enemy's armies but also his economic base. Railroads, factories, mills, and cotton gins, as well as crops and livestock, increasingly became the targets of military operations. To some extent both sides embarked on a program of economic destruction, but of the two the North had both the greater need and the greater opportunity to attack the enemy's war resources.

Some Northerners had urged such attacks from the very outset of the war, but the logic of the conciliatory policy had argued persuasively against a campaign of unbridled destruction. The issuance of the Emancipation Proclamation, however, had signaled the demise of conciliation, and by early 1863 Union policy makers increasingly realized that more destructive measures were necessary. As Halleck explained to Grant in March 1863, "The character of the war has now very much changed within the last year.

There is now no possible hope of reconciliation with the rebels. . . . We must conquer the rebels or be conquered by them." Spurred by this grim logic, some Northern commanders began to claim the full extent of the destruction permissible within the existing rules of war. They were driven to this extreme not only by the changed political equation but even more importantly by their need to supply themselves and, by extension, to deny supplies to the enemy.

Attacks on the South's economic base initially arose from the practice of widespread foraging. Such foraging occurred first in the western theater, where Union armies often found themselves operating in areas where suitable rail and water communications were unavailable. When that occurred, normal supply lines proved inadequate, and Union armies had to augment their official rations with crops and livestock taken directly from local farmers. This foraging soon made them very aware that Confederate forces also drew supplies from the countryside, and western armies began a policy of destroying unneeded crops in order to prevent the Confederates from using them.

For a considerable period large-scale foraging and supply-denial policies remained mainly confined to the western theater. Union armies in the east, it turned out, were far slower to adopt similar policies. This was probably because they were much less successful than their western counterparts at capturing Southern territory. Thus their supply lines simply never lengthened. Since eastern armies seldom experienced serious logistical problems, they underestimated the impact supply denial might have on the enemy. It seldom occurred to them to destroy those supplies at their source, despite the fact that the Southern forces in the east drew considerable food and forage from local districts. Western armies, by contrast, had far greater sensitivity to logistical matters.

Extensive foraging, Union commanders recognized, inevitably meant hardship for civilians. Commanders attempted to minimize such hardship by forbidding abuses and by issuing instructions that Southern families should be left enough supplies for their own use. Even so, civilians suffered a great deal. Partly in an attempt to justify the hardship thus inflicted, Union commanders began to see it as a form of punishment. Eventually they deliberately sharpened the effects of foraging in order to produce political effects: for example, by stripping crops as much as possible from the farms of known secessionist sympathizers.

The next logical step in supply denial was to destroy the mills that processed agricultural products and the railroads that transported them, as well as factories that manufactured militarily useful goods. Destruction of this sort had occurred on a modest scale even during the early months of the war. Nevertheless the year 1863 marked a significant watershed, for it was during that year that one can see the emergence of large-scale destruction carried out, in fairly routine fashion, by large bodies of troops. By mid-1863, then, both sides were trying to mobilize fully to prosecute the war, and the North, at least, had embarked on a program of economic warfare. The Civil War had truly become a total war.

Vicksburg and Gettysburg

In April 1863 a mob of housewives, furious that they could not find enough to feed their families, rioted in the streets of Richmond. The incident underscored a serious disturbance in Confederate morale, born of privation and endless casualty lists, that would only grow worse without some decisive victory to offset it. The win at Chancellorsville a few weeks later was encouraging but incomplete. The Federal Army of the Potomac had retired intact to lick its wounds; it would surely resume the offensive within a few months. Out west the situation had grown disquieting: Grant's army had come down the Mississippi River, cast about for a viable means to attack the fortress city of Vicksburg, and discovered one late in April.

Vicksburg

After the failure of his overland campaign in the fall of 1862, Grant had brought most of his army to Milliken's Bend, a bleak piece of bottomland a few miles north of Vicksburg. Although Grant was now much closer geographically to the Confederate fortress, the biggest operational problem remained unsolved: how to get into a position from which the bastion could be attacked successfully. From January through April he tried a number of alternatives. First his engineers attempted to connect a series of creeks, old river channels, and bayous into a waterway that would enable Union vessels to get around Vicksburg to the south, after which Grant would march his army down and have those vessels ferry him across the river to the dry ground on the eastern shore. This scheme became known as the Lake Providence Route, after its central feature, but after weeks of backbreaking labor the project was abandoned. Next, hundreds of troops and escaped slaves attempted to dig a canal across the neck of the great river bend directly opposite Vicksburg in hopes of changing the course of the Mississippi so that its main channel would bypass the city. This project sparked the imagination of many people—Lincoln expressed particular fascination with the idea—but it failed as well. A third attempt—similar in concept to the Lake Providence Route—called for creating a waterway through the Yazoo Delta country via Steele's Bayou. It produced the spectacle of Union gunboats steaming through a narrow channel in what amounted to a huge flooded forest, but constant harassment by Confederate snipers eventually forced its abandonment. A fourth effort aimed at creating a waterway running down from the Yazoo Pass at the northern end of the Delta. This too failed when the Confederates erected a fort to block it.

Four attempts, four failures—yet Grant was not discouraged. Later he would claim that he never expected these efforts to yield results and agreed to them largely in order to occupy his men and create the illusion of action—an illusion necessary to allay his critics in the North while he

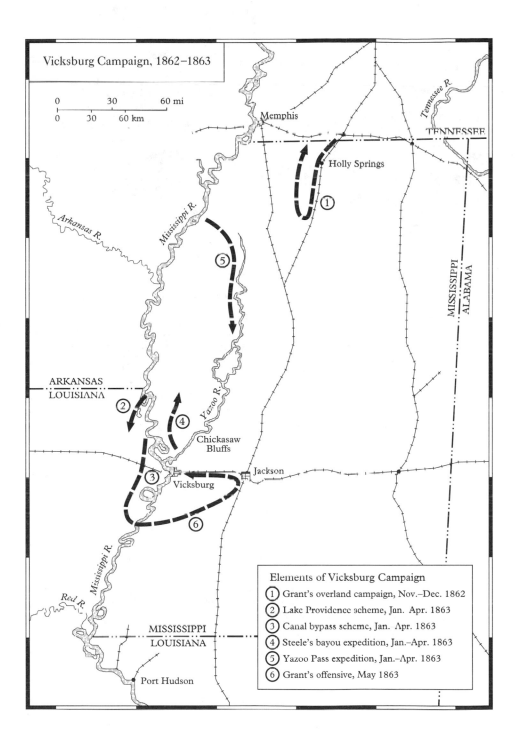

Vicksburg Campaign, 1862–1863

| 0 | 30 | 60 mi |
| 0 | 30 | 60 km |

Memphis

Holly Springs

TENNESSEE

Tennessee R.

Arkansas R.

Mississippi R.

①

⑤

MISSISSIPPI
ALABAMA

ARKANSAS
LOUISIANA

②

④

Yazoo R.

Chickasaw
Bluffs

③

Jackson

Vicksburg

⑥

Mississippi R.

Red R.

MISSISSIPPI
LOUISIANA

Port Hudson

Elements of Vicksburg Campaign

① Grant's overland campaign, Nov.–Dec. 1862
② Lake Providence scheme, Jan.–Apr. 1863
③ Canal bypass scheme, Jan.–Apr. 1863
④ Steele's bayou expedition, Jan.–Apr. 1863
⑤ Yazoo Pass expedition, Jan.–Apr. 1863
⑥ Grant's offensive, May 1863

Grant confers with Admiral David D. Porter during the campaign against Vicksburg, the Confederacy's bastion on the Mississippi River. Close army-navy cooperation was indispensable to the Union victory there in July 1863.

concocted a plan that would work. By early April he had done it. The ensuing campaign sealed his reputation as a great commander.

On the night of April 16, Admiral David Dixon Porter, the naval officer in charge of the riverine flotilla cooperating with Grant's army, led some of his vessels on a midnight run directly past the guns along the Vicksburg bluffs. Darkness shielded Porter's vessels part of the way; even after the Confederates spotted them and opened fire, the Union boats escaped with the loss of only one transport. More steamers made the dash five nights later. Once below the Vicksburg batteries, Porter's fleet awaited the arrival of Grant's army, which took barges and shallow-draft steamers through a series of bayous that wound past Vicksburg on the Louisiana side of the river. That done, Grant's troops began crossing the Mississippi at Bruinsburg, fifty miles south of Vicksburg, on April 30.

The landing at Bruinsburg placed Grant's army squarely between Vicksburg and the secondary river fortress of Port Hudson, Louisiana. Forty miles eastward lay Jackson, the state capital, and a point at which four railroads converged. One of these led to Vicksburg and formed the bastion's main line of supply. If Grant meant to seize Vicksburg, he would first need to choke off those supplies; for that reason Jackson became his first important objective. Yet to march upon Jackson necessarily meant exposing his own line of supply to ruinous interdiction from Pemberton's army at Vicksburg. Consequently, Grant decided to maintain no supply line at all. Just as his troops had done after the disastrous raid upon Holly Springs in December 1862, they would live off the country, except that this time the choice was deliberate.

At the beginning of May his three army corps headed east, hugging the south bank of the Big Black River and guarding the ferries against any attempted crossings by Pemberton's troops. With them rattled along several hundred wagons loaded with ammunition and a few staples like salt and coffee. They fought two minor preliminary battles with detachments from Pemberton's army and by the evening of May 13 had reached the vicinity of Jackson.

Vicksburg fell only after a siege of forty-seven days, much of it under shelling from Union gunboats and field artillery. Confederate civilians huddled in shelters like these. Cut off from the outside world, they were reduced, in some cases, to eating rats.

Ahead of them, a small Confederate force under General Joseph E. Johnston barred entrance to the city. The next day two Union corps attacked the rebels and pushed them north. In weeks to come Johnston would hover to the northeast of Grant's army, gather additional troops, and look for a way to help Pemberton defeat Grant. Grant never gave Johnston the opening.

After burning Jackson's war manufactories, the Union forces swung sharply west and headed for Vicksburg. Pemberton, meanwhile, moved east in search of Grant's nonexistent supply line. On May 16 elements of the two armies clashed at Champion's Hill, a commanding ridgeline about midway between Jackson and Vicksburg. Grant's troops managed to beat Pemberton and send his force in full retreat to the powerful Vicksburg fortifications. After a sharp action along the Big Black River with the Confederate rearguard, Grant's army reached the outskirts of the river city on May 18. There Grant resumed contact with Porter's gunboats, reestablished a solid line of supply, and began to invest the town.

Once Grant surrounded Vicksburg he made two quick tries to take the city by assault. The first attempt came on May 19, but the Confederates smashed it within minutes. A second, much more determined effort followed three days later. This time most of Grant's army rolled forward against the Confederate trenches that crowned the steep hillsides around Vicksburg, only to be stopped almost at once by a wall of musketry and artillery fire.

Grant suspended the attacks and settled down to a siege. In Washington, General-in-Chief Halleck funneled reinforcements to Grant's army as fast as possible. The Confederate government, meanwhile, met to consider how to avert impending disaster.

Gettysburg

The Confederate high command met in Richmond, weighed alternatives, and struggled to find a solution to the crisis. Secretary of War James Seddon favored dispatching reinforcements from Lee's army to help Pemberton throw Grant back. Then, with the threat to Vicksburg removed, Confederate forces could concentrate to help Bragg win decisively in central Tennessee. Davis agreed; so did James Longstreet, Lee's senior corps commander, although Longstreet reversed the priority: reinforcements should go first to Bragg, then Pemberton. Joe Johnston, P. G. T. Beauregard, and an informal network of other Confederate generals all concurred that some variation on this strategy should be attempted.

Lee, however, did not agree. Troops dispatched to succor Vicksburg, he said, could not reach the city in time to do anything if the fortress were in danger of imminent surrender. In Virginia, on the other hand, the Army of the Potomac could renew its advance at any time. Far from being in a position to donate troops to others, Lee insisted, "[U]nless we can obtain some reinforcements, we may be obliged to withdraw into the defences around Richmond."

The enormous prestige enjoyed by the South's greatest general compelled respect for his views. Davis called Lee to Richmond for a strategy conference on May 15. There, before the president and his assembled cabinet, Lee unveiled his own proposal. He would embark on an invasion of Pennsylvania. Such an offensive would remove the threat to Virginia and open the way to decisive victory on Union soil, with concurrent prospects for foreign recognition and a negotiated peace. At a minimum, he insisted, an invasion of the North would produce such consternation that the Federals would have to relax their grip on Vicksburg.

From anyone else, Lee's scheme would have seemed like the hallucination of an opium addict. But repeated success had given him the reputation of a miracle worker, and Davis saw Lee's point when the Virginian objected that the scheme to reinforce Vicksburg was highly problematic at best. "The answer of General Lee," he decided, "was such as I should have anticipated, and in which I concur."

Lee thus won permission to embark on his invasion of the North. Within three weeks his army was underway; by the end of June his troops had fanned out across southern Pennsylvania, where they courteously but thoroughly plundered the local population. In the meantime, Hooker brought the Army of the Potomac northward in pursuit.

By June 28 the Union army had entered Maryland, always keeping between Washington and Lee's forces. On that date, irritated by a rash of complaints from Hooker, Lincoln relieved him of command and replaced him with Major General George G. Meade, a well-respected but

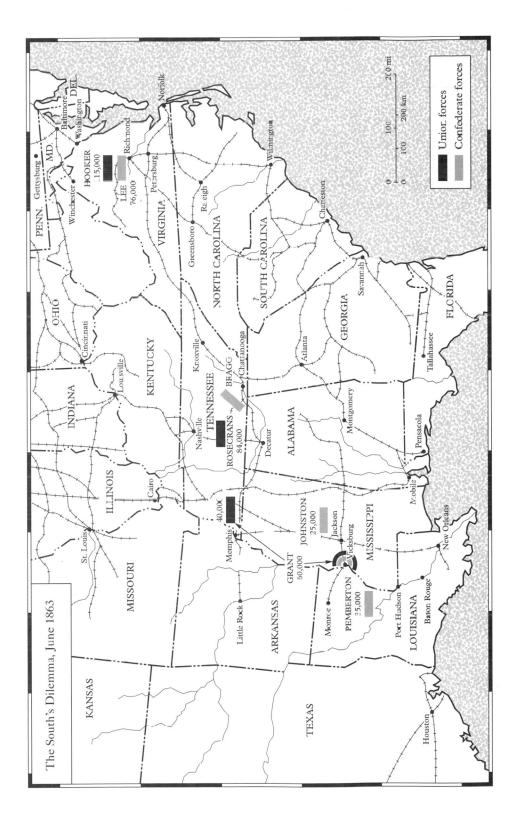

The South's Dilemma, June 1863

Union forces
Confederate forces

200 mi
200 km

HOOKER
15,000

LEE
76,000

Gettysburg

PENN.

MD.

DEL.

Baltimore
Washington
Winchester

Norfolk

Richmond
Petersburg

OHIO

VIRGINIA

Greensboro
Raleigh

NORTH CAROLINA

Wilmington

Cincinnati

INDIANA

KENTUCKY

Louisville

Knoxville

Nashville

TENNESSEE

BRAGG

Chattanooga

ROSECRANS
84,000

Decatur

ALABAMA

GEORGIA

Atlanta

Montgomery

SOUTH CAROLINA

Charleston

Savannah

FLORIDA

Tallahassee

Pensacola

ILLINOIS

Cairo

St. Louis

MISSOURI

40,000

Memphis

GRANT
50,000

JOHNSTON
25,000

Jackson

Vicksburg

MISSISSIPPI

PEMBERTON
25,000

Monroe

ARKANSAS

Little Rock

Port Hudson

Baton Rouge

LOUISIANA

New Orleans

Mobile

KANSAS

TEXAS

Houston

comparatively unknown corps commander. Meade thought it bad business to replace an army commander on the eve of battle and tried to decline; Lincoln, however, forced him to accept. Thus the Army of the Potomac approached its greatest battle with an untried leader at the helm.

Lee, meanwhile, did not realize that the Union army was so close to his own. Jeb Stuart—the "eyes" of the rebel army—had taken three brigades on a spectacular but pointless raid around the Union army and was far out of position. Not until June 30 did a spy inform Lee of the Union army's proximity. Lee promptly gave orders to reconcentrate his scattered divisions. The point chosen for the rendezvous was Gettysburg, a small town in south-central Pennsylvania, where a number of good roads converged.

On July 1 the first of Lee's troops approached Gettysburg. Elements of A. P. Hill's Confederate corps ran into Federal cavalry, which already occupied the town. Before long a sizable battle rocked and swelled amid the tidy farm lots north, west, and south of the town. Soon Union infantry came up. Both sides fed additional troops into the fight as soon as they arrived, but the Confederates had the advantage: their troops were closer and came onto the field more rapidly. A second Confederate corps under Lieutenant General Richard S. Ewell happened upon the Union right, north of Gettysburg, and pitched into it furiously. The Federal line cracked under the pressure. By late afternoon the Confederates had routed one corps, pummeled another, and driven the surviving Federals through Gettysburg. Hundreds of Northerners surrendered to closely pursuing rebels while the remaining Union troops withdrew south of the town to Cemetery Ridge.

Lee arrived on the field shortly after noon on July 1 but found the action so fluid and confused that he refrained from giving any orders. As daylight waned, however, he made two fateful decisions. First he elected to fight a general engagement around the fields and hills below Gettysburg, despite earlier doubts that his army was strong enough to fight a pitched battle against the larger Union army. Second, although he instructed Ewell to capture Cemetery Hill "if practicable," he failed to insist upon it. Ewell did not consider the move practicable and therefore did not attack. His reluctance to attack enabled the Federals to use Cemetery Hill, the northernmost point on Cemetery Ridge, as the foundation on which they constructed their entire defensive line.

During the night both sides received reinforcements as additional units took their places in the battle lines. The Union line south of Gettysburg began to take on its famous "fishhook" appearance: the barb at Culp's Hill southeast of the town, the curve at Cemetery Hill, and then a long shank that ran for a mile or so south along Cemetery Ridge. The Confederate II Corps faced Cemetery and Culp's hills while III Corps on its right faced Cemetery Ridge. Behind it lay I Corps under Lieutenant General James Longstreet. Recently arrived on the field and as yet unbloodied, I Corps would make the morrow's main attack. The target would be the Union left flank.

For the Confederates, the attack did not begin auspiciously—it was made without adequate reconnaissance and began only at 4:30 P.M. But the

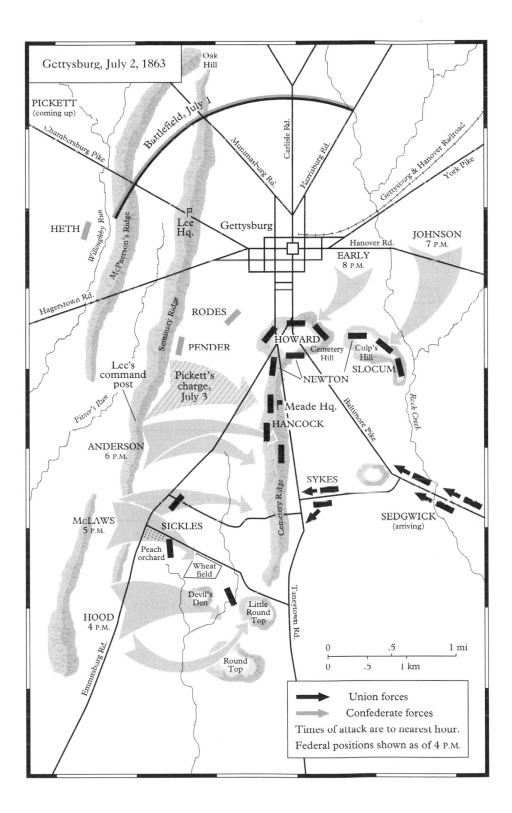

Gettysburg, July 2, 1863

Oak Hill

PICKETT
(coming up)

Chambersburg Pike

Battlefield, July 1

Mummasburg Rd.

Carlisle Rd.

Harrisburg Rd.

Gettysburg & Hanover Railroad

York Pike

HETH

Willoughby Run

McPherson's Ridge

Lee Hq.

Gettysburg

Hanover Rd.

JOHNSON
7 P.M.

Hagerstown Rd.

Seminary Ridge

RODES

PENDER

EARLY
8 P.M.

Lee's command post

Pitzer's Run

Pickett's charge, July 3

Cemetery Hill

Culp's Hill

SLOCUM

HOWARD

NEWTON

Baltimore Pike

Rock Creek

Meade Hq.

ANDERSON
6 P.M.

HANCOCK

SYKES

SEDGWICK
(arriving)

McLAWS
5 P.M.

SICKLES

Cemetery Rdge.

Peach orchard

Wheat field

HOOD
4 P.M.

Devil's Den

Little Round Top

Taneytown Rd.

Emmitsburg Rd.

Round Top

0   .5   1 mi
0   .5   1 km

Union forces

Confederate forces

Times of attack are to nearest hour.
Federal positions shown as of 4 P.M.

blow fell like a thunderclap when it came. Afterward, Longstreet would call this attack "the best two hours' fighting done by any troops on any battle-field." It certainly showed both armies at the height of their powers. As such, the engagement well illustrates the dynamics of a Civil War battle.

Longstreet's attack began with massed artillery fire. The cannoneers fired solid shot to disable enemy batteries and shell to strike his foot soldiers. The artillery was still firing when the rebel infantry advanced: two divisions from Longstreet's own corps, supported by a third from another corps. The divisions advanced *en echelon*—that is, one after another, from the right end of the line toward the left—a tactic designed to mislead the enemy as to the actual focus of the assault. The infantry regiments marched steadily, try-ing hard to maintain their two-line, shoulder-to-shoulder battle formation despite the hilly, wooded terrain. Brigade and regimental commanders supervised their units closely. Their main duty was to preserve the troops' linear formation and to prevent their units from crossing in front of one another or spreading out too far.

In severe fighting the Confederates smashed a badly positioned Union corps and plunged up the steep, rocky slopes of Little Round Top, a hill at the end of the Union left flank. Last-minute reinforcements beat back the Confederates there and restored the front; particularly memorable was the famous defense by the 20th Maine Regiment under Colonel Joshua Lawrence Chamberlain. But the fighting swirled back and forth until night-fall. Amid the deafening noise of musketry and cannon fire, each side strug-gled to secure local superiority at several key points. For the commanders the job was mainly to "feed the fight"—finding and throwing in whatever reinforcements became available—while encouraging their soldiers and rally-ing them when a short retreat became necessary. For the individual soldiers, the job was to maintain "touch of elbows" with the man on either side, follow the regimental colors—in the smoke and din the movement of these flags often became a primary means of communication—and fire low. Despite the greatly increased range of the rifled musket, this engagement, like many Civil War battles, was actually fought well within smoothbore range. The two sides were often only a few dozen yards apart. Sometimes they collided; when they did, a desperate close-quarters struggle with clubbed muskets and even bare fists would result.

Several times Longstreet's men came close to victory. But ultimately the combination of rough terrain and tough Union resistance exhausted them, and the attack fell short of success. Things were no better on the bat-tlefield's opposite end. Ewell failed to begin a secondary attack until dusk and won little but casualties for his pains. The Union position had proven too strong, the Confederate thrusts too late or too weak.

Lee remained determined to continue the offensive. The great stub-bornness that had displayed itself at the Seven Days, Antietam, and Chancel-lorsville seemed more entrenched than ever at Gettysburg. Despite the fail-ures on July 2, Lee perceived amid the reports glimmerings of potential success: good artillery positions *had* been seized, charging divisions had *almost* broken through, probing brigades had come *close* to breaching the Union center. Then reinforcements arrived in the form of Stuart's long-lost

The recently invented technique of photography captured the grisly aftermath of Civil War battles. Nearly 620,000 Americans died in the Civil War, far more than in any other conflict.

cavalry and an infantry division under Major General George Pickett. Morale remained good, and Southern valor could still be counted upon. Lee ordered Longstreet to renew the attack the next day.

Longstreet, however, opposed the plan and urged that the Confederate army try an envelopment or a turning movement instead. Lee listened courteously, then instructed Longstreet to attack the Union center with three divisions spearheaded by Pickett's men. After a long preliminary bombardment by Confederate artillery, the climactic attack began on the afternoon of July 3. Fifteen thousand rebel soldiers in battle lines that stretched nearly a mile from flank to flank surged from the wooded crest of Seminary Ridge and headed toward a clump of trees that marked the center of the Union line. The gallant men in whom Lee vested such outsized confidence charged bravely and died bravely but never had a chance. Napoleonic assaults of that sort could no longer win against veteran troops firing rifles that could kill at ranges of 300 yards or more. Nor could they prevail against canister—artillery rounds made up of lead slugs that transformed cannon into huge sawed-off shotguns. Valor was not at issue, for as a general who helped lead the charge claimed, "If the troops I commanded could not take that position, all Hell couldn't take it." What lay at issue were the tactical realities of 1863. By that time, the balance of strength had tilted sharply from the offensive to the defensive.

Pickett's charge illustrated both the lethal effectiveness of artillery on the defensive and a corresponding weakness on the offensive. Although Union cannon scythed down the Confederate attackers in droves, the preliminary Confederate artillery bombardment, although massive and intense, signally failed to create the conditions for a successful infantry assault. In the days of Napoleon, artillery batteries might have advanced to a point just outside smoothbore musket range and battered down the enemy infantry line, but the extended range of the rifled musket—coupled with effective counterbattery fire from the new rifled artillery—made such a tactic impossible. Some Confederate batteries did, in fact, move forward in support of Pickett's attack but nowhere near as far as their Napoleonic counterparts might have gone.

The survivors of what became known as "Pickett's Charge" came streaming back across the field, leaving their dead and dying comrades strewn across the shallow valley that separated the rival positions. Lee rode among the returning troops, shaken, saddened, and moved to a strange, almost wistful tenderness. "It's all my fault," he would tell Longstreet later. "I thought my men were invincible."

Lee lost nearly 20,000 men at Gettysburg. During the retreat he nearly lost his entire army. Summer storms caused the Potomac to rise, barring passage to the retreating Confederate forces. With the fords unusable and the bridges long since destroyed, the beaten Confederates faced annihilation if Meade's Federals caught up with them and launched a determined assault. Meade, however, pursued cautiously. Minor skirmishing ensued, but no major attack. While a jury-rigged ferryboat shipped handfuls of men across, Lee's engineers built a pontoon bridge—a crazy patchwork of planks, scows, and barges completed on July 13. The wagons crept across it, and the infantry waded to safety through chest-high water. The Army of Northern Virginia was saved, scarcely twenty-four hours before Meade planned to launch a belated attack.

Captured during Lee's retreat from Pennsylvania, three rebel soldiers await transportation to a Union prison camp. The Confederate defeats at Gettysburg and Vicksburg occurred within a day of each other and together marked the war's military turning point.

Lincoln was disappointed. He thought Meade had blown a spectacular chance to wreck Lee's army for good. But Meade had probably done as well as was possible. For one thing, at Gettysburg his army had suffered tremendous casualties of its own. For another, the Confederate bridgehead on the Potomac was heavily fortified; an attack against it would most likely have failed. Most important, Meade's successful defense at Gettysburg had inflicted 33 percent casualties on Lee's army and, as it turned out, blunted forever its offensive capability. And coupled with Grant's victory at Vicksburg, Gettysburg offered important new proof that the North was winning the war.

Vicksburg fell on July 4, 1863, after a siege of nearly seven weeks. Inside the town food had grown desperately short; toward the end of the siege, soldiers and civilians started eating horsemeat and rats. Outside, Grant's army bided its time, dined comfortably on the plentitude of supplies arriving at their new river base, and grew steadily stronger as additional troops reinforced those already on the scene. (Grant had conducted his May offensive with about 44,000 men; by the end of the siege he had over 70,000 men in all.)

The capture of Vicksburg reopened the Mississippi River and severed Arkansas, Texas, and much of Louisiana from the rest of the Confederacy, but these results were largely symbolic. The midwestern states had learned to ship their goods by rail, and they continued to do so even after the "Father of Waters" again became an available conduit. The real significance lay in the capture of Pemberton's entire army—nearly 31,000 Confederate troops became prisoners, together with 172 cannon and about 60,000 small arms. The Confederacy could scarcely afford such losses.

Struggle for the Gateway

While Grant was besieging Vicksburg and Lee was advancing and retreating in the East, a third campaign, more prolonged than either of the other two, was underway along the southern fringe of the Appalachian highlands. From June until November 1863 Union and Confederate armies grappled for possession of Chattanooga, a strategic railroad city in southeastern Tennessee. In addition to its significance as the place where three major railroads met, Chattanooga also formed the principal gateway into Unionist Tennessee, whose occupation had been a cherished objective of the Lincoln administration since the war's outset. Even more important, it was the northern end of a corridor that led a hundred miles south to Atlanta, Georgia.

In a real sense, the capture of Chattanooga was more important than that of Vicksburg. With the seizure of the latter city, the Mississippi River was reopened and the strategic purpose of a thrust in that direction reached its logical culmination. But Chattanooga was not only a major objective in its own right; it opened the way to further attacks into the Southern

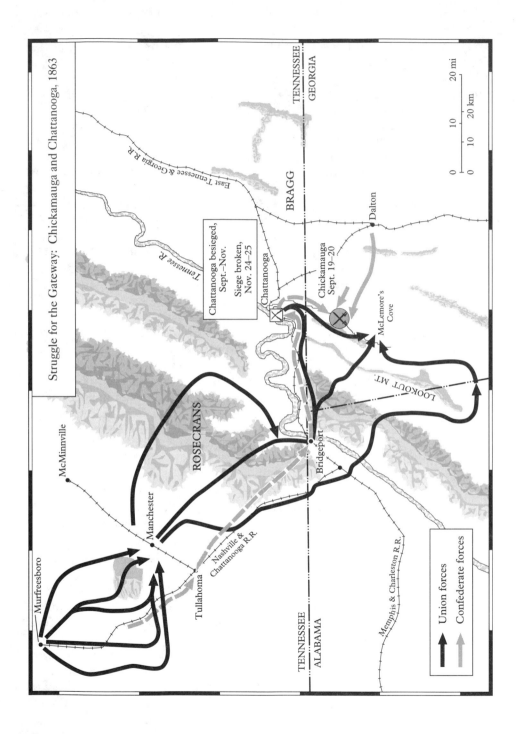

Struggle for the Gateway: Chickamauga and Chattanooga, 1863

TENNESSEE
GEORGIA

BRAGG

East Tennessee & Georgia R.R.

Tennessee R.

Dalton

Chattanooga besieged, Sept.–Nov.

Siege broken, Nov. 24–25

Chattanooga

Chickamauga
Sept. 19–20

McLemore's Cove

LOOKOUT MT.

ROSECRANS

McMinnville

Manchester

Bridgeport

Tullahoma

Nashville & Chattanooga R.R.

Murfreesboro

TENNESSEE
ALABAMA

Memphis & Charleston R.R.

Union forces

Confederate forces

0   10   20 mi

0   10   20 km

heartland. As events developed, the most fatal blows to the Confederacy would originate from this modest town, hugging a bend in the Tennessee River in the massive shadow of Lookout Mountain. Small wonder that for five months, well over 150,000 men struggled for possession of this city, a struggle in which some 47,000 of them became casualties.

Prologue to Chickamauga

The drive toward Chattanooga did not begin until the year 1863 was almost half over. After the bloody stalemate at Stone's River around New Year's Day, 1863, both the Army of the Cumberland and the Army of Tennessee entered a long period of quiet recuperation. Bragg lacked the numbers to undertake an active campaign. Rosecrans, despite much cajoling from his superiors in Washington, stubbornly refused to begin an advance until he was certain that his army was ready for a sustained offensive that promised decisive results. His subordinates agreed. "We certainly cannot fight the enemy for the mere purpose of whipping him," wrote a division commander. "The time has passed when the fate of armies must be staked because the newspapers have no excitement and do not sell well. I think our people have now comprehended that a battle is a very grave thing."

This was particularly the case if the battle under consideration promised to do no more than push the enemy back a few dozen miles, which was all the carnage at Stone's River the previous winter had done. Instead, Rosecrans hoped that an adroit campaign of maneuver could compel Bragg to fall back all the way to Chattanooga without major fighting. The climactic struggle, when it came, would then be fought for possession of the city itself. Such a thrust, however—effective *and* bloodless—required Rosecrans to place his entire army in Bragg's rear while maintaining his own communications intact. It was one of the most difficult maneuvers in warfare; no Civil War general had managed the feat (although at Second Manassas Lee had come close).

Rosecrans, then, was playing for very high stakes. To win, he believed, required two things. First he must not advance before he was ready. Second, the advance, when made, must be swift and unswerving. It turned out that Rosecrans had a very exacting idea of what it meant to be ready. Not until June 23 did he believe he possessed sufficient cavalry and supply reserves to advance. But when he did he conducted one of the Civil War's most remarkable campaigns. In little more than two weeks of hard marching—punctuated by minor skirmishes in which his army lost just 560 men—Rosecrans seized a key gap in the Cumberland Plateau, turned Bragg's right flank, and forced him to retreat all the way to Chattanooga, a distance of eighty miles. The rough terrain and great difficulty in supplying his army then compelled a pause of several weeks while Rosecrans consolidated his gains. In August he resumed the advance, this time turning Bragg's left flank. While Union artillery kept up a brisk demonstration against Chattanooga, distracting Bragg's attention in that direction, a Union infantry corps crossed the Tennessee River below the town. With his communications now in imminent jeopardy, Bragg abandoned Chattanooga.

The strategic railway city and gateway to the Confederate heartland fell without a fight on September 9.

Predictably, the loss of Chattanooga spurred the Confederate high command to dramatic action. Even before Rosecrans had resumed his advance in August, President Jefferson Davis had considered the possibility of strongly reinforcing Bragg with troops drawn from Joe Johnston in Mississippi. Subsequently Davis conducted a series of conferences with Lee over a two-week period, at the end of which Lee agreed to detach two divisions from his Army of Northern Virginia. These divisions would go by railroad to support Bragg's army; then, with luck and skill, the Army of Tennessee might destroy Rosecrans's force, retrieve Chattanooga, and possibly advance into middle Tennessee.

The most direct line, the Virginia and Tennessee Railroad, was unavailable because of the recent loss of Knoxville, and the two divisions were forced to travel by a circuitous route that doubled the beeline distance. Led by James Longstreet, the reinforcing Confederates rattled along no fewer than ten railroads on dilapidated cars, with frequent transfers and attendant delays. They left Lee's army on September 9, the same day that Chattanooga fell. It took ten days for the first troops to reach Bragg's army. Two-thirds made it in time for the battle then brewing. With their assistance, the Army of Tennessee won its greatest victory.

Chickamauga

The apparent ease with which he had shoved Bragg out of middle Tennessee and Chattanooga made Rosecrans overconfident. Although inordinately careful in his preparations, once on the march Rosecrans tended to be aggressive. As Rosecrans's Union troops swung into northern Georgia in early September, he believed Bragg's Confederates were demoralized and on the defensive. In his judgment, it was important to keep up the pressure and give his opponent no opportunity to sort things out. Bragg, however, was hardly demoralized. Secure in the knowledge that he was about to be reinforced, the Confederate commander kept looking for chances to strike the Federal invaders a resounding blow.

The mountainous Georgia countryside gave Bragg several opportunities, for it forced Rosecrans to send his columns through widely separated gaps. On two occasions the Union commander inadvertently gave the Confederates an excellent chance to concentrate against one or another exposed segment of his army, but on each occasion Bragg's subordinates botched the opportunity. Finally alert to the danger his army was in, Rosecrans ordered his scattered units to concentrate near West Chickamauga Creek about twelve miles south of Chattanooga.

On September 19, Bragg attacked. The two-day battle that ensued was fought in a dense tangle of second-growth timber broken at intervals by small open fields. Both sides had difficulty effectively controlling their units in such terrain; the engagement was really more a series of individual firefights than one concerted battle. The Confederates, for once, had the edge in manpower: about 66,000 rebel effectives against roughly 56,000 Federals. But in the first day's fighting this advantage was largely nullified by Bragg's faulty grasp of the Union dispositions and the confused nature of the fighting, which led to his troops being committed piecemeal. Late in the evening, however, he reorganized his army into two informal wings, placed them under his senior commanders—Lieutenant Generals Longstreet and Leonidas Polk—and made plans to resume the battle next morning.

The fighting on September 20 began about 9:30 A.M. and consisted of a series of sequential attacks made from north to south. None of these charges made much headway, however, and by 11 A.M. Bragg abandoned this *en echelon* approach in favor of a straightforward thrust by his remaining force. Until this moment the Federals had waged a capable defense and by and large had rebuffed every Confederate attack. In the process, however, Rosecrans was forced to shift some of his units from one threatened point to another—much as Lee had done at Antietam. But where Lee had conducted this delicate operation almost flawlessly, Rosecrans—in part confused by the terrain—made a major mistake. Seeking to plug a small hole in his line, he ordered a division shifted from one part of the field to another. That, in turn, created a very large hole: a hole, it turned out, just where four divisions under Longstreet were moving to attack.

The result, of course, was a shattering defeat for the Union army as some 20,000 Confederates poured into the gap. Three entire Union divisions ceased to exist as organized units; two more divisions had to withdraw from the field and could not return to the fray until evening. Rosecrans himself, crestfallen and dispirited, virtually abandoned the field. Two of his corps commanders did the same. Only a magnificent stand by a Union corps under Major General George H. Thomas saved Rosecrans's army from complete disaster. In a masterful defense of Snodgrass Hill in the center of the battlefield, Thomas blunted the momentum of the Confederate attack and enabled the rest of the army to withdraw intact. For that achievement he was known ever after as the "Rock of Chickamauga."

Confederate casualties in the battle totaled 18,454; the Union lost 16,170. Rosecrans's army fell back exhausted into Chattanooga. Bragg refused to pursue vigorously and elected to besiege the Union army by holding the high ground south and east of the town. Despite the victory, most of his subordinates were disgruntled with Bragg's battlefield performance and the way in which he tamely let Rosecrans escape enraged at least one of them. "What does he fight battles for?" growled Confederate cavalry leader Nathan Bedford Forrest. Still, the Army of the Cumberland had suffered a signal defeat, and if it were starved into surrender at Chattanooga, the Union disaster would undo most of what the victories at Vicksburg and Gettysburg had achieved.

Missionary Ridge

In this crisis the Lincoln administration turned to Grant. At the end of September, Secretary of War Edwin M. Stanton arranged an emergency conference with Grant at Louisville, Kentucky. There he gave Grant an order placing him in charge of substantially the entire western theater—everything from the Mississippi River to the Appalachian Mountains except Louisiana. Stanton also asked Grant to decide whether Rosecrans should be relieved. Grant thought he should, and Rosecrans was replaced by Major General George H. Thomas.

The Lincoln administration took one other decisive step as well. It withdrew two entire corps—20,000 men—from Meade's Army of the Potomac and sent them west to reinforce the beleaguered troops in Chattanooga. Railroads had been used throughout the conflict to shuttle troops about, but this September 1863 movement was a logistical tour de force. Within forty hours of the initial decision, the first units were on their way west. Eleven days and 1,200 miles later practically all the detached troops, together with their artillery, horses, and wagons, had reached Bridgeport, Alabama, staging point for the relief of Chattanooga.

Late in October, Grant personally went to Chattanooga to have a closer look at the situation. His party rode on horseback via the only route that remained open into or out of the city—a narrow road, hardly more than a bridle path in spots, that wound about sixty-five miles from Bridgeport to Chattanooga through a desolate stretch of mountains. This road formed the only means by which the besieged Army of the Cumberland could receive supplies. The supplies amounted to hardly more than a trickle, and once at Chattanooga Grant discovered that the horses were starving and the men not far from it.

Efforts to repair the situation got under way as soon as Grant arrived. Within days the Union troops broke out of their encirclement enough to reestablish a solid supply line through the Tennessee River valley—a "Cracker Line," the men called it. Along with a welcome deluge of rations, thousands of reinforcements arrived to help drive away the Confederate army. In addition to the two corps from Virginia, most of Grant's own Army of the Tennessee, now led by red-bearded General Sherman, came up from Mississippi. A new spirit entered the beleaguered army at Chattanooga. "You have no conception of the change in the army when Grant came," one soldier testified. "He opened up the cracker line and got a steamer through. We began to see things move. We felt that everything came from a plan. He came into the army quietly, no splendor, no airs, no staff. He used to go about alone. He began the campaign the moment he reached the field."

By mid-autumn the Union armies were ready to attack, and on November 24–25 they conducted a series of offensives aimed at breaking the Confederate grip on Chattanooga. The unexpected climax of these battles occurred on the second day of fighting, when Thomas's Army of the Cumberland transformed what had been planned as a limited thrust into a wild, hell-for-leather charge up the rugged slopes of Missionary Ridge, smack into the center of the whole Confederate line. It seemed impossible that such a charge could succeed, and Grant, watching the impromptu attack, remarked that if it failed whoever had ordered the assault was going to sweat for it. Yet, incredibly, the Union troops made it to the top and routed the astonished Confederates.

At first glance the victory appeared, if not a "visible interposition of God," as someone remarked, then at least a vindication of continued faith in the frontal assault. In fact it could more accurately be seen as the harvest of sloppy Confederate planning. Most of the Confederate defenders had been placed, not at the military crest of the ridge—the highest point from which a marksman could hit what was below him—but at the topographical crest, where he generally could not hit much of anything. In addition, a good number of rebel soldiers had been deployed at the foot of the ridge, where they were too few to stop the Federal advance, but sufficiently numerous, when they retreated, to force their comrades at the summit to hold their fire. Finally, the Confederates had neglected to cover the numerous ravines that led to the top, so that the assaulting Federal columns found numerous covered avenues as they scrambled up the slope.

Thus through Bragg's failure to pursue Rosecrans after Chickamauga and his mismanaged siege of Chattanooga, the Federals were able to restore the situation, secure permanent control of this gateway city, and win a glittering autumn victory at surprisingly low cost. The Union lost 5,800 men, slightly more than 10 percent of the total engaged. The Confederates lost 6,700 out of 46,000, and embarked on a retreat that did not end until they reached Dalton, Georgia, some twenty-five miles away. The road into the Southern heartland was now open.

Even after the North decided to recruit African Americans as soldiers, fears persisted that blacks would not make effective soldiers. As units like the 54th Massachusetts demonstrated, such fears were misplaced. Its assault at Fort Wagner, South Carolina, in July 1863 was one of the most famous of the war.

★   ★   ★   ★

By the end of 1863 the Confederacy had lost not only two key strategic points—Vicksburg and Chattanooga—it had also lost a great deal of its ability to counterpunch effectively. Lee's great victory at Chancellorsville and his great disaster at Gettysburg had, between them, cost the South about 33,000 men. Roughly the same number went into the bag with Pemberton's capitulation at Vicksburg. The Confederacy simply could not afford to sustain such casualties. It had nearly reached the bottom of its manpower pool, and the losses of 1863 included many of its most experienced and motivated soldiers. The North, by contrast, still had ample manpower reserves. It also had begun to reap one advantage of the Emancipation Proclamation by recruiting and fielding thousands of African-American troops. The first black units had their baptism of fire in 1863 and, to the surprise of white men North and South, performed with courage and élan. Ultimately a full 10 percent of the Union army—180,000 men in all—would be composed of black soldiers.

The reversals of 1863 also began a long-term decline in Confederate morale. The South had endured at least one previous crisis of confidence, during the first six months of 1862, but this second crisis was just as bad. Desertions swelled in the months after Gettysburg and Vicksburg as soldiers decided that "we are done gon up the Spout." A Confederate war department clerk described Chattanooga as an "incalculable disaster," while the wife of a prominent Southern leader wrote that "gloom and unspoken despondency hang like a pall everywhere." As the New Year approached, Southerners knew that the most terrible trial of the war was at hand.

SUGGESTED READINGS

Black, Robert C., III. *The Railroads of the Confederacy* (Chapel Hill: University of North Carolina Press, 1952).

Catton, Bruce. *Grant Moves South* (Boston: Little, Brown, 1960).

———. *Never Call Retreat* (Garden City, N.Y.: Doubleday, 1965).

Coddington, Edwin A. *The Gettysburg Campaign: A Study in Command* (New York: Charles Scribner's Sons, 1968).

Connelly, Thomas L. *Autumn of Glory: The Army of Tennessee, 1863–1865* (Baton Rouge: Louisiana State University Press, 1970).

Cornish, Dudley Taylor. *The Sable Arm: Black Troops in the Union Army, 1861–1865* (New York: Longmans, Green, 1956).

Cozzens, Peter. *This Terrible Sound: The Battle of Chickamauga* (Urbana and Chicago: University of Illinois Press, 1992).

Escott, Paul D. *After Secession: Jefferson Davis and the Failure of Confederate Nationalism* (Baton Rouge: Louisiana State University Press, 1979).

Furgurson, Ernest B. *Chancellorsville 1863: The Souls of the Brave* (New York: Alfred A. Knopf, 1992).

Geary, John. *We Need Men: The Union Draft in the Civil War, 1861–1865* (DeKalb: Northern Illinois University Press, 1990).

Glatthaar, Joseph T. *Forged in Battle: The Civil War Alliance of Black Soldiers and White Officers* (New York: Free Press, 1989).

Griffith, Paddy. *Civil War Battle Tactics* (New Haven, Conn.: Yale University Press, 1989).

Hagerman, Edward. *The American Civil War and the Origins of Modern Warfare* (Bloomington: Indiana University Press, 1988).

McWhiney, Grady, and Perry D. Jamieson. *Attack and Die: Civil War Military Tactics and the Southern Heritage* (University, Ala.: University of Alabama Press, 1982).

Paludan, Philip S. *A People's Contest: The Union and the Civil War, 1861–1865* (New York: Harper & Row, 1988).

Royster, Charles. *The Destructive War: William Tecumseh Sherman, Stonewall Jackson, and the Americans* (New York: Alfred A. Knopf, 1991).

Weber, Thomas. *The Northern Railroads in the Civil War, 1861–1865* (Westport, Conn.: Greenwood Press, 1952).

7

THE CIVIL WAR, 1864–1865: TOTAL WAR

The Virginia Campaign

To Atlanta and Beyond

The Naval War, 1862–1865

The War Ends

The final year of the Civil War witnessed the full bloom of total war. No western state in centuries had waged a military contest more comprehensively than did the Union and Confederacy. Determined national efforts the world had seen: during the Napoleonic Wars the Spanish and Russian people had fought relentlessly against the French invaders; and in 1813 the Russians had pursued the retreating French for nearly a thousand miles. Yet neither the Spanish nor the Russians had mobilized their populations and economies as systematically as did the North and South. Also, when the allies carried the war into France in 1814, they did not make a sustained effort to destroy the French people's capacity to make war. By 1864, however, the North was not only bringing pressure against the Confederate field armies but was also striking powerfully at the material and psychological resources of the South.

In strictly military terms, the South now had little chance to win the war. With Lee's offensive power blunted, the trans-Mississippi isolated, and Chattanooga in Union hands, the Confederacy's strategic situation was bleak. Moreover, the battles of previous years had bled rebel manpower so heavily that by early 1864 the Confederate Congress was forced to pass a new conscription law that abolished substitutes and "robbed the cradle and the grave" in an effort to secure more troops. Even this did not help. In desperation, a few Confederate leaders began to ponder the previously unthinkable option of using slaves as soldiers—and, in exchange, to emancipate those slaves who agreed to fight for the South.

Most, however, continued to regard this last step as anathema. Instead they pinned their hopes on the fact that in November 1864, Lincoln faced reelection. If the South could only hold out until then, the war weariness of Northerners might result in his losing the White House. "If we can break up the enemy's arrangements early, and throw him back," noted one Confederate general, "he will not be able to recover his position or his morale until the Presidential election is over, and then we shall have a new President to treat with." Presumably this new president would be receptive to a compromise peace.

Lincoln, of course, understood the rebel hope as well as anyone, and he had no intention of permitting a prolonged stalemate. Instead he did what most observers had assumed he would do since the triumph at Chattanooga: he gave Ulysses S. Grant command of all the Union armies. With the new job came the three stars of a lieutenant general, a rank not held by any U.S. officer (except honorifically) since George Washington. In March 1864, Grant came to Washington, met Lincoln for the first time, received his promotion, and settled down to win the war.

The Virginia Campaign

Now installed as general-in-chief (with Halleck retained as army chief of staff), Grant began planning at once for the 1864 campaigns. The content of those plans and the way in which he devised them provide a good lens through which to examine the salient features of his generalship.

To begin with, Grant saw the war as a whole. Until that time most Union generals had viewed the conflict in terms of separate theaters; no one placed much premium on cooperative effort. As a result, the outnumbered Confederate forces had been able to shift troops from one place to another, shoring up one threatened point by diverting strength from quiet sectors. In this way Johnston had gathered over 30,000 soldiers for his vain but bothersome effort to relieve Vicksburg; in this way as well, troops from all over the Confederacy had gathered to administer the near-crippling blow to Rosecrans at Chickamauga. To prevent the Confederates from shifting troops from quiet to threatened sectors, Grant planned for a simultaneous advance along the entire front.

Second, Grant was less interested in occupying "strategic points" than in destroying the enemy's main forces. He believed that when no armies remained to defend them, the strategic points would fall as a matter of course. Important cities like Richmond and Atlanta were useful chiefly because the main Confederate armies would fight for them, and in the course of fighting they could be destroyed. Grant put this concept succinctly in a letter to Major General George Gordon Meade, commander of the Army of the Potomac: "Lee's army is your objective point. Wherever Lee goes, there you will go also."

Third, Grant wanted the 1864 spring offensive to be as strong as possible. He regretted the detachment of so many Union troops on passive occupation duty. Some of this could not be helped—by this period of the

The architect of victory. Appointed to command the Union armies in March 1864,
Ulysses S. Grant quickly applied a strategy of maintaining constant military pressure on the
Confederacy through coordinated offensives to wear down Southern armies and destroy
Southern war resources.

war the Federal armies had to contend with well over 100,000 square miles
of captured hostile territory—but it struck Grant that all too often the passive stance was unnecessary. At an April conference with Lincoln, Grant
expressed the view that these detachments could do their jobs "just as well
by advancing as by remaining still; and by advancing they would compel the
enemy to keep detachments to hold them back, or else lay his own territory
open to invasion." Lincoln grasped the point at once. "Oh, yes!" he said. "I
see that. As we say out West, if a man can't skin he must hold a leg while
somebody else does."

Finally, Grant expected to combine destruction of Southern armies
with destruction of Southern war resources. Although Sherman would
become the general most identified with this policy, Grant had a profound
understanding of the fact that Civil War armies had become too large and

too powerful to destroy in battle. Their annihilation required not only military defeat but also the elimination of the foodstuffs, forage, ammunition, and equipage necessary to maintain them in the field. His instructions to Sherman reflect this: "You I propose to move against [Joseph E.] Johnston's army, to break it up, and to get into the interior of the enemy's country as far as you can, inflicting all the damage you can against their war resources."

Grant refused to direct operations from Washington and decided to make his headquarters with the Army of the Potomac. He had good reason

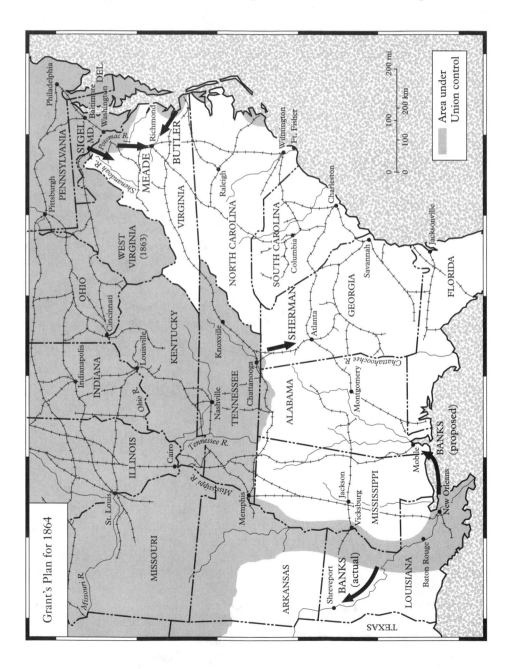

Grant's Plan for 1864

for doing so. That army formed one of the two primary concentrations of Union force; as such it would play a decisive role in the campaign to come. But except for its single defensive victory at Gettysburg, the Army of the Potomac had a depressing record of stalemate or defeat; in its entire existence it had never won a clear-cut offensive victory. Worse, the army had traditionally suffered from its close proximity to Washington, which made it strongly susceptible to political pressures and even to factionalism among the officer corps. In short, the Army of the Potomac seemed to need first-hand attention far more than the other reservoir of Federal striking power—the combined armies of the Cumberland, the Tennessee, and the Ohio—which Sherman had assembled at Chattanooga. Sherman, in any event, enjoyed Grant's entire confidence.

Grant also came to think highly of General Meade, leader of the Army of the Potomac. He had never met Meade before his arrival in Virginia and did not know what to expect, but Meade impressed him by offering to step aside immediately if Grant wished to put someone in his place. Grant declined the offer and Meade remained in command; even so, Grant exerted such close supervision over the Army of the Potomac that it quickly became known, erroneously but enduringly, as "Grant's army."

Grant's final plan for the great 1864 campaign pressed the Confederacy on all sides: in the eastern theater, the Army of the Potomac would advance against General Robert E. Lee's Army of Northern Virginia. Two smaller forces would "hold a leg": Major General Franz Sigel would advance up the Shenandoah Valley while Major General Benjamin F. Butler would conduct an amphibious operation against the Richmond-Petersburg area. Unfortunately, Sigel and Butler were political generals, men of little or no military ability who held important commands exclusively because they had strong influence with constituencies important to the Union war effort. (Sigel was a hero among the German-American community, Butler an important Democrat.) Grant would have been justified in expecting nothing at all from these men. Instead he pinned many of his hopes for the upcoming Virginia campaign on the belief that both would perform capably. Grant gave Butler an especially significant role: he anticipated that Butler's army would be able to seize the important railroad town of Petersburg and perhaps even capture Richmond itself.

Out west, Sherman's three armies would move upon Johnston's Army of Tennessee. Grant had hoped that yet another force, under General Banks, might advance from Louisiana against Mobile, Alabama, but for political reasons Banks marched up the cotton-rich but strategically irrelevant Red River valley. Except for Banks, who had already made—and lost—his campaign by early April, the remaining operations were timed to jump off simultaneously in early May 1864.

The Wilderness and Spotsylvania

Grant, of course, paid closest attention to the offensive against Lee. On May 4 the Army of the Potomac crossed the Rapidan River into the

Wilderness, the same region where Hooker had come to grief the year before. Some miles to the west lay Lee's Army of Northern Virginia. By crossing here, Grant hoped to turn Lee's right flank and compel him to retreat. But that same day Lee got his troops in motion and came thundering east; early the next morning he hurled them into action against two Union corps as they struggled along the narrow lanes of the Wilderness.

Outnumbered nearly two to one (64,000 men against Grant's 119,000), Lee wanted to force a battle in the Wilderness where thick woods would dilute the Union numerical advantage and make it difficult for the Federals to use their numerous and well-trained artillery. During the next two days he savaged the Union army with a sustained intensity Grant had never experienced in his previous campaigns. Those who *had* experienced it were not slow to offer advice. On the second day of the fighting one Union general told him, "General Grant, this is a crisis that cannot be looked upon too seriously. I know Lee's methods well by past experience; he will throw his whole army between us and the Rapidan, and cut us off completely from our communications." Usually phlegmatic, Grant permitted himself a rare show of annoyance. "Oh, I am heartily tired of hearing what Lee is going to do. Some of you always seem to think he is suddenly going to turn a double somersault and land in our rear and on both of our flanks at the same time. Go back to your command," he snapped, "and try to think what we are going to do ourselves, instead of what Lee is going to do."

This kind of thinking brought something new to the Army of the Potomac. The fighting in the Wilderness cost the Union nearly 17,000 casu-

In Virginia, Grant's 1864 campaign began with two bitter days of fighting in the densely wooded Wilderness. Many wounded men on both sides were burned to death when the trees and undergrowth caught fire. Despite harrowing losses, Grant maintained pressure on Lee's army.

alties; Lee, by contrast suffered no more than about 10,000. In earlier days the Army of the Potomac would have retreated after such a battle to lick its wounds. Grant, however, decided simply to disengage and continue his effort to get around Lee's flank. After suffering for years from a chronic sense of inferiority, the Army of the Potomac found itself led by a man who never thought in terms of defeat and who did not lose his will to fight when confronted by casualties.

The army began moving during the evening of May 7, heading for Spotsylvania Court House, an important crossroads, ten miles southeast of the Wilderness, whose swift possession would allow the Union forces to interpose between Richmond and Lee. Confederate troops got there first, however, and in a series of sharp little engagements held the crossroads long enough for Lee's army to arrive in strength. For twelve days (May 9–21), the two armies grappled inconclusively in the fields north and east of Spotsylvania.

Unlike the Wilderness, where Lee had counterattacked early and often, at Spotsylvania the Army of Northern Virginia fought almost entirely behind entrenchments. Grant viewed this as a confession of Confederate weakness. At the same time, however, he found it very difficult to crack the rebel line. On May 10, for example, an imaginative young West Point graduate named Emory Upton managed to break into the Confederate entrenchments using a new tactical scheme of his own devising. His division advanced in column formation, without pausing to fire en route—Upton took the precaution of having his men charge with muskets uncapped except for the leading rank. The attack indeed broke the rebel line, but supporting Federal troops failed to arrive and Upton reluctantly withdrew.

Grant, however, was sufficiently impressed with the new tactic to try it again, this time using an entire corps. Shortly after dawn on May 12 the corps struck a prominent salient in the Confederate position known as the "Mule Shoe." As in Upton's charge, the Federals broke through the enemy trenches, this time capturing more than 4,000 prisoners. Lee was forced to counterattack in a desperate attempt to restore the breach, resulting in some of the most ferocious combat of the entire war. In many places the fighting was hand to hand, and at one point the bullets flew so thick that an oak tree nearly two feet in diameter was completely cut in two. By evening Lee managed to complete a new line of entrenchments across the base of the Mule Shoe, and the surviving Confederates withdrew. In a pattern that would be repeated endlessly during World War I, the defenders had managed to repair a breach in their fortified line faster than the attackers could exploit it.

To the Banks of the James River

Initially Grant was determined to break the Confederates at Spotsylvania— he wired Washington, "I propose to fight it out on this line if it takes all summer." But by mid-May it had become obvious that both secondary offensives in Virginia had failed. A hastily assembled rebel force defeated Sigel on May 15 at the Battle of New Market. Butler landed at the tip of a peninsula

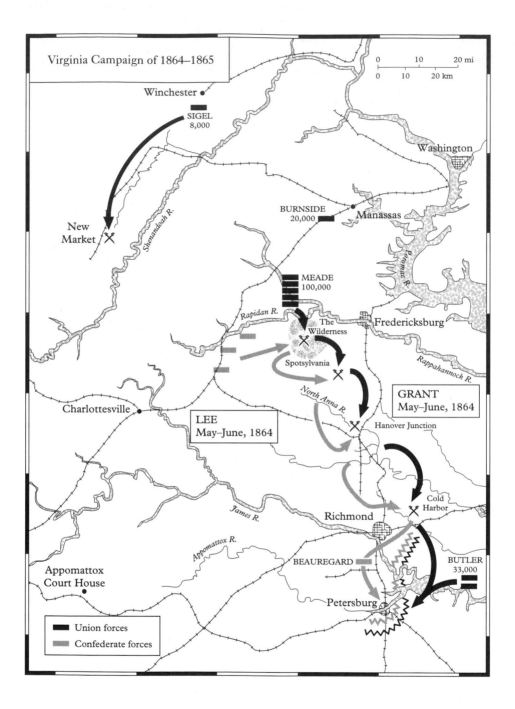

Virginia Campaign of 1864–1865

Winchester

SIGEL
8,000

Washington

Shenandoah R.

BURNSIDE
20,000

Manassas

New
Market

Potomac R.

MEADE
100,000

Rapidan R.

The
Wilderness

Fredericksburg

Spotsylvania

Rappahannock R.

North Anna R.

GRANT
May–June, 1864

Charlottesville

LEE
May–June, 1864

Hanover Junction

Cold
Harbor

James R.

Richmond

Appomattox R.

BEAUREGARD

BUTLER
33,000

Appomattox
Court House

Petersburg

Union forces
Confederate forces

formed by the James and Appomattox rivers, advanced a short distance inland, then stalled. A much smaller Confederate detachment soon sealed off the neck of the peninsula with entrenchments. This left Butler's force, in Grant's scornful words, "as completely shut off from further operations against Richmond as if it had been in a bottle strongly corked." Designed to place additional pressure on Lee and siphon troops from his army, these efforts to "hold a leg" wound up having the opposite effect: with Sigel beaten and Butler neutralized, Lee received 8,500 reinforcements from the forces that had opposed the two Union generals.

Lee's increased strength made "fighting it out" at Spotsylvania no longer such a good idea. Unable to dislodge the Confederate commander, Grant attempted once again to slide past Lee's right flank and continue his advance southward. The formula he had given Meade before the campaign—"Wherever Lee goes, there you will go also"—became reversed: wherever Grant went, Lee went also, and Lee invariably got there first. Yet in every previous campaign, Lee had found a way to wrest the initiative from his opponent. Grant gave him no such opportunity. The Union general-in-chief had both the military strength and the moral determination to keep moving on.

The campaign in progress resembled nothing that had come before. Previous Civil War operations had usually followed a fairly classic pattern: long periods of preliminary maneuver, careful sparring as the opposing forces located one another, then a major battle that ended in clear-cut victory or defeat. Grant's campaign, on the other hand, amounted to a six-week brawl in which the armies seldom broke contact for more than a few hours and from which no clear decision emerged. The losses it generated horrified the Northern population. In the long months since Shiloh the North had grown used to casualty lists on the same scale as those of that bloody struggle; but the fighting in May and early June 1864 produced 55,000 Union dead, wounded, and missing—about five times the cost of Shiloh. Confederate losses exceeded 20,000: much fewer than those of the Federals, but about the same in proportion to the forces engaged.

The campaign differed in one other respect as well. Both sides had learned the value of field fortifications; indeed, the soldiers had gotten so that they would dig in without orders and practically every time they halted for more than a few minutes. "It is a rule," wrote one Union officer, "that when the Rebels halt, the first day gives them a good rifle-pit; the second, a regular infantry parapet with artillery in position; and the third a parapet with abatis [sharpened stakes] in front and entrenched batteries behind. Sometimes they put this three days' work into the first twenty-four hours." These entrenchments had the effect of making it almost impossible to carry a defensive position; those who attempted it generally got slaughtered, while their killers found almost total protection behind rifle pits and earthen parapets.

Though the generals did not quickly grasp the full significance of this, the Battle of Cold Harbor provided a final, chilling lesson. By early June, Grant's army had gotten within seven miles of Richmond, but it had not yet beaten Lee's army and it had nearly run out of room to maneuver:

further efforts to turn the Confederates would run into the tidal estuary of the James River. Partly because of this situation, and partly because Grant thought he discerned a weakness in Lee's line, he ordered a frontal assault against Lee's entrenched defenses. The attack jumped off at about 4:30 A.M. on June 3. It was really nothing more than a succession of charges made along different parts of the line, most of which collapsed within minutes, smashed beneath an annihilating storm of rifle and artillery fire. The abortive and bloody attack cost nearly 7,000 Union casualties. Grant later called it one of two attacks during the war he wished he had not ordered.

 With no prospect whatever of breaking through to Richmond, Grant then went forward with an operation he had pondered even while the armies were still fighting at Spotsylvania. He would shift the Army of the Potomac south of the James River, use the river as his line of supply, and try to get at Petersburg, a city about twenty miles south of Richmond through which the Confederate capital—and Lee's army—received most of its supplies. Between June 12 and 16 the Union forces made the crossing, with Grant managing the feat so adroitly that for several days Lee did not know what was being done. As a result the Army of the Potomac almost seized Petersburg before an adequate rebel force could arrive to hold the city. Through misperception and bad management on the part of Meade's subordinates, however, the fleeting opportunity vanished. Lee's army scrambled down to Petersburg, entered fortifications already in place to defend the city, and once again forced a stalemate. The Army of the Potomac settled in for a siege; for the next ten months, Lee and Grant faced one another across a trench-scarred landscape.

The Siege of Petersburg

Militarily the stalemate at Petersburg suited Grant just fine. Although ideally he would have preferred to destroy Lee's army outright, at a minimum he expected the Army of the Potomac's advance to pressure Lee so strongly that the Confederate would be unable to send any troops to support Johnston in his defense against Sherman. This the Army of the Potomac had accomplished. Sherman, meanwhile, was steadily pushing Johnston's army back toward Atlanta, and Grant regarded the Georgia offensive as crucial. Once Sherman had gained control of Atlanta, the entire Southern heartland would lay open, and therein lay the ultimate key to Union victory.

 Politically, however, the stalemate in Virginia was sheer poison. Northerners considered it unacceptable that the bloody campaign to reach the Richmond-Petersburg area should have yielded nothing better than a deadlock. War weariness had set in, and although on the map the Union armies had made great gains, none of them seemed to have brought the conclusion of the struggle one whit nearer. Many Northerners began to feel that perhaps the only way to end the war lay in a negotiated, compromise peace. Worse, with the 1864 presidential election approaching, they might well register their discouragement at the polls if the stalemate continued.

Summer brought no reversal in Union fortunes. Grant could not get into Petersburg; Sherman drew nearer to Atlanta but found that the city's fortifications firmly barred entry. Meanwhile Lee managed what looked like a real victory: in June he detached a corps under Lieutenant General Jubal Early and sent him swinging northwest toward the Shenandoah Valley. After clearing the valley of Union troops, Early's men crossed into western Maryland, sliced southeast toward Washington, and by mid-July actually carried their raid to within sight of the Federal Capitol building. Although the Confederates could not penetrate the powerful fortifications that ringed Washington and Union reinforcements soon arrived to drive them away, this seemed less significant than the sheer fact that, in the summer of 1864, a major Confederate force could still successfully threaten the Union capital. Early's raid, coupled with the apparent lack of Union success in Virginia and Georgia, boded ill for the upcoming November election. In August 1864 Northern morale reached its nadir, and Lincoln gloomily predicted that he would shortly lose the presidency.

To Atlanta and Beyond

What saved Lincoln was the capture of Atlanta—another potent demonstration of the close connection between battlefield developments and politics. The chief author of his salvation was Major General William Tecumseh Sherman, Grant's most trusted lieutenant and his choice to head the Military Division of the Mississippi. The triumph came after four months of steady campaigning along the one-hundred-mile corridor that separated Chattanooga and Atlanta. It probably destroyed what remained of the Confederacy's chance to win the Civil War.

Northern Georgia

The Atlanta Campaign pitted Sherman against Joseph E. Johnston, the Confederate general chosen to replace Bragg after the humiliating Chattanooga fiasco. Sherman led approximately 100,000 men, divided into three parts: the Army of the Cumberland, commanded by Major General George H. Thomas; the Army of the Tennessee, led by Major General James B. McPherson; and the corps-sized Army of the Ohio, commanded by Major General John M. Schofield. To oppose the Union forces Johnston had just 50,000 men (although he was shortly reinforced to about 60,000). Although outnumbered, the Confederates had the advantage of fighting on the defensive in rugged mountain country well-suited to the purpose.

Ever since Chattanooga, the Confederate Army of Tennessee had been posted at Dalton, Georgia, and had strongly fortified Rocky Face Ridge just northwest of the town. Sherman called this position "the terrible door of death." A direct attack was out of the question. Instead, in early May he sent McPherson's army on a long swing around the rebel left flank while Thomas and Schofield distracted Johnston. McPherson managed to penetrate into the Confederate rear through a carelessly guarded mountain gap. This penetration forced Johnston to abandon his first line and retreat about ten miles to Resaca. Sherman had taken the first trick, but in retrospect he realized that McPherson had missed a great opportunity. Had he acted more aggressively he might have cut Johnston's line of retreat, but instead McPherson had obeyed the letter of Sherman's orders and avoided this daring but risky move. "Well, Mac," Sherman told his protegé, "you missed the opportunity of your life."

The rival armies lingered three days at Resaca while Sherman vainly searched for a weakness in Johnston's line. Finding none, he sent McPherson on a second wide sweep around the Confederate left flank. This time Johnston withdrew another twenty-five miles until he reached Cassville on May 19. Thus, in twelve days' time the Army of Tennessee had yielded about half the distance from Dalton to Atlanta. President Jefferson Davis was considerably disgruntled by this development, but given the great disparity in troop strength Johnston felt he had little choice.

One of his key subordinates disagreed, however. Lieutenant General John B. Hood, a former division commander in the Army of Northern Virginia, had come west during Longstreet's September 1863 redeployment and had remained with the Army of Tennessee. A gallant fighter—he had lost an arm at Gettysburg and a leg at Chickamauga—Hood had been befriended by President Davis and his wife and had been given command of a corps in the Army of Tennessee. He knew Davis and Johnston despised one another and, as a good Davis ally, sent the president a stream of private letters critical of the army commander. Trained in the offensive school of warfare favored by Lee, Hood considered Johnston far too cautious. Sherman, he believed, should be dealt a whole-souled counterpunch of the sort that had bested McClellan, Pope, and Hooker. Davis agreed and considered relieving Johnston of command if he continued to retreat.

Johnston, however, remained true to his Fabian tactics. (Ironically, on the one occasion when he did plan a counterstroke, Hood proved unready and urged that the attack be called off.) The Army of Tennessee occupied one well-entrenched defensive position after another. Sherman, meanwhile, made yet another swing around the Confederate left flank. The move brought him a few miles closer to Atlanta but no closer to "breaking up" Johnston's army as Grant had instructed.

Unfortunately for Sherman, his three armies relied for supply on a single railroad coming down from Chattanooga. Johnston destroyed the railroad as he withdrew and although Sherman's engineers quickly repaired the damage, Sherman realized the vulnerability of this line. He particularly feared that Confederate cavalry raiders—especially the fearsome Bedford Forrest—might damage his communications in Tennessee, and he diverted thousands of Union troops to forestall them. Consequently, instead of making Confederate raids, Forrest spent the summer of 1864 largely responding to Federal raids into Mississippi. The tactic worked: although Forrest racked

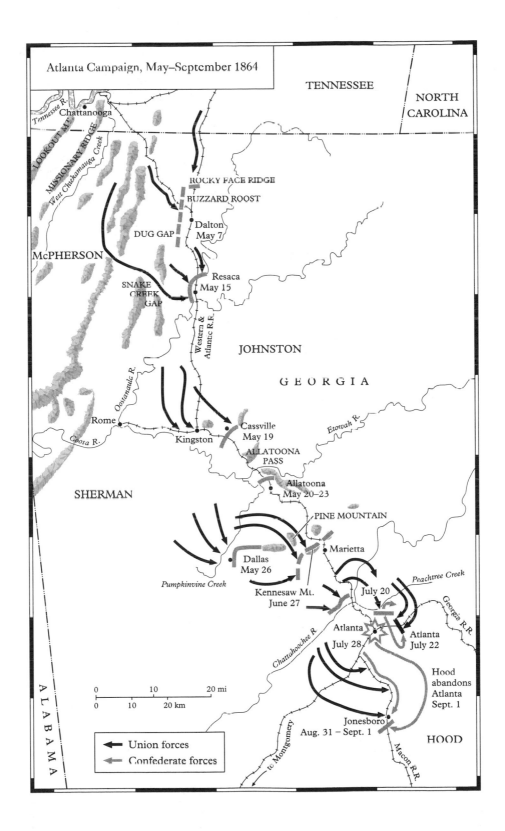

Atlanta Campaign, May–September 1864

TENNESSEE

NORTH CAROLINA

Tennessee R.
Chattanooga

LOOKOUT MT.

MISSIONARY RIDGE

West Chickamauga Creek

ROCKY FACE RIDGE

BUZZARD ROOST

DUG GAP

Dalton
May 7

McPHERSON

Resaca
May 15

SNAKE
CREEK
GAP

Western & Atlantic R.R.

JOHNSTON

GEORGIA

Oostanaula R.

Rome

Cassville
May 19

Etowah R.

Coosa R.

Kingston

ALLATOONA
PASS

SHERMAN

Allatoona
May 20–23

PINE MOUNTAIN

Dallas
May 26

Marietta

Peachtree Creek

Pumpkinvine Creek

Kennesaw Mt.
June 27

July 20

Georgia R.R.

Chattahoochee R.

Atlanta

Atlanta
July 22

July 28

Hood
abandons
Atlanta
Sept. 1

ALABAMA

0   10   20 mi
0   10   20 km

Jonesboro
Aug. 31 – Sept. 1

HOOD

to Montgomery

Macon R.R.

⬅ Union forces
➡ Confederate forces

up an impressive series of victories against these raiding forces, he was forced to leave Sherman's communications alone.

For the first two months of the Atlanta Campaign neither side risked a major battle. As a result, neither side lost heavily; the Union armies, indeed, suffered casualties only marginally greater than the Confederates. Finally, on June 27, Sherman mounted a major assault upon Johnston's center at Kennesaw Mountain. This part of the Confederate line appeared weak to Sherman, who thought a breakthrough might be possible. Moreover, recent rains had reduced his army's mobility so that the alternative to an attack was delay. Then too, Sherman believed, "The enemy as well as my own army had settled down to the belief that flanking alone was my game." By attacking, he hoped to convince Johnston that he might strike anywhere and thus that Johnston must hold his entire line in strength. He also thought it would restore some aggressiveness to his own troops. They had become so chary of fortifications, he complained, that a "fresh furrow in a plowed field will stop a whole column, and all begin to entrench." But the Battle of Kennesaw Mountain cost his army 2,000 casualties, against just 450 for the Confederates, and gained not an inch of ground.

Sherman then reverted to the flanking game. He made a fourth move around Johnston's left flank, breached the line of the Chattahoochee River—the last real barrier separating him from Atlanta—and followed up with a fifth turning movement, this time around the Confederate right flank. By mid-July, Johnston had withdrawn behind the outer fortifications that ringed the city itself. Although the Army of Tennessee remained intact, it had run out of room to maneuver.

Battles for Atlanta

At about this time a visiting congressional delegation warned Johnston that Davis would surely remove him if he continued his passive defense. Artlessly, one of the congressmen quoted a story that was then making the rounds in Richmond, to the effect that the president had said that "if he were in your place he could whip Sherman now." "Yes," Johnston harrumphed. "I know Mr. Davis thinks he can do a great many things other men would hesitate to attempt. For instance, he tried to do what God failed to do. He tried to make a soldier of Braxton Bragg, and you know the result. It couldn't be done."

Johnston might have heeded the delegation's warning. On July 17, Davis removed him and substituted Hood. He made the change despite misgivings expressed by Lee, who of course had once commanded Hood. Asked for his opinion, Lee was candid: "It is a bad time to release the commander of an army situated as that of Tennessee. We may lose Atlanta and the army too. Hood is a bold fighter. I am doubtful as to other qualities necessary." In perhaps the most controversial military decision Davis made during the war, he went ahead with the replacement anyway. Johnston, despite his excessive caution, had been a canny tactician and frugal with his limited supply of manpower. Hood did exactly what the president wanted:

As this photo attests, the Confederate manufacturing center of Atlanta, Georgia, was one of the most heavily fortified cities in America by mid-1864. Its capture by Sherman's army in September 1864 electrified the North, dismayed the South, and helped ensure Lincoln's reelection two months later.

he fought. The result, as Lee had suspected, was the loss of Atlanta and the crippling of Hood's army.

On July 19, Hood struck the Union Army of the Cumberland while its two sister armies were attempting another of their inevitable turning movements. He achieved little. Two days later he struck again, this time against McPherson's Army of the Tennessee. The attack was adroitly made, but as usual the defending side had the resilience and flexibility to recover and restore the line. A third assault on July 28 resulted in a virtual massacre. Although McPherson was killed in one of these battles (one of only two army commanders to suffer such a fate), Hood's army lost about 15,000 of its 40,000 effectives; Federal casualties numbered just 5,400.

Hood, like his predecessor, now withdrew into the Atlanta fortifications. Sherman inaugurated a quasi-siege, lobbing shells into the beleaguered city, and meanwhile planned to cut the railroads connecting Atlanta with the rest of the South. In late August he carried out this operation. Leaving one corps to distract Hood, he took the rest of his armies on one last turning movement, this time to a point well south of the city. Hood recognized the move and turned to meet it, but he was too late. Sherman had gotten squarely across the Confederate line of communications. When a desperate Confederate counterstroke at Jonesboro failed to dislodge Sherman, Hood had no choice but to abandon the city. It fell on September 2, 1864.

Hood's army, badly weakened, drew off into northern Alabama and tried with limited success to destroy Sherman's extended supply lines.

The fall of Atlanta sealed the fate of the Confederacy. Until then the possibility existed that Lincoln would lose his bid for reelection that year because the North, like the South, had grown increasingly frustrated with a war that seemed to go on interminably. If Lincoln lost, it seemed likely that some sort of negotiated peace might be arranged. But Sherman's victory gave Union morale an enormous boost. The North now was clearly winning.

Union Raids

September brought additional triumphs. In the middle of that month, a Union army under Major General Philip H. Sheridan confronted Early's veterans in the Shenandoah Valley. Badly outnumbered, the Confederates suffered defeat in two sharp battles that forced them to yield the entire valley to Union domination. In October, Sheridan won a third shattering victory that destroyed Early's army for good, but by that time the valley that Early defended had already become "a smoking, barren waste." Its destruction illustrates an important dimension of Grant's strategy.

General Philip H. Sheridan was one of the Union's most implacable "hard war" generals. As commander of Northern forces in the Shenandoah Valley, he defeated the Confederates in two sharp battles, then destroyed the valley's barns and crops to end its days as a source of Confederate supply.

Sometimes called the "breadbasket of the Confederacy," the rich Shenandoah Valley had long served as a major source of supply to Lee's army. Consequently, Grant regarded destruction of the Valley as a legitimate military objective. Once Early's force had been beaten, he believed, the pursuing troops should "eat out Virginia clear and clean as far as they go, so that crows flying over it for the balance of the season will have to carry their provender with them." As he explained to Sheridan, "[N]othing should be left to invite the enemy to return. Take all provisions, forage and stock wanted for the use of your command. Such as cannot be consumed, destroy."

During the early weeks of autumn Sheridan carried out these instructions with grim enthusiasm. By mid-October he could report, "I have destroyed over 2,000 barns filled with wheat, hay and farming implements; over 70 mills, filled with flour and wheat; have driven in front of the army over 4,000 head of stock, and have killed and issued to the troops not less than 3,000 sheep. . . . The people here are getting sick of the war."

The final sentence in Sheridan's dispatch alluded to a new element in the struggle, one that Grant had begun to see as early as 1862 but that had required two more years to reach maturity. The war for the Union had become not only a war against the "slave aristocracy" but against the Southern people as a whole. Typical of this tough new mindset was Sherman's decision, shortly after his capture of Atlanta, to order the evacuation of its entire civilian population. When the city's mayor protested the inhumanity of this action, Sherman responded witheringly: "[M]y orders are not designed to meet the humanities of the case but to prepare for the future struggles. . . . War is cruelty, and you cannot refine it. . . . You might as well appeal against the thunder storm as against these terrible hardships of war." Although Grant never came close to Sherman's desolating eloquence, his own orders as well as his endorsement of Sherman demonstrate that he felt exactly the same way.

For several weeks after the fall of Atlanta, Sherman made no further advances. He was too busy protecting his greatly overextended supply line. No longer obliged to defend Atlanta, Hood had shifted into northwest Georgia and now drew his supplies from neighboring Alabama. With his own lines of communication secure, Hood spent October threatening the vulnerable Western and Atlantic Railroad that was Sherman's lifeline with the North. Sherman's armies spent several frustrating weeks fruitlessly chasing Hood's army as it bedeviled the tenuous Union supply line through the northern part of the state. The Federals, in effect, were having to fight twice for the same real estate.

Clearly some new solution must be found, and Sherman believed he knew what it was. He wanted to cut loose from the Western and Atlantic Railroad entirely, abandon Atlanta, and strike out for a new base on the coast. On October 9 he wrote Grant, "I propose that we break up the railroad from Chattanooga forward, and that we strike out with our wagons for Milledgeville, Macon, and Savannah." The mere occupation of Georgia, he argued, was useless given the hostile population. "[B]ut the utter destruction of its [rail]roads, houses, and people, will cripple their military resources. . . . I can make the march, and make Georgia howl!"

Grant delayed before giving Sherman permission for the operation. Noting that the Confederate leadership might send Hood's army to recover middle Tennessee, he thought it best to eliminate Hood before doing anything else. Lincoln, for his part, confessed that Sherman's idea made him "anxious, if not actually fearful." But Sherman stuck to his guns. He could detach enough troops to protect Tennessee, he argued, and in any event the change of base could accomplish an important purpose in its own right. "If we can march a well-appointed army right through his territory," Sherman argued, "it is a demonstration to the world, foreign and domestic, that we have a power which [Confederate President Jefferson] Davis cannot resist. This may not be war but rather statesmanship; nevertheless it is overwhelming to my mind that there are thousands of people abroad and in the South who reason thus: if the North can march an army right through the South, it is proof positive that the North can prevail. . . ."

Eventually Grant approved Sherman's proposal. Sherman sent about 35,000 troops under General George Thomas to defend Tennessee, then abandoned Atlanta after destroying everything that might support the Confederate war effort. On November 15, advancing against almost no opposition, Sherman and 60,000 veterans began to carve a sixty-mile swath across Georgia. "[W]e had a gay old campaign," declared one of his men. "Destroyed all we could not eat, stole their niggers [sic], burned their cotton & gins, spilled their sorghum, burned & twisted their R. Roads and raised Hell generally."

By Christmas Eve 1864, Sherman had entered the city of Savannah on the Atlantic coast. In February 1865 he headed northward into the Carolinas, repeating on an even grander scale the pattern of his March to the Sea. Ultimately these marches, more than anything else, destroyed the Confederacy. They ruined Southern morale, smashed the remainder of the Confederate rail network, eliminated foodstuffs and war resources, and caused the desertion of thousands of Confederate soldiers who had resisted valiantly for years.

The Naval War, 1862–1865

Shortly after Sherman's army began its march northward into the Carolinas, a Union fleet appeared off Fort Fisher, North Carolina. This sprawling, improvised earthwork commanded the approaches to Wilmington, the last Confederate port open to blockade runners. When, on February 22, 1865, a combined landing party of 6,000 Federal soldiers and sailors successfully stormed the fort, it marked the culmination of a four-year naval campaign aimed at isolating the South from the outside world.

Until 1861, the U.S. Navy had played only a peripheral role in America's wars. During both the War for American Independence and the War of

1812, the Royal Navy had easily predominated; American naval contributions were confined to commerce raiding, a few single-ship encounters, and showing the flag in neutral ports. During the Civil War, however, the U.S. Navy for the first time bore a major strategic responsibility. Not only was it expected to control the open sea—a relatively simple task—it was also required to maintain a close blockade of the Confederate shore, to transport Union military might wherever it was needed, and to fight for control of the Confederate inland waters.

Since the American navy had never before faced such a task, it obviously had to improvise. But at least it had the advantage of existing when the war began. The Confederate navy also had to improvise, but more than that, it also had to create itself and devise a coherent mission under the immediate pressures of war. Although both sides did well with the resources available, the disparity in industrial might between North and South was never more lopsided than in the contest between the two navies. The North had an enormous advantage throughout the conflict. The South was never able to mount a serious challenge to Union seapower.

The Blockade

Sheer numbers convey something of the North's advantage. In April 1861 the Federal government possessed about ninety warships. By December 1864, under the outstanding leadership of Secretary of the Navy Gideon Welles, the North had expanded this total to 671 vessels, including 236 steam-powered ships constructed during the war. Although much of this new navy was used in riverine warfare and to track down commerce raiders, most of it went to enforce the Union blockade.

The blockade served two important functions. First, in economic terms it greatly reduced the South's access to outside markets, making the import and export of goods much more difficult. Second, diplomatically it helped reinforce a sense of the North's iron determination to crush the rebellion and caused European powers to think long and hard before recognizing the Confederacy. But maintaining the blockade was certainly a huge task. The rebellious states had a combined shoreline of roughly 3,000 miles, with 189 inlets and river mouths into which a blockade runner might dart. Blockade duty was dreary. Months might pass without action; during that time the main enemies were discomfort and boredom. One naval officer tried to give his mother some idea of the rigors of blockading duty: "[G]o to the roof on a hot summer day," he advised, "talk to a half-dozen degenerates, descend to the basement, drink tepid water full of iron rust, climb to the roof again, and repeat the process at intervals until [you are] fagged out, then go to bed with everything shut tight."

When a blockade runner was sighted, it enjoyed every advantage. Typically such a vessel would choose a moonless night to make its run, during which time its slate-gray hull would be nearly invisible. Swift and almost silent, the blockade runners would also burn smoke-free anthracite coal to heighten the difficulty of sighting them and would sometimes fire decoy signal flares to mislead the blockaders. Such tactics, coupled with an intimate knowledge of the shoal waters just outside the harbor entrances, resulted in a high rate of success. By one estimate, 84 percent of the runners that attempted the port of Wilmington made it through (1,735 out of 2,054), with a similar ratio prevailing along the rest of the Confederate coastline.

Some historians offer these figures as evidence of the blockade's ineffectiveness. Others, however, maintain that such statistics miss the point. The true measure of comparison, they maintain, should be difference in Southern sea trade before the war and during it. By this criterion the blockade was quite effective. Twenty thousand vessels cleared in or out of Southern ports in the years 1857–1860, compared with just 8,000 during the entire Civil War. Moreover, since blockade runners typically carried less cargo than an average merchantman, the wartime tonnage of goods imported or exported was probably less than one-third of the prewar figure.

That still leaves the question of the role played by the blockade in inflicting Confederate defeat. Here statistics have much less meaning. The issue turns, in part, on such intangibles as the blockade's impact on the Confederacy's morale. A more concrete way to look at the matter is to note the concern (or lack thereof) with which the Confederate government regarded the blockade. Certainly it never saw breaking the blockade as a priority (even if this were in its power, which it was not), and as late as 1864 the government required that only one-half the blockade runners' space be given over to military cargo. Then too, it is difficult to see what the Confederacy required that it could not produce. Food? It had plenty of that; the difficulty there lay in shipping local surpluses to points of need via the Confederacy's inadequate rolling stock. Arms and ammunition? The Confederacy, under the able leadership of ordnance czar Josiah Gorgas, managed to supply these wants to the end of the war.

Ultimately one must concede that the blockade was scarcely decisive in its own right. Still it did have an effect—not just in terms of reducing the South's volume of trade but also in terms of exacerbating high prices for consumer goods that helped fuel a ruinous inflation. But the Confederacy had enough territory to provide for its own needs—and did an ingenious job of exploiting its resources. Perhaps, then, the Union navy's most pronounced contribution to victory came in the support it gave the land forces.

Joint Operations and Riverine Warfare

Throughout the war the Union exploited its great superiority in sea power to throw troops ashore at various points along the Confederate coastline. These operations scarcely resembled the amphibious warfare of World War II, for in the great majority of cases they met little or no opposition directly on the beaches. It was much more usual for the troops to go ashore unopposed, establish a solid, fortified enclave, and only then advance inland. On only two important occasions during the conflict did troops try to fight their way ashore. The first, a Union night attack on Fort Sumter in September 1863, failed miserably. The second, against Fort Fisher in January 1865, was of course a success.

The relative dearth of opposed landings owed mainly to the fact that much of the Confederate coastline was undefended. The rebels maintained troops and artillery only at a few dozen key points. Thus it was easy for Union forces to find places to land without having to fight simply to get ashore. Their troubles came later, for although Union troops had little difficulty establishing a coastal enclave, they found it far more difficult to penetrate very far inland. For one thing, once the Union troops were ashore the Confederates knew exactly where they were and could dispatch sufficient troops to block them. The more important reason, however, was that there were almost never enough Union troops based along the coast to undertake offensive action.

Indeed, for most of the conflict the Lincoln administration neglected to use ocean-based sea power as a major instrument in the land war. McClellan's Peninsula Campaign appears to have permanently soured Lincoln, Stanton, and Halleck on this option. When Grant proposed in January 1864 that 60,000 troops be dispatched to occupied North Carolina, whence to raid the railroads that supplied Richmond, the administration vetoed the plan.

If one excepts the Peninsula Campaign—which functioned, in most respects, like a conventional land campaign—the most sustained joint operation of the war was the siege of Charleston, South Carolina. Although this campaign nominally began as early as November 1861, it did not start in earnest until April 1863, when a Union flotilla composed entirely of ironclads tried to bombard the Charleston forts into submission. The forts pummeled them instead, achieving over 400 direct hits—without, however, doing great injury to the heavily armored vessels. Then throughout the balance of 1863, the army and navy cooperated in a series of attacks upon the forts, but achieved limited success. The geography of Charleston harbor made it an extraordinarily difficult nut to crack. Both the entrance and the approach channel were narrow, so that Union warships had little room to maneuver, while forts protecting the harbor were themselves protected by salt marshes and swamps. Indeed the prolonged campaign was almost certainly a venture not worth the gain, except that Charleston had been the original cockpit of secession and many Northerners ached to see it destroyed. (The city fell only in February 1865, after Sherman's advancing army had cut its communications with the rest of the South.)

In contrast to the relatively limited cooperation between land forces and the bluewater navy, the army and brownwater navy worked hand-in-glove throughout the war. The two services cooperated effectively to reduce Forts Henry and Donelson, Island No. 10, Vicksburg, and a number of lesser Confederate fortresses in the Mississippi valley. Union naval control of the navigable rivers enabled land forces to supply themselves far from their main bases, and the riverine lines of communication proved much more difficult for rebels to disrupt than the highly vulnerable railroads. Moreover Federal gunboats could also interdict long stretches of these rivers, rendering it next to impossible for large Confederate forces to cross. This interdiction significantly impeded Southern mobility, particularly in terms of transferring units across the Mississippi River.

The most striking feature of the coastal and riverine war was the use made of ironclad vessels. When the war broke out the American navy possessed no armored ships of any kind; only Britain and France owned a few experimental ironclads. The Confederacy, however, soon began to construct an ironclad using the hull of the captured frigate USS *Merrimack*, partially scuttled when the Federals abandoned the Norfolk Navy Yard in April 1861. Rechristened the CSS *Virginia*, the new ironclad rode so low in the water that it resembled the roof of a floating barn. It mounted ten 11-inch cannon and, in a throwback to the days of galleys, an iron ram on the bow below the waterline.

Designed to break the Union blockade and protect the James River estuary, the *Virginia* briefly struck terror in Union hearts. During its maiden voyage on March 8, 1862, it steamed from Norfolk into Hampton Roads, rammed one Union frigate, destroyed another with gunfire, and ran a third warship aground before retiring for the night. The next day it steamed forth to wreak further havoc, only to be confronted by an oddly shaped vessel that looked exactly like a cheesebox on a raft. It was in fact the USS *Monitor*, the North's answer to the *Virginia* and a remarkable answer at that. Created by the brilliant naval designer John Ericsson, the heavily armored *Monitor* boasted no fewer than forty patentable inventions, most prominently a rotating turret (the "cheesebox") that mounted two 11-inch smoothbore cannon

In March 1862, the USS *Monitor* clashed with the CSS *Virginia* at Hampton Roads, Virginia, in the world's first battle between ironclad warships. Although the combat ended in a draw, the *Monitor* caused the *Virginia* to return to port, thereby saving Union wooden warships in the area from further damage.

and could fire in any direction. Built in just one hundred days, the Union ironclad managed to wallow down from New York City just in time to save the fleet in Hampton Roads from complete disaster. In a two-hour battle on March 9, the two revolutionary vessels pumped shot after shot at one another, only to see the heavy cannon balls merely dent the enemy's armor and ricochet into the sea. Neither ship was seriously hurt, although the *Virginia* eventually broke off the action and withdrew into Norfolk harbor. Two months later it was scuttled to prevent capture when the Confederates withdrew from the area. (The *Monitor* eventually sank in heavy seas in December 1862.)

Both the *Virginia* and the *Monitor* served as prototypes for further armored vessels. The South ultimately built twenty-one ironclads (and laid the keels for twenty-nine more), mostly patterned after the *Virginia*. The North, which constructed fifty-eight ironclads, tried several designs but concentrated on vessels patterned after the *Monitor*. Every one of these ships was intended either for coastal defense or attack; none fought in the open ocean. Together they confirmed a major technological shift in naval warfare. As the London *Times* remarked shortly after the fight at Hampton Roads, the British navy had suddenly dropped from having 149 first-class warships to exactly two, its twin experimental ironclads. Apart from those two, "[t]here is not now a ship in the English navy . . . that it would not be madness to trust in an engagement with that little *Monitor*."

Commerce Raiders

In addition to its ironclads, the South also built, or purchased, a number of commerce raiders, the perennial resort of weaker maritime powers. It tried privateers as well—privately owned vessels given "letters of marque" and permitted to attack enemy shipping. In older times privateering was a lucrative business, but most European powers had officially disowned the practice by the mid-nineteenth century, and would-be privateers found it too difficult to bring captured prizes into Southern ports. Thus the Confederacy had to use warships manned by regular naval crews and designed primarily to destroy, not capture, enemy merchantmen.

The South deployed only a relative handful of commerce raiders, but they achieved great notoriety and in some respects great effectiveness. They sank a large number of Union merchantmen, forced hundreds more to seek refuge by reregistering under neutral flags, and sent insurance premiums soaring. The CSS *Shenandoah* managed to cripple the New England whaling fleet in the Bering Sea—it did this, incidentally, in June 1865, unaware that the war was over—but the greatest rebel sea raider was the CSS *Alabama*, commanded by the rakish Captain Raphael Semmes.

Like many Confederate commerce raiders, the *Alabama* was built in England, having been covertly commissioned by the tireless Confederate agent, James Bulloch. (Bulloch also tried to get British shipyards to build several ironclads as well, but Her Majesty's government eventually blocked the attempt.) The warship mounted eight guns and could make better than

Although the Confederacy could not begin to match the Union's naval might, it still managed to deploy a number of commerce raiders, including the CSS *Nashville*, shown here burning a captured Northern merchant vessel.

thirteen knots under steam. In its twenty-two-month voyage it destroyed a total of sixty-eight Union vessels—without, however, injuring the crews. Instead the rebel sailors (many of them actually British subjects) boarded the enemy merchantmen, removed whatever they wanted, and took their seamen prisoner. Only then would the enemy vessels be burned or blown up. When the *Alabama* grew too overcrowded with reluctant guests, Semmes would designate the next captured merchantman a "cartel ship," place the prisoners aboard, and let them sail to the nearest port. In that way he accomplished his mission without bloodshed.

The *Alabama* continued its colorful career until June 1864, when the Union frigate USS *Kearsage* cornered the raider while it was in a French harbor for repairs. The *Kearsage* hovered outside the entrance to the port, barring escape. The *Alabama* gamely came forth to do battle, but in a spirited one-hour engagement the Confederate vessel was sunk. Semmes himself went over the side, was picked up by a yacht filled with admiring sightseers, and thus eluded capture.

The commerce raiders exerted a surprising influence on subsequent naval policy. After the war the American navy regarded them as a vindication of its historic emphasis on raiding as opposed to major fleet actions. Despite his own wartime experience with ironclads, Admiral David Dixon Porter led the U.S. Navy throughout the 1870s in its continuing rejection of a battle-fleet orientation. "[O]ne vessel like the *Alabama* roaming the ocean, sinking and destroying," he wrote, "would do more to bring about peace than a dozen unwieldy iron-clads. . . ." Some European navies concurred. Inspired in part by the exploits of Confederate raiders, many French and Italian navalists touted a maritime strategy that emphasized coastal defense and commerce destruction. In any event, not until the 1890s would the United States move decisively toward a naval strategy based unequivocally on the battleship and command of the sea.

All in all, the naval conflict remained a constant and indispensable feature of the Civil War. But the two contending forces compiled very different records. Stephen R. Mallory, the South's highly capable secretary of the navy, certainly did a superb job of creating a navy, yet it must be questioned whether this navy managed to achieve results commensurate even with the relatively slender resources expended on it. The ironclad program produced a number of formidable vessels but usually failed to prevent Union warships from capturing a Southern port when they mounted a major effort to do so. Land fortifications, not armored vessels, seemed the most effective way to defend Southern harbors. The commerce raiders, for their part, did considerable damage but never enough even to deflate the North's will to continue the war. Considering the vast amount of commerce carried by Northern ships, Southern raiders were really little more than a nuisance.

By contrast, the Union navy played a major role in defeating the Confederacy. Union blockaders sharply curtailed the amount of Confederate shipping and may have contributed to a decline in Southern morale. Union gunboats and ironclads vied with their rebel counterparts for control of Southern rivers, sounds, and ports. The Union naval contribution richly deserved Lincoln's wry compliment to Federal seamen in 1863: "At all the watery margins they have been present. Not only on the deep blue sea, the broad bay, the rapid river, but also up the narrow muddy bayou, and wherever the ground was a little damp, they have made their tracks."

The War Ends

Sherman's marches were only the largest of many Union raids that characterized the final six months of the conflict. The Federals, in essence, had abandoned any attempt to hold Southern territory. Instead they simply ravaged it, destroying anything of military use and in the process convincing thousands of white Southerners that the Confederate government could not protect them. The Davis administration, meanwhile, grew increasingly out of touch with the darkening strategic picture. Instead, in the autumn of 1864, Davis made an energetic circuit of the Deep South and argued that if the Southern people would only redouble their efforts, the Confederacy might yet plant its banners on the banks of the Ohio. This visionary thinking actually produced one of the strangest campaigns of the war, Hood's disastrous invasion of Tennessee.

Franklin and Nashville

Conceived in early October 1864, Hood's operation had two main purposes. Strategically it was supposed to recover middle Tennessee and cut off Sherman from the North; Hood even fantasized that he might eventually combine with Lee's army and overwhelm Grant. Politically it was intended to bolster flagging Southern morale; Jefferson Davis hinted on several occasions that Hood's thrust might reach as far as the Ohio River. The fulfillment of either objective was clearly well beyond the reach of Confederate resources.

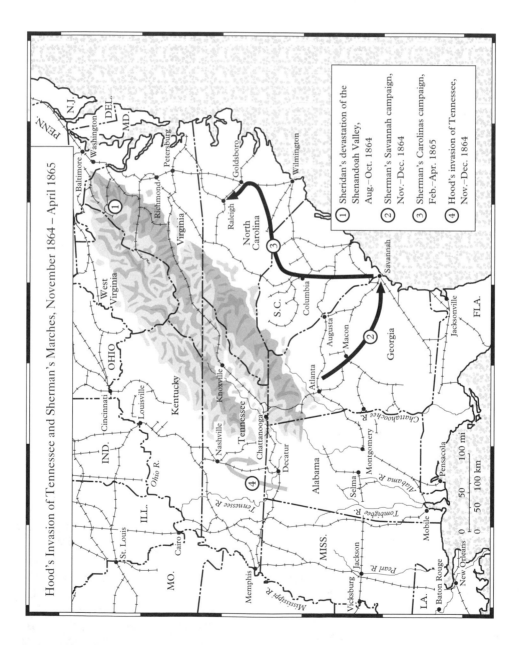

Hood's Invasion of Tennessee and Sherman's Marches, November 1864 – April 1865

① Sheridan's devastation of the Shenandoah Valley, Aug.–Oct. 1864

② Sherman's Savannah campaign, Nov.–Dec. 1864

③ Sherman's Carolinas campaign, Feb.–Apr. 1865

④ Hood's invasion of Tennessee, Nov.–Dec. 1864

For one thing, Hood lacked anywhere near enough troops to do the job. For another, he was not able to begin his campaign until mid-November, by which time his well-advertised invasion had brought thousands of Union troops into position to oppose him.

Even so, the Tennessee gambit gave the Union high command a fairly acute case of heartburn. Grant fretted that Hood's eccentric expedition might somehow disrupt his otherwise promising plans to finish off the Confederacy. Thomas, the Federal commander tapped to oppose Hood, believed the quality of Hood's veterans much superior to that of his own men, many of whom were either recently enlisted or garrison troops with little combat experience. (Thousands of his own veterans had either left the service by this time or had been retained by Sherman for his march to the sea.) Grant wanted Hood stopped as quickly as possible, before he had time to do mischief. Thomas, on the other hand, considered it best simply to delay Hood while he gathered his disparate forces into some kind of cohesive whole.

As a result, Thomas concentrated most of his troops at Nashville. In the meantime he sent Major General John M. Schofield, with 28,000 troops, to delay the Confederate advance. Hood managed to make an end run around Schofield's flank and came close to gobbling up the entire Union force. But somehow his army failed to strike Schofield, and the Federals retreated intact to Franklin, about thirty miles south of Nashville. There Hood caught up with them. Although the obvious move was to turn Schofield's flank again, Hood—enraged by his army's failure—ordered a frontal assault on November 30. In a larger and even more disastrous attack than Pickett's Charge at Gettysburg, 18,000 Confederates lunged into the teeth of Union field entrenchments, artillery, and rapid-fire carbines. More than half of them became casualties. Five Confederate generals lay among the dead.

The Battle of Franklin shattered whatever offensive potential Hood's army retained. Now reduced to about 30,000 men, its remnants continued to the outskirts of Nashville, which after thirty-one months of Union occupation was one of the most heavily fortified places on earth. Behind the scowling entrenchments were about 70,000 Federal troops. Though Hood made a feeble show at "besieging" the city, he had no chance for success.

Despite his formidable numerical advantage, Thomas delayed two full weeks before delivering the counterstroke, largely because of a major ice storm. But on December 15 the weather broke and Thomas attacked. After effectively deceiving Hood about the location of his main thrust, Thomas executed a massive flank attack that by nightfall overwhelmed the Confederate left. The following morning he put Hood's entire army to flight. On both days, massed Federal cavalry played a pivotal role in providing the speed and power necessary to achieve success and pursued Hood tirelessly for several days afterward. Although the casualties were not especially high—the Union forces lost about 3,000 men, the Confederates about 7,000 (three-fourths of them captured)—the Army of Tennessee practically went out of existence, leaving Lee's army as the Confederacy's only substantial remaining military force.

In March 1865, Lincoln met with Sherman, Grant, and Admiral David D. Porter aboard the USS *River Queen* to discuss the closing operations against the Confederacy. Here the president listens as Sherman recounts his destructive marches through Georgia and the Carolinas.

The Collapse of the Confederacy

In the waning months of the war, large columns of swiftly moving Union horsemen slashed through the Confederacy almost at will, crippling what remained of its railroad grid, burning war factories, and spreading despair among the Southern population. Meanwhile the Army of the Potomac patiently maintained its siege of Petersburg. As the long months passed, Grant extended his lines steadily to the west, never quite able to get around Lee's flank but forcing the Confederates to stretch their lines to the breaking point. In March 1865, Sheridan came from the Shenandoah Valley with most of his cavalry. Grant gave him an infantry corps and told him to break Lee's western flank. On April 1, in the Battle of Five Forks, Sheridan did exactly that. As soon as he learned of the victory, Grant ordered a general attack all along the Petersburg front. This final assault forced Lee to abandon the city, which fell on April 3. Union troops entered Richmond the same day.

Lee had only one move remaining: he could try to get his army—now reduced to barely 50,000 men—into central North Carolina, where Joseph E. Johnston with 20,000 troops was fruitlessly attempting to halt Sherman's advance north from Savannah. Grant understood this perfectly, and as he placed the Army of the Potomac in pursuit he made certain that Sheridan's cavalry thwarted every attempt by Lee to turn southward. As a result, Lee was forced to retreat to the west, hoping to reach a Confederate supply dump at Lynchburg, reprovision his famished men, and then somehow get into North Carolina.

On April 6 Union forces caught up with Lee's rear guard and destroyed it, capturing 6,000 prisoners. The following day Grant sent Lee a summons to surrender. Lee declined, but by the evening of April 8, Sheridan managed to get ahead of the beleaguered Confederate army and cut off its retreat. After one last effort to open an escape route—valiantly made but easily repulsed—Lee felt he had no choice but to surrender. On April 9, 1865, Palm Sunday, he requested a conference with Grant. The two commanders met at Appomattox Court House, a small village about eighty miles west of Richmond. There, in the parlor of a modest two-story home, Lee surrendered the Army of Northern Virginia. Early that evening, as word of the surrender spread like wildfire and Union soldiers began to cheer and touch off cannon in salutes to the victory, Grant told his staff officers to put a stop to the celebrations at once. "The war is over," he told them. "The Rebels are our countrymen again."

Although magnanimous, Grant's declaration was also premature. Some rebels continued to resist, among them Jefferson Davis. Not yet ready to submit, Davis had told the Southern people on April 4 that the war had merely entered a "new phase": "Relieved from the necessity of guarding cities and particular points, . . . with our army free to move from point to point, and strike in detail the detachments and garrisons of the enemy, . . . nothing is now needed to render our triumph certain, but the exhibition of our own unquenchable resolve. Let us but will it, and we are free."

Davis and his cabinet fled Richmond and established a new temporary capital at Danville, Virginia. Then, on the afternoon of April 10, he learned that Lee had surrendered at Appomattox Court House the previous day. The news, wrote Secretary of the Navy Stephen Mallory, "fell upon the ears of all like a firebell in the night." Later that evening, Davis and his cabinet left by train for Greensboro, North Carolina. Their famous "flight into oblivion" had begun.

Still determined, Davis met with Beauregard and Johnston and told them that the army could be fleshed out by gathering conscripts and deserters. Both men found this suggestion utterly devoid of realism; in a second meeting the next day, Johnston bluntly informed Davis that "it would be the greatest of human crimes for us to attempt to continue the war." After a prolonged silence, Davis asked for Beauregard's opinion. Beauregard basically agreed with Johnston; so, it turned out, did most of those present.

Afterward the discussion turned to the question of possible surrender terms. Davis still seemed not to grasp the enormity of the occasion, for the terms he suggested substantially failed to acknowledge that the South had lost the war. Realizing that the Federals would not treat with him, however, he authorized Johnston to carry out the negotiations. Yet even so, he obviously thought the contest could be continued and asked Johnston to give his favored line of retreat so that supplies could be stockpiled along the route. The hopelessness of the situation became apparent, however, when a dispatch from Lee arrived, officially announcing his surrender. Until that moment, Davis had seemed at ease and confident. But after reading it, he passed it along and "silently wept bitter tears."

While Johnston opened negotiations with Sherman, Davis and his cabinet made preparations to continue their flight. The president had a vague idea of making it to Alabama, where Confederate troops remained in the field, or possibly to the trans-Mississippi; but his cabinet members were more concerned with getting him safely out of the country. On May 10, 1865, Federal horsemen captured Jefferson Davis near Irwinville, Georgia, about fifty miles from the Florida state line. After a few days he was incarcerated at Fort Monroe, Virginia, where he spent the next two years.

By that time, Johnston had capitulated to Sherman and General Richard Taylor had surrendered most of the remaining Confederate troops east of the Mississippi. On May 26, the last Southern troops laid down their arms when General Edmund Kirby Smith, commanding the trans-Mississippi theater, surrendered his department. The Civil War was over.

The Legacy of the War

In terms of its impact on the United States, the Civil War remains the pivotal episode in American history. Like the near-contemporaneous wars of Italian and German unification, the American conflict took a fairly loose gathering of states and welded them into a nation. Politically it destroyed the concept of extreme states' rights and established the principle that the Union was perpetual. Its impact on American society was no less great. Not only did it result in the emancipation of 3.5 million African-Americans, it also ensured that thenceforward the mainstream of American civilization would be the industrial North, not the agrarian South.

Its significance in the history of warfare was no less great. Even more than the campaigns at the end of the Napoleonic Wars, the Civil War displayed the ascendancy of the defense over the offense, the inability of armies to destroy one another in battle, and the corresponding need to think in terms of a strategy of exhaustion or attrition rather than annihilation. The increased size of armies accounted for part of their enhanced resiliency; so too did the use of the corps, which enabled separate army wings to fight effectively on their own until reinforcements could come to their assistance. Only when Civil War armies allowed themselves to be surrounded and besieged (as at Vicksburg), or when they had previously exhausted themselves through prolonged offensives (as at Nashville) did it prove possible to destroy them.

A second important feature of the conflict was such sociopolitical factors as mass armies, conscription, and the mobilization of entire societies for war. The wars of the French Revolution and Napoleon had also witnessed these developments, but the Civil War carried them to a higher pitch, perhaps because both the Union and the Confederacy were among the most political societies then on earth. Both Northern and Southern soldiers were motivated in no small measure by strongly held beliefs about the causes for which they were fighting. The Western world had seen something like this during the wars of the American and French revolutions and, more recently, the struggles for Greek and Italian liberation. Otherwise one would have to reach back into the sixteenth- and seventeenth-century wars of religion for a parallel.

Third, the Civil War also saw the harnessing of the Industrial Revolution to the emergent forces of popular sovereignty and nationalism. New technologies played an enormous role in the conflict: railroads, rifles, and the telegraph, not to mention such naval innovations as turret-firing guns, iron-clad warships, and so on. Both the Union and the Confederacy worked diligently to exploit their industrial resources to the fullest; the North in particular evolved effective ways to organize and distribute their industrial output to armies in the field. The U.S. Military Railroads under Brigadier General Daniel C. McCallum, for example, achieved a record of energy and efficiency that any European army would have envied.

The Civil War also witnessed the great marches of destruction undertaken by Union forces during the war's final years and highly reminiscent of the English during the Hundred Years' War, numerous armies during the Thirty Years' War, and the French in 1688–1689. Often mistaken for an anticipation of twentieth-century strategic bombing, the Union raids against Southern war resources had much stronger continuities with past experience. The chief difference was that whereas the soldiers of the *ancien régime* in Europe had inflicted much indiscriminate mayhem, the greater political and moral awareness of the Civil War soldier—still thoroughly rooted in the ethical norms of his community—meant that Union armies conducted their attacks on Southern war resources with much greater discrimination. Depredations occurred, but wholesale killing of Southern civilians certainly did not. Private homes were rarely destroyed except in retaliation for guerrilla activity, and rapes—at least of white women—were uncommon. A much larger number of African-American women were assaulted and sexually abused. Taken together, the extensive mobilization of Northern and Southern societies, coupled with the large-scale union attacks on Southern crops and war resources, marked the first appearance of the total war dynamic that would become a pronounced characteristic of many twentieth-century struggles.

Finally, a word is in order about the strategic and operational conduct of the war. In general its quality, on both sides, was quite high. Both governments responded intelligently to the nature of the conflict and adopted realistic strategies. Of the two commanders-in-chief, Lincoln was clearly more able than Jefferson Davis, but then Lincoln was probably one of the three or four greatest statesmen of the past two centuries. Union and Confederate generalship was about equal. If the South had Lee and Jackson, it also had Bragg and Pemberton. Similarly, such lackluster Northern commanders as McClellan and Burnside were more than offset by Grant, Sherman, and Sheridan. Both sides fought according to the Napoleonic model, but both learned to adapt to the rather different logistical conditions of warfare in the vast, largely rural South. Each side eventually grasped the greatly changed tactical environment created by the rifled musket, and each made extensive use of field fortifications. This sound defensive solution, however, was not matched by an equivalent solution on the offensive. Both armies, despite scattered experiments with more open formations and tactics, continued to rely heavily on the traditional, practically shoulder-to-shoulder battle line.

Ultimately, however, the harsh realities of the Civil War battlefield did give a major impetus to the increasing professionalism of officers. It was obvious that largely untrained citizen-officers could not adequately cope with the demands of mid-nineteenth-century warfare, nor could regular officers whose imaginations were geared to skirmishing with Native American war parties. Deeply impressed by the failures of Civil War officership and the attendant waste of manpower, military reformers like Lieutenant Colonel Emory Upton waged a passionate crusade in favor of better professional education and standards. Upton's peers and disciples studied European armies, lobbied for advanced military schools and war colleges, and attempted to drag the United States Army thoroughly into the modern industrialized age. Although it required decades to complete, the result was a new cycle of military reform that prepared American armed forces, albeit imperfectly, to meet the challenges of a violent new century.

SUGGESTED READINGS

Barrett, John G. *Sherman's March Through the Carolinas* (Chapel Hill: University of North Carolina Press, 1956).

Beringer, Richard E., et al. *Why the South Lost the Civil War* (Athens: University of Georgia Press, 1986).

Castel, Albert. *Decision in the West: The Atlanta Campaign, 1864* (Lawrence: University Press of Kansas, 1992).

Catton, Bruce. *Grant Takes Command* (Boston: Little, Brown, 1969).

———. *A Stillness at Appomattox* (New York: Doubleday, 1952).

Donald, David H., ed. *Why the North Won the Civil War* (Baton Rouge: Louisiana State University Press, 1962).

Fowler, William M. *Under Two Flags: The American Navy in the Civil War* (New York: Norton, 1990).

Glatthaar, Joseph T. *The March to the Sea and Beyond: Sherman's Troops in the Savannah and Carolinas Campaigns* (New York: New York University Press, 1985).

Horn, Stanley F. *The Decisive Battle of Nashville* (Baton Rouge: Louisiana State University Press, 1956).

Marszalek, John F. *Sherman: A Soldier's Passion for Order* (New York: Free Press, 1992).

Matter, William D. *"If It Takes All Summer": The Battle of Spotsylvania* (Chapel Hill: University of North Carolina Press, 1988).

Reed, Rowena. *Combined Operations in the Civil War* (Annapolis: Naval Institute Press, 1978).

Rhea, Gordon C. *The Battle of the Wilderness, May 5–6, 1864* (Chapel Hill: University of North Carolina Press, 1994).

Still, William N., Jr. *Iron Afloat: The Story of the Confederate Armorclads* (Baton Rouge: Louisiana State University Press, 1970).

Sword, Wiley. *Embrace An Angry Wind: The Confederacy's Last Hurrah: Spring Hill, Franklin, and Nashville* (New York: HarperCollins, 1992).

Trudeau, Noah Andre. *Bloody Roads South: The Wilderness to Cold Harbor, May–June, 1864* (Boston: Little, Brown, 1989).

———. *The Last Citadel: Petersburg, Virginia, June 1864–April 1865* (Boston: Little, Brown, 1991).

———. *Out of the Storm: The End of the Civil War, April–June 1865* (Boston: Little, Brown, 1994).

Wert, Jeffry D. *From Winchester to Cedar Creek: The Shenandoah Campaign of 1864* (Carlisle, Penn.: South Mountain Press, 1987).

Wise, Steven A. *Lifeline of the Confederacy: The Blockade Runners* (Columbia: University of South Carolina Press, 1987).

8

MAKING WAR MORE LETHAL, 1871–1914

New Technologies,
Institutions, and Ideas

Small Wars and Regional
Wars Before 1914: Mixing
the Old and the New

              The wars of the late nineteenth century shattered the hopes of those who believed that the world was entering an era of enduring peace. Instead of peace, the Western world experienced increased tension and heightened nationalism and endured a wave of "new imperialism." As Western states added to their territorial possessions, particularly in Africa and Asia, industrial production increased, and numerous technological advances occurred. At the same time, the powers of central governments expanded, and more resources became available to the military. Important changes also occurred in the methods, organizations, and equipment for waging war. Of the many changes taking place in the military in the late nineteenth century, some of the most important stemmed from the introduction of much more effective and lethal weapons. Advances in artillery, rifles, and machine guns profoundly affected the waging of war on land, while improvements in naval technology and design—particularly the introduction of the HMS *Dreadnought*—made the older battleships of the world's fleets obsolete. Other changes came from improved military organizations. As recognition of the expanding scope of war became apparent, some nations attempted to copy the example of the Prussians in the fielding and employment of mass armies and in the functioning of a general staff. New ideas—such as those of Captain Alfred Thayer Mahan on the importance of sea power—also had an effect. By 1914, the world's armies and navies bore little resemblance to those of 1815.

        The decades before World War I did not include a war between two of the major Western powers, but numerous conflicts did occur as regional wars broke out and as the Western powers used their military advantages to expand their control over the globe. Between 1800 and 1914 they expanded their global empires from about 35 percent of the world's land surface to about 84 percent. Among the conflicts occurring before World War I, the Spanish-American War of 1898, the Boer War of 1898, and the Russo-Japanese War of 1904–1905 tested and demonstrated new methods of waging war across a broad spectrum of conflict. The victory of the Japanese over the Russians, however, signaled the eventual end of the Western monopoly over the new methods. That same war also provided hints about the future scale and destructiveness of the two world wars of the twentieth century.

New Technologies, Institutions, and Ideas

Throughout the nineteenth century, the effects of the industrial revolution profoundly influenced the waging of war. Important technological advances began to affect military weapons and equipment and eventually altered the way in which wars were fought. In the latter part of the century, steam power replaced sails on the oceans. At the same time, the Bessemer process permitted the making of cheap steel, and chemists produced powerful new explosives. Along with the technological advances came substantial increases in population. In Europe alone, the population went from about 266 million in 1850 to about 401 million in 1900. With industries capable of producing massive amounts of advanced weapons and ammunition, with countries having many more citizens available for military service, and with steam locomotives and ships capable of moving huge quantities of men and equipment, the wars of the late nineteenth century assumed new dimensions in scale and lethality.

One of the most incisive observers of these changes was Ivan S. Bloch, a Polish banker and railway magnate. In 1897–1898 he published an elaborate, multivolume treatise on modern warfare, *The Future of War in its Technical, Economic, and Political Relations.* Bloch recognized that the character of war had changed as many nations had passed from agricultural into industrial societies. Believing that war had become "impossible, except at the price of suicide," Bloch argued that technological advances had transformed war into an endless cycle of attrition and had made warring nations vulnerable to social upheaval. He warned of the dangers of unparalleled slaughter and noted:

> The outward and visible sign of the end of war was the introduction of the magazine rifle, . . . smokeless powder, . . . the quick-firing gun, . . . and higher explosives. . . . The first thing every man will have to do . . . will be to dig a hole in the ground, and throw up as strong an earthen rampart as he can to shield him from the hail of bullets. . . . When you must dig a trench before you can make any advance, your progress is necessarily slow. Battles will last for

days, and at the end it is very doubtful whether any decisive victory
can be gained.

In most countries, the military ignored the warnings of Bloch, who was not
a professional soldier and whose emphasis on the destructiveness of war
aroused strong pacifist sentiments. Most armies and navies experimented
with new technologies and ideas and adopted new weapons and methods,
but almost none recognized the extent of the profound changes occurring
in warfare.

Smokeless Powder

Most of the new weapons introduced in the decades before World War I cap-
italized on the perfection of a noncorrosive smokeless powder that gave its
user significant tactical advantages. In the 1860s a smokeless powder was
introduced, but it was often unstable and dangerous in storage. Then in
1884 a French chemist, Paul M. E. Vieille, invented a safer, more powerful,
and more stable powder. By primarily producing gases and almost no solid
byproducts, the new powder eliminated the cloud of smoke that accompanied the firing of black powder, enabling soldiers to see and fire more effectively. It also allowed soldiers to conceal their firing position from the
enemy. The clouds of smoke from burning black powder, which had been a
conspicuous feature of previous battles, all but disappeared.

The smokeless powder had other important technical advantages.
As a clean-burning propellant, it left the firing mechanism and bore of a
weapon relatively clear of the residue that had plagued weapons using black
powder. In contrast to the extremely rapid burning of black powder, the
new powder burned more evenly and produced a prolonged power impulse
with a relatively low chamber pressure. This yielded greater range and penetrating power. The introduction of smokeless powder proved to be one of
the most important steps in the wave of innovations occurring at the end of
the nineteenth century.

Advances in weapons at the end of the nineteenth century, however,
depended on improvements other than the introduction of smokeless powder. For example, after the development of picric acid as a high explosive
(also known as mélinite or lyddite) in the late 1880s, the military began
using it as a bursting charge in shells. During the next two decades, TNT
(or, trinitrotoluene) replaced picric acid in artillery shells, thereby increasing
the bursting power of shells more than twenty times over the pre-picric acid
versions. Additionally, the development of better and more dependable steel
was particularly significant, for it enabled technicians to improve the design
of weapons. The result was lighter weapons with greater lethality, longer
ranges, better accuracy, and vastly greater rates of fire.

Artillery

Significant changes in the technical characteristics and role of artillery occurred at the end of the nineteenth century. Instead of projectiles following

a fairly flat trajectory, they began following a high, round trajectory; and instead of batteries firing from positions alongside the infantry, they began firing from behind it. The major changes in artillery began in the middle of the nineteenth century. Although the Germans used steel breech-loading cannon in the Franco-Prussian War, the guns lacked a recoil mechanism and thus had to be pushed forward and relaid after each firing. After firing, a gun could roll backwards for several yards depending on its size and the force of the propelling charge. By the end of the nineteenth century most cannon had a recoil mechanism that absorbed much of the shock from firing and that permitted repeated firings without having to relay the piece.

The perfection of a recoil system using a hydrostatic buffer and recuperator system enabled the French to build their first 75-mm field gun in 1893 and adopt it as standard in 1897. This extremely light and highly mobile piece became the first of many "quick-firing" guns. Since the gun recoiled into its cradle, the breech could be easily opened and the gun reloaded and fired in a matter of seconds. Though the standard rate of fire was six rounds per minute, a much higher rate of twenty rounds per minute could be attained in an emergency. The introduction of the French 75-mm gun soon forced most armies to spend vast sums modernizing their artillery.

Although the French remained content with their revolutionary 75-mm gun and neglected the development of heavier, longer-range artillery, the Germans recognized the need for heavy artillery. Before 1870 the Krupp steel-making firm had prodded the German military into capitalizing on the use of steel in making breech-loading artillery; and in the late 1870s the firm gave several spectacular demonstrations on the capabilities of extremely large artillery pieces. For a time the German navy took more advantage of the large Krupp pieces than did the army, but after carefully studying the Russo-Japanese War of 1904–1905 and observing the vulnerability of guns in the open, the German army increased its heavy artillery in its divisions, corps, and field armies. By 1914, the possession of this heavy artillery and its long-range and plunging fire gave the Germans an advantage over most other armies.

Machine Guns

As artillery was shifted from a short-range, direct-fire role to a longer-range, indirect-fire role, the machine gun began providing close-range fire support for the infantry. Just as the French failed to recognize the potential of the *mitrailleuse* in 1870, however, most armies failed to recognize the potential of the machine gun and eventually entered World War I with only a small number in each infantry division. Before 1914, most military leaders had reservations about the reliability and utility of the awkward, heavy weapons. Prior to 1884, machine guns depended on some sort of external power source, such as the hand-cranking motion required to fire the Gatling gun. When the American Hiram S. Maxim produced the first self-powered machine gun in the spring of 1884, the weapon became truly automatic for the first time.

Actuated by the recoil that came from the firing of the shell, the new gun attained a rate of fire of over 600 rounds per minute.

One of the first nations to recognize the potential of the machine gun was Russia. After testing two Gatling guns in 1865, the Russians ordered more than one hundred and then began manufacturing their own. By the time of the Russo-Turkish War of 1877–1878, they had over 400 Gatling guns and used them extensively in that war. By the time of the Russo-Japanese War of 1904–1905, each Russian division had its own machine-gun company. The Japanese were not as enthusiastic about the new weapon, but its use by the Russians convinced them of its value and they too soon supplied each of their divisions with twenty-four machine guns.

By 1914, most armies had supplied their infantry divisions with machine guns and often organized them into separate companies or batteries, rather than integrating them into regiments or battalions. Though not completely portable, the new weapons were much more mobile than the older ones. In 1912, for example, the British adopted the new Vickers Maxim, which was water-cooled but weighed only thirty-eight pounds, significantly lighter than the sixty pounds of the older model. The Vickers was Britain's principal heavy machine gun in both world wars.

At the beginning of World War I, each British, French and German infantry battalion had two heavy machine guns. By the end of 1918, British and German battalions had about fifty light and heavy machine guns, while French battalions had about forty. This dramatic increase clearly illustrates how battlefield experience overcame the reservations most armies had about machine guns.

Gatling guns at their Washington trials, May 6, 1866. Dr. Richard Gatling invented the gun, which consisted of rifled barrels revolving around a central fixed axis. Hiram S. Maxim's automatic machine gun soon made the Gatling gun obsolete.

Rifles

Even though breech-loading, bolt-action rifles were used in the Franco-Prussian War, the introduction of smokeless powder, adoption of magazines, and perfection of metallic cartridges greatly improved the rifle before 1914. The first widely used European breechloader was the Prussian needle gun, which used paper cartridges and a bolt. Its design provided the basis for future improvements. In 1871, a German, Peter Paul Mauser, introduced one of the first successful metallic-cartridge, bolt-action rifles. The next fifteen years saw other important advances. One of the most significant improvements came with the introduction of magazines that increased a rifle's rate of fire. Instead of a soldier having to load each round awkwardly by hand, magazines enabled him to load another round by simply opening the bolt and then pushing it forward. In 1885, an Austrian inventor, Ferdinand Ritter von Mannlicher, introduced the clip-loading magazine system that soon became a common feature on many modern rifles.

After the French in 1886 adopted the Lebel rifle, which used smokeless powder, most states recognized the need to improve their rifles. By the early 1890s, every major army in the world—except the United States—had adopted bolt-action, magazine-fed rifles that used smokeless powder. In 1893, after a decade of tedious testing, the U.S. Army finally adopted its first general-issue magazine rifle, the .30-caliber, 5-shot Krag-Jorgensen. Named for its Scandinavian designers, the bolt-action rifle used smokeless powder and rivaled in range and accuracy most European rifles of its time. Despite the sturdiness of the "Krag," the Spanish-American War revealed it was not as good as the Spanish Mauser, and in 1903 the United States adopted the bolt-action Springfield, which quickly earned a reputation for excellence and reliability.

Improvements in weapons were not the only technological advances that affected the waging of war. As the telegraph and telephone became more common, commanders no longer had to rely solely on messengers or semaphores to communicate. Decades would pass, however, before reliable wireless telegraphy became commonplace. Despite the wave of new weapons that began to appear at the end of the nineteenth century, most armies made only moderate changes in their methods at the beginning of the twentieth century and did not make more extensive changes until after August 1914. Most remained content with incremental rather than radical change.

The Example of the Prussian System

While technological advances exercised great influence over the waging of war, changes in the social and political structures of Western states expanded the scale and scope of modern war throughout the nineteenth century. At the same time, the expanding influence of governments over the lives of their citizens contributed to a greater reliance on mass armies. As governments grappled at the end of the nineteenth century with the complexities of organizing and fielding mass armies, intense debates occurred over the question of creating more modern military systems and a more professional corps of officers.

After Germany's quick victories over the Austrian Empire and France in 1866 and 1871, most states attempted to copy or at least borrow from the Germans. Every major power studied the German system of mobilizing and fielding a mass army as well as their system of higher military education. Military leaders recognized that the German general staff provided new levels of expertise and effectiveness to military administration. Some even credited the Germans with having achieved a revolution in military organization.

In the years following the Franco-Prussian War, the German general staff expanded greatly in influence and size, increasing from 64 in 1857, to 135 in 1871, to 239 in 1888, to 625 in 1914. At the *Kriegsakademie*, technical studies were completely under the control of the general staff. Similarly, its influence over the railway system increased as intricate plans for the mobilization and concentration of armies were completed. Another important step in its growing influence occurred in 1883, when the chief of the general staff received permission to have direct access to the kaiser, even in peacetime. The wine-red stripe on the collar and trousers of the uniform of the general staff officers became a symbol not only for the highest standards of competence and professionalism, but also of an elite and highly influential group.

After the Franco-Prussian War, Great Britain finally initiated long-overdue reforms to overcome weaknesses that had become apparent in the Crimean War. These reforms are normally associated with the name of Edward Cardwell, the secretary of war, and included abolishing the purchase of commissions, shortening the term of service for soldiers, creating a larger reserve, and streamlining the army's command structure. Although the reforms did not establish a carbon copy of the German army in Great Britain and did not create a general staff, they did permit the British army to function more efficiently and effectively in the later years of the nineteenth century.

France borrowed ideas more heavily from the Germans than did the British. Following its defeat in 1871, France carefully studied German methods of education and organization and made several important reforms. Among these were improvements in its military schools and in the preparation of its general staff officers. France was reluctant, nevertheless, to give its general staff officers special responsibilities and authority, and its reorganized military schools became even more technical than those in Germany. Staff officers remained technicians and never had the influence of German general staff officers.

Though French military leaders supported the adoption of conscription and accepted the necessity to create a mass army, they were reluctant to rely as extensively on reserve units as did the Germans. They did create reserve units and developed a more efficient system of mobilization, but reserves were relegated to a secondary role. Similarly, France made some changes in the command structure of its army, but republican leaders refused to appoint a single commander-in-chief who could provide firm leadership. They appointed one officer to be chief of the general staff and designated another to assume command of the army in the event of war.

In the United States, some fears surfaced about the wisdom of following the German model of a general staff and a massive army. The U.S. Congress debated the ideas of Brevet Major-General Emory Upton about organizing an expansible army with a large cadre of professional soldiers, but many congressional leaders remained fearful of "Germanizing" the U.S. Army and giving it influence over other governmental institutions. The few military reforms that occurred in the United States came through the efforts of Elihu Root, who served as secretary of war from 1899 to 1904. Root succeeded in increasing the size of the army and in partially reorganizing and reforming the War Department general staff, but he accomplished these reforms only after encountering numerous difficulties during the Spanish-American War.

While the United States remained uninterested in establishing a large military force, General William Tecumseh Sherman made advanced education for U.S. Army officers possible with the establishment of the School of Application for Infantry and Cavalry at Fort Leavenworth, Kansas, in 1881. During the next two decades, officers such as John F. Morrison, Eben Swift, and Arthur Wagner guided the transformation of the school from a technical school of tactics to a true staff college preparing officers for high-level duties. Sherman also influenced Commodore Stephen B. Luce who persuaded the navy to establish the Naval War College at Newport, Rhode Island, in 1884. Among Luce's most important accomplishments at the Naval War College was his selection of Alfred Thayer Mahan to join the faculty. In 1901, two of Sherman's protégés, Tasker H. Bliss and William H. Carter, played key roles in the establishment of the Army War College. The establishment of advanced military schools by the army and navy demonstrated American recognition of the requirement for officers to study their professions in depth. In the broadest sense, however, American improvements in professional military education and high-level staffs were part of a wave of reforms that swept most military forces of the industrialized world at the turn of the century.

Throughout the Western world, the years between 1871 and 1914 witnessed the emergence of a more professional corps of officers who devoted their lives to mastering the highly technical skills of their profession. Almost none of these professionals, however, anticipated the sort of fighting that would be encountered after the opening battles of World War I. Most believed that improvements in technology favored the offense and made battle more decisive. Expecting heavy casualties in future battles, they demanded larger armies and prepared them to fight in highly mobile and short campaigns. They refused to believe that any country would endure for very long the huge costs of fielding and supporting large forces or would accept the heavy casualties modern weapons could inflict. Despite their increased professionalism, the campaigns they foresaw in the future resembled those of 1870 more than they did those of 1914–1918.

The New "Navalism"

Throughout the 1870s and part of the 1880s, most Western nations placed a stronger emphasis on armies than on navies. Expenditures on navies remained relatively moderate in the years following the American Civil War and the Franco-Prussian War. Nations remained indifferent to overseas empires from the end of the Napoleonic Wars through the mid-1870s, but beginning in the mid-1870s many began placing an increasing emphasis on naval power.

As Western powers expanded their navies, intense rivalries emerged between the British, on the one hand, and the French and Russians, on the other. At the end of the nineteenth century the Germans also applied their considerable industrial capabilities to the creation of a powerful naval force. The emergence of a strong German fleet came from the efforts of Admiral Alfred von Tirpitz, who dominated the German navy from the early 1890s through 1916. The British in particular became concerned about the growth of naval power in other countries, and in 1888 a special committee of British admirals recommended that "no time should be lost in placing the British navy beyond comparison with that of any two powers." The British government endorsed this proposal and by 1890 had considerably increased its naval expenditures. France and Russia reacted promptly by increasing their naval budgets as well. A second British building program began in 1893–1894 and a third in 1904 after Germany decided to build up its navy.

The United States also became deeply involved in the naval rivalry. In the short period from the early 1880s through 1908, the United States went from having a navy inferior to many second-rate powers to having the second-largest fleet in the world. In 1890 the United States decided to build three battleships, the *Indiana*, *Massachusetts*, and *Oregon*. By 1898, the U.S. Navy had four "first-class" battleships, plus numerous other modern ships. In keeping with the tenor of the times, the navy was designed as a "blue-water" force for controlling the sea.

The naval competition and buildup that emerged at the end of the nineteenth century was a result not only of competition over the size of fleets but also of the technology used in ships. With the greatly increased use of steel and the almost universal adoption of better gunpowder, navies concentrated on improving the size and firing range of guns, the thickness of armor protection, and the speed of their ships. Advances occurred in the development of new armor-piercing shells and the adoption of hydraulic recoil mechanisms for the powerful weapons. Changes also occurred in ship design with the introduction of turrets and barbettes that permitted all-around fire and significantly increased the firing power of the battleship.

In 1906 the launching of the HMS *Dreadnought* by the British admiralty made all other battleships obsolete. Older battleships had carried a mixture of guns of varying ranges and calibers. The *Dreadnought*, however, was an "all big-gun" ship. Although it did have an antitorpedo-boat battery of twenty-four 12-pounders, its main armament was ten 12-inch guns, each of which could fire an 850-pound projectile. With firepower on the new ship being more than double that of other battleships, most navies had no choice but to build "dreadnoughts" if they hoped to maintain their status as naval powers. Ironically, the idea for an all big-gun ship came from an Italian designer, and the United States and Japan were already moving in the direction of larger, faster, more heavily gunned ships when the British launched the *Dreadnought*.

Naval Theorists

As naval officers reflected on the effects of the changes occurring in naval warfare at the end of the nineteenth century, new ideas began to emerge. In France, Admiral H. L. T. Aube became the main spokesman for what was known as the *Jeune École*. According to members of this school of thought, technological advances in mines and torpedoes had rendered the older and much more expensive approaches to naval warfare obsolete and had ended the dominance of the battleship over the sea. Aube and his followers believed that relatively inexpensive torpedo boats, mines, and small warships could launch raids on commercial shipping (*guerre de course*) and could thereby have a significant strategic effect. Most of the proponents of the *Jeune École* came from France, where the allure of a technological alternative seemed to offer a way of establishing France as a naval power without having to build an extraordinarily expensive fleet based on battleships.

Despite the appeal of a less costly alternative, the most important theorist of naval power during this period of profound change was the American Captain Alfred Thayer Mahan, whose work, *The Influence of Sea Power upon History* (1890), became the bible for most navies at the turn of the century. Instead of focusing on the technology and costs of war, Mahan concentrated on history. As one of the few original American theorists on military or naval affairs, he studied history to determine the experience and characteristics of nations that had been great sea powers. While arguing that the greatest nations had been those with sea power, he observed that certain natural factors affected the ability of a state to become a sea power. These factors included geographic position, extent of territory, availability of ports, size and character of population, and attitude of government. According to Mahan, England was especially well-suited to be a great sea power because it was surrounded by water and thus had little need for a large army; it also had numerous ports, an expanding population interested in trade and commerce, and a government favoring industrial, commercial, and naval activities. Mahan concluded that the United States also possessed most of these factors and had the potential to be a great sea power.

Mahan looked beyond the factors influencing the development of sea power and addressed how it should be used. The principal purpose of a navy was to gain "command of the sea" by controlling the areas of sea communication. This could be attained by securing sea communications for one's own cargo vessels while denying their use by an enemy. Rejecting completely the ideas of the *Jeune École*, which stressed raids on commercial shipping, Mahan argued that only the destruction or neutralization of an enemy's fleet with a more powerful fleet could lead to securing the sea for one's own use. Mahan's message was clear: no nation could maintain world-wide influence and commercial greatness without a large battle fleet. He also insisted that concentration was the "predominant principle" of naval warfare and concluded, "Never divide the fleet!"

Although Mahan's ideas initially were not well received in the United States, his works were read widely throughout the world, particularly in Britain, Germany, and Japan. Indeed many naval officers agreed with Mahan's theory. As for the practicality of *guerre de course*, naval officers agreed that such ideas were appropriate only for inferior powers who did not have the resources or will to construct powerful fleets.

One of the most important alternatives to Mahan's ideas came from Sir Julian S. Corbett, a lecturer at the British Royal Naval War College who made significant contributions to the concept of maritime strategy. In 1911 he published *Some Principles of Maritime Strategy*, which became very contro-versial in naval circles. He defined maritime strategy as the "principles which govern a war in which the sea is a substantial factor." He added, "The paramount concern . . . of maritime strategy is to determine the mutual rela-tions of your army and navy in a plan of war." Corbett argued that it was "almost impossible" for a war to be "decided by naval action alone." He explained:

> Since men live upon the land and not upon the sea, great issues between nations at war have always been decided—except in the rarest of cases—either by what your army can do against your enemy's territory and national life, or else by fear of what the fleet makes it possible for your army to do.

Corbett differed from Mahan in that he believed command of the sea was only a means to an end. In the decades before 1914, when Western states used naval and land forces to project power around the globe, the role of naval power more closely resembled the ideas of Corbett than those of Mahan or the *Jeune École*. Most naval officers, however, preferred Mahan's arguments, for his emphasis on sea power and the clash of battle fleets, rather than maritime strategy, suggested that the fleet was the most crucial element of national power.

Small Wars and Regional Wars Before 1914: Mixing the Old and the New

At the end of the nineteenth century, Western states greatly enlarged their territorial possessions around the world in what has been called the "new imperialism." With Social Darwinism encouraging the notion of competi-tion between races, the French often spoke of their "civilizing mission," and

Rudyard Kipling passionately exhorted the British to "take up the White Man's Burden." The hope of converting people to Christianity encouraged numerous missionaries to seek converts. Economic considerations also had an effect. Though the new possessions often proved unprofitable and expensive, the Western powers sought natural resources and new markets in their far-flung empires. With tariff barriers rising in the late nineteenth century, they feared being locked out of vast areas of the globe. Many of those who participated in the new imperialism believed foreign possessions enhanced the prestige of their country, adding to its status as a world power. After the completion of the Suez Canal in 1869, the British aggressively safeguarded this important link to their imperial possessions in South Asia; and for similar reasons the United States established firm control over the Panama Canal in 1903.

The expansion of steam power contributed to the expansion of the Western powers' territories. As screw propellers replaced paddle wheels, more efficient steam engines reduced fuel consumption and increased ships' range. With transportation costs declining, the shipment of goods and low-priced raw materials between continents became common, and large passenger liners frequently plied the oceans. As intercontinental trade prospered, the capability to transport troops and supplies improved, and the projection of power across vast portions of the globe became more efficient. Without this naval capability, the Western states could not have expanded their influence and territories so easily.

As the Western powers expanded their empires around the globe, they became involved occasionally in what were called "small wars" to conquer or to police their colonial possessions. In some cases, a show of naval strength—gunboat diplomacy—enabled them to influence or gain control over a city or a region. When a show of force did not work, the threat of a bombardment (such as American Commodore Matthew C. Perry's threatening Tokyo in March 1854) or the actual bombardment of a city (such as the British shelling of Alexandria, Egypt, in July 1882) sometimes compelled a ruler to yield to Western demands. In many cases, however, the Western powers used land forces to achieve their objectives. In *Queen Victoria's Little Wars*, for example, Byron Farwell listed some 230 "wars, military expeditions, and campaigns" conducted by the British from 1837 through 1901.

By the end of the nineteenth century, the French and British had developed highly effective methods for conducting operations in distant regions. The French often conducted offensive operations with what they called "mobile columns"; these were heavily armed, highly mobile forces, consisting primarily of professional soldiers and members of the French Foreign Legion. The mobile columns would conduct forced marches deep into enemy territory, seize key terrain or important enemy leaders, and seek to end the fighting in a swift, sure strike. In 1899, Major Charles E. Callwell of the British army wrote a book entitled *Small Wars: Their Principles and Practice*. He focused on the operations of well-equipped and well-trained forces against poorly equipped and trained opponents and suggested that such conditions led intervening forces to rely primarily on offensive operations. While advocating methods similar to those used by the French, Callwell warned of the difficulty of striking a decisive blow against a foe who operated by different rules and who probably had greater mobility. He also warned of the difficulties of obtaining adequate information about the enemy. Nonetheless, he argued that intervening forces would face their greatest challenges in dealing with questions of transport and supply. According to Callwell, the nature of such campaigns was completely different from that of "modern regular warfare."

Not all wars at the end of the nineteenth century resulted from attempts by Western states to expand their colonial empires; some stemmed from traditional power politics, economic rivalries, and long-term animosities. Examples of these wars are the War of the Pacific in 1879–1884 between Chile, Peru, and Bolivia, the Russo-Turkish War of 1877–1878, the Sino-Japanese War of 1894–1895, the Greek and Turkish War of 1896, the Tripolitan War of 1912 between Italy and Turkey, and the First and Second Balkan Wars of 1912 and 1913. Though most of the "small wars" were short and did not involve new methods or weapons, military leaders studied them carefully. Unfortunately for the soldiers of 1914, most armies would learn little about future warfare from the numerous conflicts at the end of the nineteenth century.

The Spanish-American War

Of the several wars fought around the turn of the century, the Spanish-American War represented a transition between the old and the new. This was due in part to Spain's declining power and the rising world power of the United States. The Americans expected to achieve a quick and relatively painless victory, but while the navy performed superbly, the army, which was unprepared for war, experienced significant difficulties during the early days of the conflict. The fighting against Spain lasted only four months with the most important land fighting lasting only one month. But the United States also became involved in putting down the Philippine insurrection, a bitter guerrilla war that lasted more than three years. What was supposed to be a "splendid little war" turned out to be something far different.

The war began because of American concern over Spanish presence and activities in Cuba. After the outbreak of a rebellion in Cuba in 1895 and another in the Philippines in 1896, American sentiment strongly supported the Cubans against the Spanish, who were accused of employing barbarous methods to suppress the rebellion. President William McKinley hoped to achieve a diplomatic solution to the Cuban problem, but two events occurred that aroused a storm of public indignation in the United States. One of these was the publication of a private letter from the Spanish minister in Washington expressing strong criticisms of President McKinley. Another was the sinking of the battleship *Maine* in Havana harbor with the loss of 260 lives. Though the explosion that sank the ship may have come from ammunition in its hold, an outpouring of demands for war literally overwhelmed the American government, leading it to make a formal declaration of war on April 25, 1898.

The U.S. Navy was well prepared for the war because it had five battleships, four of which were new and rated as first class. The Spanish could not match American sea power since they had only one battleship and it was rated as second class. The American advantage in sea power greatly affected the outcome of the war, because, as suggested by Corbett, it enabled the United States to land and support armies in Cuba, Puerto Rico, and the Philippines. It also blocked Spain from reinforcing and resupplying its threatened possessions.

Compared to the preparedness of the navy, the army was not ready to fight a modern war. With a regular army of about 28,000 and a National Guard of about 100,000, the United States was neither organized nor trained to fight a war outside the mainland. The army had an inefficient staff in Washington, no system of effective mobilization, no up-to-date knowledge of the Spanish forces, no accurate maps of Cuba or the Philippines, and very few modern weapons. With no unit larger than a regiment, the regular army was accustomed to operating in small units and employing tactics that worked well against the Indians but not against a foreign power. The National Guard was especially unprepared, for its units had little practical experience other than close-order drill. Subsequent difficulties and misfortunes stemmed primarily from this unpreparedness and from the complexities of implementing policies rapidly with too few trained soldiers and inadequate supplies.

Except for a naval plan that called for blockading Cuba, isolating Spanish forces on the island, and attacking a Spanish squadron in Philippine waters, no war plans existed. With no clear strategic objective in mind, the army prepared to send a corps under General William R. Shafter against Havana. Shafter was supposed to capture a port city near Havana and, after the arrival of additional forces, attack the capital city.

The outpouring of volunteers and demands for use of the National Guard quickly swamped the War Department, and by July the United States had mustered more than 270,000 troops and rushed them to camps in the southern states. Since the supply services had maintained stockpiles for a force of only 40,000, the assembled forces could not be issued essential items such as uniforms, shoes, socks, and underwear. For weapons, the regular forces were armed with the newly adopted Krag-Jorgensen rifle, but the National Guard and the volunteers carried the obsolete .45-70 Springfield, a single-shot breechloader that used black powder.

The Spanish navy was reluctant to engage the U.S. Navy, but in April a small Spanish fleet under Admiral Pascual Cervera y Topete sailed slowly from Spain toward the Caribbean. When information about the sortie became known in Washington on April 29, a panic spread along the American east coast, and for a time the navy and army were overwhelmed with calls for coastal defense. The response of the navy was to divide the North Atlantic Squadron into two main parts, even though the action violated Mahan's precept about never dividing a fleet. Under the command of acting Rear Admiral William T. Sampson, the first part prepared for offensive action against Cuba and Puerto Rico. The second, known as the "Flying

Squadron," was under the command of Commodore Winfield Scott Schley and prepared itself to protect the Atlantic seaboard.

While the U.S. Navy searched the Atlantic for Cervera's ships, Commodore George Dewey audaciously steamed into Manila harbor in the Philippines on the night of April 30; the following morning in a battle lasting only a few hours, he destroyed the entire Spanish fleet in the harbor. Dewey had an overwhelming advantage: the seven Spanish vessels outnumbered his six, but his were more modern, had armored decks, and carried longer-range guns. More importantly, intense training before the fight had made American guns much more effective than they otherwise may have been. His crushing victory made him a national hero overnight.

Meanwhile, in the Caribbean, Cervera could not get sufficient coal at other ports, so he put into the harbor of Santiago de Cuba, the only unblocked Cuban port. By chance the Americans discovered him, and soon the squadrons of Sampson and Schley assumed blockading positions off the harbor. By blockading Cervera, the navy had secured the fundamental objective of the naval campaign in the Caribbean—command of the sea. The United States could now operate at will against Cuba and Puerto Rico. The Spanish fleet, however, could not be destroyed without the elimination of the Spanish shore batteries around the harbor. Admiral Sampson soon called for army troops to eliminate these batteries.

General Shafter's corps received the mission of landing in Cuba, and he chose to land at Daiquiri, about twenty miles from Santiago's harbor, rather than storm the 250-foot bluffs at the harbor's entrance. Though unopposed, the landing did not go smoothly. The lack of coordination, the unwillingness of the civilian transport captains to bring their vessels close to shore, and the lack of sufficient lighters to carry troops and equipment from ship to shore caused the landing to drag on for four days.

As soon as a sizable contingent of troops was on shore, Shafter ordered his advance guard to occupy Siboney (about eight miles closer to Santiago), which was better suited than Daiquiri for landings. After assembling sufficient forces and supplies, he planned on pushing westward from Siboney toward the high ground known as San Juan Heights, overlooking Santiago. But his advance guard disregarded his orders and advanced quickly toward the city; the Americans brashly attacked the Spanish rear guard about three miles northwest of Siboney and suffered severe casualties.

News of the clash forced Shafter to move forward and take personal command of his forces. After analyzing the situation and terrain, he decided to launch a two-staged attack, first clearing his right flank by assaulting the fortified village of El Caney, two miles to the north, and then advancing west toward the San Juan Heights, which consisted of San Juan Hill and Kettle Hill. He asked local insurgents to block a road running north out of Santiago and thereby prevent the arrival of Spanish reinforcements. Anticipating the easy capture of El Caney and the San Juan Heights, Shafter expected to enter Santiago quickly.

Unfortunately for the Americans, the Spanish were strongly entrenched and fortified at El Caney. Using their excellent Mauser rifles with

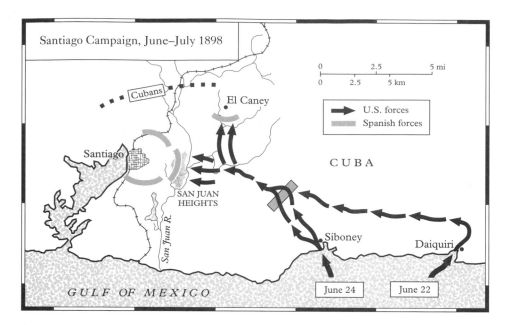

great effectiveness, the 521 Spaniards held off the 5,400 Americans for more than eight hours. American artillery, which consisted of four light guns, provided some support, but only in the final hours of fighting, when the guns concentrated their fire against a stone fort, did they open the way for a final charge against the Spanish position.

Meanwhile, two divisions moved slowly along the road to Santiago. They raised an inflatable, hot-air balloon to improve observation, but the Spanish used it as an aiming point for their artillery and inflicted heavy casualties on the Americans who were struggling to move forward. Similarly, the Americans opened fire on the San Juan Heights with four light guns, but smoke from the guns' black powder revealed their location to the enemy and brought in highly effective counterbattery fire. With plunging fire coming from the heights to their front, the situation became even more confused when the leading regiment—the 71st New York Volunteers—panicked and refused to advance.

The Americans finally began their attack even though they did not have artillery support and had to move through barbed-wire entanglements. The attack on San Juan Hill succeeded only because of the fortunate placing of fire on the Spanish position by six Gatling guns under the control of Second Lieutenant John H. Parker. Kettle Hill, which was just north of San Juan Hill, fell under the assault of the African-American troops of the Ninth Cavalry with the First Cavalry and Rough Riders following closely behind.

Instead of continuing on to Santiago, the Americans immediately halted and prepared for a counterattack. Shafter reinforced the San Juan Heights and abandoned all thoughts of moving quickly toward Santiago. The Americans were disorganized and shaken. They had taken 1,385 casualties at El Caney and the San Juan Heights, but the strongest defenses still

African-American troops in the Spanish-American War. Members of the Ninth Cavalry distinguished themselves in the fighting and led the assault on Kettle Hill.

lay to their front. Colonel Theodore Roosevelt, who had participated in the charge, wrote to a friend, "We are within measurable distance of a terrible military disaster."

Concluding that he could not penetrate the Spanish second line of defense, Shafter cabled the War Department and asked permission to withdraw toward Siboney until the arrival of reinforcements and additional supplies. After the secretary of war ordered him to hold his position, he turned to the navy and asked Admiral Sampson to force his way into the harbor. This seemed a ridiculous request to Sampson, who argued that his ships could not enter the harbor until the army destroyed the shore batteries at its mouth.

While the admiral and general debated what was to be done, the entire situation changed abruptly on July 3 when Admiral Cervera received orders from Spanish authorities in Havana to flee the harbor at Santiago. Though such a move would be suicidal, Cervera obeyed, and American naval forces soon destroyed his entire fleet in a running fight that lasted less than four hours. Knowing the destruction of the Spanish fleet had completely isolated the defenders of Santiago, Shafter demanded their surrender. After a long-range naval bombardment on July 10 and 11, the commander in Santiago agreed to surrender his garrison and all troops in eastern Cuba. On July 17, 1898, American troops entered Santiago. Less than a month later, forces under General Nelson Miles easily secured Puerto Rico.

As for the Philippines, an American army corps under the command of General Wesley Merritt had departed for Manila on May 25, before the landing in Cuba at Daiquiri. With about 8,500 troops, Merritt's corps took

Capron's battery firing on the morning of July 1. The battery provided support in the assault on the Spanish fortified position at El Caney. Note the clouds of smoke caused by the burning of black powder.

up positions behind a Filipino insurgent army under Emilio Aguinaldo, who had proclaimed himself the leader of the independence movement and whose forces surrounded the Spanish in Manila. After a sharp fight on August 13, in which the Americans lost 17 killed and 105 wounded, the Spanish surrendered. Tragically, the battle occurred two days after Spain and the United States agreed to an armistice.

After the United States formally proclaimed possession of the Philippines in January 1899, Aguinaldo and other insurgent leaders were outraged, for they did not intend meekly to accept the exchange of one foreign ruler for another. Their insurrection proved to be much more difficult and prolonged than the war against Spain. After several years of fighting, the collapse of the Filipino resistance accelerated rapidly in 1901 when American soldiers captured Aguinaldo in a daring raid. Though the insurrection continued, resistance eventually collapsed. On July 4, 1902, President Roosevelt announced that the war had ended.

Public outrage at the difficulties encountered in the Philippine Insurrection and in the Spanish-American War led to several reforms, most notably the creation of a War Department general staff by Elihu Root. Clearly, modern war required trained staffs and technicians who could plan and execute complex operations. Root also improved the army's school system, making it more comprehensive and adding the War College. Recognizing the difficulties encountered in organizing forces for the war, Congress passed the Dick Act of January 1903, which ensured better coordination between the active army forces and the National Guard. Tactically, the war demonstrated the advantages of smokeless powder, but it also demonstrated the difficulty of overcoming a well-organized defense. Neither the Americans nor the Europeans, however, learned very much from the fighting in Cuba.

The Boer War

Of the numerous wars fought around the turn of the century, the Boer War in South Africa had a significant influence on military thinking because of the demonstrated effect of firepower. The Boers were hardy people whose ancestors were Dutch colonists. When Great Britain annexed the Cape of Good Hope after the Napoleonic Wars (subsequently naming it Cape Colony), many Boers made the "Great Trek" north to avoid the British mandate of 1834 to emancipate their slaves. They soon established the two republics of Transvaal and the Orange Free State, and between 1852 and 1854 Britain recognized their independence.

The discovery of vast quantities of diamonds in the Transvaal renewed Britain's interest in the region. In 1877, it annexed the Transvaal as the first step in an attempt to expand its control over South Africa. In December 1880, however, the Boers proclaimed their independence and inflicted several defeats on the British. Prime Minister William E. Gladstone was unwilling to continue the war and in April concluded a treaty that gave the Transvaal its independence.

The discovery of huge gold deposits in the southern Transvaal soon precipitated another crisis. Waves of British people and capital poured into southern Africa, and the mistreatment of some of the immigrants by the Boers caused great concern in London. When negotiations collapsed, Great Britain sent reinforcements to Cape Colony. As British troops arrived in Cape Town, the two Boer republics decided to attack instead of waiting for an invasion. They hoped to capture several key ports and enormous quantities of artillery and supplies before the British had sufficient forces in place to defeat them. They also hoped that a rapid strike against key points would shake the entire British Empire.

With a strength greater than 40,000, the Boers initially swept easily through British Rhodesia, Natal, and Cape Colony in October 1899 and besieged British garrisons at several key cities. In addition to being extremely fine marksmen, the Boers had a small number of modern artillery pieces, including 75-mm, 120-mm, and 155-mm guns and howitzers. Even though the British slowly increased their strength from about 15,000 to more than 60,000, they suffered several sharp and costly defeats in their attempts to relieve the besieged garrisons.

The British commander, General Sir Redvers Buller, recognized the Boers' strengths and began altering his tactics among which were modifications in old-fashioned methods of using artillery. Given the range and accuracy of modern rifles, the artillery pieces could no longer deploy on line in the open and fire over open sights at a visible target. Against exposed artillery, a rifleman could conceal himself and deliver deadly, accurate fire. Artillerymen quickly learned the advantages of firing from a concealed position or behind folds in the ground. To deliver their fire accurately from these concealed positions, they had to develop new and improved methods of indirect fire. They also learned how to fire rounds behind ridges and hills where an enemy had previously been safe from artillery projectiles. Another important advance was the coordinating of artillery and infantry actions more closely. British infantry learned to crawl along the ground with a slowly advancing curtain of shell fire to their front. These and other improvements, such as better use of cover and advancing by rushes, soon enabled the British to move more effectively against the Boers.

While the British improved their tactical methods, Field Marshal Frederick S. Roberts, who had gained fame in the second Afghanistan War, replaced General Buller as commander of British troops in December 1899. General Horatio H. Kitchener became his second-in-command. During 1900, Roberts' forces increased to some 200,000, and they attacked deeply into Boer territory, relieving several besieged garrisons. After the defeat of the main Boer forces, Roberts departed for England, leaving Kitchener in charge. As he left, he was certain the war was practically over.

Unwilling to concede defeat, however, the Boers changed their strategy. The arrival of large numbers of British troops and the loss of several important battles convinced the Boers that they could not attack their enemies directly and that instead they had to employ guerrilla tactics. With the supply lines of the British spread over thousands of square miles, the Boers struck again and again at vulnerable points and inflicted significant losses.

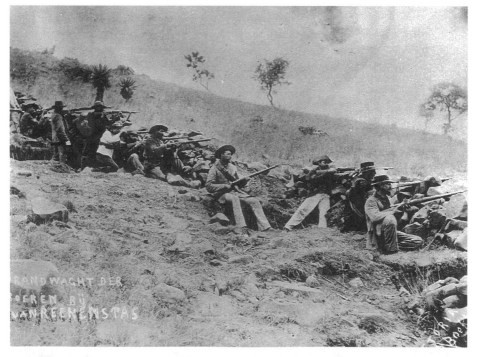

Boer soldiers proved to be excellent marksmen. Their long-range, smokeless, magazine rifles proved highly effective against British soldiers who were wearing gleaming insignia, stars, buttons, and buckles.

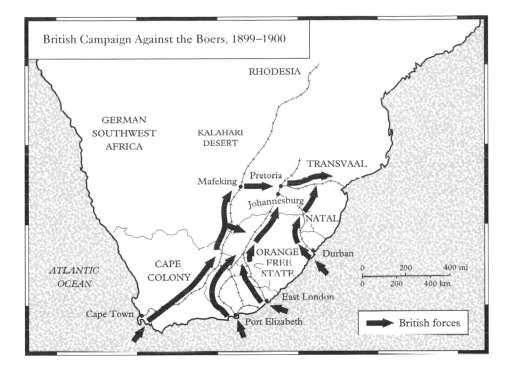

British Campaign Against the Boers, 1899–1900

RHODESIA

GERMAN SOUTHWEST AFRICA

KALAHARI DESERT

TRANSVAAL

Mafeking   Pretoria

Johannesburg

NATAL

ATLANTIC OCEAN

CAPE COLONY

ORANGE FREE STATE

Durban

East London

Cape Town

Port Elizabeth

0   200   400 mi
0   200   400 km

➡ British forces

Kitchener believed he had little choice but to conduct large operations in search of his elusive enemy. He and his men began defining success in terms of the number of enemy killed and captured. He also decided to sweep the countryside clear of anything that could give sustenance to the guerrillas. As part of this effort, he concentrated women and children in protected "laagers" alongside railway lines and even resorted to reducing their rations to force their husbands and fathers to surrender. Because of poor diet and inadequate sanitation practices, thousands of Boers died in these concentration camps. By the time the fighting ended, the cost in lives was about 22,000 British soldiers, 7,000 Boer soldiers, 18,000 to 28,000 Boers in the camps, and more than 12,000 black Africans.

In addition to learning more about the coordination of artillery and infantry, the British left the Boer War with a greater respect for rifle fire. They recognized the importance of accurate, rapid fire from modern rifles and concentrated on improving the marksmanship of their infantry. Well-trained British soldiers prided themselves on being able to fire as many as fifteen rounds a minute. By 1914, Great Britain placed a stronger premium on rifle fire than any other European nation.

Even though the experience of the Boer War taught most British officers the importance of firepower and impressed on them the difficulty of crossing an area covered by small arms and machine-gun fire, they tended to downplay the effect of firepower on tactics and concluded that a war on the European continent would be different from the Boer War. Most believed the effect of modern weapons could be overcome by stronger discipline and better training rather than improvements in infantry tactics and in coordination between the artillery and infantry. Although the British military did institute some changes, they brushed aside their most important experiences in the Boer War.

The Russo-Japanese War

In the Far East, the Russo-Japanese War of 1904–1905 demonstrated both the complexities of employing large mass armies and the effect of the new, highly lethal weapons. The root of that conflict came from the intentions of both Russia and Japan to expand into the territory of the declining Chinese Empire. Japan was particularly interested in Korea's serving as a base for further expansion into China and a way to prevent a rival nation from transforming the jutting Korean peninsula into "a dagger pointed at Japan's heart." Russia wanted to expand its influence into neighboring Manchuria, Korea, and perhaps Mongolia as part of its centuries-old expansion toward the Pacific. Convinced that a partition of China by the Great Powers would soon occur, both Russia and Japan hastened to establish themselves in Korea and Manchuria.

After Japan soundly defeated China in the Sino-Japanese War of 1894–1895, it won control over part of the Liaotung Peninsula in the southern extremity of Manchuria, lying just west of Korea and projecting into the Yellow Sea. The diplomatic intervention of Russia, France, and Germany, however, forced Japan to relinquish its control over the Liaotung Peninsula and Port Arthur on the southern tip of the peninsula. Russia soon gained permission from China to build the eastern section of the Trans-Siberian Railway through Manchuria and in 1897 acquired a lease over the Liaotung Peninsula and Port Arthur. In addition, Russia extended a spur of the Trans-Siberian Railway south to Port Arthur. Amidst growing resentment over being "robbed" of their victory over the Chinese, the Japanese became even more angry when Russian designs on Korea became apparent; many Japanese officials regarded war as inevitable.

Russia had several advantages—primarily its huge army and relatively large fleet. However, it could reinforce its troops in east Asia only by moving them along the lengthy, single-track trans-Siberian Railway; and its fleet was split between the Baltic, the Black Sea, and the Far East. Though Japan had a smaller army and navy, it had the advantage of being close to the Liaotung Peninsula. If the Japanese could concentrate their forces and defeat the Russians before the arrival of reinforcements, they had a solid chance of victory.

Around midnight on February 8, 1904, the Japanese launched a surprise attack against the Russians at Port Arthur. Using destroyers in a night torpedo attack, Vice Admiral Togo Heihachiro struck the force of Russian battleships and cruisers. Though he hit two battleships and one cruiser, he failed to destroy the fleet, and for the next six months, the Russian fleet remained trapped in Port Arthur.

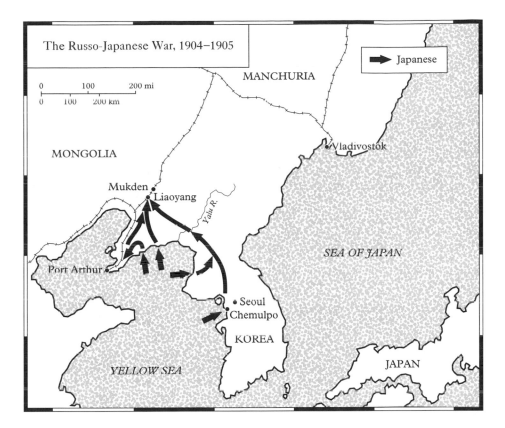

The Russo-Japanese War, 1904–1905

Shortly after the attack on Port Arthur, elements of the Japanese First Army began landing in Korea at Chemulpo (near Seoul) and moving north toward the Yalu River. Despite the bitter cold of the Korean winter, the Japanese reached the Yalu River at the beginning of April. After defeating the Russian forces along the river, the First Army began moving northwest toward Liaoyang. In early May, the Japanese Second Army landed about seventy-five miles north of Port Arthur under the protection of Togo's fleet and moved down the Liaotung Peninsula toward Port Arthur. The Japanese hoped to reduce Port Arthur quickly and then to concentrate against the remaining Russian forces.

After Japanese forces closed in on the area around Port Arthur, the Russian fleet in the port made a dash for safety. Though the Russians escaped the Japanese fleet, Togo soon forced most of the ships back into Port Arthur. Initially believing they could capture Port Arthur as easily as they had in 1894, the Japanese drove what were described as "waves of living flesh and blood" against the modern weapons and trenches of the Russians. After suffering fearful losses, they turned to using parallel trenches and mining to soften the Russian defenses, but the Russian will to resist did not collapse until the Japanese began using 11-inch howitzers firing 485-pound shells. In January 1905, after a siege of 240 days, the Russians surrendered at Port Arthur, but not before scuttling the last of their ships. During the fighting

To capture Russian defensive positions the Japanese relied on massive infantry charges. Japanese infantry are shown here forming lines prior to a charge.

around the port, the Japanese suffered about 60,000 casualties and the Russians about 30,000.

Before the fall of Port Arthur, the Russian commander, General Aleksei N. Kuropatkin, hoped to gain time for reinforcements and supplies to arrive. He decided to withdraw without fighting so the Japanese could be drawn inland and be weakened by their extended supply lines. Late in August, the Russians concentrated about 150,000 soldiers in entrenchments near Liaoyang (about 200 miles northeast of Port Arthur), and the Japanese concentrated about 120,000. After a confusing battle in which each side sustained about 20,000 casualties, the Russians withdrew toward Mukden. Following a disastrous Russian counteroffensive at Sha Ho in which they

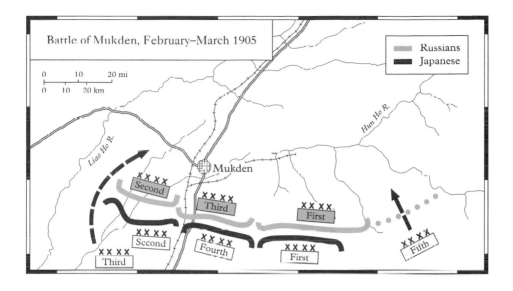

suffered 41,000 casualties, Kuropatkin continued withdrawing his forces toward Mukden. The stage was now set for the final battle.

By the end of February, the opposing forces faced each other along a line at Mukden that extended about seventy-five miles but that had heavy concentrations of troops along forty miles. The Russians had 275,000 infantry, 16,000 cavalry, and 1,219 artillery pieces; the Japanese had 200,000 infantry, 7,350 cavalry, and 992 artillery pieces. The only area in which the Japanese had an advantage was in machine guns, for they now had more than the Russians.

Kuropatkin attempted to attack first, but a Japanese attack on February 26 preempted him. The Japanese commander, Field Marshal Oyama Iwao, decided to attack all along the front with three field armies and then, in a feint, to move one of his five armies against the Russians' eastern flank. As Russian reserves moved toward the east, Oyama intended to send another army around the Russians' western wing, enveloping their flank and cutting their line of retreat. The Japanese endured heavy casualties in their frontal attack against the Russians, but they managed to envelop the western flank of the Russians. They failed, however, to cut off the enemy's line of retreat. At the end of the three-week battle, the Russians had suffered about 65,000 casualties and 20,000 prisoners, while the Japanese lost about 41,000. Despite their victory, the Japanese did not pursue the defeated Russians. Oyama had used up much of his army and was aware that only a small portion of the Russian forces had arrived in east Asia.

The final blow against the Russians came with the defeat of their Baltic Fleet near Tsushima Strait between Japan and Korea. Departing from the Baltic in October 1904, the Russian fleet set out for Vladivostok, 18,000 miles away. The Russians were ostensibly more powerful at Tsushima than the Japanese, yet Admiral Togo's superior leadership and actions proved decisive. Following the crushing victory of the Japanese on May 27, 1905, only a cruiser and two destroyers from the fifty-three ships that had departed

Admiral Togo Heihachiro was the Japanese
naval hero of the Russo-Japanese War. His
defeat of the Russian fleet near Tsushima
Strait enabled the Japanese to maintain a sea
link to their forces in Manchuria.

from the Baltic managed to reach Vladivostok. Much in accordance with
Mahan's ideas, Togo's decisive victory prevented the Russians from severing
Japan's sea link to its armies in Manchuria and provided the Japanese a sig-
nificant advantage.

The defeats at Port Arthur, Mukden, and Tsushima angered the
Russians, but their resentment focused more on their own government than
on the Japanese. Rebellion soon forced the Russians to seek peace and on
September 5, 1905, at Portsmouth, New Hampshire, the two nations signed
a treaty ending the conflict. Under the terms of the treaty, Japan gained control over Port Arthur and the Liaotung Peninsula and acquired a preferred
position in Manchuria and a protectorate over Korea. It also received the
southern half of the island of Sakhalin. The first war between major powers
since 1871 had ended with an Asian power defeating a Western power. As a
result of an intense period of industrialization and modernization, the Japanese had successfully learned about Western military organization, equipment, and methods and had defeated the largest power in Europe. They had
mastered the technologies and techniques that previously had given only the
Western powers the capacity to dominate other areas of the world, and they
had interrupted three centuries of Western success.

☆   ☆   ☆   ☆

The years before 1914 profoundly changed warfare. The introduction of
new weapons, the adoption of new techniques of organizing and controlling

armies, and the outbreak of numerous small wars required members of the military to reconsider many of their methods and the structure of their forces. In 1866 and 1870, the Prussians had demonstrated new ways of organizing, supplying, and moving a mass army, but advances in weapons had caused only small changes in tactics and organizations. By 1914 improvements in rifles, machine guns, and artillery had greatly increased the lethality of weapons. Moreover, increased industrial production and the enhanced power of central governments over bigger populations made even larger military forces possible; improved staffs and communications also made their organization and employment more efficient and effective. Total war of unparalleled lethality had become possible.

Beyond the importance of the rise of a new power in east Asia and the subsequent outbreak of revolution in Russia in 1905, the Russo-Japanese War provided valuable insights into how the waging of war had changed at the beginning of the twentieth century. Increases in firepower from artillery and machine guns had compelled the opposing forces to disperse and make wide use of entrenchments and barbed-wire entanglements. Communications had improved with the introduction of the telegraph and field telephone, which linked forward positions to headquarters. As most armies analyzed the Russo-Japanese War, they concluded that despite the advantages provided to the defense by the new weapons, the offensive remained supreme. The deadly effect of Boer marksmanship had shaken faith in the offensive, but Japanese success restored confidence in the offensive. The superior morale and determination of the Japanese to advance often enabled them to seize positions defended by Russians who usually waited passively behind their entrenchments. Tragically for many of the soldiers who would die in futile charges in 1914, European military leaders concluded erroneously that superior morale could prevail against modern firepower.

Similarly, the Russo-Japanese War provided ammunition for those arguing that future wars had to be short. Many believed, as did Ivan S. Bloch, that no nation could endure such losses for a long period. After all, the Japanese had experienced significant financial difficulties and the Russians had had a revolution at home. Many military leaders believed that the effects of increased industrialization, the introduction of the mass army, the perfection of new, more lethal weapons, and the vastly increased costs of waging war could lead only to shorter, not longer wars. Rarely have military leaders been so wrong.

SUGGESTED READINGS

Abrahamson, James L. *America Arms for a New Century* (New York: The Free Press, 1981).

Armstrong, David A. *Bullets and Bureaucrats: The Machine Gun and the United States Army, 1861–1916* (Westport, Conn.: Greenwood Press, 1982).

Bidwell, Shelford, and Dominick Graham, *Fire-Power: British Army Weapons and Theories of War 1904-1945* (London: George Allen & Unwin, 1982).

Callwell, C. E. *Small Wars: Their Principles and Practice* (London: Her Majesty's Stationery Office, 1899).

Corbett, Sir Julian Stafford. *Some Principles of Maritime Strategy* (London: Longmans, 1911).

Cosmas, Graham A. *An Army for Empire: The United States Army in the Spanish-American War* (Columbia, Mo.: University of Missouri Press, 1971).

Crowl, Philip A. "Alfred Thayer Mahan: The Naval Historian," in Peter Paret, ed., *Makers of Modern Strategy* (Princeton, N.J.: Princeton University Press, 1986), pp. 444–477.

Ellis, John. *The Social History of the Machine Gun* (Baltimore: Johns Hopkins University Press, 1975).

Farwell, Byron. *Queen Victoria's Little Wars* (New York: W.W. Norton, 1972).

Gates, John Morgan. *Schoolbooks and Krags: The United States Army in the Philippines, 1898–1902* (Westport, Conn.: Greenwood Press, 1973).

Goerlitz, Walter. *History of the German General Staff, 1657–1945*, trans. Brian Battershaw (New York: Frederick A. Praeger, 1953).

Gudmundsson, Bruce I. *On Artillery* (Westport, Conn.: Greenwood Press, 1993).

Headrick, Daniel R. *The Tools of Empire: Technology and European Imperialism in the Nineteenth Century* (New York: Oxford University Press, 1981).

Hogg, Ian V. *The Guns, 1914–18* (New York: Ballantine Books, Inc., 1971).

Huntington, Samuel P. *The Soldier and the State: The Theory and Politics of Civil-Military Relations* (Cambridge, Mass.: Harvard University Press, 1957).

Hutchison, G. S. *Machine Guns: Their History and Tactical Employment* (London: Macmillan & Co., 1938).

Mahan, Alfred T. *The Influence of Sea Power upon History, 1660–1783* (Boston: Little, Brown, & Company, 1894).

McNeill, William H. *The Pursuit of Power: Technology, Armed Force, and Society Since A.D. 1000* (Chicago: The University of Chicago Press, 1982).

Pakenham, Thomas. *The Boer War* (New York: Random House, 1979).

Potter, Elmer B., and Chester W. Nimitz, eds. *Sea Power: A Naval History* (Englewood Cliffs, N.J.: Prentice-Hall, Inc., 1960).

Ralston, David B. *The Army of the Republic: The Place of the Military in the Political Evolution of France, 1871–1914* (Cambridge: M.I.T. Press, 1967).

Trask, David F. *The War With Spain in 1898* (New York: Macmillan, 1981).

Westwood, J. N. *Russia Against Japan, 1904-1905: A New Look at the Russo–Japanese War* (Albany: State University of New York Press, 1986).

9

THE GREAT WAR:
AN INDECISIVE BEGINNING

Planning for a Short,
Decisive War

Failures of Conception and
Execution: The Western
Front, August-September 1914

Stabilizing the Eastern
Front, August–December
1914

$\mathbb{B}$efore the war of 1914–1918 became known as the World War, and later as World War I, it was known to those who experienced it as the Great War. It occurred in an era when increases in population, growth of industry, expansion of roads and railroads, and increases in the powers of central governments permitted the mobilizing and equipping of huge armies. Nearly 50 million men served in military units during the war, and millions more men and women supported them by working in factories, transportation systems, hospitals, and numerous other war-related positions. The major campaigns of the Great War pitted the Central Powers (Germany and Austria-Hungary) against the Allies (Great Britain, France, Russia, Italy, and eventually the United States), but more than thirty states ultimately became belligerents, including several from Asia, South America, and Africa. In every sense the Great War was the first world war.

When the war began, most participants expected it to be short; they believed no country would be able to endure for very long the huge costs of fielding and supporting large forces or accept the heavy casualties modern weapons could inflict. The first battles, however, proved indecisive, and as the war progressed both sides found themselves struggling to meet the voracious demands of their armed forces. As the Great War evolved into a total war, many of the belligerents had to commit a significant portion of their population and resources to the war effort, surpassing the commitments of the Napoleonic Wars and the American Civil War. Never before had so many countries and large armies engaged in battles of such magnitude and with such lethal and numerous weapons. Compulsory military service became the norm, and centralized economic planning and industrial mobilization became an essential aspect of most governments' war efforts. Throughout the war, both sides devised new strategies and tactics and shifted the focus of their efforts among the various fronts; they also made significant progress in the development of new weapons such as the airplane, submarine, and tank. Rarely have so many important innovations in warfare occurred in such a brief period.

The Great War witnessed vastly larger armies, unparalleled industrial output, and numerous innovations in technology and methods. Momentous changes stemming from the war initiated an era of remarkable political, economic, and social change throughout Europe and the world. But the costs were high: until the even larger losses of World War II, the unequaled material destruction and loss of lives of World War I surpassed those of any other war in human history. Casualties numbered about 8.5 million killed and 20 million wounded.

As chief of the German general staff, Count Alfred von Schlieffen did not win great victories like Moltke the Elder or execute grand plans as Moltke the Younger did, but he did devise Germany's war plan of 1914.

Planning for a Short, Decisive War

World War I was the first war in which the opponents went to war prepared with detailed and precise plans that had been written in the years preceding the outbreak of hostilities. Most of the plans used in 1914 were based upon the assumption that a future war would be short and that decisive results could be achieved only through the offensive. Of these war plans, none was more ambitious than Germany's.

Count Alfred von Schlieffen, who served as the chief of the German general staff from 1891 until 1906, was primarily responsible for originating the war plan used by Germany in 1914. For some time the general staff had recognized the difficulties inherent in waging a two-front war against France and Russia. Germany's initial strategy sought to cripple both opponents by a sequence of attacks first against Russia and then against France. With the conclusion of the Franco-Russian Alliance in 1894, however, the threat of a two-front war against Germany intensified, and the search for a response to this danger led to a daring strategy—Germany would use its central position and the excellent striking power of its armies to gain a decisive victory over France and then to turn against Russia.

Schlieffen initially planned for German forces to move through eastern Belgium and around the French fortress system on its northeastern frontier (along the Meuse River between Verdun and Toul). By 1905, however, he planned to have the "hammer," or right wing, of the German army march through western Belgium, the Netherlands, and northern France before circling to the west of Paris and driving the opposing armies against the "anvil" of the German forces in Lorraine. By sending the right wing of his army through Belgium and the Netherlands in a gigantic wheeling movement, he sought a huge *Kesselschlacht* (battle of encirclement) and a quick, decisive victory in the west. He intended to destroy France before Russia could mount an effective offensive against the weak forces on Germany's eastern frontier.

To concentrate sufficient power on the right flank of his attack against France and to make the wheeling movement possible, Schlieffen planned on placing five armies on his right wing and two on his left. The mission of the right wing was to pivot on a point north of Metz and to deliver the decisive blow, while the mission of the left wing was to mislead the French and draw them toward the east. Schlieffen expected the French to attack into the difficult terrain of Alsace and Lorraine and thus wanted the German left wing to oppose this advance without becoming decisively engaged and by withdrawing if necessary. When the heavily weighted right wing reached the Franco-Belgian border, the left wing would hold its ground, enabling the extreme tip of the right wing to speed around Paris and fall upon the flanks and rear of the French army.

After General Helmuth von Moltke (the Younger) became chief of the general staff in 1906, he maintained the basic thrust of the Schlieffen Plan but made several important modifications to it. As evidence began to

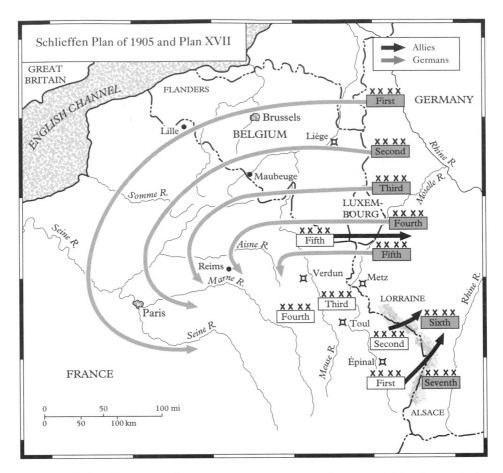

mount of the Russians' having recovered surprisingly quickly from their defeat in 1905, Moltke moved four-and-one-half corps from the west to the east to protect East Prussia. He also had reservations about the wisdom of violating the Netherlands' neutrality and soon modified the sweep of the right wing so the Germans would not enter the Netherlands. After changing the path of the right wing, he also modified the mission of the left wing. Not wanting to lose the valuable coal and iron mines of the Saar and Rhineland, Moltke ordered his left wing to delay the advance of the French initially but then to counterattack and drive them back. In essence, he weakened the right wing and strengthened the left wing without abandoning the idea of sweeping around Paris. As a result of these changes, the plan departed sharply from its original spirit, which was exemplified in Schlieffen's supposed dying words, "Keep the right wing strong."

Despite these modifications, the plan retained its fundamental inadequacies and contradictions, one of which was the German army's never having sufficient forces for a two-front war against a numerically superior coalition. Moltke's hasty shifting of forces from one front to the other might not have been necessary if he had had additional forces. The lack of sufficient forces could have been partially offset through better coordination with

Austria-Hungary, but both states jealously pursued their own strategies. After Germany decided to follow its highly risky strategy, much depended on the enormous logistical effort of moving hundreds of thousands of men and horses, as well as their equipment, from Aachen to around Paris in slightly more than five weeks. The intricate plan ignored the possibility of every lucky break not being in the Germans' favor.

The plan also deprived German political leaders of any flexibility; in fact, the German Chancellor and War Ministry remained ignorant of the new plan until 1912. Since the general staff had prepared only for attacking France first and then Russia, no changes could be made on the afternoon of August 1, 1914, when Kaiser William II asked for the army to be deployed in the east instead of the west. Because of the technical difficulties associated with changing the location and movement of armies, the Germans had no alternative other than a two-front war, and they had to launch their attack— military leaders believed—before the Russians or the French could snatch the initiative from their hands.

Germany thus accepted the waging of "war by timetable," and it chose to ignore many of the factors that might disrupt the timetable. That Germany came so close to victory in 1914 comes more from France's having played into its hands than from the brilliance of the plan itself.

War Plans: France

In the decades after 1871, the French army became increasingly influenced by the idea of the offensive, and on the eve of the Great War adopted an extreme doctrine, known as the *offensive à outrance*, according to which commanders would break the enemy's will to fight by an aggressive infantry assault. After gaining superiority of fire from their rifles, machine guns, and 75-mm cannon, the attacking French infantry would charge the enemy soldiers and finish them with their bayonets. The key to success, in the French view, lay in the will of the attacking commander and in the courage and determination of his troops to complete the attack regardless of losses.

French strategy in 1914 also emphasized the offensive, but unlike the Schlieffen Plan, their Plan XVII provided few details on operations and no clear strategic objective other than to fight a decisive battle with the Germans. General Joseph Joffre, commander of the French forces, retained the flexibility to shift his attacks, for his goal was to bring about a decisive battle. Nonetheless, his principal option was a two-pronged offensive with forces advancing into Lorraine on each side of the Verdun-Toul line. Forces in the southern attack would move from the vicinity of Toul toward the east, and those in the northern attack would move from the north of Verdun toward the east. One field army served as a strategic reserve and had the mission of moving on order and entering the anticipated decisive battle. If the Germans attempted to envelop their left flank, the French intended to attack north into Belgium, but they had to depend on assistance from the Belgians and the British. Despite the absence of any clear strategic objectives, the French firmly believed that their offensive would be successful.

By charging into Lorraine, however, the French played directly into the Germans' hands. As has often been said, the situation was somewhat analogous to a revolving door. While the French pushed hard on one side, the Germans would push on the other and seek to strike them in the rear.

War Plans: Other Powers

In contrast to France and Germany, Great Britain was foremost a naval power with the world's finest navy and a small yet capable army. Though reluctant to become embroiled in a war on the Continent, Britain became increasingly committed to France during the years before 1914, particularly through naval agreements.

As the size and capability of the German fleet increased, Britain began orienting its strategy and war plans toward concentrating its naval forces in the North Sea and withdrawing them from the Mediterranean. On the eve of the war, France agreed to concentrate its naval forces in the Mediterranean, while Britain concentrated its forces in the north near the main ports of the German fleet. The British also accepted the moral obligation of defending France's coast along the English Channel, since France had concentrated its naval forces in the Mediterranean.

Beginning in 1906, secret Franco-British military staff talks obliged the British to send the small British Expeditionary Force (BEF) to the Continent and for it to operate on the left of the French army. Though no formal commitments existed, these arrangements bound Britain to France in the event of an attack from Germany. Like France, Britain had no clear strategic objective other than the defeat of Germany.

In the east, the Russians intended to follow a strategy that, in consonance with the actions of France, would force a two-front war upon Germany and Austria-Hungary. Unlike France and Germany, which had only single strategies, Russia prepared two major plans, one offensive and the other defensive. In Plan G, which assumed Germany would attack Russia with the bulk of its forces, Russia prepared to defend against attacks coming from East Prussia and Austria-Hungary while it completed its mobilization and prepared to counterattack. In Plan A, which assumed Germany would attack first toward France, Russia prepared to advance into Austria-Hungary and East Prussia, followed by an advance into Silesia (eastern Germany). The Russian military hierarchy viewed this plan as the more likely alternative. When faced with the choice of concentrating in the southwest against the Austro-Hungarians or in the northwest against the Germans, the Russians prepared—in accordance with Plan A—to launch serious offensives on both fronts, thereby dispersing their first efforts. Adding to their difficulties, they also accepted France's demand to place some 800,000 soldiers in the field by the fifteenth day of mobilization and to begin offensive operations against Germany as soon as possible.

Prior to the outbreak of war, Austria-Hungary confronted especially difficult strategic problems, because it faced potentially hostile powers in three different directions: Italy in the southwest, Serbia in the south, and

Russia in the east. Austrian military leaders divided the army into three major groups and made plans for a large war (designed as Case I for Italy and Case R for Russia) and a small war against Serbia and Montenegro (Case B). The main force could be deployed against either Italy or Russia; the second could be deployed against Serbia; and the third could reinforce either of the other two forces. The situation of the Austrians was made even more complicated by the existence of a dozen nationalities in the army and the absence of a common language, except for a limited vocabulary of German words used in giving commands. Despite these complexities, Field Marshal Franz Conrad von Hötzendorf, chief of the general staff, failed to complete detailed plans for coordinated actions with the Germans. Not until May 1914 did the Germans tell him they would turn their main strength from France toward Russia six weeks after beginning operations.

The strategies and war plans of the major powers thus strongly emphasized the offensive. Confident of their armies and their leaders, most Europeans greeted the beginning of hostilities in 1914 with relief and in some cases with celebration. The long period of tension and crisis had ended, and many now believed that long-festering problems would soon be resolved. Consequently, thousands of soldiers marched or rode off to battle amid cheering crowds who expected their sons and neighbors to return soon as heroes. The soldiers, however, soon found themselves trapped in a long and brutal war with no apparent route to victory. Despite years of preparation and planning, the armies of Europe were unprepared for the situations they faced and surprised at the nature of the fighting they encountered.

Failures of Conception and Execution: The Western Front, August–September 1914

The rush to war began on June 28, 1914, with the assassination in Sarajevo of Archduke Francis Ferdinand, heir apparent to the Habsburg throne of Austria-Hungary, by a young Bosnian revolutionary. Convinced that the assassination had occurred with the knowledge and perhaps assistance of Serbian officials, Austria-Hungary decided to punish the Serbs. After Kaiser William II provided unconditional assurance of German support, Austria-Hungary issued an ultimatum to Serbia on July 23 that insisted upon Austrian participation in the investigation and punishment of the assassins.

In the following week, the chain of alliances and the web of military plans expanded a single terrorist act into a vast war. When Serbia received support from Russia, which refused to allow Austria-Hungary to destroy Serbia, the possibility of a limited Austro-Serbian conflict was replaced by a much more dangerous Austro-Russian one. After Serbia rejected part of the ultimatum as being an infringement on its sovereignty, Austria-Hungary declared war on July 28. Attempting to curtail expansion of the conflict, Russia first began a partial mobilization against the Austrians, but then on July 30 ordered a complete mobilization.

Since military leaders believed that the first nation to mobilize would have the advantage, Germany demanded an end to the Russian mobilization on its border. It also sent an ultimatum to France asking what actions it would take in the event of a Russo-German conflict. Receiving no response from Russia, Germany began its own general mobilization on August 1, followed the same day by a declaration of war against Russia. When France replied that it would follow the dictates of its own interests, Germany declared war on it on August 3.

As the first step in its move toward France, Germany demanded that Belgium acquiesce in its crossing Belgian territory, but the small country refused to permit the violation of its neutrality. Following the violation of Belgian neutrality, Great Britain declared war on Germany on August 4. Finally, on August 6, Austria-Hungary declared war on Russia.

The Great War had begun, and Europe was divided into two opposing camps. Germany and its allies became known as the Central Powers; and Great Britain, France, Russia, and other participating powers were known as the Allies.

The Opening Battles in the West

During the first month of the war, things went pretty much as military leaders had imagined they would before August 1914. The bulk of the German army moved through Belgium in an attempt to envelop the French flank; most of the French army attacked German positions in Alsace and Lorraine. The Russians moved against East Prussia and Austria-Hungary; the Austrians attacked Serbia and Russia. On all fronts, gigantic offensives threw millions of men into strategic maneuvers. Yet not until after the first month did the real character of the war become apparent and the errors in conception become evident.

The campaign in the west began with the attack into Belgium, and despite some difficulties in the initial fighting, adhered relatively closely to the tightly constructed schedule. The Germans did not expect significant opposition from the Belgians, but the decision by Moltke to avoid violating the neutrality of the Netherlands carried with it the decision to crowd the German First and Second armies, which constituted the heavy end of the right wing, through a bottleneck that included the fortification system around Liège. While the fighting elements of the two field armies could have bypassed the Liège fortress system, the all-important logistical elements behind them could not. The system of six main forts and six smaller forts arranged in a circle around the citadel in the city blocked the important railway and road network that passed directly through it.

The Germans had long recognized the importance of the obstacle formed by Liège and organized a special task force of six infantry brigades and three cavalry divisions to reduce the area. They planned on clearing the Belgians from the fortress system in the two weeks required to mobilize the entire army. Shortly after the Germans issued on August 4 a final note to the Belgian government that amounted to a declaration of war, elements of the special task force crossed the Belgian frontier and moved toward Liège. When German cavalry threatened to encircle the Belgians in Liège, the Belgians pulled their infantry out of the intervals between the forts on August 6, leaving the forts as the only opposition to the Germans. The Germans had foreseen the necessity to employ heavy siege artillery against the forts, and on August 12, the Krupp 420-mm howitzer, soon to become known as the "Big Bertha," and the 305-mm Skoda guns, which had been borrowed from the Austrians, began shelling the forts. Since the forts had been designed to withstand only 210-mm fire, the siege artillery easily destroyed them, the last two forts falling on the morning of August 16.

The Germans completed the mobilization and concentration of their army on August 14 and began moving forces forward before the capture of the last fort. The German First Army, commanded by General Alexander von Kluck, advanced on the extreme right of the entire German force, and the Second Army, commanded by General Karl von Bülow, moved forward on its left. Because of the great distance between Moltke (the German chief of staff was in Koblenz but soon moved to Luxembourg) and his subordinate army commanders, Moltke attempted to ensure coordination between his two right-wing armies by placing Kluck under the operational control of Bülow. By August 20, Louvain and Brussels had fallen to the First Army, and the remnants of the Belgian army were withdrawing toward Antwerp.

The French Offensive

Despite reports of heavy fighting around Liège, the French remained focused on executing Plan XVII. General Joffre dismissed the attack on Liège as a feint and expected the Belgians and the soon-to-arrive British to halt what he believed to be a relatively small German force moving through central Belgium. As a precaution, a French cavalry corps moved north into Belgium on August 6 but failed to penetrate the German cavalry screen.

Oblivious to the giant sweep of the Schlieffen wheel, Joffre pressed forward with his plan for a two-pronged attack—one south and the other north of the Verdun-Toul Line. The First and Second armies prepared to launch the southern attack, while the Third and Fifth armies made ready to launch the northern attack. Joffre ordered the southern attack to begin on the thirteenth day of mobilization, August 14. Conscious of the importance of convincing the French public that their army was confident and prepared, he also launched a small offensive on August 7 by elements of the First Army. Meanwhile, he ordered the Fourth Army, which could have functioned as a strategic reserve, to enter the line between the Third and Fifth armies and to advance with the northern attack. If the unexpected occurred, he had little or no means of response.

On the morning of August 14, Joffre's First and Second armies began the southern attack and advanced into Lorraine. Just as planned, the German Sixth and Seventh armies fell back skillfully, making the advancing French columns pay dearly. Attack after attack, the French infantry gallantly moved forward, charging in the open with their bayonets fixed, often without artillery support, but German artillery and machine guns killed and wounded thousands of them. The two French armies crossed the frontier on August 15, but their forward progress was halted by August 19.

As the attack of the French First and Second armies ground to a halt, the German Sixth and Seventh armies under Crown Prince Rupprecht of Bavaria launched a surprise counterattack at noon on August 20. While the First French Army withdrew in relatively good order, the Second Army had two corps that were almost routed, and by August 22, the two French armies had withdrawn to their starting positions.

The second French offensive was supposed to move in a northeasterly direction from Verdun into the Belgian Ardennes and then turn east. To protect his center, Joffre formed the "Army of the Lorraine" out of reserve divisions on August 19 and placed it between the forces launching the northern and southern attacks. As the southern attack came to a halt on August

As the French marched into battle they wore blue coats, red trousers, and soft caps. The reality of combat soon compelled them to don steel helmets and more subdued uniforms.

20, he issued orders for the French Third and Fourth armies to attack in a northeasterly direction toward Longwy, Virton, and Neufchâteau. Although Joffre was beginning to realize that significant numbers of Germans were sweeping north of the Meuse through Belgium, he steadfastly refused to change his plan, for he believed the Germans were pursuing retreating Belgians. He thought the Third and Fourth armies had the advantage of surprise and numbers and could strike the flank of enemy forces moving west through Belgium.

As the French Third Army moved forward through difficult terrain, it did not expect to encounter large German forces. Meanwhile, the German Fourth and Fifth armies advanced into eastern Belgium and occupied new positions as they waited for the German First, Second, and Third armies to sweep through the central part of Belgium. And as they waited, they organized strong defenses. On August 22, the French Third Army blindly bumped into the German Fifth Army in eastern Belgium. Hoping to hit an advancing German army in the flank, Third Army instead stumbled into a killing zone and suffered thousands of casualties. The French Fourth Army was no luckier than the Third. Just as in the Lorraine offensive, the French infantry failed to coordinate its actions with those of the artillery and often did not bother to suppress enemy fire before advancing. Following several disastrous actions, Joffre reluctantly permitted the two armies to withdraw.

A final French offensive came from Fifth Army. General Charles L. M. Lanrezac, who commanded Fifth Army on the French left, convinced Joffre to send his army north toward the Sambre River. On August 21 Bülow's Second Army collided with elements of the French Fifth Army on the Sambre and secured a foothold south of the river. While the French launched a series of unsupported, uncoordinated assaults against Bülow's forces, the German Third Army crossed the Meuse River on Lanrezac's right flank on August 23 and forced him to retreat.

The defeat of the French Fifth Army on the Sambre was the final step in the collapse of Plan XVII. Instead of concentrating superior force against a weak or decisive point, Joffre had diffused his offensive power in three separate and almost unrelated attacks. Everything now depended on the small British force on the French left flank and on Joffre's ability to shift his demoralized forces from his right to his left.

The Battle of Mons

As part of the military staff conversations between the French and British before the war, the British had agreed to dispatch an expeditionary force to France four days after Great Britain declared war on Germany. With the first troops embarking on August 9 and the bulk moving on August 12–17, the British landed a cavalry division and four infantry divisions under Field Marshal Sir John D. P. French at Boulogne, Le Havre, and Rouen. Using trains, the entire force then concentrated near Le Cateau on the left flank of the French Fifth Army. Despite the small size of the BEF, it was a well-trained, capable force. On August 19, the Kaiser issued an order to General

Kluck to "exterminate the treacherous English and walk over General French's contemptible little army." Because of this order, the small British force tagged themselves the "Old Contemptibles," a name they carried with great pride.

As late as August 20, Moltke believed no important landings of British troops in France had taken place. On August 21, however, the British began marching toward Mons, directly in the path of the German "hammer." After reaching the small Belgian mining town, they occupied a position to the left of the French Fifth Army. The first German encounter with the BEF occurred when Kluck's First Army changed direction and moved south to support the Second Army's attack on Lanrezac's Fifth Army. A small skirmish between German and British cavalry patrols occurred on August 22, but the next day Kluck launched a full-scale attack against the BEF's II Corps which had solidly dug in along the Mons-Condé Canal. Despite heavy casualties from massing their infantry and charging the rapidly firing British, the Germans managed to push back the British in several places along the canal by mid-afternoon.

Around midnight Sir John French learned that Lanrezac's Fifth Army on his right had pulled back and opened his flank. Having little choice, he ordered his two corps to withdraw south. Unfortunately for the British, the Germans followed the retreating soldiers closely and inflicted a major defeat on II Corps at Le Cateau on August 26 when its commander, General Sir Horace Smith-Dorrien, chose to fight rather than continue withdrawing. Shaken and demoralized, the BEF joined the French Fourth and Fifth armies in retreat.

The German Advance

As the German field armies moved forward, the forced diversion of troops (strategic consumption) gradually weakened them. The First Army had to leave a corps to cover the Belgian army in Antwerp. Second Army left a corps to besiege the fortress of Maubeuge, just south of Mons. Third Army left a division to besiege a small fortress near Givet. After receiving bad news from the east about the Russians attacking into East Prussia, Moltke dispatched two corps to the eastern front from the Second and Third armies.

Though his right wing was becoming overextended, Moltke refused to weaken his left wing. Instead of moving forces from his left to his right, as Schlieffen had envisaged, he directed the Sixth and Seventh armies on his left wing on August 27 to continue their attack against the French, directly into their strong defenses between Toul and Épinal. The French fortifications proved to be strong enough to withstand the enemy's attacks, providing Joffre the opportunity to begin shifting forces from his right flank to his left.

The Germans also began having problems with their transportation system. While they had had the advantage of using their own national railway system to transport and concentrate troops and equipment for the attack into Belgium and France, only a small portion of the Belgian and French railway networks remained intact or could be repaired as the Germans advanced. Nonetheless, the railways carried forward the requisite supplies, for even during the time of greatest demand the Germans managed to have about six trains a day arrive with supplies for each army. Because of the fast rate of advance of the armies, the distances separating units from their railheads gradually increased, as did the difficulties of moving supplies forward from these railheads. Much of the ammunition was moved from railheads to units by motor-transport companies, but by September 1, many of the trucks had broken down, primarily because of shortages in spare parts and tires. Despite occasional ammunition shortages, the Germans managed to provide sufficient supplies to units; no German unit lost a battle in the fall of 1914 because of supply shortages.

The long distances covered in the march of the German right wing across Belgium and France severely tested the soldiers' endurance. Many suffered from the sheer exhaustion of having to march twenty to twenty-five miles a day for many days, with those in the First Army on the right wing marching some 300 miles to the Marne River. During the advance, each German corps consumed about 130 tons of food and fodder each day, and their rapid advance and distance from railheads soon forced them to subsist off the countryside. Though the soldiers had to contend with an occasional hungry day, they did manage to live reasonably well on the food they foraged. The horses were not so fortunate. The Germans brought forward or foraged some fodder for their horses, but exhaustion and starvation soon took their toll. On the eve of the battle of the Marne, German heavy artillery—which was horse-drawn like the rest of the artillery—could no longer keep up with the still-advancing columns.

As logistical difficulties mounted, confusion increased. Even though Moltke moved his headquarters from Koblenz to Luxembourg, he still found himself swamped with messages that were invariably out of date. Communications between him and his subordinate commanders remained problematic because he insisted on using the wireless telegraph, even in cases where messengers would have moved faster. Unfortunately, radio links proved to be inadequate, and overloaded relay stations soon became incapable of handling messages without intolerable delays. To add to these difficulties, messages sometimes had to be transmitted three or four times before they were received correctly. Hot summer storms and interferences emanating from the Eiffel Tower in Paris frequently disrupted transmissions. At lower levels, commanders relied primarily on messengers and an extensive system of liaison officers. As the Germans moved farther into France, communications problems became progressively more difficult.

The Allies, too, became exhausted and hungry, but unlike the Germans, they did not have the exhilaration of victories to sustain their morale. They did have, however, the advantage of Joffre's maintaining close contact with his subordinates and staying abreast of the rapidly changing situation. On several occasions, he moved forward and met with some of his subordinate commanders. Also, the passing of information between headquarters occurred more quickly and dependably. Another key advantage pertained to the Allies falling back on their lines of communication. With French roads and railways radiating out from Paris and with the French railway system continuing to function, Joffre managed successfully to shift troops and equipment from northeastern to northern France.

The French Response

As the German forces pressed forward, Joffre carefully recast French strategy and tactics. German strategy had finally become apparent to him; he abandoned hopes of holding along the frontiers and attempted to establish a second defensive line deeper in France. On August 25, he ordered First and Second armies on his right to hold in place, while Third, Fourth, Fifth, and British armies on his left withdrew to the south, pivoting on Verdun, to a defensive line extending westward from Verdun, to Laon, and almost to Amiens. Joffre also began strengthening his left flank and forming two new armies. Composed primarily of troops transported from Lorraine, the new Sixth Army assembled near Paris under General Michel Maunoury and had the mission of preventing the Germans from enveloping the French flank. The new Ninth Army assembled under General Ferdinand Foch behind the retreating Third and Fourth armies but soon entered the line when a gap opened between the Fourth and Fifth armies.

Joffre also took steps to improve the performance of French units. He informed his army commanders that the infantry should attack only after artillery preparation, and he forbade large attacks. Recognizing the need for

General Joseph Joffre commanded French forces in 1914. Though his initial attacks proved costly and wasteful, he succeeded in shifting his forces from northeastern France and in halting the Germans in the battle of the Marne.

new leadership, Joffre began ruthlessly weeding out officers who had not performed to his expectations, among whom were the commanders of the French Fifth and Third armies. Within a short period he relieved dozens of brigade and divisions commanders, sometimes unjustly, but he wanted hard-nosed, self-confident fighters as commanders.

Still the Allies did not halt the Germans. After learning of the British defeat at Le Cateau on August 26, Joffre ordered Lanrezac's Fifth Army on August 27 to attack westward and strike the flank of the Germans who were pressing the British. Despite Lanrezac's pessimism, he managed to move most of his army to face west, but Bülow's Second Army unexpectedly hit his right flank on August 29 near Guise. Though the Germans initially pushed back the French, a spirited counterattack by a corps under General Louis Franchet d'Esperey momentarily halted Bülow's army. With the rapidly advancing German First Army threatening to envelop Lanrezac's flank, however, Joffre gave him permission to withdraw.

When General Maunoury's Sixth Army began unloading from trains east of Amiens, it encountered the leading elements of the German First Army. Kluck's forces drove Sixth Army southwest toward Paris. With his left flank being pressed hard by the Germans, Joffre had no choice but to abandon the attempt to establish a new line between Verdun and Amiens, and on September 1, he ordered his forces to continue their withdrawal.

As the Allied situation became increasingly difficult, coordination between the French and British worsened. After the shattering loss at Le Cateau and after several instances of the French withdrawing and exposing the British flanks, Sir John French lost confidence in the French army and its leaders. Refusing Joffre's appeals, he hurried his army to the south with the intention of going past Paris. When the possibility of a huge gap in the Allied lines appeared, Lord Horatio H. Kitchener, the British secretary of state for war, hastened to France and convinced Sir John to stop withdrawing and to take part in halting the German advance. These actions left Joffre uncertain about the role the BEF would play in the next phase of the campaign.

The Miracle of the Marne

After Franchet d'Esperey's surprising counterattack, the German Second Army remained in place for about a day and a half, thus enabling the French and British on the left to retreat without interference and allowing the German First Army to move ahead of Second Army. On August 27, Moltke released Kluck's First Army from Bülow's operational control and told him to resume his march in a southwesterly direction and to pass around the western edge of Paris. He also ordered Kluck to be prepared to go to the aid of Bülow's Second Army. On August 30, Kluck received a message from Bülow announcing the defeat of the French at Guise in a "decisive manner" and later received another message from Bülow requesting him to move his army southeast to exploit the victory. Aerial reconnaissance also revealed that the still-forming French Sixth Army was pulling back toward Paris and did not pose a threat to the flank of Kluck's First Army.

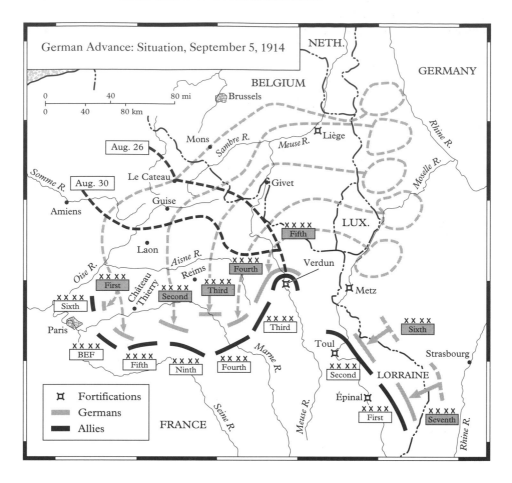

German Advance: Situation, September 5, 1914

Kluck felt torn between Moltke's order on August 27 to move his army to the west of Paris and Bülow's request on August 30 to move his army in a southeasterly direction to the east of Paris. Because of ineffective communications with Moltke and lack of time, Kluck knew he had to make a decision on his own. Certain that a great victory was about to be won, Kluck decided to turn his army toward the south and go around Paris on the east rather than the west. This was a decision that was to have a profound effect on the outcome of the campaign.

By September 2, Kluck's First Army was northeast of Paris, more than a full day's march ahead of the Second Army on its left. To Kluck's amazement, he received a message from Moltke that evening ordering the First Army to follow the Second Army in echelon. When Kluck learned that one of his corps had seized the bridges over the Marne River at Château Thierry about forty miles east of Paris, he did not know whether he should pull back the corps or reinforce its success. Choosing to act boldly but also choosing to violate Moltke's order, he ordered his army forward and left one reserve corps to defend against an attack from Paris. He dispatched a message to Moltke, explaining his decision, and in the last paragraph complained about not receiving "regular information" about the other German armies.

As the Germans approached Paris, the French government departed from Paris for Bordeaux on September 2, leaving General Joseph Gallieni in charge of its defenses. As the strength of the Sixth Army in Paris increased, and as the German First Army's turn to the east of Paris exposed the right flank of the entire German line, Joffre recognized the possibility of an attack against the German flank. He remained uncertain, however, about the willingness of the British to participate in a counterattack. Since the BEF was located just east of Paris and to the left of the French Ninth and Fifth armies, a counterattack probably would have failed without British assistance. Joffre also had reservations about the fighting abilities of the Ninth, Fifth, and Sixth armies under Foch, Franchet d'Esperey, and Maunoury, respectively.

On September 4 the vulnerability of the Germans became apparent to Gallieni in Paris after several aircraft reported that large German forces had crossed the Marne northeast of Paris and had left only one corps behind to protect the entire German flank. Later that evening, Gallieni had a heated telephone conversation with Joffre and urged an immediate attack on the German flank. After visiting the British and convincing Sir John French to participate, Joffre finally decided to launch a counterattack on the morning of September 6.

With reports of French troops being moved from east to west, Moltke recognized by September 4 that the right flank of the entire German line was exposed to an attack from the French Sixth Army in Paris. To avoid a disaster, he halted the advance of the First and Second armies on his right wing and ordered them to face Paris and protect the Germans' right flank. Kluck's First Army was ordered to pull back from its exposed position and stay north of the Marne. Still hoping for a victory, Moltke also ordered the Third, Fourth, and Fifth armies to continue attacking in the center, while the left-wing armies continued attacking in the south.

At 0700 hours,* September 5, eleven hours after Moltke's message had been dispatched, Kluck received the order to pull back. The order included no information about the enemy and made no sense to him; he still believed French forces in Paris were only beginning to assemble and posed no threat to his flank. Convinced that Moltke was poorly informed, he let his army continue moving south of the Marne until the end of the day, but he did take the precaution of ordering one corps to halt where it stood. This left two German corps in the vicinity of Paris and two south of the Marne.

On that same day, September 5, the French Sixth Army began moving east so it could launch the counterattack against the German flank on the following morning. The German reserve corps, which had been left behind by Kluck on September 2, became aware of French units advancing from

---

*The use of a twenty-four-hour clock by the military became common during World War I.

Paris and launched an attack to develop the situation. This bold action prevented the Germans from being completely surprised and provided Kluck time to shift his forces from south of the Marne to face the French attack. As Kluck pushed back the French attack, he stopped Joffre's attempt to roll up the German flank, but the movement of two corps to the north opened a large gap between the German First and Second armies.

Abandoning his effort to destroy the German right, Joffre pushed the BEF and the left of d'Esperey's Fifth Army into the gap that was occupied by only a thin line of German cavalry. The Allies advanced slowly, but the British crossed the Marne near Château Thierry on the morning of September 9, thereby threatening to envelop Kluck and Bülow's flanks. An officer from Moltke's staff had visited Bülow's headquarters and authorized the withdrawal of the Second Army if the enemy actually crossed the Marne. As Bülow's army began pulling back, the First Army had no choice but to pull back as well. The Germans hoped to withdraw only a short distance, but by September 12 the First and Second armies had reached the Aisne River. The concurrent withdrawal of the other armies on their left resulted in a long defensive line running roughly from Noyon east to Verdun, and then extending southeast toward Colmar. The opening campaign of the war on the Western Front had ended.

The Race to the Sea

While Joffre had not saved France from a long and bloody war and had made some terrible mistakes in the opening phases of the campaign, he had won a victory that some have classified as one of the most important battles in military history. If Joffre can receive credit for a victory, Moltke must receive some of the blame for the defeat. In contrast to the more energetic and personal role played by Joffre in rallying his forces and successfully modifying his strategy, Moltke had exerted little influence over several key actions and decisions on his right wing. On September 14 the Kaiser relieved him and secretly replaced him with General Erich von Falkenhayn, the Prussian minister of war.

Though the change did not become official until November 3, the new commander of the Germany army immediately began to amass a strong force on his right wing and attempted to roll up the Allied left. As the Allies also moved to outflank the Germans, a series of bloody struggles occurred with every battle moving farther north. The so-called "Race to the Sea," a "leapfrogging" action as each side tried to outflank the other, had begun.

During these struggles, the British moved farther to the north so they could shorten and secure their lines of communication. Also, the small Belgian army, which had been reinforced by three British marine brigades, remained under siege at Antwerp until the first week of October, when they successfully escaped from the Germans and made their way to the northernmost point of the Allied lines. There they occupied a defensive position on the extreme left of the Allies and remained for the duration of the war. By the second week in October, the two opposing positions stretched from the Swiss border to the English Channel.

As winter approached, the new character of the war on the Western Front became obvious. Barbed wire, entrenchments, and mud became pervasive along the 350-mile front from the English Channel to Switzerland. A war of movement in the brisk autumn air had yielded to a war of trenches in the cold winter wind.

Stabilizing the Eastern Front, August–December 1914

Geographic considerations greatly affected the war on the Eastern Front, which extended more than 1,000 miles from the Baltic Sea, around East Prussia, along the protruding Polish salient, and along the Austro-Hungarian border to the northern tip of neutral Romania. The Eastern Front was much longer than the Western Front and extended even farther after Romania entered the war in August 1916 on the side of the Allies. All the major powers in eastern Europe (Russia, Austria-Hungary, and Germany) confronted the question of military operations in the vast area along this front and worried about the problem presented by the Polish salient. The question of the Eastern Front was magnified for Austria-Hungary by the additional question of the Balkan front that extended from the western tip of Romania, between Austria-Hungary and Serbia, to the Adriatic sea. After Italy entered the war in May 1915 on the side of the Allies, Austria-Hungary's strategic situation became even more difficult.

Though military operations on the Eastern Front often relied heavily on the same types of entrenchments and strong defenses as those on the Western Front, the war of grand maneuvers never disappeared from the Eastern Front. Battles in this region frequently assumed a mobile character that did not exist on the Western Front except for the opening and closing battles of the war. Part of the explanation for this stems from the much greater length of the Eastern Front and the existence of vast plains, but the lack of extensive roads and railways also affected the flow of battles. While large formations could be moved easily in the west to fill a gap, the more primitive lines of communication in the east substantially delayed the movement of operational reserves and hampered efforts by a defender to halt a successful enemy offensive.

The large size of the Russian army also contributed significantly to making the Eastern Front different from the Western Front. During the war the Russians mobilized some 12,000,000 men, as compared to 11,000,000 in Germany and 8,410,000 in France. Immediately after mobilization the army numbered about 6,300,000 men, but almost 5,000,000 had received little or no training. The Russian infantry relied on simple, mass tactics, and

Eastern Europe, 1914

even though they had about as much artillery as the Germans, the Russians had placed much of their most modern heavy artillery in fortresses. Achieving cooperation between the infantry and the artillery was a constant problem for the Russians throughout the war. Despite the large size of their army, the Russians did not have a strongly centralized command system. They referred to their supreme headquarters as *Stavka*, a name given to it by Grand Duke Nicholas Nicholaievich when he arrived there on August 14 and took command; the Grand Duke derived the name from an ancient

Russian chieftain's camp. Real power, however, was held by the generals who commanded the two separate fronts, or army groups (the Northwestern Front faced Germany and the Southwestern Front faced Austria-Hungary). The Grand Duke was reluctant to interfere with their decisions or actions.

Prewar disagreements in Russia between officers who wanted to concentrate either against Germany or against Austria-Hungary were accentuated by the maneuvering of several cliques and by the effects of personality clashes; rivalries among the infantry, artillery, and cavalry worsened the problem. It was common for commanders to dislike their chiefs of staff or not to talk to their neighboring commanders. Amidst an environment of intrigue and status-seeking, military efficiency often was sacrificed for personal gain. In the end, faulty planning and poor command decisions had more to do with the initial Russian disasters than unpreparedness or weakness in equipment and supplies.

The Battle of Tannenberg

The most decisive actions initially occurred in East Prussia and were greatly affected by the chain of Masurian Lakes near its eastern frontier. The lakes channeled advancing armies into two avenues of approach—the first through the gap to the north of the lakes and the second through the Polish salient to the south of the lakes. The Russians eventually decided to send two armies into East Prussia; the First Army under General Paul V. Rennenkampf moved north of the Masurian Lakes, while the Second Army under General Alexander V. Samsonov moved south of the lakes. The two armies were placed under the control of the Northwestern Front commanded by General Yakov G. Zhilinski. The Russians had agreed with France before the war to put 800,000 men in the field fifteen days after mobilization, but after the war began, the French pressured them into sending the two armies of the Northwestern Front into the field on August 15, a week earlier than prewar estimates of readiness.

The goal of German strategy in the east was to avoid defeat and to maintain as stable a front as possible. To delay the Russian advance, the Germans placed the Eighth Army in East Prussia under General Max von Prittwitz. Although Prittwitz's forces were better led, disciplined, and equipped, they had the difficult mission of holding back the Russians' overwhelming numbers until reinforcements were shifted from the Western Front. Prittwitz's initial plan was to spread his forces across the frontier of East Prussia and—depending on the circumstances—to concentrate against the Russians coming either north or south of the Masurian Lakes. When monitoring of the enemy's radio traffic revealed the slow movement of the Russian First Army north of the lakes, Prittwitz decided to concentrate most of the Eighth Army against the Russian Second Army, which was moving south of the lakes. Unfortunately, an overly aggressive corps commander boldly pushed his forces forward and engaged Russian forces north of the lakes, thereby upsetting Prittwitz's plan.

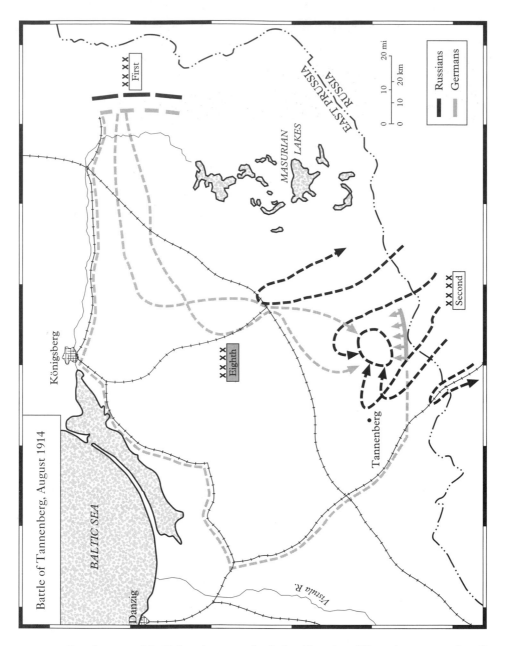

Battle of Tannenberg, August 1914

On August 20, Prittwitz attacked the Russian First Army north of the Masurian Lakes with nine divisions. By that evening it was clear that the Russians were winning at Gumbinnen, but more disturbing to Prittwitz were reports of two Russian armies (one of which did not exist) entering East Prussia to his rear, south of the Masurian Lakes. In a telephone communication with the German high command, Prittwitz said he would have to retreat across the Vistula River, more than 125 miles to the west of Gumbinnen. Such a withdrawal would have abandoned East Prussia to the Russians.

After the conversation with the German high command, several of Prittwitz's principal staff officers convinced him to use the superior lateral communications of the German forces to concentrate the bulk of his forces against the slowly advancing Russian Second Army to the south. They suggested leaving only a small force behind in the north to slow the advance of the Russian First Army and to move as many forces as possible by rail to the south. Reassured by his staff, Prittwitz agreed to the moves and thereby set into motion the sequence of events that would lead to the battle of Tannenberg and an important German victory.

Disturbed by Prittwitz's initial proposal to abandon much of East Prussia and by his apparent move to divide his forces in the face of a superior enemy, however, Moltke decided to replace him. On the afternoon of August 22, 1914, the 66-year-old retired General Paul von Hindenburg received a telegram from German headquarters offering him the possibility of returning to active duty. After telegraphing his acceptance, he received a second telegram informing him that Major General Erich Ludendorff— fresh from a remarkable performance at Liège—would visit him that night. Subsequent telegrams informed him that he was to command the German Eighth Army on the Eastern Front and that Ludendorff was to be his chief of staff.

As the two men traveled east to take command of Prittwitz's army, their styles and skills began to meld into an extraordinarily well-matched team. On the one hand, Hindenburg, as the commander, was a solid leader who was loyal, dependable, capable of maintaining morale and confidence, but not extremely intelligent; on the other, Ludendorff, as his chief of staff, had one of the finest minds of the war. A skilled technician, he was tough, aggressive, and attuned to detail. The team functioned smoothly with remarkably few clashes until the end of the war.

Though Prittwitz did not learn of his relief until the last moment, Hindenburg and Ludendorff arrived on August 23 to take over the Eighth Army. Hindenburg concurred with the movement orders and the plan for attacking the Russian Second Army, which had already been initiated by Prittwitz. After the slow advance of the Russian First Army in the north became apparent, Ludendorff rushed four corps toward the south so they could attack Samsonov's Second Army. During these moves Moltke decided to reinforce the Eastern Front by withdrawing two German corps from France. Though the two corps did not participate in the battle of Tannenberg, their departure weakened the German effort in France and thereby lessened the chances of German strategy succeeding.

Despite some confusion among troop units and some ignoring of orders by subordinate commanders, the German attack began on August 26. After repulsing an attack by a Russian corps, two German corps drove south toward the right flank of the Russian Second Army. On Samsonov's left flank, a German corps attacked on the 26th with only limited success but moved forward more energetically on August 27. Failing to recognize the operational goal of the Germans and remaining ignorant of what was happening on his flanks, Samsonov launched an attack toward the northwest on August 28 with his center. This attack thrust the neck of his forces into a

A German machine-gun crew in East Prussia. Though the Eastern Front had many more mobile operations than the Western Front, the Germans, Austrians, and Russians often used strongly fortified positions with entrenchments and barbed wire.

noose. After the attack ground to a halt, the Germans struck the Russian left flank, causing it to disintegrate. As German forces on both Russian flanks moved forward, they surrounded Samsonov's force, allowing only a few units to escape.

After some valiant efforts to escape, the Russian troops began surrendering on August 29. The Germans eventually captured about 92,000 prisoners; the Russians apparently lost about 50,000 killed and wounded; and the Germans lost 10,000–15,000. Samsonov shot himself. The Germans had annihilated the Russian Second Army, but they had gained an operational, not a strategic victory. They had destroyed two Russian corps and almost destroyed two others, but the Russians had mobilized at least thirty-seven corps, as well as several other independent brigades and reserve units.

The Russian defeat was due more to a compromised communications system, confused commanders, and inadequate intelligence about the enemy than to the brilliant performance of Hindenburg and Ludendorff. In reality, Russian soldiers had performed better than their officers, who had been unable to take advantage of their superior numbers or of their soldiers' willingness to fight. Similarly, higher commanders had done very little to coordinate the actions of the two Russian armies battling the Germans in East Prussia. Although opposed by small forces, the Russian First Army moved forward slowly and provided no support to the ill-fated Second Army.

As Hindenburg turned the Eighth Army toward the north he hoped for another Tannenberg, but when the Russian First Army commander recognized the danger facing his forces, he pulled them back across the Russian border on September 13. One week later the Germans encountered stronger opposition, and on September 25 the Russians drove the Eighth Army back to the frontier of East Prussia.

Operations in Galicia and Poland

While the Russians were being driven out of East Prussia, the main Russian forces became heavily engaged with the Austrian forces farther to the south on the Galician front. The Russian Southwest Front was under the command of General Nikolai Ivanov; the Austrian forces were under the command of the elderly Archduke Friederich in theory but actually were under the command of Field Marshal Franz Conrad von Hötzendorf, the chief of the general staff. After the first encounters on August 23, 1914, the Austrian First Army achieved some success at Krasnik in the southern part of the Polish salient, and on its right the Fourth Army pushed the Russians back at Komarov. But poor communications and mobility prevented them from taking advantage of their success. To their right, the Austrian Third Army was routed south of Lemberg by two stronger Russian armies.

To halt the Russian advance in the area of the Third Army, Conrad von Hötzendorf turned the Fourth Army to the south toward Lemberg, hoping to strike the advancing Russians in their flank. The movement of the Fourth Army, however, opened the way for a Russian advance between the First and Fourth armies. When Conrad learned to his horror that large Russian forces were moving through his center, he ordered the withdrawal of his forces. After leaving behind a strong force to defend the fortress of Przemysl, the Austrians pulled back about one hundred miles to the Carpathian Mountains. The Austrians would have suffered even worse defeat had the Russians not been so sluggish in their advance. Nevertheless, the Austrians lost nearly 250,000 killed and wounded, plus an additional 100,000 taken as prisoners. Conrad had little choice but to ask for and await German

Operations in Galicia and Poland, 1914

assistance. Thus by September 11 the Russians had gained an important victory against the Austrians and had inflicted more casualties on the Austrians than they had lost at Tannenberg. The Austrian collapse ended any chances of exploiting the German victory at Tannenberg.

In late September, the Russian *Stavka* began preparations for launching an offensive through the Polish salient into Germany (Silesia) after the Austrian army pulled back toward the Carpathian mountains. Hindenburg recognized the danger of such an attack and moved the newly formed German Ninth Army to the northern flank of the battered Austrian First Army. In subsequent fighting, the Germans and Austrians pushed the Russians back sixty miles, reaching the Vistula-San line and relieving Przemysl. But the Russians counterattacked, pushing back the Germans and the

Austrians by the end of October to their original positions. As the Russians rolled through Poland almost to the German border, Hindenburg and Ludendorff moved the Ninth Army to Thorn on the northern edge of the Polish salient and attacked deep into their rear toward the city of Lodz; the Russians held, almost encircling one German corps. Though fearful of suffering their own Tannenberg, the Germans nonetheless managed to halt the Russian drive toward the west.

The Russian offensive made more gains against the Austrians than against the Germans, and in November the Austrians faced the prospect of

Thousands of soldiers died trying to cross no-man's-land, which was often criss-crossed with miles of barbed wire. When measured against the reality of artillery, machine guns, and barbed wire, prewar notions of bayonet charges and élan seem ridiculous.

the Russians' penetrating into Hungary. With some German assistance, they managed to push the Russians back in early December but were too exhausted to exploit their success.

The Austrians had performed no better against the Serbs. When the Austrians entered Serbia on August 12, the two sides were about equal in numbers, but the Serbs were better trained and led, had combat experience from the Balkan Wars, and had modern artillery. The Austrians achieved some success, but by the end of August the Serbs had driven them back. Another Austrian attack occurred in early September, but it too failed. A third Austrian offensive drove the Serbs back, but a desperate counterattack pushed the Austrians out of Serbia by December 15. Not until late 1915 did the Central Powers return in force and overrun Serbia.

☆   ☆   ☆   ☆

In the broadest sense the Central Powers had failed despite their holding the Russians in the east. German strategy had depended on swift victory in the west, but Joffre had indeed achieved a miracle at the Marne when he shifted sufficient forces to face and then turn back the strong right wing of the German forces. In the east, the Germans had achieved remarkable success at Tannenberg, but with the Austrians' being mauled by the Serbians and the Russians, the situation remained grim for the Central Powers.

All the energy spent on the preparation of plans before 1914 had proved futile; no one had achieved quick victory, and all now faced a long, arduous war. With a stalemate settling on the Western Front and with the Eastern Front momentarily stabilized, both sides struggled desperately to meet the needs of their military forces. All armies were consuming previously unimaginable amounts of ammunition and supplies, forcing the warring states to organize nearly all their citizens and their economies to meet these formidable needs; and military leaders on both sides began searching for new strategies and methods for winning the war.

SUGGESTED READINGS

Barnett, Corelli. *The Sword-Bearers: Supreme Command in the First World War* (New York: William Morrow & Company, 1964).

Bucholz, Arden. *Moltke, Schlieffen, and Prussian War Planning* (Oxford: Berg, 1991).

Howard, Michael. "Men against Fire: The Doctrine of the Offensive in 1914," in Peter Paret, ed., *Makers of Modern Strategy* (Princeton, N.J.: Princeton University Press, 1986), pp. 510–526.

Isselin, Henri. *The Battle of the Marne*, trans. Charles Connell (Garden City, N.Y.: Doubleday & Company, Inc., 1966).

Kennedy, Paul, ed., *The War Plans of the Great Powers, 1880–1914* (London: Allen & Unwin, 1979)

Marshall-Cornwall, James. *Foch as Military Commander* (New York: Crane, Russak & Company, 1972).

Morrow, John H., Jr. *The Great War in the Air: Military Aviation from 1909 to 1921* (Washington: Smithsonian Institution Press, 1993).

Ritter, Gerhard. *The Schlieffen Plan: Critique of a Myth*, trans. Andrew and Eva Wilson (New York: Frederick A. Praeger, 1958).

Rothenberg, Gunther E. "Moltke, Schlieffen, and the Doctrine of Strategic Envelopment," in Peter Paret, ed., *Makers of Modern Strategy* (Princeton, N.J.: Princeton University Press, 1986), pp. 296–325.

_____. *The Army of Francis Joseph* (West Lafayette, Ind.: Purdue University Press, 1976).

Showalter, Dennis. *Tannenberg: Clash of Empires* (Hamden, Conn.: Archon Books, 1991).

Stone, Norman. *The Eastern Front, 1914–1917* (New York: Charles Scribner's Sons, 1975).

Terraine, John. *Mons: The Retreat to Victory* (New York: Macmillan, 1960).

10

ATTEMPTING TO END THE
STALEMATE, 1914–1916

**1914–1915: Adjusting to the
Unexpected and Searching
for Alternatives**

1916: The Battles of Attrition

**Tactical and Technological
Innovations**

$\mathbb{T}$he failure of the belligerents in 1914 to end the war transformed it into a long total war and ultimately into a world war. As the war became deadlocked at the tactical and operational levels, and as the battling armies consumed vast supplies, the belligerents mobilized nearly all their people and economic resources. Despite the terrible casualty lists and huge costs, none of the belligerents chose to quit fighting; instead, other powers, such as Italy and the Ottoman Empire, entered the war. Because of the enormous demands of the war, resources and access to them became crucial, and sea power for obtaining these resources or conversely for preventing an opponent from acquiring them assumed greater importance. The war soon became a vast conflict on air, land, and sea in major portions of the globe.

In the search for ways to win the war, the participants reconsidered their strategies. For the Central Powers, an intense debate began in late 1914 about how Germany should focus its efforts. As Austria-Hungary's situation became more desperate, Falkenhayn reluctantly shifted forces from the Western to the Eastern Front. By remaining on the defensive in the west and moving forces to the east, he hoped to neutralize Russian military power and then to return to the west and deal with the Allies. For the Allies in the west, the alternatives seemed more numerous. While some political and military leaders perceived weakness in Austria-Hungary and the Ottoman Empire and called for the opening of new fronts on the flanks of Europe, others argued for concentrating efforts against German defensive positions on the Western Front and breaking through them. And almost all recognized the importance of blocking the flow of resources to the Central Powers. With the launching in 1915 of major offensives on the Western Front and several peripheral operations, the Allies tried simultaneously to break through German defensive positions on the Western Front and to open new fronts on the flanks of Europe.

The many battles of the war's first two years left the Western Front deadlocked and almost static, while armies on the Eastern Front moved great distances. On the Western Front both sides focused their energy and resources on making a breakthrough and restoring mobility but failed. After the Central Powers broke through Russian defenses at Gorlice-Tarnow and drove forward two hundred miles on the Eastern Front, the Germans turned west and in a grinding battle of attrition at Verdun tried to force France from the war. As the combatants searched for alternatives, they began developing new technologies and methods capable of breaking the stalemate. Though the common view of World War I is one of stagnation, this search for new tactics and technologies resulted in the introduction and development of new methods, weapons, and equipment on a remarkable scale.

1914–1915: Adjusting to the Unexpected and Searching for Alternatives

As fall turned into winter in 1914, the dreams of a highly mobile, short war were replaced by the realities of a destructive, consuming war of position and attrition. The changing situation forced both sides to address fundamentally different problems than the ones they had anticipated. When General von Moltke, who was Chief of the German General Staff, received a letter early in the war outlining the need for better economic planning and controls, he responded, "Don't bother me with economics. I am busy conducting the war." Moltke's views were common among political and military leaders, but it did not take long for them to realize that the waging of modern war demanded the mobilization and marshaling of economic resources.

Germany in particular was in no position to wage a long drawn-out war, for it had to import many raw materials and goods. As soon as the war began, the British navy established a blockade of Germany's coastline and severely curtailed its access to overseas suppliers. Though other navies contributed, the subsequent war at sea was essentially a conflict between the navies of Great Britain and Germany. Although the Germans were not yet willing to give up the possibility of receiving supplies from overseas, they immediately recognized the importance of obtaining resources from the heart of Europe; Walther Rathenau, one of Germany's leading industrialists, led the effort to set up a mixture of government and privately owned companies for obtaining raw materials. He began with no clear plans, but by the spring of 1915 he was able to report to the minister of war that the supply of essential raw materials was sufficient. Germany's industry could supply the army with thousands of items in sufficient numbers and quality. Not until August 1916, when simultaneous battles were being fought on the Somme, on the Meuse, in Galicia, and in Italy did serious shortages again occur. Nonetheless the Allied blockade had an effect; though no substitutes for food could be found, the German government established meatless days and initiated a rigid system of price controls and rationing. When wheat supply grew short, the Germans learned to make "war bread" out of potatoes and turnips. And to take the place of supplies unavailable to the German war economy, scientists created *ersatz* (substitute) materials. The perfection of the nitrogen-fixation process, for example, permitted the manufacture of explosives even though nitrates could no longer be imported. Similarly, cellulose was developed as a substitute for cotton.

In the beginning of the war, France also faced particularly acute problems, for it had conscripted most of its factory and farm workers because of its expectations of a short war. Ammunition shortages appeared almost immediately, and barely two months into the war France began releasing soldiers so they could return to factories and farms and begin producing desperately needed food and matériel. To make matters worse, when the front stabilized, some of France's most important sources of coal and iron lay behind enemy lines; however, it eventually managed to increase the manufacture of war matériel and to lead the Allies in the production of all types of weapons except rifles and machine guns. Nonetheless, France depended on Great Britain and the United States for raw materials and fuel and became increasingly reliant on them for food.

Throughout Europe centrally planned and directed economies emerged as each government set up a system of boards and commissions to coordinate its war effort. The British, for example, formed a ministry of munitions in June 1915 with David Lloyd George as its first head. A large increase in output soon resulted. With many men in the armed services, women—particularly in Britain and France—played an increasingly important role in manufacturing crucially needed war matériel. The industrialization of war had arrived, and each country committed almost all its resources to the war effort. Meeting the demands of the military while simultaneously maintaining popular support for the war in the face of failure and horrendous casualties, however, created many problems for governments and often caused stormy confrontations between political and military leaders.

Searching for Tactical and Strategic Alternatives

As political and military leaders feverishly labored to increase the size of their armies and navies, replace casualties, and obtain sufficient weapons, munitions, equipment, and supplies, both sides continued their attacks on the Western Front. After they failed to outflank each other in the "Race to the Sea," they concentrated on breaking through their opponent's defenses. Before the trench lines reached the English Channel, the Germans attacked

The industrialization of war transformed the
home front as well as the battlefield. Many
women found jobs in factories that produced
vast amounts of weapons, equipment, and
ammunition.

around Verdun in September 1914 but did little more than create a salient
east of the city of St. Mihiel. Other German attacks near Soissons and in
Lorraine in January 1915 also failed to yield substantial results.

The first major opportunity to prevent a deadlock came to the Germans when the escape of the Belgians from Antwerp released the German
forces that had besieged them. After combining these forces with other
newly formed divisions, the Germans made a strong attack against the
extreme western end of the front near the English Channel. When in the
middle of October the Belgians opened the sluices and allowed the sea to
flood the area, the Germans attempted to break through Allied defensive
lines east of Ypres. The Germans threw newly formed divisions—consisting
primarily of 17-to-20-year-olds—into the battle, but these poorly trained
but enthusiastic youth suffered such horrendous casualties that the Germans used the phrase "The Massacre of the Innocents at Ypres" to describe
the action.

Despite the initial failures, both sides continued to seek a breakthrough. They believed that if they could reach the open fields behind the
trenches and barbed wire, a decisive battle could be fought and victory
attained. The attacks, however, invariably failed. The length of the opposing
lines and the strength of the defensive positions seriously limited the combatants' ability to maneuver. With no open flanks and with barbed wire,
entrenchments, machine guns, and artillery creating a significant barrier,
most attacks quickly ground down to muddy and bloody halts. On those

rare occasions when an attack managed to break through the enemy's position, sufficient forces could not move quickly enough through the opened gap to take advantage of the momentary opportunity. Both sides quickly recognized the advantages of using heavy concentrations of artillery fire to blast their way through the enemy's lines. Reliance on massive amounts of artillery, however, increased the demand for munitions and complicated coordination of infantry and artillery actions.

After the first battle of Ypres ended in the middle of November 1914, the Allies launched several attacks. In December, Joffre attacked unsuccessfully north of Arras and supported this attack with another one in Champagne, but neither attack yielded important results. The French blamed their failures on the absence of sufficient artillery preparation and on inadequate coordination between the artillery and the infantry. In February 1915 the French again attacked in Champagne, and in April they attempted to reduce the German-held salient around St. Mihiel. Both attacks failed despite the improved use of artillery.

The Germans initially had the upper hand in artillery exchanges, for they had considerably more heavy artillery than the Allies. Each German corps had 16 150-mm howitzers, 18 105-mm howitzers, and 126 77-mm field guns, a total of 160 tubes, while a French corps had only 120 75-mm guns. Though the British had fewer artillery pieces than the French, each of their infantry divisions did have four 60-pounders that could reach the Germans' 150-mm howitzers. For months the Germans skillfully used their more numerous and longer-range artillery to shatter Allied attacks, disrupt their artillery, and inflict large numbers of casualties.

In March 1915 the British attacked at Neuve Chapelle in their first serious attempt to break through the German trench system. To make a penetration, the British concentrated 40,000 men and sixty-two light artillery batteries along a front of about 2,000 yards. Their objective was to seize Aubers Ridge, which was behind the German line and being used to observe their positions. Hoping to surprise the Germans, the British moved their guns forward at night and registered them surreptitiously by firing only a few rounds. This provided sufficient firing data for all the guns to fire more accurately and effectively. Relying heavily on aerial photographs to identify targets, they intended to fire an intense, thirty-five-minute preparatory bombardment which would also include cutting the barbed wire with shrapnel from 18-pounders. When the attack began, the British made some advances but could not exploit their advantage before the attack bogged down because of inadequate coordination between the artillery and the infantry. As the British advance slowed, the Germans moved reinforcements into the gap and halted the attack. Future attacks usually relied on much more extensive and longer artillery preparation.

A momentary advantage appeared for the Germans in April 1915 when they employed chlorine gas on the Western Front. The use of poisonous gasses had been proposed during the Crimean War and the American Civil War, but none had been used. As early as 1899 at the Hague Conference, the international community passed a declaration prohibiting the use of shells filled with asphyxiating gasses. By 1915, the desire to overcome the

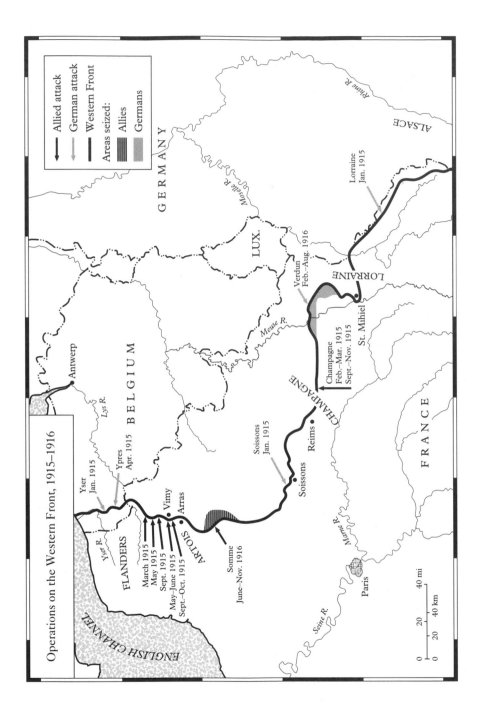

Operations on the Western Front, 1915–1916

Legend:
Allied attack
German attack
Western Front
Areas seized:
Allies
Germans

GERMANY

Rhine R.

ALSACE

Lorraine
Jan. 1915

LORRAINE

Moselle R.

Verdun
Feb.–Aug. 1916

St. Mihiel

LUX.

Meuse R.

Champagne
Feb.–Mar. 1915
Sept.–Nov. 1915

CHAMPAGNE

Antwerp

Lys R.

BELGIUM

Yser
Jan. 1915

Ypres
Apr. 1915

Soissons
Jan. 1915

Reims

Soissons

FRANCE

Yser R.

FLANDERS

ARTOIS

Vimy
Arras

March 1915
May 1915
Sept. 1915
May–June 1915
Sept.–Oct. 1915

Somme
June–Nov. 1916

ENGLISH CHANNEL

Marne R.

Paris

Seine R.

0   20   40 mi
0   20   40 km

bloody tactical stalemate had led both sides to employ tear gas. On January 31, 1915, the Germans fired over 18,000 artillery rounds filled with asphyxiating gas at the Russians, but the rounds had little or no effect because of the cold weather.

On the morning of April 15, 1915, the Germans released a cloud of yellowish-green chlorine gas against French positions about three miles north of Ypres. Though the equipment consisted of little more than commercial cylindrical containers, the unexpected appearance of gas in the trenches led to panic and the French troops ran away, leaving a huge hole in their defensive line. The Germans, protected only by cotton wadding tied over their faces, moved forward into the opening, but were soon stopped by their own gas and then by the heroic fighting of the Canadians and French. The Allies reestablished their defensive lines, but the Germans had made significant gains.

Poisonous gasses were used throughout the war, but they never again came so close to providing a decisive edge for victory. In fact, very few soldiers actually died from poisonous gasses. Thus chemical warfare added to the terror and casualties of the war but did little to shorten it. One of the interesting byproducts of the use of gasses was the introduction of smoke-making devices to simulate gas. These soon provided the smoke screens that would be used in attacks for the remainder of the war.

Despite the use of chemicals and despite extremely high casualties, the Allies continued to attack and to seek a breakthrough of the enemy's defensive lines. On May 9, 1915, a combined Franco-British attack began in Artois between Neuve Chapelle and Arras. The main objective was to seize Vimy Ridge, which dominated the entire region, but neither the French nor the British came close to breaking through the enemy's defenses.

The opposing armies quickly recognized the difficulty of moving across terrain where massive artillery barrages had fallen. The heavily churned and broken ground slowed the advance of follow-on forces and in particular delayed the forward displacement of artillery batteries. An attacker sometimes had to build roads through positions previously held by the enemy before heavy artillery pieces could be advanced. Since the infantry could hardly move without the protection of artillery, the depth and pace of penetrations were severely limited by the moving of artillery across the devastated ground. The Germans learned that they could rush reinforcements by light railway to a threatened sector faster than the Allies could push through devastated terrain. As a consequence, attacks rarely advanced more than a mile or two, and thousands of Allied soldiers lost their lives in vain attempts to achieve the much-desired breakthrough.

After a summer of recuperation and accumulation of supplies and equipment, the Allies attacked in Artois and Champagne in September. In Artois, the British attacked toward Loos, while the French again attacked toward Vimy Ridge. In Champagne, the French attacked midway between Reims and Verdun. The Allies were particularly optimistic about the attack in Champagne, for they attacked with two armies against twelve German divisions along a front of fifteen miles. With gasses being used, with follow-on infantry ready to move, with cavalry available for the exploitation, and with a violent artillery preparation from 2,500 guns lasting three days, the Champagne attack seemed a sure success. But like the attacks in Artois, it too failed, even though it initially made significant gains. For the first time in the war, the Germans had prepared a second belt of defenses and withdrew part of their artillery behind this belt before the French attacked. Though the German defenders were shaken and Falkenhayn feared a breakthrough, the second belt managed to hold. The French had made extensive preparations and suffered huge losses, but they had nevertheless failed.

The year of costly Allied attacks came to a close with the failure of the Champagne offensive. Despite numerous attacks and the loss of thousands of lives, the defensive lines on the Western Front never moved more than three miles in either direction. Hoping a new commander would bring an end to the slaughter, the British replaced General Sir John French with General Sir Douglas Haig at the end of 1915. The French also sought to reduce their casualties. During the sixteen months from August 1, 1914, to November 30, 1915, 664,000 French soldiers had died; during the thirty-five months from December 1915 until the armistice another 683,000 would die. Instead of replacing Joffre in 1915, however, the French intensified their efforts to devise operational methods that would save French lives.

From the Allies' viewpoint, the only positive development in the first year of fighting was some progress in improving cooperation between the British and French armies. The Allies, however, did not establish a clear chain of command; with neither a supreme war council nor a supreme commander, the best the Allies could do was to coordinate their strategy and operations.

Life and Death in the Trenches

More so on the Western than on the Eastern Front, the trench came to symbolize the new type of warfare now facing the participants. Its appearance and use changed greatly during the first two years of the war. The first trenches to appear on the Western Front were little more than long, shallow ditches about waist deep; but after the Western Front stabilized, they became much deeper and much more extensive. Initially consisting of only one or two lines, trenches eventually consisted of two or three lines and in some cases two or three belts, each with multiple lines of trenches. As the terrifying effects of artillery became apparent, the trenches became deeper and much more elaborate. Except for those areas where high water tables prevented deep digging, most trenches became deeper than a man's head and one or two yards wide. Instead of being straight lines, trenches quickly assumed a zigzag appearance. Turns and bends in a trench prevented an enemy from using enfilading fire down the entire length of a trench if a small portion of it was captured. Between the opposing lines of trenches and thousands of rolls of barbed wire, a "no-man's-land" quickly appeared. Depending on the terrain, the separation between the opposing trenches varied from a few dozen to several hundred yards.

Trenches running perpendicular to the main lines were also used. These zigzag-shaped trenches, known as communication trenches, connected one line of trenches to another and enabled troops to move back and forth between lines in relative safety. Messengers and reserves frequently

An extensive network of trenches quickly appeared on the Western Front. Those who lived in the trenches used boardwalks to keep their feet dry and sand bags to keep the walls of the trenches stable. Signs provided directions to the front lines as well as to other points.

moved back and forth between the connecting trenches. Shallow trenches were also placed ahead of the front lines. These trenches extended to observation posts or early warning positions.

As the effects of firepower became more apparent in the second and third years of fighting, the opposing armies often used strong points, rather than continuous lines of trenches. Scattered in depth, the strong points were usually organized for all-around defense and strengthened by numerous machine guns. With enormous amounts of artillery churning and plowing the ground, neat lines of entrenchments quickly disappeared in a moonscape of shell holes and mine craters. Though entrenchments remained important, defensive positions came to resemble a checkerboard, rather than a system of lines. The use of strong points was particularly prevalent after late 1916.

Commanders found it extremely difficult to feed and care for their soldiers in the trenches; indeed, providing a hot meal to soldiers in the trenches proved to be a most arduous task. The Germans made special efforts to shelter their soldiers when they were not occupying the front line and often prepared deep dugouts that could protect platoons and companies from Allied artillery fire. By Allied standards, many of their dugouts were almost luxurious—some even included beds and electric light systems. The Germans also made wide use of concrete pillboxes, often camouflaged and hidden from artillery fire. One can still often identify the location of German positions by the presence of these rudimentary but effective concrete bunkers.

Life in the trenches was grisly—the overpowering stench of decaying bodies of men and animals, of human excrement, and of chloride of lime to combat odors and disease could not be escaped. Soldiers had to coexist with huge rats feeding off the dead. The constant threat of death also weighed against the trench occupants. In addition to the danger of an attack or raid, random artillery rounds sometimes fell among soldiers who had to endure incessant sniper fire. A simple hot meal and cool beverage in a place safely to the rear must have seemed like heaven to a soldier who had survived a long stretch in the trenches.

Peripheral Operations

From the earliest days, it was clear that the Great War would not be confined to the European continent. As early as August 7, 1914, British and French troops invaded German Togoland on the coast of west-central Africa. Other German possessions in Africa, including Southwest Africa and the Cameroons, soon came under pressure. By November 1914, German possessions in the Pacific had been seized by Australia, New Zealand, and Japan. A notable exception to the relatively rapid defeat of Germany's forces in its colonial possessions occurred in East Africa, where a small detachment managed to resist Allied forces until the end of the war.

The entry of the Ottoman Empire into the war on the side of the Central Powers, as well as growing discontent—particularly among the British—with the deadlock on the Western Front, however, prompted the Allies to launch operations on the periphery of Europe. To some, the Ottoman Empire appeared easier to break than the German defenses on the Western Front. The British split into two schools of thought—one seeing western Europe as the decisive theater and the other calling for attacks on the enemy's strategic flanks. Joffre strongly objected to attacks on the periphery of Europe, for he believed that victory could be achieved only on the Western Front and that the diversion of resources to other theaters would delay a decision. Nevertheless, between 1915 and 1916 the Allies sought gains in peripheral operations while simultaneously seeking a breakthrough on the Western Front. Whether one views the peripheral operations as B. H. Liddell Hart did as a "Strategy of the Indirect Approach," or as J. F. C. Fuller did as a "Strategy of Evasion," significant forces became involved in campaigns in the Middle East and on the periphery of Europe.

In January 1915 the British defended Egypt against a Turkish invasion, and over the next three years of fighting gradually moved into Palestine with British forces eventually fighting under the command of General Sir Edmund Allenby. In March 1915 the British began the Dardanelles campaign in an abortive attempt to open the narrow straits between the Aegean and Black seas. In the spring of 1915, British forces expanded their control over Mesopotamia and moved courageously up the Tigris River against overwhelmingly larger Turkish forces. In October, British and French forces launched the Salonika campaign into Macedonia in an attempt to aid the Serbian army.

Of these campaigns, the Gallipoli campaign in the Dardanelles was the most poorly conducted. The objective of the operation was to seize the Straits of the Dardanelles. In doing so, the Allies could expand seaborne lines of communications with Russia and sever links between the Central Powers and most of the Ottoman Empire. Although the Turks had managed to block the Straits with minefields, shore batteries, and two German ships, the Allies expected the Turkish defenses to crumble under only light pressure. The Allies initially dispatched a sizable naval squadron with orders to seize the Gallipoli peninsula and Constantinople, but after three of the eighteen Allied battleships were sunk and three others badly damaged, the naval forces pulled back and awaited the arrival of ground forces. During this delay, the Turks formed a separate army for the defense of the Dardanelles and placed it under the command of General Otto Liman von Sanders, the head of the German military mission. The new commander quickly located his forces in central positions where they could react rapidly to any Allied landings.

When an Allied force consisting of British, French, and Australian–New Zealand (ANZAC) troops attacked on April 25, 1915, the operation began as planned but soon degenerated into a disaster. The Allies landed at several different points near the southwestern tip of the long Gallipoli peninsula. With troops disembarking from barges towed by rowboats and from colliers that had been converted into infantry landing craft, the British and ANZAC forces encountered strong opposition and were prevented from moving inland. The British landing at Cape Helles at the tip of the peninsula met particularly strong resistance; on one beach 70 percent of the first 1,000

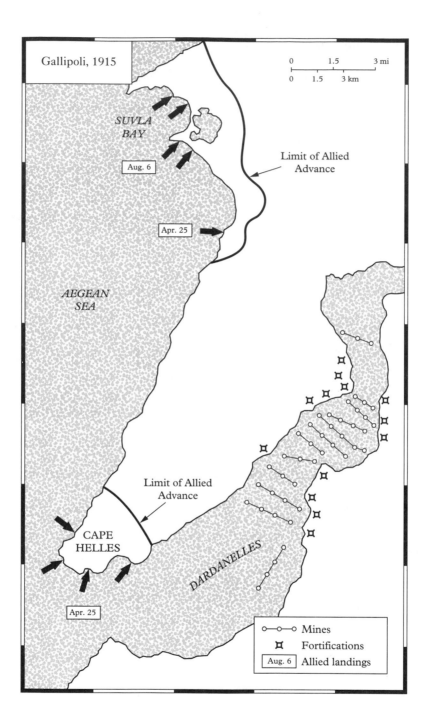

Gallipoli, 1915

0   1.5   3 mi
0   1.5   3 km

SUVLA
BAY

Aug. 6

Limit of Allied
Advance

Apr. 25

AEGEAN
SEA

Limit of Allied
Advance

CAPE
HELLES

DARDANELLES

Apr. 25

○—○—○ Mines
¤ Fortifications
Aug. 6 Allied landings

troops to land became casualties. Attacks on subsequent days made only minimal gains and within two weeks of the first landings, Gallipoli resembled the Western Front with its entrenchments and fortified positions.

On August 6, the British landed additional forces at Suvla Bay, about fifteen miles north of Cape Helles, and attempted to outflank the Turkish defenders to the south. Despite being unopposed initially, the slow advance of the British and the rapid reaction of the Turks soon resulted in another stalemate. The Allied operation suffered from numerous deficiencies including lack of experience in amphibious operations, water shortages, poor fire support, misused communications, and muddled commanders. In December 1915 the Allies abandoned the Suvla Bay beaches, and in January 1916 the last Allied soldiers withdrew from Cape Helles and thereby from the Dardanelles peninsula. The British alone had suffered more than 200,000 casualties. Neither the Gallipoli campaign nor the other peripheral operations contributed significantly to shortening the war.

The Eastern Front

After the failure of the Schlieffen Plan in 1914, the Germans reconsidered their strategic alternatives. For a short time in November–December 1914 they temporarily relied on a defensive strategy, later described by Falkenhayn as a "transition to trench warfare." Emphasis on the defense enabled the Germans to protect their frontiers, increase the manufacture and supply of matériel, expand the capacity of their railways, take advantage of interior lines, and rest, train, and reequip their troops. As the Germans analyzed their alternatives, the military hierarchy was split by a debate between the "Westerners" (led by Falkenhayn) and the "Easterners" (led by Hindenburg and Ludendorff) about whether the German effort should be focused in the east or the west. Hindenburg and Ludendorff believed the shifting of divisions from the west to the east would enable the Central Powers to defeat Russia and induce the other Allied powers to end the war. Insisting the war could be won only in the west, Falkenhayn rejected this argument.

Friction between the Germans and the Austrians complicated Falkenhayn's dilemma. Much like the Allies, the Central Powers had no supreme command. Though the Germans slowly assumed the role of "senior partner" in the alliance, the Austrians did not enter into a clearly secondary role until late 1916. Despite the better performance of the German military and the need to use German forces to stiffen the Austrians, Conrad von Hötzendorf, the chief of the general staff, refused to relinquish Austria-Hungary's freedom of action in making strategy or conducting military operations. Relations between Falkenhayn and Conrad became particularly strained in early 1915 when the Germans pressured the Austrians to yield territory to the Italians in order to keep them from entering the war on the side of the Allies. Conrad, nevertheless, continued to demand additional support from Germany.

Despite his desire to focus German efforts in the west, Falkenhayn soon found himself compelled to come to the aid of the Austrians. In January 1915, he gave four corps to Hindenburg for an attack from East Prussia that would force the Russians to divert forces to the north and provide the Austrians in the south some relief. Meanwhile, Conrad launched an attack from the Carpathian Mountains, but the Austrians suffered heavy casualties and made no progress. On February 7, Hindenburg's Eighth Army defeated the Russian Tenth Army in the second Masurian Lakes campaign, but most of the Russians escaped and established new defensive positions to the east. On February 27, Conrad launched another attack and failed again. About one month later, about 120,000 Austrians surrendered at the fortress of Przemysl, which had been surrounded for months. In April, the Russians began a new offensive and seized the important Dukla Pass, thereby threatening to break through the mountains into the heart of Austria-Hungary.

As the Austrian situation deteriorated, Falkenhayn concluded that the Central Powers had to cripple Russia's offensive capability. After Allied offensives on the Western Front failed in February–March 1915, he believed that the Allies could not yet force a decision on that front and that he had the freedom to focus on the east. Instead of allowing Hindenburg to attack from the north, however, he decided to strike the Russian center. After initiating preparations, he contacted Conrad in the middle of April and coordinated the upcoming attack.

The Gorlice-Tarnow Breakthrough and Russian Withdrawal

To increase the chances of success against the Russians, Falkenhayn directed the formation of Eleventh Army and appointed General August von Mackensen as its commander. Mackensen chose Colonel Hans von Seeckt as his chief of staff. Consisting of eight German and three Austrian divisions, Eleventh Army moved into position north of the Carpathian mountains between the Austrian Third and Fourth armies. Conrad refused to give the Germans overall command of the operation. Though Mackensen also controlled the operations of the Austrian Fourth Army, the German and Austrian high commands jointly approved all major directives, and the Austrians issued them.

Most of the German divisions in Eleventh Army had recently served on the Western Front, as had Colonel von Seeckt, one of the most outstanding officers in the German army. Von Seeckt had played a key role in the January 1915 attack at Soissons and had learned important lessons about the need to modify infantry tactics and achieve better cooperation between infantry and artillery. He now applied some of these ideas on the Eastern Front. The subsequent German success, however, was due less to the introduction of fundamentally new methods than it was to Russia's shortage of machine guns and the inability of its artillery to work closely with its infantry. That the Germans had not yet solved the riddle of breaking through an enemy's defensive position is best illustrated by several of the regiments in the Gorlice-Tarnow attack taking casualties at the same rate as in the disastrous Ypres offensive of the previous fall.

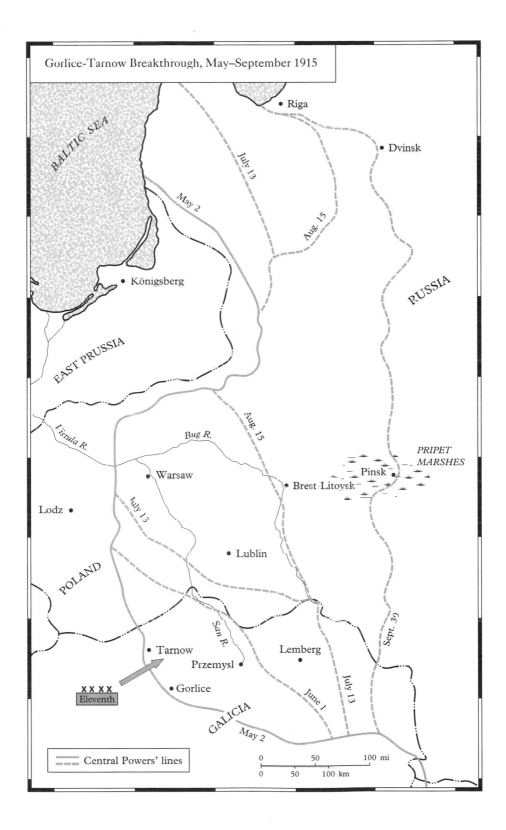

Gorlice-Tarnow Breakthrough, May–September 1915

BALTIC SEA

• Riga

• Dvinsk

May 2

July 13

Aug. 15

RUSSIA

• Königsberg

EAST PRUSSIA

Vistula R.

Bug R.

Aug. 15

PRIPET
MARSHES

• Warsaw

Pinsk •

Brest-Litovsk •

Lodz •

July 13

• Lublin

POLAND

San R.

• Tarnow

Przemysl •

Lemberg •

Sept. 30

XXXX
Eleventh

• Gorlice

June 1

July 13

GALICIA

May 2

Central Powers' lines

| 0 | | 50 | | 100 mi |

| 0 | 50 | 100 km |

The two Russian corps opposing Eleventh Army between Gorlice and Tarnow were not prepared for the onslaught that struck them on May 2, 1915. Four hours of preparatory fire from German artillery reduced their trenches, opened holes in their sparse barbed wire, cut communications lines, and disrupted their artillery. Pushing forward rapidly and advancing almost eight miles in the first two days, the Germans quickly punched through the shallow defenses of the Russian Third Army. With few Russian reserves available, the Germans continued moving forward rapidly, but the Russian *Stavka* refused to give General Ivanov, the commander of the Southwest Front, permission to withdraw; Russian leaders feared the Germans would outflank their forces as they pulled out of the Carpathian Mountains. This refusal condemned Third Army to staggering losses. On May 10, Third Army finally received permission to withdraw to the San River, which was about seventy-five miles east of their original position.

After arriving at the San River, the Russians found themselves in an extremely weak position; they had lost 80 percent of Third Army. Almost no defensive positions had been prepared, and much of the barbed wire and timber seized from the Austrians that could have been used to strengthen their positions had been sold to the local population. Supplies of artillery ammunition were extremely limited; the Russians had only 100,000 rounds in reserve while the German Eleventh Army alone had more than one million. To add to the Russians' difficulties, German positions on the western bank of the narrow river completely dominated the eastern bank in several key areas.

The battles along the San River followed the Gorlice-Tarnow pattern with the Germans establishing a large bridgehead across the river between May 16 and 19. Meanwhile, the Russians pushed back the Austrians, and the Germans had to rush to their assistance. In mid-June, the German offensive began anew, and on June 22 Austro-German forces captured Lemberg, fifty miles east of the San River. The Russians began a full-scale retreat and fell back; by the time they stopped some units were seventy-five miles east of the San River and 150 miles east of Gorlice-Tarnow. The Central Powers once again controlled most of Galicia.

Between June 3 and July 1, a debate occurred between Falkenhayn, Conrad, and Hindenburg over the Central Powers' strategy. With Italy entering the war on May 23 on the Allied side, Conrad wanted to concentrate against Italy, but Falkenhayn preferred to concentrate against the Allies in France. He believed that the offensive against the Russians had achieved its purpose and had neutralized Russian military power. Hindenburg and Ludendorff aggressively opposed the movement of divisions away from the Eastern Front and argued for a continuation of the attack in the east. Conrad and Falkenhayn finally agreed that the best course of action was to continue the offensive against Russia.

As the Central Powers pressed the Russians, they shifted the direction of their attack in Galicia from the east to the northeast toward Brest-Litovsk. In a gigantic pincer movement, other forces attacked toward Brest-Litovsk from the north. With pressure coming from the south and the north, the Polish salient was quickly overrun. Lublin fell on July 30, Warsaw on August 4. By August 30 the Russians had withdrawn east of the Bug River and Brest-Litovsk, and the Central Powers had established a vast front across the base of the Polish salient.

The Russian withdrawal continued. By September 30, the Central Powers had moved deep into Russia. They occupied a line running from Riga on the Baltic Sea, to Dvinsk, to Pinsk, to the Romanian border. This line was about 200 miles east of Gorlice-Tarnow where Mackensen's forces had made the first breakthrough in May 1915. Except for the moves associated with Brusilov's offensive in 1916 and the Russian collapse in 1917, the opposing forces on the Eastern Front remained generally along this line for the remainder of the war.

The Central Powers had gained a victory of immense proportions and had inflicted more than 2 million casualties on the Russians. Their success was due as much to the ineptitude of the Russian army as it was to the professionalism and preparedness of the German army. With more advanced techniques of artillery and infantry coordination, a more effective command and staff structure, and more supplies, the Central Powers had significant advantages. The Russians were hampered by an inefficient and fragmented high command and were outnumbered in machine guns and artillery pieces. Nevertheless, the Russians did not quit fighting, and thousands of them lost their lives.

The disaster provoked an immediate outcry in Russia, and complaints focused on crippling shortages in rifles and in artillery shells. In reality, however, the Russians needed more than an increase in the number of weapons and shells. Russian leaders recognized the poor organization of the army and the ineptitude of some of the commanders; they soon began streamlining their command structure and replacing weak commanders. Having reduced the Russian threat, Falkenhayn shifted forces to the west where the buildup of Allied troops posed a greater threat.

1916: The Battles of Attrition

Even though the Allies had the common goal of defeating Austria-Hungary and Germany, they had no common, agreed-upon strategy for achieving this goal. The first meeting of Allied military leaders occurred in July 1915, but no supreme command or common staff structure emerged, and almost no agreements—except for a call for future meetings—were reached on the conduct of coalition warfare. In December 1915, military leaders of France, Great Britain, Belgium, and Italy and representatives from Russia and Japan met at Joffre's headquarters.

This was the first and only time that the major Allies formulated and attempted to carry out a coordinated strategy; but the strategy was neither detailed nor tightly coordinated. To regain the initiative from the Germans, which they had seized in the west in 1914 and on the Eastern Front in 1915, the Allies agreed to launch offensives on the principal fronts in France,

Russia, and Italy, but they did not establish formal mechanisms for coordinating strategy and operations. The Allies preferred personal meetings and coordination among the military leaders rather than a formal command and staff structure that could have impinged on their sovereignty.

Of all the Allies, the French and British cooperated the best, but the British were reluctant to subordinate their small and still expanding army to the French. They preferred to make their main effort in Flanders, close to the Belgian coast, which they believed to be "an objective of great political and naval as well as military importance." In February 1916, the French and British finally agreed to conduct a combined offensive on both sides of the Somme River and tentatively scheduled the offensive for the late summer of 1916. This agreement was overcome by events when the Germans launched an offensive on February 21 at Verdun.

While the Allies reconsidered their strategy, Falkenhayn shifted his main effort from east to west. By late 1915, the Central Powers had successfully reoccupied Poland and Galicia and had seriously weakened the Russians. Similarly, the Allied attack in the Balkans through Salonika had been stymied, and the Allies were withdrawing from Gallipoli after the failure of their attempted invasion. The only area in which the war was not going well for the Central Powers was on the sea, for the naval blockade was beginning

General Erich von Falkenhayn became Germany's chief of the general staff in September 1914. He presided over the shifting of German strategic focus from the Western to the Eastern Front in 1915 and back to the Western Front in 1916.

to cause shortages (particularly of food) and to affect military operations. The sea power of the Allies also enabled them to add to the men and matériel on the Western Front. If the Central Powers did not act quickly, the buildup of Allied troops and matériel would soon provide them an important advantage in what clearly had become a war of attrition.

The Battle of Verdun

In Falkenhayn's analysis of his options on the Western Front, which he completed in December 1915, he described England as Germany's "arch enemy" and the war on the Continent as a "sideshow" for the English. If the Germans defeated France, he said, England's "best sword" would be removed from its hand, and the "strong probability" existed that it would "give up." He also argued that France was "almost exhausted" and that an attack on Verdun would force France to "commit every man available" since Verdun anchored the center of the entire Allied line. Given the closeness of Verdun to German railway connections (only twelve miles), the Germans could, theoretically, make a "relatively small effort" in which the forces of France could be "bled white." Thus Falkenhayn consciously chose a battle

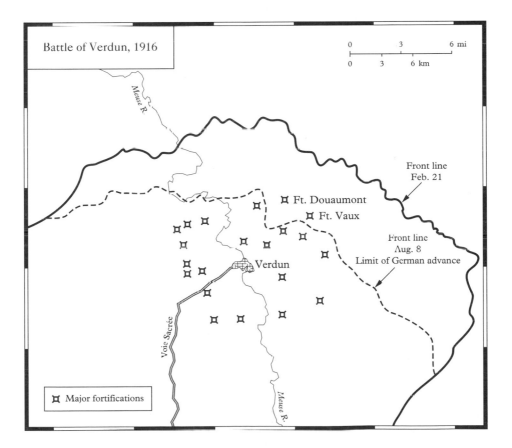

Battle of Verdun, 1916

0   3   6 mi

0   3   6 km

Meuse R.

Ft. Douaumont

Ft. Vaux

Front line
Feb. 21

Front line
Aug. 8
Limit of German advance

Verdun

Voie Sacrée

Meuse R.

◘ Major fortifications

of attrition; he intended to weaken French morale significantly and to force them to the breaking point. In believing Germany had to make only a relatively small effort, however, Falkenhayn forgot that attrition is a two-edged sword. France and Germany were about to become embroiled in a gigantic battle that would consume hundreds of thousands of lives.

When the Germans attacked on February 21, 1916, Falkenhayn ordered the German crown prince, William, whose Fifth Army had the mission of making the assault on Verdun, to confine his attack to the eastern side of the Meuse River. This river split the fortress system around Verdun through its center. With the city in the center, the fortress system consisted of more than twenty smaller forts arranged in a circle with a radius of about four to five miles. By insisting that the crown prince not attack on both sides of the Meuse, Falkenhayn intended to minimize casualties by attacking on a narrow front. Unfortunately for the German infantry, his order sent them forward into the roughest terrain around Verdun.

The German attack on February 21 began with a twelve-hour bombardment from 1,400 guns firing about 100,000 shells per hour into the small area. Late in the afternoon the infantry moved forward with scouts in the forefront; they located areas not destroyed by artillery fire and directed further fire against them. If they encountered a strong point, they bypassed or encircled it. Centers of resistance fell one by one, but the Germans succeeded in advancing only three miles after two days of fighting. Despite the Germans' overwhelming advantage in infantry and artillery, the French delayed their advance by a heroic defense and by highly effective artillery fire from across the river into the German flanks.

The Germans continued to attack over the next several days, and in one of the greatest coups of the war managed to capture Fort Douaumont, the most important fortification in the fortress system, without firing a shot. In the heat and confusion of battle, French commanders on both flanks of the fort assumed that a permanent garrison was holding it, but in fact only a few soldiers were manning it. A handful of Germans surprised the few occupants and captured the fort easily. The fall of Fort Douaumont was one of the most tragic blunders of the war and cost France thousands of lives as it attempted to regain the fort.

To ensure Verdun did not fall, Joffre placed General Henri-Philippe Pétain in charge of its defense. Though hampered by a severe bout of double pneumonia, Pétain managed to strengthen Verdun's defenses and to reoccupy and rearm the forts still in French hands. Early in the war, the French had removed much of the artillery from the forts when they were desperately seeking longer-range artillery. Pétain assigned garrisons to the forts and ordered them to fight to the last man. Simultaneously, he began improving transportation links to the threatened sector. The two main rail lines to Verdun were unusable, for one was cut off by German forces in the St. Mihiel salient and the other by enemy artillery fire a dozen miles west of Verdun. Almost all the supplies for Verdun had to move along the narrow road from Bar-le-Duc. Soon an almost endless stream of trucks moved constantly up the important road that became known as the *Voie Sacré*, or Sacred Way.

Pétain also reorganized his defenses, breaking down his sector into four corps areas, each with its own artillery support. Part of this effort included the strengthening of the western bank of the Meuse. Recognizing the awesome power of the German artillery, he modified the defensive scheme by placing an advanced line of resistance in front of the principal line of resistance. The forward line did not have to be held at all costs and provided some elasticity for the defense; it also limited the number of soldiers coming directly under enemy fire.

By the end of February, the German Fifth Army's attack on the eastern bank had ground to a halt, so Falkenhayn approved expanding the fight to the western bank. On March 6, the Germans launched a powerful attack on the western bank and made their largest gains along the Meuse. Another attack began on March 20, followed by another on March 28 after fresh reserves were brought up. Despite the huge concentration of men and matériel, the Germans advanced only two miles.

On April 9 the Germans launched attacks on both sides of the Meuse, but again the French somehow managed to stop them. The next two months witnessed several bitter battles that resulted in only small changes in the location of the lines. After one final attempt to break through French lines on the western bank, which witnessed a huge expenditure of ammunition and lives, the Germans shifted away from the western bank and for the remainder of the battle concentrated on the eastern bank.

The bloody attacks and counterattacks continued through August when Falkenhayn was relieved as chief of staff of the German army. Hindenburg replaced him, and one of his first orders halted the attacks at Verdun. During the next three months the French launched several carefully controlled attacks with the infantry advancing by bounds as enormous artillery concentrations flattened German defenses to their front. These methodical attacks with limited objectives succeeded in pushing the Germans back slowly from their expensively gained terrain.

Though some innovations occurred in artillery and infantry tactics, the bulk of the fighting at Verdun was characterized more by its brutality than by its sophistication or subtlety. With hundreds of thousands of men jammed into a relatively small area and with the skies constantly filled with falling artillery shells, the Germans called Verdun the "sausage grinder" and the French called it the "furnace." A typical battle began with an artillery bombardment to obliterate the enemy's forward defenses. As reinforcements rushed forward to strengthen the defenses, many died under enemy artillery barrages before they could reach the forward positions. The survivors in forward positions, as well as the reinforcements, often fought desperately from destroyed shell-holes and trenches until friendly artillery and machine-gun fire repulsed the attackers.

By the time the fighting ended, the struggle had indelibly marked both armies. No one knows the exact number of casualties, but the French acknowledged having 377,231 casualties, with 162,308 soldiers killed or missing. Although the Germans probably suffered fewer casualties than the French, the combined losses of both countries may have been over 700,000.

Despite the sufferings of hundreds of thousands of soldiers, the front lines had barely moved.

The Battle of the Somme

Just prior to the attack on Verdun, the French and British had agreed to make a combined attack on the Somme, but the German attack derailed Allied plans. As enemy pressure on Verdun increased, Joffre asked the British to launch a diversionary attack in the Somme region and thereby relieve some of the pressure on Verdun. Haig delayed the attack, however, so he could complete the training of newly arrived divisions. He also recognized the considerable strength of the German defenses to his front and wanted his units as well prepared as possible.

Although the plan for the Somme attack was ambitious, it was fairly simple. Along a front of about twenty miles, the Allies intended to attack with the British Fourth Army in the north making the main attack and the French Fifth Army in the south making a supporting attack. After reaching the high ground between Bapaume and Péronne, the Allies would expand the gap by having the British turn north and northeast and the French east. Large cavalry forces would exploit the breakthrough by moving northeast in the direction of Cambrai.

British infantry leaving a forward trench on the first day of the Battle of the Somme. Many of the British never made it through their own barbed wire even though nearly 250,000 artillery shells exploded on German trenches in the hour just prior to the assault.

The key to the British attack was the overwhelming use of artillery. Massive preparatory fires rained on the German positions from June 24 until the attack on July 1. With 1,437 guns firing, the British sent 1,508,652 shells into the German lines. British leaders confidently believed the artillery would destroy the wire entanglements to the infantry's front and annihilate the German defenders. To ensure control by their officers, the heavily burdened British infantrymen were told to march slowly and steadily toward the enemy's lines; no one expected any serious opposition. Tragically for the British, the 1.5 million rounds of artillery did not obliterate German defenses. After the preparatory fire had ceased and the barrages had shifted from the front lines to the rear, German infantry emerged from their dugouts and delivered withering fire against the surprised and helpless British. Hurrying forward to join the attack on time, many British soldiers never even made it to the front lines of their own position.

Within the first hour of the attack, the British suffered 30,000 casualties; by the end of the day they lost 57,400—the highest rate of casualties ever experienced by the British army. The losses exceeded the total British combat casualties in the Crimean, Boer, and Korean wars combined. But despite these tremendous losses, General Haig continued to attack. Remaining optimistic about the possibility of making a breakthrough and determined to divert the Germans from Verdun, he pressed forward. With his forces taking large numbers of casualties at Verdun and the Somme, Falkenhayn ordered his commanders not to give up any terrain. German casualties also mounted alarmingly.

In mid-November the offensive on the Somme finally ended. Ludendorff noted in his memoirs that both sides were "utterly exhausted." The Allied blockade that prevented trade between the Central Powers and the rest of the world had weakened Germany. The effect of so many losses in 1916 and of large shortages of foodstuffs and other important goods greatly complicated Germany's continuing to press for a military victory in the war.

The Brusilov Offensive

The situation also became increasingly difficult in Russia. To support the offensives that were supposed to be launched by the Allies in the late summer of 1916 on the Western Front, Tsar Nicholas II agreed to launch an offensive on the Eastern Front. That he would do so is more an indication of his loyalty to his allies than of his army's preparedness. Nevertheless, the Russians had worked hard to improve their army following the disasters of 1915. In addition to greatly expanding the army's size, military leaders made the supply system more efficient and issued additional rifles, machine guns, field artillery pieces, and ammunition. Despite the increased supplies of ammunition, the number of rounds available per artillery piece remained significantly lower than that of the Allies on the Western Front.

As part of the effort to reinvigorate the Russian army, the tsar dismissed his uncle, Grand Duke Nicholas, as commander-in-chief, and on September 18, 1915, he personally assumed command of the entire front. While this caused some distress among the officers who admired the Grand

Duke, the tsar also appointed General Michael V. Alexeyev as his chief of staff, the officer who actually ran the army. Alexeyev was neither brilliant nor extremely talented, but he brought in additional officers to the *Stavka* and improved its functioning. Despite improvements in military effectiveness, the domestic situation deteriorated, for with Tsar Nicholas deeply involved in military operations, the direction of the government was left in the hands of Tsarina Alexandra and the mysterious holy man, Gregory Novykh, better known as Rasputin, who had a great deal of influence over the tsarina.

As part of the tsar's reforms, General Aleksei A. Brusilov replaced General Ivanov as commander of the Southwest Front. From the beginning, Brusilov recognized the necessity to resume the offensive and make numerous changes in techniques and organization so attacks could succeed. More than other Russian leaders, he tried to learn from the experience and methods of the Germans and the Allies. Among the points he emphasized were the use of surprise, the need to move reserves forward secretly and to protect them in deep dugouts, the need to coordinate artillery and infantry more closely, and the importance of improving front-line trenches and moving them closer to enemy lines. Brusilov also believed the Russians should attack on multiple axes—rather than mass in one sector—to prevent the enemy from concentrating all his reserves in a single sector.

What mattered most, however, was the diversion of German troops from the Eastern to the Western Front for the Verdun offensive. The Austrians also diverted some nine divisions to the Italian front for an offensive in Trentino. By May the inferno at Verdun was in full blaze, and the Austrians were making gains against the Italians.

An initial offensive in the north by the Russians on March 18, 1916, failed, but after Joffre pleaded for the Russians to launch their promised attack, the tsar asked Brusilov to attack in the south. Along a front of more than 175 miles, Brusilov's offensive began on June 4 with a one-day artillery preparation, followed by an infantry assault by his four field armies. The attack was a huge success. By June 12 Brusilov's forces had captured more than 190,000 Austrians, 216 guns, and 645 machine guns. Counting other casualties, the Austrians lost more than half their forces facing the Russians. On July 2 the commander of the northern Russian front began his attack, supported by far more artillery than had been available to Brusilov's forces. Though the northern front made only small gains, Brusilov continued advancing, and the Central Powers began rushing in reinforcements to halt him. As Germans and Austrians poured into the Galician area, Brusilov slowly lost the momentum of his attack since he had no reserves. Nevertheless, his forces captured more than 390,000 prisoners by the end of July and advanced more than fifty miles at their deepest point of penetration. But his advance did not sever the important railway line from Kowel to Lemberg that provided lateral communications for the Germans and the Austrians, and the offensive ended toward the end of September. Russian casualties for the year approached one million.

Along with the casualties and losses suffered by Germans on the Western Front at Verdun and the Somme, Brusilov's offensive had far-reaching

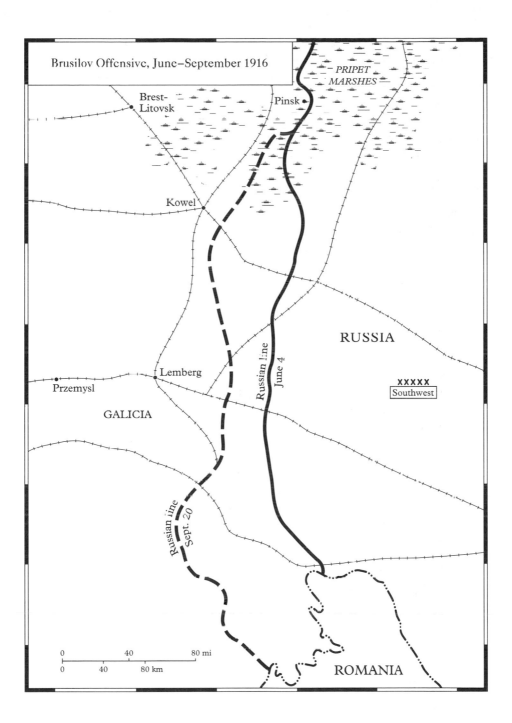

Brusilov Offensive, June–September 1916

PRIPET
MARSHES

Brest-
Litovsk

Pinsk

Kowel

RUSSIA

Russian line
June 4

Lemberg

XXXXX
Southwest

Przemysl

GALICIA

Russian line
Sept. 20

0   40   80 mi
0   40   80 km

ROMANIA

effects. The Austrian attack into Italy and the German attack against Verdun had been weakened. Falkenhayn's position as chief of staff had also eroded; and not surprisingly Hindenburg's position had strengthened since the
Russians had achieved little or no gains in the north. In August 1916, Hindenburg replaced Falkenhayn; Ludendorff accompanied him to Berlin. The
Russians' success against the Austrians also encouraged the Romanians to
join the Allies, but a German army under General Falkenhayn, who had been
demoted to commanding the combined forces of the Central Powers in Romania, quickly crushed the Romanian army. German and Austrian forces
entered Bucharest on December 6, 1916. Although Brusilov's offensive was
Russia's greatest victory of the war, its huge casualties contributed to the
Russian people's growing disillusionment with the war and ultimately to the
outbreak of revolution in Russia.

Tactical and Technological Innovations

Throughout the disastrous early years of the war, the participants continued
to seek better methods of attacking or defending. Some advances came from
improvements in tactical methods. For example, one of the most important
innovations of 1916 was the "rolling barrage," or "creeping barrage." Both
the French and British have claimed they introduced it. Whatever its origins,
previous methods of artillery support for attacking infantry consisted essentially of a barrage of fire falling on the infantry's successive objectives. As
communications and fire-control techniques improved, artillerymen devised
methods for keeping a barrage moving forward about one hundred yards in
front of advancing infantry. With the artillery barrage and the infantry moving about one hundred yards every three to five minutes, attacking infantrymen could move into an enemy's trench line before the defenders could
come out of their shelters and occupy their firing positions. Despite the significant advantages the rolling barrages provided an attacker, the new methods did not enable anyone to achieve a breakthrough on the Western Front
in 1916.

Innovations in defensive techniques nullified innovations in offensive
techniques. Indeed, the French finally learned at Verdun the importance of
adopting a more flexible defense. The Germans made the most important
innovation in defensive tactics, however, when they adopted the "elastic
defense" on December 1, 1916. The keys to this new German defensive tactic were fewer soldiers in the front line, a willingness to yield terrain, and a
reliance on counterattacks. When an attacker was extended and vulnerable,
a timely counterattack could destroy him when he was most off balance and
before he consolidated his gains. To launch local counterattacks, the Germans placed small units behind the front lines and worked hard to develop
the initiative and judgment of the small-unit leaders upon whom the success

Even more than the machine gun, artillery dominated the World War I battlefield. The French estimated that three quarters of their casualties in the first three years of the war resulted from enemy artillery.

of the counterattacks depended. Commanders of much larger units, such as corps and field armies, also designated units for counterattacks. By the time the Allies launched their offensives in 1917, the Germans had this new defensive system in place.

As the opposing sides sought methods of breaking through their opponents' defenses and achieving a decisive victory, they devoted considerable resources and time to developing new technologies. Soldiers hoped some new weapons would give them an edge and provide them a means of ending the stalemate that gripped the battlefield, particularly on the Western Front. Of the many types of new technologies that were tried and developed by the military, one of the earliest was gas. Both sides on the Western Front frequently used it, but it became clear that gas could only add to the terror of a stalemate not end it. Other innovations included the flamethrower, trench mortar, bangalore torpedo, and light machine gun.

The Airplane

One weapon that exercised an important influence over the fighting and whose use increased dramatically during the war was the airplane. Although airplanes had been used in combat in Libya and in the Balkans before World War I, most armies had reservations in 1914 about the utility of flying machines, and some believed the airship (the dirigible) had more potential than the airplane. Officers argued that the dirigible had greater range, speed, and load-carrying ability than the fragile airplane, which could not carry a large military load. By January 1915 German Zeppelins, which could

carry about 5,000 pounds of bombs, were flying out of Belgium and dropping their bombs on London.

Though dirigibles and balloons remained in use, the airplane proved
more useful and was enthusiastically developed by most participants in the
war. During the first battle of the Marne, both sides relied on airplanes to
provide them information about the enemy, and by late 1914, aerial photography was widely used on the Western Front. Problems with communications continued, for until the planes were equipped with the Marconi wireless, the pilot had to land and pass on important information personally or
had to drop handwritten messages. Nevertheless, constant reconnaissance
flights made it extremely difficult to conceal preparations for a major offensive, and by the end of 1914, no ground commander would consider an
operation without aerial assistance.

To prevent the enemy from acquiring damaging information, both
sides devoted considerable effort to destroying enemy reconnaissance planes.
The first weapons used in aerial combat were pistols and rifles, but within
weeks after the beginning of the war, observers in two-seater airplanes were
firing crudely mounted machine guns. After the introduction of the inter-
rupter gear, which synchronized the firing of a machine gun with the spinning of a propeller, machine guns were mounted on the front of airplanes
and fired directly at the enemy. Huge "dogfights" quickly became common
over the Western Front.

During the four years of the war, numerous technical advances provided the airplane with greater speed, range, climbing power, maneuverabil-
ity, and structural strength. The British launched bombers against Zeppelin
hangars in Germany in September 1914. When the war began, none of the
participants had a mechanism that would release a bomb from an airplane,

Use and control of the air remained a high priority for the combatants of World War I. The
value of the airplane is evident in the British producing 25,685 airplanes in 1918, the French
24,652, and the Germans 17,000.

but by the end of the war, the British had produced a bomb weighing 3,360 pounds and a mechanism for releasing it.

Of all the nations involved in the war, the British—under the prodding of General Sir Hugh Trenchard—placed the strongest emphasis on strategic bombing directed at the enemy's civilian population, industrial capacity, and lines of communication. Trenchard believed airplanes could do more than serve as fighters or support ground operations; he believed long-range, high-payload bombers could blast Germany out of the war. The Germans also developed strategic bombers, which carried out their first raid on Great Britain in June 1917, but the war ended before ideas about strategic bombing could be fully tested.

Aircraft also played an important role in naval warfare, where they provided important advantages in aerial spotting and reconnaissance. Prior to World War I, navies often floated airships high above their fleets, and they quickly developed the ability to hoist seaplanes over the sides of ships, where they could land and take off from the water. The first flight of an airplane from a ship occurred in November 1910 off the USS *Birmingham*. In December 1914, the British launched a seaplane carrier raid on the German North Sea base of Cuxhaven but inflicted little or no damage. In late 1914 and early 1915 the British placed long, downward sloping ramps on several ships and thereby enabled seaplanes to take off without being hoisted over the side. The seaplanes could not land on the ships, however, and had to land on the sea before being hoisted back on the ships. In 1918 the British added a landing deck on the rear of a ship, permitting planes to take off and land on the same ship. Numerous accidents, however, limited the use of the landing deck; the new ships would make much more significant contributions in World War II.

The Tank

Another weapon introduced during World War I was the tank. In October 1914, Lieutenant Colonel Ernest D. Swinton began British efforts to develop an armored vehicle, but he failed to generate any enthusiasm for his idea among British military leaders. After Winston Churchill, First Lord of the Admiralty, encouraged the British army to investigate the idea, the British began working energetically in 1915 to create an armored fighting vehicle. The French effort was led by General Jean B. Estienne who had an idea similar to Swinton's. After the two nations became aware of each other's efforts, they agreed to delay using the new weapon until enough were available for a mass assault. Both recognized the tank's ability to move across the devastated and deadly battlefield and hoped for a surprise introduction of the new weapon.

Despite the agreement between the two nations, the British threw their small number of tanks into an offensive on the Somme on September 15, 1916, and achieved very little. The French used their tanks for the first time on April 16, 1917, as part of the ill-fated Nivelle offensive in Champagne, but they were hardly more successful than the British. The Germans

Mark IV tank stuck in a trench. Tanks helped the infantry advance across no-man's-land, but they failed to live up to their proponents' exaggerated claims because of their slow speed, low power, and inexperienced crews.

did not begin developing tanks until the British and French had used tanks against them. After the dismal failure of the French tanks in Nivelle's offensive, Ludendorff dismissed tanks as being almost useless. Not until November 20, 1917, did the British at Cambrai make the first successful attack with tanks in large numbers.

★   ★   ★   ★

From late 1914 to 1916, the combatants expended thousands of lives and enormous resources trying new methods, technologies, and strategies in desperate attempts to end the war. Along with the appearance of tanks, planes, and gasses came better methods for attacking and defending, such as the Germans' use of the elastic defense. And all the combatants gradually improved their methods of coordinating infantry and artillery actions. While the Allies simultaneously sought a breakthrough on the Western Front and success on the periphery of Europe, Germany changed its strategy from a focus on the west in 1914, to the east in 1915, and back to the west in 1916. By 1916, Falkenhayn had abandoned hopes of a breakthrough in the Western Front and unwisely hoped a gigantic battle of attrition would force the Allies to yield.

By the end of 1916, the strains, disruptions, and costs of total warfare had seriously affected all the participants. In the waning days of 1916 hopes for peace flickered but soon faded. As the new year began, the belligerents renewed their efforts to achieve victory. Much as if the exhausted combatants were tied to death itself, none chose to leave the struggle. To surrender was unthinkable; to withdraw without victory after the loss of so many lives was impossible.

SUGGESTED READINGS

Ashworth, Tony. *Trench Warfare 1914–1918: The Live and Let Live System* (New York: Holmes & Meier, 1980).

Bidwell, Shelford, and Dominick Graham. *Fire-Power: British Army Weapons and Theories of War, 1904–1945* (London: George Allen & Unwin, 1982).

Clark, Alan. *The Donkeys* (New York: William Morrow and Company, 1962).

Heller, Charles E. *Chemical Warfare in World War I: The American Experience, 1917–1918* (Fort Leavenworth, Kans.: Combat Studies Institute, 1984).

Horne, Alistair. *The Price of Glory: Verdun, 1916* (New York: Macmillan Co., 1962).

Keegan, John. *The Face of Battle* (New York: Viking Press, 1976).

King, Jere C. *Generals and Politicians: Conflict Between France's High Command, Parliament, and Government, 1914-1918* (Berkeley: University of California Press, 1951).

Leed, Eric J. *No Man's Land: Combat and Identity in World War I* (Cambridge: Cambridge University Press, 1981).

Middlebrook, Martin. *The First Day on the Somme: 1 July 1916* (New York: W. W. Norton & Company, 1972).

Moran, Charles M. W. *The Anatomy of Courage* (London: Constable, 1945).

Remarque, Erich Maria. *All Quiet on the Western Front*, trans. A. W. Wheen (Boston, Mass.: Little Brown, 1929).

Siney, Marion. *Allied Blockade of Germany, 1914–1916* (Ann Arbor: University of Michigan Press, 1957).

Stone, Norman. *The Eastern Front, 1914–1917* (New York: Charles Scribner's Sons, 1975).

Terraine, John. *Douglas Haig: The Educated Soldier* (London: Hutchinson, 1963).

Travers, Tim. *The Killing Ground: The British Army, the Western Front, and the Emergence of Modern Warfare* (London: Allen & Unwin, 1987).

11

1917: THE YEAR OF DESPERATION AND ANTICIPATION

Unrestricted Submarine
Warfare

The Disastrous Allied
Offensives of 1917

Creating the American
Expeditionary Force

Cambrai: The Final Allied
Offensive of 1917

For both the Allies and the Central Powers, 1917 was a crucial year in the war. The Central Powers faced a particularly serious situation at the end of 1916 as discontent increased in the civilian populace and food shortages and health problems worsened. After Woodrow Wilson was reelected President of the United States in 1916, he attempted to mediate peace by asking the belligerents to make public the conditions under which they would conclude peace. The Germans finally provided the conditions under which they would accept peace, but their response was accompanied by notification of their intent to resume unrestricted submarine warfare on February 1, 1917. As German submarines began sinking hundreds of thousands of tons of Allied shipping, France launched an offensive in April 1917. This offensive failed miserably and led to the outbreak of mutinies in the French army. Thereafter, France concentrated on rebuilding the morale of its shattered army, while Great Britain assumed an increasingly larger role in the land war. The British attack at Passchendaele in the summer and fall of 1917, however, did little to end the war. Amidst the growing sense of desperation in Europe, the overthrow of Tsar Nicholas in March 1917 and the seizure of power by the Bolsheviks in November contributed to the Russians' eventually leaving the war. Though the entry in April 1917 of the United States into the war renewed hope among the Allies for winning the war, the task of organizing, equipping, and transporting more than 2 million soldiers to Europe proved to be one of the most difficult and significant accomplishments of the entire war.

While sweeping changes altered the list of participants in the war, some innovations occurred in the waging of war. The disastrous offensives of 1917 drove the Allies to rely more and more on limited offensives, rather than to seek a complete breakthrough of German defenses. And at Cambrai the British launched a large armored attack supported by aircraft in November 1917. The year ended with the belligerents anticipating the entry of a massive American force into battle and the launching of a major German offensive in 1918.

Unrestricted Submarine Warfare

The German decision to resume unrestricted submarine warfare greatly affected the conduct of the war. Though the decision did not bring immediate disaster for the Germans, it resulted in the United States' entering the war at a time when Russia was forced to withdraw. The Americans began arriving in substantial numbers about the same time the Russo-German armistice of Brest-Litovsk ended active operations on the Eastern Front. Although the Americans did not win the war for the Allies, their entry ensured that the Allies would not lose.

The decision by Germany in early 1917 to resume unrestricted submarine warfare came after several years of discussions about the relationship between naval and land operations. In the first days of August 1914, German military leaders considered using sea and aerial forces to end Great Britain's participation in the war. Most plans on the subject lacked substance, for despite Germany's monopoly of the Zeppelin, it lacked the forces to make continuous, effective attacks against the British. About all it could do was lay some minefields and send out some light ships to bombard a few coastal towns. Great Britain effectively used its superior sea power to deliver supplies to its armies and those of its allies while denying seaborne supplies to the Central Powers. By the end of 1914 British naval forces cut Germany off from the high seas and imposed a blockade that severely restricted their supply of war matériel. In March 1915, the Allies added foodstuffs to the list of contraband, making the blockade total.

Since Great Britain had almost twice as many capital ships available in the North Sea, Germany was hesitant to challenge British sea power, and its High Seas Fleet remained bottled-up along the short coastline between the Netherlands and Denmark. Not until May 31, 1916, did the German fleet venture out of its heavily mined and fortified bases and engage the British Grand Fleet in the Battle of Jutland. Although the battle involved 254 ships and was the largest naval battle ever fought up to this time, the strategic situation did not change, for the German fleet escaped without being annihilated and the blockade of Germany continued.

More than one year before the Battle of Jutland, Germany declared the waters around Great Britain and Ireland to be a "war zone." On February 4, 1915, it published a notice about the establishment of the war zone and warned of the destruction of enemy merchant vessels within it even though it would not always be possible "to avert danger . . . to the crew and passengers." The same notice also warned of possible unintentional attacks on neutral ships. Germany's main weapon for attacking Allied shipping was the submarine, or the U-boat, which most navies previously had ignored.

When Germany established the war zone, it had only twenty-one submarines in the North Sea. The actual number at sea at any one time was usually no more than one third of its fleet. Despite complaints from neutral nations, particularly the United States, and despite a widespread belief that the Germans could not actually establish a war zone, submarines began sinking an average of more than one ship a day for the remainder of 1915.

The sinking of the *Lusitania* on May 7, 1915, and the death of more than one hundred American citizens on the British ship created a great stir in the United States, but the Germans insisted that the vessel was carrying munitions and was therefore a legitimate target. After the sinking of another British ship, *Arabic,* in which two Americans lost their lives, American protests became more vehement. Unwilling to face war with the United States, Germany retreated and abandoned unrestricted submarine warfare on September 20, 1915. It shifted the focus of its submarine operations to the Mediterranean.

But at the end of 1915, the German army and navy joined forces to place renewed pressure on the German chancellor, Theobald von Bethmann Hollweg, to resume unrestricted submarine warfare. Bethmann Hollweg feared an expansion of submarine warfare would bring the United States into the war on the side of the Allies. When Kaiser William II supported the chancellor, the secretary of state for naval affairs, Admiral Alfred von Tirpitz, resigned in protest. He and other naval officials had argued that unrestricted submarine warfare would force Britain to surrender in two to four months. At last yielding to the pressure, the kaiser decided to resume submarine attacks but not in an unrestricted manner. Attacks would be launched only within the war zone and only against merchant ships carrying weapons for protection against submarines.

In late 1916 the question of using unrestricted submarine warfare rose again. Except for its narrow North Sea coast, Germany remained confined within central Europe, cut off from the world's markets by Allied armies and navies. The British blockade had wrecked Germany's export trade, had denied it essential raw materials, and was affecting its citizens' morale. The shortage of foodstuffs made Germans go hungry and raised the death rate of the elderly and of infants. Moreover, the heavy losses at Verdun, on the Somme, and in the Brusilov offensive convinced the army's new leaders, Hindenburg and Ludendorff, that Germany could not endure the military stalemate much longer.

When the Germans began their unrestricted submarine warfare campaign in 1917, they had about 150 U-boats but kept only 30 to 35 operating in the Atlantic at any one time. This small number of U-boats nevertheless sank more than 3 million tons of shipping in the first five months of the campaign.

Over Bethmann Hollweg's objections, Hindenburg and Ludendorff convinced the kaiser to resume unrestricted submarine warfare. They determined that Great Britain could be forced out of the war before the United States could intervene decisively on the continent of Europe. The kaiser's decision rested on the navy's promise of a war of attrition at sea in which German submarines would sink an average of 600,000 tons of shipping each month and would force Britain to come to terms in five months. Although Germany's submarines managed to sink an even larger amount of shipping for a short period, its military analysts had woefully miscalculated British self-sufficiency and resilience; they also underestimated the effect that the United States' entering the war would have on the Allies.

On January 31, 1917, Germany notified the United States of its resumption of unrestricted submarine attacks. President Woodrow Wilson broke off diplomatic relations and ordered the arming of American merchant ships. Meanwhile, the publication of the infamous Zimmermann telegram appalled most Americans. Germany's foreign secretary, Arthur Zimmermann, sent instructions to the German ambassador in Mexico to work toward an alliance with Mexico and Japan in the event of war with the United States. In return, Germany would restore to Mexico the states of New Mexico, Arizona, and Texas. After German submarines sank several U.S. ships in February and March, Wilson concluded that war was unavoidable and he obtained a declaration of war from Congress on April 6, 1917.

The Disastrous Allied Offensives of 1917

In late 1916 and early 1917, the Allies continued their efforts to break through German lines and win the war with an offensive strategy. Despite the losses at Verdun and the Somme in 1916, the debate between France and Great Britain focused less on strategy than on command relationships. Although the role of the British forces on the continent gradually expanded between 1914 and 1917 and by the summer of 1917 rivaled those of France, no centralized command structure for controlling British and French operations emerged, primarily because the British refused to play the subordinate. Consequently, many aspects of military operations and strategy on the Western Front remained loosely coordinated. A similar situation existed among the other allies as well.

Soon after David Lloyd George became prime minister of Britain in December 1916, however, he succumbed to French persuasion and agreed to place the entire BEF at France's disposal for offensives on the Western Front in 1917. Lloyd George did this reluctantly, for he strongly believed the Allies should concentrate against the weaker of the Central Powers, Austria-Hungary, and make their main attack along the Italian front. General Douglas Haig, who had replaced Field Marshal Sir John French as commander of the BEF in December 1915, strenuously objected to his forces being controlled by the French, but he finally agreed to tailor the conduct of his operations to those of the French—but only during the upcoming campaign.

The Allied plans for 1917 were greatly influenced by the appointment on December 12, 1916, of a new commander for French forces. Joffre was promoted to the rank of marshal of France and appointed as an advisor to the government, and General Robert G. Nivelle became commander of the French armies on the Western Front. In essence, Joffre was promoted out of his position, so a younger, more vigorous leader with new ideas could take charge. Nivelle was appointed commander only of those forces in northern and northeastern France, not all French forces, but his political masters expected much from the new commander who promised a major breakthrough.

When Nivelle and Haig coordinated the operations that would take place in 1917, the British commander agreed to launch a limited offensive near Arras to divert enemy attention and forces from the main French attack on the Chemin des Dames between Soissons and Reims. The French attack would occur after the British attack. The idea was to draw the German reserves toward the northwest so they could not be used against the attempted breakthrough by the French. Following the attacks at Arras and the Chemin des Dames, Haig intended to launch an attack on Messines Ridge, the high ground occupied by the Germans in the salient south of Ypres.

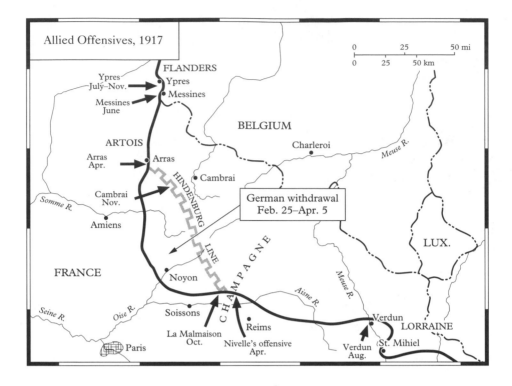

Allied Offensives, 1917

The British had to capture this high ground before they could launch Haig's main effort, an attack around Ypres. Haig did not want the attack at Arras or Messines Ridge to drag on for too long, for his main goal in the Ypres attack was to push the German lines back and capture the key submarine bases at Ostend and Zeebrugge in Belgium. He also hoped to drive the German flank farther along the Belgian coast, thereby opening it to further attacks. Thus Haig and Nivelle envisaged a series of attacks: Arras, Chemin des Dames, Messines Ridge, and then Ypres.

The Germans did not docilely await the Allied attack. Since Hindenburg and Ludendorff anticipated large Allied offensives in 1917, they decided to retire from the huge Noyon salient and occupy a shorter, stronger position to its rear. The newly fortified zone was named the "*Siegfried Stellung*" but was soon tagged the "Hindenburg Line" by the Allies. A key aspect of the Hindenburg Line was the establishment of reverse slope positions and the use of elastic defenses. The elastic defense sought to prevent a breakthrough and to inflict maximum casualties on the enemy by bending but not breaking in the face of an attack. Establishing defensive positions in depth, the Germans placed small forces forward to avoid heavy losses from enemy artillery fire and relied on a network of mutually supporting strong points to halt the enemy. Large numbers of machine guns and carefully planned artillery fires strengthened the defenders. The construction of the Hindenburg Line enabled the Germans to shorten their defensive lines and to increase the size of their reserves. Commanders at all levels prepared to use counterattacks to disrupt the enemy's advance or to push him back before he could consolidate his hard-won gains.

The British launched their limited offensive near Arras on April 9. After five days of preparatory artillery fire, First and Third armies met great success. Most notable was the Canadian seizure of Vimy Ridge, an important piece of terrain that the Germans had held for more than two and a half years. Because of the nature of the terrain, the German commander had not organized an elastic defense but instead had placed strong defenses along the heights of the ridge and held large reserves to its rear. Though fighting under unfavorable circumstances, the Canadians finally captured the much-contested ridge.

General Edmund Allenby, who commanded Third Army, ordered his cavalry forward so the gains could be exploited, but the efforts to parlay the gains into a breakthrough and exploitation failed. From April 12–17, the British Fourth Army attacked south of Arras, and then from April 23–28 and May 3–5, First and Third armies continued attacking. Although the later battles captured far less terrain than the first battle, the British inflicted heavy casualties on the Germans and managed to divert some units and matériel from the main French effort at the Chemin des Dames.

The Nivelle Offensive

Ten days after the Americans entered the war, the French launched their disastrous offensive at the Chemin des Dames. Instead of waiting for the arrival of large numbers of American troops, the French were persuaded by false promises from Nivelle that a breakthrough could be made. Unfortunately for France, Nivelle's "formula" for success proved to be a formula for disaster.

Nivelle was an excellent officer who quickly rose from the rank of colonel in 1914 to a corps and then a field army commander. An innovative artillery officer, he had made his reputation by being the inventor—according to the French—of the rolling barrage and had coined the slogan "The artillery conquers; the infantry occupies." Nivelle had added to his reputation by successfully launching an attack at Verdun in October 1916. After detailed rehearsals and eight days of preparatory artillery fire, he had used seven divisions along a four-mile front to capture Fort Douaumont. His forces penetrated no more than two miles, but the advance seemed spectacularly deep by the standards of the day. Two months later he launched another successful attack which managed to penetrate four to five miles. After more than three years of terrible losses, Nivelle had apparently found the formula for unlocking the riddle of trench warfare, the main feature of which was reliance on tightly controlled infantry attacks, supported by vast amounts of artillery. In his December attack at Verdun, Nivelle used more than one million rounds of artillery against German positions before beginning the rolling barrage of artillery fire in front of the advancing infantry.

After Nivelle became commander of the northeastern front in December 1916, he began work on a plan to smash through the German defenses in the Champagne sector between Soissons and Reims. His objective was the heights of the Chemin des Dames to the north of the small Aisne River. To the detriment of Nivelle's grand scheme, the Germans obtained information about his plan and reorganized their positions in preparation for his attack. One of their key changes was the use of an elastic defense that placed only a minimum number of infantrymen in forward trenches. They placed most of their troops on the reverse slope of the Chemin des Dames so they could be protected from the direct fire of the Allies, and they reinforced the threatened sector with an additional field army.

Despite indications that the Germans expected an attack on the Chemin des Dames, Nivelle remained confident of achieving a breakthrough and insisted on launching his offensive. In comparison to some attacks of the past, he had a huge force. He massed two armies along a front of approximately forty miles and kept two armies in reserve, totaling approximately 1,400,000 men in fifty-two divisions. To support the four armies, he had approximately 1,800 75-mm guns, 1,700 heavy artillery pieces, and 1,650 mortars and accompanying guns. Stocks of ammunition included 24 million rounds of 75-mm shells and 9 million rounds of heavy artillery ammunition.

Nivelle's plan was relatively simple. On the right-front of his four field armies, Fifth Army had fourteen infantry divisions, ten of which were in the front line. On the left-front, Sixth Army had fourteen infantry divisions, eight of which were in the front line. After the two armies attacked and broke through the German defenses, Sixth Army was supposed to turn

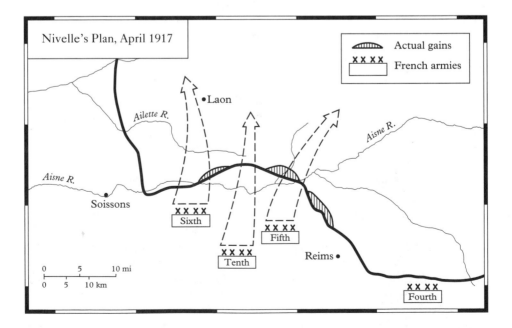

Nivelle's Plan, April 1917

Actual gains

X X X X French armies

•Laon

Ailette R.

Aisne R.

Aisne R.

Soissons

X X X X Sixth

X X X X Fifth

X X X X Tenth

Reims •

0   5   10 mi
0   5   10 km

X X X X Fourth

toward the west and Fifth Army toward the east. This would enable Tenth Army to pass through the two leading armies and advance toward the north. Despite increasing indications of German preparations, Nivelle confidently expected Tenth Army to advance fifteen miles by the end of the second day's attack. First Army remained in reserve.

Before the attack began on April 16, the French pounded the German positions with nine days of artillery preparation. After this lengthy preparation, the first wave of infantry easily occupied the initial enemy positions, which were only lightly occupied because of the elastic defense. The French soldiers also reached the geographic crest of the heights without difficulty, but as they moved over the crest of the Chemin des Dames and began descending the slope, heavy enemy fire halted their advance. The Germans had located their main positions on the reverse side of the slope, out of sight of French artillery observers. They had also placed many of their machine guns in concrete shelters or bunkers and thus had protected them from the massive French artillery concentrations.

Some of the French infantry managed to advance down the slope to their front, but German fire halted almost all of them. The following waves of infantry did not fare any better. All attempts to regain forward movement collapsed as soon as the French infantry arrived on the line covered by enemy machine guns. The only possible movement was through trenches using grenades, but this was soon stopped by the Germans.

For the remainder of the first day and for the two following days, combat atop the Chemin des Dames assumed the form of a series of limited attacks, preceded as much as possible by artillery bombardment of the enemy's positions and executed under the control of local commanders according to the availability of munitions and grenades. Many of the units who participated in the initial attacks were pulled out of the lines during the night of April 18–19.

After three days of heavy losses, Nivelle concluded that the French could not break through the strong German defenses and modified his plan. Believing that the Germans had weakened their defenses on his right so they could concentrate sufficient forces in front of his attack, he launched a limited offensive to slice off the shallow German salient above Reims. He ordered Fifth Army, which was on the right-front in the attack against the Chemin des Dames, to attack in a northeasterly direction, while Fourth Army, which was to its right and which had made some gains against the Germans, continued its attack toward the northwest. But the French had lost the initiative, and this limited offensive fared no better than the first attack.

Although the fighting continued until May 7, it was obvious within a week that the Nivelle offensive had failed dismally, particularly when compared to the successful British attack at Arras. The casualties during the first week were approximately 117,000, including 32,000 dead. Perhaps more importantly, the senseless losses plunged much of France into despair. Exhaustion, indiscipline, and low morale had replaced the exhilaration and optimism that Nivelle had engendered in the French army.

An aerial view of a battlefield in France. By 1917 thousands of artillery rounds had devastated the once-pastoral countryside and obliterated the previously neat lines of trenches.

As a consequence of his failure, the French government relieved Nivelle and named Pétain to command the armies on the Western Front. This relief signaled the end of France's efforts to break through German defenses, for Pétain would employ only limited offensives that sought mainly to capture key terrain and force the Germans back. The relief of Nivelle also signaled the end of military leaders operating without the guidance and occasional interference of political leaders. Disgusted political leaders began exercising greater control over military operations, and the assumption of power by Georges Clemenceau, who became premier of France in November 1917, symbolized the opening of a new era. He expressed its theme when he said, "War is too important to be left to the generals."

The major task confronting Pétain as commander of the French army in northern France, however, was restoring the fighting spirit of his soldiers. After more than one million soldiers had died in battle and many more were wounded, the French army seemed to be on the verge of complete collapse. Mutinies in May and June affected fifty-four divisions, more than half of the French army. Although the French had agreed to launch an offensive during the summer to support a British offensive in Flanders, Pétain reluctantly informed Field Marshal Haig's headquarters that such an offensive was impossible. To end the mutinies, Pétain initiated a program of swift and severe punishment. He also visited many of the French divisions and appealed to the soldiers' pride and patriotism. To restore the faith of the French troops in their higher-level commanders, he took steps to improve living conditions by modifying the furlough system and providing better food in the trenches. Finally, he established rest camps to provide exhausted soldiers a break from the fighting in the trenches. By the end of July most of the mutinies had ended, and in September only one act of collective disobedience occurred. Though the French army remained fragile, Pétain's efforts had succeeded in restoring discipline.

On August 20, Pétain launched a limited offensive at Verdun and achieved moderate success. As soon as the Germans brought reserves into the area and offered stiff resistance, he halted the attack. At La Malmaison at the end of October, he launched a more elaborate offensive, attacking with Tenth Army along a front of about seven miles. The objective of the attack was the high ground anchoring the German right flank along the Chemin des Dames. The attack was supported by fourteen tank companies and approximately 1,850 artillery tubes, which provided three days of preparatory fire. After advancing about three miles, the French outflanked the Germans on the Chemin des Dames and forced them to withdraw.

Pétain's gains on the much-contested terrain demonstrated that limited offensives could achieve important gains and that his reforms for reviving the morale of the French had at least partially succeeded. Instead of continuing forward in an attempt to break through the German defenses completely or beginning another major offensive elsewhere, however, he preferred to await the arrival of "the Americans and the tanks."

Messines Ridge and Passchendaele

During the period of the French mutinies, the British maintained pressure on the Germans, thereby providing the French time to rebuild their army. The British also prepared for an offensive at Ypres that would push the Germans back and permit the capture of the submarine bases at Ostend and Zeebrugge. The desire to capture these bases intensified when Admiral Sir John R. Jellicoe warned that the war could not be continued through 1918 if shipping losses persisted at such a high rate. To reach the submarine bases, however, the British had to push back or break through the German defenses, a task they had not been able to accomplish during the past three years.

Before attacking at Ypres, Haig launched a limited offensive against Messines Ridge, which dominated the plain around Ypres. Although having to contend with German countermining, British tunneling companies dug shafts deep under the ridge for more than a year and packed them with 500 tons of explosives. After a seventeen-day artillery preparation, nineteen huge mines exploded simultaneously under the ridge on the morning of June 7.

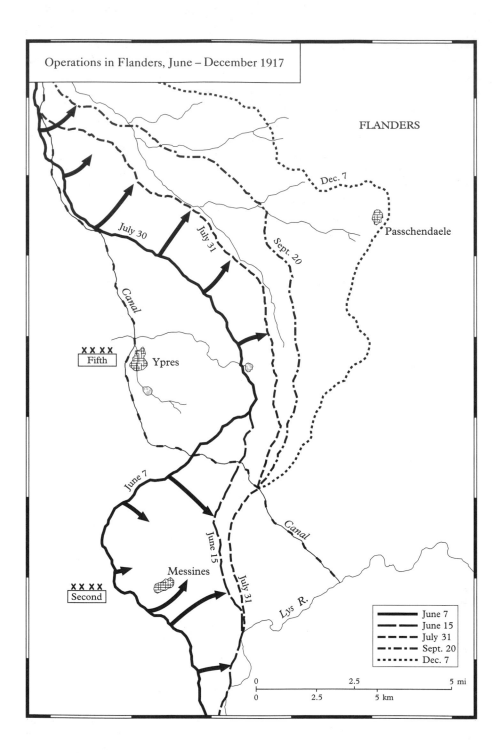

Operations in Flanders, June – December 1917

FLANDERS

Dec. 7

Passchendaele

July 30

July 31

Sept. 20

Canal

XXXX
Fifth

Ypres

June 7

Canal

June 15

Messines

July 31

Lys R.

XXXX
Second

———	June 7
—·—	June 15
— —	July 31
—··—	Sept. 20
······	Dec. 7

0   2.5   5 mi

0   2.5   5 km

With an unfavorable wind disrupting the British use of gas, a heavy artillery barrage began falling on German positions immediately after the explosion. Just behind the artillery barrage, nine infantry divisions advanced in an assault, and within twelve hours, they captured almost the entire objective, which included one of the most devastated areas ever encountered in the history of warfare.

The swift and easy success at Messines Ridge was not a portent for the future, for the British now entered one of the bloodiest and most futile campaigns of the entire war. Although the subsequent campaign was the Third Battle of Ypres, it became known as "Passchendaele," a word that has become synonymous in military history with suffering and disappointment. During the first part of the war the British had relied on volunteers to expand the size of their forces and replenish their losses. Because of severe manpower shortages, however, they adopted conscription in January 1916, but only after much debate. Many of these conscripts subsequently became casualties under the terrible conditions of Passchendaele.

With little or no thought being given to the effect on the terrain, the British began in July 1917 with one of the heaviest bombardments of the entire war. More than 3,000 guns fired more than 65,000 tons of artillery shells for almost two weeks prior to the launching of the attack on July 31. The British quickly captured their initial objectives and then prepared to move toward their main objective, the village of Passchendaele, which lay less than four miles to their front.

Then rain began to fall. Although the Ypres area in peacetime consisted of many idyllic pastures that centuries of labor had reclaimed from marshes, heavy bombardment disrupted the drainage system, and unusually heavy rains turned the area into a vast swamp. To facilitate movement, the British constructed plank roads and laid many miles of boards across the quagmire. The mud was bad enough, but the introduction and use by the Germans of mustard gas during the campaign made living conditions even more difficult to endure. On August 16 the attack began again. Except for units in the center, however, the British captured very little terrain.

Believing a change in commanders would improve British fortunes, Haig replaced Fifth Army commander, General Sir Hubert Gough, with General Sir Herbert Plumer. The new British commander began a series of attacks with limited objectives. Fortunately for his soldiers, the weather turned favorable, and several attacks occurred in huge dust clouds. The weather did not last long, and the terrain once again turned into mud. The next phase of the offensive, which began on September 20 and continued on September 26 and October 4, also yielded some success. As the British attacks continued pushing forward, the Germans stopped using an elastic defense and began placing larger numbers of troops in forward trenches. This caused them to suffer high casualties because the British used massive amounts of artillery in their carefully controlled attacks. The Germans also began taking higher casualties in their counterattacks. Close coordination between the Royal Flying Corps and the infantry and artillery often enabled the British to disrupt the frequent enemy counterattacks.

In December 1915, Sir Douglas Haig succeeded Sir John French as commander of the
British Expeditionary Force. In late 1917, Haig remained confident that he could achieve a
breakthrough at Passchendaele even though he had failed to break German defensive lines
on the Somme a year earlier.

Finally, on November 6, two divisions managed to occupy the ruins
of Passchendaele village. By November 10, the British had expanded their
control over the ridge on which the ruins of the village sat; then Haig ordered
a halt to the offensive. Both the British and the Germans had lost about
240,000 men. Despite their optimism at the beginning of the campaign, the
British had not been able to break through the German lines, and the goal
of seizing the submarine bases along the Belgian coast had long since been
forgotten.

As the Allies awaited the arrival of large American forces, the situation became even bleaker on the Eastern Front. After the overthrow of Tsar
Nicholas in March 1917 and the establishment of a provisional government,
Russia attempted to remain in the war. In July the Russians attacked into
Galicia. Though they made some gains, the Germans and Austrians counterattacked and drove them back. In subsequent weeks the Russian army
began to disintegrate completely; soldiers on the front did little or no fighting, while soldiers in the rear joined the revolutionary forces. In September
the Germans launched the last campaign of World War I on the Eastern
Front. Against only slight resistance, they crossed the Dvina River and

seized Riga. Two months later, the Bolsheviks seized power and almost immediately called for an ending of the war.

Creating the American Expeditionary Force

When the German high command assessed the dangers of resuming unrestricted submarine warfare in late 1916, it dismissed the possibility of the United States' entering the war quickly and playing a significant role. The Germans recognized that the United States had more than 100 million citizens, one of the world's richest and largest economies, and a first-class fleet that rivaled that of the British. But they also recognized that the United States faced enormous difficulties in vastly increasing the size of its small army and in transporting its forces to Europe. In the end, the Germans took a calculated risk and lost, for they failed to end the war before American soldiers and supplies helped halt their final drives and push them back to defeat.

In April 1917, the United States faced enormous challenges if it were to participate in the European conflict. Despite the reforms following the Spanish-American War, the U.S. Army had no large tactical units, few weapons, an extreme shortage of officers, and little or no training. On April 6, 1917, the War Department had only 213,557 troops at its disposal, including 127,588 active, 5,523 Philippine Scouts, and 80,446 National Guard troops. No active units larger than a regiment existed. In a matter of months, the Americans not only had to expand the size of their army but also equip and supply it, train it for modern warfare, and transport it to Europe. Rarely has any military force faced such a huge challenge.

The first challenge faced by the small American army was the induction and training of millions of recruits. After six weeks of spirited debate, the United States passed the Selective Service Act of May 18, 1917, that provided for the conscription of males. Meanwhile, a wave of volunteers enlisted in May and June. The first draft did not occur until July 20, and the first large contingent of conscripted soldiers did not arrive until September. Thereafter, a steady stream of inductions and voluntary enlistments swelled the size of the American armed forces. At the time of the Armistice in November 1918, the United States Army consisted of 3,685,458 soldiers, an increase of more than seventeen times the number of soldiers available in April 1917.

Amidst a great outpouring of public support for the war, waiting for the manufacture and delivery of weapons and equipment severely constrained the rapid expansion of the army. Prior to the declaration of war, no one recognized the complexity of mobilizing sufficient assets to equip, train, and transport 2 million Americans overseas. As early as July 1917, the shortage of clothing, for example, was so severe that the army's quartermaster general recommended that the first induction of personnel be postponed from September to October. More severe shortages existed in weapons and ammunition. Consequently, matériel needed for expanding the army to more than seventeen times its previous size could not be met as quickly as individual soldiers could be inducted and trained. On numerous installations, combat units did not have uniforms, modern rifles, or field artillery pieces. Some newly inducted soldiers trained in coveralls and used wooden sticks to simulate weapons, while the War Department and American industry exerted a Herculean effort to overcome critical shortages.

To facilitate coordination and to enhance the effectiveness of the nation's mobilization, President Wilson created a number of boards, including the War Industries Board, the Food Administration, the Fuel Administration, and the Railroad Administration. These boards coordinated the mobilization effort, accelerated production, and contributed significantly to the eventual Allied victory. Nonetheless, some shortages proved impossible to overcome; for example, the army modified and issued its soldiers British Enfield rifles that were already being manufactured in the United States, as well as Allied machine guns and mortars. French factories produced much of the heavier weapons and equipment for the Americans.

Additional challenges appeared in distributing goods to appropriate units. Even after weapons and equipment were manufactured, the logistics apparatus for controlling their distribution suffered serious flaws. Every conceivable problem appeared, from the provision of wrong supplies, to the frequent arrival of defective or useless equipment, to the loss of badly needed equipment. Among complaints about the logistics system, commanders in Europe sharply criticized the arrival of lawn mowers, cuspidors, and floor wax when other critical supplies were needed. In October 1917 when soldiers of the 1st Infantry Division entered the trenches, severe shortages of winter clothing and blankets kept them in their summer uniforms. Despite complaints in Congress about the supply system having "almost stopped functioning," sufficient equipment and supplies somehow did find their way to the right units. Considering the tremendous increase in the size of the army and the huge requirements associated with transporting and supplying the AEF in Europe, one should perhaps marvel that the system managed to function as well as it did.

Transporting the AEF to Europe

Although significant challenges continued to exist in inducting and training military personnel and in providing them with adequate equipment, American soldiers could contribute to the war effort only if they traversed the Atlantic Ocean. Unfortunately for the Americans, the U.S. merchant marine lacked sufficient ships to carry the entire AEF across the Atlantic. This problem existed before German submarines began destroying shipping faster than it could be replaced. One historian has observed that the Norwegians had a larger capability in 1917 for transporting an army overseas than the Americans. To overcome this serious deficiency, the United States took extraordinary steps to add ships to its fleet, including using seized German ships. Nonetheless, more than half the AEF eventually traveled to Europe on British troop transports. To ensure the best utilization of existing shipping, the United States set up a Shipping Board to acquire the necessary ships, a Shipping Control Committee to coordinate the use of shipping, and an Embarkation Service to supervise the shipment of munitions, supplies, and personnel. Though some persistent problems continued, most were solved by the end of the war.

The entry of the United States coincided with the highest rate of shipping loss experienced by the Allies during the war. While losses on short voyages such as across the English Channel were low, losses in long-distance ocean shipping amounted to about one-fifth of all ships undertaking such voyages. After the Americans entered the war, the possibility of a large engagement between fleets remained extremely small, for the only large-scale engagement of opposing fleets during the war had occurred at Jutland in May 1916 with indecisive results. It quickly became apparent that the mission confronting the U.S. Navy differed significantly from the task for which it had been prepared. Instead of relying on battleships and battle cruisers to fight enemy vessels, the navy found itself needing more destroyers and antisubmarine craft to protect and assist the movement of forces to Europe.

When Rear Admiral William S. Sims, who was commander of U.S. naval forces operating in European waters, arrived in Great Britain in early April 1917 to discuss the employment of the American navy, he was surprised at the high rate of loss for ocean shipping and disturbed by pessimistic assessments from British authorities who considered the situation "hopeless." As a younger officer, Sims had impressed his superiors with his ability and willingness to adopt new ideas, and he soon demonstrated those same creative qualities by recognizing the requirement to establish a convoy system. British admirals had long before rejected convoys; they believed convoys served merely to group ships as targets, increased the chances of collisions, and reduced the efficiency of ocean transport. After convincing the British to study more systematically the advantages of convoys, he urged his superiors in the United States to send as many antisubmarine vessels as possible to Europe. The Department of the Navy reluctantly accepted the use of convoys on July 2, for it favored defending specific ocean routes—preferably by offensive action—rather than concentrating defenses around slow-moving and difficult-to-control convoys. As the use of convoys became common, the rate of losses began to decline immediately and by the end of the year was only one-fifth of what it had been in April 1917.

Except for extremely fast ships that continued to sail independently, most ocean convoys had twenty or thirty ships, moving in four to six columns. Naval escorts patrolled the flanks of these convoys, as well as the front of especially slow convoys. Heavily escorted troop convoys regularly made the transatlantic run, and by the summer of 1917, about 50,000 troops a month began reaching Europe. By 1918 about one-quarter of a million troops were arriving each month. Many of those who made the passage safely owed their lives to the wisdom and energy of Admiral Sims and to the professional skills of the U.S. Navy.

The Issue of Amalgamation

On June 13, General John J. Pershing, the commander of the AEF, arrived in France. Within days he and his staff began preparing for the arrival of a huge American force. They faced a formidable task, for neither Pershing nor any other living American had any experience in employing the large number of troops that would eventually comprise the AEF. A veteran of the Indian wars and the Spanish-American War, Pershing had commanded the punitive expedition against Mexico in 1916 and had the personal qualities to meet the challenges confronting him, but he had never participated in a major war and naively believed American attacks could break the deadlock on the Western Front. In future months he would emphasize open rather than trench warfare and would impose high standards of marksmanship, drill, and discipline on his soldiers.

While attempting to come to grips with the difficulties of transporting a huge American army across the Atlantic, Pershing had to face the sensitive issue of Great Britain and France's request to attach American units to the armies of other nations. Instead of awaiting the organizing, transporting, and training of American divisions and corps, the Allies wanted to rush Americans into combat as small units; such use of American troops would enable them to participate in the fighting much more quickly. Since the

General John J. Pershing (seated, second from the left) and the staff of the American Expeditionary Force in June 1917. Pershing faced the twin challenges of preparing the AEF for combat and keeping it autonomous from the French and British.

Allies had suffered the great bulk of their casualties in infantry squads, platoons, companies, and battalions, it made sense in their eyes to "amalgamate" small American units into already existing command and support structures in Allied regiments and divisions. Considerations of timing, efficiency, and logistics also strongly argued against their awaiting the organization of an independent American army. Some Allied officers insisted it was a foolish expenditure of lives to train division and corps commanders instead of using already experienced Allied commanders; one argued that a division commander had to lose 12,000 casualties before he became sufficiently proficient at his job.

Despite grave problems in transporting and preparing his large force, Pershing adamantly refused to accept amalgamation. President Wilson's desire for the United States to play an independent and important role at the postwar peace conference buttressed his position. Pershing frequently pointed out the strong disadvantages of amalgamation: language problems with the French, Irish-American dislike of the British, effect on the subsequent peace negotiations, and potentially disruptive resentment against Allied commanders responsible for high American casualties. He also recognized the sensitivity of national pride and the significance of having a separate American army contribute to Allied victory in the Great War.

After Prime Minister Lloyd George exerted diplomatic pressure on President Wilson to accept amalgamation, Pershing found himself almost alone in resisting Allied pressure for sending Americans directly to the trenches. He bent only once under the pressure when he assigned the four African-American regiments of the 93rd Division to the French. Although Pershing stipulated that the regiments were to be returned when he asked for them, they remained with the French throughout the war. After receiving French weapons and uniforms, one of the regiments, the 369th, spent 191 days in the front lines.

The Americans Enter the Trenches

Despite the vast industrial capability and military potential of the United States, it had to act as a junior partner in its efforts to contribute to the war. The fighting had been in progress for thirty-two months, and the Americans had to construct their plans and commit their forces within the framework of already existing Allied plans and dispositions. One of the most important strategic questions was the placement of the American forces in France. Though Pershing had his choice on the location of the American front, his options were limited by the British desire to cover the channel ports and by the French being reluctant to have any army but their own defend Paris. Consequently, the main area available to him was in Lorraine near the St. Mihiel salient. Placing the Americans in Lorraine also had the advantage of enabling them to route their supply lines away from the channel ports being used by the British and around the potential bottleneck of Paris. Moreover, an offensive toward the north by the Americans could sever the important railway line through Metz (which the Germans used to support the western

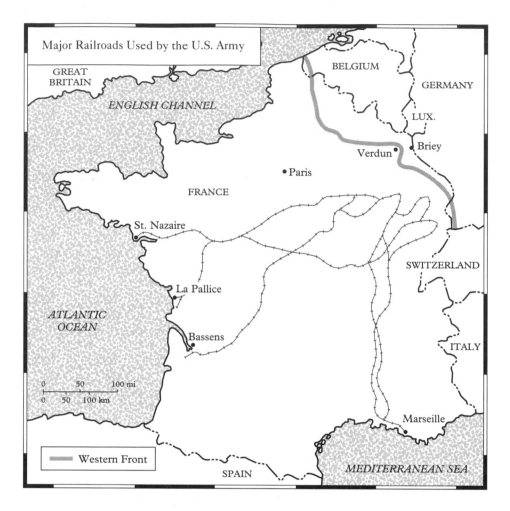

Major Railroads Used by the U.S. Army

extension of its front across France) and capture the huge iron mines of the Briey Basin and the coal mines near Saarbrücken. Thus, when offered a choice of sectors, Pershing chose for logistical and strategic reasons the area the Allies wanted him to take.

Before American troops began arriving in large numbers, their logistics system began to take shape. Known as "Services of Supply," the system proudly trumpeted its mission of relieving "the combatant field force from every consideration except that of defeating the enemy." To accomplish this mission, about 670,000 men eventually became involved in the myriad tasks associated with supporting a large army in the field; everything from hospitals, to schools, to replacement centers, to maintenance shops, to storage depots came under the large thumb of the Services of Supply.

To demonstrate its resolve, the United States hurriedly dispatched a combat division to Europe. Since no organic divisions existed, the U.S. Army brought the 16th, 18th, 26th, and 28th infantry regiments from the Mexican border, formed them into the 1st Infantry Division, and promptly shipped them to Europe. Shortly before departing, a period of disruptive personnel turbulence occurred when many of the regular soldiers from the four regiments were transferred to training camps and replaced by raw recruits. By the time the regiments steamed for France, more than half the personnel were recruits. After arriving in the port of St. Nazaire in late June 1917 and having a detachment march through Paris on the Fourth of July, the division rode boxcars to Lorraine and began intensive training.

Though assisted in its training by the French 47th Division, the 1st Division was not ready to enter the trenches until October 21. Beginning that day individual battalions began moving into a quiet sector of the trench line for ten days. Early on the morning of November 3, three American soldiers from Company F, 16th Infantry Regiment, died during a German raid on their trenches. These were the first soldiers in American units to die in the Great War. By November the AEF had four divisions in France (the 1st, 2nd, 26th, and 42nd), but they were not yet ready to play a large role in the fighting. At the end of November, the 1st Division began further training, but not until January 18, 1918, six months after its arrival in France, did it assume responsibility for a sector on its own.

One month later the 26th Division occupied a sector at Soissons and the 42nd moved into the trenches near Lunéville. The following month the 2nd Division occupied part of the line near Verdun. By the middle of March 1918, the Americans had made no significant contribution to the actual fighting, and Allied disappointment and resentment reached a peak. The Allies were particularly concerned, because they were convinced—correctly—that the Germans were shifting forces and preparing for a major offensive on the Western Front. Nevertheless, from June 1917 until May 1918, American combat units in France concentrated on training. Pershing refused to allow them to enter the trenches in large numbers until their training was complete and until sufficient combat units and support had arrived for the Americans to operate independently.

The Air Service of the AEF

The challenge of creating an air service to support the AEF was as difficult as any faced by Pershing. Among the reasons for this, as Pershing explained to King George V on June 9, 1917, was that the United States had only fifty-five military planes, almost all of which were obsolescent when it entered the war. Yet during the punitive expedition to Mexico, the new American commander had recognized the importance of aviation. He soon acted to improve American aviation in Europe and appointed Colonel Billy Mitchell as the aviation officer of the AEF.

Before the United States declared war, Mitchell had been in Europe for almost two months, studying the role of aviation in the war. For a time he had used his own money for setting up an official aviation office. He quickly recognized that American aircraft were decidedly inferior to European models because three years of warfare had accelerated the development of aviation far beyond the models available to the American military, most of which were similar to the ones available in Europe in 1914. Despite the best efforts to produce modern aircraft in the United States, organization and technical problems hampered production, and the Americans soon turned to the Europeans for delivery of aviation equipment.

As months passed, very little equipment arrived for American aviators. The failure to produce adequate aircraft in the United States was compounded by the failure of French industry to meet promised delivery dates. Moreover, the number of aviation personnel increased very slowly. The shortage of shipping and the according of a higher priority to the shipment of infantry in the spring of 1918 resulted in no aviation personnel arriving in May and June. Of the small number of airplanes received by the air service, almost all were French fighters.

A year after the declaration of war, the first air squadron was formed in April 1918 with American pilots who had served with the Allies. Soon, the number of American-trained pilots began to increase slowly. After Major General Mason Patrick arrived in France and became chief of the air service, Mitchell found himself directing the American planes in combat. Though the number of aircraft slowly increased until there were forty-five squadrons at the front at the time of the armistice, Mitchell never had more than 650 planes, almost all of which were fighters. The American aerial forces never had the capability for strategic bombing and remained primarily concerned with supporting the land battle or fighting against enemy aircraft.

Cambrai: The Final Allied Offensive of 1917

As the Americans slowly built up and transported their forces to the European continent, the bloodbath continued. Following the French disaster at Chemin des Dames and the British losses at Passchendaele, the Allies were in no shape to deliver a knockout blow to the Germans, but they became concerned in late 1917 that the balance would tilt in favor of the Germans before the Americans arrived. Believing that the position of the Provisional Government in Russia (which had seized power in March 1917) had become increasingly precarious, the Allies foresaw the complete collapse of Russia and feared a flood of German divisions moving from the Eastern to the Western Front.

Allied fears were heightened when Austro-German forces won a brilliant victory over the Italians in the Battle of Caporetto during October–November 1917. The Italians lost more than 3,000 guns and about a million soldiers killed, wounded, or captured. Although the assistance of six French and five British divisions seemed momentarily to hold off disaster, the Allies faced the disconcerting specter of complete collapse on the Eastern and Italian fronts and the subsequent concentration of all the Central Powers' forces on the Western Front. Meanwhile, German submarines continued to gnaw at the lifeline of Allied shipping.

While fighting was still going on at Arras and the Chemin des Dames, Haig and Nivelle agreed that the Allies had to clear the submarine bases in Belgium either by advancing directly from Ypres or "indirectly" by attacking toward Charleroi-Liège. Haig soon directed the completion of a study on breaking through the Hindenburg Line in the vicinity of Cambrai. Since the firm, rolling terrain around Cambrai was ideal tank country, Lieutenant Colonel J. F. C. Fuller of the Royal Tank Corps drew up a scheme for a quick armored raid that would plunge through German lines, capture and destroy enemy personnel and equipment, and then return to friendly lines. British commanders, however, quickly decided on a full-scale battle in which the tanks were tied to the infantry and artillery. In the middle of October, Haig approved a plan for an attack at Cambrai.

The British Third Army, which was given responsibility for the attack, concentrated its forces along a six-mile front. The attack began with five divisions on line, one division following, and three divisions in reserve. To their rear, five cavalry divisions were set to race toward Cambrai. The Royal Tank Corps of the British army, which was commanded by Brigadier General Hugh Elles and which had Fuller as chief of staff, supported the attack with three tank brigades. Of 476 available tanks, 374 were combat tanks and 98 were administrative tanks, including those specially equipped for clearing wire, communicating, or carrying bridging material. The tanks were Mark IVs, which were huge, rhomboidal-shaped fighting vehicles carrying four 6-pounder guns and four machine guns.

Though one division commander refused to use the methods devised by the Royal Tank Corps, the other divisions practiced an intricate procedure for coordinating the actions of tanks and infantry. The main feature of this procedure was to have a section of three tanks lead an infantry company across no-man's-land and through enemy wire. With one tank leading and two tanks following in echelon on both sides, the infantry company advanced under the protection of the tanks. An infantry platoon moved in a flexible column formation behind each of the following tanks. When the leading tank reached the enemy's trenches, it swept them with fire, dropped its fascines—which were rolled bundles of sticks—into the trenches, and then crossed. After reaching the enemy trenches, the two leading infantry platoons cleared out the enemy. The two rear platoons then moved forward, sealed off the captured trench, and worked on improving paths through the wire. Meanwhile, the tanks continued forward to the next trench, and the infantry quickly followed. Since each of the tanks carried a fascine, the force could cross three trenches before being halted.

The British tried several new techniques in the attack. Fourteen squadrons of the Royal Flying Corps provided air support, which included not only flying the normal observation missions and attacks on German aircraft and headquarters but also providing direct support to ground units. The flying squadrons prepared to move forward with the first wave and to fire directly into the enemy's trenches. Also the British, preferring the advantage of surprise, decided to attack without the usual prolonged artillery preparation. The bombardment was supposed to begin at the same time as the assault, without preliminary registration that might have compromised

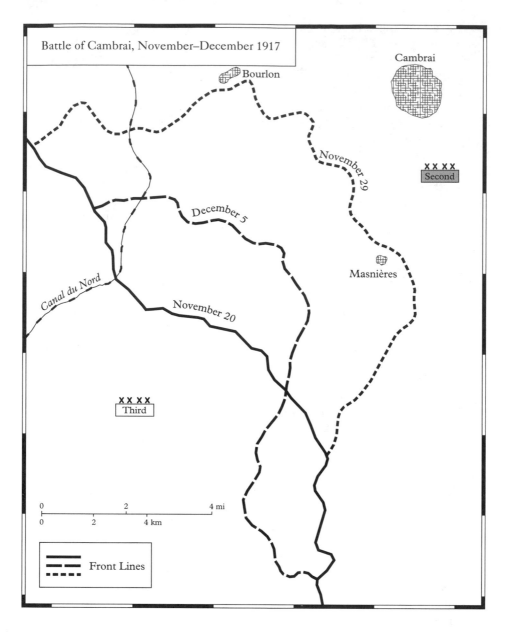

Battle of Cambrai, November–December 1917

Cambrai

Bourlon

November 29

X X X X
Second

December 5

Masnières

Canal du Nord

November 20

X X X X
Third

0 — 2 — 4 mi
0 — 2 — 4 km

Front Lines

the plan. Although the technique of using maps (rather than visual sightings) to control the firing of artillery had not been used extensively up to this point, the use of maps and what came to be known as "predicted fire" proved to be extremely successful.

The attack began early on the morning of November 20, 1917. Ludendorff noted in his memoirs that the Germans expected the Allies to continue the attacks in Flanders and on the French front and did not expect them to begin an attack at Cambrai. By the end of the first day, the British had advanced about three miles and punched through the main defenses and support line of the Hindenburg Line. This was the deepest penetration into German lines on the Western Front since the beginning of trench warfare. Of the 374 combat tanks that took part in the fighting, 179 were out of action, but only sixty-five because of enemy fire. On the second day, the British made additional gains, but the Germans brought four more divisions into the area. On the third day, very little was accomplished. In the face of determined German resistance, those battalions that made any gains at all soon lost them. For the next several days, bitter fighting swirled around the high ground in the area.

By November 30, the British Third Army was crammed into a salient about seven miles deep and eight miles wide. Having brought forward significant artillery and reserves, the Germans struck after an all-night bombardment. The strong German attack pushed the British behind their original starting point. Some sharp fighting continued, but the offensive and the counterattack were over. Of the 474 tanks that entered the battle, less than one-third returned from Cambrai. Most of them required extensive repairs, and very few ever participated in a battle again. The Battle of Cambrai was the last major battle fought by the Allies on the Western Front in 1917.

✶   ✶   ✶   ✶

As 1917 came to a close, the hopes of the Allies rested on the "Americans and the tanks." The French and British had suffered terribly at the Chemin des Dames and at Passchendaele. Their losses provided vivid evidence about the high price an attacker could pay and underlined the wisdom of using limited offensives to help reduce casualties. Limited offensives, however, held little promise for ending the war other than through attrition. Despite the introduction of the tank, the experience of Cambrai confirmed that much remained to be done before the tank could alter the nature of the battlefield. The British high command began developing a plan for 1919, but its success rested upon efforts to improve and manufacture tanks by the thousands. The most fervent Allied hope, however, was that large numbers of Americans would arrive on the Western Front before the Germans shifted forces from the east and launched a final desperate offensive.

Despite widespread starvation and shortages, the year did not end on an entirely negative note for the Central Powers. The victory against the Italians at Caporetto in October–November 1917 and against the Russians at Riga in September 1917 suggested that the Central Powers had made important steps in breaking the deadlock of trench warfare. Additionally, peace discussions had begun on December 22 at Brest-Litovsk, and on March 3, 1918, the Bolsheviks signed a treaty that yielded vast areas and important resources to the Germans. The treaty accelerated the shifting of German forces to the west and the German army's preparation for what Ludendorff called the "biggest task in its history"—the launching of the final offensives in the spring of 1918.

SUGGESTED READINGS

Braim, Paul F. *The Test of Battle: The American Expeditionary Forces in the Meuse-Argonne Campaign* (Newark, N.J.: University of Delaware Press, 1987).

Coffman, Edward M. *The War to End All Wars: The American Military Experience in World War I* (Madison, Wisc.: The University of Wisconsin Press, 1968).

Cooper, Bryan. *The Battle of Cambrai* (New York: Stein and Day, 1968).

Halperin, Paul G. *A Naval History of World War I* (Annapolis, Md.: Naval Institute Press, 1994).

Legg, Stuart. *Jutland* (New York: John Day Co., 1967).

Macdonald, Lyn. *They Called It Passchendaele* (London: Michael Joseph, 1978).

McKee, Alexander. *Vimy Ridge* (Toronto: The Ryerson Press, 1966).

Millet, Allan R. *The General: Robert L. Bullard and Officership in the United States Army, 1881–1925* (Westport, Conn.: Greenwood Press, 1975).

Ryan, Stephen. *Pétain the Soldier* (New York: A. S. Barnes and Company, 1969).

Smythe, Donald. *Pershing: General of the Armies* (Bloomington, Ind.: Indiana University Press, 1986).

Trask, David F. *The United States in the Supreme War Council* (Middleton, Conn.: Wesleyan University Press, 1961).

Watt, Richard M. *Dare Call It Treason* (New York: Simon and Schuster, 1963).

Wolff, Leon. *In Flanders Field, the 1917 Campaign* (New York: Viking Press, 1958).

Woollcombe, Robert. *The First Tank Battle: Cambrai, 1917* (London: Arthur Barker Limited, 1967).

12

BREAKING THE HOLD OF THE TRENCHES, 1918

Infiltration Tactics and the
Failure of the German
Offensives, March–July 1918

Overwhelming the Germans
with Men and Machines

The Great War

As the bloody months of 1917 drew to a close, some military leaders believed the strategic situation momentarily favored the Central Powers more than the Allies. With the Russian army collapsing in the east, with the defeat of the Italian army at Caporetto, and with the British weakened by the unrestricted submarine warfare campaign, some leaders believed Germany had an opportunity to gain military superiority on the Western Front. They also believed the German army had demonstrated during the breakthroughs at Caporetto and Riga that it could break the deadlock of trench warfare on the Western Front. With the introduction of infiltration tactics, the Germans seemed to have developed a new method for restoring mobility to the battlefield.

Despite these promising indications, long-term prospects were not favorable to the Central Powers. The German people were obviously growing more and more discontented with the war, and Americans were entering Europe by the thousands. Clearly, decisive action had to be taken quickly if Germany was to win the war militarily. In a race against time, the Germans began preparing for a huge offensive, while the Allies did all they could to accelerate the arrival and preparation of the Americans.

Infiltration Tactics and the Failure of the German Offensives, March–July 1918

The overthrow of Russia's tsarist government in March 1917 by a provisional government and the seizure of power by the Bolsheviks in November created new hope in Germany. For the military, the ending of the war in the east meant troops and equipment could be shipped from the east, but for the civilians the collapse of Russia suggested the possibility of greater food supplies and other necessities. Throughout 1916–1917, the effects of the Allied blockade reached their peak as distress and discontent caused by food shortages increased among the civilian population. Families became especially concerned about the undernourishment of their children, and misery became particularly acute among the poor. The winter of 1916–1917 was known as the "turnip winter," when German citizens were forced to eat turnips, which were usually fed to cattle.

In the army and navy, resentment grew among the enlisted men, for they were angered by a system that provided better food for officers. Also, being bottled up in ports for years with little to do made sailors discontented and vulnerable to propaganda. Dissatisfaction became most obvious when the crew of the *Prinzregent Luitpold* mutinied on June 6, 1917, and went on a hunger strike.

Opposition to the war also grew rapidly in organized labor. In January 1918, the first outbreak of widespread political strikes occurred. On January 28, some 400,000 workers in Berlin went on strike, seeking food and higher wages and demanding an end to the war. The movement spread to most of the larger industrial cities and involved more than one million workers. This growing evidence of mounting civilian discontent heightened the German military's interest in bringing the war to a close.

For some leaders, the prospect of Russia's withdrawal from the war offered the best chance of reviving flagging German morale. Leaders in German industry and commerce believed the Treaty of Brest-Litovsk would open vast areas in eastern Europe to economic exploitation. By the treaty of March 3, 1918, Russia lost one-fourth of its territory—44 percent of its population, 73 percent of its iron ore, and 75 percent of its coal. Before the treaty was signed, German leaders received optimistic projections of food shipments from the Ukraine, but actual shipments always remained below expectations. This environment of disappointment intensified German interest in a rapid victory.

Throughout this period, the German high command greatly expanded its power, and by the end of 1917, the high command—particularly Ludendorff—dominated the German government. The extent of Ludendorff's power can be seen in a meeting held on November 11, 1917, in Mons, Belgium, to discuss German strategy for 1918. Neither Kaiser William II, the chancellor, nor Hindenburg was present. Although Ludendorff later lamented the absence of a strong political figure in Berlin, he would never have tolerated the emergence of a German Clemenceau who would have argued, "War is too important to be left to the generals." Instead of military policy being subordinate to political power and objectives, the German government had become the servant of the high command.

When Ludendorff arrived at the meeting at Mons in November 1917, he did not believe that unrestricted submarine warfare had failed, but he knew that the Americans were beginning to pour into Europe and that the Allies were once again building up enormous quantities of matériel. He had already made up his mind that Germany had to achieve a major victory and force the Allied powers to recognize that continuing the war offered no chance of success, despite the involvement of the Americans. Moreover, launching a final desperate offensive would, he hoped, end the general despair in Germany about the hopelessness of the struggle as well as revive the fighting spirit of Austria-Hungary, Bulgaria, and Turkey. The key decision in the November 1917 meeting thus concerned the launching of an offensive on the Western Front in the spring of 1918. The Germans believed a series of offensives, delivered at intervals and at several different points, would restore mobility to the battlefield and end the long stalemate that had lasted for four years on the Western Front.

The Germans focused on the British front (Flanders, Arras, and the Somme); they believed Great Britain might be more eager for peace once its

Kaiser Wilhelm II with Hindenburg on his right and Ludendorff on his left. Despite the Kaiser's constitutional authority as Supreme War Lord, he was disregarded almost entirely by the real makers of policy, Hindenburg and Ludendorff.

soldiers suffered terribly. With the heavily used Channel ports to its rear, Flanders appeared to be the most favorable area for an attack, since a breakthrough could sever the BEF's communications lines to Great Britain. The possibility of rains soaking the soft terrain in Flanders, however, ruled out any offensive before May. An offensive in Arras (south of Flanders and north of the Somme) also seemed unwise because of strong British defenses.

The most vulnerable area appeared to be the Somme, where the British seemed to be overextended and their defenses the weakest. An offensive there, near St. Quentin and Cambrai, offered the possibility of splitting the British and French forces. If an advance deep into the Allied positions were made, the Germans would push the British toward the Channel coast. Ludendorff believed that the defeat of the British forces would drive them out of the war and ultimately provide a favorable peace for the Central Powers. Nevertheless, tactical considerations dominated his thinking, and he later explained, "A strategic plan which ignores tactical factors is doomed to failure."

On January 21, Ludendorff ordered preparations to begin for an offensive, code named "Michael," to be launched in the Somme area. In October 1917, the Germans had only 150 divisions on the Western Front, but by the spring offensive of 1918, they would have 192.

Infiltration Tactics

Although Ludendorff warned the kaiser that the impending struggle would be "immense" and take a "long time" and that the battle would flow from one point to another, he was confident that the German army would succeed. Since the "Massacre of the Innocents" at Ypres, the Germans had devoted considerable efforts to solving the riddle of trench warfare, and they had improved their tactical methods through a process of incremental change. German leaders recognized the unfavorable strategic situation facing them and were more willing than the Allies to take risks or consider new methods. The general staff also encouraged innovation and circulated information among units about successful methods such as the elastic defense. In Ludendorff's judgment, successful attacks in late 1917 on the Italian front and the Eastern Front had demonstrated the Germans' ability to break the deadlock of trench warfare. He recognized the difficulties, however, of changing the entire thinking of the army from trench warfare back to the offensive.

Between November 11, 1917, when the Germans decided to attack, and March 21, 1918, when the attack began, the German army worked diligently to improve its offensive doctrine and to prepare its units for the attack. After careful reexamination of their own experience with the offensive, the Germans published on January 26, 1918, the basics of their new doctrine in a pamphlet entitled *The Attack in Position Warfare*. Contained within the pamphlet was the outline of new tactics (which were not completely new) which later became known as "infiltration tactics."

The tactics emphasized bypassing enemy resistance and pushing forward as far as possible. Using specially trained assault troops, armed with light machine guns, the Germans expected small units to exploit success at weak points and to advance as far and as quickly as possible into enemy defenses. Instead of clearing pockets of enemy resistance as they advanced, the assault troops were expected to continue to advance and to reach the enemy's artillery. The January 1918 pamphlet explained, "The aim of the breakthrough should be the enemy's artillery." Follow-on units were expected to neutralize bypassed enemy strong points. If the reserves were committed, they would reinforce success, not push their way through unbroken enemy defenses.

The new tactics relied strongly on effective artillery support. Using techniques devised by Colonel Georg Bruchmüller, the Germans prepared to fire artillery in depth through the enemy's positions. They also practiced using a rolling barrage in front of the advancing infantry. Despite reservations from infantrymen who feared being fired upon accidentally and from artillerymen who wanted greater precision, the Germans adopted in January 1918 a system of predicted fire known as the "Pulkowski method." With this method of fire, an artillery unit could support infantry attacks without pre-registering and without losing the element of surprise. Technical firing tables and coordinates from improved maps provided data that could be modified for deviations caused by weather conditions or wear on an artillery tube. These methods shortened the time needed for artillery preparation before an offensive and encouraged the use of "hurricanes" of fire—short, intense, surprise bombardments immediately before an attack began. For their attacks on March 21 and April 9, 1918, the Germans used some pre-registration, but they engaged most targets using the predicted fire method. After April 9, they supported almost all attacks with the new method.

In addition to changes in infantry tactics and in coordination between infantry and artillery, the Germans recognized the error of trying to command from the rear by using a telephone. In the spring of 1918, Ludendorff ordered all division commanders in the coming offensives to command from the front lines on horseback. He recognized the importance of their presence and their personal example in motivating soldiers to continue moving forward.

To ensure the highest levels of performance, the Germans strongly emphasized training and physical fitness before the battle. Companies, battalions, and regiments followed detailed training guidelines on the conduct of assaults. As smaller units finished their training, complete divisions began conducting practice assaults. Many of the exercises included live fire, as well as the employment of rockets and flares to control artillery. Of their 192 divisions on the Western Front, the Germans trained and equipped only fifty-six in the new tactics. The remainder concentrated on holding the German line and had a lower priority for replacements, training, and equipment.

The Spring Offensive

At 0440 hours on March 21, 1918, the long-awaited spring offensive began. The Germans launched their attack in the area of the Somme with three armies: the Seventeenth Army on the right, the Second Army in the center, and the Eighteenth Army on the left. The Seventeenth and Second armies belonged to the army group commanded by Crown Prince Rupprecht of Bavaria, and the Eighteenth Army belonged to the army group commanded by German Crown Prince William. Ludendorff had decided to split the attack between two army groups so he, as he later explained, "could exercise a far-reaching influence on the course of the battle."

The German attack on March 21 struck the British Fifth Army and the Third Army to its north. For some time the Allies had expected the Germans to begin an offensive, and Haig had anticipated a strong attack on the front of Fifth Army, commanded by General Sir Hubert Gough, which faced St. Quentin in the Somme area. Nevertheless, Gough's army was spread across a forty-mile front, had done little to establish a defense in depth, and was not fully prepared to ward off a major attack. British defenses were particularly weak in the southern part of Fifth Army's front, for this area had recently been turned over to the British by the French. This was to be the area where the German Eighteenth Army made its largest advances.

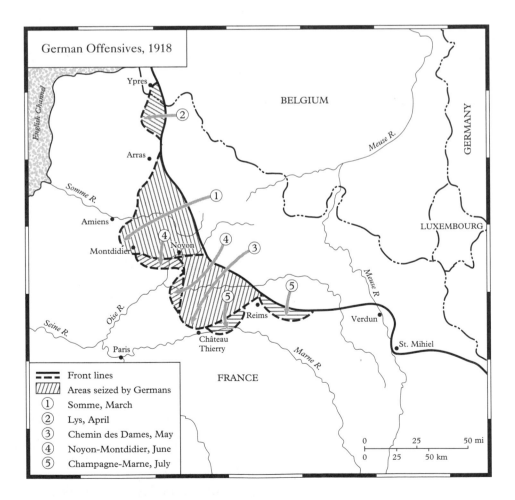

From 0440 until 0940 hours, the Germans fired an artillery bombardment that consisted of gas, smoke, and high-explosive shells. At 0940, the Germans advanced with thirty-two infantry divisions, closely followed by an additional twenty-eight. A heavy rolling barrage preceded the infantry. The Germans wanted their infantry to penetrate about five miles, the distance between the front line and the British artillery. By nightfall, Second and Eighteenth armies in the German center and left had pushed through most of the forward zone of the British Fifth Army, but Seventeenth Army on the right encountered a more stubborn resistance from the British Third Army. Ludendorff had expected Seventeenth and Second armies on the center and right to make the most progress and planned on their turning to the right and enveloping the British forces. Since Seventeenth Army was advancing slowly and Eighteenth Army on the left was advancing rapidly, however, Ludendorff decided to reinforce the Eighteenth Army's success and began sending it additional forces and supplies.

In subsequent days, the German advance continued, particularly in the center and left sectors. Pétain and Haig had earlier agreed that France would send reinforcements if a major offensive were launched against the British, and so on March 23, Pétain agreed to send sufficient forces to prevent the Germans from splitting the French and British. Pétain remained concerned, however, about the possibility of an offensive on his own front between Soissons and Reims, and he did not send reinforcements as rapidly as Haig desired.

By the morning of March 25, the fourth day of the offensive, the French Third Army with seven divisions was deployed on the southern flank of the expanding German salient, and the French First Army with six divisions was on its way. General Émile Fayolle assumed command of a provisional army group that included French and British units south of the Somme River. On March 27, the German Eighteenth Army captured Mont didier, but its forces were exhausted and running out of supplies. To the north of Eighteenth Army, the Germans made several other assaults, attempting to capture the railhead of Amiens, but on April 4, Ludendorff halted the offensive.

The first attempt to break through Allied lines had failed. This failure resulted from a variety of factors, including the Allies' successful reinforcement of the threatened area. The Germans were also stymied by the difficulties of transporting troops and artillery across the destroyed terrain of the attack, the inability of reserves and supporting units to keep up with the leading forces, and the lack of discipline among some German units. Though the Germans had made numerous tactical innovations, problems that had existed from the beginning of the war continued to limit their ability to make a breakthrough. Most notably, the Germans had not been able to prevent the enemy from moving in fresh troops by railway and roads into the endangered area. Nevertheless, the German army had advanced some thirty-five miles, the largest advance by far of any army on the Western Front since 1914.

Allied Unity of Command

Throughout the first three years of the war, the Allies had made some attempts to coordinate their strategy and operations, but concerns about relinquishing their sovereignty made them reluctant to adopt a unified command system. In early 1917, Lloyd George had agreed to (and Haig had reluctantly accepted) the British forces in France being subject to the orders of Nivelle for the 1917 offensives. The failure of these attacks ended this arrangement. Not until after the collapse of Russia and the defeat of Italy at Caporetto in late 1917 did the Allies take steps to establish a formal system of coordinating their strategies.

As French and British divisions moved into Italy to bolster their ally, Allied heads of government met at Rapallo, Italy, in November 1917 and agreed to form the Supreme War Council. Focused on the Western Front, the council consisted of each nation's head of government and one other high-ranking member of the government. The council also had a board of permanent military representatives that met at Versailles. According to the council's charter, the military representatives were supposed to "watch day by day the situation of the forces and of the means of all kinds of which the Allied armies and the enemy armies dispose." Thus, no hint of real command authority existed. The weakness of the Supreme War Council became very evident when an attempt to form a general reserve in January 1918

When General Ferdinand Foch was charged with coordinating the actions of the Allied armies on the Western Front, he responded with enthusiasm and energy. Never losing his faith in the offensive despite years of losses, he successfully coordinated the final drives that defeated the Germans.

foundered: only days before the German spring offensive, the executive committee of the Supreme War Council concluded that it was "impossible" to organize an Allied general reserve.

The crisis engendered by Germany's success along the Somme led Allied leaders to assemble in late March 1918 at Doullens, France, to consider alternatives for strengthening coordination among their military forces. After much wrangling, Foch was charged "with coordinating the action of the Allied armies on the Western Front." Although his responsibilities were only for the duration of the crisis, the Allies—including the Americans— agreed on April 3, 1918, to an extension of Foch's powers. The agreement stated, "The British, French and American governments . . . entrust to General Foch the strategic direction of military operations."

For the first time in the war, some semblance of a unity of command existed among the Allies. Upon the insistence of the British, however, the commander of each national army would have the right to appeal to his government if he thought Foch's orders endangered his army.

The Germans Continue Their Offensive

As the tactically impressive but strategically unsuccessful March offensive came to a halt, Ludendorff launched another attack, striking the Allies in Flanders, with the main attack hitting twenty miles south of Ypres, near the Lys River. This area was more than sixty miles northwest of the area in which the Somme operation occurred. Though Ludendorff's strategic objectives are not completely clear, he evidently aimed to strike a weaker portion of the British front and perhaps to capture the vital rail junction of Hazebrouck.

On April 9, the second offensive began, its main attack striking the Portuguese II Corps. By April 12, the Germans had made significant gains, and Haig desperately sought assistance from Foch. Foch sent only token forces to reinforce the British; he hoped to retain sufficient forces to create a reserve capable of responding to a larger German attack that he expected to strike in the Somme region. Haig responded with a "backs to the wall" order, and British soldiers responded with some of the most gallant and tenacious fighting of the war. The battle continued until April 29 when the German attack ground to a halt. During the fighting German operations were affected by a breakdown in discipline, particularly when the troops captured well-stocked British supply dumps. This was an early indication that the German army was beginning to deteriorate. In another ominous development for the Central Powers, the Allies began launching new ships in April at a faster rate than German submarines could destroy them.

Ludendorff launched his next blow on May 27 near Soissons against the Chemin des Dames, the scene of Nivelle's disastrous attack of 1917, which had remained quiet for more than a year. The third offensive was a diversionary attack, for the Germans sought to divert Allied reserves from Flanders and then to resume their attacks against the British. Even though the terrain on the Chemin des Dames favored the defenders, the Germans achieved surprising success. The defending forces in this region included a British corps that had been mauled in the first two German offensives and sent to recuperate in what was supposedly a quiet sector. The commander of the French forces, General Denis A. Duchêne, had refused to establish a defense in depth and had placed his meager forces along the high ground. The attackers swept through the thinly held front easily and advanced more than twelve miles on the first day of their attack. This was the largest advance made in a single day on the Western Front since the early months of the war, and Duchêne paid the penalty for his unpreparedness by being relieved of his command. As with other German attacks, the Allies moved reserves into the endangered area. This time, however, some of the reserves were Americans whose hard fighting at Château Thierry and Belleau Wood helped stop the German attack by June 4. The Germans were not prepared to exploit their gains, but they established a large salient near the Marne.

With the ending of this attack, Ludendorff's offensives had accomplished little more than the creation of three large salients (Somme, Lys, and Marne) and the depletion of the German army. Still seeking to draw Allied reserves away from Flanders, he decided to launch an attack between the Somme and Marne salients. By attacking from the neighboring flanks of the Somme and Marne salients between Montdidier and Noyon, he planned on expanding the two salients into a single larger salient and threatening Paris. Unbeknownst to the Germans, the Allies had detected preparations for the attack and had prepared strong defenses in depth. Just prior to the Germans beginning their artillery preparation for the attack on June 8, the French began counterbattery artillery fire. Although the attackers made limited gains, a French counterattack with tank support stopped them. By June 13 the fourth offensive was over.

During the month of comparative quiet that followed, Ludendorff prepared two great attacks that would comprise his fifth and final offensive: the first was an attack in the Champagne-Marne area on both sides of Reims; the second was the long-awaited offensive in Flanders. Just as had occurred in June, the Allies detected preparations for an attack in the Reims area, with much of the information coming from an ever-expanding flow of German deserters. Consequently the Allies strengthened their defenses in this area. Before the German attack began, Allied counterbattery fire disrupted their efforts. With one of the most spirited defenses coming from the U.S. 3rd Division along the Marne River, the Germans made only limited gains in their attack, which began on July 15 but ended by July 17. The final, great offensive in Flanders never occurred.

The Americans Enter the Battle

Without the moral and matériel support of the Americans, the French and British might not have survived the German spring offensive. Large numbers of Americans did not fight the Germans until the summer of 1918, but their entry into battle helped blunt the German attack. Not surprisingly, given Pershing's faith in the offense, the first important action was an attack conducted by the 1st Infantry Division at Cantigny near the tip of the Noyon-Montdidier salient, created during the first German offensive. The Americans staged a limited attack on the ruined village of Cantigny as part of a French attempt to retake Montdidier. Beginning at 0545 hours on May 28, the 1st Division attacked with its 28th Infantry Regiment and reached its objective by 0730 hours. The Germans launched six or seven counterattacks, but they failed to coordinate their artillery support with their infantry attacks and thus failed to push the Americans back. For the next several days, the men of the 28th and 16th regiments endured continued shelling and machine-gun fire. The attack was not significant strategically, but its success did bolster American confidence.

Following Pétain's appeal for assistance in halting the third German offensive at the Chemin des Dames, Pershing dispatched the U.S. 2nd and 3rd Divisions toward the Marne near Château Thierry. One of the two brigades of 2nd Division was a U.S. Marine brigade. The arrival of 3rd Division at Château Thierry on May 31 and 2nd Division at Belleau Wood-Bouresches-Vaux on June 1 demonstrated the willingness and ability of the Americans to fight. Their contributions were more important strategically than the fight at Cantigny, for their strong defenses and counterattacks played a key role in halting the third German offensive. Some French officers credited the Americans with having saved Paris.

On July 15 the fifth German offensive struck along the Marne River east of Château Thierry. Though the Germans crossed the Marne and established a sizeable bridgehead, the U.S. 3rd Division held firm, fighting in three directions. On the division's right flank, 30th Regiment was forced

An American column moving across a cratered battlefield. Throughout the war, armies on the offensive faced considerable difficulties moving across terrain that had been softened and churned by thousands of artillery rounds.

back under the German attack, but 38th Regiment on its left held firm. In an action Pershing later described as "one of the most brilliant pages in our military annals," Colonel Ulysses Grant McAlexander's regiment withstood the attack of two German divisions. The actions of 38th Regiment sealed the end of the fifth German offensive and contributed significantly to 3rd Division becoming known as "The Rock of the Marne."

Although Ludendorff still clung to his hope for a final offensive in the Flanders sector, the opportunity for decisive action had slipped away. His forces had suffered terrible losses, his reserves and supplies were depleted, and the morale of his soldiers was sinking rapidly.

Overwhelming the Germans with Men and Machines

As the fifth and final German offensive ground to a halt, the Allies accelerated their efforts to seize the initiative with strong counterattacks. Foch's initial efforts focused on three salients held by the Germans (Marne, Somme, and St. Mihiel). Since the middle of April, he had worked energetically to assemble forces for a counterstroke, and on July 18, after concentrating his forces around the Marne salient, he launched the Second Battle of the Marne. This was the first of a series of great drives that would roll back the German army.

Beginning at 0435 hours on July 18, the French Tenth Army made the main attack into the western neck of the Marne salient near Soissons, while Sixth, Ninth, and Fifth armies pushed against the salient on its other sides. Nine American divisions participated in the Allied attempt to push the Germans out of their positions. The American divisions attacked as part of three French field armies and did not operate as an independent force. The actions of 1st and 2nd divisions as part of the French Tenth Army were particularly important, for when their attacks threatened Soissons and the main German supply line running through it, the Germans had no choice but to withdraw. Though the Germans were forced out of the salient, their withdrawal was conducted skillfully and orderly. Nonetheless, the success at driving the Germans out of their Marne position clearly demonstrated that the initiative had passed to the Allies.

Foch's next attack struck the northern part of the Somme salient and is sometimes called the Battle of Amiens. The date of its launching was later described by Ludendorff as the "black day of the German army." The attack marked a turning point in the conduct of Allied operations and inaugurated the form of relatively open warfare that characterized the last months of the war.

The attacking forces consisted of the British Fourth Army under General Henry Rawlinson and the French First Army under General M. Eugène Debeney. The British Fourth Army was responsible for the main attack, and Rawlinson had the Canadian Corps of four divisions and the Australian Corps of five divisions lead it. Both corps were renowned for their fighting abilities. As one indication of how the war was changing, Rawlinson's army was reinforced by twelve battalions of tanks (414 combat tanks and 120 administrative tanks).

After a concerted effort to prevent the Germans from detecting the Allied preparations, the British attack began at 0420 hours on August 8 without any preparatory fire and with almost no prior registration of the artillery. Since the French had only two battalions of tanks (seventy-two tanks) to support their attack, they began their artillery preparation at the same time as the British began their attack, and then sent their infantry forward forty-five minutes later. They had delayed their artillery preparation and infantry attack to avoid warning the Germans of the impending Allied attack.

The attackers, particularly the Canadians, advanced swiftly. By noon they had advanced up to ten miles and captured some 16,000 prisoners. Though the French advance was slower, they also captured many prisoners and weapons. For the remainder of the month, Haig continued pressing on the Somme salient. For a short time he shifted the main attack to the British Third Army on the left of Rawlinson's Fourth Army, but then ordered an advance by both field armies. By the end of the month the Germans began pulling back to the Hindenburg Line, where they had started their Somme offensive in March.

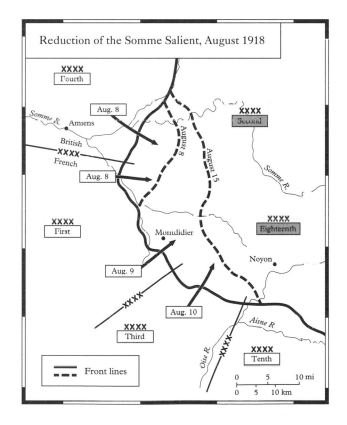

Reduction of the Somme Salient, August 1918

The counterattack by the French and Americans on July 18 against the Marne salient had been a rude shock to the Germans, but the success of the Allies against the Somme salient was the beginning of the end. German losses on the Marne and on the Somme had not been large, but the Allied victories had sent a clear signal that Germany's power could only get weaker while that of the Allies could only get stronger. The kaiser held a conference at Spa on August 14, and German military leaders acknowledged that the war no longer could be won militarily. They concluded, "We have reached the limits of our endurance."

Reduction of the St. Mihiel Salient

The swiftly changing situation was as much a surprise to the Allies as it was to the Germans. Most Allied leaders had anticipated some gains in the campaigns of 1918 but expected the final blow to occur in 1919. In June, Marshal Foch had encouraged the British and Americans to prepare their forces for the final effort in 1919. And when Haig launched the offensive against the Somme salient on August 8, he planned only on conducting a limited offensive and did not expect to make dramatic gains. He too had expected the decisive battles to occur in 1919.

As the deterioration of the Germans became apparent to the Allies, Foch recognized the importance of continuing pressure on the enemy. If the Germans succeeded in making an orderly withdrawal to their own frontiers, they could destroy roads, bridges, and railways and thereby force the Allies to rebuild lines of communication before they advanced. The Germans could also carry much of their supplies and equipment with them and perhaps reestablish their defenses near their own border. Consequently, Foch began preparations for two simultaneous attacks that would advance and then turn inward as if they were giant pincers. A combined Franco-British force would advance in the west toward Cambrai, Le Cateau, and the railway junction at Aulnoye, while a Franco-American force would advance in the east toward the railway junction at Mézières. While these attacks drove forward, Foch would launch a series of staggered attacks along the entire front to confuse the Germans and prevent them from concentrating their reserves against the two pincers. What was eventually to be the American Meuse-Argonne offensive would be the main component of the eastern pincer.

As events accelerated on the Western Front, the Americans had to change some of their long-standing plans. In June 1917, Pershing and Pétain had agreed that once an American army was formed, its first mission would be the reduction of the St. Mihiel salient. In the following months many of the recently formed American divisions served in that sector so they could familiarize themselves with the terrain. By July 1918, Pershing had sufficient forces to form First Army officially; he then named himself its first commander. Amidst the important changes of August 1918, Foch told Pershing that he wanted to split the American forces and to commit substantially fewer forces against the St. Mihiel salient, which he considered less important than the launching of an offensive toward Mézières in the

Meuse-Argonne area. But as before, Pershing strongly objected to dividing his forces.

The two leaders finally compromised by agreeing that First Army would attack the St. Mihiel salient but would then participate in a major offensive farther west in the Meuse-Argonne area. This plan was extremely ambitious, for it called upon the American First Army, whose staff had no experience in large operations, to engage in a major battle and then to disengage and move about thirty miles west for another major battle. Such a task would have been difficult for an experienced army; for the untested First Army, it was a superhuman task.

The offensive against the St. Mihiel salient began at 0500 hours on September 12 after a four-hour artillery preparation. Pershing attacked with four corps, composed of four French and eight-and-one-half American divisions. Seven of the American divisions were on the southern face of the salient; the other one-and-one-half divisions were on the western face. The

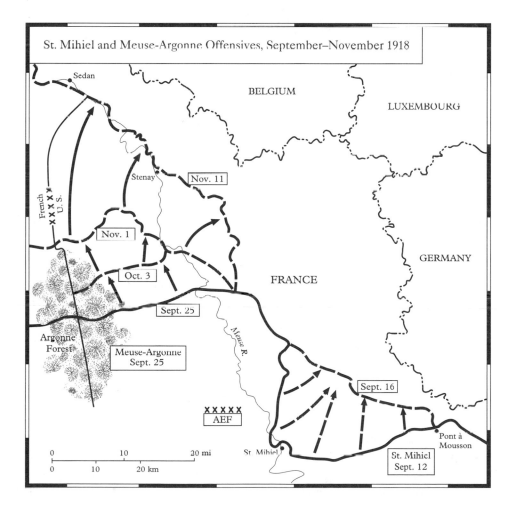

St. Mihiel and Meuse-Argonne Offensives, September–November 1918

French divisions concentrated against the high ground at the southwestern tip of the salient. To support the attack, there were 3,010 artillery tubes and 267 light tanks, almost half of which were manned by French soldiers. The attack on St. Mihiel was the first on the European continent by an entire American field army, and it relied heavily on Allied assistance.

Above the battlefield, Colonel Billy Mitchell achieved the greatest concentration of aircraft during the war. The 1,481 Allied airplanes, not one of which was American built and many of which were flown by British, French, and Italian pilots, overwhelmed the German force of 283 planes. Colonel Mitchell, who had only loose control over the planes flown by Allied pilots, wanted to attack the lines of communication and supply system deep in the Germans' rear, but Pershing insisted that the huge armada of planes be subordinated to the needs of the ground battle. The performance of Mitchell and his pilots in the subsequent fighting delighted Pershing and resulted in Mitchell's promotion to brigadier general.

Despite heavy rains that made the soldiers miserable, movement over muddy terrain dificult, and aerial operations risky, the attack went as planned. Fortunately for the Americans, the Germans were in the process of evacuating the salient, and the advance went forward much more easily than expected and without heavy casualties. By the time First Army stopped on a line at the base of the salient, it had captured 450 guns and 16,000 prisoners, while taking 7,000 casualties. Flushed with success from having reduced the salient in two days, the Americans could have continued to attack and perhaps reached Metz, but Pershing had agreed with Foch to halt the attack at the base of the salient and begin preparations for the offensive farther west. Several high-ranking officers within the AEF, including Brigadier General Douglas MacArthur, complained that a marvelous opportunity for an important advance and perhaps even a breakthrough had been missed.

The Meuse-Argonne Offensive

For the Meuse-Argonne offensive, Foch ordered the American First Army to relieve the French Second Army in its sector, which included the Argonne Forest and the area east to the Meuse River. He also assigned the French Fourth Army to a sector west of the Argonne Forest. The French Fourth and the American First armies were to attack northwest and either cut or interdict the railway line that ran east–west through Sedan and Mézières. The railway line had great strategic importance, for by cutting it the Allies not only could prevent the Germans from moving laterally along the Western Front, but also prevent the Germans from carrying many of their supplies with them as they withdrew in the face of Allied pressure. The loss of many tons of supplies would greatly weaken the Germans' ability to continue their resistance until 1919.

After relieving the French Second Army and occupying the Meuse-Argonne sector, the American front extended some ninety miles from the eastern edge of the St. Mihiel sector to the western edge of the Argonne Forest. For the headquarters of First Army, the requirement to concentrate the huge American force in the Meuse-Argonne sector was doubly difficult, because it had to direct the St. Mihiel operation while simultaneously beginning the concentration of other forces to the west. Inexperienced commanders and staffs at army, corps, and division levels had to control the complicated operation of replacing the French Second Army in the Meuse-Argonne area before the attack began. None had any experience with such a huge and complex operation. The staff officer in First Army headquarters who planned the vast movement of Americans and their supplies was Colonel George C. Marshall Jr. Working unbelievably hard and with rare attention to detail, Marshall handled the difficult task brilliantly. Beyond a doubt, it was one of the most difficult staff operations of the war.

The fact that most of those who participated in the battle had very little combat experience complicated First Army's task. Having used the most experienced divisions in the St. Mihiel offensive, the Americans had to commit a number of untried divisions in the Meuse-Argonne offensive. Of the nine divisions scheduled for the Meuse-Argonne offensive, only four had participated in combat operations, and the other five had had almost no combat experience. Moreover, the experienced divisions contained large numbers of recent replacements, some of whom had been in the army for only six weeks and had never fired their rifles.

Using only three small roads, the French pulled back eleven divisions, plus support units and headquarters, while the Americans moved in fifteen divisions, plus support units and headquarters. To make the operation even more difficult, most of the moves occurred at night. The transfer of the American forces to the Meuse-Argonne area required the movement of more than 600,000 soldiers and many hundreds of tons of equipment and supplies over a long distance. Some troops and equipment began moving toward the Meuse-Argonne area ten days before the beginning of the St. Mihiel offensive.

Once the offensive began, the Americans faced extremely strong enemy defenses. The Germans recognized the strategic importance of the railway to their rear and had worked diligently for more than three years to create a strong defensive zone in the Meuse-Argonne sector. Beginning with terrain that was strongly defensible because of many hills and thick woods, the Germans built three major belts of fortifications and established a lightly manned defensive position to their front. The belts of fortifications included numerous trenches, concrete dugouts, concrete machine-gun emplacements, and strong points. Miles of barbed wire reinforced these defenses, and the thick vines and brush that had grown up during the four years of German occupation concealed them from the attackers until the Allies were on top of them.

As the first part of the multistaged operation, Pershing planned on moving forward ten miles with a quick thrust. While a French and an American corps made a feint with artillery fire and raids in the old St. Mihiel sector to the east, the main American attack would be made by three corps (nine divisions) moving on line across a front of about twenty miles. Since Pershing's forces initially faced only five under-strength German divisions, he counted on the element of surprise to increase his advantage of attacking with superior numbers. However, German commanders learned of the up-coming attack and began reorganizing their front-line troops and moving reinforcements forward before the Americans launched their attack.

After a six-hour preparation fired by some 4,000 artillery pieces, American infantry and 189 light tanks moved forward rapidly at 0530 hours on September 26; they overwhelmed the forward defenses of the Germans easily, with a few units advancing as much as four miles. But from then on, things became disorganized and confused. Because of the Americans' inex-perience, numerous problems appeared: officers failed to coordinate prop-erly the infantry and artillery, soldiers tended to attack and die in bunches, and tanks lagged behind. As traffic-control problems increased, march disci-pline disappeared, and convoys got mixed together on the heavily traveled roads. The Americans continued to attack on September 27, but they suf-fered frightful casualties. In contrast to the other Allied offensives farther west, the American offensive achieved disappointing results.

On October 4, after regrouping, First Army attacked again, seeking the same objective as the September 26 attack. As in the previous attack, the infantry charged ahead bravely, performing many heroic acts, but their courage did not deflect the bullets and artillery fire of the well-prepared Ger-mans. On October 8, First Army attacked east of the Meuse River, but this attack also ground to a halt.

On October 12, Pershing split First Army, which was becoming too unwieldy, into two armies. He appointed Major General Hunter Liggett as

Not having experienced three years of trench warfare, the Americans had an almost naive faith in the offensive. Pershing insisted that American soldiers wear their uniforms correctly and train for mobile operations.

the commander of First Army and Major General Robert L. Bullard as commander of Second Army. Pershing became an army group commander.
While First Army focused on the Meuse-Argonne area, Second Army
focused on the base of the old St. Mihiel salient.

From October 14–19, First Army attacked again but soon halted
because of high losses. After three weeks of heavy fighting, the Americans
had suffered about 55,000 casualties and had advanced no farther than
where they had hoped to be on the first day's attack. Criticism against Pershing from Clemenceau, the French premier, became particularly sharp after
the American attack had halted. In his characteristically blunt fashion,
Clemenceau spoke of a "crisis" in the AEF and complained of many excellent American troops being "unused." Foch reacted to these criticisms by
defending Pershing. He explained that the Americans problems were not
due solely to Pershing but to the inexperience of lower-level commanders
and staffs.

Using the latter part of October to reorganize the forces of First
Army, Liggett attacked again on November 1 with seven veteran divisions.
After a two-hour artillery preparation, the attack began at 0530 hours with
only eighteen tanks accompanying the infantry. The attack proceeded much
more smoothly than previous attempts, and most divisions quickly reached
their first objectives. As the demoralized Germans began withdrawing, the
rate of advance by the Americans increased. The German commander attempted to withdraw behind the Meuse River, but on November 3–5, the
U.S. 5th Division fought its way across before the Germans could reestablish
their defenses. The end of the war was clearly near.

The armistice on November 11 finally ended the Meuse-Argonne
offensive in which more than 850,000 Americans had participated. During
the forty-seven-day campaign, First Army suffered about 117,000 casualties
while capturing 26,000 prisoners, 875 cannon, and 3,000 machine guns and
inflicting about 100,000 casualties.

The Final Allied Offensives

While the Americans delivered their attacks in the St. Mihiel and Meuse-
Argonne sectors, the other allies were also making several important attacks.
To the north, Belgian, British, and French units attacked in Flanders in late
September and eventually seized the Ypres ridge. As German resistance
dwindled, rain and mud delayed the Allies' continued advance. In perhaps
the most important attack along the front, one French and three British field
armies attacked in the Somme sector. By the first week in October, these
armies had fought their way through the Hindenburg Line and forced the
Germans to withdraw. To their right, three French armies advanced slowly
in the Allied center and maintained pressure on the Germans.

As the Allies advanced, the situation of the Central Powers became
hopeless. While American moral and matériel support strengthened Allied
resolve, the morale of the Central Powers was drained by four years of
bloody losses and weakened by the Allied blockade; their will to fight had

collapsed after the failure of the spring offensives. On September 29, Hindenburg and Ludendorff told Kaiser William II that Germany had to request an armistice; and they urged that a new democratic government be formed in Berlin. Several days later, the German and Austrian governments appealed to President Wilson for an armistice based on his Fourteen Points, but the Allies had not yet agreed on the particulars of a peace settlement. In late October, Austrian defenses along the Piave River collapsed completely; the Italians advanced quickly and captured several hundred thousand prisoners. Recognizing the inevitable, the Austrians notified President Wilson that they were willing to conclude a separate peace. On October 26, when Ludendorff showed signs of wanting to continue the war, the kaiser dismissed him.

By November 1, the Allied armies were prepared for their final offensive against the Germans. Foch's plans for continuing the attack were similar to his original concept. With the major thrusts coming from British-French forces in the west and American-French forces in the east, and with French forces maintaining pressure in the center, he intended to prevent the Germans from conducting an orderly withdrawal. As the Allies resumed their attack and as their rate of advance accelerated, German interest in concluding the war intensified.

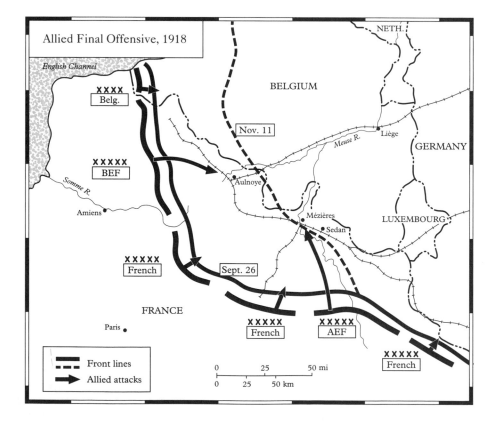

On the evening of November 7, members of a German armistice commission departed for France and drove toward a secluded forest near Compiègne, forty miles north of Paris. The following morning they met Foch in a railway car. He had been granted authority to offer the terms of an armistice. The German commission was dismayed to find that the terms bore little resemblance to Wilson's Fourteen Points. But when they complained to Foch, he informed them that hostilities would not cease until an armistice was concluded. The next few days were a whirlwind of activity; revolution broke out in various German cities, the kaiser abdicated and fled to Holland, and the German delegates finally received permission to sign the armistice. The Great War ended at 1100 hours on November 11, 1918.

The Great War

In terms of military developments, the events of World War I had corroborated many of Ivan Bloch's pessimistic predictions. The nations of Europe— both the winners and the losers—had paid remarkably high prices. The chief combatants had lost 8.5 million soldiers killed and 20 million wounded. As Bloch had predicted, the providing of unlimited resources to the military and the introduction of new weaponry had transformed war into an endless cycle of attrition. The huge costs and terrible sacrifices eventually brought on revolution and ruin. Bloch had been mistaken, though, in his underestimation of the willingness of belligerents to commit their resources and the lives of their people to the demands of total war.

Though all changes were not yet evident by 1918, it soon became apparent that the Great War was a turning point in the history of the world. The German, Austro-Hungarian, Russian, and Ottoman empires were among the victims of the war, and the structure of the European state system was fundamentally altered. With Europe distracted by four years of war, the rest of the world speeded up its industrialization and modernization and brought the age of European economic supremacy closer to its end. Among other changes, the necessity for governments to plan and direct the activities of their people cast them into arenas from which they would not depart. With so many men in military service, women worked in jobs that previously had been closed to them and in doing so took an important step in modifying their role in society.

The Great War added new meaning to the term "total war," as entire societies were mobilized and committed to the war effort. The major belligerents used conscription to provide millions of men for their armies, but many other men and women contributed to the war effort in factories, fields, mines, and offices. Almost the entire resources of states were committed to the war effort, particularly those of industry. Factories poured out thousands of rifles, mortars, trucks, airplanes, typewriters, telephones, and other items, as well as millions of artillery and rifle rounds and millions of uniforms, blankets, helmets, and boots. Huge logistical systems had to be organized to obtain, allocate, and deliver these products. The "nation in arms" had become a reality.

The war also fundamentally altered the nature of land warfare. Nineteenth-century battles, which sometimes appear almost quaint in comparison to those of 1914–1918, were a thing of the past. As military leaders confronted the unexpected challenges of the Great War, much of their thinking and many of their long-established practices had to change. New methods for organizing, equipping, supplying, and moving huge armies had to be devised. Nonetheless, most armies adapted slowly to the new conditions of the battlefield, and thousands of soldiers died in vain attempts to apply methods that might have worked in the past but that were no longer sufficient for the new conditions. As is all too often the case, the tragedy of huge casualty lists forced most armies to adapt.

As armies adjusted to the new conditions, numerous innovations occurred. New weapons, such as the tank, flamethrower, and light machine gun, provided means for punching through strong defenses. And for the first time, war became truly three-dimensional because of the airplane. From the first battle to the last, commanders on both sides depended on aircraft to provide information about the enemy, adjust artillery fires, attack enemy targets, and control the air above the ground forces. The war also affected naval forces. Though rudimentary, the aircraft carrier became a reality, and the submarine proved deadly against surface shipping.

Conceptual changes also occurred. Gradual improvements in coordination between artillery and infantry enabled attacks to succeed with fewer

Artillery, machine guns, and poison gas transformed the battlefield of World War I into a moonscape of destruction and carnage.

casualties, and new techniques, such as rolling barrages and predicted artillery fire, enhanced the performance of artillery. Similarly, the use of the elastic defense and infiltration tactics provided new methods for attacking and defending. The development of new tactical methods and the use of limited offensives provided advantages that were not foreseen in the early days of the war. By 1918, soldiers had uniforms, weapons, equipment, and methods that differed significantly from those of 1914.

Despite intense efforts by most belligerents, some military questions had not been resolved by November 1918, particularly those relating to breaking through soundly prepared defensive positions—as the failure of the Germans in 1918 demonstrated. Nevertheless, the Great War had witnessed the introduction of many concepts and weapons that would dominate twentieth-century warfare.

SUGGESTED READINGS

Asprey, Robert B. *At Belleau Wood* (New York: Putnam, 1965).

Braim, Paul F. *The Test of Battle: The American Expeditionary Forces in the Meuse-Argonne Campaign* (Newark, N.J.: University of Delaware Press, 1987).

Coffman, Edward M. *The War to End All Wars: The American Military Experience in World War I* (Madison, Wisc.: The University of Wisconsin Press, 1968).

De Groot, Gerard J. *Douglas Haig, 1861–1928* (London: Unwin Hyman, 1988).

Fischer, Fritz. *Germany's Aims in the First World War* (New York: W. W. Norton & Company, 1967).

Goodspeed, D. J. *Ludendorff, Genius of World War I* (Boston: Houghton Mifflin Co., 1966).

Gudmundsson, Bruce I. *Stormtroop Tactics: Innovation in the German Army, 1914–1918* (New York: Praeger, 1989).

Hurley, Alfred F. *Billy Mitchell: Crusader for Air Power* (New York: F. Watts, 1964).

Lupfer, Timothy P. *The Dynamics of Doctrine: The Changes in German Tactical Doctrine During the First World War* (Fort Leavenworth, Kans.: Combat Studies Institute, 1981).

Middlebrook, Martin. *The Kaiser's Battle, 21 March 1918: The First Day of the German Offensive* (London: Allen Lane, 1978).

Millet, Allan R. *The General: Robert L. Bullard and Officership in the United States Army, 1881–1925* (Westport, Conn.: Greenwood Press, 1975).

———. "Cantigny, 28–31 May 1918," in Charles E. Heller and William A. Stofft, *America's First Battles, 1776–1965* (Lawrence, Kans.: University Press of Kansas, 1986), pp. 149–185.

Pitt, Barrie. *1918, The Last Act* (New York: W. W. Norton & Company, 1963).

Prior, Robin, and Trevor Wilson. *Command on the Western Front: The Military Career of Sir Henry Rawlinson, 1914–1918* (Oxford: Blackwell Publishers, 1992).

Samuels, Martin. *Doctrine and Dogma: German and British Infantry Tactics in the First World War* (Westport, Conn.: Greenwood Press, 1992).

Smythe, Donald. *Pershing: General of the Armies* (Bloomington, Ind.: Indiana University Press, 1986).

13

GERMANY TRIUMPHANT: RESTORING MOBILITY TO WAR

Military Developments
Between the Wars

The Outbreak of
World War II

Poland

The Scandinavian
Campaign

The French Campaign

World War II was the largest and most costly conflict in human history. It began with the German invasion of Poland on September 1, 1939; it ended on the decks of the battleship *Missouri* on September 2, 1945. By its conclusion the war in Europe had killed approximately 15 million military and 35 million civilians. The Nazis had exterminated 6 million Jews and countless others; 25 million Soviets were homeless; and Allied strategic bombing had wrecked every major German city. In Asia the casualty bill was equally horrendous. No one knows how many died as a result of the Sino-Japanese war; famine, military actions, disease—all combined to raise the Chinese losses to tens of millions. The firebombing of Tokyo and the dropping of the atomic bomb on Hiroshima, *each* killed well over 100,000 Japanese.

In a real sense World War II resulted from the desire of three of the major powers to overturn the legacy of the nineteenth century. Germany, Japan, and Italy had come late to the division of the world; World War I served only to exacerbate their frustrations. In the case of all three nations, ferocious ideologies emerged out of national historical experiences and economic collapse in the depression, and extreme ideological nationalism led them to wage merciless war against their enemies. Though initially hesitant to mobilize all its resources, Nazi Germany defined the terms within which it would fight World War II as a total war. In reply, the democracies had to go to equal extremes in order to survive. The cost was terrifyingly high, and if the world that emerged in 1945 was less than perfect, at least it was a world in which the three great tyrannies of Germany, Japan, and Italy no longer existed.

Perhaps the best way to understand warfare during World War II is to think of the period 1914–1945 as a single continuum, for the battlefields of 1939 to 1945 represented a continuation and an amplification of the developments that had occurred in World War I. Except for the final explosion of the atomic bomb, there was little that was revolutionary about World War II. Even the seemingly revolutionary operational employment of tanks by the Germans in 1940 represented the fruition of tactical and operational concepts the Germans had developed in the latter part of World War I. Technological developments largely followed the paths laid out by the last conflict, even though advances in communications, radar, sonar, jet power, proximity fuses, rockets, and other equipment raised technology to new levels. The mobilization of men, women, machines, and raw materials also largely followed the paths laid out in the last conflict. What was different was the harnessing of all resources to the war effort at unprecedented levels and the unparalleled destruction, particularly of civilians and their possessions, in the course of the war. It was not revolutionary tactics or exotic weapons but rather the greater industrial potential and economic strength that won the war. God, as Napoleon had suggested, was indeed on the side with the biggest battalions.

Military Developments Between the Wars

Ground War

With the end of World War I, Europe and the world settled into an uneasy period of peace lasting barely twenty years. With huge arsenals remaining from the Great War, the thinking of most armies remained constrained by the capabilities of weapons left over from the war. As weapons like the tank became more capable, most military leaders simply integrated the improved weapons into old concepts and prepared to fight tightly controlled and relatively static battles reminiscent of the Great War. The Germans, however, prepared to fight mobile battles. By carefully studying the experiences of World War I (particularly the doctrinal developments of the war's last years), they identified the most important innovations of that war and concluded that those innovations provided the conceptual framework for restoring mobility to the battlefield. They also recognized how improved tanks and airplanes could magnify the effect of infiltration tactics and make them even more dramatic. Thus the Germans adapted more successfully than their opponents, devised concepts for mobile warfare, and inflicted crushing defeats on their enemies in the early years of World War II.

Historians have often pictured development of the *Blitzkrieg* as a revolutionary step that took place in the late 1930s; it was not. Almost immediately after the Weimar Republic had settled down, the *Truppenamt* (the title of the disguised general staff) finished a doctrinal manual that crystalized the World War I experience. Completed in 1924, *Die Truppenführung* expertly distilled the tactical and operational methods of World War I and provided the basis of the German "way of war." The doctrine emphasized a number of crucial ideas: (1) the nature of the modern battlefield demands decentralized, mission-oriented orders; (2) speed and exploitation of enemy weaknesses demand that whether on the offensive or defensive, troop commanders use initiative and take advantage of developing situations without waiting for orders; (3) modern warfare demands a close integration and cooperation between combat branches; and (4) commanders must exercise leadership from the front.

The German success in preparing for the next conflict reflected personal as well as intellectual factors. The first commander-in-chief of the *Reichswehr* (the German army during the Weimar Republic), General Hans von Seeckt, was a general staff officer. When the Western Powers dictated a reduction of the German army to 5,000 officers and 100,000 men after World War I, Seeckt confronted the necessity of drastically reducing the officer corps. In so doing he insured that members of the general staff controlled all key positions. This was a crucial step because general staff officers had developed the offensive and defensive doctrine in 1917–1918 that had

Despite the constraints imposed by the Treaty of Versailles, General Hans von Seeckt prepared the German army for highly mobile, offensive operations.

altered the World War I battlefield. Seeckt also focused the army on the offensive. With only 100,000 soldiers, the Germans could not wage a long defensive campaign; instead, the army would become a powerful striking force relying on mobility and surprise, rather than enormous amounts of firepower. In essence, Seeckt shaped the army for what came to be known as the *Blitzkrieg*, and he did this before the Germans had panzer divisions.

Shortly after Adolf Hitler came to power on January 30, 1933, the German military began a massive rearmament program. Given Hitler's program for extensive conquests on the European continent, the army was the centerpiece of German rearmament. In particular, the army's commander-in-chief, Colonel General Werner von Fritsch, and the chief of the general staff, General Ludwig Beck, set the tone and direction of the army effort. They aimed at creating a modern military force and incorporating the experience of World War I in its doctrine, training, and preparation. In no sense was their approach revolutionary. The focus of the buildup emphasized traditional combat branches, infantry and artillery. But their doctrine concentrated on decentralized authority, flexibility, speed, and exploitation, a framework that eventually translated into the basis of modern mechanized warfare.

Between 1933 and 1939, the Germans greatly expanded the size of their army and armored forces. Beck backed the establishment of the first three panzer divisions in 1935, and during the same period he ordered the general staff to conduct a war game on the employment of panzer corps. By 1936 the Germans were studying the employment of a panzer army and in 1938 began forming two more panzer divisions. By the start of the war in September 1939, they had fifty-four active divisions, six of which were armored. But for economic reasons as well as the shortage of petroleum available to the Third Reich, the *Wehrmacht* remained a traditional infantry-dominated army. Nevertheless, its leaders had shaped it into a highly mobile and capable force, the perfect tool for Hitler's aggressive policies.

On the basis of their experiences in Poland, the Germans converted four light divisions into panzer divisions, with motorized infantry divisions backing them up. Still, the army that invaded France in May 1940 consisted of less than twenty motorized and mechanized divisions and over one hundred regular infantry divisions. Nevertheless, all these divisions, including the armored, possessed a common doctrinal conception, and all were prepared to fight highly mobile battles.

German preparation went beyond developing a doctrine for mobile warfare and forming panzer units. The Germans expected all officers to be thoroughly familiar with doctrinal and tactical concepts. Whether in exercises or on the battlefield, units had to live up to the spirit of doctrine. When they did not, commanders instituted rigorous training programs to ensure that standards rose. German officers, however, did not learn to apply doctrine blindly; rather they learned to solve tactical and operational problems by using doctrine as a framework or guide, not as a formula. In accordance with their tradition of *Auftragstaktik*, or mission-oriented tactics, commanders were expected to understand the *intent* of their leaders and to take initiative when necessary to accomplish the mission. Thus in an environment that emphasized decentralization and initiative, the Germans prepared their officers and units to function smoothly on a mobile battlefield.

In Britain the educated elite rejected the possibility that their army might ever again fight on the European continent. Nevertheless, Britain produced two of the more original military thinkers during this period: J. F. C. Fuller and B. H. Liddell Hart. Fuller, a tank officer in World War I, wrote extensively on the potential of the tank. Liddell Hart, an infantry officer in the war, extended Fuller's ideas to suggest the possibility of using tanks not only to break through enemy lines but also to drive deep into enemy rear areas as an exploitation force and disrupt its command and control. Under these two men's influence in the 1920s and early 1930s, the British army carried out experiments with armored test forces. Limited defense budgets, however, made it difficult to fund extensive experiments or

form armored units. Additionally, the general unwillingness of the British even to consider another war in Europe made the formation of armored units unnecessary and unlikely. It was difficult to see what armored divisions would do for an army that was going to fight only colonial wars. In the end even Liddell Hart abandoned his advocacy of mechanization and argued for an army that would have no continental role.

Nevertheless, the problems confronting the British army resulted from more than a lack of public interest or funds; some were of its own doing. Not until 1932 did the army establish a committee to study the lessons of World War I. When that committee presented its findings, the chief of the imperial general staff prevented the report from circulating in the army. Throughout the interwar period, the officer corps reflected the stratification of British society; social standing contributed more to advancement than did professional competence and tactical proficiency. The army had no common doctrinal framework within which it prepared for war, and the combat branches went their own separate ways.

The British army did conduct a series of remarkable experiments in the late 1920s and early 1930s to examine the potential of armored warfare. Those tests underlined the potential that tanks offered as well as some of the limiting factors. The British failed, however, to incorporate the lessons of these experiments into the development of their armored forces. Ironically, the Germans learned the most from these efforts and began their armored forces in 1933 based on much of what they had learned from observing the British experiments.

The French developed forces and doctrine very different from those of Germany. Facing a potential enemy with nearly twice the population and much greater economic means, they devoted considerable efforts and resources in the interwar period to ensuring their security. Most noteworthy among their accomplishments was the building of the Maginot Line along the northeastern frontier of France. Composed of huge underground fortresses with elaborate electrical, ventilation, and communications systems, the Maginot Line protected key natural resources and large industrial and population centers along the frontier. Though historians have sometimes blamed the disaster of 1940 on a "Maginot Line" mentality, the defensive line accomplished its strategic purpose of shielding vulnerable areas and permitting the concentration of forces along other parts of the frontier.

The French also spent considerable sums on the development of armored forces; by 1940 they had approximately the same number of tanks as Germany. Instead of concentrating their tanks in large armored formations, however, they spread them thinly across the army. They developed large cavalry divisions that resembled German panzer divisions, but they did not form their first armored division until after the Germans overran Poland in September 1939. After devoting years to careful analysis and experimentation, the French prepared to fight methodical battles in which infantry, artillery, and tanks remained under the tight control of higher commanders and moved short distances from phase line to phase line. Thus the French tried to control the battlefield and their troops in a fashion that the battles of

1918 had already proven unrealistic. Their excessive emphasis on firepower robbed subordinate commanders of initiative and flexibility and ruled out the possibility of any grand maneuvers.

The Soviets provide an interesting and tragic contrast. Arising out of the collapse of 1917, the Red Army, largely created by Leon Trotsky, had beaten back both its Russian opponents and invading Poles in 1919–1921. The Soviets then had to create a military organization loyal to the revolutionary regime. Even within the Red Army, serious disagreements existed as to what kind of forces the Soviet Union required for its defense in a hostile world. A substantial group, centered around former tsarist officer Mikhail N. Tukhachevskii, pushed for creation of an elite force on the leading edge of emerging technology and military thinking. Under Tukhachevskii's leadership the Red Army created its first armored divisions in 1931 (four years before the Germans) and organized large-scale paratrooper drops for the 1935 and 1936 maneuvers.

But the idea of a mass conscript army still appealed to many; as a result, the Soviets vacillated and followed both paths. A series of five-year plans, launched by Stalin in 1927, forced the industrialization of Russia and aimed at providing an economic base to support great military forces. But in May 1937, Stalin loosed his secret police on the Soviet military. A devastating purge savaged the army; Tukhachevskii and virtually all of the modernizers died in front of firing squads. The doctrine developed by these "traitors" also had to go; 1939 found the Soviets busily dismantling the Red Army's armored divisions at the moment that the Nazi panzer divisions were winning their first successes.

In many ways the experiences of the U.S. Army in the interwar period reflected those of the British army. In the early 1920s, Congress had passed the National Defense Act which, had it been implemented, would have provided a framework for developing coherent military forces. But it was not implemented. Instead, as "normalcy" tightened its grip on the American public, defense budgets steadily declined in the 1920s; the arrival of the depression in 1929 further decreased funding available to the military. In the 1920s, with a relatively benign international climate, there was some justification in the disinterest that politicians and public displayed toward the military. But the continuing disinterest in the 1930s as war approached is indeed difficult to explain.

The army in the interwar years confronted no opponents. The Indian wars had ended years earlier, and the Filipinos awaited independence. In small, isolated posts scattered around the United States and its possessions, the interwar army possessed neither equipment, nor funding, nor force levels to prepare seriously for war. As one historian of the army has suggested, "The Army during the 1920s and early 1930s may have been less ready to function as a fighting force than at any time in its history."*

---

*Russell F. Weigley, *History of the United States Army* (New York: Macmillan, 1967), p. 402.

So parsimonious was Congress that the army's annual report for 1934 indicated that it possessed only *fourteen* post–World War I tanks.

Nevertheless, if the army had little chance to experiment with new ways of war, it did develop extraordinary officers who emerged in World War II to lead great citizen armies. Its educational system also provided a framework within which to think about the next war. If its intellectual preparations were weaker than those in Germany on the tactical and operational levels, it is clear that American officers developed an understanding of strategy and logistics that the German officer corps never possessed. Virtually all the important commanders of World War II served lengthy terms in the army's various schools. That intellectual preparation paid enormous dividends when war arrived.

Air War

All of the missions that make up the employment of air power had appeared by 1918. Strategic bombing, interdiction, close air support, reconnaissance, air defense, and air superiority had all played roles in aerial combat during World War I. Yet the full potential of air power, as well as its limitations, remained unclear. Despite the ambiguities that existed within the body of military experience, advocates of air power argued that air forces would be the dominant military force in future wars and that armies and navies would be of little significance. They believed that air power offered a cheap and easy path to victory and an alternative to the costly attrition of the trenches, but only if nations employed air power as a unified force to break the enemy's will. Air forces, in the view of theorists, must not fritter away their strength in supporting ground forces in defending one's own territory, or even in gaining air superiority; instead of "tactical" missions to support the army (or navy), the single proper role for air power must be "strategic" bombing.

Yet within this dogmatic framework, British and American views diverged significantly on the choice of targets. Like Guilio Douhet (the Italian air power theorist), Sir Hugh Trenchard (the first commander of the Royal Air Force after World War I) argued that the most vulnerable target to air attack was the enemy's civilian population. Trenchard believed that the working class could not stand up to the pressures of bombing; under air attack civilians would rebel and demand peace.

In the United States, Brigadier General Billy Mitchell shaped the tone of relations between airmen and the traditional services. That tone was intolerant and uncompromising. Mitchell and fellow enthusiasts denied that the older services would have a role in future conflicts. Unlike other airpower theorists, however, Mitchell recognized that enemy air forces represented a significant hindrance that an air force would have to defeat *before* it could execute successful bombing operations.

In the 1930s, that basic principle disappeared from the American Air Corps Tactical School. The army school was a hotbed of theoretical musings that created an American strategic bombing doctrine. Its approach did not

Father of the Royal Air Force in Britain, Sir Hugh Trenchard believed civilians were a legitimate target of bombers. Destruction of civilian lives and property, according to Trenchard, would destroy civilian morale and alter the entire course of a war.

seek attacks on enemy population centers, but rather on vulnerable sectors of what planners called the enemy's industrial web. Its argument rested on the premise that large formations of bombers, unescorted by defensive fighters, could fly deep into enemy territory and drop their bombs on key industrial targets (such as ball-bearing plants or oil refineries), the destruction of which would cause the collapse of the enemy economy. The problem with this argument lay in the difficulty of carrying out the missions. Could bombers find their targets (particularly in bad weather conditions) and destroy them; could they fight their way through enemy air-defense systems without cover from long-range escort fighters? But the greatest fallacies lay in the arguments that the economies of modern industrialized states were fragile and easily damaged and that the bomber would always get through.

In Germany the new leader of the Luftwaffe was Hitler's ruthless and thoroughly corrupt subordinate, the World War I ace, Hermann Göring, who aimed to make his air force the most formidable in Europe. The idea of strategic bombing appealed both to Göring and to the Luftwaffe's senior leadership. In 1936, however, the Luftwaffe canceled two prototype four-engine bombers because both aircraft designs were already obsolete. Design work continued throughout the 1930s on the four-engine He 177, which the Germans regarded as their future strategic bomber, but a variety of engineering mistakes and technological problems rendered that program a disastrous failure. Thus the Luftwaffe continued to have problems in developing a strategic bombing capability.

Nevertheless, more so than the British and American air forces, the Luftwaffe developed a realistic and balanced air doctrine. Partially as a result of experienccs in the Spanish Civil War, the Germans discovered that it was difficult to place bombs accurately on target and that bombing civilians did not necessarily lead to the collapse of morale. In addition, they placed considerable emphasis in their air doctrine on supporting the army. The Luftwaffe preferred the interdiction mission to close air support, but after Spain it also developed the capability to support the army in breakthrough battles. However, through 1940 the Luftwaffe could not support the army's tanks once the exploitation phase had begun.

Naval War

Navies provide an interesting contrast. Their great prophet, the American theorist, Alfred Thayer Mahan, appeared before World War I; by and large navies saw no reason to change their operational approach because of wartime experience. Having developed sonar (called "asdic" by the British—a device that used sound waves to detect submerged submarines out to a range of about 1,500 yards) at the end of World War I, the Royal Navy believed that it had solved the submarine menace and proceeded on that assumption in its planning and preparations for a future war. In 1938, believing convoys would no longer be necessary, it quietly acquiesced to the surrender of western Irish ports essential to convoys in the eastern Atlantic. Ironically, the German navy, having read British pronouncements about ending the submarine menace, believed those reports. Despite their great success with the submarine in World War I, the Germans displayed minimal interest in the U-boat as they rearmed. Also, neither the British nor the German navy paid much attention to air power. British naval air power remained hobbled by the surrender of its assets to the Royal Air Force (RAF) in 1918. Nor did the German navy show much interest in naval air power, and squabbling with Göring's Luftwaffe ensured that the navy received little air support. In both fleets the emphasis remained firmly on the battleship and big gun.

    The interesting developments in naval operations came in the Pacific. Both the United States and Japan sensed a great naval clash in the offing. In America, naval airmen, led by Rear Admiral William A. Moffett and helped by Billy Mitchell's wild attacks, convinced more conservative admirals that naval air power represented a significant supplement to fleet capabilities. Much the same thing happened in Japan; by the mid-1930s both navies had developed sophisticated concepts for carrier operations that would soon change the face of naval war.

    The Japanese and Americans made significant advances in other areas as well. Both developed amphibious capabilities to seize bases in the wide expanses of the central Pacific. U.S. Marine Corps doctrine provided the departing point for solving the basic problems associated with amphibious war. The willingness to recognize the threat of the submarine was, however, less obvious. The Japanese expended great resources in the 1930s in building up their merchant marine to supply the home islands in case of war; however, they made *no* preparations to defend that merchant marine against

U.S. submarines. The Americans did no better in preparing themselves to meet the threat of U-boats in the Atlantic, even after watching the Germans savage the sea lines of communication to Britain in World War I.

Historians often berate military leaders for preparing for the last war. In fact they would fare better if they prepared for the next war on the basis of what had happened in the last. Unfortunately, they generally do not. Disinterested in the uncomfortable experiences of World War I, military leaders in the 1920s and 1930s preferred for the most part to study what was agreeable and what supported preconceived notions. The results would show all too clearly in the next war.

The Outbreak of World War II

World War I had not solved the German problem, even though defeat in 1918 and the Versailles Treaty hobbled the Germans in the short term. The results of World War I did not limit Germany's long-range potential, for the Reich was still the most powerful nation in Europe. To the east and south, Russia's and Austria-Hungary's collapse had left weak and politically divided states—a region open to German penetration and domination. Only in the west did the Germans have a frontier with a major power, a France weakened by the blood-letting of four years of war.

The Treaty of Versailles did attempt to shackle German potential, but in strategic terms the treaty failed before its signing. Angered by the provisions and burden of the treaty, most Germans refused the obvious explanation for the defeat of 1918 that the Reich had fought the whole world and lost; rather, they believed, erroneously, that their army had remained unbeaten in the field and that defeat had come as a result of traitorous actions by Jews and Communists who had stabbed the front-line soldiers in the back. In the early 1930s the troubles of the newly established Weimar Republic combined with a worldwide depression to destabilize German political life. In the hour of political despair, Adolf Hitler and his evil cohorts grasped the mantle of power.

Hitler brought to office a coherent and consistent ideology. Unlike Marx, Lenin, and Stalin who defined the Left's enemies on the basis of class, Hitler defined evil along racial lines. He believed the Aryan race solely responsible for creating the world's great civilizations and the Jews responsible for subverting and undermining human progress. Moreover, he argued that Germany must acquire a great European empire to provide the living space and resources for the German people; the Reich must acquire land in the east at the expense of the inferior Slavic races, particularly the Russians. In Hitler's vision, the new German empire, free of Jews, would control Europe from the Urals to Gibraltar and from the North Cape to the Alps. This ideologic vision provided the motivation behind the most catastrophic war in human history.

After becoming chancellor in January 1933, Hitler had to consolidate his power and mitigate the depression's economic and social dislocations. Despite the weakness of Germany's position, he embarked on a risky diplomatic course. In 1933, Germany withdrew from the League of Nations; in 1935 it declared conscription and creation of the Luftwaffe; and in 1936 it remilitarized the Rhineland. Hitler also provided the military services with funds to undertake a massive program of rearmament. After all, as he made clear, he was not interested in reestablishing Germany's World War I frontier, but rather in destroying the entire European balance of power.

The rearmament program, however, brought with it considerable economic dislocation. Nazi Germany was a resource-poor nation with few raw materials and limited access to foreign exchange. Consequently the rearmament program ran into trouble almost immediately. In a conference with his military and diplomatic advisors in November 1937, Hitler announced that Germany would have to take greater risks in foreign policy to escape its economic and strategic difficulties; however, he ran into substantial opposition from his ministers of defense and foreign policy and the army's commander-in-chief. Within three months he had dispensed with all three. In the resulting political storm, Hitler doubled the stakes and deliberately manufactured a crisis with Austria. In March 1938, the *Wehrmacht* marched into Austria with no opposition from the French or British. The *Anschluss* (occupation of Austria) brought the Third Reich a number of advantages. Austria possessed foreign exchange, a large untapped labor force, and a geographic stranglehold over Czechoslovakia. Hitler's triumph reduced the political crisis within Germany.

Scarcely had the dust settled on Austria before Hitler turned his attention to Czechoslovakia. Again he courted a crisis, this time to isolate the Czechs, so that the *Wehrmacht* could execute a quick campaign. Hitler's actions alarmed Germany's generals and created strong military opposition to his plans. Throughout spring and summer 1938, the chief of the general staff, Ludwig Beck, wrote a series of memoranda arguing that Germany's strategic situation was desperate; then in late August he resigned in protest. The British prime minister, Neville Chamberlain, resolved to prevent the outbreak of war; he eventually persuaded Hitler to accept the Sudetenland, the German-speaking districts of Czechoslovakia where most Czech fortifications were located. Few in England or France voiced opposition to the Munich settlement at the end of September 1938. Although Winston Churchill strongly criticized the government's policies in the House of Commons, many believed Churchill was a foolish old man for still believing in military power and strategic issues.

The nature of Germany's aims became clear in March 1939, when Hitler ordered his troops to occupy the remainder of Czechoslovakia. Germany's continued economic difficulties lay at the heart of his decision; Czechoslovakia with its foreign exchange holdings and industrial resources offered a tempting target. While the Germans gained much equipment and matériel from their seizure of the remainder of Czechoslovakia (enough to equip eight infantry and three panzer divisions), their actions prodded the

Western Powers into taking action. Hitler's move so outraged the British public that Chamberlain finally embarked on a massive effort to repair Britain's dilapidated defenses and to challenge Germany's expansionary policies. It was too little, too late.

At the end of March 1939, the British precipitously guaranteed Poland's independence. Outraged by this action, Hitler ordered his generals to draw up plans to invade Poland by September 1, 1939. Unlike the year before, the German military fell into line behind Hitler; they raised no objections about the strategic wisdom of invading Poland and unleashing a major war. On his part, Hitler seems not to have taken British and French intervention seriously. As he told his entourage, he had seen his "enemies at Munich and they were worms."

Nevertheless, at the end of August he engineered a pact with Stalin. That deal, the infamous Nazi-Soviet Non-Aggression Pact, divided eastern Europe between the two powers. Germany gained the right to destroy Poland without interference from the Soviet Union; and in return Stalin received eastern Poland, while Finland, Latvia, Estonia, Lithuania and the province of Bessarabia (in Romania) all fell within the Soviet sphere. Stalin also committed his regime to remaining neutral and removed the threat of a two-front war; the Soviet Union would soon send massive quantities of raw materials (grain, oil, manganese, etc.) to prop up a seriously strained German war economy. Stalin clearly hoped that a German-Allied conflict would result in a stalemate, as had occurred in World War I, in which the contending capitalistic powers would fight themselves to exhaustion. The Soviet Union would then be able to step in and dominate what was left of Europe. As for Hitler, the deal promised him peace in the east after he had conquered Poland and enabled him to face the Western Powers with his full strength if they intervened on Poland's behalf.

By August 1939, circumstances had set the stage for another great European war unleashed by German actions, this time motivated by Nazi ideology. Hitler had determined to create a Nazi hegemony from the Urals to Spain. The Germans, along with various lesser Aryan nations, would rule the Reich and exterminate other "subhuman" races such as the Jews and Gypsies. There would be no pity and no quarter; the racial crusade began the moment the Germans crossed the border into Poland.

Poland

On September 1, 1939, the *Wehrmacht* precipitated World War II by attacking Poland. Vigorous German offensive action broke the Polish defenses, while the Luftwaffe struck Polish air bases. Heavy air attacks also occurred against military targets in Warsaw; these attacks were accompanied by considerable collateral damage and casualties among the civilian populace—not surprising given the current technology. On September 3, the governments of Britain and France honored their obligations to the Poles and declared war on Germany. Hitler's gamble that swift military action, the Nazi-Soviet Pact, and the Western Powers' own reluctance to go to war would deter a larger war had failed.

Planning for the attack on Poland had begun in April 1939 in response to Britain's guarantee of Polish independence. Given Germany's great advantages (among others the Reich bounded Poland on three sides), operational planning did not require military genius. The OKH (*Oberkommando des Heeres*, army high command) created two army groups, North and South, to break into central Poland. Army Group North, under Colonel General Fedor von Bock, consisted of the Third and Fourth armies; its assignment was to cut the Polish Corridor—the sliver of Polish territory separating East Prussia from the rest of Germany—and threaten Warsaw from the north. Bock's army group held the 10th Panzer Division in reserve and General Heinz Guderian's XIX Panzer Corps (one panzer and two motorized infantry divisions) for its mobile operations.

The main attack came from Army Group South, commanded by Colonel General Gerd von Rundstedt; it consisted of Eighth, Fourteenth,

and Tenth armies. The first two would protect the flanks of the main drive launched by Tenth Army against Warsaw in the heart of Poland. Of the fifty-five German divisions, Army Group South had twenty-eight, including thirteen in Tenth Army and eleven in Fourteenth Army. The seven panzer divisions were spread among the five German armies.

The Poles were in an impossible strategic situation; their whole country was a flat plain. The only defensible feature was the Bug River, but it lay so far to the east that a defense along it would have forced the Poles to surrender everything of political and economic value before the fighting even began. Unwilling to surrender their territory, Polish leaders chose a forward defense, thereby allowing the Germans to divide the Polish army and defeat it in piecemeal fashion.

Not fully mobilized and spread thinly across a lengthy frontier, the Poles put up a stout resistance. Nevertheless, German armored and motorized units soon broke through. Army Group South achieved the greatest success. By the end of the first day several of its forward units had advanced fifteen miles, and within the first days, its tanks had breached frontier defenses and gained operational freedom. By September 6, its panzer units were halfway to Warsaw and had isolated Polish forces in the Posen sector. Meanwhile, Army Group North sliced across the Polish Corridor. While some elements drove toward Warsaw, Guderian's panzer corps moved across East Prussia and advanced deep behind the Polish capital; this move destroyed the possibility of a sustained resistance behind the Vistula River.

From the air, the Luftwaffe hammered enemy ground forces. In the air-to-air battle, superior numbers quickly told. Along with winning air superiority, the Luftwaffe interdicted the Polish railroad system and severely restricted frantic Polish efforts to complete their mobilization, while close air-support strikes helped the army in its efforts to penetrate Polish defenses. Thereafter, the Luftwaffe found it difficult to provide close air support in the mobile environment, largely because communications between ground and air forces were completely inadequate. Yet air strikes against Polish troops attempting to concentrate west of Warsaw were so effective that the Poles collapsed entirely in that sector.

German breakthroughs and relentless exploitation broke Polish resistance within one week. When the Polish high command moved from Warsaw on September 7, it completely lost control of its military forces. Eager to participate in the victory, the Soviet Union moved into eastern Poland on September 17 to "protect" the local population. By the end of the month Polish resistance had ceased; the Poles had lost 70,000 killed, 133,000 wounded, and 700,000 prisoners. German losses were only 11,000 dead, 30,000 wounded, and 3,400 missing.

The process by which the German army examined its performance after the Polish campaign suggests why it did so well on the battlefields of World War II. By early October, the OKH had gathered "after action" reports from the army groups down to the regimental level; it then established a rigorous training program throughout the entire army to correct the deficiencies and doctrinal weaknesses that after-action reports had highlighted. Over the next six months the OKH ensured that subordinate commands executed that program rigorously. From October 1939 through April 1940 the army trained ruthlessly and endlessly (sixteen hours a day, six to seven days a week), and when the *Wehrmacht* came west in May 1940, few armies in the twentieth century have been as well trained or highly disciplined.

German success did not come from a revolutionary secret developed in the interwar years; rather, it rested on the firm foundation of a coherent, modern doctrine emphasizing speed, exploitation, combined arms, and decentralized command and control. Nonetheless, the Germans had many improvements to make in both their doctrine and their battlefield performance. For example, they emphasized combined arms by including infantry and tank regiments in their panzer divisions, but they did not perfect the combining of those arms until the 1940 campaign in France.

From the beginning, the invaders embarked on Hitler's ideological crusade. Atrocities, unseen by Europeans for centuries, fell on Jews and Poles alike; Hitler demanded the liquidation of Poland's ruling and intellectual elite, an effort that Stalin's NKVD (secret police) pursued with equal enthusiasm in the east. Senior generals had full knowledge of what the Nazis were doing. The chief of the general staff, Franz Halder, noted in his diary after a speech by Hitler: "Poland is to have its own administration. It is not to be turned into a model state by German standards. Polish intelligentsia must be prevented from establishing itself as a new governing class. Low

The Panzerkampfwagen IV had a short-barreled 75-mm gun, weighed about twenty tons, and had a range of about 125 miles. It was the best German tank in the Polish and French campaigns. Throughout the war the Germans considered it a useful tank.

standards of living must be established. Cheap slaves." An even darker fate awaited the Jews.

The Allied Powers did almost nothing as Poland went down to defeat. They never intended to launch a major offensive into Germany this early in the war. Instead, they concentrated on mobilizing and preparing their forces and hoped to halt the Germans when they turned toward the west. A major offensive would occur only after they had halted the German attack in the west. In the meantime, the French sent out patrols that did not even reach the outpost line of the West Wall, despite the fact that one of Germany's key economic districts, the Saar, lay on the other side of the frontier. This lack of action allowed the German war economy to utilize the Saar's industries unhindered for the first nine months of the war. Similarly, Allied politicians and military leaders refused to undertake any action against German imports of Scandinavian iron ore, and they found numerous reasons to allow the Italians to escape into neutrality. Quite rightly the Western media dubbed the period between the defeat of Poland and the following spring as the "phony war." Failure to exert any pressure on the Germans allowed the Nazis to husband their military strength and mitigate their serious economic problems until the great throw of the dice in spring 1940.

The Scandinavian Campaign

While the Germans and the Western Powers faced off inconclusively in central Europe, the Soviets moved against the Baltic states. In fall 1939 they demanded that the Baltic republics allow Red Army garrisons on their territory. Lithuania, Latvia, and Estonia acceded. The Soviets then demanded that Finland cede territory and make similar concessions. The Finns agreed to the cession of territory but refused any terms that compromised their independence. A furious Stalin ordered the invasion of Finland; the time of year (late November) speaks volumes for Stalin's arrogance as well as a misplaced belief that the Finns could hardly wait to join his "workers and peasants' paradise."

Instead of an easy victory, the Red Army suffered humiliating defeat. From December 1939 through March 1940, the Soviets hurled tens of thousands of troops against the Finns. Relying on massive amounts of artillery and human wave attacks, the Soviets finally broke Finnish resistance. The poor performance of the Red Army in the Winter War underlined its weaknesses, particularly in terms of leadership and initiative, direct results of the purges from 1937 to 1939. Soviet troubles in Finland also reflected a hasty mobilization, lack of preparations, and the difficult conditions in the theater. The Red Army's performance in Finland misled the Germans who overlooked the skillfully executed operations of the Soviets against the Japanese at Nomonhan in August 1939.

The Winter War focused attention on Scandinavia. In February 1940, British destroyers sailed into a Norwegian fiord to rescue Allied merchant sailors imprisoned on a German supply ship. The commander-in-chief of the German navy, Admiral Erich Raeder, had been pressing for a campaign to seize Denmark or Norway to outflank Britain and provide U-boat bases to strike deeper into the Atlantic. Hitler now gave his enthusiastic approval for an attack on Scandinavia in early spring.

Denmark represented no significant problem because of its proximity to the Reich; the attack on Norway, however, required an intricately coordinated operation. The Germans had to capture the major harbors and airfields in Norway before the Royal Navy could react. Supply ships and oilers had to move out in advance of attacking forces—transported by warship— and arrive concurrently with naval units. For one of the few times in the war the Germans placed a joint operation under control of the OKW (*Oberkommando der Wehrmacht*—armed forces high command). General Nikolaus von Falkenhorst commanded the landing and ground operations.

All in all, *Weserübung* (code name for the attack) was a risky operation. On D-1 the Norwegians and British possessed clear intelligence that the Germans were launching a major operation in the North Sea. The former, however, failed to mobilize despite the fact that German soldiers had washed ashore on a beach in northern Norway from a supply ship sunk by a Polish submarine. The Royal Navy picked up the German navy's movement into the North Sea but interpreted the intelligence as indicating that the Germans were breaking out into the Atlantic.

Denmark fell with hardly a shot—not so for Norway. Even before the operation began, a British destroyer had rammed and seriously damaged the heavy cruiser, *Hipper*. The naval force running the Oslo fiord met unexpected opposition from the ancient forts guarding the passage and had to retreat and land its remaining troops at the mouth of the fiord after losing the new heavy cruiser, *Blücher*. The Norwegians failed to utilize the respite. Their cabinet ordered a mobilization by mail; and no one thought to block Oslo's airport. By mid-morning German paratroopers had seized the Oslo airfield and the Luftwaffe rushed in troops by Ju 52s (the German transport aircraft); within five or six hours the Germans had bluffed their way into the capital. By that time, the Norwegian government had fled and resistance had begun throughout the country. The Germans achieved greater success elsewhere in Norway. Luftwaffe strikes silenced coastal defenses, paratroopers seized major airports, and the navy grabbed other ports without serious losses.

In the early morning hours of April 10, however, a small force of British destroyers followed the German picket destroyers up the Narvik fiord; in a fierce gun duel they sank four out of ten of the enemy destroyers and all the German tankers. The surviving ships were trapped. Within the week, the battleship *Warspite* sank the remaining German destroyers in Narvik, a force that contained half the destroyers in the German navy.

Despite these losses, the Germans held all the cards, for they controlled the major ports and airfields. The Allies launched two unsuccessful expeditions to drive the Germans from northern Norway. Near Trondheim 240 miles from Oslo, British troops landed but accomplished little. Farther north, an Anglo-French expedition enjoyed more success against German

Scandinavia, April 1940

mountain troops in Narvik, but by the time the Allies took the port (early June) disasters in Western Europe had led to the collapse of the entire effort in Scandinavia.

Meanwhile in early June, despite intimations that an invasion of Britain might be necessary, the German navy launched its two battle cruisers, the *Gneisenau* and *Scharnhorst*, to influence what it regarded as the coming postwar budget debates. They did sink the British aircraft carrier *Glorious*, but both received such extensive damage that they remained in dry dock until December 1940. Whatever its success in Norway, the German navy had suffered irreplaceable losses. At the end of June 1940, it had only one heavy cruiser and four destroyers operationally ready, a force totally inadequate to support a successful landing on the British Isles.

Norway provided few strategic gains for Germany. In the short run the campaign ruled out an amphibious operation against the British Isles; in the long run, it represented a drain on resources that the Germans could have better utilized elsewhere. By 1943, Norway was tying down hundreds of thousands of troops to no useful purpose. After the fall of France, neither the submarine bases nor the secure route for Swedish ore proved to be of crucial strategic importance in the unfolding war.

The French Campaign

Victory over Poland confronted the Reich with serious economic and strategic difficulties. Underlining the Germans' predicament was the fact that the military had done little contingency planning for a campaign in the west. Therefore, Hitler's demand that the *Wehrmacht* launch a fall campaign against the Western Powers caught his senior military advisors with no operational plans and an army unprepared for a major campaign. Consequently, German military leaders argued furiously with their Führer to delay the fall campaign until the following spring; they did not, however, dispute Hitler's strategic or political assumptions. Instead they argued their case entirely on operational and tactical grounds.

Hitler had no clear conception or objective for a campaign in the west; rather, he believed that the Western Powers lacked the political stomach for a great war. Thus he directed the OKH to seize the Low Countries and northern France to the Somme River so that the Luftwaffe and navy could attack the British Isles. Hitler obviously hoped that such a strategy would drive Britain, led by Chamberlain, from the war. Once Britain withdrew from the war, Hitler believed France would not continue the fight alone. In no respect did the initial directive aim to destroy Allied ground power on the Continent; nor was it a replay of the Schlieffen Plan.

When the OKH completed its plan for taking the Low Countries and driving the French back to the Somme, no one concerned, neither Hitler nor the generals, was happy with it. Nevertheless, arguments between Hitler and his generals focused on the readiness of the army for a campaign in the west rather than on German strategy. German military leaders, on the basis of after-action reports from the Polish campaign, remained extremely concerned about the readiness of their forces, particularly the infantry. Despite their objections, Hitler insisted on the launching of an immediate offensive, and on a number of occasions the *Wehrmacht* rolled up on the frontier and prepared to attack with a fundamentally flawed strategy. Only bad weather prevented the Germans from making a serious mistake. Arguments in the high command continued into January, when a courier aircraft, carrying a staff officer and the German plan, went astray and crash-landed in neutral Belgium. The operational details consequently fell into Allied hands. Only at this juncture did the generals persuade Hitler to call off the attack until spring, and a fundamental operational reassessment began.

By January, Hitler had already conceived of launching a major attack through the Ardennes, the heavily forested and rolling countryside between the Maginot Line in northeast France and the flat countryside of western Belgium. His intuition received support from Army Group A's chief of staff, General Erich von Manstein, who independently concluded that a drive through the Ardennes with armored forces could split the Allied front and offer enticing operational prospects. But such a plan possessed considerable risks; if the Allies reinforced the Ardennes quickly, the Germans would not be able to fight their way into the open beyond the Meuse River.

The OKH found Manstein's proposal, supported by his commander, Rundstedt, both self-serving and risky. But after a series of debates with Hitler, a number of war games, and serious reconsiderations within the OKH, the Germans expanded the Ardennes conception to include nearly all the panzer and motorized forces. In the north, Army Group B, under Bock, would seize Holland and advance into western Belgium in order to fix Allied attention on that area. Meanwhile, Army Group A would push its panzers through eastern Belgium and the Ardennes as rapidly as possible; if all went well they would break into the open on the west bank of the Meuse River before the Allies could react. The success of the daring strategy rested on the Germans' moving large armored forces through the Ardennes and over the Meuse before the Allies could concentrate additional forces along the Meuse and trap the Germans in the Ardennes.

While the Germans hammered out their plans, British and French commanders also prepared for the coming battle. They carefully coordinated their strategy and prepared for French forces to hold along the Maginot Line while a combined French and British force rushed forward into Belgium. The Allies, expecting the Germans to launch their attack through central Belgium, much as they had done in 1914, placed few forces along the Ardennes. It was not that the French failed to see that the Germans might attempt a breakthrough in the Ardennes; rather, they believed they could concentrate reinforcements along the Meuse before the Germans could move large forces through the Ardennes and achieve a breakthrough. As the French prepared to fight a methodical battle with a highly centralized command and control system, they failed to recognize the effect that mechanized forces would have on the tempo of operations. Nothing underlines more clearly their misunderstanding of German mobility than General Maurice Gamelin's decision to move his Seventh Army (the only large reserve force available to him and consisting of some of the best mechanized and motorized units in the French army) from its central location near Reims to the far left of the Allied front. Its task now was to move forward to link up with the Dutch. Thus, for strategic reasons of dubious merit, Gamelin dispersed the French operational reserves.

The armies that clashed in 1940 disposed of relatively equal numbers of troops; the Allies, in fact, possessed more tanks, the Germans more

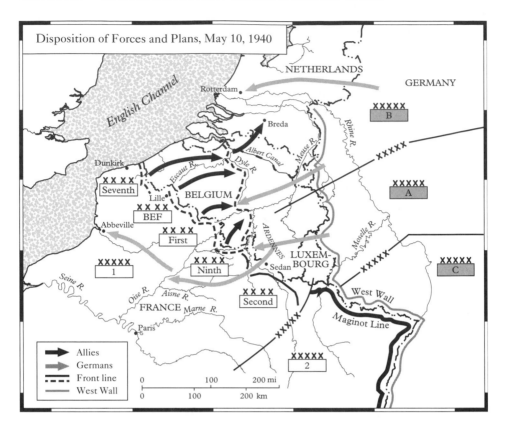

Disposition of Forces and Plans, May 10, 1940

aircraft. But equivalency in forces hid a number of German advantages. On the Allied side, British and French armies had begun to work together only in 1939. The Belgians and Dutch entered the war only after the Germans began their offensive; little or no consultation on either strategic or operational matters had occurred before the Germans struck. Consequently, under the pressure exerted by the German advance the Allied high command never operated effectively or efficiently. On the other hand, the Germans came west with a coherent operational doctrine and conception, executed with ruthless efficiency. The results reflected the thorough intellectual preparations that the German military had made since World War I.

The Opening Moves

The German attack began on May 10, 1940. The Luftwaffe struck across the length and breadth of western Europe. It aimed first to achieve general air superiority; therefore most of its first strikes hit Allied air bases. These raids achieved some successes but met ferocious resistance, resulting in heavy losses. On the first day the Luftwaffe lost more aircraft than on any other day in 1940 (including the Battle of Britain). Some strikes hit the Allied transportation system to delay movement of reserves; significantly, few attacks struck Allied forces moving forward into Belgium and Holland.

Despite heavy losses, the Luftwaffe not only gained air superiority in the first days but also provided strong support to German ground forces. At dawn on May 10, Ju 52s dropped German paratroopers on a series of major targets; the Germans attempted to seize the main airfield near the Hague and capture the government, thus ending Dutch resistance. The sudden descent failed, however, as the Dutch army responded and drove the paratroopers off the airfield. Nevertheless, the strike at the Hague thoroughly distracted the Dutch. Meanwhile other paratroopers seized the major bridges leading into fortress Holland, so that the 9th Panzer Division could sweep through Dutch defenses and into the middle of the country. By May 15, the Dutch position was hopeless. After the Luftwaffe destroyed the center of Rotterdam, the Dutch, fearing that the Germans would repeat such attacks, surrendered. At the time German propaganda was not slow to draw a connection between terror bombing and the Dutch collapse. But the real credit for the success in Holland rested on the courage and operational imagination with which fewer than 5,000 German paratroopers seized crucial communication points in Holland.

To the south of Holland, Army Group B rolled swiftly into Belgium. Airborne forces aided its advance. In one particularly daring and important operation, 180 German troopers landed by glider on top of Eben Emael, the large fortress in the center of the major avenue of approach into central Belgium. Within hours, they had blinded the fort and opened the way for Army Group B, which consisted almost entirely of infantry divisions. The swift collapse of the Dutch and of Eben Emael, as well as the hammering advance of Bock's infantry in central Belgium, captivated the attention of the French high command and convinced the Allies that the Germans were attacking as they had expected.

The drive through the Ardennes proceeded flawlessly. Because of Belgian neutrality, the French could do little to hinder a German move through the difficult Ardennes terrain. By the evening of May 12, the three panzer corps had arrived on the Meuse; in the north Hoth's XV Panzer Corps reached the river south of Dinant; Reinhardt's XLI Panzer Corps arrived at the mid-point of the panzer fist; and in the south Guderian's XIX Panzer Corps reached the Meuse near Sedan. The first to cross was Hoth's corps. The 7th Panzer Division, driven by its commander, Erwin Rommel, achieved the first lodgement on the west bank of the Meuse. At great cost to its infantry, 7th Panzer battered the French back and began building a bridge for its tanks to cross. Rommel's success opened the way for Hoth's other division, 5th Panzer, to cross; consequently the northern flank of French forces holding the Ardennes began to dissolve. In the center, tenacious resistance savaged the infantry of Reinhardt's panzer divisions; they made a small lodgement but could not get their tanks across.

In the south, Guderian crossed late on the afternoon of May 13 as sustained, heavy air attacks punished French defenders. Of the three attacking divisions, 10th Panzer Division on the left got less than a company across and lost forty-eight out of fifty of its assault boats. On the right 2nd Panzer ran into equal difficulties; only 1st Panzer Division in the center, led by the 1st Infantry Regiment and the army's *Grossdeutschland* Infantry Regiment,

General Heinz Guderian strongly and enthusiastically supported the Nazis. Though his influence over the development of German armored forces is often exaggerated, he possessed a sophisticated understanding of mobile warfare.

fought its way across and onto the heights overlooking the Meuse and Sedan. This gain allowed German engineers to build pontoon bridges, and in the early morning hours of May 14, 1st Panzer began moving its tanks across the river. The 1st Panzer Division's success opened the way for both the 10th and 2nd Panzer divisions to cross.

The French response to Guderian's crossing was late and uncoordinated. Although some infantry units fought with considerable bravery, others offered only token resistance. French artillery units, whose morale had been eroded by Luftwaffe attacks, panicked and ran; reserves in the area, a few battalions of infantry, dissolved. By the time French commanders launched a halfhearted counterattack, units from the XIX Panzer Corps were across in strength. Several divisions, including the 3rd Armored and 3rd Motorized, were available to the French. The corps commander of these two divisions, General Jean Flavigny, ironically a proponent of tanks in the interwar period, failed to launch a counterattack; instead he parceled his forces out along the disintegrating front, where the growing German tide swamped them. On May 14, Allied air launched a massive effort to knock out the pontoon bridges across the Meuse at Sedan; they met tenacious opposition from German fighters and antiaircraft batteries. The RAF lost forty out of seventy-one obsolete "Battle" bombers attacking the bridges; French losses were as heavy. By now Guderian's forces were rolling west in full flood.

The German leadership suffered several cases of bad nerves. On the evening of May 15–16, Colonel General Ewald von Kleist, commander of Reinhardt and Guderian's panzer corps, intervened to stop the exploitation to the west. Kleist was clearly acting at the behest of the OKW, which feared an attack against the flank of the advancing German forces. Guderian objected strongly and received permission to continue his advance. By evening on the 16th, XIX Panzer Corps had reached Marle, fifty-five miles from Sedan (traveling forty miles on that day alone). That evening Guderian received a peremptory order to halt; infuriated, he reported that he was resigning from command of XIX Corps. At that point, Rundstedt stepped in and worked out a compromise that ordered the corps' headquarters to remain in place while Guderian's panzer divisions continued a "reconnaissance in force"—in effect a license to steal.

The French Collapse

Guderian's breakthrough in the south combined with Hoth's success near Dinant to uncork Reinhardt's panzer corps. Once Reinhardt had crossed near Monthermé, the Germans had achieved a breakthrough of massive proportions, one that ran from Dinant to Sedan, a distance of almost forty miles. A giant fist of seven armored divisions then pushed toward the Channel. Throughout the drive to the Channel, Hitler, OKW, and OKH worried that everything had gone too well. Meanwhile small Allied counterattacks on the flanks of the panzer wedge exacerbated German worries. On May 19, Charles de Gaulle's 4th Armored Division caused some temporary dislocation on the southern flank. On the 21st a more substantial strike by British armor hit 7th Panzer and *SS Totenkoph* divisions, but the intrepid Rommel soon restored the situation. In reality the flanks were solidifying faster than the Allies could respond. Behind the armored advance, German infantry divisions pounded down the roads at over twenty miles per day to relieve the screening forces on the flanks. On May 19, 1st Panzer Division reached Péronne on the old Somme battlefield; the next day 2nd Panzer reached the coast near Abbeville. Ecstatic over reaching Abbeville, neither OKW, OKH, nor Army Group A thought to order Guderian to capture the Channel ports. But the Germans had cut off the whole Allied left wing.

Not until after the Germans crossed the Meuse did the French recognize the location of the main attack. But as Gamelin admitted to Churchill on May 15, they had no reserves. In this desperate hour paralysis gripped French leaders. Unable to deal with the speed of German moves, the French high command collapsed. Thus, there was no effective response as the panzer divisions drove relentlessly toward the Channel. Gamelin's failure to halt the Germans resulted in his removal. His replacement, General Maxime Weygand, arrived from Syria tired and incapable of wresting the initiative from the Germans.

By May 23, Guderian was moving up the Channel coast supported by Reinhardt's panzers to the east. The next day both threatened Dunkirk, the last port through which an Allied evacuation could take place. At that point, the OKW issued one of the most controversial orders of the war—its infamous "stop order," halting German armor. After the war German generals singled Hitler out as responsible for the failure to finish off the Allied left wing. In fact, besides the Führer, a number of senior generals, including Rundstedt and Guderian, shared the blame. The German senior leadership worried that the campaign thus far had proceeded too flawlessly and that their armor had suffered heavy losses; consequently it seemed best to preserve the panzer divisions for the final task of destroying France. At the time there was much that supported the decision: the panzer forces were a strategic weapon of decision, not a siege force, that had suffered heavy losses; much of France had yet to be conquered; and the panzer divisions would have to change their axis of advance substantially for the upcoming campaign.

The halt, however, allowed the British and French to establish a defense line around Dunkirk and provided the commander of the British Expeditionary Force (BEF), Lord Gort, time to save the British army. As early as May 19, Gort had warned London that his forces might have to withdraw from the Continent. Hardly happy with that communication, the War Cabinet instructed the navy's command at Dover to gather vessels for a possible evacuation.

For the next four days Gort maintained the position of a loyal army commander faithfully executing the orders of the French high command. On the evening of May 23–24, however, he broke with that role without fully informing the French and ordered his 5th and 50th divisions (nearly surrounded at Arras) to pull back to the coast. On the next day he used those two divisions to bolster his left flank, where the Belgians were collapsing. Gort's decision ended the prospect of an Allied counterattack from the pocket—an action that French leaders sharply criticized. Despite the con-

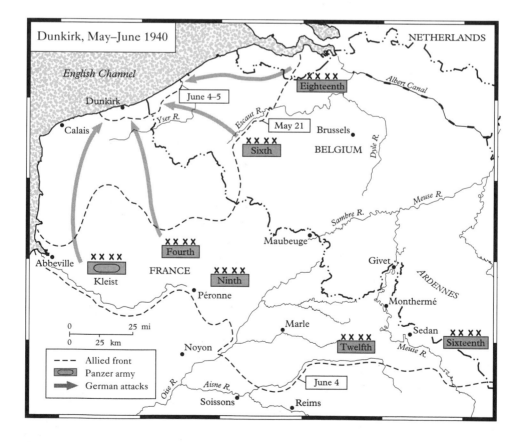

Dunkirk, May–June 1940

troversy surrounding his decision, Gort managed to cover his northern flank and make the Dunkirk evacuation possible.

As Allied forces streamed into the pocket, the British set in motion a full-scale evacuation, Operation "Dynamo." They had already evacuated 28,000 noncombat troops. Evacuation proceeded at full speed, but the British at first failed to extend a helping hand to the French. The French high command exacerbated the situation by refusing to authorize its commanders to participate in the evacuation; nor did it alert the French navy that such an operation was imminent. By afternoon May 29, the British had evacuated a large number of troops, the French none. At this point Churchill stepped in and ordered that British ships share space on a one-to-one basis with the French; but the damage had already been done.

Fortunately for the Allies, things began to go wrong for the Germans. By May 26, no less than two army groups and four army headquarters were controlling attacks on the Dunkirk perimeter. Not until May 30 did the Germans reorganize their command structure and place Eighteenth Army in control of the Dunkirk perimeter. And it was only on that day that they realized the British were getting away. On May 31, 68,000 Allied troops escaped, raising the total evacuated to 194,000. On June 1 a further 64,000 came out; by now virtually all the BEF had escaped. By the time Operation Dynamo ended on June 3, no less than 340,000 Allied troops had evacuated Dunkirk.

The German failure at Dunkirk was also a Luftwaffe failure. Most of its aircraft were still operating from bases in western Germany; as a result they were farther from Dunkirk than British fighters operating from the British Isles. Spitfire and Hurricane attacks were a nasty surprise to the Luftwaffe, which had had pretty much its own way in the campaign. Altogether the RAF lost 177 aircraft during the air battles over Dunkirk, the Luftwaffe 240. The successful withdrawal should not, however, obscure the extent of the catastrophe. As Churchill commented: "Wars are not won by evacuation." While the evacuation spared the British army and permitted it to fight again, the Germans had completely destroyed the balance of power in Europe.

One should not lose sight of the moral parameters of the Nazi conquest in the west. On May 27 a company of the *SS Totenkoph* Division captured one hundred men of the British Royal Norfolk Regiment. They lined the British soldiers up against a barn wall and machine-gunned them; afterward they bayoneted the wounded. German military authorities brought no charges against the soldiers involved in the incident. Along with the destruction of Rotterdam, this murder of British prisoners suggests the brutality of Nazi conquest.

The End in France

By now a deep malaise had spread throughout the French high command and the government. Premier Paul Reynaud had relieved Gamelin, appointed Weygand as his successor, and brought the aged Marshal Pétain back from Spain. But the change in leadership could not halt the expanding disaster, as the *Wehrmacht* turned to deal with the remainder of France. Its panzer divisions, extricated from Dunkirk, redeployed to jump off positions in north central France. Three army groups (Rundstedt's Army Group A, forty-five divisions; Bock's Army Group B, fifty divisions); and Wilhelm Ritter von Leeb's Army Group C, twenty-four divisions; plus twenty-three divisions in OKH reserve fell on a French army of barely fifty divisions.

Army Group B jumped off on June 5. The French had improved their methods of fighting and, despite overwhelming German superiority, put up tenacious resistance. So tough were the defenses in front of Kleist's panzer group that the OKH pulled the entire group out on June 7 and moved it farther east. Not surprisingly, Rommel's 7th Panzer Division captured two railroad bridges on the lower Somme and in a matter of hours was hustling down French roads toward the Seine River. By the end of the campaign, Rommel's forces had swept to Rouen, sidestepped to the coast to put the French IX Corps (including the British 51st Division) in the bag, and then driven on to Cherbourg. In six weeks 7th Panzer Division captured 97,648 prisoners, 277 guns, 458 armored vehicles, and 400 tanks. Rundstedt's Army Group A attacked on June 9 and rapidly swept the French off the battlefield. Guderian drove to the Swiss frontier, while Paris fell on June 14.

The Anglo-French alliance, barely patched together in the late 1930s, collapsed under the weight of defeat. Late on June 16, Reynaud resigned, and Pétain assumed power. Within two hours he asked for an

The British used more than 850 ships of all shapes and sizes to evacuate Allied troops from Dunkirk. They had hoped to rescue 45,000 men but managed to evacuate 340,000.

armistice. A few days later in the forest of Compiègne, representatives of France signed an armistice in the same railroad car in which the Germans had capitulated in November 1918.

✳   ✳   ✳   ✳

In the campaigns of 1939 and 1940, the Germans restored mobility to the battlefield and swiftly defeated Poland, Norway, and France. Their success rested less on a revolutionary idea than on an evolutionary process that had begun in 1917–1918. Through intelligent, careful analysis of the experience of World War I and of the possibilities of improved technology, they developed a doctrine for mobile warfare that rested as much on artillery and infantry as it did on tanks. Placing a greater value on maneuver than on firepower, the Germans shaped their army for mobile operations. Unlike the British and French forces, the armor, artillery, and infantry in the German army spoke the same language—one of speed, exploitation, decentralized authority, and ruthless, aggressive leadership.

Yet, the victory over France did not solve Germany's problems. Despite the doctrinal coherence and effectiveness of the German way of war, the *Wehrmacht* remained a hybrid military organization. Of the divisions that invaded France in May 1940, only eighteen were modern motorized and mechanized units; the remainder, over 80 percent of the force, were World War I–style infantry who marched on foot and depended on horse-drawn transport to bring up their artillery, supplies, and baggage. Additionally, German units possessed diverse equipment, most clearly demonstrated by three panzer divisions' being equipped primarily with Czech tanks. And there was scant prospect that the armament industry would be able to replace horse-drawn wagons with trucks or foreign equipment with German-made matériel. German logistics remained weak at best; the devastating nature of their victory in 1940 hid the sloppiness with which the support structure was able to move supplies forward. Some of Guderian's units, for example, had to depend on French gas stations for their fuel in the drive to the Channel.

Nevertheless, the Germans had achieved an important victory that allowed them to escape the economic constraints under which they had operated thus far. To maintain Germany's newly won position in the world, the Germans would have to recognize how vulnerable they remained in the center of Europe. But they did not; instead Hitler, his generals, and many of the German people drew the conclusion that nothing was impossible for the Third Reich. Instead of using caution, they would now reach out to expand the boundaries of greater Germany to the limits of their dreams.

SUGGESTED READINGS

Bond, Brian. *British Military Policy between the Two World Wars* (Oxford: Clarendon Press, 1980).

Corum, James S. *The Roots of Blitzkrieg: Hans von Seeckt and the German Military Reform* (Lawrence: University Press of Kansas, 1992).

Dcist, Wilhelm. *The Wehrmacht and German Rearmament* (Toronto: University of Toronto Press, 1981).

Dennis, Peter. *Decision by Default: Peacetime Conscription and British Defense, 1919–1939* (Durham, N.C.: Duke University Press, 1972).

Doughty, Robert A. *The Seeds of Disaster: The Development of French Army Doctrine, 1919–1939* (Hamden, Conn.: Archon Books, 1985).

———. *The Breaking Point: Sedan and the Fall of France, 1940* (Hamden, Conn.: Archon Books, 1990).

Erickson, John. *The Soviet High Command: A Military-Political History, 1918–1941* (Boulder, Col.: Westview Press, 1984).

Glantz, David M. *Soviet Military Operational Art: In Pursuit of Deep Battle* (London: Frank Cass, 1991).

Hurley, Alfred F. *Billy Mitchell: Crusader for Air Power* (Bloomington: Indiana University Press, 1975).

Knox, MacGregor. *Mussolini Unleashed: Politics and Strategy in Fascist Italy's Last War* (Cambridge: Cambridge University Press, 1982).

Liddell Hart, B. H. *History of the Second World War* (New York: G. P. Putnam's, 1978).

Millett, Allan R., and Williamson Murray, eds. *Military Effectiveness*, Vol. II, *The Inter War Period* (London: Allen and Unwin, 1988).

Murray, Williamson. *The Change in the European Balance of Power, 1938–1939: The Path to Ruin* (Princeton: Princeton University Press, 1984).

———. *Luftwaffe* (Baltimore: Nautical and Aviation Publishing Co., 1985).

Murray, Williamson, and Allan R. Millett. *Calculations: Net Assessment and the Coming of World War II* (New York: The Free Press, 1992).

Taylor, Telford. *The March of Conquest: The German Victories in Western Europe, 1940* (New York: Simon and Schuster, 1958).

Trythall, Anthony J. *"Boney" Fuller: The Intellectual General, 1878–1966* (London: Cassell, 1977).

Winton, Harold R. *To Change an Army: General Sir John Burnett-Stuart and British Armored Doctrine, 1927–1938* (Lawrence: University Press of Kansas, 1988).

14

GERMANY ARRESTED:
THE LIMITS OF EXPANSION

The Battle of Britain

The War in the
Mediterranean, 1940–1942

Libya and Egypt, 1941–1942

Operation "Barbarossa"

$\mathbb{T}$he conquest of France in the stunningly short period of six weeks capped seven years of diplomatic, strategic, and military successes for Adolf Hitler's regime. Though nothing seemed impossible to the victorious Germans, the Third Reich could not strike decisive blows at any of its potential future opponents. Indeed, a careful assessment of Nazi Germany's political and strategic position in summer 1940 would have left cause for sobering doubts; at a minimum it would have concluded that preparations for a long world war, utilizing the entire economic structure of central and western Europe, must begin at once. Instead, the Germans first made a halfhearted stab at solving the British problem by aerial assault, then struck at the Soviet Union, and finally foolishly declared war on the United States. Italian failures also drew the Germans into expensive campaigns in North Africa and the Balkans.

The Germans encountered substantial difficulties in the campaigns against Britain and the Soviet Union. Despite aerial attacks of unparalleled intensity and size, the British proved resilient to air attack and the campaign proved expensive for the Germans in terms of aircrews, aircraft, and industrial resources. In the Mediterranean the British initially met success against the Italians; when more capable German forces and commanders arrived, the opposing forces raced back and forth across the 400-mile North African coastline in seesaw campaigns, but the Afrika Korps failed to drive the British out of Egypt. After the Italians blundered miserably in the Balkans, the Germans intervened and rapidly overran Yugoslavia and Greece, but they failed to extinguish resistance in remote areas. The German airborne attack against Crete also achieved success, but difficulties in the campaign made the Wehrmacht and Hitler leery of such operations in the future. In the east, the invasion of Russia propelled the war to a higher level in terms of numbers of soldiers and equipment involved. Despite initial German successes, the Soviets managed to escape defeat and to bring vast forces to bear against the invaders. As Soviet resistance continued, the Wehrmacht suffered mounting losses and encountered severe logistic problems. By spring 1942 the Germans had won impressive military victories on the ground and in the air, but they had fashioned a noose firmly around their own necks.

The Battle of Britain

Before the House of Commons on June 18, 1940, Winston Churchill warned his fellow countrymen: "What General Weygand called the Battle of France is over. I expect that the Battle of Britain is about to begin." Though most military analysts concluded that it would be a short battle, Churchill did not believe that the war was over. He concluded that crossing the English Channel represented a complex operational problem, which the Germans probably could not solve. Moreover, he recognized that neither the United States nor the Soviet Union could allow a Nazi hegemony over Europe and that Germany's newly won position carried with it inevitable frictions that would result in conflict between the Reich and those two great neutral powers.

Not surprisingly, the British made approaches to both governments. The Soviets, busily engaged in gobbling up the Baltic Republics, in stealing the provinces of Bessarabia and Bukovina from Romania, and in congratulating the Nazis on their successes, exhibited little interest in cooperating with Britain. The United States was another matter. Franklin D. Roosevelt, making an unprecedented bid for a third term with an American people deeply divided over foreign policy, nevertheless made clear over summer 1940 that America was deeply committed to Britain.

By early July, Churchill felt sure enough of Roosevelt to move. With Italy's entrance into the war, the naval balance in the Mediterranean was tipping against the British; not only had the French withdrawn from the alliance, but the British feared that the new regime in France and its fleet might join the Axis Powers. On July 5 the British acted: the Royal Navy seized French ships in British ports; in Alexandria it demobilized and disarmed units of the French navy. Finally, Force H, operating out of Gibraltar and led by battle cruiser *Hood*, appeared off Mers el Kébir in North Africa. The British issued an ultimatum with three options: sink or abandon their ships, join Britain, or be destroyed. The French refused negotiations and were building up steam when the ultimatum expired; Force H opened fire and a deluge of 15-inch shells fell on the French fleet. The attack sank battle cruiser *Dunkerque* and three older battleships and killed 1,250 French sailors. Ironically only two weeks before, French and British troops had been fighting against the Germans.

The attack underlined Churchill's resolve. Not until the end of July, however, did the German high command take the British problem seriously. They then prepared two approaches: first, "Sea Lion," a joint-service, amphibious landing on the British coast; and second, a great air offensive to gain air superiority and wreck Britain's industrial infrastructure. One wonders how seriously Hitler considered the landing in Britain. The Luftwaffe hardly participated in Sea Lion's planning, while the army planned for an invasion the navy could not have supported, even at full strength. The navy, left with only one heavy cruiser and four destroyers after Norway, proposed a landing the breadth of which would not have supported a brigade. Rhine river barges would have transported the landing force. The whole planning process also involved considerable interservice bickering and gross misjudgments. Army planners proceeded as if a Channel crossing were just another river crossing!

None of this bothered the Luftwaffe; Hermann Göring and his commanders planned to win the war against Britain by themselves. At the end of June the Luftwaffe turned to the problem of winning air superiority over the

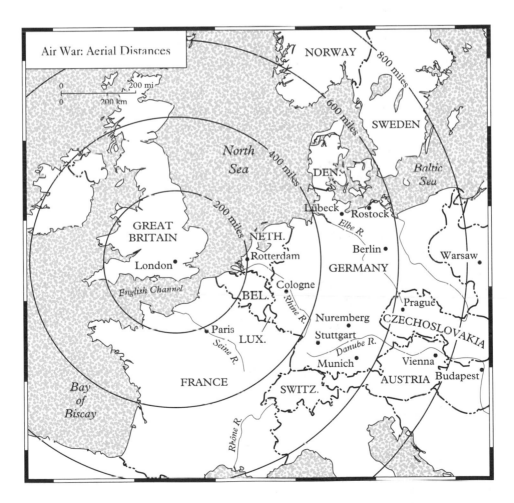

British Isles. On June 30, 1940, Göring issued general instructions. After redeployment, the Luftwaffe would begin a sustained effort to achieve air superiority. Initial targets would be Fighter and Bomber commands, ground-support echelons, and the aircraft industry. Above all, Göring underlined, the Luftwaffe must attack the RAF ceaselessly.

Unfortunately for the Luftwaffe, it entered battle with an intelligence picture that was faulty in every respect. German intelligence calculated that the Spitfire and Hurricane were inferior to German fighters and that British fighter production was between 150 to 300 machines per month. In fact the Spitfire was equal to the Bf 109, and both British fighters were superior to the Bf 110. British fighter production had also reached nearly 500 machines per month by late summer 1940. Moreover, the Germans failed to recognize the importance of British radar and ground control systems.

Building on faulty intelligence, Luftwaffe operational estimates forecast that four days' fighting would break Fighter Command, and that four weeks would destroy the rest of the RAF and the factories on which British air strength rested. Then the Luftwaffe, bombing enemy cities day and night, could protect Sea Lion, if the British still refused to surrender.

Two German *Luftflotte*, Second and Third, deployed in northern France with 2,600 bombers, dive bombers, and fighters; *Luftflotte* Five with 300 bombers and fighters in Norway would strike at northern Britain. One significant weakness affected German strategy from the start: the Bf 109 could barely reach London, while the Bf 110, a long-range escort, could not face RAF fighters in air-to-air combat. Consequently, the Germans could mount daylight strikes only to London; beyond the capital German bombers could fly only under cover of night.

The British victory in the Battle of Britain resulted from years of thought and scientific preparation. Air Marshal Sir Hugh Dowding deserves credit for much of that preparation.

The fact that the Germans confronted a well prepared opponent was due almost completely to the foresight of Air Marshal Sir Hugh Dowding. As the RAF's head of research and development in the mid-1930s, Dowding supported development of radar; he also put together the specifications and contracts that resulted in procurement of Spitfires and Hurricanes. In 1937 he took over Fighter Command and in that position created a doctrine and force structure to defend Britain from attack. Thus Dowding fought and won the Battle of Britain with a force whose development he had overseen and whose doctrine and organization he had developed—surely one of the most impressive achievements in twentieth-century military history.

Both air forces had suffered heavily in the Battle of France; the Luftwaffe had lost 30 percent of its bomber force, while the RAF had lost nearly 20 percent of its fighter pilots. But the British enjoyed important advantages. They were defending their homeland; since most air battles would occur over Britain, many British pilots who parachuted would return to operations. Moreover, Fighter Command needed only to hold on until fall when bad weather arrived. To succeed the Germans had to win a decisive victory; even then it was doubtful whether Sea Lion could achieve a successful lodgement across the Channel.

To oppose the Luftwaffe, Dowding possessed approximately 900 fighters, between 500 and 600 aircraft serviceable on any given day. Nevertheless, the disparity between Fighter Command and the Luftwaffe was not as great as it might seem; the Luftwaffe possessed a bare equivalency in Bf 109s and the success or failure of air superiority fighters would determine the outcome. Dowding aimed: (1) to keep his command in being; (2) to fight a sustained battle of attrition; and (3) to prevent the Luftwaffe from impairing Britain either economically or militarily. Half of his fighters defended southern England; a substantial number remained north of London. Throughout the battle Dowding could feed in fresh squadrons and pull back the exhausted.

Over July and early August the Germans built up their tempo of operations. They hoped to clear the Channel and achieve a measure of psychological superiority. They succeeded in the former but failed in the latter. Dowding eventually concluded that committing fighters to cover convoys was too costly; in the meantime Fighter Command achieved valuable experience in how German raids built up and how its own system would react.

On July 21, Göring advised his commanders that the objectives of Luftwaffe attacks should be the RAF and its production base. He also underlined that they should strike Fighter Command's morale and urged that the German fighters possess maximum latitude in protecting bombers. Thus bomber raids would bring up enemy fighters, while Bf 109 sweeps sought out and attacked those fighters. Three days later *Fliegerkorps* I mapped out four distinct missions for the campaign. First would be attacks on Fighter Command. But it also singled out Bomber Command and attacks on imports; finally, independent of the first three missions, it urged ruthless "retaliatory" terror raids against British cities.

Officially the Battle of Britain began on August 13, although the RAF noted a sharp increase in operations on the preceding day. On "Eagle

Day" the Germans directly attacked Fighter Command. The most dangerous attacks struck at radar sites along the coast, but the Germans soon abandoned this avenue as unproductive. By mid-August the British had lost 148 fighters to 286 aircraft for the Luftwaffe (only 105 Bf 109s). German intelligence, however, failed to perceive how British defenses were working. The early air battles should also have alerted the Germans to the weaknesses of their own intelligence; *Luftflotte* Five from Norway received a savage beating from fighters that its intelligence had described as nonexistent.

Adding to Luftwaffe discomfort was a consistent lack of focus and direction. Göring finally recognized the vulnerability of the *Stuka*, a dive-bomber whose lack of speed made it an easy target for British fighters. He made, however, the crucial mistake of tying Bf 109s more closely to the bombers, thus robbing the fighters of their flexibility. Finally, Göring concentrated Bf 109s under Field Marshal Albert Kesselring's command near Pas de Calais. While this shift enabled the Luftwaffe to pressure RAF bases in front of London, it also relieved the pressure on Fighter Command's structure over the rest of southern England.

As the air campaign developed, Dowding altered his operational conceptions. British fighters no longer pursued enemy aircraft over the Channel but now concentrated exclusively on attacking bombers. In the ten days after Eagle Day, Fighter Command lost 126 fighter pilots killed, wounded, or missing, a 14 percent loss. But enemy fighters and bombers were scarcely in better shape. Throughout the last week of August and into early September, the Germans severely damaged British airbases and sector stations in southern England. Fighter Command struggled desperately to maintain its equilibrium despite mounting losses.

The Germans broke first. Discouraged by British resistance, Hitler and Göring, with Kesselring's wholehearted support, switched from an air superiority strategy to strategic bombing in the hope that it would destroy London and sap British morale. The shift came suddenly. On September 7, Kesselring launched nearly 1,000 aircraft on London (348 bombers and 617 fighters). The raid caught British defenses by surprise; Fighter Command's response was ragged; controllers at sector stations initially concluded the Luftwaffe was striking at southern England. As a result, British fighters failed to attack until enemy bombers were on the way back. In swirling dog-fights, Fighter Command lost twenty-two more fighter pilots, but the Germans lost the same number along with numerous bombers. Damage in London was frightful, and night raids worsened the loss. But the respite allowed Fighter Command to recover.

One week later, Kesselring launched a second blow at London. This time he ran into a well-prepared and rested enemy, eager to attack the raiders. From the moment the Germans crossed the coastline, British fighters slashed into Luftwaffe formations. Both sides lost equivalent numbers of fighters; the Germans, however, lost forty-one bombers. What made September 15 decisive was the fact that many Luftwaffe bomber crews cut and ran, dropping bomb loads all over Kent. Deceived again by intelligence experts who had erroneously concluded that Fighter Command was beaten, and having suffered heavy losses since May, Luftwaffe crews had had

The British were outraged by the bombing in November 1940 of the cathedral at Coventry and the killing of 554 civilians. Three years later in July 1943, 30,000-40,000 German civilians died under Allied bombs in Hamburg.

enough. Though air attacks would continue, the Battle of Britain was over. The Luftwaffe had not won anything approaching air superiority, and Hitler postponed Sea Lion on September 17. Winston Churchill eloquently expressed the triumph: "Never in the field of human conflict was so much owed by so many to so few."

In retrospect it is hard to see how the Germans might have made a success of Sea Lion, considering the state of their navy and the problems besetting the Luftwaffe. That should not, however, diminish Dowding's accomplishments or the psychological importance of the British victory. Those responsible for Munich and appeasement in the 1930s possessed neither the strategic understanding nor the toughness of spirit needed to make the frightening decisions necessary for the defense of Britain in summer

1940. Only Churchill, called to be the prime minister on May 10, 1940, as German spearheads slashed into western Europe, possessed those qualities. His monumental eloquence and driving leadership imbued the British with the belief that they could win. On the other hand, Dowding's solid, professional leadership ensured that British air defenses made few mistakes. Britain's success made it clear to the world that the Nazis were not omnipotent—a factor of immense importance.

Though the Germans had lost the Battle of Britain, their efforts to cow Britain by terror attacks did not cease; rather, they shifted their emphasis to night bombing. Of all the world's air forces only the Luftwaffe had actually developed the navigational means to bomb in bad weather or at night. Luckily British intelligence provided warning that the Germans possessed such a capability. Through examination of crashed bombers, decryption of German message traffic, and imaginative analysis by a young scientist, R. V. Jones, the British unraveled the German system. Jones convinced his superiors and eventually Churchill of the danger, and as a result British scientists developed effective countermeasures that warped the radio beams on which German navigational systems operated. All this was of enormous importance because British defenses were blind. Air defenses could scramble single-engine fighters in the general direction of incoming bombers, but once airborne the fighters could not intercept their opponents at night. By late 1940 the first experiments with airborne radar were underway, but the sets on which interception depended were unreliable, bulky, and often inaccurate.

The problem confronting German planners in the nighttime offensive was target priority: should the Luftwaffe attack specific segments of British industry such as aircraft factories, or systems of interrelated industries such as imports and distribution, or even popular morale? The nighttime bombing offensive attempted all three strategic aims; not surprisingly it failed. As with daylight attacks, the Luftwaffe lacked either the strength or capability to achieve such wide-ranging objectives, and direct attacks on the British population only spurred the British to pay the Germans back in kind.

The *Blitz* underscored a number of important points. First, the resilience of modern economies and states allowed them to absorb great punishment. Second, the air weapon was a difficult one to wield with precision; achieving accuracy or sustained levels of damage was not easy. Finally, despite claims by airmen that air power would provide an easy solution to the costs of modern war, it was in fact extraordinarily expensive in terms of aircrews, aircraft, and industrial resources.

The War in the Mediterranean, 1940–1942

The focus now shifted to the Mediterranean. For the British the Suez Canal and Gibraltar held the key to their empire in India and the Far East. But

Italy's increasing hostility in the late 1930s forced the British to turn to the route around the Cape of Good Hope. Nevertheless, the greatly increased distances that British shipping had to travel with Italy's entrance into the war gave the British considerable incentive to open the Mediterranean.

The Italians viewed the Mediterranean as *mare nostrum* (our sea) and as the basis for the restoration of the Roman Empire. As such, Benito Mussolini recognized that he would have to expel Britain from Gibraltar and Suez. But fearful of German ambition, he hesitated to request Hitler's aid. Italy would, therefore, begin by fighting its own "parallel war." On the other hand, the Germans, with Hitler's dreams of living space in eastern Europe, had little inclination to look to the Mediterranean for strategic advantage.

Mussolini's Parallel War

On June 10, 1940, Mussolini declared war on the hard-pressed Western Powers. This was a popular move for most Italians, who believed that the British and French had robbed them of the fruits of their victory in 1918. Mussolini's conceptions, as with those of Hitler, were revolutionary. He aimed to use foreign conquest to create a Mediterranean empire and in turn to exploit that "success" to revolutionize Italian society. Mussolini's wars were murderously effective against poorly armed African peoples, but the Italians made only superficial preparations to meet their better armed and prepared opponents. The army focused on defending the Alps rather than preparing for an ambitious and difficult campaign; the air force dreamed of strategic bombing but possessed no ability to intervene in a naval war in the Mediterranean; and the navy felt thoroughly inferior to the Royal Navy.

Because of a lack of strategic and operational planning, the Italians floundered despite opportunities created by the French collapse and British weaknesses. The army's inadequate planning and preparations were symptomatic of all services: Marshal Rodolfo Graziani, army chief of staff, proclaimed in the last prewar conference that "when the cannon sounds everything will fall into place." Such wishful thinking did not make up for inadequate preparation. In the last desperate days of French resistance, the Italians launched a series of ill-prepared attacks on France; lack of success prevented them from taking advantage of the armistice with Vichy France. In early July a force of Italian battleships escorting a convoy to Libya ran into the British eastern Mediterranean fleet escorting a convoy to Malta. Despite advanced warning, greater numbers, and air superiority, the Italians fled in disarray. Arriving late, the Italian air force bombed both fleets indiscriminately but damaged nothing seriously since it possessed no armor-piercing bombs or aerial torpedoes. In September the Italian commander in Libya, Graziani, finally moved on Egypt. A lackadaisical advance got his forces to Sidi el Barrani, fifty miles from his starting point.

Meanwhile, events in the Balkans picked up momentum. Emboldened by the collapse of Europe's equilibrium, the Hungarians determined to regain Transylvania, lost to Romania in 1918. The Germans, given their dependence on Romanian oil, had no desire to see a conflict break out

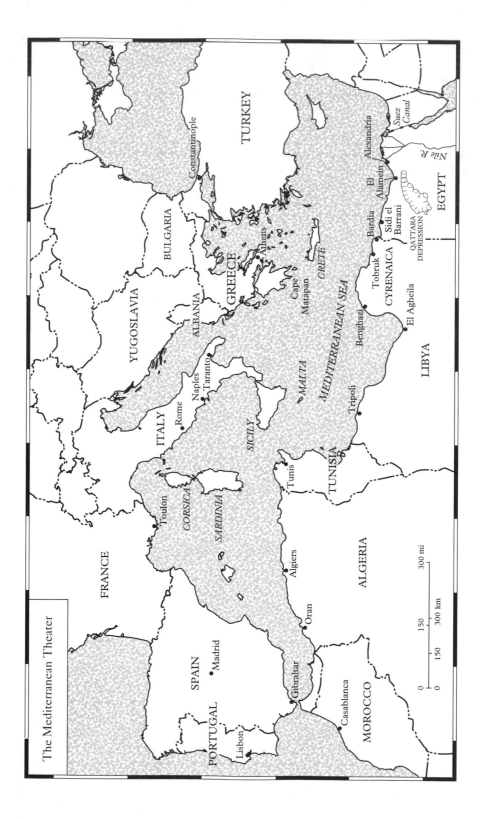

The Mediterranean Theater

between those two states. Therefore, with help from the Italians, they imposed a settlement that returned most of Transylvania to Hungary. Rebellion resulted in Romania; the king abdicated and General Ion Antonescu established a military dictatorship. The Germans, confronting a possible Romanian collapse, stepped in to stabilize the situation. At Romania's request, Hitler sent a military mission—one that by December consisted of no less than a panzer division, a motorized infantry division, two flak regiments, and two fighter squadrons. Ostensibly the German "advisors" were there to help the Romanian military; in fact they were there to guard the oil and warn the Soviets against fishing in troubled waters.

The Italian Collapse

Whatever the positive benefits from the move into Romania, it backfired on the Germans, for Mussolini viewed it as a cavalier disregard of Italian interests. As he told his foreign minister Count Galeazzo Ciano, "Hitler always confronts me with a fait accompli. This time I am going to pay him back in his own coin. He will find out that I have occupied Greece." Mussolini then ordered hurried preparations for an attack despite the lateness of the season.

Launched into northern Greece in early November 1940 from Italian-occupied Albania with little logistical support, in most cases with no winter clothing, and with numerical inferiority, the Italians marched straight into defeat. After initial successes, a combination of bad weather and Greek numerical superiority led to a general collapse. The Italian air force, with neither the inclination nor the preparation to support the army, confined its efforts to terror attacks on Greek cities. A string of incompetent commanders, including General Ubaldo Soddu—who whiled away evenings in Albania by writing musical scores for movies—failed to rectify the situation. Not only had Mussolini upset the delicate balance in the Balkans, but he also had made British, and perhaps Soviet, intervention possible. The threat to Romanian oil was obvious; given winter conditions, Germany could do little.

Mussolini's run of troubles, however, had barely begun. On the evening of November 11–12 British torpedo aircraft from the carrier *Illustrious* struck the naval base at Taranto and sank half the Italian battle fleet. With this stroke the balance in the Mediterranean swung permanently in Britain's favor. One month later the British army attacked in North Africa. What the theater commander, General Sir Archibald Wavell, intended as a mere raid resulted in a complete rout of Italian forces. Mutually unsupporting positions around Sidi el Barrani collapsed before the onrush of the British 7th Armored and 4th Indian Divisions driving rapidly westward. Though Italian forces were on the run, Wavell pulled 4th Indian out of the line and transferred it to the strategically useless campaign in Ethiopia. The two-week period during which British forces reorganized was not enough for the Italians to recover; but it did, however, allow the Germans to get across the Mediterranean to Tripoli.

In early January British forces resumed their advance into Libya. Tobruk fell with startling suddenness. As the Italians hustled down the coastal road past Benghazi in a desperate retreat toward Tripoli, the 7th Armored Division sliced across the desert, caught the Italians at Beda Fomm, and destroyed what was left of Mussolini's African army. British forces advanced to El Agheila, where they halted; they had advanced more than 400 miles. There Wavell helped others persuade Churchill that his troops could not reach Tripoli and that the British should aid Greece as quickly as possible. Nevertheless, the British, for a loss of only 2,000 men, had captured 130,000 Italians and stripped the last pretensions of competence from Mussolini's military forces.

The Germans Arrive in the Mediterranean

Italy's disasters in early 1941 threatened to undermine the Axis position in the Balkans and Mediterranean. In response, Hitler's strategy had strictly limited aims: restore a collapsing situation in the Mediterranean; prevent Italy's collapse; and protect the southern flank of German forces gathering for the invasion of the Soviet Union. Since conquering the Soviets represented the heart of Hitler's revolutionary goals, there was no serious consideration among the Germans of alternatives to the eastern campaign.

The commander of the forces deployed to North Africa in early 1941, soon called the Afrika Korps, was a newly promoted lieutenant general, Erwin Rommel. Rommel had had a spectacular career in World War I. In the interwar period he remained in the infantry, but after the Polish Campaign, assumed command of 7th Panzer Division. In the French campaign, Rommel played a crucial role in the breakthrough along the Meuse River. As a reward, he received command of the corps-sized force deploying to aid the Italians. Rommel's orders were defensive; he was to protect Tripoli and support the remnants of the Italian army in North Africa. But Rommel believed that he must strike or be destroyed; he would soon emerge as the war's premier field commander.

Characteristically, Rommel disregarded his instructions and attacked even though only one division had arrived. Coordination between British units new to the theater collapsed in confusion, and Rommel surged east across Libya. By the end of April the Germans had chased Commonwealth forces almost 400 miles and driven them out of Libya except Tobruk. By holding that port, the British complicated the Germans' logistical problems; for the next six months Rommel found himself caught between Egypt's frontier defenses and Tobruk; he was unable to deal with either satisfactorily. Nevertheless, with only one motorized division he had restored the Axis position in North Africa and rocked the British; he had driven his opponents back to where they had begun.

In the Balkans geography constrained Axis actions. Given the limited logistic capacity of Albania, the Italians could not funnel sufficient troops and equipment directly to the front facing the Greeks. To advance against the Greeks, the Germans had to move through Yugoslavia or Bulgaria. The need for action became more critical in March 1941 when British troops arrived at Athens to reinforce the Greeks.

After Erwin Rommel arrived in North Africa in February 1941, he demonstrated a remarkable mastery of mobile operations, but he could not overcome the greater numbers of the Allies and his own shortages of supplies and fuel.

As the Germans built up Field Marshal Sigmund Wilhelm List's Twelfth Army in Bulgaria for its April attack, German diplomats assuaged Turkish fears and intimidated the Yugoslavs into joining the Axis on March 25. But on the evening Yugoslav negotiators returned to Belgrade, Serbian officers overthrew the government. Wildly cheering crowds in Belgrade, bedecked with French and British flags, underlined the mood. Within hours, Hitler ordered the OKW, the armed forces high command, to "smash Yugoslavia." By evening, after conferences with Field Marshal Walther von Brauchitsch (the army's commander-in-chief) and Göring, the Führer signed Directive 25 requiring that Yugoslavia be "beaten down as quickly as possible." Hitler also ordered the Luftwaffe to destroy Belgrade.

German planning rapidly adapted to changing circumstances. Within one week, OKH, the army high command, had altered Twelfth Army objectives to include southern Yugoslavia. Meanwhile, Second Army established itself in Austria and Hungary so it could execute a major attack from the north. As panzer forces from the two armies concentrated their thrusts from the south and north on Belgrade, German infantry would overrun the remainder of Yugoslavia. Along with ground deployments came extensive Luftwaffe redeployments. The code name for the aerial assault on Yugoslavia was "Punishment," an accurate reflection of Hitler's fury. By the time the Luftwaffe had completed attacks on Belgrade, 17,000 people had died.

From the onset the Balkan campaign split into two separate operations: the conquest of Yugoslavia and that of Greece. Fortunately for the Germans, the Yugoslavs failed to mobilize; the ferocious air attacks on Belgrade shattered the government; and the Yugoslavs attempted to defend their

Messerschmitt Bf 110 fighters supporting German operations in Yugoslavia in March 1941.
The Germans had great hopes for the Bf 110 as a multi-role "strategic" fighter, but numerous
design flaws limited its effectiveness except as a night fighter.

entire country. But Nazi forces easily broke through their defenses. Within
five days the Germans had seized Belgrade as the Yugoslav army collapsed in
disarray. Ironically the extent of the success contributed to the undoing of
long-range Nazi interests in Yugoslavia; almost immediately, the OKH began
recalling units for the operations against the Soviet Union. That process left
substantial numbers of armed Yugoslavs in mountains and remote areas.
Though the government had ceased to exist, the German victory did not
extinguish resistance.

The campaign against Greece was a replica of Yugoslavia; XXXX
Panzer Corps outflanked Greek defenses and sent Allied forces pell-mell to
the south. The Greek army collapsed, and the British withdrew by sea in
the face of the Luftwaffe's overwhelming air superiority. Nevertheless, at
the end of April the Royal Navy managed to evacuate nearly 51,000 of the
62,000 British soldiers in Greece.

The Fall of Crete

In retrospect, the strategic prize in the Mediterranean was not Greece but
Crete. Possession of that island would have provided a base for RAF raids
on Romanian oil fields, as well as a base from which to supply partisan
movements throughout the Balkans. The Germans recognized the threat,
and as their forces pushed the British and Greeks southward, German planners under paratroop general Kurt Student were already preparing a strike at
Crete. Student envisioned an airborne attack on Crete's airfields, supported
by coastal landings. But the Italian naval disaster at Cape Matapan at the
end of March, where the British sank three heavy cruisers, indicated that any
attack on Crete must rely almost exclusively on airborne forces. The final
plan was simple: seize the airfields at Maleme, Rhethymnon, and Herakleion
with the Luftwaffe's 7th Airborne Division and then reinforce as rapidly as

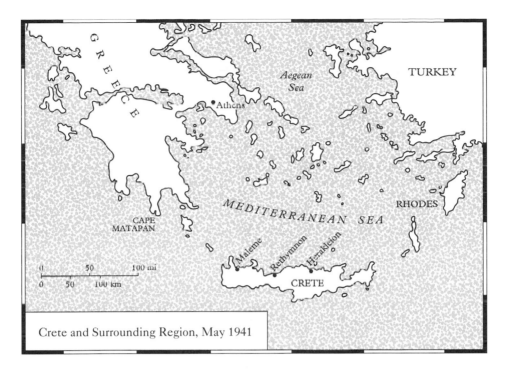

Crete and Surrounding Region, May 1941

possible with the 5th Mountain Division by using Ju 52 transport aircraft. But there were obstacles: the Allies had more troops on Crete than German intelligence reported; the local population proved distinctly hostile; and "Ultra" intelligence informed the British as to the coming attack.

The British had their own problems: many defenders had just been evacuated from Greece; they were short of equipment; and their morale was hardly solid. And despite signals from intelligence indicating that the Germans would launch an airborne assault on the airfields, Major General Bernard Freyberg, commander of Commonwealth forces, emphasized a defense of Crete's shores from the sea rather than from the air. Nevertheless, the attack on Crete, starting on May 20, almost failed. After its towrope parted, the glider carrying the 7th Airborne's commander crashed well before reaching the island. New Zealand troops at Maleme inflicted prohibitive casualties on the paratroops and retained control of the airfield. Without radios, the Germans at Maleme could not notify Student of their desperate situation. Airborne drops at Herakleion and Rhethymnon that afternoon resulted in an even greater disaster. Finally, Italian naval forces, escorting two convoys of reinforcements, ran into the Royal Navy and lost the troop ships they were convoying.

But the British lost the battle for Crete as a result of decisions taken at the end of the first day. The battalion holding the hill overlooking Maleme retreated, despite the fact that it had suffered no more heavily than its opponents. Freyberg's attention remained fixed on the sea, and few reinforcements reached the airfield's defenders—a period during which German paratroopers were particularly vulnerable to counterattack. Once the paratroopers controlled Maleme, however, they could receive reinforcements and heavier weapons; then the balance slowly but inexorably tilted against Commonwealth forces. Despite ferocious Luftwaffe attacks, the Royal Navy eventually evacuated most of Crete's defenders, but the British had lost a crucial geographical position in the Mediterranean. Romanian oil flowed to the Reich throughout spring 1944, hindered by nothing more than a smattering of air raids.

The German victory cost the paratroopers heavily. Nearly 60 percent of the transport aircraft were destroyed or badly damaged in the attack. Attacking airborne forces suffered such heavy losses that Hitler refused to employ them again as airborne forces until 1944. Ironically the allies reaped the lessons of Crete. On the receiving end of the aerial assault, they were far more impressed by the attack than were the Germans. As a result, much of the doctrine and concepts for British and American paratroop forces were derived from German airborne operations against Crete.

Libya and Egypt, 1941–1942

By late spring 1941 the Germans had achieved their short-term strategic goals in the Mediterranean. Rommel had restored the situation in Libya; intervention in the Balkans had repaired the damage done by Mussolini's invasion of Greece; seizure of Crete had driven the Royal Navy out of the Aegean Sea. But there were long-range drawbacks to these successes. While the Nazis had smashed the Greek and Yugoslav governments, they failed to achieve control of the countryside as the withdrawal to support Operation "Barbarossa" began, nor had they disarmed substantial numbers of the troops in remote Balkan areas—precisely the areas most likely to support guerrillas. On the strategic side, the Germans could not exploit their successes in the Mediterranean because they had already decided to invade the Soviet Union.

As Germany turned from the Mediterranean, the Middle East became a strategic backwater. Hitler now aimed to ensure that Italy remained in the war and to prevent the British from achieving a success that might threaten the Reich's southern flank. Rommel was chiefly responsible for meeting these objectives. Despite confronting considerable odds and having to operate at the end of long, tenuous supply lines, he emasculated much of the British military effort and by early summer 1942 even threatened to destroy Britain's position in the eastern Mediterranean.

Rommel on the Defensive

The British enjoyed a number of advantages that make Rommel's success even more remarkable. With the help of Polish cryptanalysts, they broke into the high-grade cipher transmissions of the German armed forces, particu-

The Western Desert

larly those of the air force, in 1940. This message traffic contained information about the plans, combat readiness, and intentions of the German high command, Hitler, and senior commanders in the field. The breaking of German codes for much of the war thus provided the British with clear insights into German strengths and weaknesses. "Ultra" (the code name for decrypted messages from the German "Enigma" cipher machine) often provided the British with pinpoint information on the timing and tracking of supply convoys from Italy to Libya, thus allowing the British to intercept and destroy them. The losses kept the Axis forces desperately short of supplies. Sometimes, however, intelligence from Ultra could be misleading because Rommel frequently disobeyed orders from Italian as well as German high commands. The second British advantage lay in air power. Not only did the RAF posses numerical superiority, but its doctrine, developed by openminded airmen like Sir Arthur Tedder, enabled the RAF to render effective close air support. Unfortunately, that air support could not rectify the weaknesses of British ground forces.

In June 1941, the British held the port of Tobruk in Libya and a front-line position just inside the Egyptian border. British armored forces held a four to one superiority in tanks over the Germans, whose armor was split between Tobruk and the Egyptian-Libyan frontier. Rommel, however, had created a number of tank traps, using 88-mm guns, and German defenses were carefully and skillfully sited. On June 15, Wavell launched "Battleaxe," an operation characterized by caution and inflexibility. Hoping to achieve a breakthrough before Rommel could concentrate his forces, the British attacked along the coastal road to drive straight on to Tobruk. Rommel's shrewdly prepared defenses, however, wrecked the attackers' momentum. By nightfall the British had lost half their tanks, while Rommel's armor, still shielded by antitank guns, had not come into play. A sweeping German counterattack around the British flank then drove British armor back in headlong retreat to its starting positions in Egypt. Battleaxe cost the

British ninety-one tanks, while the Germans lost only twelve (most of which they recovered and repaired).

The failure led to Wavell's removal. His replacement as Middle East commander-in-chief was General Sir Claude Auchinleck whose experience had been with the Indian army. From June through November 1941, Auchinleck prepared for another go at the Afrika Korps. For the first time, the British received substantial American aid to supplement their own equipment. Meanwhile Rommel had received barely sufficient supplies to keep his forces going. The German high command gave highest priority for supplies and reinforcements to the battles in Russia, and British air and naval attacks, aided by Ultra intelligence, proved deadly to Axis sea lines of communication. By mid-fall 1941 the British had established a considerable superiority in weapons and divisions in Africa; the RAF had nearly 700 aircraft against 120 for the Luftwaffe and 200 for the Italians; in tank strength the British had 710 against 174 German and 146 Italian vehicles. British weaknesses had more to do, however, with the intangibles of battle, and those came close to causing another defeat.

Operation "Crusader" began on November 11, 1941. One of Eighth Army's two corps, XIII, was to pin the Germans along the frontier, while XXX Corps swept around Rommel's flank to link up with Tobruk. The plan appeared clever, but in reality it split British armor, already weakened by diversion of a brigade of heavy tanks to support XIII Corps' infantry.

The attack got off to a slow start—so slow in fact that Rommel missed what was happening. When he reacted, he moved with usual dispatch; he screened off XXX Corps with antitank guns. Meanwhile, the British committed their armor piecemeal, and the Germans mauled it badly. In one action, Italian forces, showing considerable improvement, imposed a heavy toll on 22nd Armored Brigade, which lost 40 out of its 160 tanks. On November 24, Rommel pulled most of his tanks out of the main battle and dashed for the Egyptian frontier.

The balance on the swirling battlefield, however, slowly tilted to the British. Once Rommel's strike at British rear areas had failed to shake his opponents, he had to withdraw. Moreover, pressure exerted by the British from Malta placed extraordinary strains on the Afrika Korps: air and naval attacks sank nearly 80 percent of Axis supply ships crossing in October and November. Rommel's retreat took his forces back all the way across eastern Libya to El Agheila. Though Crusader appeared to represent a considerable turn in the desert war, the success rested on numerical superiority and German logistical difficulties, not from equality in tactics or battlefield performance.

As German forces retreated through Libya, the balance shifted back in their favor. *Luftflotte* Two (Second Air Force) transferred to the Mediterranean from Russia and launched a massive aerial assault on Malta. Consequently Rommel's forces now received most of the supplies dispatched from Italy. Retreat through Libya also enabled the Germans to fall back on supply dumps and restore their strength while it stretched British supply lines. Finally, Crusader resulted in heavier losses among combat veterans in Eighth Army than in the Afrika Korps.

Rommel Counterattacks

As the British halted near El Agheila in late 1941, having advanced some 400 miles, they repeated their mistake of February 1941: they pulled experienced forces back for rest and refit and pushed brand-new units to the front. Strengthened with new tanks and quick to take advantage, the Afrika Korps came boiling out of its defensive positions in January 1942 and struck the newly arrived 1st Armored Division. That division's three cavalry regiments, newly converted to tanks, knew little about armored operations and less about desert combat; the three British regiments came into play separately and were destroyed separately. The deadly combination of German panzers and 88-mm antitank guns leapfrogging from position to position ruled the battlefield. Rommel's thrust pushed the British back to Gazala, just west of Tobruk, and allowed his troops to reoccupy Benghazi, where both sides, exhausted by two months of combat and movement, settled down to build up for another battle.

In spring 1942, Churchill vociferously pressured his commanders in Libya to attack; Ultra indicated an enormous British superiority in every category of weapon. What intelligence failed to reveal, however, were enemy advantages in leadership, doctrinal coherence, and tactical proficiency. British generals resisted Churchill's urgings and set the date for their offensive in early June; it was too late. On the evening of May 26, Rommel moved, hooking around the British left flank and piling directly into the middle of the Eighth Army.

The British deployment possessed a number of weaknesses. The Gazala Line, approximately forty miles west of Tobruk and held by XXX Corps, reached deep into the desert with its infantry concentrated in strong points, called boxes, protected by minefields and barbed wire. The Bir Hacheim fortress anchored the southern tip of the line. Eighth Army commander, General Neil Ritchie, mistakenly believing that a German attack would come against his center, dispersed his armor to cover both his flank and the expected attack on his center. Auchinleck did suggest a concentration of armor, but Ritchie disregarded the suggestion.

Rommel's move underlines the extraordinary risks he was willing to run; he aimed to encircle the entire Gazala Line and Eighth Army. But things failed to work as he expected. The Germans began on May 26 with a diversionary attack on the center of the Gazala Line where Allied commanders expected an attack; that night the main body of the Afrika Korps moved around the Allies' southern flank. As he moved deep into the Allied rear, Rommel ran into heavy opposition; American M-3 Grant tanks had arrived in quantity and provided a nasty surprise. By the second day, the Germans were in serious trouble. Having moved around the British flank, the Afrika Korps found itself trapped against the Gazala Line with no route through which its supplies could flow; and it was rapidly running out of food, water, and ammunition. Fortunately for the Germans, the British launched a series of piecemeal attacks. Rommel's screen of antitank guns once again devastated British armor, while the panzers remained skillfully camouflaged in hull-down positions. Finally, the Afrika Korps overwhelmed Bir Hacheim

Rommel's operations in the desert relied on the mobility of his tanks, such as the Panzerkampfwagen III. He often massed his armored forces and delivered lightning-like blows against the more numerous but less flexible British forces.

and cleared a passage for supplies. The British had turned a promising situation into a catastrophe after two weeks of fighting.

On June 11, Rommel attacked eastward; on the next day his armor trapped two British armored brigades and destroyed them. A third armored brigade intervened to help its comrades, but again it ran into well-sited German defenses and was also destroyed. Such heavy losses cost the British their advantage in tanks; the Germans now had numerical superiority. Rommel turned north toward the coast and attempted to cut off British infantry withdrawing from the Gazala Line. Though most escaped, their retreat carried them straight to and over the Egyptian frontier in headlong flight.

Chewing its way through the collapsing British, the Afrika Korps headed eastward. On June 19 German forces brushed past Tobruk in pursuit of Ritchie's troops. The port's defenders consisted of 2nd South African Division, the Guards Brigade, and 32nd Tank Brigade with seventy tanks; confident that Rommel was going elsewhere, the defenders settled down. At dawn on June 20 a massive artillery bombardment hit the southeast side of the fortress, followed by the Afrika Korps, which had doubled back overnight. By mid-morning the garrison commander had decided the situation was hopeless and surrendered himself and 35,000 troops.

The Germans confronted the question of what to do next. Luftwaffe air attacks had severely battered Malta, and German paratroopers were preparing to give the coup de grâce. Given Rommel's extraordinary successes, however, did it make sense to stop just as the Afrika Korps rolled up on the frontier with the British in a state of complete demoralization? Rommel argued that he had an opportunity to drive the British from Egypt. Moreover, casualties on Crete, strong British defenses on Malta, and doubts about Italian reliability made an attack on the island a risky affair. Hitler sided with Rommel.

Rommel's pursuit carried him deep into Egypt. Yet his attempt to drive the British out of Egypt ultimately failed. Auchinleck relieved Ritchie and assumed command of Eighth Army. Halting his forces at El Alamein, he established a defensive position between the Mediterranean and the Qattara depression. The new position had no open flank because the Qattara depression, located thirty-five miles south of the coast, was a great salt sea impassable to heavy vehicles. Distances from Libya also complicated the German logistical situation. There at El Alamein in early July 1942 the British held, only sixty miles from Alexandria, and Rommel's slim chances of conquering Egypt faded.

Operation "Barbarossa"

At the end of July 1940, Hitler determined to destroy the Soviet Union. Strategic and ideological reasons lay behind his decision. On the one hand, he recognized that the United States and the Soviet Union represented significant strategic factors that explained British intransigence. But ideology underlay Hitler's decision as well; to him the Soviet Union represented an amalgamation of his greatest enemies, the Jews and Slavs. Not until he had destroyed Stalin's "Jewish-Bolshevik" regime would the biological revolution of Nazi Germany be safe. Finally, according to the Führer's *Weltanschauung*, the Third Reich desperately needed the agricultural and raw material resources of European Russia so that it would no longer have to depend on maritime trade for raw materials and foodstuffs. Without land and space, the German nation, Hitler believed, would never realize its full potential.

Because ideology played a crucial role in "Barbarossa" (the invasion's code name), the Germans came as conquerors, not as liberators; their conquest would bring slavery for Slavs and extermination for Jews. In its wake "special action" task forces of the Waffen SS accompanied each invading army group (three in number) to liquidate Jews, Communists, and other undesirables; these SS units received the wholehearted cooperation of most army commanders. Moreover, the army made its own contribution to the hideousness of war in the east; out of the approximately 3 million Soviet soldiers captured in summer and fall 1941, barely 100,000 survived the war— virtually all were under Wehrmacht, not SS, jurisdiction. The fanatical resistance of the Soviet population in defense of Stalin's malevolent regime largely resulted from the criminal behavior that marked German actions from the onset of Barbarossa.

Planning

By fall 1940 the Germans were deep into planning. The general staff accepted Hitler's assumption that the Wehrmacht could destroy the Soviet Union within one year. Basic to the Nazi approach was a belief that an invasion would catch and destroy the Red Army in the border areas. If that did not occur, several factors would have a negative effect on the course of subsequent operations. The theater itself broadened almost immediately, which would spread out the invaders; moreover, the depths of European Russia would allow the Soviets to trade space for time, while the campaign season itself would be short. Logistic war games gave clear warning that the Wehrmacht would face difficulties in supplying forces beyond a line running from Estonia to Smolensk and into the central Ukraine.

Operational planning by the OKH focused on Moscow as the strategic goal. However, the OKW emphasized that an advance on Moscow would depend on successes on the flanks—clearing the Baltic states to Leningrad and occupying the Ukraine. While differences between OKW and OKH conceptions remained relatively small, Hitler opposed the suggestions of his military advisors. He minimized Moscow's importance and argued that the invasion must achieve success on the flanks: in the north, Leningrad, cradle of the Bolshevik revolution; and in the south, the Ukraine, heartland of Soviet agriculture. To avoid Hitler's ordering a focus on the flanks, Colonel General Franz Halder (chief of the army's general staff) completed the final plan for Barbarossa without addressing this fundamental divergence of views. He obviously hoped that after the first stage of the invasion, the army leadership could persuade Hitler to go for Moscow. Consequently, German conceptions for the invasion contained a significant divergence that the high command refused to resolve until the campaign's mid-point. All of the planning also assumed that the Germans would destroy the Red Army in the border areas.

For the invasion the Germans deployed three army groups. Army Group North, under Field Marshal von Leeb, consisted of Fourth Panzer Group and Sixteenth and Eighteenth armies (three panzer, three motorized infantry, nineteen infantry, and four security divisions). Army Group Center, under Field Marshal Fedor von Bock, contained Second and Third Panzer groups as well as Fourth and Ninth armies (nine panzer, six and one-half motorized infantry, thirty-seven infantry, and one cavalry divisions). Finally, Army Group South, under Field Marshal Gerd von Rundstedt, consisted of First Panzer Group and Sixth, Eleventh, and Seventeenth armies (five panzer, four motorized infantry, twenty-eight infantry, two mountain, four light, and three security divisions). The OKH held two panzer, one motorized infantry, and eleven infantry divisions in reserve.

The objectives for the army groups reflected the planning: Army Group North was to clear the Baltic states; Army Group Center was to advance to Smolensk; and Army Group South was to push toward Kiev and then down the Dnieper bend, while Eleventh Army covered Romania and its oil. Consequently, Leningrad, the Ukraine, and Moscow were all objectives, but there were no clear priorities, no alternatives, and no examination of what the Wehrmacht would do should the Soviet Union not collapse. Even at the operational level, German field commanders were unsure whether the first objective of Army Group Center was encirclement of Soviet forces around Minsk or those farther east at Smolensk.

The German army that invaded the Soviet Union was an extraordinary military instrument. It was thoroughly trained; its doctrine was balanced and realistic; it had honed its battlefield skills by two years of campaigning; and its officer corps was flexible, adaptive, and professional. Nevertheless, its successes hid significant weaknesses. The inadequacies of rearmament in the 1930s forced the army to equip many units with foreign and obsolete weapons. Its panzer and motorized infantry divisions acquired many of their support vehicles by stripping western Europe of civilian trucks—vehicles that were neither designed nor built for the rigors of primitive Soviet roads. Moreover, the Germans were unprepared for the logistic demands of a theater that possessed continental dimensions. Finally, German intelligence did as bad a job in judging Soviet capabilities as it had done in judging the RAF. It underestimated the Red Army and its reserves considerably, miscalculated the recuperative powers of Soviet industry and military organizations, and underestimated the technological sophistication of Soviet weaponry.

The Soviet Union had its own weaknesses. Stalin understood the political vulnerability of his own regime only too well and consequently refused to trade space for time. He moved much of the regular army to the frontier to prevent the Germans from driving into the interior and then refused military commanders permission to make defensive preparations for fear of provoking the Germans. Using estimates more in tune with the tempo of the French army of 1940 than of the Wehrmacht, the Red Army calculated that it could hold the Germans close to the frontier and then counterattack.

Even more disastrously, Stalin's murderous purges of the Red Army had created a legacy of timidity, fear, and incompetence. The Soviet high command was incapable of understanding the German system of warfare or reacting to it. Any Soviet officer who dared to question the great leader's assumptions ran the risk of being accused of defeatism. In June 1941 the Soviet Union and its Red Army awaited the German invasion almost totally unprepared for what was to come.

The First Weeks of Barbarossa

At 0330 hours on June 22, 1941, German artillery from the Baltic Sea to the Black Sea opened fire; large numbers of Luftwaffe aircraft had already crossed the frontier to attack the Red Air Force. The Germans found Soviet aircraft parked wing tip to wing tip. By noon Soviet aircraft losses on the ground and in the air had reached 1,200. Field Marshal Erhard Milch, the Luftwaffe's chief logistics officer, recorded that the Soviets lost 1,000 aircraft on the 22nd, 800 on the 23rd, 557 on the 24th, 351 on the 25th, and 300 on the 26th. German air successes came at the expense of ill-trained and

German Invasion of USSR, June 22 – December 5, 1941

German advance
Encircled Soviet forces
Front line

ill-equipped Soviet aircrews, floundering in impossible tactical formations. Within the first week, the Luftwaffe had gained such a degree of air superiority that for the next five months it could support the army's advance with interdiction and unhindered close air support.

On the ground the Germans were equally successful. Stalin's obdurate refusal to allow his forces to make defensive preparations or to raise their alert status resulted in much of the Red Army's being surprised in indefensible positions. The warning that an invasion was imminent did not go out from Moscow until midnight. Thus few front-line units received any kind of warning. Across the Eastern Front the Red Army, staggered by the ferocity of the blow, struggled to adjust as communications collapsed, rear-area headquarters lost control, and chaos and confusion reigned.

German armor quickly clawed its way into the open; behind it German infantry pounded down the lanes of western Russia sometimes at the rate of thirty miles per day. Manstein's LXVI Panzer Corps, assigned to Army Group North and attacking from East Prussia into Lithuania, broke loose and in four days drove two hundred miles to seize the bridges across

The Germans used self-propelled guns, such as this Sturmgeschütz, to support infantry attacks. They manufactured about 10,500 throughout the war.

the Dvina River at Dvinsk. Manstein then urged commander of Fourth Panzer Group, Colonel General Erich Hoeppner, to push the other panzer corps forward, while LXVI Panzer Corps moved deeper into Latvia. Hoeppner was not sure, however, whether his mission was to sweep the Red Army out of the Baltic states or to guard the flank of the advance on Moscow. Leeb, commander of Army Group North, also remained in the dark as to his next objective but settled on a conservative broad-front advance that allowed Soviet forces to recover their balance and escape from Lithuania and Latvia.

By mid-July, Army Group North had advanced three-quarters of the way to Leningrad, but serious difficulties had emerged. While it had smashed Soviet resistance and driven the Red Army from the Baltic States, the advance of its mechanized units had split into two separate axes: the first to protect the advance on Moscow, the second to push toward Leningrad. Furthermore, spearhead units were at the end of long and tenuous lines of communication, while supporting infantry were far behind and food, fuel, and ammunition were in short supply at the front.

Army Group South ran into serious difficulties from the start. Part of the problem was the fact that many of its formations had fought in the Balkans and had not had time to recuperate. Moreover, the Soviets deployed a high percentage of their forces and best units in the Ukraine, and their commander largely ignored Stalin's order not to undertake preparatory measures. As a result, Soviet troops delayed First Panzer Group's advance.

The Germans did succeed in battering Soviet defenders back to Kiev, but Hitler ordered Rundstedt, the commander of Army Group South, not to attack the city. Not until early August did First Panzer Group break clear and encircle twenty Soviet divisions near Uman. That victory resulted in the capture of 103,054 prisoners and the destruction of three Russian armies, 858 artillery pieces, and 317 tanks.

If advances by Army Group North and Army Group South failed to achieve complete success, Army Group Center's Second and Third Panzer Groups won stunning victories. Here one of the worst sycophants in Stalin's military system, General Dmitrii G. Pavlov, played a major role in the collapse. After service in the Spanish Civil War, Pavlov had persuaded Stalin that mechanized warfare represented a dead end. Consequently, Stalin directed the Red Army to disband its armored formations in late 1939. Despite the fact that German panzer groups had achieved operational freedom at the end of the first day, Pavlov, echoing orders from the *Stavka* (Soviet high command), persisted in shoveling Soviet forces forward to deliver hopeless, pointless counterattacks. Communications between his units died as the Germans rushed forward. The Red Army stood in place, moved forward deeper into the encircling pincers, or simply collapsed. Second and Third Panzer groups swung in and met at Minsk on June 28 to complete the first encirclement. Within the larger Minsk encirclement, Fourth and Ninth armies completed a smaller one around Bialystok. Somewhere around 324,000 prisoners fell into German hands; along with the prisoners went heavy Soviet casualties with 3,300 tanks and 1,800 artillery pieces knocked out or captured.

In early July German successes led Halder to note in his diary:

> On the whole, one can already say that the task of destroying the mass of the Russian army in front of the Dvina and Dnieper has been fulfilled. I believe the assertion of a captured Russian general to be correct that we can calculate on meeting east of the Dvina and Dnieper only disjointed forces which alone do not possess the strength to hinder German operations substantially. It is, therefore, truly not claiming too much when I assert that the campaign against Russia has been won in fourteen days.

In early July Army Group Center's panzer groups renewed their drive. By late July the Germans had completed encirclement of Smolensk despite desperate and often successful Soviet efforts to break out. Waves of Soviet counterattacks from the outside attempted to loosen the German hold on the pocket. Only by August 5 did the Germans complete destruction of the Smolensk cauldron; another 300,000 prisoners fell into their hands, with 3,205 tanks and 3,000 artillery pieces destroyed or captured.

Difficulties

But the German advance came to a halt. At this point the extent of Nazi miscalculations and Halder's overoptimism emerged. Neither the Soviet state nor its military institutions had collapsed, and the logistic realities of

Russian distances exacted a high price on the invaders. Armored spearheads were at the end of over-extended lines of communication. Supplies of ammunition and fuel barely made it to the front, while virtually no rations arrived. Finally a series of savage Soviet counterattacks struck the German spearheads. Though these attacks were uncoordinated and often badly led, they imposed a heavy toll.

Exacerbating German problems was the fact that the Soviets mobilized far more troops than German intelligence had calculated. By July 1, as a result of mobilizing all reservists between the ages of twenty-three and thirty-seven, the Red Army possessed 5,300,000 additional soldiers. The reserve formations these men joined were desperately short of equipment, lacked experienced officers and noncommissioned officers, and were often ill-trained and ill-prepared. They represented, however, a numerically formidable force whose counterattacks fell on the German mechanized spearheads—units already exhausted by the advance, short of ammunition and fuel, and separated by wide distances from supporting infantry units.

The heaviest fighting occurred against Army Group Center. In mid-July, Second Panzer Group had seized the high ground around Yelnya, fifty miles east of Smolensk, as a jumping off point for the attack on Moscow. Eleven Soviet armies attacked across the entire front of Army Group Center, but the nastiest fighting occurred around Yelnya, where no less than six Soviet armies attacked in efforts to break the Smolensk encirclement. Despite considerable doubts as to whether Moscow would be the next objective, the Germans decided to hold the salient. Nevertheless, by early September the Soviets had forced the Germans to abandon Yelnya, inflicted over 40,000 casualties, and wrecked five infantry divisions. The Soviet attacks had an effect beyond the casualties inflicted; heavy, unrelenting attacks forced the Germans to expend virtually all ammunition and fuel that the overextended logistic system brought forward. Consequently the Germans failed to establish the supply dumps necessary for resumption of the advance; nor could they refit the panzer and motorized infantry divisions for the next stage of the campaign.

Despite prodigious marches (in some cases twenty to twenty-five miles per day), German infantry were still far to the rear, and armored and motorized infantry received the brunt of Soviet attacks. Fighting in August increased losses among those units that had borne the brunt of fighting and on whose shoulders further advances depended. Halder's diary entry for August 11 underscores the shifting mood within the German high command:

> The whole situation shows more and more clearly that we have underestimated the colossus of Russia—a Russia that had consciously prepared for the coming war with the whole unrestrained power of which a totalitarian state is capable. This conclusion is shown both on the organization as well as the economic levels, in the transportation, and above all in the infantry divisions. We have already identified 360. The divisions are admittedly not armed and equipped in our sense, and tactically they are badly led. But there

they are; and when we destroy a dozen the Russians simply establish another dozen.

Moreover, Stalin's hand remained firmly on the helm of what had become a ruthless, desperate effort to survive. In mid-July he reimposed the commissar system and turned his NKVD—the secret police—loose on "slackers and defeatists." Nevertheless, the defects that had caused the early defeats continued to permeate the system. The Soviet military style did not tolerate failure and rewarded initiative with savage punishment. In the north tens of thousands of Leningrad civilians dug anti-tank ditches and bunkers to protect the city, but local authorities refused to stockpile foodstuffs for a siege or to allow evacuation of the old or even the young. To do so smacked of defeatism.

Along with a darkening operational situation and supply difficulties, the Germans magnified their problems by engaging in debate over the campaign's next objectives. Halder and Brauchitsch (commander-in-chief of the army) argued for a resumption of the advance on Moscow as soon as sufficient supplies arrived. Hitler in turn pressed for an advance on Leningrad and the Ukraine; nevertheless it was not until the end of August that the Führer finally forced the military to accept his decision. Only at that point were German forces in a position to resume their advance. But as the Wehrmacht entered the final stages of the campaigning season, there were dangerous signs. By September 1, it had suffered 409,998 casualties out of an average strength of 3.78 million. Moreover, the eastern army was short 200,000 replacements; OKH had committed twenty-one out of the twenty-four divisions in its reserve and virtually nothing remained, while only 47 percent of the armored force remained "in commission."

In accord with Hitler's decision to advance on the Ukraine, Guderian's Second Panzer Group turned south to slice behind Soviet forces near Kiev. At the same time Kleist's First Panzer Group, which had advanced down the Dnieper bend, crossed that river and swung north. As the German drives gathered steam, Russian commanders desperately appealed to *Stavka* for permission to abandon Kiev. Stalin still refused to countenance withdrawals. On September 16, German spearheads met at Lokhvitsa in the eastern Ukraine, one hundred miles east of Kiev; the encirclement encompassed four Soviet armies. By month's end after final destruction of the pocket, the Germans claimed 665,000 prisoners, 824 tanks, 3,018 artillery pieces, and 418 antitank guns.

While Army Group South completed destruction of the Kiev pocket, Army Group North advanced to the gates of Leningrad and almost entirely encircled the city; only a tenuous lifeline remained across Lake Ladoga. The siege of Leningrad fell on a city that possessed a peacetime population and minimal supplies of food and fuel; in the first winter over one million of its citizens would die of starvation.

The Battle of Moscow

With successes in the north and south, Hitler concluded that Stalin's regime was about to collapse. He therefore authorized an advance on Moscow before the onset of winter. With Army Group Center launching the main effort, the objectives for Operation "Typhoon" were to destroy the rest of the Red Army and capture Moscow. Hitler and his army commanders expected that Typhoon's success would result in the long-awaited collapse of the communist regime.

Combined with the lateness of the season and the failure to make up for losses suffered over the summer, the supply situation should have caused the Germans great worry. On September 13, commander of Fourteenth Army reported: "at the moment [the supply system meets] current consumption only. The transport situation [has] not thus far allowed establishment of depots sufficiently large to enable the troops to receive what they need in accordance with the tactical situation. The army lives hand to mouth, especially as regards the fuel situation." In effect Wehrmacht units were not in a position to build up crucial supply dumps (including supplies required for winter weather) because the logistical system could barely supply sufficient ammunition and fuel to meet current demands.

In the last half of September, the Germans regrouped for Typhoon, the final push. Second and Third Panzer groups rejoined Army Group Center, along with much of Fourth Panzer Group. To unhinge the Soviets before the other panzer groups moved out, Guderian began Second Panzer Group's offensive two days early and advanced rapidly. Soon after, the other panzer groups also blasted their way into the open. *Stavka* appears to have believed that the lateness of the season precluded further German advances on Moscow. Stalin's demand that the Red Army defend every square inch of Soviet soil spread the defenders out, and there were few reserves to counterattack German breakthroughs. Not until October 5 did Stalin and his advisors recognize that major operations were occurring on the central front. Ironically the Soviets awoke to the danger only through a speech by Hitler in Berlin declaring that a great offensive had begun. Within one week the Germans had ripped open Soviet front lines and encircled two enormous groups of Soviet armies. West of Moscow, near Vyazma, they encircled six armies; near Bryansk, about 150 miles to the south, they encircled three more. When the battle was over, the Germans claimed another 600,000 prisoners. The German advances caused outbreaks of panic and looting in Moscow as the Red Army seemed on the brink of collapse. So great was the booty in material and prisoners that Goebbel's Propaganda Ministry announced that the Wehrmacht had won the war in the east.

At this point the weather broke. Autumn rains arrived to turn roads and countryside into seas of mud. The German advance halted in its tracks, while the *Stavka* desperately hurried forward reinforcements from the interior. The German situation became increasingly desperate. The farther forward the Wehrmacht advanced, the greater the strain on its logistics. The demands of Typhoon and subsequent advances consumed forward stockpiles as well as the ammunition and fuel that arrived through the supply system. That consumption in turn meant that the Germans possessed virtually no stockpiles of fuel, ammunition, or winter clothing.

Despite dropping temperatures, Halder, Brauchitsch, and Bock supported continuing the Moscow drive. German intelligence estimated that

Georgi Zhukov was the Soviet Union's premier expert in mass mechanized warfare. Victor at Moscow, Leningrad, Stalingrad, and Kursk and "liberator" of Berlin, he usually commanded over one million soldiers organized into more than a dozen armies.

the victories at Bryansk and Vyazma had exhausted Soviet reserves. Bock concluded that "the Germans could now afford to take risks." In early November, Halder expressed the pious hope that it would not snow until January so that the advance could continue. Colder weather did in fact allow the advance to begin again, but worsening conditions took a terrible toll on troops, still dressed in summer uniforms. As the weather turned cold, conditions reduced the German soldiers to desperate expedients such as lighting gasoline fires under the crankcases of tanks to warm engines sufficiently to turn over.

The Soviet Counterattack

As the Soviet situation deteriorated, Stalin rushed his most competent commander, Georgi Zhukov, to defend Moscow. Zhukov was as ruthless and effective a practitioner of the operational art as World War II produced; he was one of the few competent Soviet officers to survive the purges. Now in front of Moscow, he waged a delaying defense and for the first time effectively traded space for time. Meanwhile he built up a substantial reserve from reinforcements arriving to defend Moscow (some from as far away as Siberia). Zhukov believed that the Soviets could go over to the offensive once the Germans had exhausted themselves. Not surprisingly, German intelligence picked up little of this threatening situation. By December 4 the Germans had clawed their way to Moscow's outskirts, but they possessed neither the strength nor will to continue. That night temperatures fell to −25° Fahrenheit; one infantry regiment suffered 300 frostbite casualties. On December 6 the Soviets counterattacked.

The Germans had already lost the initiative elsewhere in the east. In the north, savage Soviet attacks kept open their fragile supply line across Lake Ladoga to Leningrad. In the south the Germans had taken Rostov at the end of November; however, Soviet counterattacks threatened to envelop the German spearheads. Rundstedt, the commander of Army Group South, ordered a withdrawal to the Mius River, but Hitler countermanded the retreat, fired the field marshal, and appointed Field Marshal Walther von Reichenau as his replacement. The new commander reaffirmed Rundstedt's retreat order and then suffered a heart attack. Events in the south presaged a crisis throughout the German high command and the collapse of Hitler's confidence in his generals.

As German forces teetered, Hitler made a crucial decision that sealed the Reich's fate. On December 7, 1941, the Japanese struck both British and Americans in the Pacific. Despite his own troubles in the east, Hitler decided to support his ally by declaring war on the United States. In so doing, he enabled Roosevelt to picture the Japanese attack on Pearl Harbor as part of a larger Axis plot; consequently American strategy, developed in consultation with the British in early 1941, identified the Third Reich as the greatest danger. Hitler's decision sprang from several factors: frustration at the desperate situation in the east, anger at Roosevelt's aggressive actions over summer 1941, and a contempt for the United States and its "mongrelized," racially mixed population. Hitler, as with most German leaders, ignored America's economic potential and encountered no objections to his decision. The army, desperately concerned over its situation in Russia, hardly cared about the consequences of America's entry; the navy on the other hand had actively pushed Hitler for a declaration of war on the United States throughout summer 1941 because such a declaration would increase operational possibilities for its U-boats. The Luftwaffe expressed no opinion.

Soviet forces that counterattacked the Germans in front of Moscow on December 6 were well prepared for the harsh conditions of winter. Nevertheless, Zhukov recommended limited objectives for the offensive: namely the destruction of one or two German armies lying in front of Moscow. Stalin, however, ordered a general offensive to destroy German forces across the whole breadth of the Eastern Front. For a period in December and January it appeared that Stalin was right. The headquarters war diary of one German unit recorded the desperate conditions of its troops:

> Discipline is breaking down. More and more soldiers are heading west on foot without weapons, leading a calf on a rope or pulling a sled loaded with potatoes. The road is under constant air attack. Those killed by the bombs are no longer being buried. All the hangers on (cargo troops, Luftwaffe, supply trains) are pouring to the rear in full flight. Without rations, fleeing irrationally, they are

pushing back. Vehicle crews that do not want to wait out the traffic jams in the open are drifting off the roads and into the villages. Ice, inclines, and bridges create horrendous blockages.

The desperate situation resulted in a crisis between Hitler and his generals, with the latter arguing for sweeping withdrawals to more defensible positions. Hitler believed that any retreats could turn into a rout that would repeat the fate of Napoleon's Grand Army in 1812. The Führer, therefore, demanded the army stand firm. Those who ordered retreats found themselves relieved from command or court-martialed. Brauchitsch (commander-in-chief of the army), Bock (commander of Army Group Center), Leeb (commander of Army Group North), Rundstedt (commander of Army Group South), Hoeppner (commander of Fourth Panzer Group), and Guderian (commander of Second Panzer Group) all found themselves summarily relieved. Hitler named himself commander-in-chief of the army. From this point, the German military functioned with the OKH in charge of the east, the OKW in charge of the Mediterranean and west, the Luftwaffe high command in charge of the air war, and the naval high command in charge of the U-boat war. Nowhere except in Hitler's mind did the threads of German strategy come together.

Halder's diary suggests the difficulties that German troops encountered on the Eastern Front:

> 25 December: A very bad day . . . ; 27 December: desperate attempts to check the enemy east of Sukhinichi . . . ; 29 December: *Very bad day!* . . . ; 31 December: *Again an arduous day* . . . ; 3 January: Another dramatic scene with the Führer, who calls in question the generals' courage to make hard decision . . . ; 8 January: *Very grave day.*

By early January Zhukov had driven back both flanks of Army Group Center, but the Germans hung on desperately. In retrospect, Hitler's demand to stand fast saved the Wehrmacht from collapse. The Soviets on their part attempted too much, and their advance flowed into areas possessing little operational or strategic significance. At times their forces cut lines of communication on which the German front depended, but the Germans held the crucial roads and supply centers. Slowly they recovered their equilibrium, while the Red Army, bled white from the fighting of the summer of 1941, found it difficult to maintain momentum. Unlike the German advances over the summer and fall, the Soviet winter offensive failed to gain any significant operational success except to batter the Germans back from Moscow. Yet when the winter was over, the Germans had suffered losses from which their army never recovered. By mid-March the fighting died down as the spring thaw arrived; the two armies began preparations for the summer battles of 1942.

☆   ☆   ☆   ☆

The fall of France in 1940 had not translated into an immediate strategic success for the Germans. The British had possessed an effective and competent air defense system, while the Wehrmacht had possessed neither doctrine, nor training, nor the understanding to make an amphibious assault on the British Isles. Sea Lion was stillborn from its conception. Britain's successful defense raised a number of intractable problems the Germans were incapable of addressing, problems that Italian incompetence only exacerbated. Forced by Italian defeats to move in strength into the Balkans and to support Libya, the Germans repaired the damage for the short run. But since they had little interest in the area, they failed to turn British defeats into a strategic rout.

1941 was the crucial year on which the fate of the world turned. In this year the Germans made a number of crucial mistakes. They failed to mobilize the European continent for the long haul. Then they embarked on an ill-prepared and poorly conceived crusade against the Soviet Union, one in which their operational and tactical excellence could not redress the political and strategic mistakes inherent in their approach to war against the Soviets. Finally, in desperation because of difficulties in the east, they declared war on the United States. Even more quickly than they had in World War I, the Germans had turned the war into a conflict in which everyone was against the Reich.

For Germany's opponents in 1941 the problem was quite different. For them it was a matter of hanging on until their superior resources changed the course of the war. The enormous logistical shortcomings displayed by the Wehrmacht in its invasion of Russia underlined German vulnerabilities. While the Germans could fight battles extraordinarily well, they were less capable of fighting a war of prolonged duration. Unfortunately for them, the outcome of the war ultimately would rest on the capacity to mobilize and project military power over an extended period and over extreme distances. With Nazi expansion halted, the Allies at last possessed the reason, time, and energy to mobilize fully their popular and economic resources. The war that now emerged would increasingly become a clash of economic strength, in which the Allied powers enjoyed significant advantages.

SUGGESTED READINGS

Barnett, Correlli. *The Desert Generals* (Bloomington: Indiana University Press, 1982).

Bartov, Omer. *Hitler's Army: Soldiers, Nazis, and War in the Third Reich* (New York: Oxford University Press, 1991).

Erickson, John. *The Road to Stalingrad* (New York: Harper & Row, 1975).

Fugate, Bryan. *Operation Barbarossa* (Novato, Calif.: Presidio Press, 1984).

Howard, Michael E. *The Mediterranean Strategy in the Second World War* (New York: Praeger, 1968).

Irving, David. *The Trail of the Fox* (New York: E. P. Dutton, 1977).

Knox, MacGregor. *Mussolini Unleashed, 1939–1941: Politics and Strategy in Fascist Italy's Last War* (Cambridge: Cambridge University Press, 1982).

von Manstein, Erich. *Lost Victories*, ed. and trans. by Anthony G. Powell (Chicago: H. Regnery, 1958).

Millett, Allan, and Williamson Murray. *Military Effectiveness*, vol. 3 (London: Allen and Unwin, 1988).

Murray, Williamson. *Luftwaffe* (Baltimore: Nautical and Aviation Press, 1985).

Overy, R. J. *The Air War, 1939–1945* (New York: Stein and Day, 1980).

Pogue, Forrest. *George C. Marshall* (New York: Viking Press, 1963–1987), 4 Vols.

Taylor, Telford. *The Breaking Wave: The Second World War in the Summer of 1940* (New York: Simon and Schuster, 1967).

Ziemke, Earl F., and Magna E. Bauer. *Moscow to Stalingrad: Decision in the East* (Washington: Office of the Chief of Military History, 1987).

15

THE ATLANTIC AND THE PACIFIC:
PRODUCING AND PROJECTING
MILITARY POWER

The Pacific War, 1941–1942

Mobilizing and Projecting
Military Power

The European War at Sea,
1939–1945

The Air War

With the entry of the United States and the Soviet Union, the war became a conflict of global dimensions and unprecedented scale. The process of defeating the Axis involved not only translating large populations and economic resources into military means and combining complex technologies into effective production of weapons but also—particularly for the Americans and British protecting long and vulnerable lines of communication and projecting military power across great oceans. Throughout 1941 and 1942 German U-boats threatened the entire Allied war effort. With forces scattered across the face of the earth, the Allies halted the Japanese, mobilized the resources to fight massive battles, overcame the U-boat threat, and finally began projecting the military power on which victory rested. As the battle of the Atlantic escalated, the British, later joined by the Americans, waged a great air offensive against the Reich. Until the means for a successful assault on Fortress Europe became available, strategic bombing remained the primary means for the United States and Britain to strike Germany.

The naval wars in the Atlantic and Pacific differed greatly. Except for a few unsuccessful raids by surface ships, the battles in the Atlantic revolved around attacks by or attacks on German submarines. In the Pacific numerous large engagements of surface ships, supported by aircraft, occurred. Early in the war, however, it became apparent that the Pacific required a balance of land, air, and sea forces; geography dictated a solution different from that in the Atlantic. Though accepting the Allied strategy of "Germany first," the Americans found themselves shifting more and more resources into the Pacific, and with the attacks on Guadalcanal and New Guinea, they made the first tentative steps in what would become a massive assault across the Pacific. Nonetheless, many dark days remained before the Allies could translate their manpower and industrial advantages into sufficient military power to push the Japanese back in the Pacific and assault Fortress Europe.

The Pacific War, 1941–1942

Origins of the Pacific War

The origins of the Pacific war lay in the deeply rooted expansionist desires of Japan. When Western traders first reached the Home Islands in the mid-sixteenth century, the Japanese proved receptive to European ideas and permitted trade to occur for much of the next century. Beginning in the mid-seventeenth century and continuing for the next two centuries, however, they drove most foreigners out and isolated themselves from the West. But by the mid-nineteenth century they could no longer maintain their isolation and undertook a remarkable transformation to remake Japan. Using the British as models for their navy and the Prussians for their army, they built up effective and efficient military institutions, which defeated the Chinese in 1895 and tsarist Russia in 1905. Those wars gave the Japanese hegemony over Korea, which they annexed in 1910.

A lack of natural resources constrained the Japanese economy as it modernized and expanded, and imports became dependent upon the foreign exchange that exports earned. Until 1929 trade and industry prospered due to the upswing in the world economy. But the burden of industrialization rested on the back of Japanese peasants, and that burden was heavy, especially considering the poverty of the countryside. In 1929, when the world market collapsed and the Great Depression began, all the industrial nations, especially Japan, were hit hard. The reaction of an already xenophobic and nationalistic elite was extreme. The army's officer corps, which drew many officers from the countryside, found the idea that Japan must conquer larger markets most attractive.

Since the Russo-Japanese War, nationalists had considered China an obvious area for Japanese expansion. In 1931, the Japanese army in Korea took matters into its own hands and seized Manchuria, which it then renamed Manchukuo. The League of Nations condemned the action, as did the United States, but no one undertook serious reprisal. For the next six years intermittent military action and political intrigue continued in north China. An army memo explained: "The natural resources of Manchuria are far exceeded by those in North China. There are limitless deposits of iron

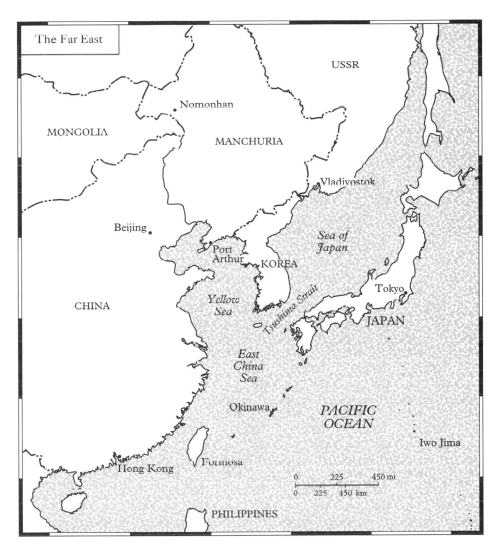

The Far East

USSR

MONGOLIA

Nomonhan

MANCHURIA

Vladivostok

Beijing

Port Arthur

KOREA

Sea of Japan

CHINA

Yellow Sea

Tsushima Strait

Tokyo

JAPAN

East China Sea

PACIFIC OCEAN

Okinawa

Iwo Jima

Hong Kong

Formosa

0   225   450 mi

0   225   450 km

PHILIPPINES

and coal in Shansi province. If we are careless, these resources will end up in English or American hands."*

In summer 1937, the army manufactured an incident at the Marco Polo bridge (near Beijing) between Manchuria and China and initiated major military operations against the Chinese. The home government had no advance warning but approved the operation due to fear of radical nationalists. Thus without addressing the political or strategic ramifications, the Japanese engaged in a full-scale yet undeclared war in northern China. The Chinese factions could not withstand ruthless Japanese assaults, but the

---

*Ienaga Saburo, *The Pacific War, World War II and the Japanese, 1931-1945* (New York: Pantheon Books, 1978), p. 68.

A Japanese infantry squad advances in China. Japanese soldiers distinguished themselves by their stamina, aggressiveness, and obedience. A British field marshal said, "We talk a lot about fighting to the last man and the last round, but only the Japanese soldier actually does it."

Japanese never possessed the strength to occupy all of China. While they occupied major ports and cities along the coast, much of the countryside remained beyond their control. Chinese guerrillas, especially Mao Zedong's Communists, made life miserable for the occupiers.

As if the "China incident"—the Japanese euphemism for their war against China—were not enough, the Japanese army courted several direct confrontations with the Red Army in Manchuria. In summer 1939 the Japanese seized a disputed area in western Manchuria; in late August the Red Army, under the future marshal Zhukov, counterattacked and destroyed a reinforced Japanese division at Nomonhan. Not surprisingly, after that defeat the Japanese army exhibited less interest in fighting the Soviet Union—at least until it had dealt with its China problem.

Americans watched Japanese behavior in China with growing outrage, but even the direct attack by Japanese aircraft on a clearly marked U.S. gunboat in China in December 1937 failed to elicit any American commitment to the Chinese. Moreover, American defense expenditures in Asia remained minimal: the Philippines received little funding, and none of the Pacific islands, on which a naval war depended, received sufficient resources from Congress to defend themselves.

The collapse of the Western Powers in spring 1940 turned Japanese attention toward the colonial empires of Southeast Asia. In June 1940 their foreign minister advocated inclusion of portions of Southeast Asia in a "New

Order in East Asia." The Japanese subsequently pressured the French to permit the stationing of troops in northern Indochina, and in July 1941 they occupied southern Indochina. This move placed them in a position to advance against British and Dutch colonial possessions in Southeast Asia and the Southwest Pacific. Viewing the Japanese move southward as a threat to the Philippines, the Americans finally reacted by embargoing exports to Japan, including oil, and by freezing Japanese assets in the United States. Oil was the essential element in the embargo, for without oil the Japanese economy and military machine would collapse. In October General Tojo Hideki became premier and one month later called for the elimination of British and American influence from the Orient.

Strategy and Plans

American strategy for a war in the Pacific changed dramatically in the inter-war period. Planning initially rested on the "Orange" plan, which the U.S. military developed before World War I as one of the "color" plans (black for Germany, red for Great Britain, green for Mexico, orange for Japan). The "Orange" plan resurfaced after 1918 and called for an "offensive war primarily naval in character" in the Pacific. It emphasized a naval drive through the central Pacific and a great clash of battle fleets. Throughout the 1920s and 1930s, students and faculty at the Naval War College tested and refined aspects of the American plan for the Pacific. In the late 1930s, as international tensions increased, the Americans began modifying these war plans. Designated "Rainbow" to distinguish them from the "color" plans, the new plans faced the possibility of the United States' having to meet the combined threat of Germany, Italy, and Japan. At a meeting of British and American staffs in January 1941, the future allies agreed that the main effort had to be made in the Atlantic, not in the Pacific, and that Germany and Italy had to be defeated first, not Japan. The new plan, "Rainbow 5," provided the main outline of strategy for World War II, but it changed Pacific strategy at the onset of a war from offensive to defensive.

American strategy changed because the combination of German, Japanese, and Italian power confronted the United States with significant threats from both east and west. President Franklin Roosevelt seems to have recognized the danger far earlier than most other Americans including his advisors. The problem then for him was how to push the buildup of U.S. forces to meet the threat without occasioning a political revolt from a population still drunk on isolationism. The fall of France made the danger greater, exacerbating American vulnerabilities in both the Atlantic and Pac-ific. In summer 1940 the president took the extraordinarily courageous dec-ision in an election year to support Britain; but that support could only re-tard the American buildup in the Pacific. Moreover, Roosevelt also 16determined that the United States would pursue a Germany-first strategy, given that nation's potential—a decision he maintained even after war began. But the problem for American planners lay in the fact that at least until 1943, when American industry would finally be producing vast quantities of weapons, equipment, and munitions, they would possess scant military means to deal with immensely complex logistic demands, not to mention opponents far better prepared to fight in the immediate future.

Defense of the Pacific proved difficult. The United States refused to send naval forces to help defend Singapore, which the British viewed as the "Gibraltar" of the Far East. With Japanese-held islands lying across the central Pacific, the Philippines seemed surrounded. Though planners anticipated problems maintaining contact with the Philippines, the United States began pouring units and resources into the islands. After the arrival of additional air and ground units, American strategists hoped to continue fleet operations from Manila and placed great faith in the buildup of heavy bombers in the Philippines both for their deterrent as well as their combat value. Nevertheless, planners did not expect the outbreak of war before spring 1942 and did not anticipate a swing in the balance in the Pacific toward the United States until 1943 when ships authorized in the 1938 building program came into service. Despite heightened tensions and extensive preparations, American commanders refused to believe that the Japanese would actually launch a surprise attack against the United States, particularly against the Pacific fleet at Pearl Harbor in the Hawaiian Islands.

In Japan the army and navy had developed substantially different strategic visions. The army looked toward Asia for expansion; as the dominant service, it had acquired a peculiarly parochial viewpoint, largely ignorant of the outside world. The Imperial navy, however, looked to Southeast Asia; it had acquired a better appreciation for Japan's vulnerability and for the most part urged greater caution in national strategy. Tied down in China, with major commitments in Manchuria on the Soviet frontier, the army could put only a small portion of its forces into the drive that overwhelmed the Western colonial empires in Asia. The navy would have to carry the bulk of the burden.

For decades the Japanese navy had planned for a war in the Pacific against the United States. Even before World War I, the Japanese planned on seizing control of the Philippines and Guam and intercepting and destroying the U.S. fleet when it crossed the Pacific and attempted to protect American possessions. Expectations of a decisive naval battle required highly proficient forces, and the Imperial navy became one of the best peacetime navies in history. It trained long and hard under the most strenuous of conditions; its pilots were outstanding. No other navy was as well-trained to fight at night. As for its technological capabilities, the "long-lance" torpedo was by far the best in the world, while its super battleships, *Yamato* and *Musashi*, were truly awesome representatives of a dying age. Finally, its conception and preparation for carrier warfare fully equalled that of the U.S. Navy, and its aircraft and pilots were initially superior to their American counterparts.

In late 1941 the army and navy established the broad outlines of Japanese war plans. They would attack Malaya and the Philippines simultaneously, seize the Dutch East Indies, and then launch a major offensive into Burma. After capturing Wake and Guam and thereby cutting America's lines of communication across the Pacific, they would establish a defensive perimeter extending west to Burma, east through the Dutch East Indies and

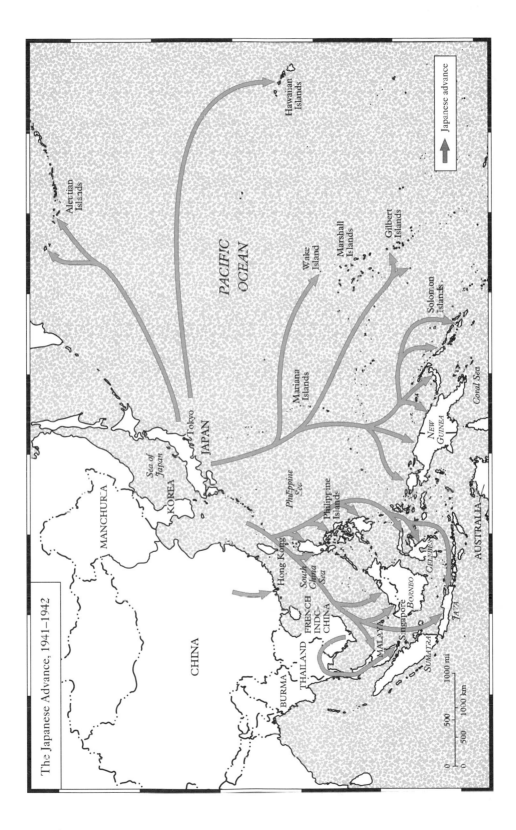

The Japanese Advance, 1941–1942

Japanese advance

Aleutian Islands

Hawaiian Islands

PACIFIC OCEAN

Wake Island

Marshall Islands

Gilbert Islands

Mariana Islands

Solomon Islands

MANCHURIA

KOREA

Sea of Japan

JAPAN

Tokyo

CHINA

Philippine Sea

Philippine Islands

NEW GUINEA

Coral Sea

Hong Kong

South China Sea

BURMA

THAILAND

FRENCH INDO-CHINA

MALAYA

Singapore

SUMATRA

BORNEO

CELEBES

JAVA

AUSTRALIA

500   1000 mi
0
500   1000 km

New Guinea to the Gilbert Islands, and north to Wake and the Kurile Islands. The Japanese initially hoped to lure the U.S. fleet into the central Pacific where submarines and aircraft could reduce its strength; their main fleet would administer the coup de grâce in the seas near Japan. But the commander of the Japanese fleet, Admiral Yamamoto Isoroku, unveiled a daring operational plan; his carriers would cross the northern Pacific and attack the American fleet at Pearl Harbor. Yamamoto hoped that the strike at Pearl Harbor would destroy or immobilize the American fleet and allow time for his forces to seize the resources that Japan's war economy needed and to construct an island barrier against an American counterattack. Then, he assumed, the United States would sue for peace, as tsarist Russia had done in 1905. Nevertheless, Yamamoto had had extensive exposure to America, including a year at Harvard University, and recognized the dangers that Japan would run in fighting a long war with the United States.

American intelligence picked up much of the Japanese movement in the weeks before war; historians have pointed to intercepts and other signals that suggested Pearl Harbor as a possible target. As in Europe, decrypts of Japanese signals (in the Pacific called "Magic") would play a crucial role in the eventual Allied victory. But no intercepts or other intelligence could overcome American perceptions of the Japanese as having an inferior military; the subsequent disaster at Pearl Harbor resulted more from this attitude than from poor or mishandled intelligence.

The Japanese Triumphant

In the morning hours of Sunday, December 7, 1941, American peacetime assumptions collapsed. The Japanese carriers had crossed the northern Pacific unobserved. From a point north of the Hawaiian Islands, they launched two waves of aircraft. The attackers reached Pearl Harbor at 0800 hours to discover the American battle fleet at anchor and the defenses at a minimal level of readiness. Japanese torpedoes and bombs found inviting targets, while their fighters destroyed the American aircraft parked wing tip to wing tip on Hickam Field. U.S. opposition was light, and Japanese losses were minimal. By the time it was over, the battleship *Arizona* had blown up; *Oklahoma* had capsized; *West Virginia* and *California* lay buried in mud; and *Nevada* got underway but had to be beached because of extensive damage. Japanese bombs damaged the *Pennsylvania* in dry dock and exploded destroyers *Cassin* and *Downes*. American casualties totaled 2,403 dead and more than 1,000 wounded.

Despite its results, the attack on Pearl Harbor proved to be an operational failure and strategic disaster for the Japanese. On the strategic level, the "sneak" attack united American support to enter the war. On the operational level, the Japanese sank an obsolete battle fleet but failed to destroy either fleet repair facilities or the gigantic fuel reserves, over one million tons. That fuel supply supported U.S. fleet movements for most of 1942; had the Japanese destroyed it, the Americans would have been forced to operate from the West Coast for the next year. Furthermore, American carriers were not in the harbor at the time of attack and thus escaped to fight another day.

Worse disasters soon befell the Allies; Japanese air attacks in the Philippines caught the Far Eastern Air Force deployed in peacetime fashion on Clark airfield. American air strength in the Philippines went up in smoke, even though eight hours had passed since Pearl Harbor. Two days later Japanese aircraft operating from southern Indochina caught and sank the British battleship *Prince of Wales* and battle cruiser *Repulse*. That success, even more than the attack on the American battle fleet, underlined the vulnerability of ships to air attack; the day of the battleship was over. Coupled with losses at Pearl Harbor, the loss of two British capital ships shifted the balance of naval power in the Pacific decidedly in favor of the Japanese.

Another disaster occurred in Malaya where nearly 200,000 British and Commonwealth troops defended the peninsula and Singapore. Despite nearly a two-to-one superiority, the British found the enemy skillful at infiltration and exploitation; the Japanese had little experience in jungle fighting but their tactical skills were outstanding. Under command of General Yamashita Tomoyuki, they outflanked the British from one position to another; by early February they had reached Singapore. On February 15, 1942, barely two months after Japanese landings, Lieutenant General A. E. Percival surrendered the city and its garrison in one of the most humiliating defeats ever suffered by British arms. That defeat reflected the gross overconfidence of British leaders and their failure to prepare their troops to fight in the jungle. It also demonstrated superb leadership and performance by the Japanese.

In the Philippines, American defensive efforts were no more successful, although they lasted longer. When General Douglas MacArthur assumed command of Philippine defenses, he convinced Washington that he could do more than simply defend Manila Bay. With additional reinforcements and supplies, he planned on meeting the invaders on the beaches and driving them into the sea. Shortly after the attack on Pearl Harbor, the Japanese made initial landings on the northern and southern tips of the main island of Luzon; then on December 22 they made their main landings in Lingayen Gulf about 125 miles north of Manila. They easily drove the defenders back, and on December 24, MacArthur ordered his forces to withdraw to the Bataan Peninsula. Abandoning much of their ammunition, equipment, and rations, which had been stockpiled forward near the beaches, the combined American and Philippine force established a twenty-mile defensive line on the northern part of the peninsula, while MacArthur's headquarters and the Philippine government moved to the island of Corregidor in Manila Bay.

By the time MacArthur's forces reached Bataan, they were on half rations; within a few weeks they were receiving less than one thousand calories per day. This inadequate diet largely resulted from MacArthur's faulty prewar strategy that had attempted to defend all of Luzon. By April, Bataan was finished, and in early May, Corregidor surrendered. In the meantime Roosevelt, realizing that he would have a public relations disaster on his

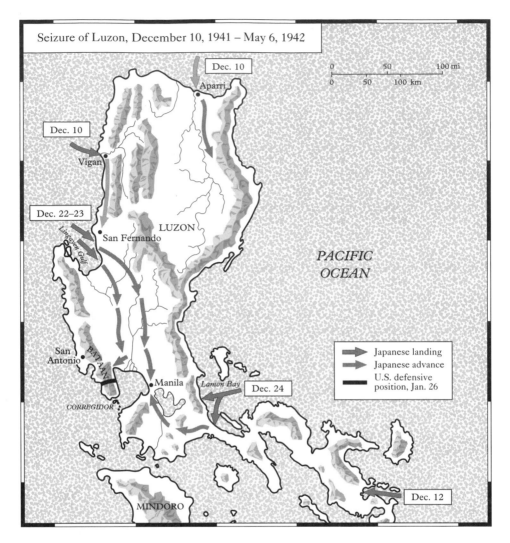

Seizure of Luzon, December 10, 1941 – May 6, 1942

hands if MacArthur fell into Japanese hands, ordered the general to relinquish command to Lieutenant General Jonathan M. Wainwright and move to Australia. There MacArthur assumed command of American and Australian forces in the Southwest Pacific.

Meanwhile, as Japanese forces reduced the Americans in Bataan, they continued their rampage in Southeast Asia and the Southwest Pacific. On January 21 they attacked Borneo with its rich oil resources. At the end of February they destroyed Allied naval forces in the East Indies (present-day Indonesia) in the battle of the Java Sea. On March 1 the Japanese landed successfully on Java, and the collapse of the Dutch colonial empire followed shortly thereafter. The Imperial navy moved at will through the waters in the Southwest Pacific. In late March, Japanese carriers struck into the Indian Ocean; in a one-week operation their forces chased the Royal Navy to Madagascar, while sinking a light carrier and two heavy cruisers.

The Japanese Checked

In spring 1942, the Japanese decided not to halt and erect a defensive perimeter, as their previous strategy suggested, but to use their fleet more aggressively and extend control over the Pacific. To this end they planned two major operations: against Australian forces in New Guinea near Port Moresby and against Midway (1,300 miles northwest of Honolulu) with the hope of destroying the remainder of the American fleet. Both Japanese operations aimed to extend the defense ring of island bases around their conquests and the Home Islands. American fleet intelligence from Magic, however, warned Admiral Chester W. Nimitz, Commander-in-Chief, Pacific (CINCPAC) and allowed him to deploy his weaker American forces against both threats.

To meet the strike against Port Moresby, Nimitz concentrated carriers *Lexington* and *Yorktown* in the Coral Sea off the eastern tip of New Guinea against an enemy force of two fleet carriers and one light carrier. The subsequent battle of the Coral Sea on May 4–8, 1942, was a new type of sea battle, waged by exchanges of air strikes, without the opposing surface ships ever making direct contact. American air attacks sank light carrier *Shoho* and damaged the larger *Shokaku*; even more significantly the air battles severely weakened the air components of both Japanese carriers so that neither would be available for operations in the immediate future. Japanese air attacks lightly damaged the American carriers; both, however, continued launching and recovering aircraft. But, a series of massive internal explosions wracked the *Lexington*. The ship's position was soon hopeless, and it had to be sunk by escorts. With the *Yorktown* also damaged, American losses in the Coral Sea were heavier, but the Japanese called off the amphibious attack on Port Moresby.

Approximately three weeks earlier, the Americans had launched an audacious raid against the Japanese Home Islands by flying B-25 bombers off the carrier *Hornet*. The operation was the brainchild of navy and army planners; it soon received the support of General Henry H. "Hap" Arnold, chief of army air forces. A relatively junior air reserve officer, Lieutenant Colonel James H. Doolittle, who had a reputation as one of the great flyers in the interwar period, put the force together. The navy provided the *Hornet*, and by the end of April 1942 the force was at sea ready to launch its aircraft. The plan was to launch the bombers close enough to the Home Islands so that the B-25s could reach China and reinforce the Chinese air force. However, the task force ran into a Japanese picket line of fishing vessels. Fearing compromise, the attackers launched early. Although they surprised the Japanese, they did not have the range to reach friendly airfields, and most crashed in China. The damage caused by Doolittle's bombers was minimal; however, an outraged and humiliated Japanese high command advanced the date for the Midway operation and set in motion the crucial confrontation in the Pacific war.

The Japanese designed an excessively complex plan to lure the American fleet to its destruction and to seize Midway by amphibious assault. No less than six different divisions of the Imperial fleet had separate responsibilities. In a diversionary operation, a strike force of two light carriers would attack American bases in Alaska and occupy two islands in the Aleutian chain, Attu and Kiska. Four battleships would provide a screening force to cover that raid. On the next day, the main carriers under Admiral Nagumo Chuichi would pound Midway, while behind them Admiral Yamamoto with superbattleships *Musashi* and *Yamato* would move up to destroy the American fleet, if it intervened. Finally another fleet moving from the southwest with two battleships, six heavy cruisers, and a small aircraft carrier would protect amphibious forces on their way to Midway.

The Japanese plan, even given its excessive complexity, might have worked. Intelligence from Magic, however, gave the game away even before the enemy left port. As a result, the feint at Alaska failed to fool Nimitz; the Midway garrison received extensive reinforcements of air and ground forces; and the American fleet, including the carriers *Yorktown*, *Hornet*, and *Enterprise*, was at sea ready to intercept the Japanese carrier force. The American battleships remained in San Francisco because they were not fast enough to keep up with the carriers—an indication of how rapidly the battleship had declined in American naval eyes. The *Yorktown*'s presence underlines the importance of Magic; the carrier returned to Pearl at full speed from the Coral Sea. Initial estimates were that it would take ninety days to repair damage it had suffered in battle; however, given the emergency, the *Yorktown* steamed out of Pearl Harbor forty-eight hours later after desperate emergency repairs.

The Japanese suspected nothing about these preparations. For the first time in the Pacific, luck turned against them. On June 4, their carriers and supporting vessels arrived north of Midway; all of the scouting aircraft took off on time except for the aircraft scheduled to search the sector where the American fleet lay waiting. Nagumo launched half of his aircraft for an attack on Midway, while the other half, armed with torpedoes and armor piercing bombs, remained on the carrier decks. Two hours later with no hostile reports from search aircraft, he ordered these weapons changed to high-explosive bombs to execute a second strike on Midway. As rearming proceeded, the search aircraft suddenly reported American fleet units. Additional moments passed until the aircraft reported one American carrier; with this warning, Nagumo decided to rearm the aircraft on the decks with the weapons needed to strike the American fleet. Meanwhile, heavy air attacks from Midway-based aircraft exacerbated Japanese problems. The attacks did no damage, but they made the task of rearming more difficult, as Japanese ships maneuvered at full speed.

Here again luck intervened. The first American carrier aircraft to find the Japanese were torpedo bombers, first from the *Hornet*, then from the *Enterprise* and *Yorktown*. Japanese fighters and antiaircraft guns slaughtered the American aircraft, which failed to achieve any hits; but low-flying torpedo bombers pulled Japanese fighters down to sea level. Shortly after the last torpedo bomber had gone in and just as the Japanese carriers turned into the wind to launch aircraft, the dive bombers from *Yorktown* and *Enterprise* arrived overhead. With no interference, they attacked the Japanese carriers, whose decks remained full of armed and fueled aircraft, high-explosive bombs, and ammunition for land targets (the munition handlers had not yet returned the downloaded weapons to the magazines). In a remarkably brief period they wrecked three carriers (*Akagi*, *Kaga*, and *Soryu*). Shielded by a rain squall, the last carrier, *Hiryu*, escaped damage for the moment and then launched aircraft against *Yorktown*, achieving a measure of revenge; three bombs and two torpedoes from the *Hiryu*'s aircraft severely damaged the American carrier and eventually contributed to its loss. Later that afternoon, pilots from the three U.S. carriers (those from the *Yorktown* were flying off other carriers) found the *Hiryu* and left it sinking as well. In early evening, the U.S. fleet pulled off to the east to avoid a night surface engagement.

Midway was a major success for the U.S. Navy; American aircraft had destroyed four Japanese carriers. Even more important the Japanese lost most of their flight crews—the best trained in the world—in the flaming wreckage. The threat to Midway was gone, and initiative in the Pacific now swung tentatively to the Americans.

The Counteroffensive

By this point, command relations in the Pacific had solidified. The size of the theater—the entire expanse of the Pacific and Indian oceans—made some division inevitable. But interservice as well as political realities resulted in the creation of two distinct American efforts. There was some irony in this state of affairs, because in Europe the Americans were preaching to their British allies about the need for a single, united command against the Germans. In the Pacific, however, they waged anything but a unified effort.

The division of responsibility resulted as much from personalities as from strategic necessity. MacArthur's escape from Bataan presented

After World War II Douglas MacArthur complained in a somewhat self-serving fashion, "[F]ailure to unify the command in the Pacific . . . resulted in divided effort, the waste, diffusion, and duplication of force, and the consequent extension of the war with added casualties and cost."

Roosevelt with a difficult decision. To bring him back to America would have caused considerable pressure to place him in a high military position; if left in a united Pacific command, his date of rank made him superior to any American officer, a state of affairs unacceptable to the navy, particularly since the Pacific was an ocean and MacArthur was a soldier. As a compromise, the Joint Chiefs of Staff (JCS) divided the Pacific in half and gave MacArthur command of the Southwest Pacific and Admiral Nimitz the Central Pacific. The two separate commands would cooperate as necessary.

Immediately after Midway, MacArthur proposed to attack the main Japanese base at Rabaul on New Britain; to achieve that goal, he argued that he needed two carriers and an amphibious division (marines). This self-seeking proposal met a self-seeking response. Admiral Ernest King, the chief of naval operations, proposed that Nimitz take command of all MacArthur's ships and aircraft; the army would merely provide forces to garrison islands that the navy and marines captured. After a week of acrimonious debate, the JCS hammered out a compromise that it published in a directive on July 2, 1942. The decision represented a less risky approach and reflected the real balance of American and Japanese forces in the Pacific. An advance on Rabaul would take place, but in three stages. The first included a landing in the southern Solomons on the islands of Guadalcanal and Tulagi (a tiny island twenty miles off the northern coast of Guadalcanal). Seizing them would protect communications to Australia. Stage two would involve an advance along the northeast coast of New Guinea and culminate in the third stage, a direct assault on Rabaul.

The Tulagi-Guadalcanal operation in August 1942 opened the American counteroffensive. When marines landed at Red Beach on Guadalcanal on August 7, they encountered little resistance because Japanese construction crews had no protecting troops. Outside of the initial landings and seizure of the airfield, nothing else went right. The lack of beach personnel and suitable landing craft resulted in supplies being unloaded on the beach haphazardly; congestion also prevented some landing craft from discharging their cargo. Then the commander of the naval task force, Vice Admiral Frank J. Fletcher, pulled his carriers out of the area almost immediately after the landing.

Disaster followed. An Allied force of heavy cruisers and destroyers under command of Rear Admiral V. A. Crutchley of the Royal Navy guarded the landings. As Fletcher's carriers exited the area, an Australian patrol aircraft spotted Japanese warships heading south from Rabaul into "The Slot" which was formed by the parallel lines of islands making up the Solomons. However, the pilot failed to report his sighting immediately. Moreover, he described the enemy force as three cruisers, three destroyers, and two sea plane tenders. In fact it consisted of five heavy cruisers, two light cruisers, and a destroyer, all of which were heading at full speed towards Guadalcanal. The report did not get to Allied fleet commanders until 1700 hours, even though the initial sighting had occurred at 1030.

Five Allied heavy cruisers and five destroyers protected the anchorage near Guadalcanal where the merchant ships were still unloading sup-

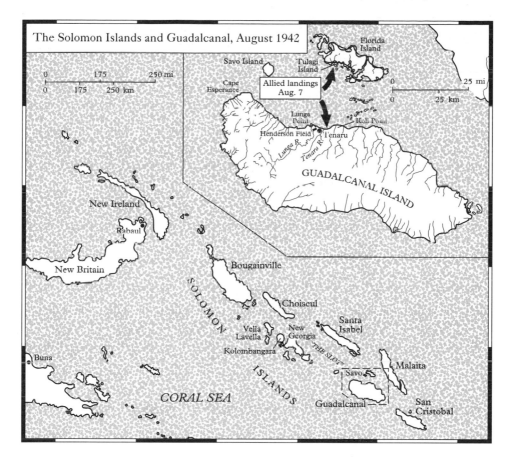

The Solomon Islands and Guadalcanal, August 1942

plies. Around 0130 hours, the attackers struck. None of the Allied vessels spotted the Japanese until it was too late. Though one lucky American shot caused minor damage on an enemy cruiser, the Japanese sank four cruisers and damaged two destroyers and one heavy cruiser. Fearing Allied aerial attacks at dawn, the Japanese admiral broke off the action and retreated; by so doing he permitted the invasion to continue.

The battle of Savo Island was a disaster for the U.S. Navy. It was even more humiliating than Pearl Harbor, for at least in December 1941 the United States had been at peace. The next morning after dumping some supplies on the beach, the support vessels weighed anchor and abandoned the marines who consequently had no barbed wire, no construction equipment, and only minimal supplies of ammunition and food. They were at the end of long and tenuous lines of supply, but they enjoyed one priceless asset: Japanese engineers had almost completed construction of Guadalcanal's airfield. On August 15, four U.S. destroyers slipped into Guadalcanal with aviation fuel, ammunition, and ground crews. Five days later, twelve dive bombers and nineteen fighters arrived at the newly named Henderson Airfield. Possession of the airbase gave marines a crucial advantage in coming weeks.

The Pacific war had exploded on the United States and the colonial empires of Southeast Asia. Now with Hitler's declaration of war, the Americans were in a two-front war. Given the reaction of the American people to Pearl Harbor, the Pacific theater represented a strong and continuing area of interest to American military planners. Yet in the long run, Germany was the greater danger. For Roosevelt and the JCS, strategy became a delicate balancing act between the requirements of a "Germany first" strategy and the political realities of public demands that U.S. forces avenge Pearl Harbor. In early 1942, the Japanese sweep through Southeast Asia and the Southwest Pacific had threatened the entire theater; only the Coral Sea and Midway provided a breathing spell. Now with the commitment to Guadalcanal and New Guinea the Americans had made the first tentative steps forward. But shortages of resources and heavy demands of a two-front war represented strategic and logistical problems that the Americans could not fully solve until 1944.

Mobilizing and Projecting Military Power

The United States

The Japanese attack on Pearl Harbor caught the United States in the first stages of a massive mobilization of its industrial and manpower resources. In no sense was the nation or its military prepared for war. In the 1920s and 1930s the United States had spent less than 2 percent of its gross national product on defense; even with the start of World War II, U.S. defense expenditures were less than five billion dollars. In 1940 those expenditures ballooned to nearly twenty billion, while the peacetime proposals of both army (which included the air force) and navy for expansion reached over one hundred billion dollars. In summer 1940, the fall of France led Congress to pass the first peacetime draft in American history. But the draft and buildup of American military power met strong opposition from many. In summer 1941 with Britain still isolated in western Europe, with the Japanese pursuing an evermore threatening policy in the Pacific, and with Nazi armies slicing through the Soviet Union, the Congress of the United States renewed the peacetime draft by *one* vote. Those drafted were hardly much happier; a movement among draftees called themselves the "Ohio" gang—"over the hill in October."

Anger over Pearl Harbor dissolved opposition to American involvement in the war; Americans rallied behind the president and the military in support of the war effort in a fashion that has never been seen, before or after, in U.S. history. The problem was how to translate economic strength and popular enthusiasm into military power. American leaders, political as well as military, had the experience of U.S. mobilization in World War I to use as a model and therefore avoided some of the mistakes that had beset mobilization in that conflict. Economic mobilization began in August 1939 when Roosevelt created several boards to plan for conversion of industry to war production, to control consumer prices, and to coordinate use of scarce materials. Prewar efforts functioned poorly, but by early 1943 the nation's economy had converted to a wartime footing and functioned relatively smoothly. Though the United States relied on numerous controls and boards, the many voluntary measures of its mobilization contrasted sharply to the mandatory approach of the Soviet Union, Britain, Germany, and Japan.

In May 1943, the Office of War Mobilization under James F. Byrnes, a former Supreme Court justice, received complete control over establishing priorities and prices. Strict regulation of rents, food prices, and wages went into effect, as did rationing of items such as meat, shoes, sugar, and gasoline. The combined effects of conscription and expanded industrial production produced a labor shortage and increased bargaining power for workers. The National War Labor Board, created after Pearl Harbor, served to arbitrate disputes and hold wage rates down. As a result, prices and wages soared during 1942, but they leveled off in 1943 and remained steady until the end of the war.

The labor shortage also encouraged large numbers of American women to join the work force. In addition to those serving in the military, many women found jobs in hospitals, factories, transportation, offices, and farms. Though most withdrew from the labor market after 1945, their participation during the war contributed to significant changes in the economic status of women in American society. African-Americans also benefited from the labor shortage; many found previously closed jobs open to them. They also found more opportunities in the military; one (Benjamin O. Davis) became an army general for the first time and more than 600 became pilots. Though treated somewhat better than they had been in World War I, they continued to suffer from prejudice and mistreatment, and the practice of segregating blacks from whites continued.

When the Japanese struck Pearl Harbor, American mobilization had been underway for about a year and a half. As U.S. industry strained to meet the needs of its allies and its own rapidly expanding forces, severe shortages appeared. By 1943, however, the dividends of the economic mobilization and the strengths of American industry became apparent. The results of that effort were truly awesome. In 1944 alone the U.S. aircraft industry produced 73,876 combat aircraft. In *all* of World War II the Germans produced only 86,311. In 1941, two years *after* Nazi Germany had started World War II, its factories produced 3,256 tanks for the entire year, including 698 made in Czechoslovakia. In 1943, two years after it entered the war, Soviet industry was producing over 1,300 tanks per month; American production that same year was over 2,400 per month. Similarly, the naval buildup in the Pacific reached extraordinary levels; by 1944 a new *Essex* class fleet carrier or an *Independence* light carrier was arriving in Pearl Harbor every month, and in some months one of each. By the battle of Leyte Gulf in October 1944, the attacking U.S. fleet possessed no less than seventeen fleet carriers. One also needs to recognize that in addition to

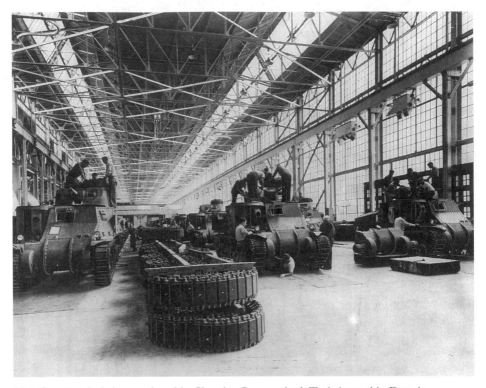

M-3 Grant tanks being produced in Chrysler Corporation's Tank Arsenal in Detroit, Michigan. During the war, the Detroit Tank Arsenal produced 22,234 tanks, or about 25 percent of all tanks produced in the United States.

projecting power around the world and supplying huge quantities of weapons to Allies, Americans also grew, processed, and transported large amounts of food and foodstuffs that prevented their allies from starving. Finally, the United States bore the immense financial and economic costs involved in the Manhattan project, which resulted in production of the atomic bomb. No other nation or economic system could have financed such a development during the war.

But there were difficulties in the early years of American mobilization. The shipment of military equipment to Britain and then the Soviet Union in 1940 and 1941 provided a shield for American preparations. Such shipments, however, also deprived U.S. military forces of equipment that was vital to preparations for war. Even in 1943, lend-lease shipments were a significant drain on equipment stocks. Other difficulties included priorities. In 1942 German successes in the battle of the Atlantic threatened to cut the sea lines of communication between Britain and the United States by sinking many merchant vessels. That same year, the American shipbuilding industry produced three million tons of merchant vessels; in response to Britain's desperate plight as well as the demands of military forces deployed around the world, industry increased production to nine million tons in 1943. Nevertheless there was a cost: production of such large numbers of merchant vessels adversely affected the production of landing craft essential for Allied amphibious attacks on Fortress Europe *and* the Japanese island empire in the Pacific.

The production of weapons represented only part of the problem; turning millions of young men into efficient and effective combat units was another. Critics of the tactical and operational competence of American forces in World War II often use as their model of comparison the performance of German soldiers. Such a comparison is fundamentally false. German rearmament began in 1933; it represented an effort that government as well as the officer corps knew would lead to a major conflict. The Germans had six years of peace and one and a half more of relatively light combat to prepare their ground forces. Moreover, they usually were on the defensive when they faced the Americans.

But the Americans, beginning the mobilization of their economy and their military in September 1939, found themselves in heavy combat on land, sea, and in the air within two years of the initiation of their effort. On the day that Germany invaded Poland, the U.S. Army possessed 14,486 officers and 175,353 enlisted men. Six years later at the end of World War II, the army possessed 891,663 officers and 7,376,295 enlisted personnel. Over those six years, the performance of American ground forces steadily improved as commanders and units gained combat experience. And there is no doubt that American naval and air forces were distinctly superior in qualitative as well as quantitative terms to their enemies by 1943. Though the ground forces may have lagged qualitatively behind their naval and air contemporaries, particularly in the early part of war, there were exceptions. The 88th Infantry Division in the Italian campaign consistently proved itself superior to its German opponents, as did the American airborne divisions. Nevertheless, there is considerable evidence that many American combat units did not match their German opponents on the ground.

A number of reasons explain this state of affairs. On the negative side, U.S. forces initially relied on the M-3 Grant but then in 1942–1943 replaced it with the M-4 Sherman tank, which was more mobile and mechanically reliable than German tanks, but which could not match German Panthers or Tigers in killing power. Recognizing the need for a heavier tank, the Americans built the M-26 Pershing but manufactured only 700 before Germany surrendered. Consequently, American armored-fighting vehicles remained qualitatively inferior to those of their opponents. Additionally, the system of manpower allocation to the armed forces sifted out too many of those who scored highly on intelligence tests into the army air forces, the navy, and innumerable technical positions and left too few among those who had to do the fighting on the ground. To make matters worse, the army all too often regarded soldiers as interchangeable parts that it could shift from one unit to another with little regard for unit cohesion.

Manpower demands on the U.S. population limited the options of military leaders. The war required that millions of Americans be involved in the manufacture of military matériel. Then the services needed millions more; at the war's end the army possessed 5.9 million men and women, the army air forces 2.3 million, the navy 3.4 million and the marine corps nearly half a million. All these military forces required enormous support to get overseas and then to fight a massive *two-front* war over distances that no other combatant had to consider. Originally army planners had foreseen the need for ground forces in excess of two hundred divisions. The realities of fighting the war in the Pacific and the air assault on the Reich forced the Army's chief of staff, General George C. Marshall, to scale back the program to ninety divisions.

That decision resulted in serious but unavoidable consequences. By the end of the war eighty-nine out of those ninety divisions had been committed to combat—scarcely much margin of security. In Europe the fighting forced American commanders to commit infantry and armored divisions to sustained combat, often beginning with Normandy and continuing through Nazi Germany's collapse. Consequently, there was little opportunity (with the exception of airborne divisions) to pull divisions out of the line to rest, refit, and retrain and to give combat units a chance to absorb replacements outside the front lines. In the Battle of the Bulge, this situation had the serious consequence of leaving General Dwight D. Eisenhower, the Allied supreme commander, with a reserve pool of two airborne divisions for the *entire* front—from Holland to Switzerland—on which American troops were fighting. Nevertheless, the main concern for American planners was balancing between the requirements for manpower in the work force and the military in order to sustain the economy as well as operations in the field. Whatever the drawbacks of having only ninety army divisions, it reflected serious choices with which American leaders for the most part grappled more effectively than did their German counterparts.

Great Britain

No country mobilized more extensively than did the British. The nature of the German threat, which lay across the straits of Dover, barely twenty miles away, underlined the desperate situation confronting Britain in June 1940. In 1939 the British had devoted 2.8 percent of their labor force to military service; by 1944 that number had grown to 24.1 percent. Similarly in 1939, 6.4 percent of the labor force worked in defense-related industries; by 1944 the number had grown to 17.7 percent. The hardship and pressures that this unprecedented mobilization placed on the British is captured by a 1944 report.

> The British civilian has had five years of blackout and four years of intermittent blitz. The privacy of his home has been periodically invaded by soldiers and evacuees. In five years of drastic labor mobilization, nearly every man and every woman under fifty without young children has been subject to direction to work, often far from home. The hours of work average fifty-three for men and fifty overall; when work is done, every citizen who is not excused for reasons of family circumstances, work, etc., has had to do forty-eight hours a month duty in the Home Guard or Civil Defense.

Supplies of all kinds have been progressively limited by shipping and manpower shortage; the queue is part of normal life. Taxation is probably the severest in the world, and is coupled with continuous pressure to save. The scarce supplies, both of goods and services, must be shared with hundreds of thousands of United States, Dominion, and Allied Troops; in the preparation of Britain first as a base and then as a bridgehead, the civilian has inevitably suffered hardships spread over almost every aspect of his daily life.

The war effort raised enormous problems. Britain's industrial plant and processes were antiquated and out of date. Yet on a relatively weak economic base the British produced almost as many aircraft as did Nazi Germany, which had all of western and central Europe upon which to draw. In armored fighting vehicles the British produced 27,896 to 46,837 for the Reich. When one considers that the Americans produced 88,410 armored fighting vehicles, and the Soviets 105,251, one gets a sense of how extraordinarily outnumbered the Germans were. But no matter how extensive Britain's mobilization, there were factors they could not overcome. Weaknesses in the industrial base placed limitations on what they could do; the antiquated nature of British industries, particularly the motor industry, had serious consequences. The inadequacy of British tanks throughout the war was one glaring example; the failure of much of the truck fleet on which General Sir Bernard Montgomery's advance in 1944 depended was another.

Germany

Of all the national economic performances, however, it was that of Nazi Germany that left the most to be desired. Hitler's Reich had launched World War II on a most inadequate economic base, one that had contributed to Hitler's belief that the Third Reich must expand to gain the economic resources required for its long-term security. Through the fall of France in spring 1940, Germany lived a precarious economic existence; only the incorporation of Austria in March 1938 and the seizure of Czechoslovakia in September 1938 and March 1939 prevented economic collapse and allowed rearmament programs to proceed. By 1938 the Reich was devoting 18 percent of Germany's gross national product to military spending.

The conquests of Poland, Scandinavia, the Low Countries, and France placed their economic and industrial resources at the disposal of the Reich and brought the Balkans and neutrals like Switzerland, Sweden, and Spain within the Nazi economic orbit. Germany possessed economic resources and industrial capacity the likes of which the Reich had never had before. But Hitler and his senior leadership drew the inaccurate conclusion that the existing production levels in Germany were sufficient to win the war. Moreover, fearful of Nazi Germany's political stability, they hesitated to bring into effect the kind of complete mobilization that Churchill instituted in Britain from 1940 until 1943. Consequently the Germans refused to introduce measures that would have mobilized their population and manpower for total war. At the precise moment that their actual (Britain) and potential (the United States and the Soviet Union) opponents were setting in motion massive mobilization and rearmament programs, the Germans continued business as usual with eight-hour shifts and six-day work weeks. Neither aircraft nor tank production, nor any other crucial indicators showed significant upward movement. Even more important was the fact that the Germans made few efforts to draw on the European economy to expand future production; instead they busily stripped factories in western Europe of machine tools and shipped them back to industrial plants in the Reich that were still working only single shifts.

This short-sighted approach continued through December 1941. However, defeat in front of Moscow, accompanied by loss of much of the army's equipment, and collapse of the Luftwaffe's logistic system (exacerbated by the brutal Russian winter) finally awoke German leaders to the fact that they needed to undertake desperate measures to fight a world war. The death of the armaments minister, Fritz Todt, in February 1942, led Hitler to make one of his more inspired decisions: the appointment of his personal architect, Albert Speer, as Todt's replacement. The thirty-six-year-old Speer possessed extraordinary managerial and leadership skills, as well as keen commonsense. He set about to allow Germany's industrial magnates and firms maximum latitude to expand production. Nevertheless, severe constraints limited options in the economic sphere. Despite the seriousness of the situation, Hitler refused to allow total mobilization of Germany's resources. For ideological reasons, he forbade mobilization of German women to support the war effort; consequently a substantial labor source remained untapped throughout the war in stark contrast to what was occurring elsewhere in the world.

Hitler's decision limiting economic mobilization also reflected his misreading of the lessons of World War I. He believed that the severe pressure in 1918 for armaments production had resulted in the collapse of morale and revolution in Germany. Nevertheless, the Nazi regime undertook extraordinary measures to stoke the war economy; it mobilized slave labor from across Europe; and Nazi authorities soon dragooned millions of French, Russians, Italians, Poles, and other nationalities into German factories.

From spring 1942 a steady and impressive upswing of weapons and munitions production occurred. That growth proceeded through summer 1944 despite Allied strategic bombing attacks. Nonetheless, increases in German production from 1942 to 1944 remained substantially behind those occurring in the United States, the Soviet Union, and Britain. The lost years of 1940 and 1941 were years that the Germans could not make up.

Equally important was the fact that Allied strategic bombing severely retarded German production. Across the Atlantic the Americans increased aircraft production by use of mass-production techniques; the Willow Run aircraft plant of Ford in Michigan possessed a factory floor over two miles long. B-24s began at one end as a tail assembly and rolled out the other as completed aircraft. In Germany the exact opposite occurred as air attacks forced the Germans to decentralize aircraft production into small, inefficient manufacturing operations. Moreover, the quality of the work significantly declined over the course of the war as more slave workers occupied crucial production positions. These unwilling slaves, undernourished and subjected to horrendous treatment, were hardly eager to turn out first-class products for their rulers. The result was a significant decline in quality of weapons produced by German industry.

Defeat at Stalingrad in February 1943, followed shortly thereafter by collapse in North Africa, finally persuaded Hitler to allow Joseph Goebbels and Speer latitude to extend war and mobilization measures throughout German society. But the Führer still held back on some measures, particularly regarding the wider employment of women in German industry. Meanwhile, strategic bombing attacks destroyed German cities and disrupted industries. By 1944 the impact of enemy bombing caused serious consequences in oil, aircraft, and transportation. Desperate efforts to squeeze the last products out of the German economy prolonged, but could not alter, the final result: catastrophic national defeat.

The European War at Sea, 1939–1945

While the opening campaigns of the war were unfolding on land, the crucial campaign of World War II had already begun in the North Atlantic. From the outbreak of war, German U-boats waged a tenacious struggle to sever lifelines between the British Isles and the rest of the world. Had they succeeded, there would have been no second front, no air campaign against the Third Reich, and few supplies for the hard-pressed Soviets; and Britain itself, confronted with starvation, might well have sued for peace. As Churchill commented: "The only thing that ever really frightened me during the war was the U-boat peril."

First Battles

Neither the British nor the Germans had prepared for the battle of the Atlantic. Having developed sonar (called asdic by the British) at the end of World War I, the Royal Navy comfortably assumed that it had solved the submarine menace. During the interwar period it did little serious preparation for protecting convoys; and it constructed few antisubmarine vessels. With the outbreak of war, it could protect only the most important shipping routes.

The Germans for their part displayed no more foresight. Before the war, the commander-in-chief of the navy, Admiral Erich Raeder, emphasized creation of a great battle fleet that would eventually be capable of challenging Britain on the seas. When the war began, the Germans had two battleships and two near completion, three pocket battleships, three heavy cruisers, and five light cruisers. They also had fifty-seven submarines, about half of which were capable of sustained operations at sea. With the outbreak of war in September 1939, Raeder recognized that since war had come early, the navy could not challenge Britain on the surface; it had to use its ships as raiders, while its submarines executed attacks on British commerce.

In fall 1939 German submarines achieved some notable successes; they sank the aircraft carrier *Courageous* and battleship *Royal Oak*. But their number was so small that after an initial wave of attacks, they inflicted minimal damage. The picture was not much rosier for the surface navy. The Scandinavian campaign cost it virtually all its strength, either sunk or damaged. Nevertheless, German successes in spring 1940 altered the Reich's strategic position. The commander of the U-boats, Admiral Karl Dönitz, moved submarine bases to the west coast of France and then launched an energetic anticommerce campaign.

By fall 1940 the U-boat force, while not significantly larger, had achieved a high level of effectiveness. Dönitz spread the submarines in patrol lines across the most likely lanes approaching the British Isles. When one made contact, it reported by radio the location, size, and direction of movement to Dönitz, who then concentrated his submarines in wolf packs against the enemy. Eventually, overcontrol by radio would cost the Germans dearly, but now it worked.

On October 5, 1940, Convoy SC-7 departed Canada with thirty-four slow merchant vessels. Its escort for much of the journey was a single sloop; its opponents were some of the great U-boat aces of the war. In mid-ocean another sloop and a corvette joined up. Eventually two more corvettes arrived. None of the escorts possessed radar; they had not trained together; and the sonar on some of the corvettes was obsolete. The result was a slaughter; SC-7 lost twenty ships with two others damaged. At the same time that U-boats were savaging SC-7, the fast convoy HX-79 departed Halifax for Britain. This convoy had a larger escort, including two armed merchant cruisers, two destroyers, four corvettes, a minesweeper, and three trawlers. But the escort fleet was no better trained. Attacking U-boats sank nearly 25 percent of HX-79's merchant vessels.

The arrival of winter provided a covering blanket over convoys. But in spring 1941 shipping losses in the Atlantic began an ominous upswing. In March losses were 243,020 tons; in April 249,375 tons; in May 325,492 tons; and in June 310,143 tons.

While British losses mounted in the U-boat war, the Germans moved to change the surface equation. Raeder hoped to make a great raid against British shipping by uniting the new battleship *Bismarck* and heavy cruiser *Prinz Eugen* (in the Baltic) with battle cruisers *Scharnhorst* and *Gneisenau* (in Brest). But *Scharnhorst* needed repairs, and an RAF Coastal Command aircraft torpedoed *Gneisenau*. Nevertheless, the Germans launched *Bismarck* and *Prinz Eugen*, as well as a number of supply ships and weather ships, on the raid. As the heavy German ships approached the Denmark Straits, British cruisers picked them up and began shadowing. On May 24 battle cruiser *Hood* and the new battleship *Prince of Wales* attacked, but the Germans destroyed *Hood*, while mechanical problems forced *Prince of Wales* to break off action. *Prinz Eugen* escaped to the south and eventually entered Brest. Crippled by a rudder jammed by British attacks, the *Bismarck* did not get away and on May 27 was finally sunk by the British battle fleet. This ended German attempts to challenge British dominance of the ocean.

Intelligence Intervenes

As a consequence of the *Bismarck* breakout, the intelligence equation in the Atlantic underwent a drastic change. On May 8, 1941, escorts of convoy OB-318 damaged a U-boat and forced it to the surface. After capturing the crew, British sailors boarded the badly damaged submarine and extracted the Enigma enciphering machine and its settings for the next seven weeks. Seizure of a weather trawler at the end of May (sent out to support the *Bismarck*) provided further access to Enigma settings, allowing teams at Bletchley Park (headquarters of British code-breaking efforts) to break into the German naval codes for the first time in the war. The first information from decrypted German transmissions allowed the Royal Navy to sweep up German supply and weather ships; the British destroyed six German tankers and three supply ships after determining their positions. Recognizing that such a clean sweep could hardly have been the result of luck alone, the Germans executed a major enquiry into the security of the message traffic but concluded that destruction of the tankers and supply ships resulted from the efforts of the British secret service.

The Germans had recognized that the British might capture Enigma settings and read transmissions for short periods of time, but they never believed that the British could do this on a sustained basis. They were wrong. Bletchley Park soon began reading U-boat message traffic on a regular basis. The opportunity came from Dönitz's close control of the U-boat war and the numerous transmissions to and from boats at sea, which provided the British with the cribs needed to break into the codes. The intelligence from these decrypts then allowed the British to maneuver convoys around U-boat patrol lines. Sinkings due to submarines dropped dramatically: in July 1941 down to 94,209 tons; in August to 80,310 tons; in September 202,554 tons; in October 156,554 tons; in November 62,196 tons; and in December 124,070 tons. The rise of losses in September reflected the fact that Luftwaffe long-range aircraft picked up the movement of Gibraltar convoys. This British success in the last half of 1941 is the only time in the war where intelligence was decisive by itself. In December 1941 the Germans introduced an additional rotor into the Enigma machine, and the British could not read U-boat message traffic for most of 1942.

The German High Point

The situation in the Atlantic took a drastic turn when Hitler declared war on the United States on December 11, 1941. Dönitz immediately sent a few long-range boats to the east coast of the United States. By mid-January five boats were off the coast from New York to Cape Hatteras, and the slaughter began. The Americans were totally unprepared. No convoy system existed. American destroyers plied up and down coastal waterways like clockwork, so that U-boat commanders always knew where they were. Some American cities along the coast refused to darken their lights. The five U-boats achieved stunning success; between the onset of Operation "*Paukenschlag*" on January 12 and the end of the month, the Germans sank forty ships, all sailing independently. Totals rose rapidly as the Germans reinforced and extended operations to the Caribbean and then to the north coast of South America. In February, U-boats sank 65 ships in American waters, in March 86, in April 69, in May 111, and June 121.

Despite the losses, the Americans stubbornly refused to establish convoys. The commander of defensive operations off the eastern seacoast believed "that a convoy without adequate protection is worse than none." Consequently he concentrated defensive forces in hunting down submarines by patrolling. Such efforts were uniformly unsuccessful; not until April did the Americans sink their first U-boat. The Americans also did not possess a system to integrate intelligence into operations. The British Operational Intelligence Center provided a guide for what was needed, but the U.S. Navy refused to heed British advice until late spring. Equally harmful was the lack of training and doctrine among the naval forces deployed against the U-boats. Initially in 1942 the Americans blamed their failures on a lack of resources, but as a veteran of the effort later admitted, the key factor was human error.

At the beginning of May, the U.S. Navy adopted convoys off the East Coast. That change led Dönitz to shift his emphasis to the Caribbean. Again the U-boats enjoyed a rich harvest of ships sailing independently. In May 1942 U-boats sank forty-one vessels of nearly 250,000 tons in the Gulf of Mexico; thirty-eight more of 200,000 tons went to the bottom in the Caribbean. The Germans had extended the range of U-boats into this area by use of submarine tankers, known as "milk cows." In May and June twenty U-boats operating in the West Indies and Caribbean sank nearly three quarters of a million tons of shipping, virtually all of it sailing independently. This catastrophe forced the Americans to begin convoys throughout the Caribbean; losses again dropped dramatically. The Germans now had to turn back to attacking convoys crossing the North Atlantic; the easy war was over.

The use of U-boats for purposes other than attacking sea lines of communication hampered the campaign in the Atlantic. In winter 1942, Hitler ordered a number of submarines to move into the Mediterranean to help Rommel. Similarly in spring and summer 1942, Hitler held back some U-boats to cover Norway. Then in November 1942, in response to Allied landings in North Africa, he ordered U-boats to attack the landing force. This redeployment cut down on the boats available in the Atlantic precisely at the moment when Allied convoys had lost many escorts to protect the North African landings.

But German difficulties in the North Atlantic were not entirely due to the diversion of submarines. Dönitz's method of controlling his boats created a situation advantageous to Allied intelligence, both in fixing enemy

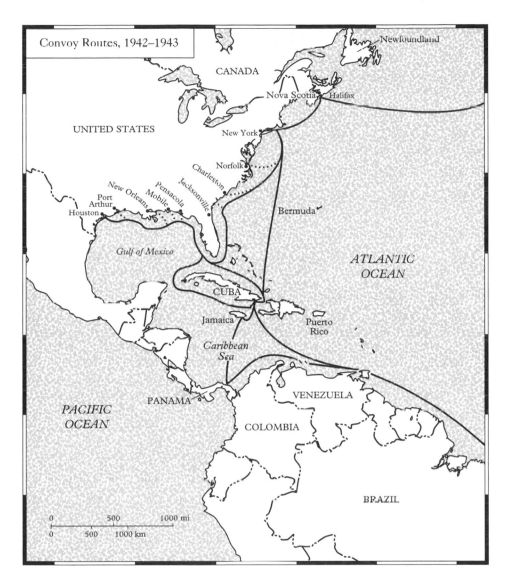

Convoy Routes, 1942–1943

boats by direction finding and in breaking German naval codes. Further-more, Dönitz attempted to win the war in the Atlantic with a minuscule staff. For the first several years of the war that approach sufficed, but with no organic research unit, with a narrowly focused intelligence effort, and with its small number of officers immersed in day-to-day operations, the German submarine command fell behind the smoothly running organization that the Allies eventually put together. As one opponent remarked, Dönitz's system was "an eighteenth-century way of war in a twentieth-century age of technology."

During 1942, nevertheless, the Germans sank no less than 8 million tons of shipping and suffered few losses. Dönitz possessed approximately 150 U-boats in commission or being constructed in September 1941, and the operational fleet reached 212 boats by September 1942, with an additional 181 preparing for sea duty. By mid-1942 approximately thirty new boats joined the fleet each month. In November total sinkings reached 729,000 tons despite the diversion of many U-boats to North Africa. The climactic moment was now approaching in the Atlantic.

Allied Victory

Despite the large numbers of German submarines, several factors favored the defenders. In December 1942, Bletchley Park again broke into German naval codes, but that intelligence became available sporadically. On some days code breakers could break in quickly, on other days only after long delays. Nevertheless the British and Americans could build up a more complete picture of German operations in the Atlantic, and they now cooperated daily in exchanging intelligence about U-boat operations. The presence of so many U-boats in the Atlantic, however, made it difficult for the Allies to slip a convoy through without its being sighted.

But in 1943 other factors also affected the balance. The number of escorts increased dramatically; nearly all now possessed radar. An improvement to radar—the shifting of microwave frequencies to higher levels—rendered the German detection and jamming equipment useless. Sonar capabilities had considerably improved; depth charges were also better, and some escorts possessed "Hedgehog" rockets that allowed them to attack submarines without losing sonar contact. Allied antisubmarine doctrine and training had also noticeably improved, so that escort groups worked as effective and efficient teams. Finally, escort carriers provided air cover throughout the mid-Atlantic gap where land-based air power had not reached, while long-range aircraft equipped with radar proved a deadly danger to U-boats caught on the surface.

In January 1943 evasive routing of convoys, based on Ultra intelligence, combined with bad weather to lower shipping losses to 200,000 tons. In February losses rose to 360,000 tons, and in March they reached 627,000 tons. In March a series of convoy battles favored the Germans. In a period during which no Ultra intelligence was available to Allied naval commanders, forty German U-boats concentrated on convoys SC-122 and HX-229. In a four-day battle they sank twenty-one merchant ships for the loss of only one boat.

April saw more great battles, but this time the Germans were the losers. In the last week of April, two wolf packs totaling forty-one boats attacked convoy ONS-5. The attackers sank twelve merchant vessels, but the reinforced escort group sank seven U-boats, while severely damaging another five. In April the Germans lost the same number of boats as in March, fifteen. Then in May the battle went completely in favor of the defenders. A combination of escort and air attacks imposed an unacceptable level of losses on U-boats. Allied antisubmarine forces sank forty-one boats during the month. Dönitz concluded that his submarines could no longer meet the Allies on an equal footing; he withdrew them from the North Atlantic.

The battle of the Atlantic was by no means over. Unable to attack Allied convoys in mid-Atlantic, U-boats sought targets in distant waters. Here again, intelligence played a crucial role in leading Allied escort groups to German supply submarines on which long-distant voyages depended. But raids by U-boats off the coast of South Africa and into the Indian Ocean represented only pinpricks that did little overall harm to the Allies. Dönitz had to wait for technological changes to alter the balance. By mid-1945 the Germans were on the point of launching submarines that could move at fifteen knots underwater for short periods of time. Had these boats been available in 1944, the Germans might have negated Allied advantages and resumed a full-scale offensive against Allied commerce.

Allied success in the North Atlantic in May 1943 came at a point at which the American shipyards had begun turning out 10,000-ton *Liberty* ships in enormous numbers. The opening of the Mediterranean, which destruction of Axis forces in Tunisia had made possible, freed up millions more tons of shipping. Through the sea lanes of the world, America could now project its immense military and industrial power in both European and Pacific theaters. With their failure in the Atlantic, the Germans lost their only hope of blocking American troops and industrial products from the coasts of Europe. Significantly, the German navy had played a major role in persuading Hitler to declare war on the United States to prevent such movement. Just as in World War I, the German submarine campaign had failed to live up to the navy's expectations.

The Air War

The Opening Moves

The air war began later than prewar theorists had expected and took much time to work into high gear. Through May 1940, RAF Bomber Command found itself hamstrung by rules of engagement forbidding attacks even on warships tied up at dock. With the German onslaught in May 1940, these restrictions disappeared. For the next ten months, Bomber Command attacked precision targets in Germany, especially oil plants and transportation. But Bomber Command, because its past experiences in the war indicated clearly that daylight bombing attacks would suffer prohibitive casualties, decided to make its attacks at night for most of the rest of the war. The hope was "that the accuracy of night bombing [would] differ little from daylight bombing." Not until summer 1941 did the British discover how unrealistic such hopes were. Then an analysis of mission photographs indicated that only one in three bombers was hitting within five miles of the target; in other words, Bomber Command had a difficult time even in hitting cities.

Such inaccuracy pushed the British toward what they euphemistically described as "area bombing" to "dehouse" the German population. The British decided to undertake a bomber offensive because they wanted to escape the terrible casualties of the last war and because the collapse

Air Marshal Sir Arthur T. Harris fervently believed that only a strategic air offensive could win the war for the Allies in a reasonable amount of time and at an acceptable cost. He also believed, "One cannot win wars by defending oneself."

of France made strategic bombing the only avenue for striking Germany directly. The meager results obtained in 1941 led to pressure for utilization of bomber aircraft in other areas, such as the battle of the Atlantic. Moreover, by the end of 1941 loss rates for bombers had risen significantly as German night defenses improved.

In January 1942 disenchantment with bombing results led to appointment of Air Marshal Arthur T. Harris to head Bomber Command. Harris possessed an unshakable belief in strategic bombing. Fortified by a strong personality and intolerant of differing views, he was an ideal candidate to shake the command's lethargy. Harris understood the need for operational successes both to bolster the morale of his crews and to counter those who argued for diversion of bombers to other tasks. The development of the first significant navigational aid, Gee, allowed the British to bomb with greater accuracy for short distances onto the Continent. In March 1942, the first demonstration of Gee's effectiveness came when Bomber Command took out the Renault factory near Paris. One month later, Bomber Command destroyed Lübeck; postraid reconnaissance indicated that the attack had destroyed 40 to 50 percent of the city. At the end of April, British bombers blasted Rostock and a nearby Heinkel factory.

But Harris's greatest triumph of the year came in May. By scraping together training units and every bomber in his command, he put 1,000 aircraft over Cologne and swamped the night defenses. The British achieved an unheard-of concentration in bombing; with a low loss rate (3.8 percent), Bomber Command devastated the city but killed only 384 civilians, small casualties compared to what was to come. Photo reconnaissance indicated the attack destroyed 600 acres of Cologne. Bomber Command, nevertheless, did not achieve a similar success for the remainder of the year, and the cost remained high. From May to September the British lost 970 bombers; in May 1942 the Command's average number of aircraft had been only 417. The loss rate for the period was 233 percent.

Selected Aerial Targets in Germany

As the bomber offensive expanded, the Luftwaffe responded. In September 1939, Germany did not possess an air-defense system similar to that of Fighter Command. To defend the Reich, the Germans deployed a large number of searchlights and antiaircraft guns. The Luftwaffe also possessed single-engine fighters but committed few of them to home defense because it saw the mission of its fighters as winning air superiority over enemy airspace. In July 1940 the Luftwaffe established the 1st Night Fighter Division under General Joseph Kammhuber. Its mission was to protect Germany from RAF incursions. Kammhuber received a disparate group of aircraft, none of which carried radar. He introduced intruder missions into British airspace to attack RAF bombers taking off; this line of attack showed promise until Hitler ordered it discontinued in summer 1941. Thereafter the Germans never resumed intruder attacks in British airspace.

Throughout 1941, Kammhuber introduced an increasingly effective air-defense system that soon posed a formidable threat to British night operations. Using a belt of radar stations from Denmark to northern France, the system provided early warning as well as ground-control intercept to night fighters equipped with radar. It possessed one considerable weakness: each ground-control site controlled only one fighter and thus one intercept at a time. If the British concentrated their bombers in time and space, they could swamp defenses; but through the end of 1941, that occurred rarely.

In 1942 Bomber Command became a formidable weapon. Despite the heavy damage to Lübeck and Rostock, the OKW did not become alarmed. The devastating attack on Cologne was another matter. Believing these raids signaled a British attempt to start a second front, the Führer decided to reply to the attacks with retaliatory raids and "revenge" weapons such as the wasteful V-2 rocket. Regardless of the vulnerability of the Allied bombers, the Germans remained faithful to Douhet's theories about the futility of countering offensive air power and refused to devote significant resources to their night-fighter defenses.

The Bombing Campaign in Full Gear: Bomber Command

1943 saw an upswing in Allied air attacks on the Germans. Beginning in March 1943 Harris's force battered the Ruhr for three months. These raids marked the beginning of a series of Bomber Command successes. In May 1943 a highly select bomber group took out several dams in the Ruhr River valley, but German air defenses imposed a loss rate on attacking bombers that was close to unbearable. Then in July 1943 the British introduced "Window" (strips of aluminum that reflected to German radar the same signature as a bomber). By dropping out bales of these strips the British blinded the air-defense system. Combined with the arrival of new four-engine bombers, the Halifax and Lancaster, the British dealt out sledgehammer blows.

On the evening of July 27–28, Bomber Command delivered a devastating attack against Hamburg. Conditions were perfect. Hamburg was easy to find; the weather was warm and dry; Window blinded German defenses; and the city's firefighters were on the west side of the city putting out persistent, smoldering coal and coke fires. The marker flares went down perfectly in the center of the city, probably on the great lumberyard where Baltic timber arrived for distribution to Germany. Most of the following bombers dropped their loads of incendiaries and high explosives into the glowing cauldron. The fire then pumped superheated air straight up into the stratosphere, at the same time sucking in fresh air from outside the city. Winds approached 300–400 miles per hour, while temperatures reached close to 1,000 degrees. The raid burned a four-mile hole in the city's center; between 30,000–40,000 perished. After the war Speer claimed that if Bomber Command had repeated its Hamburg success four or five times in succeeding weeks, Germany would have collapsed. But Bomber Command could not repeat its success. In August it took out the bomb research and experimental station at Peenemünde on the Baltic coast. Since German night defenses were recovering from Window, the attacking force of

Destruction in Hamburg. Sir Arthur Harris believed such destruction pointed the "certain, the obvious, the quickest, and the easiest way to overwhelming victory."

597 lost forty bombers (6.7 percent). In October Harris's forces created another firestorm at Kassel.

At this point Harris determined to destroy Berlin. Though his offensive did not win the war, it came close to destroying his command. Berlin lay deep in Germany and Luftwaffe defenses could pick up and follow the great bomber stream throughout its course over the Reich. Rather than guide individual fighters to bombers, the Germans now guided night fighters into the bomber stream and then allowed the fighters to identify and attack individual aircraft. Also, a new German radar, SN2, allowed night fighters to tear away Window's veil. The weather in winter 1943–1944 was appallingly bad, so that virtually all bombing took place through clouds. Although Harris's attackers damaged Berlin extensively, their target was enormous, and the British did not attain the concentration achieved over Hamburg.

British losses rapidly rose. In December 1943 the British lost 170 bombers; in January 1944, 314; in February, 199; and in March, 283. Considering that the Command had a front-line bomber strength of 1,224 in January 1944, such losses were staggering. On the evening of March 30, 1944, Bomber Command struck Nuremberg; many of the attackers hit Schweinfurt instead; the Germans shot down 108. Such disastrous losses forced Harris to call off nighttime area bombing attacks on central Germany. While Bomber Command had dealt out devastating blows, it had not broken enemy morale, and by March 1944 its rate of attrition had reached unsupportable levels.

The Bombing Campaign in Full Gear: The American Effort

In summer 1942 the first bomber units of the U.S. Army Air Forces (USAAF) arrived in England to begin daylight operations on the Continent. The Americans brought with them a belief that during daylight hours they could fight their way through German defenses with great formations of heavily armed B-17s. These bombers would then attack the vital centers of Germany's industry and, by destroying certain crucial targets, cause the collapse of the enemy's economic system. While American air commanders recognized that the Luftwaffe was a formidable force, they believed that their numbers and disciplined flying could overwhelm the German air defenses without the support of long-range escort fighters. Initially, however, they had too few bombers to launch B-17s into German airspace; American raids thus initially struck at Nazi-occupied France within supporting range of friendly fighters. Nevertheless, this rather limited experience led Brigadier General Ira C. Eaker, Eighth Air Force commander, to write his superiors that "bombardment in force—a minimum of 300 bombers—can effectively attack any German target and return without excessive or uneconomical losses." Eaker's strength, however, did not reach that level until late spring 1943 because of the diversion of bombers to support "Torch" and operations in the Mediterranean.

The question of what to attack became a divisive issue. The German aircraft industry had to be a primary target because the Luftwaffe was a far more ferocious opponent than expected. Attacks on other industries offered the possibility of weakening the German economy, but most industries, such as oil, contained a larger number of targets than Eighth Air Force's force structure could attack. Consequently, through a selection process largely determined by the number of targets, the Americans settled on the ball-bearing industry as the weak link in the German economic structure.

At Casablanca in early winter 1943 British and American political and military leaders agreed that Allied air forces should wage a "combined bomber offensive" by day and night to put relentless pressure on the Reich's population and industry. Unfortunately the agreement in principle proved difficult to implement, at least as far as finding a common focus for the offensive. Harris stood firm in his belief in "area bombing" and in his contempt for attacks on specific targets, which he derisively described as "panacea targets." The Americans, on the other hand, persisted in their belief that by making precision attacks on industrial targets they could cause the collapse of the German economy. There was thus little room for a common approach until 1944.

American raids began reaching into Germany in early summer 1943. Heavy blows fell on the Ruhr in July; on August 17, Eaker dispatched a massive force to take out the Messerschmitt factory at Regensburg and the ball-bearing works at Schweinfurt. The latter complex produced half of Germany's ball bearings. But the attacks ran into a slew of German fighters. Of 146 bombers in the Regensburg force, the Germans shot down twenty-four

(16.4 percent). Because the bombers continued on to North Africa, thereby disconcerting the defenses, they avoided higher losses, but sixty of the bombers that reached Africa had to remain to be repaired or salvaged. The forces attacking Schweinfurt (230 bombers) lost thirty-six more aircraft (15.7 percent). Twenty-seven more bombers had to be written off after returning to England because of extensive damage.

From August through October 1943, Eaker threw great unescorted formations of B-17s into German territory without support from long-range escort fighters. Surprisingly the provision of such fighters remained low on his list of priorities. American aircraft continued to attack Luftwaffe production facilities and ball-bearing factories. Losses, however, were horrendous. In maintaining its aerial offensive, Eighth Air Force suffered a nearly 30 percent crew loss each month—a rate ensuring that few bomber crews ever completed the twenty-five missions required to return home. On October 14, "Black Thursday," Eighth again attacked Schweinfurt; the long flight across Germany took a terrible toll. Luftwaffe fighters and antiaircraft shot down sixty bombers, seventeen more were written off, while 121 were damaged but repairable. So heavy were the losses that Eighth had to call off deep-penetration raids. The Luftwaffe had won one of the last, but temporary, victories achieved by Germany in the war.

The Schweinfurt raids of 1943 against the ball-bearing industry represented a terrible threat to the German war economy. After the war, Speer admitted that continued attacks on the industry would have brought the economy to a halt. But Eighth Air Force could not endure such losses from continued attacks. Moreover, the Germans discovered that their industrial concerns possessed large backlogs of ball bearings, that the Swedes and Swiss were willing to sell them to the Reich, and that in some weapons they could substitute roller bearings (easier to manufacture) for ball bearings.

Yet for all its failings in 1943, the air offensive provided substantial benefits to the Allied cause. Attacks on the aircraft industry caused German production of new fighters to fall by an average of 200 fighters per month from its peak in July 1943. In November 1943 new fighter production was 300 under the total for July (576 versus 873). While attacking American forces suffered high losses, they inflicted heavy casualties on the enemy. Admittedly, they could not maintain that effort in the face of such losses, but the attacks seriously affected the Germans.

The British raids also had a serious, though indirect, impact. Well into 1944 the Germans emphasized production of bombers to strike back at the Allies. Moreover, by 1943 they embarked on an enormously costly program to build V-1 and V-2 rockets to pay the British back for area bombing. In the end the V-1 and V-2 program used up resources equivalent to the production of 24,000 fighter aircraft.

But the largest diversion of German military strength came in the area of antiaircraft defenses. In 1940 the air-defense system consisted of 791 heavy batteries, equipped with high velocity 88-mm, 105-mm, and 128-mm guns; by 1943 the number of batteries had risen to 2,132 with over 10,000 antiaircraft guns. That total represented a considerable investment in manpower and material that the Germans desperately needed elsewhere. This was especially so since, from a German point of view, Flak was not cost effective against high-flying aircraft. The 88-mm Flak weapon, for example, required 16,000 shells to hit an aircraft at high altitude. Every night these weapons fired large amounts of ammunition into the skies over the Reich to reassure the population that the Luftwaffe was defending the country against enemy bombers.

The Luftwaffe

From the beginning of the war, the Luftwaffe suffered from a poor support structure. Göring was incapable of providing long-term guidance; General Hans Jeschonnek, the chief of staff, focused entirely on operational concerns; and intelligence was a disaster. Most seriously, the production and maintenance structure was in complete shambles. One of Göring's closest confidants, General Ernst Udet, controlled this crucial sphere of Luftwaffe activity. Udet had been a great ace in World War I, a barnstormer in the 1920s and 1930s, and then a rising star in the resurrected Luftwaffe, but he possessed few managerial skills. Göring selected him nevertheless in 1938 to run the Luftwaffe's production and design establishment. Udet soon had more than forty different offices reporting directly to him. By summer 1941 production programs were way off target; technological development had stalled; and confusion reigned. In the summer of 1941, Göring finally reinstated Field Marshal Milch in the process; soon afterward, Udet committed suicide.

Milch possessed great managerial skills, and since the air war rested on industrial management, Milch's appointment was crucial to getting the Luftwaffe back on track. But the Germans had lost one full year and were already behind the British and Americans. In a hurried trip to the Eastern Front in September 1941, Milch discovered hundreds of broken aircraft littering forward airfields because of shortages in spare parts; the supply system had almost entirely broken down in the vastness of Russia. By December operationally ready rates for German bombers had fallen to 32 percent, for fighters to 52 percent, and for the whole Luftwaffe to 45 percent. These figures underline the difficulties that the Luftwaffe, conceived in terms of central European requirements, now confronted in fighting a conflict possessing continental distances.

For the Luftwaffe the war now became one of three fronts: the Eastern Front against an increasingly effective Red Air Force, equipped not only with its own production but with American and British aircraft as well; the Mediterranean against a growing tide of Anglo-American air power; and the great night and day attacks of the Combined Bomber Offensive. Against this massive threat, Milch struggled to increase aircraft production. Since Germany controlled the industrial capacity of central Europe, he achieved considerable increases in aircraft production. But British and American bombing did retard those efforts in 1943. More important, Germany's enemies had already geared up their economies for massive production increases.

In 1942 the Germans felt the first pressure from Allied production superiority. In Russia the quality of German aircrews made up for the Red Air Force's superiority in numbers. In the Mediterranean, however, the RAF exercised increasing influence over the conduct of operations. Air Marshal Sir Arthur Tedder, perhaps the greatest airman of the war, developed a force that could gain and maintain air superiority over the battlefield, while the desert air force's interdiction and close air-support strikes rendered crucial support to the army. Moreover, its antishipping attacks, supported by Ultra, undermined Rommel's logistical support.

At the end of 1942 the roof fell in on the Luftwaffe. Hitler and the senior military leaders made two serious mistakes. In response to Operation Torch, the invasion of North Africa by the British and Americans, the OKW moved large forces across to Tunisia. To support the commitment, the Luftwaffe had to use much of its Ju 52 transport fleet; that commitment shut down the training program for bomber pilots. The air battle to protect the tenuous logistic lines to Tunisia put the Luftwaffe at a severe disadvantage, especially since Ultra intelligence kept the Allies fully informed of Axis supply movements. Undersupplied and vulnerable on North African airfields, the Luftwaffe confronted increasingly effective Allied air attacks on its supplies and base structure. By March 1943 the Germans and Italians had to stop ship movements to Tunisia; movement of supplies by transport aircraft proved equally as costly. The air battle in the Mediterranean continued through the summer, when the Germans finally conceded defeat in the Mediterranean.

Events on the Eastern Front followed a similar pattern. Almost concurrently with Torch, the Soviets launched a counteroffensive against German Sixth Army at Stalingrad. Hitler, bolstered by Göring's promise that the Luftwaffe could keep Sixth Army supplied, refused any thought of abandoning Stalin's city. The transport fleet, already stretched by Tunisia, had to rush into the breach. Despite heroic efforts, the Russian winter made airlift operations impossible. Operationally ready rates plummeted, losses mounted. The Luftwaffe never came close to providing the 600 tons per day that Sixth Army required. Throughout the winter, fighting swirled around Stalingrad and forced the Luftwaffe to provide constant support for hard-pressed ground troops. In March 1943, the spring thaw brought a short pause to ground operations in the east. The air battles, however, continued, and the Luftwaffe took particularly heavy losses over the Caucasus.

Meanwhile, Army Group Center prepared for the climactic battle of the Eastern Front, the clash of armor at the Kursk salient. The Luftwaffe concentrated nearly 2,000 aircraft over Kursk. *Luftflotte* Six supported Army Group Center's drive with 750 aircraft, while *Luftflotte* Four supported Army Group South's attack with 1,100 aircraft. In 1943 a substantial proportion of Luftwaffe frontline strength still remained committed on the Eastern Front: 84.5 percent of all dive bombers, 27 percent of all fighters, and 33 percent of bombers. On the first day of Kursk, German pilots flew 3,000 sorties and fought a great air battle over the salient. But the Germans never established air superiority, and the Red Air Force interfered significantly with German air and ground operations. After the failure of the German offensive at Kursk, the Soviets launched counteroffensives against Army Group Center and Army Group South. The Luftwaffe desperately attempted to stave off defeat on the ground but suffered heavy losses that severely affected its capabilities. At the same time, its best fighter squadrons moved from the Eastern Front to meet the American bombing offensive.

In July and August of 1943 the Luftwaffe fought three great air battles. In the Mediterranean the Anglo-American attack on Sicily and air raids into Italy cost the Luftwaffe 711 combat aircraft in July and 321 in August (1,032 for the two months); in defending the skies over western Europe, it lost 526 in July and 625 for August (1,151 for the two months); and in the east the Luftwaffe lost 558 in July and 472 in August (1,030 for the two months). The loss of 3,213 combat aircraft in two months out of a force structure of approximately 5,000 combat aircraft was simply no longer supportable. Given the threat to Germany's cities and industries, the Luftwaffe had to come home to defend its base. After September 1943, German soldiers on the Italian and Eastern fronts would seldom see their air force. The skies over the battlefield belonged to the Allies.

☆   ☆   ☆   ☆

The entry of the United States into World War II resulted from substantial miscalculations on the part of two Axis partners, Nazi Germany and Imperial Japan. In the end success in the war rested on the great industrial mobilization of the Allies' economies on which military might depended. For the Americans as well as the British the second piece of the puzzle was the ability to project military power over the world's oceans, and that required mastery over the substantial U-boat threat. Until their naval forces had mastered that threat, the economic and military potential of the Western Powers remained open to question.

For the Americans and the British, the defeat of France in May 1940 meant that their ground forces could not engage the enemy on the European Continent until 1943 or 1944. That in turn forced the Anglo-Saxon powers to rely on air power to strike at the sources of Nazi military power. From the retrospective view of fifty years, the Combined Bombing Offensive failed to achieve its stated operational objectives in 1942 and 1943. But it did at least strike the Germans hard, and it moved from being a considerable nuisance to posing a real threat to the stability of the Reich's war economy.

What was indeed remarkable was the unprecedented scale of the Allied effort in harnessing men, women, machines, and raw materials to the war effort. The successes of German and Japanese armies and navies in the first war years provided the incentive and popular support in Allied countries. The political skill and ruthlessness of the American, British, and Soviet leaders then provided the framework and means to translate large populations and economic power into military might.

SUGGESTED READINGS

Beesley, Patrick. *Very Special Intelligence. The Story of the Admiralty's Operational Intelligence Center* (London: Hamish Hamilton, 1977).

Buell, Thomas B. *Master of Sea Power. A Biography of Fleet Admiral Ernest J. King* (Boston: Little Brown, 1980).

Fuchida Mitsuo. *Midway, the Battle That Doomed Japan* (Annapolis: Naval Institute, 1955).

Hastings, Max. *Bomber Command* (New York: Dial Press, 1979).

Hayashi Saburo. *Kogun: The Japanese Army in the Pacific War* (Westport, Conn.: Greenwood Press, 1978).

James, D. Clayton. *The Years of MacArthur.* 2 vols. (Boston: Houghton Mifflin, 1970).

Millett, Allen, and Williamson Murray. *Military Effectiveness*, vol. III, *World War II* (London: Allen and Unwin, 1988).

Milward, Alan. *The German Economy at War* (London: Athlone Press, 1965).

Morison, Samuel Eliot. *The Two-Ocean War: A Short History of the United States Navy in the Second World War* (Boston: Little Brown, 1963).

Murray, Williamson. *Luftwaffe* (Baltimore: Nautical and Aviation Publishing Co., 1985).

Prange, Gordon W., with Donald M. Goldstein and Katherine V. Dillon. *At Dawn We Slept: The Untold Story of Pearl Harbor* (New York: McGraw-Hill, 1981).

———. *Miracle at Midway* (New York: McGraw-Hill, 1982).

Ienaga Saburo. *The Pacific War: World War II and the Japanese, 1931–1945* (New York: Pantheon Books, 1978).

Spector, Ronald H. *Eagle Against the Sun: The War with Japan* (New York: The Free Press, 1985).

Townsend, Peter. *Duel of Eagles* (New York: Simon and Schuster, 1970).

U.S. Army Air Forces. *Ultra and the History of the United States Strategic Air Force in Europe vs. the German Air Force* (Frederick, Md.: University Publications of America, 1980).

Webster, Sir Charles, and Noble Frankland. *The Strategic Air Offensive Against Germany, 1939–1945* (London: Her Majesty's Stationery Office, 1962).

Winton, John. *Ultra at Sea: How Breaking the Nazi Code Affected Allied Naval Strategy During World War II* (New York: William Morrow and Co., 1988).

16

THE EASTERN AND MEDITERRANEAN FRONTS: WINNING BATTLES OF MEN AND MACHINES

To Stalingrad

Defeat in the East, November 1942– October 1943

The Mediterranean, 1942–1943

The East, 1944

By early 1942 the Nazi surge toward the frontiers of Europe had exhausted itself. The Wehrmacht, nevertheless, possessed the capability to launch major offensives and represented a determined opponent, capable of defending its position with tenacity even though at the far reaches of its logistic capabilities. But the productive and mobilized strength of the Allies exercised a growing and eventually overwhelming impact on operations. Moreover, Allied superiority in personnel and logistics allowed them to fight massive battles that played to their strengths, while minimizing those of their opponents. Along with these advantages went Allied superiority in intelligence and deception. Virtually every action that the German military undertook was now open to the prying eyes and ears of Allied intelligence. Moreover, the Allies could screen their intentions and plans almost entirely. Only Hitler's "intuition" at times caught glimpses of what was coming, but the Führer possessed neither the discipline nor consistency to act coherently on such visions.

In the Mediterranean, the British defeated Rommel at El Alamein and drove Axis forces from Egypt and Libya. As the British pushed the enemy back, the Allies used their advantages in sea and air power to land on the coast of North Africa. For the first time, the Americans entered the land battle against the Germans and after some initial difficulties played a major role in the Axis defeat in North Africa and then in the landings in Sicily and Italy. On the Eastern Front, the Soviets, through the skillful use of deception, magnified their growing superiority in weapons and their improving operational performance. In their offensives, they drove the Germans back hundreds of miles. In the end the Allies battered the Wehrmacht back to the Reich and ended whatever chance the Germans had of escaping their fate.

To Stalingrad

As spring 1942 approached, the Germans surmounted the desperate situation on the Eastern Front; they had prevented the terrible conditions of the winter campaign from degenerating into a collapse. Nevertheless, they confronted difficult challenges for the upcoming spring offensive. Halder, still chief of the general staff, and senior ground commanders argued that the army should remain on the defensive, rebuild the forces shattered by the winter, and await increases in production. Hitler, however, believed that Germany must destroy Soviet military potential before American industry came into play. By this point Hitler's word almost always carried the day.

In early April the OKH issued Directive 41 for a summer campaign. In the north, German forces were to link up with the Finns and finish the destruction of Leningrad. Army Group Center would stand on the defensive, while the major effort occurred in the south. There mobile units would clear the Soviets from west of the Don River and then strike into the Caucasus. Initially Hitler accorded Stalingrad little importance. The main objective was Soviet oil with the proviso that Stalingrad's capture might block movement of petroleum up the Volga River.

Several factors underlined how much Nazi capabilities had declined since 1941. Operation Barbarossa had called for a German offensive along the entire front, but by 1942 the Wehrmacht could launch a major offensive only in the south. Moreover, as German armies advanced into the Caucasus, their left flank would become increasingly exposed to Soviet counterblows from the north, and the Germans lacked sufficient troops to cover that flank. As a result, only by persuading their Romanian, Italian, and Hungarian allies to provide armies could Hitler launch the summer 1942 offensive. More ominously, the OKH had to strip other armies in the east of equipment and troops to prepare Army Group South for its role.

Before that offensive began, however, two major battles occurred. The Soviets picked up German preparations and at Stalin's direction launched a spoiling attack at Kharkov, Army Group South's main logistics base. The *Stavka* argued against the attack, for it believed that the Red Army should hold onto its reserves until German intentions became clear. On Stalin's orders, however, the offensive began on May 12; it soon broke through the German front. For a short period it appeared that the Russians

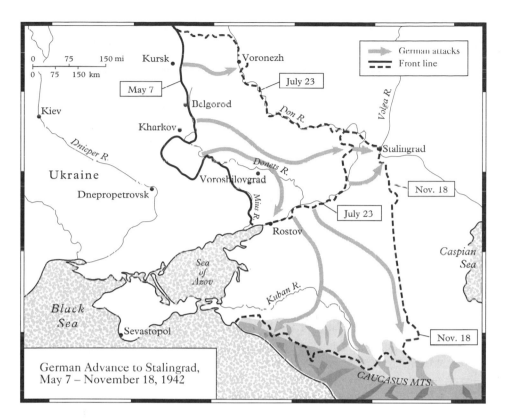

German Advance to Stalingrad,
May 7 – November 18, 1942

might reach Kharkov and its crucial supply dumps. But strong German forces contained the breakthrough and then launched a counterstrike at the salient's thin neck. Soviet commanders pleaded to retreat, but Stalin demanded that the attack continue. In effect, Soviet forces had advanced into a sack, and the German counterattack cut them off. Not only did the Germans capture 240,000 Soviet troops, but they also destroyed most of the Soviet armored reserves (1,200 tanks).

A second disaster for the Soviets followed on the heels of the first. In June 1942, Manstein, now commander of Eleventh Army, conducted a skillful attack on Sevastopol, the main Soviet naval base on the Crimean Peninsula. In ferocious fighting, German troops broke through the port's fortifications and crushed the Soviet garrison. As a reward for the successful siege, Hitler promoted Manstein to field marshal. The Führer, however, vetoed the new field marshal's suggestion that Eleventh Army form a reserve behind Army Group South's drive into the Caucasus. Instead most of the army's infantry and artillery (and Manstein) moved north to conduct siege operations against Leningrad. The few units remaining found themselves parceled out among the attacking armies of Army Group South.

On June 28 the summer offensive began. The Germans planned on launching a multiphased operation that would include sequential attacks from the left to right of Army Group South, followed by an advance into the Caucasus. On the left, in the first phase of the campaign, three panzer, three motorized, and nine infantry divisions struck due east toward Voronezh. By July 2 the Germans were on the city's outskirts, and by July 6 they had taken the city. Their success froze the *Stavka* because the German attack suggested an opening move against Moscow. However, the Germans turned south down the Don, while Hungarian divisions moved to cover the widening northern flank. On June 30, Sixth Army jumped off from the center of Army Group South and attempted to encircle Soviet units along the Don; but the *Stavka* finally persuaded Stalin to order a timely retreat and the German pincers closed on thin air.

As the Nazi advance accelerated, OKH divided Army Group South into Army Groups A and B, and on July 13 Hitler fired Field Marshal Bock for a second time. In effect, the Führer became commander of Army Group South and directed the offensive from his East Prussian headquarters. In the south Army Group A battered its way into Rostov, crossed the Don, and turned south. The gateway to the Caucasus was open. As Bock commented shortly before his relief, however, the battle had been "sliced in two." While Army Group B moved east toward Stalingrad and the Volga River, Army Group A moved south into the Caucasus. For the present, Hitler focused on the southern advance and shifted forces to Army Group A; this delayed the eastward move toward Stalingrad. Other delays came from both army groups having already encountered serious logistic difficulties, particularly the lack of fuel. The capture of Soviet oil fields in the Caucasus failed to alleviate these problems, since the Soviets did a thorough job of sabotaging wells and refining equipment.

In August, Hitler's erratic attention swung from the Caucasus to Stalingrad. On August 23, Sixth Army reached the Volga River north of the

Though the Germans occupied the center of Stalingrad, the Soviets refused to stop fighting. The Germans described the subsequent combat as a *Rattenkrieg*, a war among rats.

city; on the 24th it launched its first attacks on the suburbs and began fighting its way into the city. As fighting intensified, Hitler pulled forces out of the Caucasus and funneled them into the cauldron of Stalingrad's built-up area. The Soviet defenders prepared to hold out to the last. In the wreckage caused by constant air attacks and artillery bombardments, they established strong defenses and scattered numerous snipers. Street by street, building by building, German infantry dug the Soviets out of their defensive positions. Particularly savage fighting took place in Stalingrad's tractor works and in the city's great grain elevator. The close combat and hand-to-hand fighting, in some areas from floor to floor, maximized Soviet strengths of dogged stoicism and determination while minimizing German tactical flexibility and mobility.

Driven by Hitler's fanatical determination, the bitter battle had considerable strategic effects. The fighting ended whatever chance the Germans had to cut the Soviets off from oil supplies of the Caucasus. Moreover it reduced German reserves across the Eastern Front, while exhausting the Wehrmacht in a pointless battle of prestige. By early November Sixth Army had fought its way across the lunar landscape of Stalingrad. Although the Soviets held only a tenuous position on the banks of the Volga, they had pulled Sixth Army into a vulnerable position. Ill-equipped and poorly trained Romanian, Italian, and Hungarian formations protected its flanks; German forces in the Caucasus were exhausted; virtually no reserves were available; and winter was again closing in on a supply system stretched to the breaking point. Hitler, however, believed that the summer offensive had fought the Soviets to exhaustion. The generals were not so sure, but by this point in the war, they had learned to keep their opinions to themselves. German intelligence picked up some Soviet troop movements north of Stalingrad but reported that "only local attacks are expected."

Defeat in the East, November 1942–October 1943

Disaster at Stalingrad

In September 1942 the Soviets began preparations for a massive counteroffensive. Over the next two months, *Stavka* deployed nearly one million men, 900 tanks, and a vast array of artillery forces, including one-third of their rocket launchers, on Sixth Army's flanks. Their plan had limited aims—to break through the defenses north and south of Stalingrad and then to encircle German forces in the city. In the offensive the Soviets displayed significant improvements over the tactical and operational performance of earlier efforts.

On November 19, in the midst of a swirling snowstorm, units from five Soviet armies, including a tank army—a sign of growing Soviet operational skills—smashed into the Romanians north of Stalingrad. By early afternoon they had destroyed Romanian defenses and were in the open; their advance gained an average of fourteen miles on the first day. The XXXXVIII Panzer Corps attempted to plug the breach, but its obsolete collection of tanks had little chance against Soviet armor, equipped with T-34s. On the 20th two Soviet armies broke the Romanians south of Stalingrad. The Soviets split Fourth Panzer Army and drove some of its units into the pocket with Sixth Army. On November 23, Soviet spearheads advancing from north and south met late in the afternoon forty miles west of Stalingrad and isolated Sixth Army.

Decision making within the German high command now broke down, a sure indication of Hitler's destructive influence. On November 19 the Führer was in Berchtesgaden attempting to repair a deteriorating situation in the Mediterranean. As reports of trouble in the east arrived, he hurried north in his command train to OKH headquarters in East Prussia to deal with the Soviet emergency. During much of that trip, however, he was out of touch with the various command sections. Hitler provided no instructions to the commander of Sixth Army, General Friedrich Paulus, and by this point in the war no one remained in the high command willing to make independent decisions. On November 21, Hitler ordered Paulus to stand fast in Stalingrad "regardless of the danger of a temporary encirclement." When one of Paulus's corps commanders, General Walter von Seydlitz-Kurzbach, ordered his troops to retreat in preparation for a breakout, Hitler reacted angrily.

To deal with the deteriorating situation, Hitler created Army Group Don, consisting of four armies, and appointed Manstein to its command, but it took the field marshal nearly one week to assume control. During that period, Manstein advised Hitler that while a withdrawal from Stalingrad might be necessary, it would be best to wait until reinforcements arrived, since Sixth Army was tying down huge Soviet forces. The OKH, supported by many ground and air commanders on the scene, argued for an immediate breakout. Hitler, committed to holding on the Volga, temporized.

Göring, with the aid of some army commanders, provided the final ingredients for disaster. As early as November 21 Sixth Army had examined the possibility of an aerial bridge. The Luftwaffe's General Wolfram von Richthofen immediately warned Sixth Army that the Luftwaffe did not possess sufficient strength. Göring, however, assured Hitler that the Luftwaffe could supply Sixth Army, just as it had supported a corps and a half of German soldiers in the Demyansk pocket over the previous winter; the Luftwaffe chief of staff, despite a massive commitment of transport aircraft to Tunisia, offered no opposition to Göring's promise.

For the time being the Soviets strengthened their hold on Stalingrad. The Germans desperately attempted to patch together a relief force—not surprisingly, few of the reinforcements promised by Hitler arrived. The besieged required an airlift of 600 tons per day; under the best conditions the Luftwaffe could supply 350 tons. Airlift forces consisted of a hodgepodge of Ju 52s, Ju 86s, and He 111s. To cobble together even these aircraft the Luftwaffe stripped its bomber transition schools of their inexperienced crews; maintenance conditions were appalling, and operational rates fell to 10–20 percent during periods of bad weather. On only three days in December did transports reach a 300-ton level; on most days less than 100 tons arrived in Stalingrad.

In mid-December, Manstein launched his offensive to break through to Stalingrad; LVII Panzer Corps drove to within thirty-five miles of the city on December 19, but no farther. Manstein appears to have urged Hitler to order a breakout, but the Führer refused because neither Manstein nor Paulus would assure him that one would succeed. One observer of the Führer during this period concluded that he "seemed no longer capable of making a decision." On December 26, Paulus reported his army incapable of a breakout unless German troops outside the city first opened up a supply corridor.

In fact, it was too late. On December 16 the Soviets attacked the Italian Army along the Don northwest of Stalingrad. The Soviets ripped a one-hundred-mile gap in Army Group Don's flank, and Manstein had to shift forces to contain the breakthrough and abandon all ideas of relieving Sixth Army. The collapse along the upper Don placed an even greater burden on air supply, while Soviet capture of the airfields at Tatsinskaya and Morozovsk in early January forced the Luftwaffe to move its bases almost 200 miles from the pocket. This relocation ended any significant air bridge to Stalingrad.

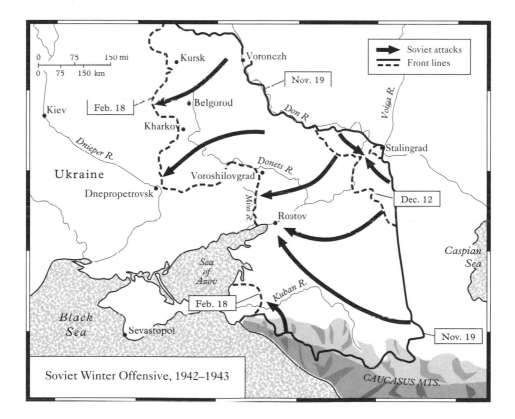

Soviet Winter Offensive, 1942–1943

Throughout January, Soviet forces drove toward Rostov and the Donets Basin. The question now was whether the Red Army would reach Rostov and cut off Seventeenth and First Panzer Armies in the Caucasus. The defenders at Stalingrad would have to hold to the end, in hopes of tying up Soviet forces, while Army Group Don desperately attempted to stabilize a collapsing situation. After Paulus rejected the final surrender ultimatum, the Soviets began their last attack on January 10. By February 2, the Germans had surrendered. Out of 250,000 soldiers trapped in the Stalingrad pocket, approximately 90,000 became prisoners; barely 5,000 survived the war.

The Germans Recover

As Stalingrad capitulated, the Germans strove to stabilize the situation along the southern front. Hitler did allow Army Group A to withdraw from the Caucasus, but part of it became shut up on the Kuban peninsula opposite the Crimea. During the third week in January, a new series of Soviet attacks ripped into Army Group B and virtually destroyed the Hungarian Second Army. The Soviets had achieved operational freedom from Voronezh to Voroshilovgrad, a distance of over two hundred miles. By mid-January, they had captured Belgorod and almost reached Dnepropetrovsk. The Germans had to abandon Kharkov on February 15.

Despite Soviet gains, the Germans managed a recovery; they were falling back on their supply dumps, while the Soviets were outrunning their supply lines. A lack of focus also worked against the Soviets; their spearheads were neither mutually supporting nor strong enough to achieve independent success. Significant German reinforcements also arrived. Hitler permitted the transfer to Manstein's Army Group of about 100,000 soldiers from Army Group A in the Crimea and seven fresh divisions from western Europe. In addition, Luftwaffe forces, reorganized under Richthofen's driving leadership, provided enhanced air support. From February 20 to March 15, Luftwaffe squadrons provided 1,000 combat sorties per day versus an average of only 350 in January. By this point the Soviet advance had left the bases of the Red air force far behind, thereby making air support incapable of intervening in the battle.

Despite Hitler's anger at the loss of Kharkov, Manstein persuaded him that Army Group South (now reformed from Army Group Don and parts of Army Group B) could reestablish control of its northern flank only by temporarily relinquishing control of that city. Supported by Richthofen's aircraft, a German counteroffensive began on February 19. The sudden eruption of the German forces caused a collapse of the overextended Soviet forces. By mid-March, Army Group South had recaptured Kharkov and driven the Soviets back to the Donets River, a gain of almost one hundred miles. The spring thaw finally arrived, and both sides, exhausted after fighting that had lasted continuously from July 1942, collapsed.

The Battle of Kursk, July 1943

Even as SS troops battered their way into Kharkov, Hitler issued a directive for the coming summer. Since the Wehrmacht no longer possessed the offensive power to win a decisive victory in a short campaign, the Führer's directive suggested instead a series of limited offensives, first at Kursk then at Leningrad, to reduce Soviet reserves and to improve defensive positions. After discarding several options, Hitler settled in mid-April 1943 on a major offensive, "Citadel," against the Kursk salient north of Kharkov.

The original conception was that Citadel would begin as soon as spring conditions provided solid ground for maneuver. But there were risks; the sectors north and south of Kursk were vulnerable to a Soviet counter-strike. The overall situation led Manstein to suggest that the Wehrmacht remain on the defensive and counterattack any Soviet summer offensive. Such an approach, however, would have entailed considerable risks and perhaps even the surrender of territory, the last thing Hitler was willing to

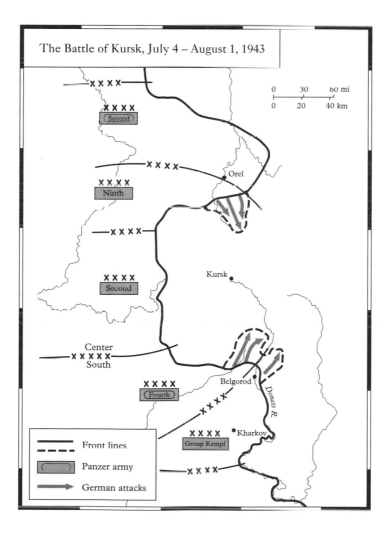

The Battle of Kursk, July 4 – August 1, 1943

countenance. In the end the plan called for the major effort to occur on the southern shoulder of the Kursk salient. Army Group South would break through Soviet positions and then drive deep behind Kursk to link up with another drive launched on the northern shoulder by Army Group Center's Ninth Army. The hoped-for result would pinch off the Kursk salient and Soviet forces defending it.

Above all, Hitler hoped to achieve a major psychological victory over the Red Army. He argued, "The victory at Kursk must have the effect of a beacon seen around the world." In May he postponed Citadel until June or July despite opposition from some generals, including the OKH chief of staff, Colonel General Kurt Zeitzler. Hitler believed the postponement would allow a buildup of the armored forces with Tiger tanks and the new Panthers. Manstein and Günther von Kluge, commanders of the army groups involved in the operation, disagreed, believing that any delay would result in Soviet countermeasures. Nevertheless, Hitler postponed Citadel to early July. An uneasy calm settled on the Eastern Front as both sides prepared for the coming battle.

The Soviets had improved considerably in operational skill and in their use of intelligence. In April they picked up German intentions to launch a major strike at Kursk and in May began preparations on both shoulders of the salient. German intelligence never divined the massive scale of Soviet defensive and offensive measures to meet the attack. By this point in the war, Stalin was displaying greater trust in his generals. Zhukov and others advised him to remain on the defensive, and he accepted their advice.

The extent of Soviet preparations underlines the trap into which the Germans were walking. Soviet first-line defenses on both sides of the salient were two to three miles deep and contained three to four trench lines with numerous bunkers and strong points. Behind this line the Soviets constructed a second defensive zone at depths varying between six and eighteen miles. Twenty-five miles farther back they laid out three more lines on a similar scale. The fortification zone extended more than one hundred miles and included more than half a million mines. On the northern shoulder the Soviets achieved a density of forty-eight antitank guns per mile of front. Four armies, including a tank army, defended the northern shoulder of the Kursk salient; six armies held the southern side, while five armies of the Steppe Front stood immediately in reserve. Three more armies stood north of Kursk and two south; these forces could reinforce the salient should things turn bad. If the front held, the Soviets intended to use these reserves in major counterattacks. German intelligence gave no indication about the extent of enemy preparations.

On the German side, the growing strength of ground forces reflected the success that Speer had had in mobilizing the European economy. The Luftwaffe possessed nearly 2,500 combat aircraft, more than half of which would support Citadel. In the north, Field Marshal Walter Model's Ninth Army contained three panzer corps with twenty-one divisions, including one panzer grenadier and six panzer divisions, as well as 900 tanks; Manstein's Army Group South contained four panzer corps with twenty-two divisions,

Konstantin K. Rokossovskii wore a set of stainless steel false teeth as a result of his imprisonment and torture by the secret police before World War II for "anti Soviet" activities. After regaining Stalin's favor he displayed a great flair for mobile warfare and played a key role in the battles of Moscow, Stalingrad, and Kursk, as well as Operation Bagration.

including six panzer and five panzer grenadier divisions, as well as 1,000 tanks. The entire battle would involve some 4,000 Soviet and 3,000 German tanks and assault guns.

On July 5, Citadel began. On the northern shoulder, Ninth Army attacked on a thirty-five-mile front and initially enjoyed limited success. Its attack broke through Soviet front-line defenses and had reached the second line by day's end. By July 6, Marshal Konstantin K. Rokossovskii, commander of Soviet forces in the north, had put in two tank corps and an infantry corps from his reserves, while *Stavka* moved additional units forward. By the next day Ninth Army's assault had stalled along a heavily fortified ridge thirteen miles beyond its start line and still well short of Rokossovskii's third defensive line; attempts to break through on July 10 and 11 failed entirely and Model could characterize the battle only as "a rolling battle of attrition"—exactly the kind of battle that played to Soviet strengths and minimized German mobility.

In the south, Manstein's offensive hardly got off to an auspicious start. As German troops moved into jump-off positions in the predawn hours of July 5, General Nikolai F. Vatutin, commander of Soviet forces in the south, unleashed a massive preemptive artillery bombardment. The surprise bombardment inflicted heavy casualties on German troops and demonstrated that the Soviets were fully informed about the coming attack. Nevertheless, the first hours went well. Fourth Panzer Army, consisting of XXXXVIII Panzer Corps and II SS Panzer Corps, attacked along a thirty-mile front. Within two hours they had penetrated front-line positions and had seemingly broken through. But by early afternoon the Germans began to recognize the weaknesses in their intelligence picture. They were, in fact, in the midst of a defensive position, the depths of which they scarcely could imagine. Moreover, in early afternoon a drenching thunderstorm flooded the battlefield and halted XXXXVIII Panzer Corps. Finally, while Fourth

Panzer Army made relatively good progress, Detachment Kempf (a temporary combination of two corps under General Werner Kempf) on its right
flank had hardly advanced. In the air the Luftwaffe provided 3,000 sorties a
day over the salient; however, even this level of effort was insufficient to eliminate Soviet aircraft that were defending their ground forces and attacking
advancing Germans.

On July 6 and 7, Manstein made some progress in the south. The
II SS Panzer Corps led the movement forward. Detachment Kempf continued to have difficulties, and Fourth Panzer Army had to detach a division to
secure its flank. The ferocious fighting and extensive mine fields throughout
the enemy's deep defensive positions imposed terrible losses on German
tank forces. By July 9, the army's *Grossdeutschland* Division had already lost
220 out of 300 tanks.

Manstein's attacks from the south finally began to show results. By
July 11, II SS Panzer Corps had advanced about twenty-five miles, and the
Soviets were forced to use reserves from the Steppe Front. On the same day
Kempf's III Panzer Corps had finally broken into the open. Despite desperate Soviet resistance, Kempf linked up with II SS Panzer Corps and trapped
a substantial number of Soviet troops. On July 12 nearly 1,800 German and
Russian armored vehicles clashed on a small battlefield near Prokhorovka in
the largest tank battle of the war. When it was over, the Germans had lost
over 300 tanks, and the Russians 400; but the Russians had held. Manstein
still had two fresh divisions and believed that his forces could reach Kursk.
He was undoubtedly wrong because the Soviets still held four armies in
reserve.

Beginning on July 10, however, events elsewhere intervened: Anglo-
American armies landed in Sicily, and Mussolini's regime teetered on the
brink of collapse. Amidst concerns about Soviet forces north and south of
Kursk, Hitler terminated Citadel to reinforce the Mediterranean. Only
Manstein urged continuation of the Kursk battle, but his reasoning largely
rested on a belief that no other alternatives existed. In retrospect, Kursk was
a disastrous failure, for it had consumed most of the German army's replenished reserves and armored forces. It was the last important German offensive in Russia.

The Soviets Counterattack

After halting Citadel, the Soviets seized the initiative and launched a series of
attacks across the breadth of the Eastern Front. They relied on methods
quite different from those of the Germans; instead of boldly relying on deep
penetrations and double envelopments, the Red Army utilized several thrusts
that aimed to push back the enemy on a broad front. If the Germans halted
one thrust, the Russians shifted to another. With a 2.5:1 advantage in the
air, the Soviets used their air forces for close ground support and air defense,
and with an even greater advantage in artillery, they used preparatory fires
on the same scale as those used in World War I.

The first Soviet move came against the Orel salient lying directly
north of Kursk. Three Soviet armies attacked the northern side of the

salient on July 12, 1943. By using forces previously committed to the Kursk battle, Model prevented a Soviet breakthrough. In this rare case Hitler sanctioned retreat from the salient, for he desperately needed troops to shore up a collapsing Fascist Italy (Mussolini fell from power on July 25).

Manstein confronted more daunting problems in the south. Soviet attacks stung his forces at their northern and southern extremities. Hitler refused to make the hard decisions demanded by the desperate plight of German forces; Manstein warned that the Führer must either provide his army group with twenty divisions or abandon the Donets Basin. The best solution might have been a phased retreat of about 150 miles to the Dnieper and reinforcement of that line. Hitler dithered, however, and the northern flank of Army Group South dissolved. Soviet forces took Belgorod on August 5, drove west, and forced the Germans to evacuate Kharkov for the last time on August 21. A desperate counterattack by two divisions finally halted the Soviet advance and permitted Eighth Army and Fourth Panzer Army to reestablish contact and new defensive lines, but the Soviets had advanced nearly eighty miles.

Soviet Offensives, July 7, 1943 – April 30, 1944

Along the Mius and Donets rivers, Soviet offensives rocked First Panzer Army and a reconstituted Sixth Army. First Panzer Army held; on August 18, however, the Soviets broke through Sixth Army by concentrating massive artillery on a narrow front. Germans attempts to pinch off the breakthrough with attacks on its shoulders almost succeeded, but fierce Soviet attacks blocked the counterattack. Manstein urged Hitler to abandon the Donets Basin. The Führer remained obdurate; not until August 31 did he approve withdrawal of First Panzer and Sixth armies forty miles to a new defensive line. As the two armies pulled back, their desperate plight finally forced Hitler to abandon the Donets Basin and permit a withdrawal of about 140 miles. Sixth Army had to hold in front of the Dnieper because its retreat would isolate the Crimea; Hitler was desperately afraid that the Russians would use that peninsula to launch air attacks against Romanian oil fields.

Despite his permitting abandonment of the Donets Basin, Hitler refused to allow Fourth Panzer and Eighth armies on Army Group South's northern flank to fall back on the Dnieper, but that flank unraveled so fast that by late September, the Red Army and the Wehrmacht were in a desperate race for the Dnieper. Many retreating Germans escaped to the far side, but the Soviets made several hasty river crossings and established bridgeheads from which they could resume their advance.

The bridgeheads made the German position desperate. North of Kiev the Soviet advance severed connections between army groups South and Center; on the lower Dnieper, the Soviets crossed the river and seized a bridgehead north of Dnepropetrovsk thirty miles wide and ten miles deep. By this time they had already won a great victory against Army Group South. Their forces had advanced an average of 150 miles on a front of 650 miles and had regained the Ukraine's most valuable agricultural and industrial areas. Despite Hitler's demands for scorched earth, the hastiness and lack of planning characterizing Army Group South's retreat minimized the damage that the Germans could inflict.

Unrelenting Soviet pressure eventually cut off German forces in the Crimean peninsula. Against thirteen German and two Romanian divisions, the Soviets on October 9 launched forty-five infantry divisions, three tank corps, and two mechanized corps, supported by 400 batteries of artillery. As the Soviet drive gathered momentum and approached the Black Sea west of the Crimea, Kleist and the Romanian dictator, Marshal Antonescu, begged Hitler to abandon the peninsula and allow Seventeenth Army to retreat. Hitler, however, refused, and by November the Soviets had isolated Seventeenth Army in the Crimea. The entire position along the lower Dnieper had now unraveled. One hundred miles to the north, Soviet forces expanded the size of their bridgehead across the Dnieper. Another two hundred miles to the north, Soviet forces seized Kiev; nowhere on the southern front could the Germans stabilize the situation. Only the arrival of autumn rains eventually brought relief to the hard-pressed Wehrmacht.

The fighting over summer and fall 1943 represented the first stage in the collapse of the Nazi position in the east. The constant battles wore German infantry down and forced the panzer divisions to act as fire brigades.

The 2.5 million German soldiers on the Eastern Front had been insufficient to alter the growing imbalance. The OKW considered conscripting women but dropped the idea because of Hitler's violent opposition. As for the Soviets, they had had about 6 million soldiers and had learned their lessons well over the past two years. Their massive attacks and multiple thrusts effectively combined armor, infantry, and artillery and overwhelmed German defenders. On the intelligence side, they enjoyed an enormous superiority, and they skillfully used deception to blind their German enemy almost entirely.

The Soviets also used partisan operations to advantage. Hitler's racial policies and brutal treatment pushed many Russians into guerrilla warfare. By early 1943 approximately 250,000 Soviets operated as partisans behind German lines. Usually organized into brigades of 1,000 men and women, the partisans extended Soviet power into Nazi-occupied territory, conducted raids, demolished roads and railroads, cut telephone lines, and provided intelligence. Those near the front lines usually took orders from the staffs of the closest Soviet armies and launched operations in coordination with major offensives. Their superiors passed commands by radio and air; supplies came from low-flying aircraft. In the two years of most intense partisan warfare, German forces suffered approximately 300,000 casualties, including thirty general officers and more than one thousand officers. Although partisan operations did not change the course of the war in the east, they compelled the Germans to diffuse their already overextended forces.

While extraordinary battles in Russia continued with savage fury, Hitler drove his police and military—willing participants—to complete the racial cleansing of eastern Europe. This extermination of the Jews and the further enslavement of the Slavic masses continued until the final collapse of the Nazis. By 1942–1943 the great killing camps such as Auschwitz and Treblinka were spewing their ashen clouds of slaughtered Jews and other unfortunates over the landscape of eastern Europe; long trains of cattle and freight cars transported the victims—a diversion of scarce transport that even affected the Wehrmacht's logistics. Meanwhile, Ukrainians, Russians, Poles, and others in slightly higher racial categories—as defined by Hitler—were dragooned by the millions to serve as slave laborers in the great industrial undertakings of the SS and German industry. If not murdered, they were brutalized, starved, and mistreated. If Germany could not win the war, then at least the Reich could live up to the Führer's promise given before the war that he would free Europe of all its Jews however the war might turn out.

Although Hitler's racial policies and refusals to abandon territory contributed to the catastrophe, the problem lay deeper. The extent of German miscalculations in planning and executing Barbarossa were now apparent. Above all, the Germans were not fighting "subhuman" barbarians, but an enormously gifted people, whose military efforts early in the war had been seriously impaired by the mistakes and prejudices of Stalin. The Soviets had now emerged as a skillful and resourceful foe.

The Mediterranean, 1942–1943

While Soviet armies had begun the arduous task of retaking territory, the Western Powers finally were able to overcome German tactical and operational performance by improved battle effectiveness of their own, as well as increasing numerical superiority in manpower and equipment. Still unprepared for a direct assault on Fortress Europe, British and American commanders undertook to push the Axis from North Africa, open the Mediterranean to Allied shipping, and drive Italy out of the war. In this they were to be successful, but only after heavy fighting. The battles of North Africa would prove particularly important to correct the significant deficiencies that had appeared with the first commitment of American troops to battle.

El Alamein

The disastrous defeat on the Gazala Line and at Tobruk in June 1942 threatened to undermine the British position in the Middle East. At this point, the British theater commander, General Sir Claude Auchinleck assumed control of Eighth Army. As its beaten remnants streamed eastward, he determined to stand at El Alamein, sixty miles west of Alexandria. Unlike other defensive positions in the desert, El Alamein had the advantage that it could not be flanked; to the south lay the Qattara Depression, a great dry salt sea that could not support heavy vehicles.

Furious at the May and June defeats, Churchill sacked Auchinleck and appointed General Harold Alexander in his place as the theater commander. On August 13, Lieutenant General Bernard Law Montgomery assumed command of Eighth Army. Montgomery was an inspired choice. Admittedly he was a careful, prudent general who rarely took risks, but his approach reflected the caliber of his forces. In his memoirs, Montgomery explained that he built up the Eighth Army by concentrating "on three essentials: leadership, equipment, and training. All three were deficient."* Other problems identified by Montgomery included discipline, confidence, and morale. As he acted to restore Eighth Army, he made the ground and air forces work closely together and ended the practice of fighting in brigade-sized units. In the future divisions would fight as divisions. As additional supplies and new weapons poured into Egypt, Montgomery overcame deficiencies in equipment and established huge supply dumps. Over a period of three months, he fought the battles of Alam Halfa and El Alamein with a flawed instrument, but his success reflected a realistic appreciation of British weaknesses.

At the end of August, Rommel began the battle of Alam Halfa with an attack similar to the one he had used along the Gazala Line in May 1942.

---

*Bernard L. Montgomery, *Memoirs* (London: Collins, 1958), p. 103.

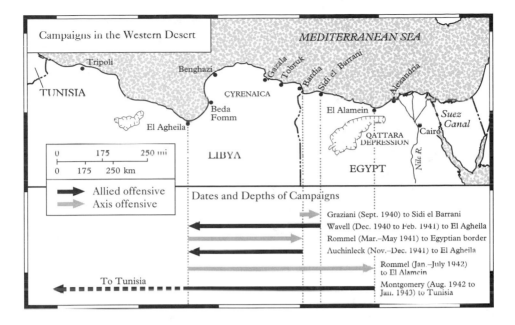

Campaigns in the Western Desert

MEDITERRANEAN SEA

Tripoli

Benghazi

TUNISIA

CYRENAICA

Gazala · Tobruk · Bardia · Sidi el Barrani · Alexandria

Beda Fomm

El Alamein

Suez Canal

El Agheila

QATTARA DEPRESSION

Cairo

LIBYA

EGYPT

Nile R.

0 175 250 mi
0 175 250 km

→ Allied offensive
→ Axis offensive

Dates and Depths of Campaigns

Graziani (Sept. 1940) to Sidi el Barrani
Wavell (Dec. 1940 to Feb. 1941) to El Agheila
Rommel (Mar.–May 1941) to Egyptian border
Auchinleck (Nov.–Dec. 1941) to El Agheila
Rommel (Jan.–July 1942) to El Alamein
To Tunisia
Montgomery (Aug. 1942 to Jan. 1943) to Tunisia

That is, he launched a diversionary attack along the coast and on the British center and then sent his main attack against their southern flank. As the Germans drove into the British rear, RAF fighter bombers hammered their columns. Extensive minefields hampered the Afrika Korps' effort to cut off British forces, while British armor fought a solid defensive battle. On September 2, Rommel pulled back after suffering heavy losses and established defensive positions between the coast and the Qattara Depression.

Montgomery now began preparing Eighth Army for what would be his most famous battle, El Alamein. His initial concept involved an attack on each flank of the German position, but reservations about the readiness of his armor to fight a mobile battle resulted in a more straightforward plan. The main attack would occur against Rommel's northern flank, while diversionary attacks pinned German units in the south. Artillery would batter enemy defenses, engineers would clear lanes through enemy mine fields, infantry would then drive through those defenses, and finally the armor would break out. It was a simple plan that relied on firepower and numerical superiority.

The operation, however, failed to go according to plan. With Montgomery having some 230,000 troops and Rommel only 80,000, the set-piece attack began on October 23 with a powerful artillery bombardment, followed by infantry assaults. But gaps cleared by the engineers were too narrow, and the infantry failed to secure the far ends of the lanes. As a result, British armor became entrapped in mine fields. Fortunately for the British, Rommel was home on sick leave, and German commanders responded slowly. They launched a series of piecemeal attacks and suffered heavy casualties; by the end of the first day 15th Panzer Division had lost three-quarters of its

General Bernard L. Montgomery usually wore a black beret, a pullover sweater, and khaki pants. Though he seemed a cranky eccentric, he improved the performance of his units, generated greater confidence among his troops, and soon drove Rommel out of Egypt and Libya.

tanks. But the Germans continued fighting, while British armor remained stuck in mine fields.

To weaken German infantry and tanks, Montgomery began what he called a "dog fight." On November 2, after one week's hard fighting, he launched a powerful thrust against the German center. With the British possessing 600 tanks and the Germans only 30, Rommel, who had rushed back to Africa, started pulling his infantry back on November 3. But Hitler stopped him. Amidst the confusion, Montgomery launched another attack and broke through German defenses. Subsequent efforts to cut off the Afrika Korps, however, failed because British forces moved too slowly. Rommel began a rapid retreat across Egypt into Libya, eventually reaching Tunisia. Montgomery's pursuit was slow and methodical as he established airfields along his route of advance and opened ports for logistical support. But he had achieved what none of his predecessors had managed; he had defeated Rommel.

Operation "Torch"

Meanwhile on the western coast of North Africa major events were in motion. During the Arcadia Conference in December 1941, Churchill had proposed a landing on the shores of French North Africa. The Americans, however, displayed scant interest; from the first, they felt that a "Germany-first" strategy demanded immediate action in Europe. In May 1942, Roosevelt even promised Vyacheslav Molotov, the Soviet foreign minister, that the Western Powers would open a second front in 1942. Planning did begin for a descent on the French coast, should the Soviet Union appear on the brink of collapse, but such a venture represented only a desperate effort to distract the Germans.

The strategy preferred by the American military leaders, particularly General Marshall, the U.S. Army's chief of staff, was to build up military capabilities for a direct assault on western Europe sometime in 1943. However, the U.S. Navy, feeding on prewar preparations and popular attitudes,

In North Africa, General Dwight D. Eisenhower gained experience and developed the skills in high-level command and coalition warfare that were essential for his future success as Supreme Allied Commander.

pushed for a Pacific strategy; and the British doubted whether a landing in western Europe could be successful in 1943. For a while, Marshall moved toward the navy's urgings that the United States turn to the Pacific. Roosevelt, however, refused to countenance such a recasting of American strategy. Instead he demanded a major initiative in Europe in 1942 if not against German-occupied France, then in the Mediterranean—because he recognized the political necessity of a commitment of American troops in Europe to keep his nation focused on defeating Germany. American military leaders eventually agreed to Torch, landings to occupy Algeria and Morocco and co-opt the Vichy French.

The commander of Torch was an obscure American general, Dwight David Eisenhower. Ike had not seen combat in World War I, but he possessed gifts of diplomacy and tact as well as operational competence. His political skills were essential to getting Anglo-American forces to work together on the operational level. Initially, he had some weaknesses as a commander, but he displayed great capacity to learn. If not Rommel's equal on the battlefield, he far surpassed most German generals in his political and diplomatic skills and in his understanding the wider aspects of war.

Considerable wrangling took place between American and British leaders about the location of the landings; the final plan focused on Algeria and Morocco. Following landings at Casablanca, Oran, and Algiers, Allied forces would advance east by land and sea against Tunisia. The initial landings in North Africa on November 8 went well, especially considering the Allied troops' lack of combat experience. The French resisted the invasion tenaciously at first; Hitler's lack of trust in the Vichy regime, however, resulted in those forces possessing obsolete matériel and inadequate ammunition stocks. Coincidentally, Vichy's number-two man, Admiral François Darlan, was present in North Africa and eventually agreed to an armistice.

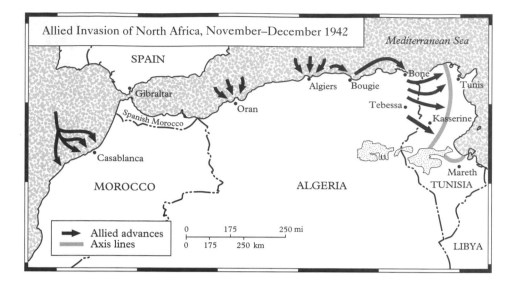

Allied Invasion of North Africa, November–December 1942

Hitler's response was, as usual, swift and ruthless. While Nazi troops occupied Vichy France, paratrooper and Luftwaffe units, flying from Sicily, won "the race of Tunisia" before the Allied forces could get there. By seizing Tunisia, the Germans kept the Mediterranean closed to Allied shipping for another six months and thereby exacerbated worldwide shipping shortages plaguing Allied logisticians. But the price was too high. The decision to fight in Tunisia resulted from Hitler's desire to support Mussolini's decrepit regime; it was perhaps the worst decision that Hitler made in 1942. It committed the remainder of Fascist Italy's military power and substantial numbers of German troops to defend a hopeless position, and it forced Axis naval and air power to fight at a severe disadvantage. The result was a defeat almost as great as Stalingrad, one entirely resulting from German miscalculations.

Though the opening moves in Tunisia had favored the Allies, German paratroopers and armor halted and then pushed the Americans and British back to Tunisia's western frontier. By January, Rommel had escaped from Libya and arrived in southern Tunisia where all the Axis forces in North Africa concentrated. However, Rommel commanded only a portion of Axis forces, while units in northern Tunisia fell under command of Colonel General Jürgen von Arnim. Immediately after his arrival in Tunisia, Rommel sensed an opportunity; Montgomery's hesitant pursuit gave the Germans a relatively free hand, while Anglo-American forces in Algeria were strung out along the Tunisian frontier. The Allied First Army included the American II Corps, commanded by Major General Lloyd R. Fredendall, who refused advice, deployed his troops badly, and located his headquarters deep underground and far behind the front lines. Rommel suggested an armored drive sweeping up from southern Tunisia to destroy Allied supply dumps in eastern Algeria and perhaps even to trap First Army against the coast. In addition, he hoped to give the Americans a severe mauling that would affect their confidence for the rest of the war. Fortunately for the

Allies, the Desert Fox received little support for the proposed attack, and much of the German armor remained under Arnim.

The battle began on February 14 when Rommel's 10th and 21st Panzer divisions punched through thinly held passes in central Tunisia. After pushing back Combat Command A of the U.S. 1st Armored Division and surrounding the 168th Regimental Combat Team, the Germans advanced west toward Kasserine. A counterattack by Combat Command C of the 1st Armored Division failed disastrously, and veteran German forces fought their way through Kasserine Pass. After Arnim had convinced Italian headquarters in Rome to deny Rommel's proposal for a deep encirclement, and after Arnim had refused to release one of his panzer divisions, Rommel advanced north in two columns. One column turned north ten miles east of Kasserine, while the other turned north at Kasserine. Both columns encountered spirited resistance from British units in prepared defensive positions and were halted; on February 22 German forces began withdrawing. Allied ground strength, Arnim's refusal to support Rommel, and German weaknesses had enabled Rommel to achieve only a tactical success.

Immediately after Kasserine, Rommel turned south against the British who had finally arrived from Egypt. Though he attempted to knock them off balance, intelligence from Ultra alerted his opponents, and Montgomery dealt the Afrika Korps a stunning defeat. German forces lost more than one-third of their tanks. Seriously ill, Rommel left Africa a few days later.

With Rommel's defeat, the Axis position in North Africa steadily deteriorated. Ultra allowed Anglo-American air power to interdict the Axis supply lines from Italy. By March the Germans had abandoned the sealift; thereafter, the Luftwaffe's hard-pressed air transports had to provide logistic support: ammunition, fuel, food, and personnel. Again Ultra provided ample intelligence, and Allied fighters destroyed protective screens of Axis fighters as well as the transports themselves. The end came in early May, as the Allies mopped up the remnants in Tunisia. The Germans had lost heavily in the air; the Wehrmacht's ground losses represented the OKH's Mediterranean reserves, while the destruction of Italian ground forces, the last to surrender, left Mussolini with little to defend the homeland. After Tunisia, the Duce's regime enjoyed neither respect nor authority among a disillusioned population.

The victory in North Africa was particularly important for American ground and air forces. Their opening exposure to combat had not been auspicious; some U.S. units in Kasserine Pass had collapsed under the pressure of what was a large-scale raid by German forces. But American commanders set about with determination to repair their deficiencies and learn from experience. As Rommel suggested shortly before his death, American ground forces had been inferior to those of the British when the Germans first encountered them, but the Americans had shown a great capacity to learn. The story of the U.S. Army was thus one of steady, consistent improvement in battlefield performance. Typical of this American improvement was that of air-ground cooperation in Tunisia. The system in place as the campaign began proved generally unworkable; but the Americans had the very effective model of the RAF-British army system to copy. Not only did they dispense with the old, but they improved the British system and subsequently used it with enormous effectiveness in Normandy.

Attack on Sicily and Italy

After the Axis surrender in Tunisia in May 1943, the Allies began preparing for the next phase in the European war. At the Casablanca Conference in January 1943, General Marshall had made a last appeal for a cross-channel invasion in 1943, but Churchill's eloquence convinced Roosevelt that the Allies should maintain their momentum in the Mediterranean and direct their efforts toward Italy. Though American military leaders still preferred an early cross-channel invasion, the advantages of defeating the Italians, opening the Mediterranean to Allied shipping, and enlarging the air offensive

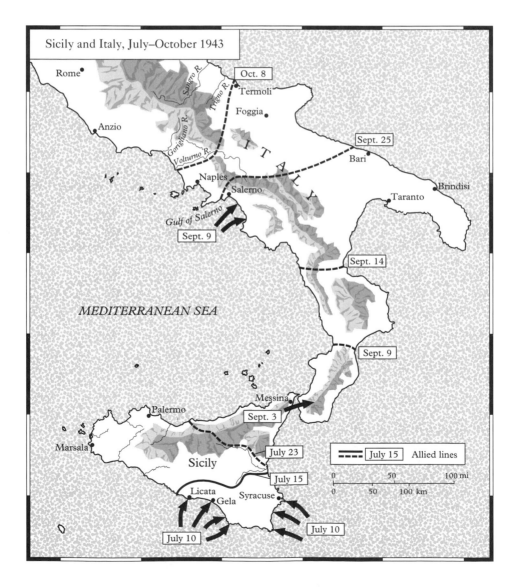

Sicily and Italy, July–October 1943

against Germany were obvious. At the Trident Conference in May 1943, the Americans accepted the strategic goal of eliminating Italy from the war but demanded that the forces involved consist only of those already in the Mediterranean. At Trident the Americans and British also agreed that planning begin for a cross-channel invasion in May 1944. The British, nevertheless, pressed for operations in the eastern Aegean and possibly in the Balkans. Finally, at the Teheran Conference in November 1943, Roosevelt, Churchill, and Stalin agreed to a cross-channel invasion—Operation "Overlord"—in spring 1944 in conjunction with an Anglo-American attack on southern France and a major offensive by the Soviets on the Eastern Front. This was the final blueprint for Allied strategy in Europe.

On July 10, 1943, the British Eighth Army under Montgomery and the U.S. Seventh Army under Major General George S. Patton stormed ashore on Sicily in Operation "Husky"—the largest amphibious assault in the war. Seven divisions made amphibious landings (compared to five divisions later at Normandy). The landings occurred on the southeast corner of the island, the British on the right, the Americans on the left. Montgomery, as the senior ground forces commander, had devised a straightforward plan for conquering Sicily; Eighth Army would drive up from the southeast corner of Sicily toward Messina, while Patton's army provided a flank guard. There seemed no reason why Montgomery could not execute his plan; only a small force of German and Italian troops defended the island. But the Germans proved as tenacious and combat-effective as usual; hilly and broken terrain aided their defensive efforts.

When Montgomery's attack slowed, Patton, who had no intention of acting as flank guard, raced west, captured Palermo, and then pushed east along the northern coast of the island. He got to Messina before Montgomery, but not before German ground forces escaped. Flak batteries on both sides of the straits of Messina protected this escape, while Allied air and naval units failed to intervene with sufficient vigor. In this operation as in everything he did, Patton projected flamboyance as well as leadership. But his political sensitivity was, unfortunately, considerably less than his military genius. He came close to ending his career by slapping two enlisted soldiers suffering from shell shock.

Whatever its failures, Husky gained considerable strategic and political advantages. It forced Hitler to shut down Citadel and confirmed his fears about the political stability of Mussolini's regime. On July 25, King Victor Emmanuel III dismissed Mussolini from office. Immediately thereafter, military police arrested the fallen dictator and whisked him away to a variety of secret locations (Luftwaffe paratroops and SS commandoes liberated him in September 1943, but he would perish at the hands of Italian partisans in April 1945). The king called on Marshal Pietro Badoglio, who had presided over the disasters of 1940, to get Italy out of the war.

By summer 1943, losses of manpower and equipment in Tunisia had destroyed the Wehrmacht's strategic reserves throughout the Mediterranean. Thoroughly distrustful of the Italians, Hitler understood the meaning of the coup against Mussolini; the new government would make a deal as soon as possible with the Allies—a deal that could place the British and Americans on the Alps and provide them bases in Italy at minimum cost. He immediately ordered the buildup of sizable forces under Rommel to intervene, while German units infiltrated to strategic locations throughout the peninsula. Hitler had every reason to worry. Though Badoglio reaffirmed Italy's loyalty, he immediately opened negotiations to switch sides. But Italy's new leaders failed to act decisively, and negotiations dragged into August and early September. By then the possibilities that Italy offered had almost slipped away.

On September 3, Eighth Army landed on the toe of Italy. Six days later an Anglo-American force under General Mark Clark in Operation "Avalanche" landed in the Gulf of Salerno, south of Naples, while the British Broadcasting Corporation, to Badoglio's horror, announced Italy's acceptance of an armistice. Italian dithering and incompetence, however, had convinced the Americans that a drop by the 82nd Airborne Division on Rome's airfields would result in disaster. The king, Badoglio, and other Italian leaders promptly decamped, leaving the army with no orders, and made their way south to Allied lines. The Wehrmacht disarmed the leaderless Italian military with minimum difficulty.

Meanwhile, Field Marshal Kesselring responded vigorously to the landings at Salerno. Well-organized counterattacks threatened to drive Clark's forces into the sea, while Montgomery's Eighth Army advanced at a snail's pace up the Italian toe. Supporting Allied naval and air forces prevented the Germans from exploiting their advantage. With the linkup of Clark and Montgomery's forces, the Germans began a slow retreat northward and eventually abandoned Naples. The Allied advance, however, turned into a nightmare as the Germans dug in on one ridge line after another. By late 1943 the advance had stalled seventy miles north of Salerno and eighty miles short of Rome. The only significant gain was Foggia and its airfields (opposite Salerno, on the eastern side of the peninsula). For the next year and a half the Allies fought their way slowly north over the peninsula and destroyed much of Italy in the process.

The East, 1944

Fall and Winter Disasters for the Wehrmacht

In October 1943 arrival of bad weather had ushered in a temporary slackening of fighting in the east. Army Group South lay battered and bleeding. Neither troops nor commanders had illusions about what was coming. Manstein, still the army group's commander, argued that the Red Army disposed of enormous reserves behind its front; on November 20, he warned OKH that in addition to the forty-four divisions and numerous armored brigades established in 1943, the Red Army had thirty-three infantry divisions and eleven tank and mechanized corps in reserve on the southern front. Only the provision of "sufficient and powerful reserves," he noted, would allow Army Group South to hold the line. He had no chance of getting such reserves given the grave state of German forces in other theaters;

Manstein's demands underline how woefully ignorant the German generals were of the Reich's strategic situation.

On Christmas Eve 1943, the Soviets launched the winter's offensive, aimed at regaining the rest of the Ukraine. South of the Pripet Marshes and west of Kiev, First Guards and First Tank armies under General N. F. Vatutin pushed Fourth Panzer Army back. Hitler again refused to authorize any retreats or to approve Manstein's request to withdraw Army Group South's right flank. By early January the Soviets had opened up a 110–mile gap between army groups Center and South. Though Army Group South's left was dissolving, Hitler refused to abandon the lower Dnieper so forces could be assembled to meet the growing emergency. As the situation became fluid, the Germans closed a small encirclement around a portion of First Tank Army and destroyed a sizable number of tanks and assault guns, while inflicting heavy casualties. But the Red Army trapped two German corps, over 56,000 troops, near Cherkassy, in the center of Army Group South. The Germans got 30,000 men out, but most had to swim to safety and were completely broken by the experience.

At the end of March 1944, Hitler finally had had enough of Manstein's streak of independence and relieved the field marshal. But Manstein's relief did not presage any fundamental changes in how the Germans fought on the Eastern Front. By this point Manstein's opponents were fully his equal, with a broader understanding of the logistic, intelligence, and deception needs for any successful operation. One must also recognize that there was little political or strategic disagreement between Manstein and Hitler, as the former's wholehearted cooperation in the murderous actions of the SS in 1941 and 1942 underlined.

Things did not go better in Army Group A along the Black Sea. The Soviets struck Sixth Army on January 10 and 11. When Hitler allowed a

Throughout the war the Germans had fewer trucks than the Allies and often used horse-drawn wagons to carry equipment and supplies.

withdrawal, the order came so late that Sixth Army abandoned much of its heavy artillery, engineering equipment, and even armored fighting vehicles. In mid-February the Soviets reorganized for a major effort to recapture the rest of the Ukraine before the spring thaw. By this point, Soviet mechanized forces enjoyed greater mobility than their German opponents. Using sturdy American trucks for logistical support, Soviet tanks maneuvered in alternating conditions of thaw, freeze, snow, and rain. Since the Germans had designed most of their vehicles for western European conditions, their trucks often broke down. For example, 24th Panzer Division lost 1,958 of its vehicles during the winter, more than half of its authorized number. Some German panzer divisions were reduced to using horse-drawn peasant carts for supply.

Over the next month and a half Soviet commanders concentrated on destroying the two enemy army groups in the Ukraine. Between the Pripet Marshes and Black Sea, the Red Army deployed from north to south First, Second, Third, and Fourth Ukrainian fronts, each about double the size of a German army. West of Kiev, First Ukrainian Front drove deep into German positions, and by late March First and Second Ukrainian fronts had encircled First Panzer Army and smashed across the Dniester River. Only a desperate counterattack extricated the encircled Germans. Meanwhile Third Ukrainian Front, having taken Nikopol, drove on to take Odessa and reach the Romanian border. Soviet advances lapped to the passes over the Carpathian Mountains leading into Hungary, but the Germans and Hungarians, aided by the spring thaw, blocked that route.

Elsewhere in the east the Red Army scored its first major advances outside of Army Group South since winter 1941–1942. In the north, the Germans still besieged Leningrad, although the Soviets had opened a corridor to the city. In late December 1943, Army Group North's commander, Field Marshal Georg von Küchler, almost convinced Hitler to authorize a withdrawal of approximately 150 miles to a newly fortified position, known as "Panther." However, Eighteenth Army's commander, Colonel General Georg Lindemann, argued that his forces could hold their well-fortified but exposed positions. Always willing to take the optimistic point of view, Hitler supported Lindemann. But the latter and his intelligence officers had missed extensive Soviet preparations for an offensive. With a three-to-one superiority, the Soviets attacked both sides of the besieging forces at Leningrad on January 14. Second Shock Army struck out from the Oranienbaum enclave west of Leningrad, while Forty-Second Army attacked south of the city. At the same time, heavy Soviet attacks put German positions around Novgorod (one hundred miles to the south) in mortal danger. When Küchler pressed Hitler to authorize a short pullback, the Führer reluctantly agreed, but the Germans could not disengage cleanly. By January 19 the Russians had surrounded substantial numbers of Germans at Novgorod. Though concerned about the fall of another important Russian city, Hitler finally authorized a breakout.

Meanwhile the situation remained desperate in front of Leningrad. Küchler begged for permission to fall all the way back to the Panther line. By the end of the month Eighteenth Army had disintegrated into three separate groups, all facing encirclement. On January 30, Hitler finally permitted Küchler to pull back about fifty miles. At that point he fired Küchler and replaced him with Colonel General Walter Model, who had gained a reputation as a great defensive expert, but who also remained a favorite of the Führer because of his fanaticism. Model immediately wired his new headquarters, "Not a single step backward."

Despite Model's optimism and the arrival of reinforcements, strong Soviet pressure forced Army Group North back to the Panther position on March 1. The Germans held in this position, which extended north and south of Lake Peipus. An early spring thaw covered the frozen lake with water and halted the Soviet advance.

One last disaster befell German forces in the spring. Since fall 1943, Seventeenth Army had clung to the Crimea. Despite the pleas of his staff and Marshal Antonescu, Hitler insisted that the peninsula, which he described as an "aircraft carrier aimed at the Romanian oil fields," hold to the last. On April 7, 1944, the new commander of Army Group A, Colonel General Ferdinand Schörner, inspected the Crimea defenses and declared them in excellent shape, so excellent that they could hold "for a long time." Schörner was one of a new breed of generals promoted by Hitler for their enthusiasm and fanaticism. His prediction proved one of the shortest lived of the war.

On April 8 the Soviets attacked the German and Romanian defenders on the peninsula. Schörner at last recognized that Seventeenth Army would have to retreat to Sevastopol and the sooner the better. Hitler, of course, refused to authorize a withdrawal. Only under intense pressure did he finally sanction retreat but then demanded Sevastopol be held indefinitely. Schörner argued for a total withdrawal from the Crimea; but Hitler marshaled counterarguments from the air force and navy that they could supply Sevastopol. In early May the Soviets broke through the city's defenses. Only at this point did Hitler authorize a pullout, but the navy, while under heavy air attack, botched the operation. Although enough ships were available to transport the troops only 38,000 out of 64,700 escaped. The original strength of Seventeenth Army had been 75,546 Germans and 45,887 Romanians.

Operation "Bagration"

At Teheran in November 1943, Stalin, Churchill, and Roosevelt approved a common strategy for the coming year: the Western Powers would land forces in France and open a second front, while the Soviets launched a great offensive to coincide with it. Roosevelt assured Stalin that the invasion would occur in spring 1944.

As the Soviets prepared for their offensive, they focused on the area north of the Pripet Marshes, the only substantial portion of Soviet territory still under German occupation, since much of the significant fighting since 1942 had occurred in the south. Consequently, as *Stavka* established priorities for summer 1944, the front opposite Army Group Center received the highest priority. Following an offensive against the Finns to fix German

attention, the Red Army would attack Army Group Center and advance to East Prussia, a distance of approximately 225 miles. After destroying Army Group Center, the Soviets would be well positioned for a move into the Balkans.

Code-named "Bagration," the upcoming operation against Army Group Center included two phases. In the first, Soviet forces would break through enemy defenses and envelop German forces at Vitebsk on the Dvina River and at Bobruisk on the Beresina River. They would then strike deeper and encircle German units east of Minsk. When Marshal Rokossovskii presented the plan to Stalin, he encountered strong doubts about the two-pronged envelopment of Bobruisk. Stalin approved the plans only after sending Rokossovskii out of the room twice to "think it over."

Preparations for Bagration began in the spring. Against Army Group Center's 700,000 soldiers, *Stavka* concentrated 1.2 million men on the front with another 1.3 million in reserve. It assembled 124 divisions, 4,000 tanks, 24,400 artillery pieces, and 5,300 aircraft. German intelligence picked up little information about the concentration; its estimates swallowed a superb Soviet deception plan that suggested another offensive against Army Group South. What few movements German intelligence picked up in the center, it dismissed as "merely a deception." This miscalculation of the situation resulted in a maldistribution of German forces. Army Group Center, defending a 488-mile front, possessed only thirty-eight divisions in the first line and five divisions in reserve; three Hungarian and five security divisions guarded its rear areas. By contrast, Army Group North Ukraine (previously Army Group South), defending a shorter front than Army Group Center, had thirty-five German and ten Hungarian divisions of which ten were panzer. Together the two southern German army groups contained eighteen panzer and panzer grenadier divisions.

But the greatest deficiency of Army Group Center lay in the slavish devotion of its commander, Field Marshal Ernst Busch, to Hitler's directives. Even in 1940, Busch had displayed a remarkable lack of imagination; by 1944 the war had entirely passed him by. Busch accepted Hitler's directive to establish "fortresses" around important centers and to hold them to the last man. He insisted on such a rigid defense that Ninth Army complained that it was "bound by orders to tactical measures which it cannot in good conscience accept and which in our own earlier victories were the causes of the enemy defeats."

By this point in the war, the qualitative as well as quantitative balance had swung against the Germans in the east. Soviet commanders down to the divisional level had mastered the conduct of the operational art; the *Stavka* could prepare, conduct, and exploit extraordinarily complex operations ranging hundreds of miles. Soviet deception entirely blinded German commanders as to Soviet operational intentions until the hammer blows fell. Once *Stavka* unleashed its forces, a skillful conduct of operations (sustained by an efficient and mobile support structure—largely due to American lend-lease trucks) enabled full exploitation of breakthroughs. Only at the tactical, small-unit level did German units enjoy some small advantage, but even here the Soviet quantitative edge gave German soldiers a sense of impending doom.

On June 22, 1944, the third anniversary of Barbarossa and two weeks after the landings in Normandy, Soviet armies attacked Army Group Center, which had its Third Panzer, Fourth, and Ninth armies deployed from Vitebsk to Bobruisk. After ripping through the Third Panzer Army's positions, Soviet spearheads closed around Vitebsk and trapped five German divisions. On the 24th, the next phase of Bagration began against Ninth Army; First Belorussian Front broke open its left flank. When Ninth Army requested permission to escape, the army group commander replied that "the army's mission was to hold every foot of ground." In fact, the speed of the Soviet offensive had already shattered Ninth Army and trapped its broken units in several small pockets around Bobruisk. At the last minute the OKH permitted a withdrawal, but again too late. The Soviets encircled two corps, 70,000 troops, and continued their drive toward Minsk. Positioned between Third Panzer and Ninth armies, Fourth Army tried to pull back, but the advancing units of Soviet armor were already closing the trap.

As the situation became increasingly confused, Hitler intervened and ordered Third Panzer, Fourth, and Ninth armies to hold east of Minsk, sixty miles behind their original positions. In fact, all three armies—or at least those units not yet captured, surrounded, or destroyed—were in desperate shape. By now OKH had finally concluded that the Soviets were launching an ambitious offensive, aimed at retaking Minsk. Hitler fired Busch, the army group commander, and replaced him with Model, but the latter confronted a catastrophic situation. On July 3, the Soviets captured Minsk amidst scenes of indescribable collapse and confusion that marked desperate German attempts to flee. In twelve days Army Group Center had lost twenty-five divisions; out of 165,000 soldiers Fourth Army alone had lost 130,000. The other armies in Army Group Center were in little better shape.

Still, OKH drew some comfort from its hope that the Soviet advance of 125 miles would cause the attackers to run out of supplies. Again the Germans were wrong. On July 8, Model reported that he could not hold a line 175 miles west of Bobruisk. A yawning chasm separated the remnants of Army Group Center from Army Group North. Model requested that Army Group North withdraw to the Riga-Dvinsk-Dvina River line, thereby shortening its front and freeing troops for use in the center. Hitler refused, this time because the Baltic coast was crucial to launching new U-boats and securing Swedish iron ore shipped through the Baltic. At the end of July the Soviet drive, having advanced some 200 miles, began to slow. The Soviets had finally outrun their supply system.

With German reserves drawn to the center, the Soviets attacked the flanks. In the south, Army Group North Ukraine lay exposed; by the end of July, Soviet forces had advanced sixty miles across a broad front. Likewise in the north, Soviet attacks unhinged Army Group North's flank and almost reached the Baltic.

Meanwhile, Soviet forces approached Warsaw. On July 30, elements of Second Tank Army reached within seven miles of the Polish capital; south of Warsaw Soviet units actually crossed the Vistula River. But at this point, short of fuel and with political concerns in mind, the Soviets stopped and refused to liberate the Polish capital. The Poles themselves had little desire for a Soviet liberation of Poland. Certainly, memories of Stalin's actions in September 1939, as well as the ferocious purges in eastern Poland in 1939 and 1940, left them none to eager to exchange one tyranny for another. Consequently, as the Red Army approached, the Poles rose in furious revolt in an attempt to liberate their capital before the Soviets arrived. Shortly before Soviet armor reached the outskirts of Warsaw, Stalin established his own Polish government, consisting of Communists obedient to him. The dictator certainly had no interest in helping anti-Communists establish themselves in Poland. Despite desperate Polish resistance, with Soviet forces totally quiescent, the Germans had little trouble crushing the rebellion.

An attempt on Hitler's life on July 20 added to the already difficult relations between the Führer and his officer corps. A small group of anti-Nazi officers placed a bomb in Hitler's daily conference. It exploded, killing a number of those present, but only slightly injuring Hitler. The SS quickly arrested the plotters and extinguished all hopes of a coup. General Guderian then became the army chief of staff and sought to rectify Germany's desperate situation by Nazi fanaticism and enthusiasm. Generals loyal to the regime, such as Guderian and Rundstedt, sat on courts of honor that stripped their comrades of rank and privilege before turning them over to Nazi "justice." Most conspirators suffered hideous deaths. Rommel was accused of cooperating with the conspiracy, but Hitler permitted him to commit suicide on October 14, 1944. Treachery and treason became Hitler's explanation for all Germany's defeats.

By early September, the Germans faced the Soviets with a patched together front. A message from the commander of Army Group North, Field Marshal Schörner, to a division commander suggests the kind of leadership that the German army had by 1944: "Major General Charles de Beaulieu is to be told that he is to restore his own and his division's honor by a courageous deed or I [the army commander] will chase him out in disgrace. Furthermore, he is to report by 2100 which commanders he has had shot or is having shot for cowardice."*

Collapse in the Balkans

In Romania the front had been quiet since April. Army Group South Ukraine had watched as a steady drain of its forces occurred. Its staff worried about the collapse of Marshal Antonescu's authority in Romania; defeats over the past two years and arrival of Soviet armies on the frontier had convinced most Romanians that they must abandon the disastrous German alliance. But commanders on the spot could convince neither Hitler nor OKH of the serious political situation since German experts in Bucharest reported all was well.

By early August the Germans had picked up indications that the quiet spell in the south would soon end. Given the catastrophes in the center and in Normandy, OKH could not reinforce Romania. On August 20, 1944, two Soviet fronts with ninety divisions, six tank and mechanized corps, and more than 900,000 troops attacked. By nightfall Soviet forces were in the open. The Romanians resisted at first but then refused to fight; Soviet spearheads were already encircling Sixth Army.

On the 23rd, worse news awaited the Germans. The young king, Michael, called Antonescu to the palace; as had happened with Mussolini, the king dismissed the marshal, arrested him, and dissolved the government. That night Michael announced that Romania would join the Allied nations and denounced the Treaty of Vienna, which had given Transylvania to Hungary. To free the German mission and overthrow the new government, Hitler authorized German air and ground forces to attack Bucharest.

*Earl F. Ziemke, *Stalingrad to Berlin: The German Defeat in the East* (Washington: Office of the Chief of Military History, 1968), p. 342.

However, fighting on the outskirts of Bucharest, as well as the bombing of the royal palace, only solidified support for the king.

As the Germans struggled to cope with political collapse, the military situation went from bad to worse. Romania's defection, followed by its declaration of war on August 25, placed every German unit in Romania at hazard. By the 27th, Army Group South Ukraine had collapsed. The Soviets cut Sixth Army into two separate pockets; in the debacle the Wehrmacht lost eighteen divisions and the headquarters of five corps. Moreover, the Romanians surrounded German forces in Bucharest, while at Ploesti they drove the 5th Flak Division from the oil refineries. Remnants of Army Group South Ukraine withdrew northwest and by September 15 had occupied positions along the spine of the Carpathian Mountains in a new line east of Budapest.

Bulgaria's defection followed on the heels of the Romanian collapse. The Bulgarians had never declared war on the USSR, and on September 2 they unilaterally ended their state of war with the Western Powers. But that was not enough for Stalin. On September 8 Third Ukrainian Front moved into Bulgaria, and the Bulgarians declared war on Germany. German forces in Greece and Macedonia were now in danger of isolation. Even Hitler recognized that there was no hope of holding the southern Balkans. A desperate retreat north began through the partisan-infested countryside of Yugoslavia. Yugoslav partisans harassed the retreating Germans but could not cut them off. The British, landing in Greece, pursued hesitantly, and Allied air power missed some substantial opportunities to interdict the escaping Germans. By mid-October most of the German forces had escaped from Greece and Macedonia.

But this temporary success did little to improve the situation. In early October the Hungarian leader, Admiral Miklos Horthy, signed an armistice with the Soviets. His government and the Hungarian army remained badly divided. Some Hungarians wanted to fight on, but many recognized Germany's hopeless position. Quick action by SS commanders overthrew Horthy's regime and installed a pro-Nazi puppet government. But Hungarian morale hit rock bottom as many senior generals, including the chief of staff, deserted. In some cases whole units went over to the Soviets.

Meanwhile the Red Army began a relentless push toward Budapest. The Germans, given their defeats elsewhere, lacked sufficient strength for a successful defense, while the Hungarians were on their last legs. In early November the Red Army fought its way into the suburbs of Budapest. By late December Soviet spearheads had closed around the city and surrounded four German and two Hungarian divisions. Hitler regarded Budapest as a symbol like Stalingrad, one that represented Germany's fanatical determination to see the war through to the end. While the Germans had made extensive preparations to withstand a siege, they did little to prepare for the needs of Budapest's one million civilians. Guderian, summing up the moral sensibilities of Hitler's military circle, commented that the requirements of the civilian population were immaterial.

✳   ✳   ✳   ✳

Events in the Mediterranean and on the Eastern Front represented a series of unmitigated disasters for the Germans from 1942 to 1944. By the winter of 1944 the Soviets had regained the Ukraine, and in the summer of 1944 they executed one of the most successful offensives of the war, Bagration, destroying all of Army Group Center and twenty-eight German divisions. In fall the Red Army liberated much of the Balkans and added that region to Stalin's empire. The Allies also made major gains in the Mediterranean, but they engaged considerably smaller German forces than the Soviets. By late 1943, British and American forces had driven Axis forces out of North Africa, captured Sicily, knocked Italy out of the war, and seized the air bases in southern Italy necessary to attack Romanian oil targets and Austria. Nevertheless, hard fighting remained before the entire Italian peninsula fell into Allied hands.

As the Allies pushed back Axis forces, the war attained new levels of scale and mechanization. At the battle of Kursk, the combatants employed about 7,000 tanks; in Operation Bagration, the Soviets committed 124 divisions and 4,000 tanks; in the landings on Sicily, the Allies launched an immense amphibious assault of seven divisions. On the Eastern Front, the Soviets overwhelmed the Germans with vast armies, supported by thousands of aircraft, while in North Africa, Sicily, and Italy, the Allies used enormous amounts of firepower to batter their way forward. As the toll of numerous battles reduced the Axis forces, the Germans slowly lost their qualitative edge, and the Allies became more proficient in planning and executing complicated and effective campaigns.

SUGGESTED READINGS

Bidwell, Shelford, and Dominick Graham. *Tug of War: The Battle for Italy, 1943–1945* (New York: St. Martin's Press, 1986).

Blumenson, Martin. *Kasserine Pass* (Boston: Houghton Mifflin, 1967).

――――. *Mark Clark* (New York: Congdon & Weed, 1984).

――――. *Masters of the Art of Command* (Boston: Houghton Mifflin, 1975).

Erickson, John. *The Road to Berlin* (Boulder, Col.: Westview Press, 1983).

――――. *The Road to Stalingrad* (New York: Harper & Row, 1975).

Hardesty, Von. *Red Phoenix: The Rise of Soviet Air Power, 1941–1945* (Washington: Smithsonian Institution Press, 1982).

Howard, Michael. *The Mediterranean Strategy in the Second World War* (New York: Praeger, 1968).

von Mellenthin, Friedrich W. *Panzer Battles: A Study of the Employment of Armor in the Second World War*, trans. H. Betzler (Norman: University of Oklahoma Press, 1956).

Sajer, Guy. *The Forgotten Soldier*, trans. Lily Emmet (New York: Harper & Row, 1971).

Wray, Timothy A. *Standing Fast: German Defensive Doctrine on the Russian Front During World War II* (Fort Leavenworth: Combat Studies Institute, 1986).

Zhukov, Georgii K. *Marshal Zhukov's Greatest Battles*, trans. Theodore Shabad (New York: Harper & Row, 1969).

Ziemke, Earl F., and Magna E. Bauer, *Moscow to Stalingrad: Decision in the East* (Washington: Office of the Chief of Military History, 1987).

Ziemke, Earl F. *Stalingrad to Berlin: The German Defeat in the East* (Washington: Office of the Chief of Military History, 1968).

17

VICTORY IN EUROPE: BRUTE FORCE IN THE AIR AND ON THE GROUND

The Air War, 1944

The Campaign in the
West, 1944

The Collapse of Germany

$\mathbb{T}$he battles on the periphery of Fortress Europe substantially wore down Germany's military forces. The Wehrmacht's battlefield excellence was no longer so sharply defined as in the earlier years of the war. Moreover, the overwhelming Allied quantitative superiority due to economic mobilization and vast resources provided a factor that no battlefield performance could match. In the west a sustained air battle began in February 1944 and continued for the next three months. When it was over, Allied air forces had broken the Luftwaffe and gained air superiority over the European continent. A successful amphibious landing on the beaches of Normandy immediately followed that success. From the east and west, Allied armies could now batter their way to and across the frontiers of the Reich.

Allied military operations, particularly those of Anglo-American forces, involved a close working of the services in a joint arena; air, sea, and land worked intimately to achieve larger purposes. Nowhere was this clearer than in Normandy and in the subsequent fighting and buildup. Naval and air forces got the ground forces ashore; naval support provided the great highway to the West's industrial might; and air power made the movement and supply of German troops a nightmare. In the end, infantry had to dig the Germans out of their positions in Normandy, hedgerow by hedgerow, but that infantry battle was possible due only to close interservice cooperation within the Allied forces.

The Air War, 1944

The Americans Defeat the Luftwaffe

Throughout fall 1943 and into early 1944, RAF's Bomber Command had waged a relentless campaign to destroy Berlin. But German night defenses recovered from the difficulties of summer 1943, and British losses mounted alarmingly. Nevertheless, as Bomber Command confronted defeat in its night offensive, the U.S. Eighth Air Force, supported by Fifteenth Air Force in Italy, returned to the attack. Not only had American bomber strength reached new levels, but now long-range escort fighters, in particular the P-51 Mustang, accompanied bomber formations all the way to targets deep in Germany. The P-51, the best piston-engine fighter of World War II, had outstanding aerial combat capabilities and the range with drop tanks even to reach Berlin.

In February 1944 the weather cleared sufficiently for Eighth Air Force to begin attacks on the German aircraft industry. The result was a massive battle of attrition that cost both sides heavily; the battle lasted until May when the German fighter force finally collapsed. Aiming to strangle production and deprive the Luftwaffe of its aircraft, the Americans initially attacked the factories manufacturing Luftwaffe fighters, but the raids failed to accomplish the objective. Despite savage pounding, the Germans raised

Due to flaws in doctrine and limitations in technology, Americans failed to develop an effective long-range day light escort fighter until early 1944. By May, however, fighters like the P-51 Mustang had won general air superiority over Europe.

fighter production by 55.9 percent during 1944, but only by shutting down production of other aircraft. The overall weight of airframes produced actually rose only 20 percent in 1944 and reflected a heavy emphasis on single-engine fighters. The new fighters also showed a marked decline in quality compared to earlier production runs.

Ironically, the offensive destroyed the Luftwaffe's air defenses, but in an entirely unforeseen fashion. The appearance of escort fighters deep in Germany represented a catastrophe for the Luftwaffe. The experience of one Bf 110 Group that scrambled twenty-one aircraft against B-17s in March was not atypical. In that incident the Germans shot down two B-17s but suffered heavily: four aircraft missing (three pilots bailed out), one crash-landing (pilot killed), another written off on landing, and three aircraft crashes on takeoff.

By early March, Eighth Air Force's new commander, Major General Doolittle, ordered his fighters to attack German airfields with low-level strikes. American fighter and bomber formations suffered heavy losses, but the Germans lost more heavily. Luftwaffe fighter-pilot losses reached an unsustainable level. In January the Germans lost 12.1 percent of their fighter pilots, killed, missing or wounded; in February, 17.9; in March, 21.7; in April, 20.1; and in May, 25 percent. From January to May the Luftwaffe averaged 2,283 pilots available in the fighter force; in that same period it lost 2,262 fighter pilots. In May 1944 the defenders cracked; the heavy losses that Allied bombers had been suffering dropped dramatically. From this point, while some daylight raids did suffer heavy losses, the Americans had won general air superiority over Europe.

Supporting the Invasion

In April, Allied air strategy changed direction. "Overlord," the invasion of the European continent, was finally ready. With achievement of air superiority over Europe, airmen had met the crucial precondition for a successful invasion. By the decision of the combined chiefs of staff, Overlord's supreme commander, General Dwight Eisenhower, commanded all air assets as of April 1, 1944. His chief deputy, RAF Marshal Sir Arthur Tedder, with advice from the scientist, Solly Zuckerman, had designed a plan to isolate Normandy by means of air interdiction. If successful, the air campaign would enable the Allies to win the logistic buildup once the battle began.

Eisenhower and Tedder ran into considerable opposition from Allied airmen. Lieutenant General Carl A. Spaatz, commander of U.S. Army Air Forces in England, argued for continuing the attack on the German aircraft industry. His planners, however, were already turning toward a new target, the German petroleum industry—which they believed represented the crucial weak link in the enemy's economy. Not surprisingly, Air Marshal Arthur Harris, commander of Bomber Command argued vociferously against air cooperation with Overlord. In particular, he worried disingenuously that attacks on French railroads would kill tens of thousands of innocent Frenchmen. Harris knew that Churchill desperately feared the postwar repercussions of such casualties.

Eisenhower and Tedder responded easily to the objections of American airmen: raids against German aircraft targets would continue, and in May attacks on oil targets would begin. Harris's claims were more difficult because of their political ramifications. However, Zuckerman discovered that Bomber Command based its estimates of French casualties on the pattern of night raids with many hundreds of bombers, when in fact French railway targets demanded attacks of no more than 100 to 200 bombers. Moreover, by this point British navigational devices were so accurate that Bomber Command could execute its attacks with great precision. The first tests showed that Bomber Command could hit targets even more accurately than Eighth Air Force. With his arguments disproved, Harris fell into line. Among the many night attacks, one on Vaires not only demolished the marshaling yard, but also caught trains from the 10th SS Panzer Division (*Frundsberg*) intermingled with a consignment of naval mines. When it was all over, the Germans collected identity disks from nearly 1,200 dead.

Out of the eighty most important transportation targets, Bomber Command attacked thirty-nine, Eighth Air Force, twenty-three, and tactical air forces, eighteen. Losses were heavy. Between April 1 and June 5, Allied air forces lost nearly 2,000 aircraft and 12,000 officers and enlisted men. But the attacks proved crucial. Beginning in early April, a precipitous drop in French railway traffic occurred. Attacks by fighter bombers on the Seine River bridges and trains further accelerated the decline. By late May, just prior to the attacks on the Seine bridges, rail traffic in France had dropped to 55 percent of January levels. By June 6, the destruction of the Seine bridges had reduced traffic levels to 30 percent, and by the end of July to 10 percent. By mid-June trains had virtually ceased to operate in western France. As the campaign progressed, Ultra intercepts and decrypts provided air commanders with crucial insights into the campaign's progress.

Air interdiction placed the Germans in an impossible situation. Since much of the Wehrmacht consisted of infantry divisions with horse-drawn equipment, the Germans depended on railroads to move reserves and supplies. Removal of that support made it difficult to redeploy forces once the invasion began. Destruction of the transportation network also forced German infantry to fight without adequate artillery support and even at times basic infantry supplies. Moreover, damage to roads and bridges made it difficult for motorized and mechanized units to reinforce the front. Thus air interdiction proved invaluable in winning the battle of France.

The Offensive Against the Petroleum Industry

Since 1939 the Germans had worried about petroleum. Romanian oil production was declining and difficult to get up the Danube River, and much of the Reich's oil came from synthetic plants that required great amounts of coal, the one natural resource Germany enjoyed in abundance. But the manufacture of synthetic fuels required refineries with miles of pipelines and production facilities, all vulnerable to air attack. In April 1944 a Luftwaffe staff officer warned that Germany's refineries and fuel plants lay within "the

The Boeing B-17 Flying Fortress was the workhorse of the American strategic bombing campaign in Europe. The normal maximum radius of action for the B-17 and B-24 was 850 miles; this range could be extended with auxiliary fuel tanks or reduced bomb loads.

zone threatened by air attack," and he found it inexplicable that the Allies had not yet attacked the oil industry—a target that would jeopardize Germany's entire war effort.

One month later his warnings came true. Eisenhower released Eighth Air Force from invasion preparations to attack oil targets. On May 12,935 B-17s and B-24s attacked the major synthetic oil plants. American losses were heavy, forty-six bombers and twelve fighters. The results were encouraging but not decisive, for the plant at Leuna, although damaged, lost only 18 percent of capacity. Ultra, however, reported a major redistribution of Luftwaffe Flak units to protect the synthetic refineries; this report alerted Allied airmen to the seriousness with which the Germans viewed the attacks. Nine days later another Ultra message indicated that Allied air attacks on oil facilities, including those in Romania, had forced the German high command to reduce fuel allocations.

After feverish efforts to repair the damage, production had almost returned to normal by the end of May. On May 28–29, Eighth and Fifteenth air forces launched another series of attacks. In the two-day air battle, both sides suffered heavy losses. The Americans lost eighty-four bombers, but the Germans lost thirty-nine single-engine fighter pilots killed or missing (twenty-one more wounded) and a further thirty-three crew members of twin-engine fighters either killed or wounded. These two attacks combined with raids against the Romanian oil fields at Ploesti to reduce German petroleum production by 50 percent. Since the Germans had virtually no oil reserves, they faced a catastrophic situation.

The attacks in May were a prelude to devastating, follow-on raids in succeeding months. New attacks in mid-June knocked out 90 percent of aviation fuel production; by the end of July successive Allied raids had lowered aviation gas production by 98 percent. When Ultra detected German efforts to restore production, follow-on attacks wrecked the repair work and what little capacity remained.

The impact of these oil attacks on Germany's strategic situation was enormous. The raids severely restricted the Luftwaffe's frontline force in its ability to defend the Reich against strategic bombers. By mid-summer, Speer's desperate efforts to restore fighter production had borne bitter fruit. New aircraft were available in increasing numbers, but insufficient fuel grounded most of them. Furthermore, without fuel the Luftwaffe could no longer train new pilots. Thus the Luftwaffe, battered into desperate condition by its mauling in the spring, could not maintain the uneven contest.

Fuel shortages were no less serious for the army. Combat operations suffered immediately; training became impossible. The Ardennes offensive, launched in December 1944, had enough fuel to get panzer spearheads only to the Meuse River; the attackers hoped to advance the rest of the way to Antwerp by capturing Allied fuel dumps. In February 1945 the German defenders of Silesia possessed over 1,100 tanks. Nevertheless, the Soviets conquered much of the province in less than one week, because the defenders had virtually no fuel. The German soldier rarely, if ever, saw the Luftwaffe overhead; throughout 1944 and 1945 he was pounded on every front by enemy aircraft, while supplies, attacked by both day and night, reached him with decreasing frequency.

The Campaign in the West, 1944

Italy

At the end of 1943 a major reshuffling of Allied commanders took place between the Mediterranean and Britain. Eisenhower became the Supreme Commander Allied Forces Europe. In every respect, he was an inspired choice. He was a first-rate strategist and operational commander, but above all he possessed political gifts that allowed him to lead and work with a quarrelsome group of senior Allied commanders. A number of other commanders moved from the Mediterranean. Tedder became Eisenhower's deputy; Montgomery became the land force commander. Among other Americans, Patton, still on probation, and Lieutenant General Omar N. Bradley journeyed to London, while Spaatz and Doolittle assumed control of American air forces in Britain. The Italian campaign, however, was not over; it continued as a secondary theater as Allied forces fought their way up the Italian peninsula.

Late 1943 and early 1944 found Anglo-American forces in Italy in a disconcerting position. The drive of the 15th Army Group under General Sir Harold Alexander had stalled well short of Rome. In four months the Allies had advanced only seventy miles beyond Salerno. The Gustav Line, a German defensive position set in the rugged Apennines, proved impervious

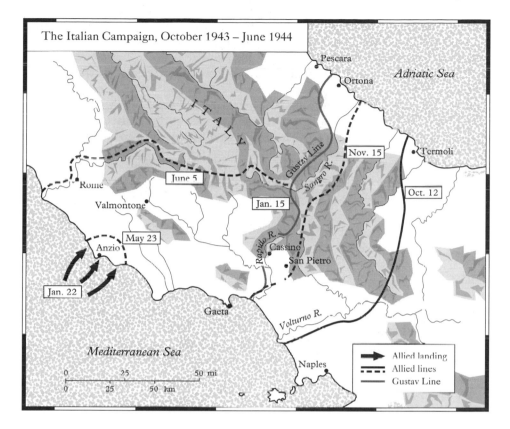

The Italian Campaign, October 1943 – June 1944

to attack. Frustrated, the Allies decided to make an amphibious landing south of Rome in coordination with another assault on the Gustav Line. They expected the amphibious assault to force the Germans to evacuate the Gustav Line and withdraw north of Rome. The target of the amphibious landing was the small town of Anzio, about sixty miles behind the Gustav Line. Chosen to command the landing was Major General John P. Lucas with his VI Corps. The attack was a combined operation with the British 1st and the American 3rd divisions making the initial landings. Assisting were commando and ranger units, a parachute regiment, and two tank battalions. Two more divisions were immediately available, U.S. 1st Armored and 45th Infantry divisions.

Unfortunately the landings in January 1944, known as Operation "Shingle," replayed the Suvla Bay fiasco of the 1915 British attack on Gallipoli. The first day went like clockwork; the landings at Anzio caught the Germans completely by surprise; the only Germans in the immediate vicinity were three drunken officers in a Volkswagen command vehicle who drove down the beach and into an LST. Within twenty-five miles of the beach were members of an engineer battalion who offered little or no resistance. By the end of the first day the Allies had landed 36,034 troops and over 3,000 vehicles. At the end of the second day VI Corps occupied a beachhead seven miles deep. The road to Rome lay open, and VI Corps was in a position to cut supply routes to the Gustav Line.

But before the invasion, Lucas expressed profound misgivings at its prospects. The Fifth Army commander, Lieutenant General Mark Clark, added to Lucas's caution by advising him not to stick his neck out. As a result, Lucas refused to exploit favorable circumstances and ordered his forces to remain inside the beachhead. The Allies did little more than consolidate their positions. But the Germans, never ones to waste time, reacted with dispatch, and by midnight on the day of landing, they had 20,000 troops closing in on Anzio. Within one week, they had concentrated elements from eight divisions and launched a series of counterattacks that nearly drove the Allies into the sea. Far from opening up the front, the Anzio landings soon represented a substantial liability.

Just prior to the Anzio landing, the Fifth Army attacked the lower half of the Gustav Line with a British, an American, and a French corps. As part of this operation, the U.S. 36th Infantry Division attacked across the Rapido River on January 20; its efforts failed miserably with almost 1,700 casualties. Neither this attack nor others broke German lines. Interdiction by Allied air forces also had little effect on the defenders; in some cases Allied air power even helped the Germans. At the abbey of Monte Casino, German paratroopers threw back every attack by Fifth Army; a major air raid on February 15 then destroyed the abbey completely. But in the scattered wreckage, German paratroopers waged an even more effective defense.

In May the balance of forces between the opposing sides finally reached the point where Allied air power, interdicting supplies from the north and pounding the front lines, combined with the overwhelming superiority of ground forces to break the deadlock. On May 11, the Allied offensive began. For three days attacks made little progress against stiff enemy resistance; but the ill-equipped Free French broke the stalemate by driving over the mountains where the Germans least expected an advance. Their success opened the Gustav Line to penetrations elsewhere. American forces at Anzio, now ably commanded by Major General Lucian K. Truscott, broke out of the beachhead, and German defenses collapsed. Truscott's VI Corps was positioned to trap many of the German defenders had it driven inland, but Clark ordered Truscott to turn north and capture Rome instead, which VI Corps did on June 5. Though Clark's capture of Rome grabbed the front pages of America's newspapers, much of the German Tenth Army escaped to fight another day.

Still, the Allies pushed the Germans northward until the front line stabilized on the Gothic Line north of Florence. In mid-August many of the U.S. and all of the Free French combat units moved off to participate in landings in southern France as part of Operation "Anvil" (later renamed "Dragoon"). The Italian theater again settled into stalemate. Some historians have claimed that Anvil prevented the Allies from driving through the Po River valley and on into the Alps and Austria. Such claims seem improbable. Not until the following April did the Allies finally break the deadlock and surge into Austria, but by that point the Wehrmacht was collapsing on every front.

What did the Italian theater contribute to victory? Through summer 1943 it proved an excellent training ground for Anglo-American forces.

The rough terrain of Italy restricted the mobility of the highly motorized American troops. In terrain where trucks could not move, mules provided valuable assistance in transporting weapons and supplies.

Moreover, the casualties the Allies inflicted on German ground and air forces in Tunisia and Sicily were a significant return on investment. After that point, however, Italy cost more than it gained. The skill and tenacity of German troops combined with difficult terrain and weather to make this a dismal theater indeed.

Northern France

In a speech to the French people in October 1940, Winston Churchill said: "Good night, then: sleep to gather strength for the morning. For the morning will come. Brightly will it shine on the brave and the true, kindly upon all who suffer for the cause, glorious upon the tombs of heroes. Thus will shine the dawn." Dawn came June 6, 1944, but only after immense preparations and a massive mobilization of manpower and resources in both Britain and the United States. The complexity of a cross-Channel invasion did not become fully apparent until after the Dieppe raid of August 1942. In that attack British commandoes and Canadian troops attempted to seize the French port of Dieppe. Anticipating less than 1,500 German defenders, they encountered three times that many, plus ample reserves, most of whom were third-line infantry. The Dieppe defeat suggested that an invading army could not gain a French port in the invasion's first days; an extremely powerful landing force would have to make the invasion over open beaches. In the end, the planners for Normandy had almost two years to absorb Dieppe's lessons, as well as those of other amphibious landings the Allies executed in the European and Pacific theaters. Consequently, the Normandy landing was perhaps the most thoroughly planned battle in the history of warfare.

A cross-Channel invasion presented enormous logistic difficulties. Not only men but also supplies would have to be down-loaded into landing craft and then moved to beaches in small boats for another unloading. Moreover, the northern French beaches fronted directly on the English Channel, which was famous for its rough and unpredictable seas. Consequently, the Allies required landing craft in far greater numbers than planners had initially envisaged. A worldwide shortage of such craft and demands from the Pacific created major hurdles. Only in 1944 did the Allies possess sufficient landing craft to make an invasion possible. Beyond landing craft, the planners decided to supply the beachhead through artificial harbors. In the first days of Overlord, Allied naval forces thus had the task of funneling hundreds of thousands of men and tons of equipment into France and of constructing two "Mulberry" artificial harbors, including breakwaters, piers, and landing facilities to speed the buildup.

The size of the invasion demanded general air superiority. During the Dieppe landing, the Luftwaffe had caused serious losses among landing

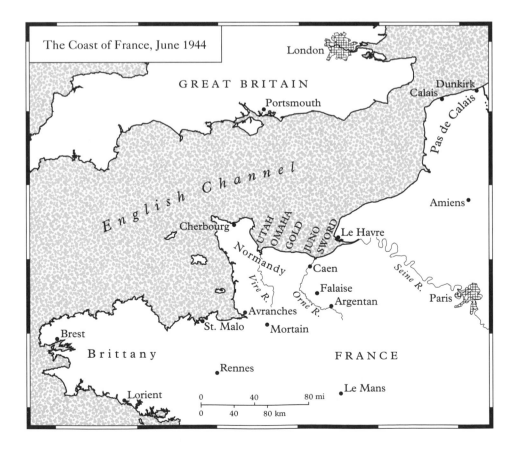

The Coast of France, June 1944

craft and naval vessels supporting the raid. But the victory of American air power over the Luftwaffe in spring 1944 removed that threat; the Luftwaffe would hardly get an aircraft over the crowded beaches of Normandy on June 6.

By summer 1943 planning was well underway; in November 1943 the planners received approval for the initial design for Overlord. They had rejected the easily accessible area around Pas de Calais, because that area was also obvious to the Germans, had received much of the effort to fortify the coast, and could be attacked from three different directions by German reserves. Instead the planners selected Normandy: it was farther removed from enemy reserves, the ocean could protect the invading force's western flank, and Allied air power could more easily isolate the battlefield from enemy reinforcements and resupply.

Logistic planning rested on a belief that once ashore the advance into France would be slow. Anticipating a methodical, rather than mobile campaign, the logisticians failed to prepare for swift movements that could consume vast quantities of gasoline. Exacerbating this miscalculation was the fact that through the end of July the battles in Normandy consumed more ammunition and less fuel than predicted. At the beginning of August, Allied logisticians increased ammunition allocations and decreased those of fuel—at precisely the moment when the campaign turned mobile.

By January the Allied high command was in place. Eisenhower commanded Supreme Headquarters Allied Expeditionary Forces, while Montgomery commanded 21st Army Group with responsibility for the landing. Under Montgomery was the British First Army (Lieutenant General Sir Miles C. Dempsey) and the U.S. First Army (Lieutenant General Bradley). Upon arrival in Britain, Eisenhower and Montgomery examined and rejected plans to land three divisions over the beaches and to drop one airborne division inland. They believed that such forces were inadequate to the task and that the initial landings would have to consist of five divisions, supported by three airborne divisions dropped inland.

The Allies would come ashore on five separate beaches; from east to west they were Sword, Juno, Gold, Omaha, and Utah. The British and Canadians would land on the three eastern beaches, the Americans on the two western beaches. On the eastern side, the British 6th Airborne would seize the Orne River bridges. On the other end of the front, the American 82nd and 101st Airborne would shield the westernmost beaches—the most exposed landing site. Above all, the Allies would have to get maximum men and equipment ashore before the Germans launched a strong counterstroke.

In the German high command, disunity and disharmony marked Nazi preparations. Field Marshal Rundstedt was in overall command in the west, but he lacked control over air and naval units and had only limited control of SS and parachute units. His chief subordinate was Rommel, who as commander of Army Group B, held responsibility for the immediate defense of western Europe. Above both hovered Hitler's disruptive influence; the Führer was determined to keep the levers for defending France firmly within his grasp. Consequently, neither Rundstedt nor Rommel had authority to move the mobile formations that made up the reserves. Moreover, they differed on how best to defend France. Rundstedt believed that German forces should conduct a mobile defense to inflict maximum casualties on the Allies; Rommel argued that superior Allied resources, air power, and manpower demanded that the Wehrmacht stop the invasion on the beaches. Should the Anglo-American force gain a foothold, he believed the war would be lost.

Rommel threw himself into the task of defending France with his usual energy. Under his inspiring leadership, German engineers laid millions of mines; beach defenses and obstacles sprouted; and "Rommel asparagus" (telephone poles with wire strung between them) spread across French fields to destroy Allied gliders. The construction of beach obstacles below the high-tide line forced the Allies to land at low tide; consequently, the landing had to take place between June 4 and 8, when low tide and dawn coincided.

The weather almost did not cooperate. After excellent weather in May, storms blew in from the Atlantic, and only on June 5 did conditions clear up sufficiently for Eisenhower to launch the invasion. However, the period of bad weather helped the Allies achieve tactical surprise. Rommel was in Germany visiting his wife, while the commander of Seventh Army and most of his corps and division commanders were away from their headquarters to participate in a war game.

Normandy

As dusk settled over airfields in England on June 5, paratroopers from three airborne divisions clambered aboard their aircraft. The first pathfinders were down in France before midnight. The British Sixth Airborne Division quickly seized the key bridges on the landing's eastern flank. The two American divisions were more dispersed on landing. In some areas heavy Flak greeted American transport aircraft; as a result troops from the 82nd and 101st divisions dropped all over western Normandy. But their spread confused the Germans, and the Americans achieved their purpose of preventing reinforcements from moving on Utah beach.

In the grey dawn of June 6, Allied troops came ashore on five different landing beaches. The assault went well on the British beaches and on Utah. Nevertheless, despite their gains, the British and Canadians failed to take full advantage of the situation. One Canadian battalion almost reached Caen but was ordered to pull back by the brigade commander because such a move was not in the plans. That night, the 12th SS Panzer Division (*Hitler Jugend*) moved into place, and the British and Canadians did not capture Caen for a month and a half. British official history attributed the failure to capture Caen on the first day to the unexpectedly high tide, congestion on the shore, strength of opposition, and a lack of urgency.

Only on Omaha did the Germans hold the attackers on the beach for a substantial period of time. Instead of encountering light defenses, the U.S. 1st Infantry Division, reinforced by elements of the 29th Infantry Division, ran head on into the 352nd Division, which had recently moved into the area. Because of strong currents and poor navigation, the Americans landed

American paratroopers prepare to jump from C-47 Dakota transport planes. Airborne forces in the enemy's rear areas in Sicily, Salerno, and Normandy confused and harassed the enemy and gave the Allies a greater chance of success.

on different parts of the beach than planned and then came under withering fire from well-placed Germans. Most of the special tanks that could supposedly "swim" sank in heavy swells, as did much of the artillery carried in amphibious trucks. For a time Bradley considered diverting follow-on forces from Omaha to other beaches. But small groups of soldiers began advancing under fire and somehow drove the Germans from the heights. By the end of the day infantry from the two divisions had pushed two miles inland, and bulldozers were clearing paths to the heights. By the morning of D+1, the Allies had over 177,000 troops ashore in four secure beachheads, and the buildup was already well underway.

The Allied success received considerable help from the Germans. As early as 0400 hours, German commanders on the scene requested release of the armor to launch a counterblow. But Hitler was asleep, and the OKW's chief of operations, General Alfred Jodl, refused to release the reserves or to wake the Führer. Not until late in the afternoon did the German high command allow 21st Panzer Division to attack, while other armored divisions were too far away from Normandy or released too late to participate in the first day's fighting.

Two distinct battles soon developed in Normandy, the British and Canadians fighting in the east, and the Americans in the west. Both efforts

While balloons provided protection against low-flying aircraft, an armada of ships poured thousands of men and tons of equipment and supplies onto the Normandy beaches.

involved a massive application of firepower, air power, and superior resources against the Germans. In the west, before driving south, the Americans were supposed to turn right, advance across and then up the Cotentin Peninsula to capture Cherbourg, but the port did not fall until June 27. To make matters worse, the Germans sabotaged the port facilities thoroughly, and Allied ships could not use its piers until August 7. In July the Allies had hoped to land some 725,000 tons of supplies but managed to land only 446,852. After capturing Cherbourg, the Americans concentrated on driving south and breaking through German defenses in western Normandy. Here they ran up against the worst of the *bocage* country and its thick hedgerows; virtually every field and village offered heavy cover for the defenders. Nevertheless, slowly, but inexorably, the Americans drove the Germans back.

On the eastern side, the British and Canadians fought in terrain more open and favorable than the hedgerow country. Dempsey, the British ground force commander, had his chances to make more substantial gains near Caen. On June 12, XXX Corps sensed a weakness in German positions. Seventh Armored Division got its lead brigade through German lines in undamaged condition. But upon reaching Villers-Bocage, the lead column consisting of tanks, soft-skinned vehicles, and supply trucks in peacetime formation came under fire on its flank from five Tiger tanks from the

501st SS Heavy Tank Battalion. In a one-sided action, the Tigers caught the British completely by surprise and destroyed almost the entire column. By the time the battle was over, the German tankers had destroyed twenty-five tanks and twenty-eight other armored vehicles and thrown 7th Armored back to its start line.

By July 1 the Allies held only a small portion of the area anticipated by Overlord planning. Caen remained in German hands. Seeking to capture that city, the British launched major offensives on July 8 and 18. Finally capturing Caen but failing to break through the enemy's positions, they drew German armor piecemeal into a battle of attrition that wore away the enemy's armored reserve.

Eisenhower identified three factors that made fighting in Normandy extremely difficult: "First, as always, the fighting quality of the German soldier; second, the nature of the country; third, the weather." The tired, weary, outnumbered, and outgunned German infantry displayed superior tactical skills and initiative compared to their opponents, and the terrain of the bocage country served only to exacerbate the imbalance. Operating in small units, they relied on an active defense and made limited counterattacks with local reserves and small groups of tanks. Soft ground limited the mobility of the highly mechanized Allied forces, and hedgerows divided the battlefield into numerous rectangular compartments that the Germans skillfully tied together. As for the weather, the amount of wind and rain in July exceeded that of any time in the past half-century and hampered air support and mobility. In the month of July, the U.S. First Army suffered about 40,000 casualties, 90 percent of whom were infantrymen. One American infantry regiment that entered combat shortly after D-day had only four officers remaining from its original complement in the third week of July.

As the Germans reinforced Normandy, extensive damage to the transportation system and road network made movement difficult. Allied fighter bombers dominated the daylight hours, while night movement was difficult. The French resistance added to German discomfiture by sniping and creating numerous obstacles. Units of 2nd SS Panzer Division (*Das Reich*) took nearly two weeks to arrive in Normandy from Limoges, a journey that should have taken two days. Along the way they committed a number of atrocities, the worst of which occurred at Oradour-sur-Glane and involved the murder of about 650 French civilians. The men were machine-gunned in open fields, and the women and children were burned to death in the village church.

As Allied forces poured into Normandy, German difficulties mounted. Ultra picked up the location of Panzer Group West's Headquarters, and an immediate strike by Allied tactical air destroyed the only headquarters in the west capable of coordinating movement of large panzer formations. The supply situation was catastrophic; only desperate measures kept the front lines from collapsing. Rommel was at his wits' end; on July 17 a fighter bomber attack badly wounded the field marshal and sent him home where Hitler would order him to commit suicide for participation in the July 20 assassination attempt. Hitler also relieved Rundstedt. In his case, in reply to Jodl's rhetorical question, "What shall we do?," the blunt old field marshal had replied: "End the war. What else can you do?" Rundstedt's replacement was Field Marshal Hans Günther von Kluge, one of Hitler's favorites. After taking over, Kluge told Rommel, "Even you will have to get used to obeying orders." After Rommel's wounding, Kluge also assumed command of Army Group B. The field marshal's experience since 1940 had been exclusively on the Eastern Front, so he had little idea of the immense superiority of Allied air power and its capabilities. He soon learned.

The Breakout

On July 25 the U.S. First Army launched Operation "Cobra," which sought to break through the German defenses at St. Lô. Major General J. Lawton Collins's VII Corps made the main attack with three infantry divisions leading and two armored and one motorized infantry divisions following. A massive bombing of German defenses was to precede the attack. On July 24, however, a major bombing went awry due to bad weather; American bombs killed twenty-five soldiers and wounded another 131. On the next day, under ideal conditions, 1,800 bombers from Eighth Air Force repeated the errors of the preceding day and dropped many bombs within American lines. This time, they killed 111 soldiers, including Lieutenant General

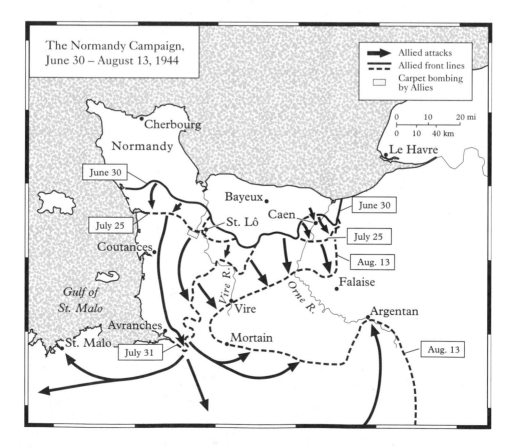

Lesley J. McNair, and wounded 490 others. The attack by the 30th Infantry Division went in anyway against the *Panzer Lehr* division. The Germans, though bloodied and battered, did not break at first. But on July 26 German resistance crumbled. VIII Corps, which was to the west of VII Corps, broke through the defenses on its front, and 4th Armored Division entered Coutances on the 28th and Avranches on the 30th. The swift advance of about thirty-five miles almost doubled the amount of terrain under Allied control.

As Cobra ended, key changes in command occurred. Under a barrage of protests from Montgomery, Eisenhower activated 12th Army Group under Bradley; with Bradley's promotion, Lieutenant General Courtney H. Hodges assumed command of First Army. Bradley in turn activated Patton's Third Army and released Patton from his role as a decoy. To trick the Germans into believing that a second invasion was coming at a location other than Normandy, the Allies had placed the flamboyant American in command of a nonexistent army group and allowed the Germans to collect information about its preparations for assaulting Pas de Calais.

On August 1, American forces poured through the bottleneck at Avranches. To secure the ports in Brittany, the first corps in Patton's Third Army turned west toward St. Malo, Brest, and Lorient. Concerned with logistical support, Overlord planners had aimed for Cherbourg to be turned over to the British as a supply base and for Brittany's ports to serve as a supply base for the Americans. To some, such as Major General John S. Wood, commander of the 4th Armored Division, the move toward the west was in the wrong direction, but the Allies remained concerned about gaining large port facilities. Recognizing the strategic importance of the ports, the Germans ordered them defended to the last man. After rushing through Avranches, 6th Armored Division raced almost 200 miles to reach Brest on August 6. Because Brest was well protected by several hills and streams, as well as numerous defensive positions, VIII Corps brought up three infantry divisions and amassed considerable ammunition reserves before it began a sustained attack on August 25, the day Paris fell. Brest finally fell on September 19, costing almost 10,000 American casualties. In retrospect, the costly siege of Brest seems wasteful and a blind adherence to plans that events had overtaken, especially since the Allies were unable to restore Brest to operating condition before the war ended.

As the area under Allied control expanded dramatically, Bradley decided on August 3, with Montgomery and Eisenhower's concurrence, to stop the movement west into Brittany and to turn American forces to the east. While the Canadian First, British Second, and U.S. First armies continued to battle the Germans in Normandy, three of the corps in Patton's Third Army raced south and then east, one corps driving south to seize Rennes (forty miles from Avranches) on August 3 and another corps driving southeast to seize LeMans (ninety miles from Avranches) on August 8.

Hitler recognized the threat posed by the breakthrough at Avranches. He ordered Kluge to pull the panzer divisions out of the battle against the British and concentrate on cutting off American forces rolling through Avranches. The target for their counterattack was the Norman village of

Mortain (twenty miles east of Avranches). Fortunately for the Allies, Ultra picked up enemy intentions, and Bradley placed strong forces on Mortain's dominating terrain to meet the attack. Moreover, American air power made German daylight movements a nightmare. The offensive failed to reach even its first objectives.

The counterattack at Mortain, however, placed German armor in danger of encirclement. With the Americans at LeMans and with the Canadians south of Caen, Fifth Panzer Army, Seventh Army, and Panzer Group Eberbach were in the middle of a rapidly closing pocket. Hitler reluctantly agreed to withdraw, but the escape exit from the pocket was narrow indeed. Neither Bradley nor Montgomery forced the closure of the pocket, or the "Falaise gap," as it became known. On orders from Bradley, Patton's forces halted at Argentan on August 13 to await the British and Canadians, driving from the north. The Canadian First Army drove south of Caen toward Falaise. On August 14, 800 heavy bombers attacked targets in front of the Canadians, but as at St. Lô, some bombs hit friendly troops, killing or wounding nearly 400. The next day the Canadians continued south but faced strong enemy resistance. At the end of the day on the 15th, they still remained two to three miles from Falaise. Meanwhile, Allied air strikes and artillery hit the mass of Germans fleeing the pocket.

Although the Germans lost more than 60,000 soldiers (killed or captured) and abandoned vast quantities of equipment in the Falaise pocket, large numbers of their best troops escaped. The loss of quantities of weapons did not create insurmountable problems, because German industry was producing vast amounts through Speer's effort. The Allies had let a golden opportunity slip through their fingers by the failure to close the Falaise-Argentan gap.

Advancing Toward the Rhine

The German collapse in France, nevertheless, was complete. Allied armies surged out across France in a wild drive toward the German frontier. On August 15, American and French troops landed in southern France in Operation Dragoon (previously known as Anvil), and German defenses collapsed as the Allies drove up the Rhône River valley. Paris fell on August 25; the Seine represented no obstacle. Unfortunately, the euphoria gripping Allied commanders and troops approaching the Reich turned into overconfidence and a belief that the war was won. The Allies correctly sensed the desperate state of the Wehrmacht, but their overconfidence carried with it seeds of failure.

As Allied forces approached the Seine, Eisenhower reconsidered his campaign strategy. The original plan had called for a halt on the Seine and buildup of supplies for three weeks before a resumption of the advance. Eisenhower knew that once a pursuit had begun, his forces should advance relentlessly, so he decided to press eastward as far as logistics would allow. But he had to decide whether to move on a broad front beyond the Seine River or whether to give priority to a single thrust into Germany.

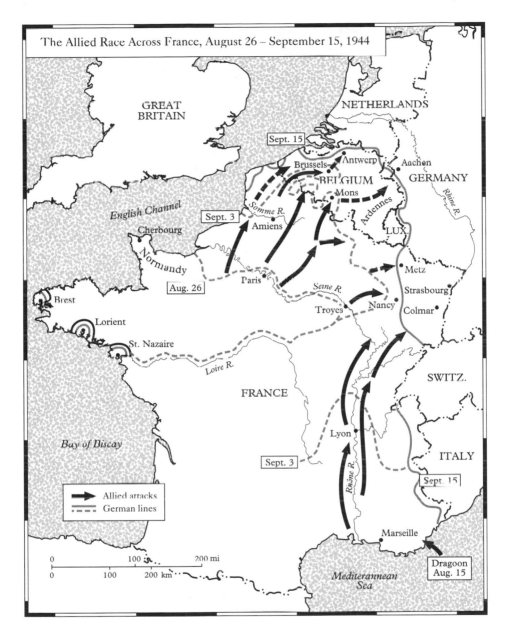

The Allied Race Across France, August 26 – September 15, 1944

GREAT BRITAIN

NETHERLANDS

Sept. 15

Brussels
Antwerp
Aachen

BELGIUM
Mons
GERMANY

English Channel

Sept. 3
Somme R.
Amiens
Ardennes
LUX.
Rhine R.

Cherbourg

Normandy

Aug. 26

Paris
Seine R.
Metz
Strasbourg

Troyes
Nancy
Colmar

Brest

Lorient

St. Nazaire

Loire R.

FRANCE

SWITZ.

Bay of Biscay

Lyon

Sept. 3

ITALY

Sept. 15

Rhône R.

→ Allied attacks
⋯ German lines

Marseille

Dragoon
Aug. 15

| 0 | 100 | 200 mi |
| 0 | 100 | 200 km |

Mediterannean
Sea

The ensuing debate about "Broad Front" versus "Single Thrust" strategy revealed much jealousy and friction between Americans and British. Prior to crossing the Seine, the Allies had envisaged their advancing along two axes into Germany. The northern route went through Amiens, Mons, and Liège to the Ruhr industrial region; the southern one went through Reims, Metz, and the Saar to Frankfurt. On August 23, Montgomery proposed that the bulk of Allied divisions and supplies concentrate under his command for a single thrust along the northern route. On August 29, Eisenhower decided to adhere to the original plan but add weight to the north by having Hodges's First Army move along the northern, rather than southern axis. Montgomery would take Antwerp and drive toward the Ruhr, while Bradley's forces spread across the Ardennes—Hodges's First Army moving north, and Patton's Third Army toward Metz. The decision angered Bradley and Patton, for it weakened 12th Army Group and gave Third Army a low priority for gasoline supplies. On September 1, Eisenhower assumed control of the ground campaign, but not before calling a press conference in London and warmly praising Montgomery. Both 21st and 12th Army groups now reported directly to Supreme Headquarters, Allied Expeditionary Force (SHAEF). Eisenhower insisted that this was not a demotion for Montgomery, who was promoted to field marshal to assuage his ego.

Montgomery drove into Belgium, all the while complaining about shortages of supplies and fuel. He still was pressing for a single thrust—under his command. Arguing that insufficient logistical support existed for more then one major drive, he proposed that Bradley's forces should halt and that all logistic support go to 21st Army Group for the last, decisive blow against a tottering Wehrmacht. Although Montgomery received nearly 80 percent of the logistical support he requested, he missed a golden opportunity to shorten the war. On September 3 British forces captured Brussels; on September 4, 11th Armored Division seized Antwerp so quickly that the Germans could not destroy the port facilities. Everything fell into British hands in undamaged condition; only the opening of the Scheldt estuary stood between the Allies and the relief of their growing supply difficulties. But Montgomery, focusing his attention entirely on the Rhine, missed the logistic implications of Antwerp's capture. Furthermore, by capturing Antwerp, the British were in position to put the German Fifteenth Army in the bag. That sizable force had guarded Pas de Calais and was now fleeing up the coast. An advance of less than ten miles beyond Antwerp would have sealed off the Walcheren and South Beveland peninsula and bottled up Fifteenth Army. But Montgomery halted at Antwerp. Consequently Fifteenth Army, ferrying across the Scheldt at night, escaped to Walcheren Island and then back into Holland.

Montgomery's pause reflected his desire to tidy up the battlefield and bring his forces under tighter control. He proposed to Eisenhower an armored thrust, supported by British and American airborne forces, across Holland and the Rhine into the Reich. Eisenhower agreed to the operation which became known as "Market Garden." From its inception it proved to be badly thought out and, moreover, plagued by bad luck. Similar in conception to the German attack on Holland in May 1940, Montgomery's plan aimed for three airborne divisions to capture the bridges leading up to and over the Rhine. Then, his XXX Corps would drive through the Dutch countryside to the north German plain. The last, crucial bridge lay across the Rhine at Arnhem. Significantly, Montgomery's proposal meant that the Allies would not be able to clear the Scheldt estuary and therefore use Antwerp to relieve growing supply difficulties.

The British needed almost two weeks to get attacking forces ready. While preparations proceeded, the Germans replenished and reorganized their beaten units back into effective fighting formations. The pause also

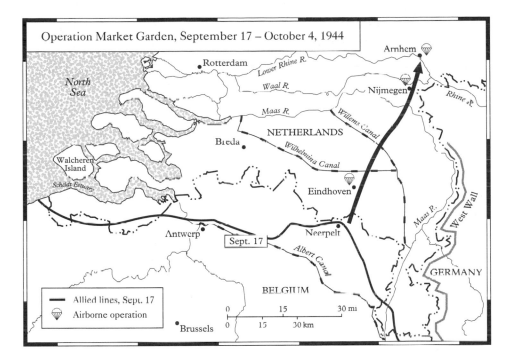

Operation Market Garden, September 17 – October 4, 1944

allowed a number of panzer divisions, including 9th and 10th SS Panzer, to withdraw for rest and refit; those two divisions went to southern Holland, while units from Fifteenth Army worked back into fighting trim in the same area. As early as September 5, Bletchley Park indicated that 9th and 10th SS Panzer were in the Arnhem area. Further Ultra decrypts, as well as intelligence from the Dutch underground, reinforced the first warning, but such intelligence made no impression on the British generals.

Montgomery and his airborne commander, Lieutenant General F. A. M. Browning, selected the inexperienced British 1st Airborne Division to capture the most difficult bridge at Arnhem. The more experienced American divisions, the 82nd and 101st, received the easier tasks of securing the bridges at Nijmegen and Eindhoven. Allied airmen then persuaded the inexperienced commanders of 1st Airborne to accept a drop zone six miles from their target because the flight path to the excellent drop zone immediately south of the bridge would expose aircraft to heavy antiaircraft fire.

Market Garden began on September 17 after extensive air attacks prepared the way. It went badly from the first; poor weather interfered with air reinforcements and supply. Despite stringent prohibitions, an American officer carried a complete set of the plans on board one of the attacking gliders; it crashed, killing him and the other occupants. Within hours, those plans were in the hands of General Kurt Student, commander of German paratroopers, who was in the area. The British 1st Airborne got only one battalion to the Arnhem bridge before the Germans sealed off the drop zone. In the south, XXX Corps advanced extremely slowly in its drive north to support the paratroopers; units from the German Fifteenth Army put up a tenacious resistance. Mud and water constrained XXX Corps' movement and forced armored vehicles to advance along a single road, an ideal killing zone for German antitank guns. Market Garden failed short of the Rhine. Though it opened a salient deep into German lines, XXX Corps never reached Arnhem, and the Allies failed to establish a bridgehead across the lower Rhine. Montgomery had prepared everything thoroughly but had wasted the most important commodity in war, time.

On September 22, Eisenhower directed Bradley to support Montgomery's operation with a drive toward Cologne. Bradley in turn ordered First Army to fight its way through the West Wall at Aachen. From October 13 to 21, some of the most bitter house-to-house fighting in the war occurred in that demolished city. As the Allied offensive slowed, it became apparent that the Germans had pulled off what Goebbels termed "the miracle of the west." The German West Wall and fighting around Arnhem, Aachen, and Metz brought the Allied offensive to a halt.

Logistic realities caught up with British and American forces who had outrun their supply system. Allied air power had wrecked the French railroad and road network in preparation for the invasion and breakout and had exacerbated the difficulty of moving Allied supplies. To shorten supply lines and ease the logistic situation, Montgomery had to open the Scheldt, but the Germans had had plenty of time to prepare defenses. Thus the failure to open the Scheldt in early September resulted in bitter and costly fighting. Not until mid-November did the Canadians finish the job. The first supply ship docked in Antwerp on November 28—nearly three months after the British had captured the port.

Weather added to Allied discomfort. British and Americans battered at weary German troops but could not break the deadlock. Swollen rivers and streams made movement difficult. The Germans hung on tenaciously in the hope that the Führer would deliver the promised miracle weapons. The widespread knowledge of the army's and Nazi Germany's criminal behavior throughout the war undoubtedly encouraged many Germans to resist to the bitter end. Moreover, the West Wall, constructed in 1938–1939 along the Reich's western frontier, provided the Wehrmacht with well-positioned defenses, although the Germans had moved most of its guns to the Atlantic Wall in 1943 and 1944.

In an attempt to move forward toward the Ruhr, Eisenhower assigned Bradley responsibility for the main effort. In mid-November the Ninth and First armies on Bradley's left launched an attack on a narrow front near Aachen in another attempt to break through the West Wall. Preceded by the heaviest close-air support bombing attack of the war, American troops encountered strong opposition, particularly in the Huertgen Forest. By early December they had advanced no more than twelve miles. Meanwhile, Patton fought his way beyond Metz. The French First Army, part of Lieutenant General Jacob M. Devers' 6th Army Group, failed to overcome strong German resistance around Colmar and created what became known as the Colmar Pocket west of the Rhine. Despite significant gains, the euphoria that had gripped Allied troops as they raced across France and Belgium had evaporated.

The Collapse of Germany

The Air Contribution

By December 1944 the Allied forces had battered the German army back to the Reich. Now the many pressures brought to bear on Germany worked in combination to broaden the effect of individual efforts. In early September 1944 control of Allied strategic bombing forces returned to the airmen. With the loss of its long-range warning network on the French coast and a sharp decline in oil production, the Luftwaffe could hardly wage an effective air defense. Moreover, Allied tactical air could also strike targets in Germany. The result was a three-pronged offensive by Allied air forces that contributed considerably to Nazi Germany's collapse.

Tedder argued strongly for a focused effort to destroy the German transportation system. His argument emphasized the Allied success in attacking French transportation. He received some support from airmen, but the strategic bombing barons had their own agenda. Harris obdurately clung to "area" bombing, but as most major railway stations lay in the center of German cities, he agreed to use them as aiming points. Spaatz still pushed for the oil campaign; nevertheless, when conditions did not permit precision bombing, he agreed to attack transportation targets. Much of the tactical air efforts also went into support for the transportation plan. The

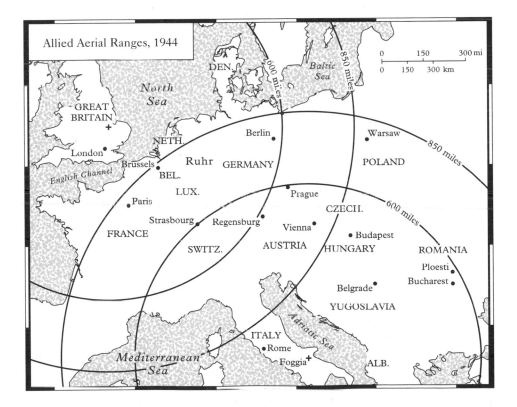

Allied Aerial Ranges, 1944

impact of such attacks on the Reich's rail and road system represented the single most effective use of air power in the war.

By early September 1944, air attacks against German transportation targets were well underway, and by October they were having considerable impact. For the week ending August 19, 1944, the German railroads had loaded and dispatched 899,091 cars; by the end of October that figure had fallen to 703,580 cars; by the end of December the total had fallen to 547,309 despite the demands of the Battle of the Bulge, the German winter counteroffensive. In that month, marshaling capacity of rail yards had declined to 40 percent of normal; in February 1945 it had fallen to 20 percent. The Battle of the Bulge indicated that attacks on transportation could not yet prevent the Germans from executing military operations. On the other hand, according to the Strategic Bombing Survey, these attacks "had reduced the available capacity for economic traffic in Germany to a point at which [the war economy] could not hope to sustain, over any period of time, a high level of military production." And, of course, the diversion of declining transport resources to supporting the Battle of the Bulge exacerbated the difficulties that German industry was already experiencing.

The steady decline of the transportation network gradually strangled the war economy by disorganizing and reducing the flow of raw materials and finished goods necessary for the production of weapons and munitions. Under such conditions neither planning nor production took place in an orderly fashion. The precipitous decline of coal transportation, essential to continued functioning of the economy, underlines the extent of the problem. In January 1944 the Essen division of the German railway system had loaded an average of 21,400 coal cars per day; by September that total had dropped to 12,000, of which only 3,400 were long-haul cars. By February 1945, Allied air attacks had cut the Ruhr off from the rest of Germany, while German railroads often had to confiscate what little coal they loaded just to keep locomotives running. The Ruhr was swimming in coal that it could no longer transport even to the industries in the region, much less to the rest of Germany.

The evidence suggests a general collapse of the war economy by mid-winter 1945. Since it was not a sudden and cataclysmic collapse, it remained difficult to discern even to those conducting the campaign. In July and August 1944 both the Eastern and Western fronts had suffered enormous defeats with great loss of equipment. Nevertheless, because German armaments production in summer 1944 remained at a relatively high level, the Wehrmacht reequipped the survivors and the new men (mostly boys) called upon to defend the frontier. There the Germans offered tough resistance and even launched the Ardennes offensive. However, beginning in January 1945 in the east, followed within a month and a half in the west, German armies again lost major battles, but this time neither on the Rhine nor on the Oder rivers were they able to reknit for a last stand. The collapse came because air attacks on the transportation network had successfully shut down the war economy, and the Wehrmacht no longer had the weapons, munitions, or petroleum necessary to fight. Even blind fanaticism could not maintain a struggle under such conditions.

Battle of the Bulge

The idea of counterattacking in the west had come to Hitler in early September 1944, even as his armies streamed back toward the German frontier. He believed that the Wehrmacht could still achieve a decisive battlefield victory that would drive the Western Powers from the war. Ever the gambler, he selected the Ardennes as the location of the main attack. The target would be Antwerp to destroy a vital logistic link for the Allies and to entrap much of the British army. But to get to Antwerp the Germans had to capture Allied fuel dumps, and the Wehrmacht possessed only enough petroleum to get to the Meuse.

On the Allied side, senior commanders remained optimistic despite German resistance on the frontier. Few could conceive that the enemy would be able to assemble the necessary resources for a major offensive. In early December, Eisenhower met with Montgomery and Bradley and outlined plans for an attack in early January 1945. The Allies would retain the broad-front strategy, but the main effort would be in the north. As Anglo-American armies prepared to launch another offensive, there were indications that the Germans were also preparing an attack. Even though the Wehrmacht faced desperate shortages of supplies, Ultra intercepts indicated major buildups of ammunition and fuel dumps opposite the Ardennes, the one place where the Allies were not attacking. But preoccupied with their own offensive and confident the Germans could not attack, Allied commanders

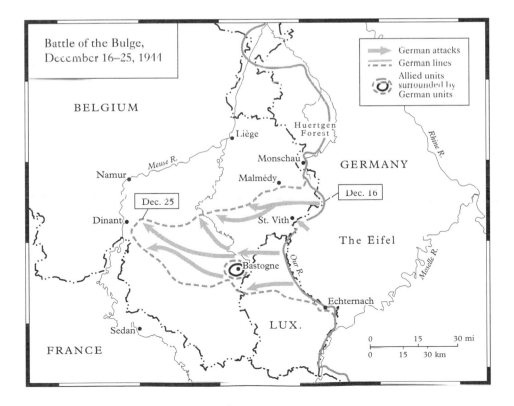

Battle of the Bulge,
December 16–25, 1944

German attacks
German lines
Allied units surrounded by German units

BELGIUM

GERMANY

Huertgen Forest

Liège

Monschau

Meuse R.

Namur

Malmédy

Dec. 16

Dec. 25

Dinant

St. Vith

The Eifel

Bastogne

Our R.

Moselle R.

Echternach

Rhine R.

Sedan

LUX.

FRANCE

0   15   30 mi
0   15   30 km

missed the warnings. In late fall the vulnerability of the Ardennes increased with the insertion of inexperienced divisions into that quiet sector. Only the 82nd and 101st Airborne divisions were in reserve; the Allied high command had committed everything else to the front.

On December 16 the Germans struck between Monschau and Echternach along a fifty-mile front in the Ardennes. The weather cooperated by providing a heavy, thick blanket of clouds to obscure the battlefield and prevent the intervention of U.S. air power. Sixth SS Panzer Army attacked in the north but met stiff resistance on its right from the U.S. 99th and 2nd divisions, part of V Corps. Fifth Panzer Army to the south, however, broke through the U.S. 106th and 28th divisions. The Germans advanced rapidly, for the U.S. divisions were spread thinly across wide fronts and were inexperienced or weakened from previous fighting.

On the northern shoulder, the 99th and 2nd divisions held the critical Monschau and Eisenborn Ridge area and thereby denied use of its critical roads to the Germans. Because of the difficult terrain in the Ardennes, the main German advance was along secondary roads, but American troops offered strong resistance at several key road junctions, most notably St. Vith and Bastogne. At St. Vith, American soldiers blocked the vital road junction for six days. At Bastogne, a small armored detachment held the Germans long enough for the 101st Airborne Division to arrive. Though surrounded, the defenders at Bastogne refused to surrender. On the southern shoulder of the penetration, U.S. forces retreated, but as in the north, they eventually held. Thus strong defenses on the shoulders and at several critical road junctions limited the width of the German penetration and disrupted the enemy's advance.

The Allied high command responded more swiftly than the Germans had expected. Since the Germans had cut off Bradley's communications with the northern flank of the Bulge, Eisenhower turned the battle there over to Montgomery, while Bradley coordinated the battle in the south. Montgomery eventually brought in his XXX Corps to help strengthen the defenses.

In the south, Patton had his finest hour. His initial reaction when told of the attack in the Ardennes was to commit all his units in heavy fighting so that he would not lose any to the fighting farther north. When he recognized, however, that a full-scale enemy offensive had begun, he shifted units of Third Army on his own authority to counterattack the breakthrough from the south. He advised Eisenhower: "Hell, let's have the guts to let the sons of bitches go to Paris. Then we'll really cut 'em off and chew 'em up." When the weather failed to cooperate, he had his chaplain compose a particularly bloodthirsty prayer. On December 23, the weather cleared, and Allied tactical and strategic air forces pounded the Germans throughout the Ardennes. Patton decorated his chaplain.

By Christmas Eve elements of Fifth Panzer Army had reached within three miles of Dinant and the Meuse River, an advance of about sixty-five miles, but that was as far as they got. Along the way Waffen SS troops under Lieutenant Colonel Jochen Peiper massacred American prisoners near Malmédy; the SS troops also murdered Belgian civilians as they advanced.

News of the atrocities and the presence of Germans in American uniforms and vehicles created considerable turmoil; sentries energetically questioned unknown Americans passing through their position about who played first base for the Cubs or how many home runs Babe Ruth had hit in 1927.

As Allied units attacked the northern and southern flanks of the Bulge, Allied aircraft raked the exposed German units. On December 26, Patton's 4th Armored Division made contact with the defenders of Bastogne. By mid-January Allied counterattacks had pushed the Germans back, and the bulge had disappeared. Hitler's desperate gamble had gained the Reich nothing. Instead he had wasted the Wehrmacht's mobile reserves and lost 100,000 men, and the Allies were on the western frontier of Germany with their forces poised for the final campaign and with their logistic base steadily improving.

Collapse in the East

The German offensive in the Ardennes led the Western Powers to request the Soviets to launch their long-expected winter offensive. The Red Army had preparations well in hand. On January 12, 1945, it struck along the Vistula; the number of forces was totally in the Soviets' favor, for the Germans had bled off most of their reserves for the Ardennes offensive. What little remained went to Hungary to fight around Budapest. The Soviets launched two concurrent offensives. The first, on the central portion of the front, saw the First Belorussian and First Ukrainian fronts break out between Warsaw and the Carpathian Mountains. They intended to drive through central Poland into Germany to the Oder River. The second, north of Warsaw, resulted in the Second and Third Belorussian fronts striking East Prussia and Pomerania. Up to now the Red Army's watchword in its conduct of operations had been "liberation"; now it was "vengeance." Soviet troops entered German territory fully encouraged to pay the Germans back for their momentous crimes in the Soviet Union.

The offensive on the central portion of the front opened with the First Ukrainian Front's attack, which hit seven weak German divisions with nearly five armies, two tank armies, and over 1,000 tanks. Within a day it had opened a forty-mile hole through which its troops and tanks poured into Silesia and raced toward the Oder River. On January 14, the First Belorussian Front launched its attack; within a day it had broken through German lines north of Warsaw. Guderian warned Hitler that Soviet attacks had shattered Army Group Center and that weakened German forces could not halt the Red Army unless reinforced. Hitler released some forces from the west but promptly shipped them off to Budapest.

By January 17, the Soviets had taken Warsaw and were approaching Cracow. Hitler sent Field Marshal Schörner to restore the situation and blamed the OKH for Warsaw's fall. After having three OKH staff officers arrested, he ordered that henceforth no command be given that could not be countermanded from above. Schörner brought unwarranted optimism and a fanatical belief in Naziism to a hopeless situation. By January 19, Army

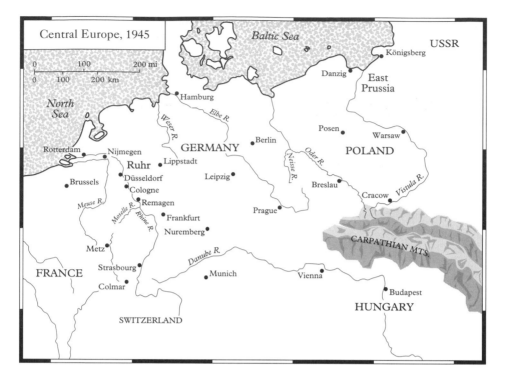

Group A, defending Upper Silesia and central Poland, had lost contact with Army Group Center. Soviet forces had ripped Army Group A's front to shreds; only logistical limitations could halt their advance. In Hitler's headquarters, the Führer appointed Heinrich Himmler to restore the front on the Oder. As commander of Army Group Vistula, Himmler's mission was to maintain an open corridor to East Prussia and prevent breakthroughs to Danzig and Posen. But his experience as the head of the SS did not translate into battlefield competence.

Before Himmler arrived to take command, the dam broke. Soviet forces attacked German units protecting East Prussia. Though Hitler had diverted divisions from East Prussia to central Poland, he refused permission for any withdrawals; German defenses again unraveled. On January 24 the Soviets reached the coast west of Danzig and the mouth of the Vistula; this advance isolated East Prussia from the rest of Germany. On the 25th the Soviets drove past Posen.

By early February 1945 the Soviets had pushed 200 miles west of Warsaw. Their leading units rested on the Oder within forty miles of Berlin; they had surrounded large German garrisons in Posen and Breslau. Though on the brink of final collapse, the Germans pulled themselves together for a final stand in front of Berlin. Not surprisingly the Soviets themselves were experiencing logistical difficulties, given the distances they had covered. In February and March, the Red Army cleaned up East Prussia, except for Königsberg and a small coastal strip. As the main body of the Russians closed on the Oder-Neisse line (the eventual Polish-German boundary), they did not resume their offensive toward Berlin. Perhaps close to the wolf's lair, they did not want any failures to dampen their triumph at war's end. Since Western ground forces still remained on the west bank of the Rhine, there seemed little need for haste.

Despite what subsequently happened to the Germans, many found it hard to sympathize with them, since they had committed such horrible crimes in the east. Nevertheless, a terrible revenge fell on eastern Germany, as Soviet troops began systematically looting and raping the territories they conquered. Soviet soldiers, often in a drunken stupor, murdered tens of thousands of civilians. Estimates of civilian casualties are as high as 3,000,000. Whatever the total, it represented the hideousness of the ideological war unleashed by the Nazis on June 22, 1941.

Collapse in the West

Meanwhile, German defenses in the west unraveled at a fast rate during January and February 1945. In the south Devers's 6th Army Group reduced the Colmar Pocket in the first week of February, while in the north and center, Allied units began closing in on the Rhine. By early March British and American units had battered their way into the Rhineland. By March 11, 21st Army Group held the Rhine between Düsseldorf and Nijmegen. Eisenhower planned on encircling the Ruhr by having Montgomery make the major crossing of the Rhine north of the Ruhr, and having Bradley make secondary crossings to the south with First and Third armies. Montgomery ordered a pause to prepare the massive assault across the Rhine, but the Americans moved more quickly.

In early March Third Army cracked German defenses in the Eifel (northeast of Luxembourg) and in three days reached the Rhine. Hodges's First Army did even better: on March 7, 9th Armored Division reached the Rhine at the moment that the Germans were blowing up the Ludendorff railroad bridge at Remagen. German engineers had placed their charges too evenly on the bridge supports. After pressing the plunger, the appalled defenders watched with amazement as the bridge, with much smoke and noise, rose several feet in the air and then settled back on its pilings. U.S. infantrymen rushed the bridge and then seized the cliffs overlooking the river. They now commanded the approaches and reinforcements surged across.

Hodges, with Bradley's support, rushed a large number of units across without fully informing SHAEF, for fear that the Allied high command might not recognize the opportunity. Eisenhower's operations officer lived up to expectations. He told Bradley: "Sure, you've got a bridge, Brad, but what good is it going to do you. You are not going anyplace down there at Remagen. It just doesn't fit into the plan."* But Eisenhower proved more flexible, allowing Hodges and Bradley to push strong forces over the Rhine.

An enraged Hitler ordered an immediate search for traitors. With no reserves, the Nazi army could do little to contain a growing American

---

*Omar N. Bradley, *A Soldier's Story* (New York: Holt, 1951), p. 500.

bridgehead. The Luftwaffe launched a number of sorties against the bridge and even fired off V-2s, while the navy floated mines and frogmen downriver in desperate efforts to cut the cord across the Rhine. Eventually the bridge collapsed, but by then the Americans had pontoon bridges and four divisions across the Rhine.

To the south Patton moved down the Rhine valley and in cooperation with Seventh Army cleaned up the left bank. To Goebbels' outrage German civilians greeted the Americans everywhere with white bed sheets displayed from windows; there was no fanatical resistance in the Rhineland. Not to be outdone by Hodges's accomplishment at Remagen, Patton threw a bridge across the Rhine at Oppenheim on March 22 and rushed everybody he could across the river. That day, in reference to Montgomery's coming assault across the Rhine on March 24, Patton's briefing officer reported: "Without benefit of aerial bombing, ground smoke, artillery preparation, and airborne assistance, Third Army at 2200 hours, Thursday, March 22, crossed the Rhine River." The rapid advance of the U.S. First, Third, and Seventh armies through the Rhineland had killed, wounded, or captured 225,000 Germans at a cost of 5,000 casualties.

After two weeks of intense preparations, Montgomery was finally ready to launch his blow. Against five ill-equipped, weakly manned divisions holding a thirty-mile front, the British used an artillery bombardment of 3,300 guns, Allied strategic and tactical air forces, and two airborne divisions. The weight of the offensive initially slowed its forward movement, but the British soon broke out into the open. The combined effect of Mont-

Allied forces made rapid progress in Germany. Many towns decked themselves in white flags whereas others offered only token resistance.

gomery's advance and the Americans' advance south of the Ruhr placed the Germans in a hopeless position. The exploitation occurred at an even faster pace than in the Normandy breakout. On April 1, the U.S. 2nd Armored Division from the north met First Army's 3rd Armored Division at Lippstadt, seventy-five miles east of the Rhine, thereby encircling the Ruhr. Within the wreckage of Germany's industrial heart lay Field Marshal Model's Army Group B. Nothing remained in western Germany except a few pockets of fanatical Nazis to hinder Anglo-American forces.

The Allied advance followed political realities as well as operational concerns. Since the political agreements at Yalta had already placed the area around Berlin within the Soviet sphere, it made little sense for Allied soldiers to die capturing territory that would end up under Soviet control. Consequently, Allied troops halted along the Elbe River. In the south the Red Army had already reached Vienna's outskirts; it made equal sense not to reach for what was within Soviet grasp. Only by seizing Prague could the Western Allies perhaps have made a difference in the postwar settlement, but Eisenhower halted Patton's Third Army before it reached the Czech capital.

One last act remained. As Anglo-American forces rampaged through western and central Germany, the Red Army launched its forces on Berlin. The Germans had no prospect for delaying the coming blow. Their Ninth Army, defending the capital, consisted of fourteen understrength divisions; Third Panzer Army on its left flank had eleven divisions. In total, the Germans possessed 754 tanks, 344 artillery pieces, and 900–1,000 antiaircraft guns. Their opponents, First and Second Belorussian fronts, disposed of 110 infantry divisions, eleven tank and mechanized corps, and eleven artillery divisions (4,106 tanks and self-propelled guns, and 23,576 artillery pieces).

The main Soviet offensive across the Oder came on April 16. Despite initial difficulties and fanatical resistance, the Soviets by April 20 had won the battle of Berlin. On the 21st, Soviet artillery shells began falling on the German capital. In the bizarre atmosphere of his bunker, Hitler maneuvered nonexistent units on his battle maps, but there was no hope of relief. On April 25, Soviet and American units met on the Elbe and cut Germany in half. On the afternoon of April 30, Adolf Hitler, having just married his mistress Eva Braun, committed suicide; he was soon followed by Goebbels and his family. The nightmare in Europe was finally over.

★   ★   ★   ★

The collapse of Germany reflected a war waged by one major industrial power against three of the world's other major industrial powers, including one that by itself could outproduce most of the world. Allied air had brought Germany's transportation network to a halt by winter 1945, which in turn caused the collapse of war production, while the destruction of petroleum facilities grounded much of the Luftwaffe and robbed the German army of its mobility. On the Eastern and Western fronts, Allied superiority wrecked the German Army. Hitler's strategic and operational direction of the war made a bad situation worse, but his fanatical will drove the German nation to fight to the end. Nevertheless, the Wehrmacht's competence at tactical and operational levels mitigated some of Hitler's decisions and prevented Allied thrusts from breaking into Germany until 1945.

The battles in Europe in the last year of the war reflected the narrowing of the gap between German battlefield performance and the performance of the opposing armies. The steadily improving tactical and operational capabilities of Allied forces was, of course, substantially aided by their overwhelming superiority in numbers and firepower. The invasion of Normandy, the expansion of the beachheads, and the breakout and surge across western Europe demonstrated the Allies' improved ability to join infantry, tanks, and artillery into effective combined arms teams and to use air power to extend the performance of their ground forces. Particularly noteworthy was the capacity of Allied forces to work together in a joint environment in which the services complemented the capabilities of each other. Combined with the advantages of superior intelligence and deception on a massive scale, these capabilities had placed the Germans in a hopeless situation.

SUGGESTED READINGS

Ambrose, Stephen E. *The Supreme Commander: The War Years of General Dwight D. Eisenhower* (Garden City, N.Y.: Doubleday, 1970).

Bennett, Ralph. *Ultra in the West: The Normandy Campaign, 1944–45* (New York: Scribner, 1979).

Blumenson, Martin. *Breakout and Pursuit* (Washington: Office of the Chief of Military History, 1961).Bradley, Omar N. *A Soldier's Story* (New York: Holt, 1951).

Eisenhower, Dwight D. *Crusade in Europe* (Garden City, N.Y.: Doubleday, 1948).

Harrison, Gordon A. *Cross-Channel Attack* (Washington: Office of the Chief of Military History, 1951).

Hastings, Max. *Overlord: D-Day and the Battle for Normandy* (New York: Simon and Schuster, 1984).

Hechler, Ken. *The Bridge at Remagen* (New York: Ballantine, 1957).

MacDonald, Charles B. *The Mighty Endeavor: American Armed Forces in the European Theater in World War II* (New York: Oxford University Press, 1969).

———. *Time for Trumpets: The Untold Story of the Battle of the Bulge* (New York: Morrow, 1984).

Montgomery, Bernard L. *The Memoirs of Field-Marshal the Viscount Montgomery of Alamein* (New York: World, 1958).

Patton, George S. *War as I Knew It* (Boston: Houghton Mifflin, 1947).

Pogue, Forrest C. *The Supreme Command* (Washington: Office of the Chief of Military History, 1954).

Ryan, Cornelius. *A Bridge Too Far* (New York: Simon and Schuster, 1974).

Weigley, Russell F. *Eisenhower's Lieutenants: The Campaign in France and Germany, 1944–1945* (Bloomington: Indiana University Press, 1981).

Wilmot, Chester. *The Struggle for Europe* (New York: Harper, 1952).

Ziemke, Earl F. *Stalingrad to Berlin: The German Defeat in the East* (Washington: Office of the Chief of Military History, 1968).

18

VICTORY IN THE PACIFIC:
NAVAL AND AMPHIBIOUS WAR
ON THE OPERATIONAL LEVEL

The Americans committed large forces to the Pacific even though U.S. grand strategy was one of "Germany first." No matter how appealing such an approach might be in strategic terms, the strategy of "Germany first" flew in the face of the fundamental political reality that it was Japan against whom the American public directed its anger. The strategy also encountered the military reality that a major invasion of the European continent could not have occurred before spring 1944. Thus throughout the war, Japan received a higher priority in terms of the commitment of U.S. military forces than the grand strategy seemingly dictated. Many of the debates about strategy focused less on strategic objectives and courses of action than on the allocation of scarce resources. In the end it worked out, but there were times when American strategy and operations in the Pacific possessed a distinctly ad hoc nature.

The war in the Pacific differed greatly from most other wars in the twentieth century. After the battle of Midway in early June 1942 halted the tide of Japanese victory, U.S. commanders in the Pacific possessed only the slimmest of resources; the move against Guadalcanal with one marine division underlined this fact. Though the Americans initially could do little more than defend the sea lines of communication to Australia, the mobilization of manpower and industrial production eventually allowed them to take the offensive. Partially due to interservice rivalries, U.S. forces made two great drives—one from the south Pacific, one across the central Pacific—to destroy Japanese military power. As the Americans confronted their Pacific enemies, the number of naval battles and ships sunk exceeded the combined totals of all other twentieth-century conflicts. Nonetheless, the Americans combined air, land, and sea forces in an unprecedented manner for giant leaps across the ocean. In the end the war in the Pacific concluded the same way it had begun, by air attack, but the explosion of two atomic bombs over Japan heralded the unleashing of new levels of destructive power.

The South Pacific, August 1942–December 1943

The Allied moves against Guadalcanal in August 1942 and into New Guinea in October–November occurred because of the strategic requirement to protect sea lines of communication to Australia. Although American leaders gave Europe first priority, they could not permit the Japanese to consolidate their position in the Pacific. Moreover, public opinion in the United States, still outraged by Pearl Harbor, demanded revenge. The South Pacific saw a series of inconclusive air and naval battles that collectively turned the tide against Japan. There were no decisive victories, but American naval, air, and ground forces emerged from these battles in greater strength, whereas the opposite occurred with the Japanese. Above all, the growing American superiority reflected the awesome industrial capabilities of the United States.

Guadalcanal

In August 1942, U.S. Marines found themselves haphazardly deposited on Guadalcanal. The naval disaster at Savo Island forced the transport fleet to leave, and marines ashore received only half the equipment they required. Fortunately for the Americans, the Japanese had almost completed the airfield on the island; within two weeks the U.S. Navy Seabees had completed it, and fast destroyers brought in fuel, bombs, and ground crewmen. Soon marine aircraft arrived, and from that point on American air reigned over the Solomon Islands. Japanese arrogance and miscalculations also aided the Americans considerably. The Imperial high command, misled by Savo Island, believed the American attack against Guadalcanal was nothing more than a raid; the Japanese army estimated that a reinforced regiment would suffice to regain the airfield on Guadalcanal. Consequently the Japanese launched an ill-prepared countermove on August 21; the marines almost wiped out the attackers in a night of savage fighting. That defeat finally woke up the Japanese high command to the seriousness of the threat; both sides rushed to build up forces on Guadalcanal—the Japanese at night, the Americans by day. Meanwhile a series of naval and air battles swirled around Guadalcanal. On August 24, in the battle of the eastern Solomons, the Americans sank the small carrier, *Ryujo*; the U.S. carrier *Enterprise* in turn received three bomb hits that put it out of action.

By the end of August, the Japanese had built their forces up to 6,000 men. In a series of ferocious attacks on September 13, they came close to breaking through to Henderson Field, but the marines held. The attackers lost 50 percent of their men; the marines lost nearly 20 percent. In early October the U.S. Navy slipped the 164th Regiment of the Americal Division into Guadalcanal. The Japanese by now had over one division ashore and prepared a three-pronged attack on the defensive perimeter despite insufficient artillery. The attacks on October 23–26 came in disjointed fashion. The main attack hit the south side of the perimeter which one marine battalion, reinforced by a battalion from the 164th, held. Throughout two nights of fierce fighting, the well-entrenched Americans beat off the attack. Nearly 3,500 Japanese died in the unsuccessful attempts. The line on Guadalcanal had held.

When American marines landed on Guadalcanal on August 7, 1942, 75-mm pack howitzers came ashore with the assault battalions to provide fire support. Heavier 105-mm howitzers landed later in the day.

From September through November, naval battles continued in furious but indecisive fashion. The Japanese sank carrier *Wasp* and badly damaged carrier *Saratoga* and new battleship *North Carolina*. Off Cape Esperance, northwest of Guadalcanal, American cruisers and destroyers bested their Japanese opponent for the first time at night on October 11–12; their success was largely a result of radar and of Japanese confusion rather than of improvement in U.S. tactical skill. As the Japanese attacks against Henderson Field failed in late October, another inconclusive naval clash occurred north of Guadalcanal. In the battle of the Santa Cruz Islands, 350 miles east of Guadalcanal, the Japanese sank carrier *Hornet* and again damaged *Enterprise*; in turn, American aircraft damaged two Japanese cruisers. Though the U.S. Navy had suffered heavier losses, both sides pulled back.

Recognizing the need for new leadership, Nimitz fired the naval commander of the South Pacific who had originally objected to the campaign in the Solomons and who had become exhausted and indecisive from the strain. His replacement was Vice Admiral William F. "Bull" Halsey, an aggressive combat sailor. As he told the marine commander on Guadalcanal, Major General Alexander A. Vandegrift: "Go on back. I'll promise you everything I've got."

By now the Japanese were not only slipping reinforcements down the Solomons by night but were also bombarding Henderson Field with heavy cruisers and battleships. In November they attempted to land large numbers of reinforcements on Guadalcanal. They began their effort on the night of November 12–13 with an attack against American ships off Guadalcanal and an attempt to land troops on the island by transports. The Americans suffered heavily but forced the enemy to turn back. They badly damaged battleship *Hiei*, and U.S. aircraft sank it the next day. The Japanese returned on November 14, but the Americans sank seven of eleven troop transports. A clash of battleships, one of the few in the entire war, also took place: on the American side battleships *South Dakota* and *Washington*; on the Japanese side, *Kirishima*. Although the Japanese had to scuttle the badly damaged *Kirishima*, they beached four transports on Guadalcanal. Thereafter they risked no more capital ships in the Solomons campaign. The Japanese attempted to send reinforcements by troop transports on December 3, 7, and 11, but heavy losses forced them to abandon the effort to reinforce Guadalcanal.

By early January 1943 the situation completely favored the Americans. The 2nd Marine Division had replaced the 1st, while the 25th Division and the remainder of the Americal Division had arrived. Under the command of Lieutenant General Alexander M. Patch, the Americans drove west to push the Japanese off the island. The Japanese conceded defeat, however, and pulled off 11,000 weary, beaten troops in the first week of February 1943. Of 60,000 American marines and soldiers who fought on Guadalcanal, 1,600 died and 4,200 were wounded; of 36,000 Japanese, 15,000 were killed or missing, 9,000 died of disease, and 1,000 were captured. The air and naval contest had also ended in an American victory; there the results were even more decisive. Air battles over the Solomons cost the Japanese 1,000 naval aircraft and a further 1,500 in defending New

Guinea and Rabaul. The fighting cost the Japanese navy nearly half its fighter pilots and an even greater percentage of dive bomber and torpedo crews; those losses, combined with Midway, undermined the Japanese navy's capacity to fight a naval air battle on anything approaching equal terms with its American opponents.

Papua

The American victory in the battle of the Coral Sea in May 1942 momentarily halted the drive on Port Moresby in New Guinea, and victory at Midway in June swung the initiative tentatively to the Americans. The Japanese, however, did not abandon their hopes of seizing Port Moresby and thereby threatening Allied lines to Australia. On July 21 they landed 11,000 troops on New Guinea and marched south over the mountains toward Port Moresby. After the Japanese got within twenty miles of their goal in mid-September, Australian forces drove the enemy back to the northeast coast where the Japanese established a defensive perimeter. They intended to renew their offensive once they had beaten the Americans on Guadalcanal.

Since MacArthur believed the best way to defend Australia was to control New Guinea, he reacted strongly. In October and early November, the Australian 7th Division and the American 32nd Division moved across from Australia to Port Moresby and on to the northeast coast of Papua (the easternmost extension of New Guinea). When the 32nd Division attacked Buna on November 19, it discovered the Japanese solidly dug in, surrounded by a huge swamp. Without heavy artillery, flamethrowers, or tanks, American attacks gained little. Unwilling to tolerate delays, MacArthur sent Lieutenant General Robert L. Eichelberger to remedy the situation.

While the Australians attacked Japanese forces west of Buna, Eichelberger replaced the 32nd Division's commander and swiftly improved the supply situation and combat power of his forces. In addition to providing better food and ensuring that his soldiers rested, Eichelberger obtained tanks to support the infantry and developed more effective methods for capturing enemy bunkers. Thirty-two days after his arrival, Buna fell. One month later Australians and Americans captured Sanananda, three miles northwest of Buna and the strongest Japanese position in Papua. The Allies had learned important lessons about reducing Japanese defensive positions, but the cost was heavy—8,500 casualties, over 3,500 dead. Nonetheless, the Allies had held at Guadalcanal and driven the Japanese from Port Moresby; they now held the initiative.

Operation "Cartwheel"

These successes raised the question of what to do next. At the Casablanca Conference in January 1943, the Americans lost most of the strategic arguments, but the Combined Chiefs of Staff agreed to retain the initiative in the Pacific. Admittedly, this decision reflected political realities; it also reflected the fact that the great fleet the U.S. Navy was assembling could

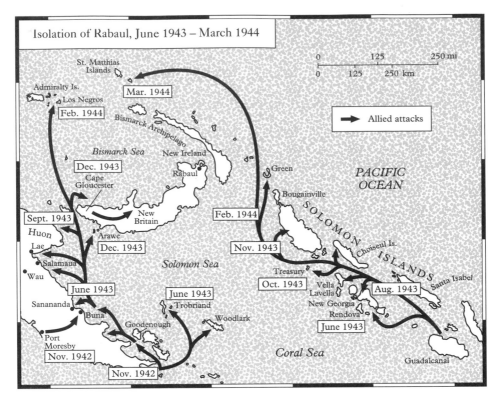

Isolation of Rabaul, June 1943 – March 1944

serve no other purpose. The Combined Chiefs of Staff, however, did not envisage a full-scale offensive against Japan until after Germany's defeat.

Soon after Casablanca, the issue of unity of command in the Pacific arose. The army favored MacArthur, the navy Nimitz. Washington had not yet reached a decision when representatives of the Pacific commanders gathered in the U.S. capital. There, MacArthur's chief of staff asked for much larger forces for a drive on Rabaul: no less than five additional divisions and 1,800 aircraft. Appalled at the magnitude of MacArthur's request, the Joint Chiefs of Staff concluded that there were not enough planes, ships, or divisions available in the Pacific to capture Rabaul in 1943. In March they postponed plans to seize Rabaul and accepted MacArthur's new proposal for a two-pronged drive converging on the Japanese base. With MacArthur in overall command of Operation "Cartwheel," Halsey would advance up the Solomons as far as Bougainville, while forces under MacArthur would move along the coast of New Guinea before attacking the western end of the island of New Britain. Whether or not to attack Rabaul on the eastern end of New Britain would depend on the availability of additional forces.

Operation Cartwheel established a model that Pacific commanders would use for the rest of the war. The Americans would advance by great bounds due to their air superiority, hit the Japanese at weak spots, seize existing airfields and ports, and then use their newly acquired bases to support the next leap forward.

Air Power

Air power played a key role in Cartwheel, as well as subsequent Pacific operations. Much of the Allied effort aimed to cut Japanese lines of communication—the air, sea, and land routes over which troops and equipment moved—and to prevent Japanese reinforcement or escape. In August 1942, MacArthur had received a new air commander, Major General George C. Kenney. Kenney may have been the premier airman of World War II; he was certainly the best in the Pacific. Unlike many other airmen, he was no ideologue; he understood the need to adapt military forces to actual conditions and to use air power to accomplish overall theater objectives. Kenney took over a weak organization: combat crews were discouraged and dispirited, maintenance was in shambles, and supply channels were inefficient and incompetent. He gave his air units a thorough housecleaning and relieved no fewer than five generals and an even larger number of colonels. But Kenney made his greatest contribution in air tactics and operations. High-level bombing of ships had thus far killed mostly fish, and Kenney determined to change his forces' tactical approach. Among other improvements, he retrained medium bomber crews and modified their aircraft to attack at low level. B-25s now carried eight .50-caliber machine guns in their noses and six 100-pound bombs that could be skipped into targets.

Meanwhile the Japanese replied to the increasing American threat in the South Pacific by moving forces from as far away as China to the theater. They placed their Eighth Army at Rabaul, Seventeenth Army in the Solomons, and Eighteenth Army in New Guinea and New Britain. In April 1943, they moved the 51st Division from Rabaul to New Guinea; eight transports and eight destroyers provided sea lift. Nearly one hundred fighters were to provide continuous cover for the convoy as it rounded New Britain. "Magic" (the breaking of Japanese codes) picked up Japanese plans. Forewarned of enemy intentions, Kenney studied past experience with Japanese convoys. These assessments along with further Magic intelligence allowed U.S. aircraft to strike with devastating effectiveness. Japanese fighters looked for high-altitude bombers; instead, B-25s attacked at low level from head on. Machine-gun fire and fragmentation bombs rained death on crowded transport decks, while 100-pound bombs skipped into the enemy ships. In one day's air attacks, Kenney's aircraft sank all the transports and four destroyers; the Japanese lost about 3,000 soldiers and most of the 51st Division's staff. Besides demonstrating Kenney's skills, the battle of the Bismarck Sea represented a decisive success for land-based air against naval power.

The Japanese concentrated much of their land-based air at Rabaul and Wewak (an island off the north-central coast of New Guinea). To halt erosion of the Japanese situation, Admiral Yamamoto Isoroku launched a series of massive air raids—the "I" operation—against New Guinea and Guadalcanal in April 1943. The raids achieved little. Moreover, by utilizing Magic the Allies learned of a visit by Yamamoto to the theater and shot down his aircraft. Despite Japanese opposition, Kenney built air bases in

New Guinea, gained air superiority above MacArthur's ground forces, and attacked the Japanese bases. American raids not only destroyed one hundred enemy aircraft on the ground at Wewak on August 17 but also wrecked the enemy's base and supply organization. Consequently the Japanese no longer could shuttle air units back and forth within the theater.

A deteriorating operational situation led the Japanese to undertake desperate remedial measures. The navy committed its new carrier pilots to defend Rabaul's airfield; code name for the counterattack was "RO." A series of savage air battles occurred over Rabaul and New Britain in October and November. Again there was no clear winner; both sides suffered heavy losses, while claiming even heavier ones for their opponents. But in the end, the Americans could replace crews and aircraft without difficulty; the Japanese, their naval air units decimated by the fighting, lost the full combat value of their carriers for the remainder of the war.

The Amphibious Campaign

By early summer 1943, MacArthur and Halsey had begun Operation Cartwheel. The arrival of additional landing craft made movement and commitment of amphibious forces far easier. Specially designed craft such as the Landing Ship Tank (LST), Amphibious Tractor (Amtrac), and Landing Craft Infantry (LCI) moved men and equipment from ship to shore. Halsey's forces had more new craft than MacArthur's forces did in the southwest Pacific, but MacArthur had an Engineer Amphibious Brigade, which carried troops and equipment to shore and organized the beachhead. Such support left the landing troops free to fight the battle.

Halsey's first amphibious strike went against the Munda airfield on New Georgia, which threatened Guadalcanal. Landing on a small, nearby island in late June, about 32,000 soldiers and 1,700 marines moved to New Georgia but took several weeks to dislodge the Japanese from the dense jungle. The next target was Kolombangara with 12,000 Japanese troops in strong defenses. Instead of attacking the enemy force directly, Halsey skipped Kolombangara and landed on the next island, Vella Lavella, where there were no Japanese. Though enemy land-based air posed some risk, the move caught the Japanese off guard. They had no choice but to evacuate the isolated troops on Kolombangara.

MacArthur's forces achieved similar success in New Guinea. Late in January a small contingent of Australian forces repulsed an attack on Wau (about 150 miles northwest of Buna). Allied reinforcements arrived by air, while Kenney's destruction of enemy transports carrying the 51st Division halted Japanese reinforcements. In late June, Allied forces landed on the New Guinea coast east of Wau. On September 5, the 503rd Parachute Regiment dropped on the airfield at Nadzab (fifty miles north of Wau); Kenney's transports then flew in the Australian 7th Division. Combined with another amphibious assault, this vertical envelopment forced the Japanese to abandon strongly held positions at Salamaua and Lae on the coast. A few weeks later the Allies grabbed the Huon Peninsula north of Salamaua and Lae.

The peninsula lay just west of New Britain, which had Rabaul on its eastern tip. Taking advantage of the favorable situation, Kenney's aircraft dropped 685 tons of bombs on Rabaul in October.

Halsey now moved against Bougainville; on November 1, 1943, 3rd Marine Division landed at Empress Augusta Bay. In eight hours both troops and equipment were ashore, a considerable improvement over Guadalcanal. Offshore, the navy, with radar's assistance, fought the Japanese on even terms at night. Staying outside the range of "Long Lance" torpedoes, American ships blasted Japanese light cruisers and destroyers that had come from Rabaul to attack the transports. The Japanese responded by sending a larger naval force to reinforce Rabaul and attack the Allied naval forces near Bougainville. On November 5, violating previous practice, Halsey sent almost one hundred carrier aircraft against Japanese ships anchored at Rabaul. The raid damaged six cruisers and two destroyers and ended the enemy threat to Empress Augusta Bay. Meanwhile the 37th Infantry Division with a New Zealand brigade arrived to assist the 3rd Marine Division in clearing Bougainville, a task not completed until the war's end. As the Allies expanded control over the island, they built an airfield that placed them in an even better position to attack Rabaul.

In mid-December, the 112th Cavalry Regiment landed on the south coast of New Britain. Two weeks later the 1st Marine Division landed at Cape Gloucester on New Britain's western tip. These landings effectively neutralized Rabaul. MacArthur saw no need to undertake a costly assault on the fortified port; the Americans could leave the Japanese to wither on the vine and move to more distant and significant targets. After mid-February 1944 no Japanese warships remained in Rabaul, and no aircraft rose from Rabaul to challenge Allied bombers.

The island-hopping campaign was underway. The Americans, where possible, now avoided Japanese strong points and struck deep into the Japanese island empire. The carriers or land-based aircraft provided air superiority to suppress enemy ground-based air in the area and to fend off enemy naval forces. The amphibious forces, army or marine, would then capture the base, and Allied logistical forces would move up to support the next jump. Without aircraft and cut off from support, the isolated Japanese posed no threat to the Allied advance.

The Submarine Campaign

While two great American drives pushed up the Solomons and New Guinea and across the central Pacific, the U.S. Navy waged one of the most effective campaigns of World War II—one that brought the Japanese to the brink of collapse. That campaign was the submarine offensive against enemy commerce. Before the war, the Japanese had recognized that commercial shipping would play a crucial role in bringing raw materials from the "Greater East Asia Co-Prosperity Sphere" to keep the war economy functioning.

Therefore, in their prewar buildup they expended considerable resources on modernizing their merchant fleet.

Ironically, the Japanese made virtually no preparations to defend commercial shipping. In fall 1941 only two junior staff officers in the naval high command were responsible for protecting the entire Japanese merchant fleet from enemy submarines. The title for their area of responsibility was "rear area" defense; within their sphere lay not only antisubmarine warfare but also antimining and antiaircraft operations. One officer with the derogatory title of "staff officer for training" was responsible for all commercial shipping along the Honshu coast and from Tokyo to Iwo Jima. Despite the obvious success of German submarines against British shipping in the Atlantic, the Japanese failed to provide escorts for merchant shipping at the onset of war. Not until six months after Pearl Harbor did they establish an escort fleet at Formosa, but it consisted of only eight destroyers.

At the beginning of the war the U.S. Navy could not take advantage of such weaknesses. It possessed excellent submarines with enough range and load capacity to operate in the wide expanses of the Pacific, but most submarine commanders were overage and lacked a killer instinct. It took the war's first year to create a cadre of younger, more aggressive skippers. But the problem was not just one of leadership; American torpedoes simply failed to work. The magnetic device designed to make them explode underneath enemy ships rarely functioned because the navy had tested torpedoes inadequately before the war. The navy's Bureau of Ordnance refused to believe reports coming from the Pacific about defects and blamed misses on the submarine commanders. When the evidence finally became too overwhelming to deny, another equally serious defect cropped up: the contact firing pin, designed to explode the torpedo by direct hit, was too delicate; direct hits jammed the firing mechanisms without an explosion. Not until July 1943 was the second problem recognized at Pearl Harbor, and not until September 1943 did U.S. submarines finally have effective torpedoes.

The failure of U.S. boats in their attacks on merchant shipping lulled the Japanese into a false sense of security; they waited until March 1943 to establish a second escort fleet. Even then their escorts numbered only sixteen destroyers, five coast-defense frigates, and five torpedo boats. In no fashion could they handle the storm that now broke. In September 1943 the Japanese lost a record 172,082 tons of merchant shipping; by November that total had climbed to 265,068 tons. Magic and other signals intelligence revealed the routing of Japanese merchant vessels; consequently U.S. submarines easily intercepted enemy shipping. In 1944, American submarines formed wolf packs in response to increasing use of convoys by the Japanese. The slaughter continued; in 1944 the submarine offensive sank more tonnage than the Japanese had lost in the entire 1941–1943 period. By the end of 1944, American submarines had sunk half the Japanese merchant fleet and two-thirds of their tanker fleet. Movement of oil from the Dutch East Indies stopped; shipments of raw material to the Home Islands slowed to a trickle.

Overall, American submarines sank 1,113 merchant vessels over 500 tons, a total of 5,320,000 gross tons. In addition they sank 201 naval vessels, including battleship *Kongo* and supercarrier *Shinano*. The total naval tonnage sunk reached 577,000 tons. All of this cost the U.S. Navy only fifty-two submarines. Considering that American losses included 22 percent of the sailors in the submarine force (the highest casualty rate of any branch), one should not minimize the cost, but the succes of the submarine campaign more than repaid the investment in resources and manpower.

Advance Across the Central Pacific, November 1943–February 1944

In May 1943 at the Trident Conference in Washington, the Combined Chiefs of Staff set long-range objectives for the defeat of Japan: while the Allies would continue to pursue a strategy of Germany first, they would maintain relentless pressure on Japan. The first aim would be to cut the Japanese Empire off from the raw materials of Southeast Asia; the second to launch a strategic bombing campaign against Japan; and the third to invade Japan and break its military power. To achieve these goals the Allies planned to build upon British efforts in Burma, American successes in the South Pacific, and Chinese military power in East Asia for a final offensive against the Home Islands of Japan.

But Admiral King had his own conception. Beginning in January 1943 he pressed for a drive across the Central Pacific by naval forces. This drive would move toward Japan over the coral atolls scattered across the

Admiral Ernest J. King believed, as a distinguished naval historian has explained, that "what was good for the Navy was good for the United States, and indeed the world." Never a seeker of publicity, he was an enormously talented officer who had a firm grasp of naval strategy and tactics.

Pacific. During the same period, MacArthur proposed an advance across the South Pacific via New Guinea and the Philippines. While King emphasized the advantages of leaping vast distances across the Pacific, MacArthur emphasized Allied obligations to the Filipinos, the advantages of maintaining pressure against an already retreating enemy, and the possibility of a renewed Japanese threat to Australia. Even Nimitz had qualms about two Pacific drives. In the end the American chiefs of staff performed a delicate balancing act; King would get his way, but the drive across the central Pacific would move first against the Gilbert Islands and then advance toward the Philippines, as would MacArthur. The move against the Gilberts and then the Philippines would leave considerable sea lift for MacArthur's forces.

Sea Power

While Halsey's and MacArthur's successes in Cartwheel were wearing away Japanese ground and air power, the naval balance swung drastically in favor of the Americans. The first Essex-class fleet carriers arrived at Pearl Harbor; at 27,000 tons, with a top speed of thirty-two knots and one hundred aircraft, they represented a major increase in naval air power. American industry was producing them at the rate of nearly one a month. At the same time the Independence-class light carriers of 11,000 tons with a similar speed and a capacity of fifty aircraft were also arriving. By autumn 1943, Fifth Fleet under Admiral Raymond A. Spruance had grown to six fleet carriers, five light carriers, five new and seven old battleships, nine heavy and five light cruisers, and fifty-six destroyers—all of which required an enormous support system of tankers, supply ships, and tenders. The carriers, moreover, possessed the F6F Hellcat fighter, which finally gave navy pilots a fighter superior to the Zero. All of this reflected design and production decisions made in the late 1930s and early 1940s. The new carriers provided the navy the capability to advance across the central Pacific toward Japan.

One of the great triumphs of the Pacific war was the fact that the U.S. fleet remained at sea on a constant basis with only individual ships returning for refit and with Halsey's and Spruance's headquarters rotating command. While Halsey's headquarters, Third Fleet, was commanding at sea, Spruance's headquarters, Fifth Fleet, would be in Pearl Harbor planning the next operations; and when Spruance and his headquarters went to sea, Halsey and his headquarters returned to Pearl.

No matter who commanded, a vast armada of supply ships sustained the fleet across the immense distances of the central Pacific. The unsung story of the drive across the central Pacific was the logistic support for that fleet, a fleet that quite literally never returned to its bases. It represented a triumph that no other nation could match. In a manner not anticipated in the 1920s and 1930s, the fleet could exist by itself in enemy waters for indefinite periods of time; it required anchorage only for resupply and refit, but more often than not the former took place while ships were underway in the open ocean. Island bases provided only the logistic structure from which the fleet drew its sustenance.

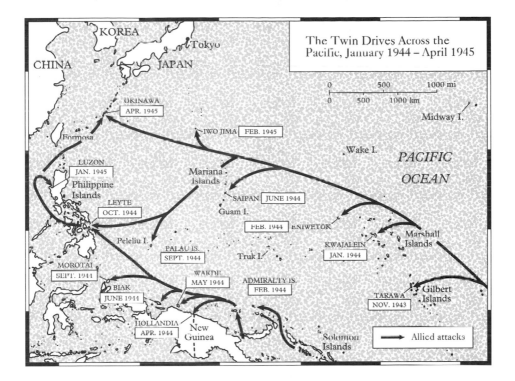

In October 1943 Nimitz created two mobile service squadrons. By the end of the year three squadrons contained thirteen large fleet oilers, innumerable stores and ammunition ships, and a whole host of smaller repair barges and tugs. These squadrons enabled the American attack fleet to cut its ties with the shore. Individual ships, of course, returned to port for overhaul and refitting, but the fleet remained at sea. The attack on the Mariana Islands in June–July 1944 suggests the immensity of the logistical operations. Some 535 combat and auxiliary ships carried 127,571 troops to island targets 1,000 miles from Eniwetok and 3,500 miles from Pearl Harbor; they then executed a massive set of landings *and* fought a series of great naval and air battles to protect the landings. By 1945 logistic capabilities of the U.S. fleet had reached an undreamed of extent. On July 21–22, for example, Task Force 38, after completing a series of air strikes on Tokyo, replenished at sea less than 450 miles from the Japanese capital. In less than two days supply ships transferred 6,369 tons of ammunition, 379,157 barrels of oil, 1,635 tons of stores and provisions, and 99 replacement aircraft. The Japanese had no chance against such capabilities.

Tarawa

The first target of King's Central Pacific drive was the coral atoll of Tarawa. The assault on Tarawa on November 21, 1943, was a costly but necessary learning experience for American amphibious forces. The preinvasion bombardment was too short, lasting only two-and-one-half hours. It stunned the enemy but failed to impair fighting capacity. Unfortunately for the attacking marines, the planners had underestimated enemy defenses. Equipped with 200 artillery pieces, including some 8-inch guns removed from the British defenses at Singapore, 5,000 Japanese troops defended Tarawa. As the landing craft moved toward shore, communications problems caused the bombardment to lift too early. Advancing in Amtracs, the first of three waves of marines reached the shore safely, but low tide prevented following landing craft from crossing the barrier reef. Some marines had to leave their landing craft 700 yards short of the beach; Japanese defenders slaughtered them as they waded ashore and pinned others into a narrow beachhead less than 300 yards deep. At the end of the first day the marines had 5,000 men on Tarawa, but 1,500 were dead or wounded. In the end, however, superior American firepower destroyed the defenders. When it was over only seventeen Japanese soldiers had survived, while the marines had lost 1,000 dead and 2,000 wounded.

As the marines suffered heavy casualties on Tarawa, the army's 165th Regimental Combat Team and 105th Infantry Regiment landed on Makin in the Gilberts. There the Japanese possessed fewer troops and virtually no heavy weapons. Nevertheless, the soldiers took four days to reduce the garrison. While their deliberate, careful approach kept the casualty rate low, naval support had to remain overly long on station. As a result, a Japanese submarine got in among the invasion fleet and sank escort carrier *Liscome Bay*, killing nearly 650 sailors. With control of Tarawa and Makin, the Americans had control of the Gilberts; the Marshalls were the next target.

Kwajalein and Eniwetok

Almost immediately after Tarawa, American naval leaders debated where to strike next in the advance across the central Pacific. Previous plans had called for a two-step operation aimed at two atolls at the eastern edge of the Marshalls, followed by seizure of Kwajalein in the chain's center. But Nimitz believed the Japanese had strengthened the eastern Marshalls and preferred Kwajalein as the next target. Spruance and Admiral Richmond Kelly Turner, commander of amphibious forces, argued that an attack on Kwajalein would expose U.S. forces to enemy air attacks from bypassed positions in the eastern Marshalls. When Nimitz insisted on moving directly on Kwajalein, Spruance received permission to seize an unoccupied atoll in the eastern Marshalls to provide a protected anchorage.

Accompanied by Task Force 58 with twelve carriers and 650 aircraft, the amphibians attacked the Marshalls at the end of January 1944. Although the defenders possessed formidable defenses, more than three-quarters of the 8,000 Japanese defenders were supply and administrative rather than combat troops. Moreover, the Americans had thoroughly studied Tarawa and other recent landings and succeeded in overcoming many problems that had occurred in earlier operations. Some improvements included a more

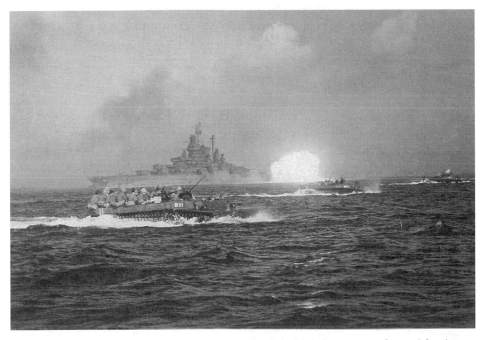

A battleship fires salvos onto a beach as Amtracs loaded with infantry move forward for the amphibious assault.

thorough reconnaissance of beaches and reefs, more extensive naval support fire, and enhanced communications between those landing and those supporting. Following three days of bombardment, the 4th Marine Division and the army's 7th Division captured Kwajalein at a fraction of Tarawa's cost in lives.

Success at Kwajalein led to a move within a month against Eniwetok, an atoll west of the Marshalls, while at the same time fast carriers neutralized Truk, 750 miles farther to the west. In a series of heavy blows, they destroyed 200 enemy aircraft, damaged the island's airfields, and then sank fifteen naval vessels and twenty-four cargo vessels and tankers. This ended Japanese use of Truk as an operating base and effectively isolated Eniwetok. On February 19, 1944, marines and soldiers hit the beaches at Eniwetok. Though a strong Japanese garrison occupied the island, the enemy had not prepared extensive defenses; and incessant air attacks hindered what efforts they did make before the invasion. Nevertheless, fighting was heavy but not nearly as heavy as might have occurred had the Japanese had time to strengthen their positions. Consequently the decision to attack Eniwetok in February 1944 rather than May saved a large number of American lives. By seizing Eniwetok the Americans had moved nearly one thousand miles from Tarawa. The Mariana Islands were next; once there, the Americans could begin aerial bombardment of Japan.

Continuing the Two Drives Across the Pacific, 1944–1945

By early 1944, relations between the army and navy were so delicate that the Joint Chiefs gave no clear priority to either drive across the Pacific. Their strongest guidance was that "due weight should be given to the fact that operations in the Central Pacific promise more rapid advance." At the Quadrant Conference at Quebec in August 1943, the British expressed concern about the twin drives and suggested that the Americans halt MacArthur. When King and Marshall defended the U.S. approach by arguing that the drives were mutually supporting, the British responded that they were also mutually competing.

MacArthur's Advance in the Southwest Pacific

While the Central Pacific thrust picked up speed, MacArthur's drive also accelerated. By avoiding enemy strong points and moving forward in leaps, he sought to advance the fighter-escorted bomber line until it could cover an invasion of the Philippines. In February 1944, Kenney reported that there was no sign of major Japanese units in the Admiralty Islands, 400 miles west of Rabaul. Anxious to complete his isolation of Rabaul and to accelerate the advance, MacArthur accompanied 1,000 assault troops from the 1st Cavalry Division to the Admiralties and landed on February 29. The attackers hit Los Negros Island, held by a Japanese garrison nearly four times U.S. strength. Fortunately for MacArthur, the enemy had deployed to protect the other side of the island. By the time the Japanese had reorganized, American destroyers had brought in 1,500 additional cavalrymen and 400 Seabees. Japanese counterattacks failed. By mid-March another brigade had landed, and the islands were securely in American hands.

MacArthur's risky but successful stroke encouraged another move. It also focused Washington's attention on the Southwest Pacific; thus MacArthur found support to strike at Hollandia, far up the coast of New Guinea. The new target, 580 miles from American bases, was barely within range of Kenney's fighters, but the capture of Hollandia would isolate 40,000 enemy troops and provide American control of three Japanese-built airstrips. Nimitz offered support from fleet carriers, but Kenney argued that his fighters could achieve air superiority by themselves. They did.

In mid-April the landing force departed from the Admiralty Islands. The main attack targeted Hollandia and a smaller force targeted Aitape (125 miles to the east of Hollandia) on the coast of New Guinea. The Japanese had 11,000 men in the Hollandia area, but few were combat troops. Achieving surprise, two infantry divisions under Eichelberger landed on April 22. By the 26th the Americans held all three airfields. The landing by a regiment at Aitape also achieved surprise. The Allies poured in additional troops, however, when they learned that the Japanese Eighteenth Army was moving west toward Aitape. After about a month's intense fighting and a loss of nearly 9,000 soldiers, the Eighteenth Army withdrew.

In late May, MacArthur's forces seized Wakde (150 miles west of Hollandia) off the coast of New Guinea, and a small beachhead on New Guinea to protect the island. On May 27 the Americans struck Biak (325 miles west of Hollandia). Both Wakde and Biak had airfields, but from Biak American aircraft could reach the Philippines.

At this point the Japanese were expecting to fight a major naval battle in the Central Pacific, but they recognized the threat posed by American land-based bombers on their southern flank. Consequently the Imperial navy assembled powerful amphibious and naval forces and moved against Biak in late May, but false reports about sizable Allied naval forces near the island convinced them to withdraw. After assembling an even larger force, including battleships *Musashi* and *Yamato*, the Japanese again prepared to move. Just before they could move, however, the Japanese received word of Spruance's strike against the Marianas in the Central Pacific. They immediately called off the attack on Biak, set in motion "A-GO," code name for a decisive fleet operation, and prepared for a battle in the Central Pacific. These events point out the risks as well as the benefits of having two Pacific drives. Had the attack on Biak begun earlier or had Spruance moved later, the Japanese might well have dealt MacArthur a serious blow—one that could have set the Pacific advance back by a number of months. Such an event would have also given Japanese morale an enormous boost.

Saipan

In the Central Pacific, the next objective was Saipan in the Marianas, one thousand miles west of Eniwetok. Even Nimitz doubted the wisdom of the move, for all the protecting air power would come off carriers. Aware of the impending landing in Normandy, King made clear that the fleet must reach for the Marianas and gain a significant victory. Only 1,200 miles from Japan, Saipan was the closest major island in the Marianas to the Home Islands; the new American superbomber, the B-29, could strike Japan from airfields located there. Along with Saipan, the Americans planned to seize Guam and Tinian as well. Protection for landing forces consisted of Spruance's Fifth Fleet. The attack force for Saipan included the marines' 2nd and 4th divisions and the army's 27th Infantry Division. After taking Saipan that force would assault Tinian. To the south 3rd Marine Division and 77th Infantry Division attacked Guam. On Saipan itself, the Japanese had 32,000 troops, but they had not completed their defenses. Again the Americans had moved faster than their enemy expected.

Overall commander at Saipan was the marine amphibious expert, Lieutenant General Holland M. Smith, referred to behind his back as "Howling Mad" Smith. The plan called for landing two marine divisions in the southwest corner of the island. New lightly armored amphibian tractors were to drive deep into the beachhead. A two-day bombardment by battleships, cruisers, and destroyers, as well as air strikes, preceded the landing.

The bombardment, however, had not concentrated sufficiently on the immediate beachhead and had been too brief; heavy enemy fire and rough terrain
prevented the amphibians from driving inland. By nightfall, June 15, 1944,
the Americans had 20,000 troops ashore, but the beachhead was 1,000 yards
deep, half the distance anticipated by planners. Within two days, Smith
brought in the 27th Division to reinforce the marines. That division had
moved too slowly at Makin Island and Eniwetok, and on Saipan with a
marine division on each flank, its performance was again marginal. At this
point, Holland Smith did what MacArthur and Eisenhower regularly did in
their theaters: he relieved the division commander. The result, however, was
a cause célèbre, one that caused unnecessary bad blood between army and
marine corps.

Outside the 27th Division and one or two other anomalies, army and
marine divisions performed similarly in the Pacific. The divisions in the
Pacific had an advantage over those in the European theaters, for once committed to the battle, army divisions in Europe remained in sustained, unremitting combat, in which replacements had to be integrated directly on the
battle front. In the Pacific, fighting for the most part involved sharp bitter
engagements over Japanese-held islands where casualties were usually high.
But substantial periods of noncombat usually followed, during which units
could adapt to new conditions, retrain their combat personnel on the basis of
lessons learned in the last campaign, and integrate replacements in a coherent and effective fashion. The result was a steady and impressive improvement in the combat effectiveness of army and marine units in the Pacific.

By early July, the Americans had pushed the Japanese to the northern tip of Saipan. From there the enemy launched the largest banzai attack
of the war. When the battle was over, the Americans had suffered 14,000
casualties, while most of the 32,000 Japanese were dead. To add to the
tragedy, many Japanese civilians committed suicide or were killed by their
own troops to avoid falling into American hands.

On July 24, 4th Marine Division attacked Tinian. The marines hit
the narrow beaches opposite Saipan (within artillery range) where the Japanese did not expect a landing. Within eight days Tinian and its valuable airfields were in American hands. Meanwhile, 3rd Marine Division and the
army's 77th Infantry Division took Guam. Here soldiers and marines got
along without difficulty; the 77th, although never before in combat, was an
exceptionally well-trained outfit, and its performance was every bit as good
as its more-experienced marine counterpart. By early August the Americans
had secured the island. Within several months, B-29s would begin the great
aerial bombardment of Japan.

Battle of the Philippine Sea

As noted earlier, the American advance on the Marianas and the landing on
Saipan caused the Japanese to halt their move against Biak and send the
First Mobile Fleet of nine carriers, five battleships, thirteen cruisers, twenty-
eight destroyers, and over 400 aircraft to fight a decisive battle in the Central

Pacific. In the subsequent battle of the Philippine Sea from June 19–21, the Americans enjoyed numerous advantages: their pilots were more experienced; their aircraft were superior; and they outnumbered the Japanese in almost every category. While the Japanese counted 222 fighters and almost 200 bombers, the Americans possessed 500 fighters and over 400 bombers. Enemy aircraft were superior only in range, but that superiority came from a lack of self-sealing fuel tanks and armored protection. Nevertheless, Japanese carriers could launch aircraft against American carriers while remaining outside the reach of U.S. aircraft from those carriers.

The battle of the Philippine Sea occurred after Spruance held his fleet between the Japanese and the American forces attacking Saipan and refused to sail west in search of the enemy. On the afternoon of June 18 the Japanese spotted the Americans. On the next morning they launched heavy air attacks but had to fight their way through a dense screen of F6F Hellcats, and then through heavy antiaircraft fire from American fast battleships before reaching the carriers. Relying on radar, American naval pilots intercepted and destroyed four successive waves of attacking aircraft; less than one hundred enemy aircraft survived out of 373. The Americans lost only twenty-nine aircraft; the pilots nicknamed their victory the "Great Marianas Turkey Shoot." Late that afternoon, American reconnaissance aircraft located the enemy carriers. Although the Japanese were almost out of range, the commander of Task Force 58, Vice Admiral Mark A. Mitscher, launched his aircraft and sank one carrier and damaged three others; U.S. submarines had already sunk two enemy carriers. Much of the Japanese fleet escaped, but it had lost the bulk of its trained aviators. As a result, enemy carriers had entirely lost their combat effectiveness.

The performance of American carriers in the battle of the Philippine Sea deserves note. No fewer than five subdivisions of Task Force 58 operated in close coordination, four containing fast carriers and fast battleships. Each carrier group contained between three and four carriers, fifteen fleet and light carriers altogether, while the fast battleship group possessed no fewer than six battleships. This conglomeration of capital ships, all completed and manned since Pearl Harbor, worked in close cooperation to provide the combat air patrols to shield the fleet, to cover the carriers with antiaircraft gunnery, and eventually to attack the Imperial fleet as it approached. In every respect the American performance reflected not only an awesome projection of military power across Pacific distances but an organizational triumph of impressive magnitude.

The Invasion of the Philippines

During summer 1944, the Americans squabbled over their next major target. King advocated a continuation of "island hopping" by seizing a foothold on Mindanao in the southern Philippines and then making a long leap to Formosa and the China coast; not surprisingly, MacArthur disagreed and argued that the United States could not leave the Filipino people under Japanese control. By and large, naval commanders in the Pacific supported MacArthur.

In September a raid by aircraft from Halsey's carriers suggested (wrongly) that the Japanese lacked strong forces in the Philippines. Halsey recommended cancellation of a number of secondary operations and a direct attack on the Philippines. Nimitz approved, moved the invasion to an earlier date, and canceled secondary attacks—except one. In September, following a three-day bombardment, the 1st Marine Division landed on Peleliu in the Palau Islands; this time, however, the Japanese had withdrawn from the beaches and established strong defenses inland. The marines that made the amphibious assault suffered more than 40 percent casualties, the highest casualty rate of any assault in the war. A joint force of soldiers and marines finally secured the island at the end of November but lost over 1,000 dead and 5,000 wounded. Unfortunately the island proved of little use in the invasion of the Philippines. Peleliu was probably Nimitz's worst mistake.

Leyte

Meanwhile, American planning and preparations proceeded for a landing on Leyte in the central Philippines as a stepping stone to Luzon, the main island in the northern Philippines, which included both Manila and the Bataan Peninsula. The invasion of the Philippines married the two Pacific drives. MacArthur's staff would control ground fighting, while his air commander, General Kenney, would be responsible for land-based air. Rear Admiral Thomas C. Kinkaid's Seventh Fleet, which had older battleships, would provide direct support. Finally, Halsey's Third Fleet with its fast carriers and new battleships would provide long-distance cover.

In early October 1944, Halsey's ships moved between the Philippines and Formosa, and a huge air battle took place. When it ended, American naval air had destroyed much of the enemy's land-based and naval air in the area. Inexperienced Japanese crews gave wildly optimistic but false reports of the damage inflicted on American ships. Meanwhile the Imperial navy returned its carriers to Japan for repairs and pilot training; the "Marianas Turkey Shoot" and Halsey's raids in October had stripped Japanese carriers of their air crews. The remainder of the fleet moved to Lingga Roads, near Singapore. Although the Japanese would have preferred to concentrate their fleet in home waters, the loss of tankers to American submarines forced the surface fleet to remain close to Borneo's oil.

The Imperial navy, nevertheless, prepared for a decisive battle. As usual, the Japanese drew an excessively complex plan, code-named "Sho-1," which was the Philippine variation of its overall defense plan called "Sho." Four separate task forces would move against the Americans: the carriers would sortie from the Home Islands and draw the American carriers away from the landings; the Japanese surface fleet, including super battleships, would move through San Bernadino Strait (south of Luzon) and attack the landing forces; a smaller task force would move through Surigao Strait (south of Leyte); and finally, another small force of destroyers and cruisers from the Home Islands would also move through Surigao Strait. For once the complex plan came dangerously close to success.

On October 20, MacArthur attacked Leyte. Under the command of Lieutenant General Walter Krueger, Sixth Army struck the northeast coast of Leyte. After the 6th Ranger Battalion cleared several offshore islands, X Corps (1st Cavalry and 24th Infantry divisions) landed near Palo, while XXIV Corps (96th Infantry and 7th Infantry divisions) landed ten miles to the south. In the face of moderate Japanese opposition American infantry fought their way inland.

The Japanese responded immediately. On October 23 two U.S. submarines reported the main Japanese fleet north of Borneo; the Americans

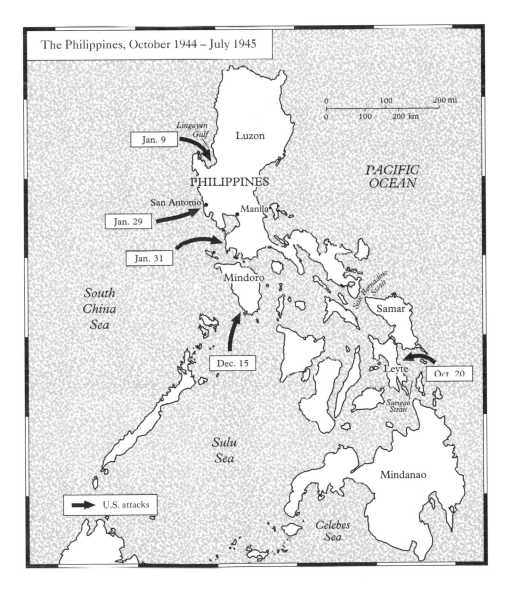

The Philippines, October 1944 – July 1945

then attacked and sank two heavy cruisers and badly damaged another. Admiral Kurita Takeo, commander of the main San Bernadino task force, was using one of the heavy cruisers, the *Atago*, as his flagship. He transferred his flag to battleship *Yamato*, but the sinking clearly unnerved him at the start of the battle.

On the morning of October 24, the battle of Leyte Gulf moved into high gear. Japanese aircraft, based in the Philippines, found Halsey's fleet and launched a series of attacks. Hellcats destroyed most of the attackers, but one enemy aircraft got through to hit carrier *Princeton*, which eventually had to be scuttled. Meanwhile, Halsey's aircraft found Kurita's battle fleet west of San Bernadino Strait and sank super battleship *Musashi*. Although most of Kurita's force escaped serious damage, the admiral lost his nerve and turned back. American pilots reported his move but considerably exaggerated the damage they had inflicted on his other ships.

Now began a series of miscalculations that nearly resulted in disaster. Halsey had finally picked up the Japanese carriers to the north. Satisfied that he had taken care of Kurita, he moved to the north and took with him all the carriers and fast battleships. He left nothing behind to guard San Bernadino Strait and failed to inform other naval commanders. Meanwhile, the Japanese naval high command communicated its displeasure to Kurita about his retreat, and Kurita reversed course to the east toward the unguarded San Bernadino Strait.

The first contact between surface fleets came on the night of October 24–25 in Surigao Strait. Two Japanese task forces entered the strait separately, but battleships from the Seventh Fleet crossed the enemy "T" and sank all of the enemy except one destroyer. Shortly after dawn on the 25th, escort carriers supporting landings off Leyte suddenly spotted Kurita's force of heavy cruisers and battleships. Kurita had passed unopposed through San Bernadino Strait and turned south toward the invasion fleet where only a few destroyers and escort carriers stood in his way. Weak American forces desperately harried the Japanese and even sank three heavy cruisers, but if the Japanese steamed on, there was no chance of stopping them. Under continuous attack from American aircraft and weary after the pounding of the previous days, however, Kurita turned back. That ended the naval battle, although it did considerable harm to Halsey's reputation.

But attacks on the American fleet protecting the Leyte invasion had not ended. On that same day, the Japanese delivered the first *kamikaze* (divine wind) attacks. Though the suicidal pilots managed to damage some American ships and sink escort carrier *St. Lô,* their attacks marked the end of the battle of Leyte Gulf.

As the invasion of Leyte proceeded, the Japanese made other responses. Reinforcements arrived through early December and more than tripled the forces defending the island to about 55,000 troops and elements of five divisions. To achieve this level of reinforcement the Japanese stripped their forces from other islands, including Luzon and Okinawa. American air power, unfortunately, failed to interfere with the reinforcement because of the battering that the kamikaze attacks were giving the escort carriers. Moreover, it took a considerable period to construct air bases for the army's

On October 25, 1944, a bomb dropped by a plane from the USS *Essex* hit the *Ise*, a Japanese battleship to which flight decks had been added.

Fifth Air Force on Leyte. Following the arrival of the Japanese reinforcements, the operation became much more difficult for the Americans.

Krueger's objective was the port of Ormoc on the western coast of Leyte through which the Japanese had shipped reinforcements onto the island. Fearing the possibility of an enemy landing in his rear, Krueger moved slowly until the arrival of additional American forces. With the arrival of the 7th Infantry, 11th Airborne, and 32nd Infantry divisions, the Americans pressed forward. Nevertheless, the Japanese had used the time to strengthen their defenses along the mountains that extended north to south through the center part of the island. On December 7, the 77th Division landed just south of Ormoc and three days later captured the city. At about the same time the Japanese made a combined ground and airborne attack against the airfield at Burauen in the center of the island. After the seizure of Ormoc, however, Japanese resistance collapsed, and on Christmas Day the Americans seized the last port on the island. The Leyte campaign had cost the Japanese dearly; in addition to losing most of five divisions, their naval and air losses had doomed their other forces in the Philippines.

Luzon

Early January 1945 saw MacArthur finally in a position to redeem his pledge to return to the heart of the Philippines: Luzon. This campaign was the largest of the Pacific war with two armies (ten divisions and five regimental

combat teams) fighting their way across a battle-scarred landscape. Nonetheless the campaign would still see Japanese forces in the field when the
emperor finally surrendered in August 1945. For his amphibious landing,
MacArthur selected the beaches of Lingayen Gulf on the western coast of
Luzon; that location offered him access to the best road and railroad network
in the islands as well as to Manila and its port facilities.

Had the Japanese attempted to defend Manila and Bataan as
MacArthur had in December 1941, they would have suffered an even
quicker defeat. But they did not. The Japanese commander in the Philippines, General Yamashita Tomoyuki, who had gained a brilliant victory over
the British in Malaya and Singapore early in the war, yielded the main cities,
particularly Manila, as well as the coastal lowlands, in favor of a prolonged
resistance in the mountainous region of northern Luzon.

In early January 1945 the American invasion fleet sailed against
Luzon. From the first, kamikazes subjected it to savage attacks; the U.S.
Navy had no fewer than twenty-five ships sunk or damaged by these suicide
attacks. Despite the kamikazes, Krueger's Sixth Army made an amphibious
assault on January 9 against the beaches of Lingayen Gulf with four infantry
divisions and a regimental combat team. Within several days the Americans
had 175,000 men ashore. Facing only light opposition, Krueger's forces
advanced south more than forty miles within two weeks.

Despite dense jungle and difficult terrain, American infantry relied on tanks for support.
Tanks often destroyed enemy pillboxes and strong points or covered enemy positions with
fire as American infantry advanced.

On January 29 the Americans made the first of two landings intended to keep the Japanese off balance. As part of Eichelberger's Eighth Army, XI Corps landed near San Antonio, sixty-five miles northwest of Manila. Two days later a regiment of 11th Airborne Division made an amphibious landing forty miles southwest of Manila. On February 3 another regiment of 11th Airborne made a parachute landing twenty miles inland. On that same day the first units from the landing at Lingayen Gulf reached Manila. Despite Yamashita's order to abandon the capital city without a fight, Japanese marines, not under his command, fought to retain the city. The resulting month-long battle wrecked Manila almost as completely as Warsaw. As many as 100,000 Filipino civilians died in the carnage.

Meanwhile, American forces rapidly liberated Bataan and Corregidor, names that still resonated from the dark days of the war. MacArthur also set in motion reconquest of the remaining Philippine Islands; in a month and a half, Eighth Army under Eichelberger made almost forty amphibious landings and swiftly liberated the remaining islands. The subsequent campaign in the mountains of northern Luzon, however, proved to be almost as difficult as the fighting in Manila. Yamashita dug his forces in and fought a skillful delaying action against the Americans. Despite severely pounding their Japanese opponents, MacArthur's forces never succeeded in breaking Yamashita's hold on the northern mountains. The end of the war would find the Japanese still tenaciously holding on, but by that time the fighting had passed well beyond the Philippines to the very gates of Japan.

The Final Campaigns

Iwo Jima

In fall 1944, B-29s began operations against Japan from the Marianas; by January 1945 the bombers were suffering heavy losses without achieving significant results. One reason was that Japanese radar on Iwo Jima (midway between the Marianas and Japan) provided the Home Islands with advance warning of impending attacks. Intending to halt this early warning, the Joint Chiefs ordered Nimitz to seize Iwo Jima. Planners also recognized that airfields on the island could provide emergency landing strips for damaged B-29s returning from Japan.

The Japanese recognized the danger; from June 1944 they had prepared to meet an American landing. The garrison commander, Lieutenant General Kuribayashi Tadamichi, utilizing already existing caves, turned Iwo Jima into a fortress with deep redoubts. As on Peleliu, the Japanese launched no suicide charges and did not attempt to hold the Americans on the beaches; instead, Kuribayashi chose to allow the attackers to come ashore and then to impose the highest possible casualties on them. The geography of the island helped the defenders. The Japanese placed their main defenses in a volcanic peak, Mt. Suribachi, which overlooked the entire island and provided an excellent view of the landing beaches.

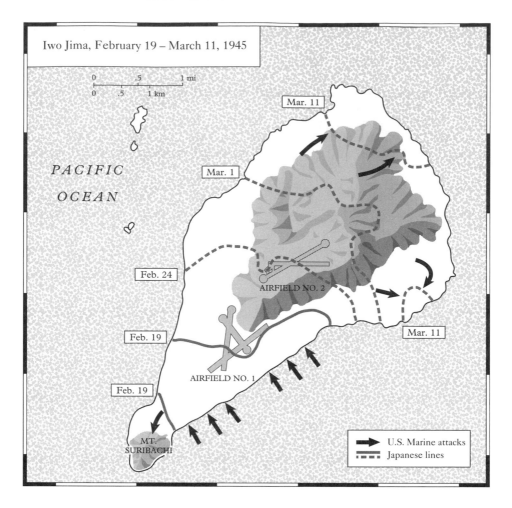

Iwo Jima, February 19 – March 11, 1945

PACIFIC

OCEAN

Mar. 11

Mar. 1

Feb. 24

AIRFIELD NO. 2

Feb. 19

Mar. 11

Feb. 19

AIRFIELD NO. 1

MT. SURIBACHI

U.S. Marine attacks
Japanese lines

Major General Harry Schmidt's V Amphibious Corps received the mission to take Iwo Jima. With the 3rd, 4th, and 5th Marine divisions, the corps was the largest force the marines had ever assembled. Though Schmidt requested a ten-day bombardment, Spruance agreed to only three days with a possible fourth. Instead of supporting the marines, Spruance used his carriers for an attack on Japanese aircraft factories; one suspects that the navy wanted to show what naval air could accomplish in comparison with the failures that B-29s had thus far encountered. On February 19, 4th and 5th Marine divisions stormed ashore after a four-day bombardment. They initially encountered light enemy fire, but soon a virtual storm swept up and down the beaches. Among the nearly 30,000 marines who had reached shore by evening, casualties were heavy, especially from artillery dug into the caves of Mt. Suribachi. The conquest of the flatter terrain was relatively easy, but the attack on Japanese troops dug in on the sides of the volcano was a nightmare. After four days of heavy fighting some marines worked their way to Suribachi's summit and planted the American flag. However, not until the end of March did the marines end Japanese resistance on Iwo Jima. The casualty bill was horrendous: 6,821 marines dead; nearly 20,000 wounded. Few Japanese from a garrison of 21,000 survived. Admiral Nimitz best described the sacrifice of the marines: "Among the Americans who served on Iwo Island, uncommon valor was a common virtue."

Okinawa

Barely had the fighting on Iwo Jima subsided when the next major amphibious assault began. This time the target was Okinawa, an obvious jumping-off position for the invasion of Japan. Defending the island was Lieutenant General Ushijima Mitsuru's Thirty-Second Army with over 70,000 troops. Ushijima recognized that he did not possess sufficient troops to defend the whole island; therefore he determined to fight for the southern portion to inflict maximum casualties on invading Americans. He also hoped that kamikazes would damage supporting naval forces sufficiently to reduce air and gunfire support. The attacking American Tenth Army, under Lieutenant General Simon Bolivar Buckner, Jr., attacked with a corps of two marine divisions and another of two army divisions. Two additional army divisions remained in reserve. Offshore no fewer than forty fleet and light carriers, eighteen battleships, and nearly 200 destroyers bolstered the landing force.

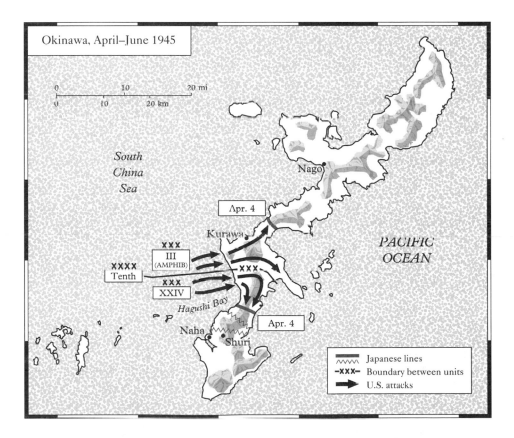

Okinawa, April–June 1945

South China Sea

Nago

Apr. 4

Kurawa

PACIFIC OCEAN

XXX
III (AMPHIB)

XXXX
Tenth

XXX

XXX
XXIV

Hagushi Bay

Naha

Apr. 4

Shuri

Japanese lines
Boundary between units
U.S. attacks

On April 1 the armada reached Okinawa and began landing soldiers and marines on the west coast of the narrow, long island. About 50,000 Americans landed the first day; by the second they had reached the east coast. While III Amphibious Corps turned north, XXIV Corps turned south. On April 6 the invasion fleet came under intense attack from kamikazes flying from Japan. On that day alone, 700 enemy aircraft—over half of them suicide aircraft—attacked the American fleet. Nine other kamikaze attacks, altogether numbering over 1,000 aircraft, hit the fleet standing off Okinawa in succeeding weeks. These ferocious attacks sank thirty ships, damaged 368 vessels, killed 5,000 American sailors, and injured a further 5,000.

On Okinawa, the marines cleared the northern half of the island in two weeks. But when XXIV Corps closed on Japanese defenses in the south, the killing began. The 96th Infantry Division ran into the main Japanese defenses first; soon three infantry divisions battered at the enemy's elaborate defenses. Some staff officers urged Buckner to use his reserve to make an amphibious assault and take Japanese defenses in the rear. Buckner believed such a landing would be difficult and costly and continued attacking straight ahead. As the Americans pressed forward, the Japanese launched two counterattacks, one of which cost them nearly 6,000 dead.

The Americans fought their way through the Machinato Line and then encountered the even stronger Shuri Line, which consisted of a web of mutually supporting strong points with artillery and mortars firing from caves. It was probably the strongest defensive position encountered by the Americans in the Pacific. But they continued pressing forward. By the end of June 1945, the U.S. Tenth Army had destroyed the Japanese Tenth Army of 70,000 troops. At least 80,000 Japanese civilians died in the fighting. The U.S. Army and Marines lost nearly 7,000 dead, with total American casualties (including the navy) 65,631 killed or wounded. Okinawa provided a frightening forecast of the coming invasion of the Home Islands.

Strategic Bombing

Strategic bombing attacks on Japan had begun in June 1944 with B-29s flying from bases in China, yet the problems in supplying that force from India over the Himalaya mountains presented insurmountable difficulties. Moreover, the Japanese army in China launched an offensive and took out the air bases, as Chinese nationalist forces proved incapable of serious resistance. But as Chinese bases fell, air bases in the Marianas (Saipan and Tinian) became available to the B-29s.

The bombing from the Marianas initially reflected the precision bombing doctrine with which U.S. Army Air Forces had entered the conflict. However, both weather and the nature of Japanese industry made such a campaign a dubious proposition. Much of the enemy's production occurred in small decentralized factories, the location of which was almost impossible to identify. In February 1945 a new commander, Major General Curtis E. LeMay, decided to launch incendiary raids on Japanese cities instead of precision attacks. Two high-altitude raids against Kobe and Tokyo proved encouraging.

Then LeMay changed the pattern of American bombing. The B-29s, now stripped of armor and defensive armament, attacked with incendiaries at night and at low altitude. In effect these attacks were indistinguishable from those of RAF's Bomber Command against Germany's cities. On March 8 the B-29s again struck Tokyo. Though attacking individually, LeMay's aircraft concentrated their bombs in the center of the capital; within minutes they had started a great firestorm. Japanese defenses were as incapable of stopping the attacking planes as the firefighting units were incapable of stopping the fires. By morning 83,000 Japanese had died, while a further 41,000 were injured; the attack burned out the center of Tokyo.

American bombers then proceeded to destroy Japanese cities, one after another. By July they had gutted the major industrial cities. Hundreds of thousands were dead, millions homeless. To add insult to injury, B-29s dropped mines and closed down Japanese shipping in the inland sea.

By summer 1945, Japan was prostrate. Industry was entirely isolated from the raw materials of Southeast Asia; cities were burning deserts; the Imperial navy no longer existed; and the tide of enemy conquest had reached Okinawa. Only the army remained intact, but much of it remained in China. If the Americans chose not to invade but rather to blockade the Home Islands, millions of Japanese would face starvation in the near future.

With this catastrophic military situation, one would expect the Japanese to seek an end to the war. They did not. They prepared, instead, to make a last-ditch stand. Some Japanese officers argued that such resistance would force Americans to concede more favorable terms. But most looked on further resistance as a matter of honor. A few Japanese, particularly in the foreign ministry, hoped to escape a final cataclysm; the Japanese did put out feelers to the Soviets, but Stalin had no interest in helping, since he had his own desiderata in the Far East. Moreover, even those interested in getting out of the war were generally unrealistic in the terms that they proposed.

Meanwhile, the Japanese military had arranged a deadly reception for the Americans. As a staff officer indicated after the war:

> We expected an allied invasion of southern Kyushu and a later invasion of the Tokyo plain. The entire army and naval air forces had volunteered for an all out Kamikaze defense, and each had from four to five thousand planes. Five thousand pilots were available with 3,000 in training. We planned to send over waves from 3–400 at a rate of one wave per hour. On the basis of Leyte and Okinawa we expected about one out of four planes to hit a ship.

The naval staff estimated that these attacks would damage somewhere between 30 and 50 percent of the attacking fleet. In addition there were nearly half a million regular troops in Kyushu, plus innumerable local militiamen. Finally the Japanese had packed hundreds of suicide speed boats with high explosives.

As the Japanese expected, the Americans planned to come ashore on southern Kyushu. In Operation "Olympic," Sixth Army with eleven army and marine divisions (650,000 troops) would execute the landing. The first wave would consist of three separate landings of three divisions each. To ensure availability of adequate forces, a steady flow of veterans from Europe began moving across the Pacific. Some senior officers in Washington estimated the conquest of Japan would double American casualties in the war, thus far approximately 700,000; even the much lower figures favored by some historians interested in minimizing the contribution of the atomic bomb would have represented a terrible price. What the Japanese casualties, civilian as well as military, would have been is unimaginable.

At this point the atomic bomb made its appearance. As the result of a warning from Albert Einstein to President Roosevelt, the Americans had started a major atomic weapons development program in the early 1940s. Code-named the "Manhattan Project," the program received vast resources from the U.S. government throughout the war. Nevertheless, U.S. scientists, aided by scientists from other nations, did not solve the intractable scientific and engineering problems until summer 1945. A successful testing at Alamogordo in New Mexico in July 1945 proved that atomic weapons had a good chance of working.

The new American president, Harry S Truman, then confronted the question of whether to use this terrible new weapon against the Japanese. Truman had learned about the A-bomb project only after succeeding to the presidency upon Roosevelt's death. In World War I he had served as an artilleryman on the Western Front and consequently had a real appreciation of the sharp end of combat. Some scientists argued against using the bomb; others argued that the Japanese should receive a warning or a demonstration of the new weapon.

In the end, Truman, influenced by the potential carnage of an invasion, decided to drop the bomb. On August 6, 1945, three B-29s flew over Hiroshima; the small size of the formation occasioned no fear among the Japanese. Over 90,000 people died in a flash brighter than the sun; three days later the Red Army rolled across the Manchurian frontier from Siberia and rampaged through Japanese defenses on the mainland of Asia. That same day another B-29 dropped the second atomic weapon on Nagasaki; another 35,000 Japanese died.

Amazingly, even after Hiroshima, the Imperial government still did not seek peace. The Japanese military had questioned whether the Americans really had such a weapon; then when incontrovertible evidence came in about Hiroshima, they claimed that the enemy could possess only one such weapon. The second bomb convincingly undermined that argument, but the Japanese cabinet remained deadlocked on whether to surrender. The deadlock, however, allowed Emperor Hirohito to take matters into his own hands. He ordered his advisors to surrender on American terms if he could retain a ceremonial position. Hirohito's decision was immensely courageous; for several weeks it was unclear whether the military, particularly the junior officers, would obey his command. In the end most did, and on

The second atomic bomb was dropped on Nagasaki on August 9, 1945. The fire-bombing of Tokyo in March 1945 killed and injured more Japanese and destroyed more square miles of urban area than either of the atomic bombs on Hiroshima and Nagasaki.

September 2, 1945, representatives of the Imperial government signed the surrender on the decks of the battleship *Missouri*. The six-year conflict was finally over.

World War II

On the decks of the *Missouri* in September 1945, World War II came to an end. By any criterion it was the most destructive conflict in human history, and the damage it had caused extended from one end of the globe to the other. Only North and South America had escaped the full impact of the fighting. Almost immediately after the war, the Cold War—overshadowed by the threat of atomic war—began. Consequently, World War II did not provide an enduring peace, yet it did see the destruction of one of the world's most pernicious and dangerous tyrannies, Adolf Hitler's Third Reich, as well as the destruction of Benito Mussolini's Fascist government and the Japanese Imperial government. Those accomplishments alone justified the war.

In the larger framework of military history, World War II was the most fluid of all major wars. Aircraft and tanks, as well as concepts for using them, restored mobility to land warfare. Gliders, parachutes, and airborne units greatly increased the reach of armies. More capable aircraft lifted larger bomb loads and flew greater distances, thereby exposing unconquered nations to sustained attack. Aircraft carriers and carrier-based planes permanently enlarged the dimensions of war at sea. Equipment and techniques for replenishing ships at sea allowed fleets to remain nearly permanently at sea and gave fleets almost unlimited range. Landing craft became large and seaworthy enough to sustain highly ambitious amphibious operations across open beaches. Improvements in sonar, submarines, and antisubmarine weapons and doctrine intensified the struggle for sea lanes. Radar helped airmen and sailors see beyond the horizon to find and destroy enemy forces. Improved communications permitted commanders to be better informed and to move units and equipment to critical areas. Altogether these developments ensured that air, land, and sea campaigns remained mobile.

Other developments gave the war a different character from previous conflicts. The Allies' ability to intercept and decode radio transmissions—Ultra and Magic—gave intelligence a timely and important effect on operations and provided the Allies significant advantages. In both the Atlantic and the Pacific, successful campaigns required an unprecedented interdependence of air, land, and sea forces—never before had large armies been transported over such great distances and landed on hostile shores with support from aircraft and warships. Waging war on a global scale also required unparalleled harnessing of men, women, machines, and raw materials. Ultimately it was the superiority of the Allies' production that gave them a decisive advantage.

World War II, nevertheless, represented an evolutionary change in the nature of warfare. Many key developments in the war that seemed revolutionary were in fact a continuation and an amplification of developments that had occurred in World War I. For example, the seemingly "revolutionary" operational employment of tanks by the Germans in 1940 in fact represented the fruition of tactical and operational concepts developed by the Germans in the latter part of World War I. Even strategic bombing, which carried the war directly to the enemy's homeland, had appeared in the last war, as had the relentless campaigns that American and German submarines executed against the commerce of their opponents. Developments did result, however, in substantially improved methods and equipment. One has only to compare the awkward armored attacks of 1918 with those of 1940, or the amateurish landings at Gallipoli in 1915 with those of 1945 to recognize the improved performance.

What was truly different about World War II was the unparalleled destruction it wrought, particularly on civilians and their possessions. Much of the devastation originated in Nazi Germany's fight for an ideology that aimed at destroying the liberal heritage of the nineteenth century and replacing it with a monstrous polity based on race. The Holocaust and the German crimes against the people of eastern and southeastern Europe were a direct result of the Nazi crusade. When the Soviets brought their own communist ideology to bear on the Eastern Front, the scene was set for an unrestrained and merciless war. The Allies added to the slaughter with strategic bombing, their air forces unleashing the whirlwind that the Axis had sowed at Rotterdam, London, Belgrade, and hundreds of other places. Raids by hundreds of bombers against German and Japanese cities killed and injured hundreds of thousands of civilians.

Adding to the devastation, the explosion of atomic bombs at Hiroshima and Nagasaki represented a true technological and philosophical revolution in war. These two explosions suggested that a war between powers possessing the bomb might lead to the annihilation not only of the opponents, but of humankind itself. By its development, the atomic bomb increased humanity's destructive power so greatly that it constricted warfare and ushered in an age where war between the Great Powers became unlikely.

The war also significantly affected political boundaries after 1945; the course of military events in the last months of the war in Europe and Asia largely established the borders between the new superpowers, the United States and Soviet Union. Soviet strategy and operations in the last years of the war had deliberately aimed at assuring firm control over much of Europe. The Yalta Conference in February 1945 occurred at a moment when Soviet forces were almost on the Oder River, a short hop from Berlin, while Anglo-American troops were barely breaking through the frontier defenses of western Germany. The resulting division seemed favorable to the West at the time, and the subsequent surge of Western forces almost to Berlin should not obscure the grim military realities of February 1945. In the Pacific the outcome reflected the consequences of military events. Since the destruction of Japanese military forces had resulted almost exclusively from American operations, the occupation of Japan became a U.S. concern and brought sweeping political and social change. On the continent of Asia, however, the hasty intervention of the Soviet Union ensured that Manchuria and northern Korea would fall into the hands of political movements favorable to the Soviets. The scene was set for future confrontations between the new superpowers.

The war also had an unexpected and crucial effect on the colonial powers and their dominions. The fall of France in 1940 loosened its control over its possessions in Africa and Southeast Asia, and the stunning successes of Japanese arms in 1941 and early 1942 against British and other colonial regimes further undermined their credibility in Asia and the Pacific. As a result, the dismantling of the great Western colonial empires began during the war and accelerated thereafter. In some cases that process was accomplished in a peaceful fashion (India and other British possessions being the foremost examples), but in other cases (Indochina and Algeria in particular), the process of decolonization proved extraordinarily costly and painful. In the long term, the war brought an abrupt end to Western political domination of Asia.

The settlement of World War II, nevertheless, proved to be surprisingly durable despite the Soviet-American confrontation in the Cold War. Conflicts would occur on the periphery and on occasion threaten cataclysmic war. But such a war never occurred. In that sense, World War II represented an enormous political and strategic success for the victors.

SUGGESTED READINGS

Appleman, Roy E., et al. *Okinawa: The Last Battle* (Washington: Office of the Chief of Military History, 1948).

Barbey, Daniel E. *MacArthur's Amphibious Navy: Seventh Amphibious Force Operations, 1943–1945* (Annapolis: Naval Institute Press, 1969).

Blair, Clay. *Silent Victory: The U.S. Submarine War Against Japan* (Philadelphia: Lippincott, 1975).

Buell, Thomas B. *The Quiet Warrior: A Biography of Admiral Raymond A. Spruance* (Boston: Little, Brown, 1974).

Cook, Charles. *The Battle of Cape Esperance: Strategic Encounter at Guadalcanal* (New York: Crowell, 1968).

Crane, Conrad C. *Bombs, Cities, and Civilians: American Airpower Strategy in World War II* (Lawrence, Kans.: University Press of Kansas, 1993).

Dower, John W. *War Without Mercy: Race and Power in the Pacific War* (New York: Pantheon Books, 1986).

Eichelberger, Robert L. *Our Jungle Road to Tokyo* (New York: Viking Press, 1950).

Frank, Richard B. *Guadalcanal* (New York: Random House, 1990).

Isely, Jeter A., and Philip A. Crowl. *The U.S. Marines and Amphibious Warfare* (Princeton, N.J.: Princeton University Press, 1951).

James, D. Clayton. *The Years of MacArthur,* 2 vols. (Boston: Houghton Mifflin, 1970).

Krueger, Walter. *Down Under to Nippon: The Story of the Sixth Army in World War II* (Washington: Combat Forces Press, 1953).

Lewin, Ronald. *The American Magic: Codes, Ciphers, and the Defeat of Japan* (New York: Farrar Straus Giroux, 1982).

Morison, Samuel Eliot. *The Two-Ocean War: A Short History of the United States Navy in the Second World War* (Boston: Little, Brown, 1963).

Potter, Elmer B. *Bull Halsey: A Biography* (Annapolis: Naval Institute Press, 1985).

———. *Nimitz* (Annapolis: Naval Institute Press, 1976).

Inoguchi Rikihei, and Nakajima Tadachi with Roger Pineau. *The Divine Wind: Japan's Kamikaze Force in World War II* (Annapolis: Naval Institute Press, 1958).

Roscoe, Theodore. *United States Submarine Operations in World War II* (Annapolis: Naval Institute Press, 1949).

Slim, William S. *Defeat into Victory* (London: Cassell, 1956).

Smith, Robert R. *The Approach to the Philippines* (Washington: Office of the Chief of Military History, 1953).

———. *Triumph in the Philippines* (Washington: Office of the Chief of Military History, 1963).

Spector, Ronald H. *Eagle Against the Sun: The War with Japan* (New York: The Free Press, 1985).

Thorne, Christopher G. *The Issue of War: States, Societies, and the Coming of the Far Eastern Conflict of 1941–1945* (New York: Oxford University Press, 1985).

19

THE COLD WAR AND THE NUCLEAR ERA: ADJUSTING WARFARE TO WEAPONS OF MASS DESTRUCTION

The Birth of the Atomic Arms Race

Placing Increased Reliance on the Bomb

Achieving Strategic Parity and Controlling Nuclear Weapons

The Cold War was a clash of interests and ideas that dominated international relations from 1945 until 1990. As antagonisms between the United States and the Soviet Union hardened in the late 1940s, a series of crises sharpened ideological differences and heightened tensions. With the Soviet Union leading communist states and the United States leading Western democratic states, the first crises occurred in Europe, but the establishment of the People's Republic of China in 1949, followed by the North Korean invasion of South Korea, intensified and expanded the Cold War. While the Soviet Union and other communist powers attempted to consolidate and expand their influence, the United States and its allies sought to "contain" communism. For more than four decades, the confrontation between the two camps yielded numerous conflicts, such as the ones in Korea and Vietnam, as well as those in the Middle East and Southwest Asia. Some of these conflicts were "campaigns" in the broader and more dangerous Cold War, and they occurred despite the threat of a small crisis escalating rapidly into a world war.

Through the decades of rivalry, the existence of atomic or nuclear weapons shaped the nature of the Cold War and influenced virtually every issue in international security. For a brief period the United States held a monopoly on the atomic bomb, but the Soviets exploded their first atomic device in August 1949. That explosion signaled the beginning of a remarkable arms race that would extend over the next four decades. From the mid-1950s to the early 1960s political and military leaders considered the effect of the new weapons and resigned themselves to the use of those weapons in an emergency. After the Cuban Missile Crisis in October 1962, the Soviet Union embarked on a massive program to modernize its nuclear arsenal. As the Soviets approached strategic parity with the Americans, both sides began accepting arms control limitations over their nuclear arsenals. Only the eventual disintegration of the Soviet Union ended the Cold War and reduced the danger of a nuclear holocaust.

Since the use of nuclear weapons created the possibility of an Armageddon, the superpowers sought to deter their use but nonetheless grappled with each other by every means short of direct combat or nuclear exchange. Each provided military and economic assistance to its allies, and each sought to gain influence in the newly emerging nations of Africa and Asia. Although direct armed conflict between the superpowers never took place, Moscow and Washington provided direct and indirect support to opposing sides in numerous conflicts around the world. Using the number of war-related deaths as the criterion for defining a major conflict, the Stockholm International Peace Institute identified more than 160 major conflicts between 1945 and 1990. Though many were regional or were civil wars with no apparent link to the Cold War, others created the possibility of escalation, superpower involvement, and the spilling over of war into Europe, where the vast forces of the North Atlantic Treaty Organization and the Warsaw Pact faced each other across the boundary of a divided Germany. Almost no one doubted that a conflict between these huge forces would escalate into a nuclear holocaust.

In the end, the introduction of atomic and nuclear weapons revolutionized the nature of strategy and imposed limitations on war to avoid the employment of these weapons. The value of nuclear weapons lay in their not being used and in their power to deter an opponent from using them or even using conventional weapons. Their introduction made the era of the Cold War unlike any other in the history of warfare.

The Birth of the Atomic Arms Race

Before the United States entered World War II, scientists had worked out the theoretical foundations of an atomic bomb. Fearful that Germany would develop and use an atomic bomb first, the physicist Leo Szilard convinced Albert Einstein to send a letter to President Franklin D. Roosevelt that explained the nature of atomic energy and how it could be fashioned into a weapon of unprecedented power. This letter led to the creation in 1942 of a highly secret program named the Manhattan Project, which became the largest, most expensive, and most secret program of World War II. Placed under the overall direction of the U.S. Army and led by Major General Leslie R. Groves, the army engineer who had just finished designing and building the Pentagon, and Dr. J. Robert Oppenheimer, a brilliant theoretical physicist, the project commanded the highest priorities for scarce wartime resources and involved many leading physicists, mathematicians, and chemists from the scientific community. Oppenheimer and his colleagues tested an atomic device for the first time in the desert of southern New Mexico on July 16, 1945.

After Germany surrendered in May 1945, some American scientists questioned whether the new weapon should be used against Japan; they believed Japan would fall inevitably to conventional forces. Political and military leaders believed, however, that using the bomb on Japan would shorten the war, save the lives of American soldiers, and perhaps influence the postwar expansionist behavior of the Soviets. The subsequent dropping

Major General Leslie R. Groves and Dr. J. Robert Oppenheimer in September 1945. The two hardly could have been less alike in appearance, personality, and politics.

of an atomic bomb on Hiroshima, Japan, on August 6, 1945, and another one on Nagasaki three days later brought the existence of the atomic bomb into the open and engendered much concern about its use. Though more people had died in some conventional bombing raids—Dresden, for example—the shock of Hiroshima and Nagasaki and the possibility of such weapons being employed in the future horrified the world.

The Americans Adapt to the Atomic Bomb

Following World War II, President Harry S Truman laid the groundwork for American atomic policy. From the beginning he regarded the atomic bomb as fundamentally different from other military arms. For a time he hoped that diplomatic initiatives at the United Nations (the Baruch Plan) would convince the Soviets to accept international control of atomic weapons, but deepening hostilities doomed the proposal. Concerned about the effects of atomic warfare, he reserved for himself the authority to order use of the bomb. Under the provisions of the Atomic Energy Act of 1946, Congress vested a completely civilian commission with control over the American atomic energy program. Scientific and technical knowledge about the atomic program, as well as production decisions, became hidden behind an unprecedented wall of secrecy. As a consequence, American war planners often worked in the early years of the atomic era without specific reference to the size, character, and capabilities of the American atomic arsenal. Recently declassified documents suggest that not even President Truman received a formal accounting until 1947 of how many weapons the United States actually possessed at any time.

As the Cold War intensified, the United States confronted the question of its role in the nuclear age. Americans watched uncomfortably as the Soviets refused to withdraw from Iran and then took over Czechoslovakia; they became even more concerned when Greek Communists attempted to overthrow Greece's government. Concluding that the United States had to take action against what seemed to be Soviet expansionist policies, Truman appeared before a joint session of Congress on March 12, 1947, and said, "I believe that it must be the policy of the United States to support free peoples who are resisting attempted subjugation by armed minorities or by outside pressures." In an attempt to revive Europe, the United States subsequently announced the Marshall Plan in June 1947. The core of the new policy of "containment" appeared in a famous article in *Foreign Affairs* in July 1947. The anonymous author, who was later identified as George F. Kennan, stated, "[T]he main element of any United States policy toward the Soviet Union must be that of a long-term, patient but firm and vigilant containment of Russian expansive tendencies." Kennan proposed opposing force with force and preventing the Soviets from expanding.

The atomic bomb provided partial answers to the question of how the United States could "contain" the USSR. In August 1947, strategic planners in the Joint Chiefs of Staff completed a war plan—code-named "Broiler"—which attempted to integrate atomic weapons into the American war machine. Recognizing that the bomb conferred a "tremendous strategic advantage" upon the United States and its allies, the planners of Broiler called for an "air-atomic campaign" very early in a war against Soviet targets that were chosen less for their military than their psychological importance. The campaign focused upon key governmental and other targets whose destruction would shock and unhinge the Soviet government. Though the target list in Broiler called for dropping thirty-four bombs on twenty-four cities, the United States had no fully assembled bombs and no capability to produce any quickly, and its more traditional means of military power had declined precipitously.

One of the first crises in which atomic weapons played a role— though an ambiguous one—occurred in the spring of 1948 when Truman responded to the Berlin Blockade. The Soviets had cut off all rail and road traffic to the western sections of Berlin, and he ordered an airlift of food and fuel supplies for the beleaguered people of the city. Part of his response included the deployment of sixty B-29s to airbases in Great Britain. Even though no atomic bombs actually left the United States, an administration spokesman pointedly announced that the aircraft were "nuclear capable." On May 12, 1949, the Soviets ended the blockade by once again permitting movement by land from West Germany into West Berlin and restoring gas and electric service. Flying more than 1.4 million metric tons of food, coal, and other supplies into Berlin apparently did more to end the blockade than deploying nuclear aircraft to Britain.

Toward the close of 1948 the United States had about one hundred atomic bombs in its stockpile, and its war plans emphasized a sudden atomic attack against the Soviet Union. Under the demanding leadership of General Curtis LeMay, the Strategic Air Command had developed the capability of delivering 80 percent of the American atomic stockpile in a single strike on the Soviet Union. One war plan—code-named "Fleetwood"—called for the delivery of 133 atomic bombs on seventy Soviet cities. Despite the emphasis on an "air-atomic campaign," the United States did not reject the possibility of a limited conventional campaign. It believed a future war would begin with a surprise attack by an enemy, to which the United States would respond with a massive atomic attack. As the aggressor reeled under an atomic attack, the United States would mobilize and employ its conventional forces. This view of future war permitted the United States the luxury of giving priority to strategic forces, while providing only minimum support to conventional forces. After all, planners argued, the employment of the bomb would provide the time necessary to prepare U.S. conventional forces.

An even greater emphasis on the atomic bomb, however, appeared in late 1949 in a new war plan code-named "Offtackle." Despite serious interservice differences, the 1950 budget reduced conventional capabilities even further. From the perspective of air-power advocates, atomic weapons seemed to need no assistance from armies except perhaps to occupy the smoking ruins of devastated cities. Air-power advocates also envisaged only limited roles for navies, including atomic bombs dropped from carrier aircraft. In what was later called the "Admirals' Revolt," the navy attempted to roll back the air-atomic emphasis, characterizing the new B-36 bombers as a "billion-dollar blunder." Nonetheless, American strategic forces flourished while conventional forces withered.

The Soviet Bomb, the Thermonuclear Bomb, and NSC-68

After failing to establish international control over atomic energy, the United States expected to maintain a monopoly over the bomb for some time and ruled out sharing scientific information with the USSR. General Groves confidently predicted it would take the Soviets ten to twenty years to produce a bomb. As early as 1939, however, Soviet scientists had started their own project to develop a bomb. By 1941, they had a cyclotron ready for experiments. The German invasion of the USSR stalled the Soviet atomic project until 1943, when the physicist Igor V. Kurchatov began directing a rejuvenated program. On August 29, 1949, in Central Asia, the Soviet Union exploded its first atomic device. The shock of America's losing its monopoly over atomic weapons was magnified by the fall of Nationalist China to the Chinese Communists in late 1949.

In response to these events, Truman formally authorized in January 1950 the building of the thermonuclear, or hydrogen, bomb—even though the Soviet Union would not have atomic weapons in large numbers or the capability to deliver them against the United States for several years. He also directed the formation of an ad hoc group of officials from the state and defense departments to conduct a review of American national security policies. This group would ultimately produce a memorandum designated NSC-68, which was to become one of the most important policy documents of the Cold War.

Presided over by Paul Nitze of the State Department's Policy Planning Staff, the ad hoc group's final report emphasized the expansionist nature of the Soviet Union and the danger such a power posed when armed with atomic weapons. Assuming the Soviets would eventually achieve atomic parity with the United States, the group considered prospects for defending Western Europe bleak. If the United States could not count on atomic weapons as its ultimate card, then conventional forces had to be ready to bear added burdens. The only recourse, Nitze's group believed, was to improve atomic and conventional forces simultaneously. The report also emphasized the adequacy "for the moment" of the American atomic retaliatory capability, but in the event of a "surprise blow," the United States had to be capable of surviving this attack and mounting an immediate counterattack. The authors of NSC-68 argued for the rejuvenation of the defense establishment so its ready combat power could deter the Soviets from a direct confrontation. With the Soviets' continuing to improve their atomic capabilities, the report signaled the eventual emergence of deterrence as a prime feature of American policy. The Americans would soon conclude that the value of their atomic weapons lay less in their actual use than in the threat of their use and that fear of retaliation would constrain an enemy from using them or creating a crisis in which they might be used.

Even though President Truman and the National Security Council formally approved NSC-68 in April 1950, chances were remote that this ambitious and expensive program would ever come to fruition. The United States still had vast superiority in atomic weapons over the Soviet Union, at least for a time, and possession of the bomb still worked as a powerful incentive for those who sought to limit government spending. To these critics, the time required for the Soviets to gain the capability to inflict significant damage on the United States seemed too long to warrant the kind of expensive defense buildup recommended by NSC-68. Truman himself was not entirely convinced of the need for rearmament.

And there the matter would have rested but for the attack, barely two months later, upon South Korea by the North Korean army on June 24, 1950. The limitations of the bomb were about to be made manifest.

The Korean War and the Truman Rearmament

Following the North Korean attack, many American political and military leaders feared that Moscow had directed the invasion as a diversionary move in preparation for a Soviet advance against Western Europe. Aware of the limitations of American power, the Joint Chiefs recommended the prompt abandonment of South Korea if the Soviets moved against Europe. Additional questions about Soviet motivations appeared in November 1950 when the Chinese Communists intervened in the war.

As a hedge against the much-feared invasion of Western Europe, Truman deployed atomic weapons to forward positions in Great Britain and the Mediterranean; however, he sent none to the western Pacific. The Joint Chiefs of Staff decided that the Korean peninsula was unsuitable for the use of atomic weapons. They believed Korea had no worthy targets, no industrial complexes or centers of military power that would warrant the use of any atomic weapon then in the arsenal. Additionally, they believed the rugged Korean terrain would limit the full effect of any atomic weapon, even against such targets as large troop concentrations. General Omar Bradley considered the idea of using these weapons in this conflict as "preposterous."

At a news conference in November 1950, President Truman nevertheless hinted broadly that atomic weapons might in fact be used in Korea. The North Koreans gave no sign they had heard, or taken seriously, the president's veiled threat, but Truman's comment alarmed the public in both the United States and Europe. British Prime Minister Clement R. Attlee immediately flew to Washington for talks with Truman, who reassured him that he would not really use the bomb. Like General Bradley and most of his other military advisors, the president feared that the real war lay elsewhere in the uncertain future and that America's atomic advantage would only be wasted on the Chinese. The Korean War thus remained limited, but it served as a catalyst for the implementation of the provisions of NSC-68, including a massive rejuvenation of the American armed forces.

The Truman administration realized that atomic weapons did not provide answers to every national security question. In fact, the brief atomic monopoly had given the United States a false sense of security and power and failed to avert military confrontation. Nor had possession of atomic weapons changed operational or tactical methods, as proven by the fighting on the Korean peninsula, which differed little from that of earlier wars.

Placing Increased Reliance on the Bomb

When Truman left office in 1953, he left nearly 1,000 atomic weapons to his successor, Dwight D. Eisenhower. Though Truman never overcame his awe of the atomic or nuclear bomb, his successor would demonstrate no such discomfort (at least in public). Nuclear weapons were about to become the centerpiece of the new administration's foreign and military policies. In the process, nuclear power would take on a much more pervasive character than what would have been believed possible in the early days of the Cold War.

During the presidential campaign of 1952, Eisenhower had campaigned on promises to end the war in Korea and to reduce the federal budget significantly. When he took office, military costs accounted for 70 percent of federal spending. Eisenhower did not think American foreign and defense policy took advantage of nuclear weapons and disagreed with the Truman administration's attempts to balance nuclear and conventional arms; reducing conventional forces would pay the bill for Eisenhower's campaign promises. By placing greater reliance on nuclear arms, Eisenhower believed the risk of reducing American conventional combat power could be minimized.

Throughout 1953, the Eisenhower administration worked to establish a "New Look" in national security policy. Hints about a new strategy suggested a stronger reliance on strategic nuclear power and less reliance on traditional ground and naval forces. In October 1953, the chiefs of the military services received a National Security document called NSC 162/2, which provided clear guidance from the Eisenhower administration. NSC 162/2 stated: "In the event of hostilities, the United States will consider nuclear weapons to be as available for use as other munitions." In an address before the United Nations, Eisenhower, reflecting his recent approval of NSC 162/2, observed that "atomic weapons have virtually achieved conventional status within our armed forces." Additional information came from Secretary of State John Foster Dulles in January 1954 when he called for "massive retaliation" in response to Soviet aggression.

"Massive Retaliation" became a shorthand description of the new strategy. It did not mean, however, that the United States would automatically respond to Soviet aggression with a massive nuclear strike; instead, it meant the Americans might reply in kind or raise the stakes by employing nuclear weapons. In other words, an American response was certain, but its nature was not. Critics of the strategy, however, perceived it as an "all-or-nothing" strategy, particularly when public comments by Dulles hinted that an aggressor had to remain uncertain about how close to the "brink" the United States would go.

Limited Nuclear War

When the Eisenhower administration adopted NSC 162/2 in 1953, the concept of "limited nuclear war" emerged as an alternative short of general nuclear war. The first concepts for limited nuclear warfare had appeared in the years immediately after World War II. One of the key figures in the development of the atomic bomb, J. Robert Oppenheimer, for example, stated in the late 1940s that existing bombs were "too big" for the "best military use." As technical advances permitted the development of smaller and more rugged nuclear devices, interest in the United States in tactical nuclear weapons accelerated. Faced with the Soviets' having significant advantages in conventional forces, analysts argued that an army equipped with tactical nuclear weapons could defend successfully against an enemy many times its

The firing of the first atomic artillery shell from a 280-mm artillery gun. Such tests demonstrated the availability of nuclear weapons and the possibility of their being employed throughout a battle area.

own size and that such weapons could enable Western military forces to halt communist aggression. Robert E. Osgood, in his influential book *Limited War*, explicitly linked tactical nuclear weapons and limited war. He wrote, "Tactical nuclear weapons, especially the low-yield battlefield weapons, can play a decisive role in supporting containment by giving the United States an adequate capacity for limited war at a tolerable cost."

Technological advances quickly provided tactical nuclear weapons. In May 1953, a U.S. Army 280-mm gun became the first artillery piece to fire a nuclear round successfully. Shortly thereafter, the army deployed half a dozen of the huge guns to Europe, even though they had a range of only seventeen miles and weighed eighty-three tons. It also equipped some of its units with Honest John rockets, which had a range of about twenty-two miles. Recognizing the need for smaller and more mobile nuclear delivery means, the army eventually introduced nuclear rounds for artillery pieces as small as 155-mm and introduced a nuclear-capable, short-range rocket, the Davy Crockett, into maneuver battalions. The Davy Crockett had a yield of .02 kilotons and a range of 650–4,400 yards.

As the army added tactical nuclear weapons to its inventory, it also reconfigured its infantry divisions by creating "Pentomic Divisions," which contained five "battle groups" (actually reinforced battalions). The new design eliminated the brigade echelon and added tactical mobility and other assets in an attempt to construct an organization that could disperse and concentrate rapidly. Theorists believed the division could survive and fight on the nuclear battlefield by spreading its forces in a "checker board," rather than linear fashion. Relying on new equipment, much of which never became available, the Pentomic Division proved to be difficult to command and not at all mobile, and its existence turned out to be mercifully brief.

Increases in the number of tactical nuclear weapons, nonetheless, created great concerns about escalation, particularly as Soviet capabilities increased. American critics argued that any tactical nuclear exchange would invariably lead to an all-out nuclear exchange. And Europeans feared the possibility of numerous tactical nuclear explosions on their crowded continent. More important, the Soviet Union paid little attention to tactical nuclear considerations, believing any use of nuclear weapons would initiate general nuclear war. In a key speech before the Supreme Soviet of the USSR in January 1960, the Soviet minister of defense ruled out "limited nuclear warfare" and "tactical use of nuclear weapons." Despite the obvious danger of escalation, tactical nuclear weapons remained an important part of the American arsenal.

Technological Advances

Eisenhower's two terms as president included not only a revolution in strategy but also a revolution in the technology of nuclear weapons and in the means of delivering them. Since the beginning of the nuclear era, air force bombers in Strategic Air Command had played the most important role in plans for delivering nuclear weapons. When Eisenhower took office, the United States had a mixed fleet of one thousand strategic and not-so-strategic bombers, and he lost no time in approving development of a truly strategic manned bomber, the all-jet B-52 Stratofortress, due to reach operational status by 1955. About 500 of these intercontinental bombers supplemented the more limited B-47 Stratojets, and by 1959 the United States had approximately 1,850 bombers.

As the United States improved its bombers, it also developed smaller, more powerful nuclear devices whose effect would be measured in megatons, rather than kilotons. In 1951, on the small Pacific island of Eniwetok, the United States detonated two small fusion devices, and the following year it detonated at Eniwetok a thermonuclear device with a force equal to 10 million tons of TNT, which was vastly larger than the bomb dropped on Hiroshima (equivalent to 14,000 tons of TNT) and the one dropped on Nagasaki (equivalent to 20,000 tons of TNT). The Soviet Union tested its own nuclear device in 1953. The United States tested an air-deliverable nuclear bomb in March 1954 but did not drop one from an airplane until May 1956. By the late 1950s, a B-52 bomber could deliver four nuclear bombs.

As technological improvements made nuclear weapons much smaller and also much more powerful, the missile began to challenge the manned bomber as the best means of delivery. By the mid-1950s, the air force was at work on two different Intercontinental Ballistic Missiles (ICBMs), the Titan and the Atlas, meant to deliver a one-megaton warhead at ranges of 5,500 and 6,250 miles, respectively. The first Atlas ICBMs became operational in the United States in 1959. The army entered the age of nuclear missiles in earnest with its own intermediate-range missiles. The Corporal became operational in 1953 with a 75-mile range, the Redstone in 1956 with a 225-mile range, and the Jupiter in 1957 with a range of 1,500 miles. Such missiles could reach far beyond the traditional area of concern of even the most senior ground commanders, leading to an intense debate between the army and air force about areas of responsibility.

The navy took a different atomic tack, investing initially in atomic propulsion for its fleet, especially its submarines. As early as 1951, however, it deployed nuclear-capable aircraft on its carriers, and three years later all carriers bore nuclear weapons and the aircraft to deliver them. Though the navy did not commission the world's first nuclear-powered aircraft carrier, the USS *Enterprise*, until November 1961, it commissioned the world's first nuclear-powered submarine, the USS *Nautilus*, in September 1954. At the end of the decade, the navy's Submarine-Launched Ballistic Missile (SLBM) program became feasible for submarines after smaller warheads and solid propellants became available. Initial plans called for the first missile-carrying submarine to be available in 1963, but increased concerns about the Soviet Union resulted in the first Polaris submarine, the USS *George Washington*, successfully launching its first missile while submerged in July 1960. Later versions of the missile increased its firing range from 1,375, to 1,700, to 2,850 miles. The age of the submarine-launched ballistic missile clearly had arrived.

The emergence of a Soviet nuclear threat made the gathering of intelligence particularly important. The United States created the National

Admiral H. V. Rickover directed construction of the USS *Nautilus*, the first nuclear-powered submarine. Its capability for sustained underwater operations was constrained only by the human limitations of its crew.

Security Agency in 1952; its mission was to conduct electronic eavesdropping on Russian communications systems. The new agency established radar stations in friendly countries along the Soviet perimeter and skirted Soviet borders with reconnaissance aircraft. As traditional sources of information—spies and refugees—began to dry up, the intelligence services resorted more and more to advanced technology to retrieve information. In 1956, the U-2, as the plane was called, became operational; it was capable of cruising above 70,000 feet, well beyond the ranges of Soviet air defenses. During the next four years, U-2s made dozens of spy flights over the Soviet Union before one was shot down by a new air-defense missile. By one informed estimate, the U-2 gleaned more than 90 percent of the West's strategic intelligence on the Soviet missile program before the flights ended. In time, satellites became the prime source of intelligence for both sides.

Meanwhile, like the Americans, the Soviets initially emphasized the long-range bomber. Their first important bomber was the Tu-16 Badger, which was similar to the American B-47 in performance. Entering into service in 1954–1955, it had the range to reach some cities in the United States on one-way flights from northern Siberia. In 1955, the Soviets introduced the Tu-20 Bear, which had a greater range and payload than the Badger, but not the American B-52. Although the Soviets had only a few hundred Bears and Badgers in service at the end of the 1950s, an intense debate erupted in the United States about the existence of a "bomber gap." A bomber gap did exist, but it was in favor of the Americans, not the Russians.

Motivated by inflated fears of Soviet bombers, the United States expended considerable effort and resources to defend itself against bombers with its Distant Early Warning line, numerous aerial interceptor squadrons, and land-to-air missiles that were nuclear armed.

As the United States prepared to defend itself against bombers, the Soviets made significant progress in the development of missiles. In August 1957 a Soviet SS-6 Sapwood ICBM traveled several thousand miles from its launch pad to its target in Siberia. Two months later, on October 4, 1957, an SS-6 rocket threw a 184-pound satellite called *Sputnik* into Earth orbit. One month later, the Soviets launched another satellite, weighing 1,121 pounds and carrying a live dog, into space. Though the Americans managed to launch a satellite, *Explorer I,* weighing thirty-one pounds, on January 31, 1958, they did not test the Atlas ICBM over its entire range for another year. Almost immediately, the "missile gap" replaced the bomber gap as Americans concluded that Soviet successes in space signaled their superiority in missile technology and numbers. Eisenhower, however, refused to panic. The U-2s, whose operations were known only to a few of the highest officials, had provided him with enough intelligence to know that the Soviets remained considerably behind the United States in strategic nuclear forces.

While Americans debated the implications of *Sputnik,* the Soviets began making slow progress in submarine-launched ballistic missiles. Between 1954 and 1957, the Soviets fitted several submarines with SS-N-4 Sark missiles, which had to be fired from the surface, rather than from underwater. The missile carried a nuclear warhead and had a range initially of 350 and later of 750 miles. Between 1958 and 1962, the Soviets equipped about thirty Golf and Hotel submarines with the SS-N-4 Sark. Not until 1968 did the Soviet navy complete a more modern submarine (the Yankee-class submarine) which carried sixteen missiles capable of being launched underwater and having a range of about 1,500 miles. The requirement for surface launching—in addition to the significant antisubmarine capability of the U.S. Navy—made the earlier Soviet submarines only a limited strategic threat to the United States. Nonetheless the Soviets had acquired the capability by the mid-1950s to inflict considerable damage on the United States, and that capability continued to expand.

Throughout much of the 1950s and 1960s, as demonstrated by the delusions associated with the "bomber gap" and the "missile gap," a significant difference existed between actual Soviet capabilities and American perceptions of those capabilities. The continued growth of Soviet missiles, however, dispelled all American hopes of fending off a Soviet nuclear strike. When the Soviets relied solely on bombers, the Americans could have destroyed many of the bombers before they dropped their bombs, but they had little or no defense against missiles. Though the United States maintained an overwhelming superiority, nuclear planners in the late 1950s recognized that the United States could not escape substantial damage in the event of a nuclear exchange.

Even though the Soviets remained far behind the Americans, a revolution in military affairs—according to Soviet writings—occurred in the Soviet armed forces between 1953 and 1960. Writers often compared the extent of the change to that which accompanied the introduction of gunpowder. In January 1960, Nikita S. Khrushchev underlined the extent of the change in an address to the Supreme Soviet of the USSR. He emphasized the decisiveness of nuclear weapons and threatened that if attacked, the Soviets would "wipe the country or countries attacking us off the face of the earth." A subsequent speech by the minister of defense highlighted the formation of new Strategic Rocket Forces and described them as "unquestionably the main service of the armed forces." In essence, the Soviets shifted from a primary focus on continental land warfare to a focus on global nuclear warfare. Military leaders believed that the revolution in military affairs compelled complete revisions in strategy, tactics, and force structure. As part of these revisions, the Soviets modified their thinking about the conduct of ground operations in the nuclear age and emphasized dispersion, mobility, high operating tempos, and multiple attacks on broad axes.

Thus, like the Americans, the Soviets acknowledged the profound effects of nuclear weapons on warfare. Changes in policy—influenced by the reduced size and increased power of nuclear weapons, the improved capabilities of manned bombers, the enhancement of missile range and accuracy, and the introduction of submarine-launched ballistic missiles—had achieved a military revolution, even if the only atomic bombs employed in combat were the two dropped on Japan at the end of World War II. For the moment the United States retained a position of superiority in nuclear affairs, but improvements in Soviet nuclear capabilities through the 1960s would eventually compel the United States to reevaluate its strategy of Massive Retaliation and to choose a different strategic path.

The Rise of the Defense Intellectuals

From the beginning, but particularly in the 1950s, much of the most important thinking in the United States about nuclear warfare was done by civilian intellectuals who traditionally had made a contribution to military thought but had never dominated the development of doctrine and equipment. Arguing that nuclear warfare was unique and answered to its own particular logic, civilian specialists provided much of the intellectual framework for nuclear thinking. They struggled to fit nuclear weapons within the framework of foreign policy and military affairs.

In a book entitled, *The Absolute Weapon*, Bernard Brodie laid down the fundamental outlines of nuclear deterrence—that the costs of retaliation in kind were too high for nations to contemplate using atomic warfare as a traditional means of defending their foreign policy interests. Brodie and his associates concluded that the real value of the atomic bomb lay not in its actual employment in war, but in the *threat* of its employment. In a now-famous passage, Brodie crafted the fundamental concept guiding what came to be called deterrence theory: "Thus far the chief purpose of our military establishment has been to win wars. From now on its chief purpose must be to avert them. It can have almost no other useful purpose." Additional thoughts came from other individuals, including J. Robert Oppenheimer, the physicist who had led the Los Alamos team during the Manhattan Project. In an essay published in *Foreign Affairs*, he depicted the Russians and Americans as "two scorpions in a bottle, each capable of killing the other, but only at the risk of his own life."

From these and other studies, the defense intellectuals conceived a wholly new vocabulary for the nuclear age and deployed it against the unconvinced defense establishment with breathtaking skill. "Counterforce" became the shorthand term for attacks against military targets. "Countervalue" was the touchstone for intentionally punitive attacks against "soft" targets such as cities and other psychologically valuable sites. "Stability" came to mean not a comfortable superiority such as the United States had enjoyed during the early years of the atomic era, but a kind of equilibrium reached when both sides were equally confident of destroying the other. Many outsiders found it difficult to accept the cold, logical language of nuclear theorists, some finding it as arcane as medieval scholasticism.

Particularly in the 1950s, Brodie and his colleagues—Albert Wohlstetter, Herman Kahn, and others—produced some of the most intellectually sophisticated work of the nuclear age. With their academic backgrounds, general contempt for traditional military thought, and quasi-official standing, the civilian strategists had a remarkable influence over nuclear thinking—and by extension, thinking about defense in general—from the Korean through the Vietnam wars.

Early Efforts to Rattle the Nuclear Saber

As for the effect of nuclear weapons on foreign policy, Eisenhower took advantage of the diplomatic power of the bomb early in his term. Attempting to unstick deadlocked negotiations with the Chinese, Eisenhower issued a discrete, ambiguous warning through the government of India that he might use atomic weapons against Chinese cities to force the Korean War to a conclusion. To back up his warning, he deployed atomic weapons to Okinawa, which was well within bomber range of both Korea and China. Though the effect of Eisenhower's atomic threat remains unclear, the Chinese did relent; several months later, the Korean armistice was announced.

The first full-fledged test of Eisenhower's new policy occurred early in 1954, a few months after the conclusion of the Korean armistice. In Indochina, the French army was gradually losing ground to a Vietnamese communist insurgency. The situation reached a crisis point in April 1954, when the French garrison at Dien Bien Phu seemed more than likely to succumb to its communist besiegers. Despite concerns about the effect of a French defeat on NATO's cohesion, Eisenhower refused to send American troops to bolster the French army in Indochina. He also refused to permit the employment of tactical nuclear weapons, even though Dien Bien Phu eventually fell.

A more direct contest with the Chinese Communists occurred over two small islands, Quemoy and Matsu, a few miles offshore from the Chinese mainland. Nationalist Chinese troops under Jiang Jieshi (Chiang

Kai-shek) had occupied the islands when they had lost the civil war in 1949. By September 1954, the Chinese Communists had concentrated troops on the mainland opposite these islands and had begun bombarding the Nationalist garrisons with artillery. Although Eisenhower never intended to use atomic weapons to solve the Quemoy-Matsu crisis, he equivocated in public. At a press conference in March, 1955, Eisenhower was asked to respond to a broad hint made earlier by Secretary of State Dulles that America would use some "small atomic weapons" if necessary. Eisenhower replied that smaller weapons could be used in such a case, "just as you would use a bullet or anything else."

The public furor that erupted over Quemoy and Matsu, along with all the talk about atomic weapons by administration officials and members of Congress, may well have been enough to dissuade the Chinese from invading the islands and attempting to take Formosa. All along, however, Eisenhower seemed to have no intention of committing American power, chiefly because he understood that the Chinese had no means of crossing the Formosa Strait against the opposition of the U.S. Seventh Fleet. The Chinese gave up their bombardment of the islands by April 1955 and agreed to diplomatic talks a while later.

The emergence of the Soviet Union as a strategic nuclear power altered the strategic equation. During the Suez Crisis of 1956, Israeli forces pummeled Egyptian forces in the Sinai while Anglo-French expeditionary forces seized the northern end of the Suez Canal and moved south quickly. With Egypt facing decisive defeat, the United States pressured the Israelis, British, and French to withdraw. Khrushchev went a step farther, however, and hinted of Soviet nuclear weapons landing in Paris and London and of Soviet "volunteers" pouring into Egypt. As with other crises, the effect of the nuclear threat was uncertain, but it was clear that more than one power could now rattle the nuclear saber.

Achieving Strategic Parity and Controlling Nuclear Weapons

Throughout the 1950s the strategy of Massive Retaliation came under severe criticism. As Soviet advances reduced American advantages in strategic arms, it no longer seemed credible to attempt to deter limited aggression by possibly escalating to a massive nuclear response. Thus, the likelihood of nuclear weapons, according to the critics, being employed against Soviet aggression decreased, as did the chances of effectively resisting communist aggression. Among those objecting most strenuously to American emphasis on strategic nuclear forces was a succession of U.S. Army general officers, including two chiefs of staff, General Matthew B. Ridgway and General Maxwell D. Taylor. To them, limited conflicts—particularly those in which conventional forces played a key role—seemed the way of the future, and they argued that the United States had to build strategically mobile conventional forces capable of meeting threats to national interests wherever they might appear.

During his campaign for the presidency, John F. Kennedy committed himself to reversing Eisenhower's Massive Retaliation strategy and substituting in its place a new strategy of "Flexible Response." Shortly after entering office in January 1961, he stated, "Any potential aggressor contemplating an attack on any part of the free world with any kind of weapons, conventional or nuclear, must know that our response will be suitable, selective, swift, and effective." In essence the president resolved to create multiple options so an American response could be tailored to a Soviet challenge. The new strategy required a larger number and variety of conventional forces, eventually leading the army, for example, to abolish its Pentomic divisions and to focus on conventional warfare.

When commissioned in 1961, the USS *Enterprise* was the largest ship ever built. It displaced 85,600 tons, measured over 1,100 feet, and carried a crew of 4,600, including 2,400 air personnel. Its vast range and great speed enabled the United States to project force over the entire globe.

The adoption of Flexible Response did not reduce the importance of nuclear weapons. Robert S. McNamara, the new secretary of defense, began developing the nuclear dimension of Flexible Response and emphasized the requirement, if deterrence failed, for greater flexibility and discrimination in the selection of nuclear targets. In June 1962, he said that "principal military objectives in the event of nuclear war . . . should be the destruction of the enemy's military forces, not of his civilian population." By refraining from an attack against enemy cities and by holding a large, strategic nuclear force in reserve, McNamara sought with a counterforce strategy to provide an adversary "the strongest possible incentive" to avoid striking American cities and to agree quickly to ending a war.

The new counterforce strategy proved to be expensive, for it required "powerful and well-protected" American nuclear forces. Additionally, the targeting of Soviet forces required more accurate and reliable delivery systems than targeting larger and more easily hit cities. The Kennedy administration took office at a time when the last of the first-generation ICBMs became operational (Atlas E in 1960, Titan I in 1962, and the Atlas F in 1962). Despite the costs involved, McNamara accelerated the entry of more accurate second-generation missiles (Minuteman I and Titan II) into the American arsenal and began eliminating first-generation missiles. He also reduced the number of manned bombers, primarily by phasing out the older B-47s. Recognizing the advantages of submarine-launched ballistic missiles, McNamara accelerated the development of Polaris submarines. The SLBMs represented the "third leg" (along with land-based ICBMs and manned bombers) of what became known as the TRIAD. To avoid substantial damage from a retaliatory or second strike, an adversary would have to destroy each leg of the TRIAD in a first strike. With the Americans' possessing three separate strategic systems for delivering nuclear weapons, however, the possibility of multiple strikes against the same target—or "overkill"— appeared, so in 1962 McNamara approved the Single Integrated Operational Plan (SIOP), which had been developed during the Eisenhower administration. By incorporating controlled options into the SIOP, the United States could hold in reserve a large strategic nuclear force and could manipulate nuclear warfighting instead of simply pulling a single trigger. By the mid-1960s, the United States had about 1,000 ICBMs, 650 SLBMs, and 650 manned bombers.

The Cuban Missile Crisis

The closest brush with nuclear Armageddon came not in the Eisenhower administration but in the Kennedy administration when the new president found few options to his liking in the Cuban Missile Crisis. The crisis grew out of Khrushchev's decision in early 1962 to place nuclear missiles in Cuba. Russian advisors, aircraft, and air-defense weapons accompanied the missiles, and in August 1962, an American U-2 spotted suspicious construction sites. As the reconnaissance flights continued, intelligence analysts identified more and more sites.

Despite Soviet assurances that no offensive missiles had been deployed in Cuba, a U-2 flight returned on October 14, 1962, bearing photographs that definitively revealed launch sites being prepared in western Cuba for medium-range (1,000 miles) ballistic missiles as well as long-range (2,200 miles) missiles. If the Soviets finished the sites and placed nuclear weapons at them, they would have the capability of covering with nuclear weapons much of the continental United States. Believing he could not permit the weapons to remain in Cuba, President Kennedy ordered a naval "quarantine" on October 22, 1962, to prevent Cuba from receiving any more Soviet equipment. He also insisted that any nuclear weapon launched from Cuba would be considered to have been launched from the Soviet Union and placed U.S. nuclear forces on the highest level of alert ever ordered, DEFCON-2 (Defense Condition 2), including the maintenance of fifty-seven nuclear bombers on a twenty-four hour flying readiness schedule. Another quarter of a million American troops also were placed in higher states of readiness. Meanwhile, Soviet commanders in Cuba received permission to use nuclear weapons in the event of an American invasion.

As the crisis intensified, Khrushchev offered to withdraw the missiles from Cuba in exchange for the Americans' removing Jupiter missiles from Turkey, lifting the naval blockade, and promising not to invade Cuba. Kennedy eventually accepted the offer but did not make his own concession public. After some tense moments at the naval picket lines, when Soviet and American ships faced off, the crisis passed. By October 27, all parties had backed off gingerly from the nuclear brink.

Both superpowers emerged from the Cuban Missile Crisis with a revitalized fear of nuclear consequences. Though Secretary of State Dean Rusk believed the Americans and Soviets came away from the crisis "more cautious and more thoughtful," the Soviets concluded that the American advantage in nuclear weapons had forced them to yield, and they subsequently embarked on an ambitious program to modernize their nuclear arsenal. Shortly after the crisis, a senior Soviet official told his American counterpart, "You Americans will never be able to do this to us again." A new period in the nuclear era had begun.

Mutual Assured Destruction

Though the American modernization program in the 1960s was impressive, that of the Soviets was even more so. A succession of new ICBMs entered the Soviets' Strategic Rocket Forces in the late 1960s. The SS-11 became operational in 1966, the SS-9 in 1967, and the SS-13 in 1969. The SS-11 became the most extensively employed Soviet ICBM. At the same time, the Soviets began to place their strategic weapons in hardened underground silos. Moreover, the Soviet Union accelerated in the mid-1960s the construction of submarines capable of launching strategic missiles. By 1970 the Soviet Union had surpassed the United States in number of operational ICBMs, 1,299 to 1,054.

As the Russians acquired a greater capability to retaliate directly against American cities, the Americans began to question a purely counterforce strategy and to look for other options. In February 1965 Secretary McNamara announced that the United States would rely on "Assured Destruction" to deter a Soviet attack. In essence, this meant the Americans would respond to an enemy nuclear attack by inflicting unacceptable damage on the Soviets, that is, an attack upon civilian as well as military targets. McNamara believed the possibility of massive destruction of Soviet cities would deter the enemy from launching a first-strike attack.

After the Soviets acquired an assured second-strike capability, the Americans modified their strategy again. In September 1967, McNamara added the word "mutual" to "assured destruction," thereby creating the unfortunate acronym, MAD, which suggested to many the insanity of holding the populations of both countries hostage. Nevertheless, Mutual Assured Destruction signaled an acceptance by the United States of its own vulnerability and the emergence of what McNamara called a "stable balance of terror." According to some analysts, the Soviet Union achieved "strategic parity" or a "rough equilibrium" in the early 1970s.

The Proliferation of Nuclear Weapons

For nearly two decades, the history of the nuclear era played out chiefly in the United States and the Soviet Union, but other powers began acquiring atomic or nuclear capability. Several months before the Soviets tested their atomic bomb in 1949, the British announced they would build their own atomic weapons. In October 1952, they tested their first atomic bomb on a small island northwest of Australia.

France's explosion of a bomb in the Sahara Desert in February 1960 signaled major changes in the nuclear arena. In his memoirs, Charles de Gaulle stated that one of his objectives had been for France "to acquire a nuclear capacity such that nobody could attack us without risking frightful wounds." It quickly became clear that the "nobody" included the United States. In November 1968, the French army's chief of the general staff published an article in which he announced that French nuclear forces, the *force de frappe*, would be capable of covering all points of the compass. In essence, he declared the independence of French nuclear forces. Other powers also acquired nuclear capabilities. In 1957, the Soviet Union agreed to provide defense assistance to Communist China, including assistance in nuclear matters. The Soviets cooperated fully with Chinese specialists who exploded their first nuclear device in October 1964.

With the number of nuclear powers increasing, many political and military leaders became increasingly concerned about the dangerous proliferation of nuclear technology. In August 1967, the United States and the Soviet Union jointly submitted to the U.N. Disarmament Commission a treaty to halt the spread of nuclear weapons. When ratified, the Nuclear Nonproliferation Treaty bound the signatory states with nuclear weapons not to supply them to other nations and those without nuclear weapons not to manufacture them. Though the pact was hailed as an epochal event, states throughout the world continued to seek nuclear technology. Communist

China denounced the treaty as a "plot," and in May 1974, India exploded its first nuclear device. Despite the sincerest of efforts, the "nuclear genie" had escaped from the bottle.

Arms Control Comes of Age

For almost two decades after World War II, little or no progress occurred in arms control. During the years when the United States had obvious superiority over the Soviet Union, Moscow often called for general and complete disarmament, but neither Moscow nor Washington accepted any real limitations or controls. In 1946, Bernard M. Baruch presented to the United Nations an American proposal for international control over the development and use of atomic energy, but the proposal foundered when the Soviets objected to on-site inspections. In 1955, President Eisenhower, hoping to lessen the danger of surprise attack, suggested having "Open Skies" over the USSR and the United States by permitting each to conduct flights over the other. The Soviets, however, denounced the plan as an espionage plot. Following the Cuban Missile Crisis, the two sides swiftly approved the Limited Test Ban Treaty of 1963. With over one hundred signatories, the treaty prohibited the testing of nuclear devices in space, the atmosphere, and underwater but allowed underground testing. Additional progress occurred as the two superpowers approached strategic parity, most notably the 1967

As the range of Polaris missiles grew from 1,375 to 2,850 miles, nuclear submarines carrying the missiles became more difficult to locate since they could hide in vastly larger areas of the ocean.

Nonproliferation Treaty. Several years of subsequent talks, however, failed to produce a breakthrough on limiting nuclear arms. In these and other efforts at arms control, distrust between the superpowers and the technical difficulties of verifying numbers and controlling technological advances created insurmountable obstacles.

Throughout the arms control discussions, verification of the number of an opponent's warheads remained impractical but became even more problematic when the United States began deploying missiles with multiple warheads. In 1964 it introduced the Polaris A-3 missile, which carried a multiple reentry vehicle (MRV) payload. When fired, the MRV would separate into individual reentry vehicles, or "bomblets," and strike an area in "shotgun" fashion. In 1968 the United States tested a multiple independently targeted reentry vehicle (MIRV) with the Minuteman III, which was an intercontinental ballistic missile with a range of about 9,300 miles. More accurate than the bomblets in the MRV warheads, the bomblets in the MIRV warheads could be directed with surprising precision against individual targets. The warhead of the Minuteman III carried three reentry vehicles, or bomblets, each with an estimated yield of about 200 kilotons. In 1970 the United States fitted its submarines with the Poseidon C-3 missile, which had a MIRV capability. The Soviet Union soon matched the technological developments in American strategic weapons. Testing of the SS-9 with a MRV warhead began in late 1968, and the fielding of Soviet missiles with MIRVs began in 1974.

The implications for nuclear strategy and arms control were enormous. Analysts contended that a preemptive nuclear strike by ICBMs with multiple warheads could inflict significant damage to fixed missile silos. Some concluded that immobile, undefended, land-based ICBMs were obsolete. Also, the existence of multiple warheads on a single missile made the number of warheads almost impossible to verify. Using satellites, both sides could detect and count missile launchers, but they could not count warheads. Technological advances had changed the rules for the nuclear game.

Despite the problems posed by MIRVs and verification, both sides slowly came to recognize in the late 1960s the "advantages" of a strategic balance and dreaded the costs of another round of nuclear improvements. For the most part, subsequent discussions between the superpowers took little notice of the increasing spread of nuclear weapons to other countries. Nonetheless, the bilateral superpower negotiations for the Strategic Arms Limitation Treaty (SALT), which began in Helsinki in late 1969, were not concluded until nearly three years later. SALT I, as it came to be known, called only for a freeze on building more ICBMs by both sides and restricted the United States and the Soviet Union to two Antiballistic Missile (ABM) sites each. The treaty did not include a limit on numbers of warheads. Despite its modest achievements, SALT I was an important first step in arms control.

The next round of SALT discussions also proceeded slowly. Meanwhile the Soviets tested a new, more powerful family of ICBMs: SS-17, SS-18, and SS-19. All of them had MIRVs. In June 1979, Jimmy Carter and Leonid Brezhnev finally signed the SALT II agreements, which capped strategic delivery systems for each side at no more than 2,250, and established a specific ceiling of 1,320 missiles with MIRVs.

Despite the apparent progress, controversy plagued the arms control process. One sensitive issue was that of U.S. plans to field the enhanced radiation bomb, which was also known as the "neutron bomb." This new device produced much greater radiation than a traditional weapon and thus had a greater effect on personnel in armored vehicles, which were relatively resistant to blast effects. This made it a useful weapon against the huge Soviet armored forces. Critics argued, however, that the new device made nuclear war more likely by blurring the distinction between nuclear and conventional war. The introduction of the cruise missile also added complexity to the nuclear equation. The missile used forward-looking radar to guide itself along the nap of the Earth to its target. Though many analysts doubted its capacity to kill hard targets such as ICBMs deep within their silos, its existence blurred the distinction between strategic and theater-level nuclear delivery systems. A protocol attached to the SALT II agreement established temporary bans on the deployment of mobile ICBM launchers and on longer-range cruise missiles. After an intense debate in the U.S. Senate about whether SALT II should be ratified, the treaty fell victim to renewed American doubts about Soviet intentions following their invasion of Afghanistan in December 1979.

Continued Innovation in Nuclear Technology

In the 1960s and 1970s, key American officials concluded that assured destruction was not enough and that the United States needed a wider range of options. In 1973, James Schlesinger, secretary of defense under President Richard M. Nixon, stated, "[W]e ourselves find it difficult to believe that we would actually implement the threat of assured destruction in response to a limited attack on military targets that caused relatively few civilian casualties." He then called for "a series of measured responses to aggression which bear some relation to the provocation." In July 1980, President Carter signed Presidential Directive 59, which incorporated many of Schlesinger's ideas; the document called for a "countervailing" nuclear strategy in which the United States would arrange its future arsenal so that it could fight a nuclear war at "any level of intensity," from limited nuclear exchange, to a theater-level war, to all-out nuclear war. Improvements in command and control, delivery systems, and accuracy had enabled the Americans to develop the capability to use their nuclear weapons in limited nuclear options against Soviet nuclear forces, conventional forces, or other military targets, and perhaps to control escalation all the way from the most limited use through an all-out nuclear exchange. In essence, the new policy signaled a move away from countervalue toward counterforce in U.S. strategy; it relied on delivery means for nuclear weapons becoming more precise and controls becoming more flexible. Nevertheless its announcement brought on a storm of criticism from those who believed the new policy increased the likelihood of nuclear weapons being employed in the future.

When Ronald Reagan became president in 1981, he was convinced that the Soviet nuclear forces were superior to those of the U.S., and he soon took steps to strengthen the U.S. nuclear arsenal. While refusing to revive SALT II, Reagan accelerated the employment of Trident nuclear submarines and Trident II missiles (an undersea long-range missile system that was begun in the early 1970s) and stood solidly behind the decision to deploy Pershing II and Tomahawk cruise missiles in the defense of Europe. He also poured money into the MX missile. Although Carter had initiated most of the new programs, it was Reagan who pushed them. From the Soviet perspective, the new president seemed to be waging economic warfare.

Among the most dramatic steps taken by President Reagan was the Strategic Defense Initiative, which initially envisaged a strategic missile defense in space using directed energy or lasers. After the use of laser weapons proved infeasible, a concept for kinetic energy interceptors replaced the notion of using lasers. Whatever its methods, the announcement of SDI created an international uproar and popular dissent. Critics saw the SDI program as a dangerous change, for the prospect of the United States' having a shield against a nuclear attack seemed to increase the chances of the Soviets' attacking before the shield was completed or to encourage the Americans to launch a first strike after the shield was erected. Either scenario could result in a nuclear holocaust. As the Soviet Union began to desintegrate and the threat of a Soviet attack receded, questions about the utility and expense of SDI increased. When Iraq's effort to develop nuclear weapons became apparent in the Persian Gulf War, however, proponents of SDI pointed out that nuclear weapons were no longer the monopoly of the superpowers and that up to fifteen states could possess nuclear weapons in the near future. They believed SDI could provide valuable protection against an attack from one of these powers.

As the 1980s ended, Mikhail S. Gorbachev, the Soviet head of state, eagerly sought additional curbs on nuclear weapons. In December 1987, Gorbachev and Reagan agreed to destroy all U.S. and Soviet intermediate-range nuclear missiles (300–3,000 miles). In July 1991, Gorbachev and President George Bush signed the long-awaited Strategic Arms Reduction Treaty (START). In essence, START cut Soviet strategic nuclear warheads from 11,012 to 6,163 and American warheads from 12,646 to 8,556. Following the dissolution of the Soviet Union, President Bush and President Boris N. Yeltsin of Russia signed START II in January 1993. The treaty limited Russia to 3,000 warheads and the United States to 3,500. The treaty also banned all long-range land-based missiles with multiple warheads. Bush concluded, "Today, the Cold War is over."

The proliferation of nuclear arms around the world, however, ensured that concerns about nuclear weapons did not disappear with the ending of the Cold War. In an indication of the increasing complexity of the nuclear environment, three of the successor states to the Soviet Union—Ukraine, Kazakhstan, and Belarus—expressed reservations about the START agreements. As the United States confronted the new strategic environment, it refocused the SDI program from providing protection against a Soviet attack to providing protection from "limited ballistic missile strikes, whatever their source." The new strategy of Global Protection against Limited Strikes (GPALS) signaled how dramatically the international situation had changed.

✱   ✱   ✱   ✱

Through the second half of the twentieth century, nuclear weapons affected many decisions and actions relating to international security and had dramatic effects on strategy and force structure. After World War II, the United States had only a few atomic weapons, but it had a monopoly over them. In subsequent years as the Cold War heated up, and as the United States adopted a policy of containing the USSR and communism, atomic weapons played an increasingly larger role in American military thinking. When the

Observers watch the explosion of an atomic shell. In mid-1955, the U.S. Army positioned a task force three kilometers from an exploding 30-kiloton atomic device and had them advance to within 900 meters of ground zero. Such exercises supposedly demonstrated the ability of ground forces to operate on a nuclear battlefield.

Soviet Union exploded an atomic and then a nuclear device, the United States lost its monopoly over the enormously destructive weapons, and deterrence became particularly important. For the rest of the Cold War, containment and deterrence remained significant American goals.

Following the Korean War, Eisenhower emphasized a strategy of Massive Retaliation, and nuclear weapons assumed a position of primacy in American military thinking. As the Soviets improved their nuclear capabilities, the Americans moved toward a strategy of Flexible Response, which relied on more balanced conventional and nuclear forces. After the Cuban Missile Crisis, the Soviet Union accelerated the development of its nuclear capabilities, and the United States adopted Assured Destruction and then Mutual Assured Destruction as its new strategy. Recognizing it could no longer maintain overwhelming superiority, the United States prepared to respond to a Soviet attack by destroying much of Soviet society.

The United States maintained its nuclear superiority until the early 1970s when the Soviet Union gained strategic parity. With nuclear forces in rough equilibrium and new technological advances threatening to upset the delicate balance or require vast new resources, political leaders became more agreeable to nuclear arms limitations. Meanwhile, the long-term evolution of American nuclear policy formally entered a new phase with the adoption of a countervailing strategy in July 1980. Instead of relying on Mutual Assured Destruction, the Americans had developed the capability to use nuclear weapons in limited nuclear options and sought to avoid an all-out nuclear exchange. Finally, the dissolution of the Soviet Union and the proliferation of nuclear weapons created a new strategic environment; the United States began shifting from an emphasis on retaliation against nuclear attack to defense against nuclear attack.

Though numerous wars occurred between 1945 and 1990, the only two bombs used in combat were those dropped on Hiroshima and Nagasaki, and thus concepts for nuclear war remained largely theoretical. The United States and the Soviet Union expended vast resources to develop strategies and forces for nuclear war, but they also devoted considerable effort and resources to avoiding such a war and to preventing a small war from escalating into a larger war. The initiation of an era of limited war thus emerged as one of the most important effects of the introduction of nuclear weapons.

SUGGESTED READINGS

Armacost, Michael H. *The Politics of Weapon Innovation: The Thor-Jupiter Controversy* (New York: Columbia University Press, 1969).

Bacevich, A. J. *The Pentomic Era: The U.S. Army between Korea and Vietnam* (Washington, D.C.: National Defense University Press, 1986).

Brodie, Bernard, ed. *The Absolute Weapon: Atomic Power and World Order* (New York: Harcourt, Brace and Company, 1946).

Brodie, Bernard. *Strategy in the Missile Age* (Princeton, N.J.: Princeton University Press, 1959).

Bundy, McGeorge. *Danger and Survival: Choices About the Bomb in the First Fifty Years* (New York: Random House, 1988).

Freedman, Lawrence. *The Evolution of Nuclear Strategy* (New York: St. Martin's Press, 1981).

Gaddis, John L. *Strategies of Containment* (New York: Oxford University Press, 1982).

Herken, Gregg. *The Winning Weapon: The Atomic Bomb in the Cold War, 1945–1950* (New York: Vintage Books, 1982).

Holland, Lauren H., and Robert A. Hoover. *The MX Decision: A New Direction in Weapons Procurement Policy* (Boulder, Col.: Westview Press, 1985).

Kaplan, Fred M. *The Wizards of Armageddon* (New York: Simon and Schuster, 1983).

Kissinger, Henry. *Nuclear Weapons and Foreign Policy* (New York: Harper, 1957).

Mandelbaum, Michael. *The Nuclear Question: The United States and Nuclear Weapons, 1946–1976* (Cambridge: Cambridge University Press, 1979).

Midgley, John J., Jr. *Deadly Illusions: Army Policy for the Nuclear Battlefield* (Boulder, Col.: Westview Press, 1986).

Neufeld, Jacob. *Ballistic Missiles in the United States Air Force, 1945–1960* (Washington, D.C.: Government Printing Office, 1989).

Newhouse, John. *War and Peace in the Nuclear Age* (New York: Alfred A. Knopf, 1989).

Osgood, Robert E. *Limited War: The Challenge to American Strategy* (Chicago: University of Chicago Press, 1957).

Porro, Jeffrey, ed. *The Nuclear Age Reader* (New York: Alfred A. Knopf, 1989).

Prados, John. *The Soviet Estimate: U.S. Intelligence Analysis and Russian Military Strength* (New York: Dial Press, 1982).

Rhodes, Richard. *The Making of the Atomic Bomb* (New York: Simon and Schuster, 1986).

Rose, John P. *The Evolution of U.S. Army Nuclear Doctrine, 1945-1980* (Boulder, Col.: Westview Press, 1980).

Rosenberg, David A. "The Origins of Overkill: Nuclear Weapons and American Strategy, 1945–1960," *International Security*, vol. 7, no. 4 (Spring 1983), pp. 3–71.

———. "American Atomic Strategy and the Atomic Bomb Decision," *Journal of American History*, vol. 66, no. 1 (June 1979), pp. 62–87.

Sherwin, Martin J. *A World Destroyed: Hiroshima and the Origins of the Arms Race* (New York: Vintage Books, 1987).

Stares, Paul B. *The Militarization of Space: U.S. Policy, 1945–1984* (Ithaca, N.Y.: Cornell University Press, 1985).

Talbott, Strobe. *Deadly Gambits: The Reagan Administration and the Stalemate in Nuclear Arms Control* (New York: Alfred A. Knopf, 1984).

————. *Endgame: The Inside Story of SALT II* (New York: Harper & Row, 1979).

Werrell, Kenneth P. *The Evolution of the Cruise Missile* (Maxwell Air Force Base, Ala.: Air University Press, 1985).

Wohlstetter, Albert. "The Delicate Balance of Terror," *Foreign Affairs*, vol. 37, no. 2 (January 1959), pp. 211–34.

20

KOREA: LIMITING WAR
TO AVOID ARMAGEDDON

Rushing to War: The High
Cost of Unpreparedness

Changing War Aims and
a Changing War

Ending the War:
Politics as War

The Korean War was the first major conflict of the Cold War; it began on June 25, 1950, when North Korean ground forces invaded South Korea. Armed forces from the United States and other members of the United Nations came to the aid of the South Koreans, and a three-year war resulted. After fighting a war of maneuver up and down the Korean peninsula for about a year, the combatants settled into deeply entrenched positions, reminiscent of World War 1. As negotiations for ending the war began and the war became a stalemate, bitter battles erupted over minor outposts for small negotiating advantages. The issue of exchanging prisoners of war became a major obstacle to final agreement, prolonging the war until an armistice stopped the fighting on July 27, 1953.

While the Korean War witnessed few innovations in warfare, it demonstrated methods for gaining national objectives in the newly born atomic era. For the United States, the war was a "limited" war. To avoid provoking retaliation from the Soviet Union, American political leaders limited the geographic areas in which military commanders could operate, the strength of their forces, and the weapons to be used against the enemy. Communist forces suffered huge losses in the fighting and sought to achieve, through prolonged armistice negotiations, what they could not gain on the battlefield. They sought an advantageous political outcome by manipulating public opinion in the United States and among its allies, as well as throughout the nonaligned nations of the world. Thus the Korean War was less about tactical evolution than about political goals, the strategy to achieve those goals, and the operations designed to make the strategy succeed.

Rushing to War: The High Cost of Unpreparedness

After World War II, antagonism between the Soviet Union and the United States grew as the two former allies became increasingly distrustful and suspicious of the other's motives. The first notable confrontation occurred in 1946 when the Soviets briefly refused to withdraw from Iran. More acute problems occurred in Turkey and Greece. The Soviets pressured the Turks for control of the straits of the Bosporus and Dardanelles and the return of territory lost at the end of World War I. When Greek Communists attempted to overthrow Greece's government, the Americans became particularly concerned, and President Truman pledged support to "free peoples who are resisting attempted subjugation by armed minorities or by outside pressures." This pledge came to be known as the Truman Doctrine. In an attempt to revive Europe, the United States established the Marshall Plan in 1947 and provided the economic base on which democratic reforms could be made. But international tensions increased with the Berlin Blockade in the spring of 1948, the explosion of a Soviet atomic device in August 1949, and the communist takeover of China in December 1949. During this series of crises, the United States adopted the policy, defined by George F. Kennan, of "a long-term, patient but firm and vigilant containment of Russian expansive tendencies."

In January 1950 President Truman directed officials from the departments of state and defense to conduct a broad assessment of American military needs. The resulting document, known as NSC-68, was the first comprehensive statement of national security policy since the end of World War II. To meet the threat posed by rapidly expanding Soviet capabilities, NSC-68 advocated an immediate buildup of U.S. and allied military strength in hopes that the United States might induce a change in Soviet policy while avoiding all-out war. The document called for the United States to have the capacity to wage either general or limited war and clearly emphasized that atomic weapons by themselves were insufficient for American national security needs. War broke out in Korea, however, before military readiness could be improved significantly.

Rapid demobilization after World War II had greatly affected American armed forces, but of all the services, the U.S. Army was in the worst shape to fight a war. In total, there were ten army divisions and eleven separate brigades on active duty in the spring of 1950. Of those forces, four infantry divisions were in Japan and immediately available to General of the Army Douglas MacArthur, Commander-in-Chief, Far East, and thereby the theater commander. But these forces were far from being combat ready. Except for the 25th Infantry Division, all were below their authorized peacetime strength of 12,500 men. Within the regiments, the number of battalions had been reduced from three to two and the tank company eliminated. The divisions' artillery was scaled down, and there were shortages of antitank mines, high explosive antitank ammunition, and spare parts for weapons. The divisions also had serious training problems. Although individual soldiers were reasonably well trained, units were not. When Lieutenant General Walton H. Walker took command of Eighth Army in the summer of 1949, training for combat finally took priority over occupation duties, but the demands of occupying and administering Japan continued to take their toll on combat readiness.

Failing to recognize the likelihood of war in Korea also had an effect on readiness. When World War II ended, the Soviets and the Americans entered Korea to administer the surrender of Japanese forces. At that time the 38th Parallel had no significance other than dividing Korea in such a way as to give the United States ports at Inchon and Pusan to facilitate the repatriation of Japanese troops. As the possibility of Korean unification became more remote, the South Koreans held elections in May 1948, and after the U.N. General Assembly recognized the newly elected government of Syngman Rhee in South Korea, the Soviets created and recognized the Democratic People's Republic of Korea. The 38th Parallel divided the two Korean states.

Throughout this period, the United States remained primarily concerned with unfolding events in Europe and demonstrated little interest in becoming deeply involved in Korea. By 1950, Kim Il Sung had risen to the top of the communist forces in North Korea and had assembled a relatively small but highly capable army of 135,000 men. With Moscow's approval, he began preparations for unifying Korea by force. Neither the Soviets nor the North Koreans expected the United States to oppose the Communists with military forces. Meanwhile the South Koreans—with American advice and assistance—organized a small ground force of about 65,000 troops equipped well enough to prevent border raids and to preserve internal security, but not to fight a hard war. Ready or not, the American and South Korean armed forces were about to be involved in a life and death struggle.

The War Begins

North Korea had completed preparations for an offensive against South Korea by June 23, 1950. The main attack, which was conducted by the 3rd and 4th North Korean divisions, aimed at Seoul on the west coast and began at about 0430 hours on June 25. Farther to the east in the mountains, the 2nd and 7th North Korean divisions drove toward Yoju and Wonju, and on the east coast, the 5th Division (reinforced) headed for Samch'ok. Second echelon regiments followed closely, prepared to attack through the lead units to objectives deep in the South Koreans' rear. Advancing on a broad front, the North Koreans achieved success everywhere. The South Korean forces, which were also known as Republic of Korea (ROK) forces and which were defending along the 38th Parallel, fell back in the face of superior enemy strength, hardly delaying the North Koreans.

As North Korean troops advanced south toward Seoul, President Truman concluded that the United States—as part of a United Nations'

President Truman reports to the nation on the actions taken by the United States. He had earlier stated, "The attack upon Korea makes it plain beyond all doubt that Communism has passed beyond the use of subversion to conquer independent nations and will now use armed invasion and war."

effort—had to oppose communist aggression in the Far East. In a complete reversal of policy, he decided American forces would intervene to save South Korea. Opposition to U.N. involvement came from the communist states, but because the Soviets had walked out of the U.N. Security Council the preceding January, their resistance was uncoordinated and ineffective. On Sunday, June 25, the U.N. Security Council adopted an American-sponsored resolution branding the North Korean attack as a breach of the peace and calling on the North Korean government to cease hostilities and withdraw behind the 38th Parallel. On the following Tuesday, the Security Council approved a follow-on resolution calling on members of the United Nations to help South Korea "repel the armed attack and . . . restore international peace and security in the area." The U.N. Security Council designated the president of the United States as its executive agent for the war in Korea. Truman, in turn, appointed General MacArthur as the Commander-in-Chief, United Nations Command (CINCUNC).

MacArthur's mission was to stop the North Koreans and eject them from South Korea. Somehow he had to slow down the North Koreans sufficiently to give him time to mount a counterattack against their flanks or rear. His first act was to delay what appeared to be the enemy's main attack on the Seoul-Suwon-Ch'onan-Taejon axis leading to the port of Pusan in the south. On the last day of June, MacArthur ordered Major General William F. Dean, commanding general of the 24th Infantry Division, to send an infantry-artillery task force to Korea as the vanguard for the division. The task force—known as Task Force Smith, after Lieutenant Colonel Charles B. Smith, commander of the 1st Battalion, 21st Infantry—consisted of about half the battalion. It reached Taejon on July 2 and moved toward a defensive position about five kilometers north of Osan. Though greatly diminished in strength, the Americans were confident that they could halt the North Koreans. One general officer told Smith, "All we need is some men up there who won't run when they see tanks." By first light on July 5, Colonel Smith's units were in place, and Battery B, 52nd Field Artillery, was prepared to provide fire support.

Beginning around 0700 on July 5, the task force received an attack from North Korean tanks, all of which tried to drive through the American position. About twenty of Smith's infantrymen were killed or wounded in the fight. Damaged but not defeated, with enemy tanks somewhere in its rear, Task Force Smith received another attack several hours later. Attacking frontally, the leading North Korean infantry units took heavy casualties; they then managed to envelop Smith's position and seize high ground on both flanks. Around 1430 hours, Smith decided that his small command had done all it could and ordered his troops to withdraw. As the infantrymen attempted to pull back, enemy pressure increased and prevented some of the Americans from making a fighting withdrawal. A few of them abandoned their crew-served weapons and their rifles. They also left some of their dead and wounded behind. Fortunately for the Americans, the North Koreans chose not to pursue aggressively. The next morning, remnants of Task Force Smith reached Ch'onan. After other survivors made their way back, the final count of missing was 148 soldiers and five officers. Any notion that the North Koreans would pull back at the sight of Americans had disappeared.

Establishing the Pusan Perimeter

Though MacArthur's knowledge of the enemy was incomplete in the first few days of the war, he formulated a broad operational plan containing three clearly identifiable phases. The first was to delay the enemy on his main approach and thereby to buy time needed to rush reinforcements to Korea. The second phase was to defend a toehold on the Korean peninsula to allow the buildup of forces through the port of Pusan. The final phase was an amphibious turning movement by a corps raised in Japan that would strike at the waist of Korea and trap the North Koreans between the new beachhead and Pusan.

For the three-phased operation, MacArthur had advantages in his air and naval forces. Aircraft from the Far East Air Force (FEAF) and the navy soon controlled the sky and provided close air support to Koreans and those few Americans then on the ground. By July 3, Australian air units joined the growing U.N. air force. U.S. carriers launched aircraft to strike targets in North Korea on July 4 and 5. Naval surface forces quickly assembled in Korean waters and secured the sea routes between Japan and Korea. Naval

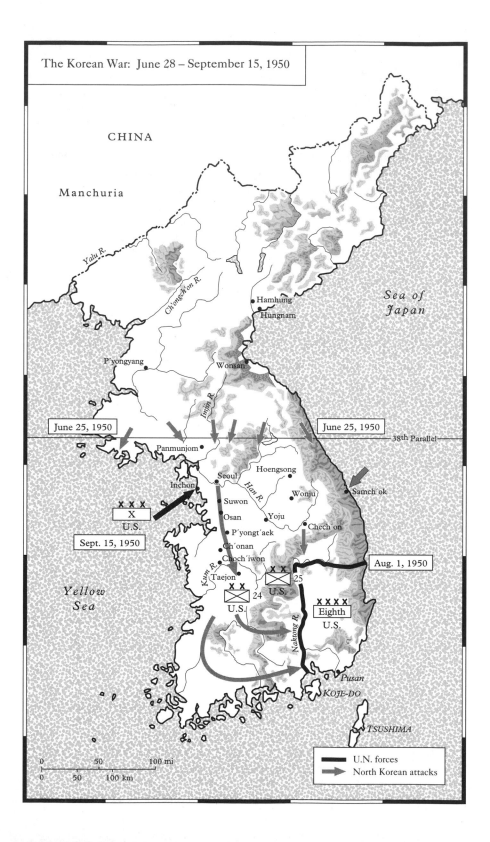

The Korean War: June 28 – September 15, 1950

CHINA

Manchuria

Yalu R.

Ch'ongch'on R.

Sea of Japan

Hamhung
Hungnam

P'yongyang

Wonsan

Imjin R.

June 25, 1950   June 25, 1950

38th Parallel

Panmunjom

Hoengsong

Seoul   Han R.
Inchon   Wonju   Samch'on
XXX   Suwon
X   Osan   Yoju
U.S.   P'yongt'aek   Chech'on

Sept. 15, 1950   Aug. 1, 1950
Ch'onan
Choch'iwon
Kum R.
Taejon   XX
XX   25
Yellow   24   U.S.
Sea   U.S.   XXXX
Naktong R.   Eighth
U.S.

Pusan
KOJE-DO

TSUSHIMA

0   50   100 mi
0   50   100 km

▬▬ U.N. forces
➤ North Korean attacks

patrols halted the movement of supplies from China and the USSR into North Korea and prevented the infiltration of troops and supplies by sea to the North Koreans south of the 38th Parallel.

U.N. air and naval superiority enabled ground forces to fight numerically superior enemy formations successfully throughout the war. Time and again, even when U.N. forces were in retreat and facing serious setbacks, tactical aircraft and naval gunfire saved the ground forces from being overwhelmed. Beyond the battlefield, supporting aircraft and ships carried war matériel to the combat zone in record-breaking time. The arrival of reinforcements and equipment around the first of August, when Eighth Army and the ROK army were backed into their defensive perimeter around Pusan, saved the whole war effort. Such was the power of air and naval superiority.

In addition to the United States, other members of the United Nations sent forces to aid South Korea. In the end fifty-three nations responded favorably even though actual contributions were slow in coming. Among those sending contingents were Great Britain, Australia, New Zealand, Canada, the Philippines, Sweden, the Netherlands, Belgium, France, Turkey, Thailand, Belgium, Greece, India, and South Africa. Some eventually sent combat forces that played significant roles fighting alongside American regiments.

While the U.N. allies marshaled forces, General Walker and his soldiers in Eighth Army shouldered the crucial task of holding on in Korea long enough to mount the amphibious counteroffensive. The North Koreans proved to be strong, numbering perhaps 80,000 troops and up to 150 tanks. Walker had four U.S. divisions at his disposal—the 7th, 24th, 25th, and the 1st Cavalry Division—but they were spread across the length of Japan and had to be transported to Korea. First he pushed the rest of the 24th Infantry Division into Korea to join Task Force Smith in blocking the enemy's main axis of advance. The division fought the North Koreans in a series of delaying actions at P'yongt'aek and Ch'onan on July 8, at Choch'iwon on the 11th, and on the Kum River between the 13th and 15th. The North Koreans pressed ahead, attacking much as they had against Task Force Smith: advancing along main roads in valleys; striking the American front with tanks, infantry, and artillery; enveloping the flanks with infantry who swarmed across the rugged hills; destroying command posts, supporting artillery, and mortars in the rear; and blocking escape with powerful roadblocks to unnerve the defenders.

When the 25th Division arrived, Walker sent it north to join the 24th in delaying the enemy. To move the 1st Cavalry Division into the country and on line with the 24th and 25th, Walker needed a delay of two days at Taejon. Dean and the 24th Division provided the two days even though they were hopelessly outnumbered. With the 1st Cavalry Division now positioned to its rear, the battered 24th gave up Taejon on July 20 and fell back to the Naktong River. Among its casualties was General Dean, who became engaged in the fight, was cut off, and escaped, only to be captured after weeks of evading the North Koreans. As the enemy continued attacking, Walker slowly gave up ground until his forces were pushed into the

"Pusan Perimeter," as it came to be known. U.S. troops occupied the western part of the defensive perimeter, while the South Koreans covered the northern part.

As reinforcements poured into Pusan and combat strength began to favor Walker, MacArthur assembled forces in Japan for his amphibious operation, now planned for mid-September. Despite the deep concern of the Joint Chiefs of Staff (JCS) for the fate of Eighth Army in the Pusan Perimeter, MacArthur was convinced that his complete superiority of air power and growing strength in tanks, artillery, and infantry would enable Eighth Army and the South Koreans to hold Pusan. His confidence was soon to be tested.

Beginning on August 5 the North Koreans launched violent, piecemeal attacks against the perimeter. Walker parried their thrusts by skillfully shifting his meager reserves between threatened points. Better organized and more savage attacks began on August 31. By this time Walker enjoyed greater combat power, particularly in tanks and artillery. By September 12, the North Korean offensive had spent itself on all fronts against Walker's skillful defense. Best of all, virtually all the enemy's units were concentrated against Pusan. The time for a counteroffensive had arrived.

The Inchon Landing

Though Inchon had the worst physical characteristics that could be imagined in an amphibious objective, MacArthur was convinced that the advantages of seizing it were worth the risk. He believed that the North Koreans, concentrated around the Pusan Perimeter in the south, would be vulnerable to an amphibious turning movement aimed so far to the north. Their vulnerability would be increased because Inchon was so close to the capital city of Seoul. Not only would the capture of Seoul be an important psychological victory, but even more important, Seoul was the intersection of most of the major roads and railroads in South Korea. To capture this intersection would force the North Koreans to surrender or escape to the mountains, abandoning all their heavy equipment.

Detractors of the plan, however, made strong arguments against Inchon as an objective. It had treacherous hydrographic conditions including nine to eleven meter tides, strong tidal currents caused by channel islands, and mud flats that stranded ships at low tide. To gain the most advantage from otherwise difficult tidal conditions, the attack had to begin on September 15. After that the weather turned cold, and rough waters made a landing more hazardous. At best, conditions required a daylight approach past the island of Wolmi-do, which if defended would be a dangerous obstacle. Even worse, a second wave could not follow the first until the next high tide, twelve hours later. Concerns about the defenders at Pusan and the risks inherent in the Inchon landing bothered the Joint Chiefs of Staff and General Walker, as well as some of MacArthur's naval and marine commanders who had to carry it out. Only MacArthur maintained a public air of confidence, so bold that it bordered on arrogance.

Beginning early in September, according to plan, naval air forces struck targets up and down the west coast of Korea; the U.S. Air Force provided general air support farther inland. As the days passed, naval air attacks converged on the Inchon area. Surface gunfire support ships took station off the harbor and began to add their weight. On September 15, Major General Edward M. Almond's X Corps made the amphibious assault at Inchon. The 1st Marine Division made the ship-to-shore landing under the cover of heavy naval gunfire and close air support. Early in the morning, marines took Wolmi-do, and on the next high tide they landed in Inchon north of the Wolmi-do causeway and then fought through the southern edge of the city. The 7th Division landed in Inchon after marines had cleared the city and then moved south of the marines to secure the south bank of the Han River and the high ground between Seoul and Suwon. Though the North Koreans were surprised, they fought fiercely to hold Seoul. Almond's X Corps nevertheless prevailed, and the city fell on September 28.

Despite the landing at Inchon, the heaviest concentration of North Koreans remained around the Pusan Perimeter, and Eighth Army had difficulty breaking out. Finally, a week after X Corps landed at Inchon, the North Koreans began to waver. On September 23, they started a general withdrawal, and Eighth Army units advanced. Within hours, the North Korean withdrawal turned into a rout as enemy soldiers sought refuge across the 38th Parallel or in the mountains of South Korea.

MacArthur's success was largely due to the confidence he had in the strategy and methods employed in the Pacific during World War II. His turning movement at Inchon completely reversed the strategic situation, giving U.N. forces the initiative for the first time. By October 1 he had expelled the aggressors from South Korea. Had nothing happened to change his mission, MacArthur could have counted this battle as a decisive victory. A change in MacArthur's mission, however, soon obliged him to continue the war with new constraints and new methods.

Changing War Aims and a Changing War

Even though the allies had achieved their strategic objectives, the war was not over. In retrospect, the turning point in the Korean War occurred when the allies decided to cross the 38th Parallel, to invade North Korea, and to pursue new strategic objectives. Conventional military wisdom demanded the destruction of the North Korean army to prevent a renewal of its aggression. On September 11—four days before the Inchon landing—President Truman approved MacArthur's pursuing the enemy into North Korea, but he adopted prudent restraints to avoid provoking the Chinese and Soviets. No U.N. troops would enter Manchuria or the USSR, only South Koreans would operate along the international border, and if the Soviets or Chinese intervened before the crossing of the 38th Parallel, the operation would be cancelled. The president also changed the national objective from saving

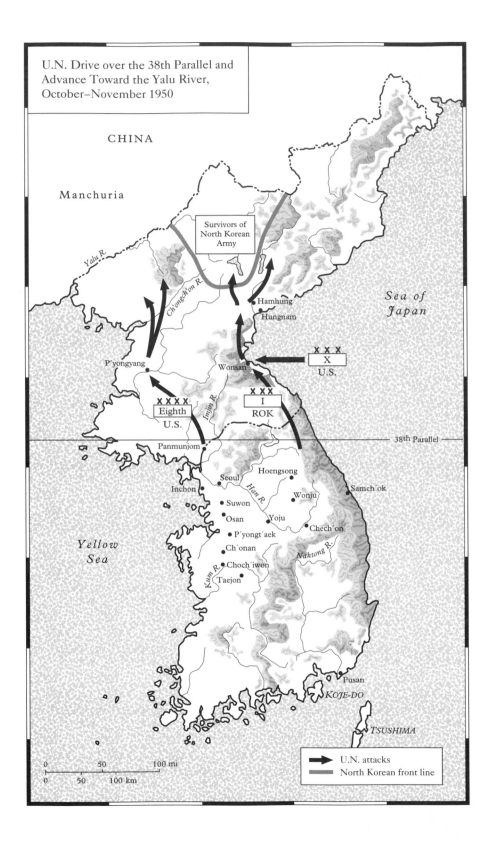

U.N. Drive over the 38th Parallel and
Advance Toward the Yalu River,
October–November 1950

CHINA

Manchuria

Yalu R.

Survivors of
North Korean
Army

Ch'ongch'on R.

Hamhung

Hungnam

Sea of
Japan

P'yongyang

Wonsan

X X X
X
U.S.

X X X
I
ROK

X X X X
Eighth
U.S.

Imjin R.

Panmunjom

38th Parallel

Hoengsong

Seoul

Inchon

Han R.

Wonju

Samch'ok

Suwon

Yoju

Osan

Chech'on

P'yongt'aek

Ch'onan

Naktong R.

Kum R.

Choch'iwon

Taejon

Yellow
Sea

Pusan

KOJE-DO

TSUSHIMA

0   50   100 mi
0   50   100 km

U.N. attacks
North Korean front line

South Korea to unifying the peninsula. After the United Nations passed a resolution calling for unification of the peninsula on October 7, MacArthur sent his forces into North Korea.

MacArthur's operations in North Korea never achieved the success of his earlier operations. He sent the exhausted Eighth Army in the main attack against the North Korean capital of P'yongyang and mounted a new amphibious assault by X Corps against the east coast port of Wonsan. Although Eighth Army advanced rapidly against light resistance, the amphibious assault by X Corps was six days late because mine sweepers ran into an elaborate mine field. Almost two weeks before the marines could land, Wonsan fell to a South Korean corps that had advanced north along the coast. After the capture of P'yongyang and Wonsan, allied troops streamed north virtually unopposed. In a conference with President Truman at Wake Island on October 15, MacArthur was optimistic about an early victory. Beginning on the 25th, however, a reinvigorated enemy struck Eighth Army and X Corps in a brief but furious counterattack. By November 2, intelligence officers had accumulated undeniable evidence from across the front that Chinese Communist Forces (CCF) from the People's Republic of China had intervened.

Before U.N. forces crossed the 38th Parallel, Chinese leaders had tried to ward off a direct confrontation with the Americans by warning them in September not to cross the 38th Parallel. American leaders interpreted these statements as bluff rather than policy. But they were wrong. Alarmed at the collapse of the North Koreans and concerned about the possible presence of American forces on China's borders, Mao Zedong—the supreme political and military leader of China—received promises of air support from Stalin and decided to intervene. Between October 14 and November 1, some 180,000 Chinese crossed the Yalu River and secretly massed in front of the U.N. Command.

Not knowing the full extent of the Chinese commitment, MacArthur believed their late October attack was a limited gesture rather than a serious intervention. After a three-week delay, while Eighth Army finally replenished its depleted supplies, the U.N. Commander resumed the advance. On November 24 the troops of Eighth Army, supported by an all-out effort by air forces, launched a rapid attack toward the Yalu River. Within twenty-four hours after Eighth Army jumped off, the Chinese struck; they aimed their main attack at the ROK II Corps on the army's right flank. Two days later the CCF hit X Corps as well. Stunned, American and South Korean units recoiled and began a long retreat that did not end until early January 1951.

Effective close air support enabled MacArthur's ground forces to escape. For days at a time, air forces were the only U.N. opposition to the advancing enemy. Timely and accurate attacks by relays of fighter bombers stopped the enemy in front of U.N. defenders. The Chinese, in their haste to close with Eighth Army in the west, abandoned their habitual concealment and marched night and day along primary and secondary roads. Casualties among men and vehicles from air attacks mounted so high that Chinese commanders had to confine road movement to nighttime, thus slowing the advance significantly. As the troops of Eighth Army put some distance

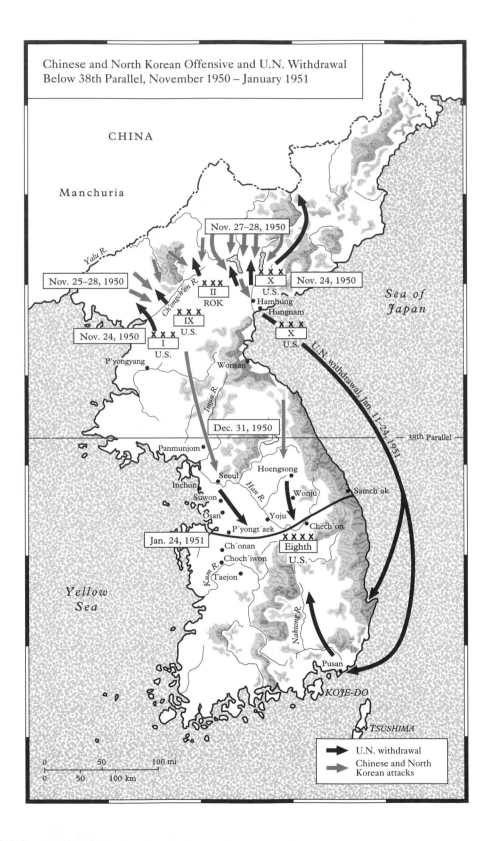

Chinese and North Korean Offensive and U.N. Withdrawal
Below 38th Parallel, November 1950 – January 1951

CHINA

Manchuria

Nov. 27–28, 1950

Yalu R.

Nov. 25–28, 1950

Ch'ongch'on R.

X X X
II
ROK

X
U.S.   Nov. 24, 1950

Hamhung

Hungnam

Nov. 24, 1950

X X X
IX
U.S.

X X X
I
U.S.

X X X
X
U.S.

P'yongyang

Wonsan

Imjin R.

U.N. withdrawal, Jan. 11-24, 1951

Sea of
Japan

Dec. 31, 1950

38th Parallel

Panmunjom

Hoengsong

Inchon

Seoul

Han R.

Wonju

Samch'ok

Suwon

Osan

Yoju

Chech'on

P'yongt'aek

Jan. 24, 1951

X X X X
Eighth
U.S.

Ch'onan

Choch'iwon

Kum R.

Taejon

Yellow
Sea

Naktong R.

Pusan

KOJE-DO

TSUSHIMA

0   50   100 mi
0   50   100 km

U.N. withdrawal
Chinese and North
Korean attacks

between themselves and the Chinese, the air forces attacked and destroyed Chinese supplies and equipment. Then in mid-December FEAF launched a coordinated interdiction campaign against railway yards and bridges, highway bridges, tunnels, and supply dumps. Eighth Army owed its survival and subsequent resurgence in January 1951 to overwhelming air support during its retreat.

Defeat in North Korea forced the United Nations to reexamine its war aims in light of Chinese involvement. MacArthur quickly charged that he was facing "an entirely new war" and that the strategy for war against North Korea did not apply in a war against China. MacArthur wanted more forces and a broader charter to retaliate against the Chinese. But even in the darkest days before the Inchon landing, American leaders believed that restraint was necessary to avoid widening the war. Within the broader scope of the Cold War, Europe remained the main concern of American policy, not Asia; attacks on China could bring on Soviet involvement and even expand the war to Europe. MacArthur's proposals to increase his forces and to retaliate against the Chinese were therefore completely at odds with those of his president and other U.N. leaders.

During the first week of December, when reports from the front were grim, President Truman met Prime Minister Clement R. Attlee of the United Kingdom in Washington. Attlee had flown to the United States after Truman had hinted publicly that atomic weapons might be used in Korea. Speaking for some other U.N. members, he questioned American direction

Chinese soldiers proved tough, skillful, and numerous. To neutralize U.N. advantages in fire power, they advanced by stealth and infiltration and often attacked at night while making wild bugle calls and barbaric screams. They steadily increased their artillery, firing a record of more than 93,000 rounds on one day in October 1952.

of the war. His principal interest was to induce the Chinese to stop fighting and withdraw. Truman entered the talks committed to sticking it out in Korea and even continuing the war against China if forced off the peninsula. Initially the two allies could not have been farther apart. After four days of intense discussions, however, the two reached a compromise solution: they would continue to fight side by side in Korea, find a line and hold it, and wait for an opportunity to negotiate an end to the fighting from a position of military strength. Moreover, they reaffirmed their commitment to "Europe first" in the face of Soviet hostility toward NATO. In essence the decision to unify Korea was abrogated and a new war aim adopted.

Significantly, the most immediate military effect of the talks was to prevent MacArthur from exacting revenge for his humiliating defeat. The Joint Chiefs limited his reinforcements to replacements, shifted the priority of military resources to strengthening NATO forces, and wrote a new directive for MacArthur that required him to defend in Korea as far to the north as possible. MacArthur was outraged. He disagreed with giving priority to Europe at the expense of the shooting war in Korea. He smoldered at the thought of going on the strategic defensive and fought determinedly against the new directive. Nevertheless, on January 12, 1951, the JCS sent him the final version of the order to conduct a strategic defensive. In essence, U.N. forces had a new war aim designed to bring about a negotiated settlement.

Ridgway's War

Just two days before Christmas in 1950, the command of Eighth Army passed to Lieutenant General Matthew B. Ridgway after General Walker died when a Korean truck hit his jeep. Ridgway arrived at his new headquarters determined to halt the retreat and to attack north as soon as possible. Somehow he had to reunite X Corps with Eighth Army, stop the retreat, and turn the army around. He also had to revive the fighting spirit of his troops.

General Douglas MacArthur and General Matthew B. Ridgway. Ridgway carefully tailored operations to correct the problems of Eighth Army. His self-assurance and his success soon restored the confidence of Eighth Army.

One of the immediate problems he faced was the separation of X Corps in Hungnam on the east coast from Eighth Army on the western flank. As Eighth Army fell back, the gap between the two forces increased, and on December 13, X Corps was evacuated by sea from Hungnam. As Eighth Army continued falling back, Ridgway's American I and IX Corps held the western sector, while a ROK Corps held the eastern end of the line. Two other ROK corps stretched themselves over the extended mountainous center. Unfortunately for the U.N. forces, Chinese and North Korean units could easily penetrate the center in a southwesterly direction and force Eighth Army to move farther south to avoid being trapped in the Seoul area by having its right flank enveloped or turned. The difficulties of this tactical situation had plagued Walker, and now, even as FEAF conducted a furious five-day air assault to halt the enemy's advance, a Chinese and North Korean penetration forced Ridgway to give up Seoul and fall below a line between Osan and Samch'ok (on the east coast).

After Ridgway pulled back, his front-line units reported only light contact with the enemy, leading him to conclude that Chinese units were unable to maintain pressure. Sensing the opportunity to turn on the Chinese, Ridgway halted on a line from P'yongt'aek in the west to Samch'ok on the east coast. When American divisions, withdrawn from Hungnam with X Corps, moved up to thicken the line in the lightly held center, Ridgway ordered his forces to patrol north and find the enemy. His offensive campaign began with an attack by the tank-supported 27th Regimental Combat Team on January 15. He next sent IX Corps units toward Inchon on the 22nd. An attack by I and IX Corps units then aimed north of Suwon and Yoju toward the Han River on the 25th. By February 10, I Corps had reached the Han River and captured Inchon and Kimp'o Airfield near Seoul.

Ridgway now looked to X Corps in the central sector to drive north against Wonju and Hoengsong. Although X Corps enjoyed early success, two CCF armies and a North Korean corps attacked south through gaps in the ROK sector to the east. They broke through three ROK divisions and forced X Corps to withdraw to Wonju. As the enemy attempted once again to drive southwest, bitter fighting raged around Wonju and Chip'yongni, the southern and northern shoulders of the penetration. Ridgway filled the gap between the two towns, defenders held the shoulders by heroic sacrifice, and the U.N. command defeated the enemy attack.

In what amounted to a renewal of his previous attack, Ridgway sent IX and X Corps north in Operation "Killer" on February 21. After Chinese and North Korean pressure subsided along the new front stretching from Chip'yongni southeastward through Wonju to Chech'on, extensive patrolling by U.N. forces disclosed that the enemy was pulling back from the salient created by their attack. Patrols reported bits of information that painted a fairly convincing picture of an army badly in need of reorganization and resupply. Though intelligence officers could not account for all the enemy forces in Korea, they nonetheless identified five Chinese armies and three North Korean corps in front of the allies. Ridgway judged the potential gains of a quick offensive to be worth the risks of an incomplete intelligence picture. He believed a rapid resumption of the U.N. offensive would take

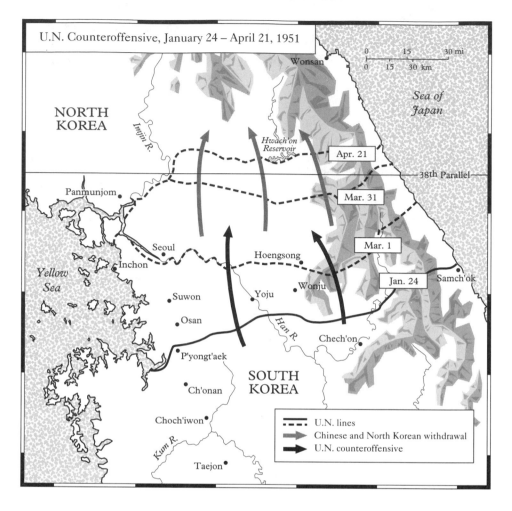

advantage of the weakened condition of the Chinese and North Korean soldiers and inflict a large number of casualties.

Ridgway's plan included an objective line known as Arizona, that ran from Yangp'yong on the Han River, to north of Chip'yongni and Wonju, and then to Kangnung on the east coast. Line Arizona was about twenty kilometers north of the U.N. front lines. The main effort would move along two axes of advance, the westernmost by U.S. IX Corps, aiming from Wonju north to Hoengsong. In the eastern sector, U.S. X Corps was to attack north to a road junction just south of Line Arizona and then attack west across the corps front to block further enemy withdrawal. The west flank of the attack was to be protected by U.S. I Corps and the east flank by the ROK III Corps. In all, eight American and ROK divisions and a British brigade would comprise the attacking force, and the rest of the army would support. The operation was code-named Killer to emphasize its main purpose.

Ridgway wanted Eighth Army units to learn from the mistakes of previous operations. He warned corps commanders to maintain tight contact between adjacent frontline units and to avoid the gaps that had doomed

South Koreans poured forth by the thousands to repel the invaders, but they initially performed poorly because of inexperienced leaders and inadequate training. Not until entire ROK divisions were withdrawn from the lines and sent through training programs did they become—to use Ridgway's words—"first rate fighting forces."

the previous attack. He wanted units to advance along the high ground and envelope enemy positions rather than assault them frontally. As was his custom in Korea, Ridgway saw the ground advance as a series of short, methodical steps, controlled by phase lines and characterized by heavy air and artillery fire on enemy positions before the infantry advanced.

Operation Killer began precisely as planned before dawn on February 21, except for one unforeseeable event. Up to that day, snow had covered the ground, roads were frozen hard, and rivers and streams were covered with thick ice. On the 21st, the temperature soared to 50 degrees Fahrenheit and remained above freezing during daylight for the rest of the month. The falling snow became rain, the ground thawed, roads turned into deep mud, melting snow filled streambeds, and breaking ice rushed downstream destroying bridges and making fords impassable. Each night the surface froze again, only to melt at sunup. Thus Operation Killer, conceived as a rapid strike to cut off enemy forces, became a plodding advance at a speed dictated by nature.

U.N. forces advanced toward Line Arizona against scattered delaying forces left behind by the enemy. By the end of February, Ridgway had made significant gains but could not catch the enemy. As the two corps labored forward, rain, mud, and high water became the real enemies. The 1st Marine Division of IX Corps finally reached the hills overlooking Hoengsong, and the 7th Infantry Division of X Corps turned west to begin sweeping across the corps front. By March 6 all the objectives had been achieved. Though the infantry of Eighth Army never closed decisively with the enemy, forward units found heavy casualties littering the hills and buried in shallow graves; most were attributable to intense artillery fire and close air support.

On March 7, Ridgway launched another carefully controlled attack. When U.S. forces crossed the Han River east of Seoul, the CCF abandoned the capital; allied forces continued moving north. In early April the U.N. advance slowed as units prepared strong defensive positions in anticipation of an enemy counteroffensive. Surprisingly, the shock came not from the enemy as expected but from Washington when Truman dismissed MacArthur.

The Relief of MacArthur

One way to view MacArthur's relief is to consider it as the last step necessary to adapt the war effort to the new war aims. MacArthur bristled under the new directive requiring him to defend South Korea rather than rebuild an offensive capability to unify the peninsula. With his outrage so close to the surface, it was only a matter of time before he gave the president good reason to dismiss him.

MacArthur had been a difficult subordinate. He had clashed with Truman over U.S. policy toward Formosa early in the war and complained about the restrictions placed on his forces and his freedom to wage the war. Occasionally he had been uncommunicative with the JCS. Then after the retreat of Eighth Army, he publicly suggested that the policies of the Truman administration had been responsible for the defeat. Truman was angered by this charge, and on December 6, 1950, he published an executive order— aimed at MacArthur—requiring all government officials to clear their public statements on foreign and military policy with the administration. Mac-Arthur then objected to the JCS directive of January 12, 1951, written to implement the Truman-Attlee agreements. By requiring MacArthur to go on the defensive, that directive squelched any hope of unifying the peninsula and defeating the Chinese and North Koreans. In February and again in March, MacArthur called for a new strategy, presumably one that would permit him to attack the Chinese in their sanctuary north of the Yalu River.

As Ridgway neared the 38th Parallel again, a position of military strength seemed near at hand. President Truman took advantage of Ridgway's success to invite the Communists to negotiate a cease-fire. After reading the text of Truman's proposed message, MacArthur broadcast a bellicose ultimatum to the enemy commander undermining the president's plan. Truman was furious; MacArthur had preempted presidential prerogative, confused friends and enemies alike about who was directing the war, and directly challenged the president's authority as commander-in-chief. As Truman pondered how to handle the problem, Congressman Joseph W. Martin, Minority (Republican) Leader of the House of Representatives, released the contents of a letter from MacArthur in which the general repeated his criticism of the administration. The next day Truman began the process that was to end with MacArthur's relief from command on April 11.

Ending the War: Politics as War

After MacArthur's relief, Ridgway took his place as Commander-in-Chief, Far East and CINCUNC. Lieutenant General James A. Van Fleet, an experienced and successful World War II combat leader, took command of the Eighth Army. On April 22, as Van Fleet's army edged north, the CCF opened the expected general offensive, aiming their main attack toward Seoul in the west. The Chinese, numbering almost a half-million men, drove the U.N. defenders south. Followed closely by this formidable force, Van Fleet had to withdraw once again below the 38th Parallel, finally halting a bare eight kilometers north of Seoul.

On May 10 the Chinese jumped off again, this time concentrating seven armies in their main effort in the east-central and eastern sector of the U.N. line. They drove X Corps and two ROK corps south of the 38th Parallel

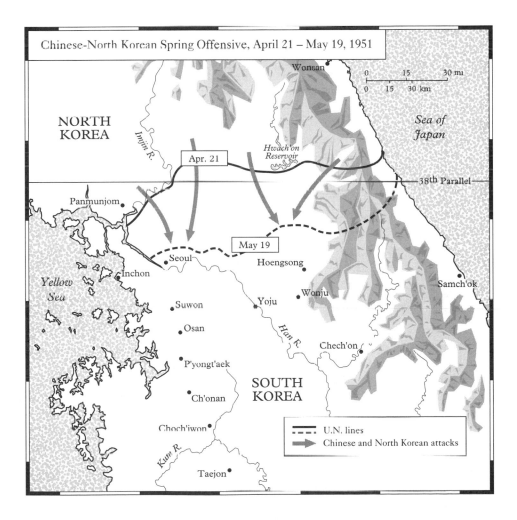

Chinese-North Korean Spring Offensive, April 21 – May 19, 1951

but paid a heavy price for thinning their front in the west. Taking advantage of the Chinese concentration in the east, Van Fleet attacked suddenly in the west, north of Seoul. The rest of the Eighth Army attacked to the front. The effect was dramatic; surprised CCF units pulled back, suffering their heaviest casualties of the war, and by the end of May found themselves retreating into North Korea. By mid-June 1951, U.N. forces had regained a line, for the most part north of the 38th Parallel. There they remained. The year-long mobile phase of the Korean War had ended, and a strange war in which most battles were fought over the control of outposts between front lines had begun. The outpost war would continue for the next two years.

Negotiations and Stalemate

Regardless of U.N. success on the battlefield, ending the war turned out to be a maddeningly long process. U.S. planners knew that because of the Truman-Attlee agreement, the war would probably not end in a conventional victory. Obtaining a cease-fire had become an implicit war aim of the United Nations. Moreover, Chinese and North Korean commanders needed a respite from the heavy casualties sustained in Van Fleet's recent offensive. Consequently both sides agreed in late June 1951 to begin negotiations. The subsequent negotiations were initially hampered by haggling over matters of protocol and the selection of a truly neutral site. On July 26, 1951, the two sides finally agreed on an agenda containing four major points: fixing a demarcation line and demilitarized zone, supervising the truce, handling prisoners of war, and making recommendations to the governments involved in the war. With an agenda in hand, negotiators at Panmunjom began the lengthy process of debating each item. Meanwhile, the fighting continued.

After receiving reinforcements in early summer, Van Fleet conducted limited attacks to strengthen his defensive line and keep pressure on the Communists. All across the front, divisions sent combat teams forward to capture key terrain features. By the end of October, Van Fleet had a new and more commanding line that provided tactical advantage to Eighth Army. He wanted to continue his attacks, but Ridgway directed him to stop and carry on an "active defense." At stake was the success of negotiations aimed at establishing a demarcation line.

On November 17 the U.N. delegation presented the Communists with a proposal to designate the current line of contact as the demarcation line, provided that all remaining agenda items were resolved within thirty days. The allies believed this proposal would make possible an early resolution of differences and a quick end to the war. But it also provided the Communists a windfall opportunity, for they could negotiate the agenda items while strengthening their defensive positions. At the end of the thirty days, the U.N. would have no agreement and would face a defensive zone too formidable to crack with the forces at hand. The communist negotiators accepted the proposal on November 27; on December 27 the United Nations faced an enemy defensive line so deeply dug in that both sides had to accept a stalemate. From that moment on, the battlefield regressed to a static kind of war, reminiscent of World War I.

As ground action waned, the United Nations turned to powerful air and naval arms for military pressure to support its negotiating team. In August 1951, air, naval, and marine commanders concentrated all available aircraft on the interdiction of Communist-controlled bridges, highways, railroad lines and yards, and supply points. Most of the air assets took part in Operation "Strangle," a road and rail-cutting scheme designed to slow down the southward movement of enemy troops and matériel. Operation "Saturate," which followed Strangle, placed even greater emphasis on the railway-interdiction effort. During the day, fighter-bombers raked the railroad lines; at night, B-26s scoured the countryside for trucks. Approximately ninety-six fighter sorties a day continued to provide close air support to the ground war. Despite the heavy bombing, enemy work details devised ingenious ways to repair the railroad overnight. The North Korean Railroad Bureau employed three brigades full time on railroad repair and, at the height of the air campaign, used as many as 500,000 soldiers and civilians to keep the lines open. The sustained bombing campaign also forced the communist air forces out of their Manchurian sanctuary in an attempt to stop interdiction of roads and rail lines. Beginning in September 1951, communist MiG-15s became more aggressive and more numerous—as many as ninety at a time entered North Korean airspace—bringing an end to the allies' uncontested control of the air. When communist fighters chose to challenge U.N. aircraft, however, they suffered heavy losses.

Beginning in May 1952, the United Nations used air power more forcefully to place greater pressure on the Communists. Despite numerous attacks on supply centers, transportation networks, and personnel, neither the North Koreans nor the Chinese acceded to the U.N. armistice terms; on the contrary, both became more intransigent and refused to yield to such pressure. As a result, aerial bombing added to the Communists' difficulties but it did not succeed in driving them from the war.

Achieving a Cease-Fire

After the winter of 1951–1952, the war in Korea became a seemingly endless succession of violent fire fights, most of them at night, to gain or maintain control of hills that were a little higher and ridges that were a bit straighter. Sharp fighting occurred over places with such names as Pork Chop Hill, Sniper's Ridge, Old Baldy, T-Bone, White Horse, and a hundred other hilltops between the two armies. In some cases, both sides piled on reinforcements until "terrain grabs" turned into prolonged and bloody fights. All of them, no matter how large the forces engaged, were deadly encounters designed to provide leverage for one side or the other in the protracted political war going on at Panmunjom. In an era when technology provided great mobility, tactical warfare in Korea went through a regression that can be explained only in terms of its close relationships to the negotiations. Constant pressure was its purpose, not victory on the battlefield. Pressure in such a stalemated war proved difficult for a democracy to maintain.

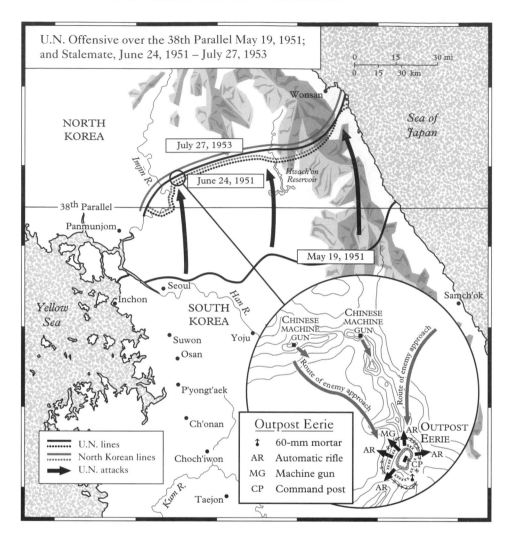

Outpost Eerie, a battle fought in March 1952, is a good example of a small-unit action typical of the fighting during the stalemate. Eerie was located on the southernmost hilltop on a T-bone shaped complex of ridges and hills. The Chinese held the top of the "T," about 1.5 kilometers to the north of Eerie. The Americans on Outpost Eerie came from Company K, 179th Infantry Regiment, 45th Infantry Division. They normally occupied the hill with two rifle squads, a light machine gun, a 60-mm mortar, and a platoon command group. Supporting fires came from .50-caliber machine guns on the main line of resistance, mortars from the K Company weapons platoon, and artillery from a direct-support battalion. To strengthen their position, the Americans on Eerie dug trenches, built bunkers, and encircled their position with three barbed-wire fences.

Lieutenant Omer Manley's 3rd Platoon of Company K occupied the outpost on March 21. At about 2300 hours, Manley received reports of the Chinese setting up a machine gun on a hill about 600 meters from Eerie. An

American patrol also encountered a platoon-sized enemy formation moving south. After two trip flares went off, the Chinese poured machine-gun fire onto the American position and began trying to break through the wire in two places. Lieutenant Manley called for artillery support and illuminating rounds, while his soldiers fired at the oncoming Chinese. By 0100 hours, the Americans had run out of illuminating rounds, and the Chinese had breached the wire. The Chinese seized the north end of the outpost and advanced across the top of the bunkers. The Americans were pushed to the southern end of the position and soon ran out of ammunition. Manley disappeared after throwing his empty carbine at a Chinese soldier.

At 0120 hours, communications with Eerie ended, and the commander of Company K called for artillery concentrations directly on the outpost. As soon as the artillery firing began, the Chinese withdrew. Company K then advanced to clear the outpost and search for survivors. Of the twenty-six men in Eerie, eight were dead, four wounded, and two missing. Manley could not be found. After discovering thirty-one enemy bodies inside and around the position, Company K repaired the defenses of the outpost and prepared to defend it against the next attack.

As fights such as the one at Outpost Eerie continued nightly, negotiators in Panmunjom plodded through the remaining agenda items. Results came slowly. One extremely contentious issue pertained to the supervision of the armistice agreement. Ridgway wanted an armistice commission with free access to all of Korea and an agreement to ban reinforcement of men and matériel. The Communists countered with a proposal that denied free access and contained no provision for reinforcements or replacements of any kind. Finally a compromise emerged that permitted rotation of 35,000 troops and supplies each month through specified ports of entry. Both sides accepted Swedish, Swiss, Polish, and Czech membership on an armistice commission. The last agenda item on political recommendations was settled quickly; both sides called for a conference to convene three months after a cease-fire. All political issues not settled during the negotiations would be discussed at that conference.

What to do about prisoners of war became the final obstacle to an agreement to end the war. Fearing mistreatment by the Communists, the U.N. Command wanted prisoners to decide for themselves whether or not they would return home. The Communists insisted on forced repatriation as was called for in the Geneva Convention. To restore movement to the talks, the U.N. delegation proposed that prisoners be polled by the International Red Cross about where they wanted to go. The Chinese and North Koreans agreed. When the Red Cross made interim results of the screening known early in April 1952, the data surprised everyone. Of 132,000 Chinese and North Korean prisoners screened, only 54,000 North Koreans and 5,100 Chinese wanted to go home. The communist delegation was incredulous and accused the United Nations of influencing the poll. From that moment on, negotiations bogged down on the prisoner-of-war issue.

At about this same time, May 1952, General Ridgway left Tokyo to become Supreme Allied Commander, Europe. General Mark Clark, who

A U.S. rifle squad attacks. As the stalemate continued, fighting often degenerated into clashes between patrols. Eighth Army sometimes conducted raids by concentrating artillery and air strikes and then sending in small ground forces against the enemy.

had made his reputation during World War II in Italy, replaced Ridgway as CINCUNC. Ridgway's last problem, and Clark's first, was to settle an uprising by hard-core prisoners on Koje-do, an island off the coast of South Korea. In an attempt to derail screening of all prisoners, leaders inside the prisons deliberately provoked their guards. Their crowning success was capturing the camp commander in an unguarded moment and forcing him to terminate forcible screening and to negotiate for humane treatment of prisoners. The Communists trumpeted acceptance of these terms as an admission of inhumane treatment and tampering with the Red Cross poll. Clark was furious and relieved the camp commander. After being reinforced with combat troops, the new camp commander stormed the compounds with tank-infantry teams and isolated the hard-core communist leaders in separate compounds.

The Koje-do incident hurt the negotiating position of the U.N. delegation. Friends, enemies, and neutrals decried the violent suppression of the prisoners, and communist negotiators became intractable on the prisoner-of-war issue. Over the summer of 1952, the language of negotiation became more abusive and inflammatory. Clark had had enough. In exasperation, he ordered the U.N. delegation to walk out of Panmunjom on October 8. With no one to refute their assertions, the Communists gained a major political victory and hammered away at U.N. treatment of prisoners and alleged U.N. violations of the neutral zones surrounding the negotiating site.

Early in 1953 the newly elected president, Dwight D. Eisenhower, increased pressure on the Communists. He believed that the Truman strategy was the only practical one but also believed that something had to be done to give the Communists an incentive to reach agreement. He permitted the air force to bomb dams in North Korea and to flood the countryside. He instructed the JCS to prepare plans for more intensive and mobile battles should negotiations break down. He deployed atomic delivery aircraft to the Far East and ordered them to train for low-level attacks with atomic bombs. And he let it be known that the United States was prepared to renew the war at a higher level unless progress was made at Panmunjom. As the Americans signaled their intentions to expand the war, the death of Joseph Stalin on March 5, 1953, brought on a deadly power struggle in the Kremlin that probably focused Soviet leaders' attention on internal problems rather than a prolonged war. With economic problems adding to political and military concerns, communist leaders in the Soviet Union, China, and North Korea had sufficient reasons to question the continuation of the war.

On March 28, 1953, China and North Korea agreed to an exchange of sick and wounded prisoners and suggested that this might lead to settlement of the entire prisoner-of-war issue and a cease-fire. On April 20, 684 Americans returned to U.N. control and 5,194 North Koreans, 1,030

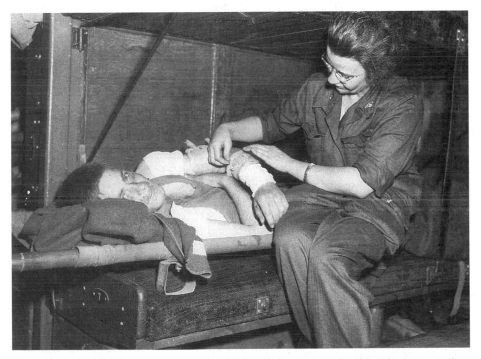

An army nurse providing care to a soldier. With its helicopters, radio dispatch system, and treatment facilities, the Mobile Army Surgical Hospital (MASH) provided better medical care than what had been available in previous wars.

Chinese, and 447 civilians went over to the communist authorities. On April 26, negotiating sessions resumed at Panmunjom. In the following months, negotiators agreed that repatriation was to be offered to all prisoners and that those who chose not to return home were to be turned over to a neutral commission that would hold them for interview by their respective countrymen before releasing them.

While the United Nations worked diligently toward an armistice, Syngman Rhee, the South Korean president, became obstructive; he had long demanded the withdrawal of the Chinese from the Korean peninsula and the disarming of the North Korean army. On the night of June 18, Rhee ordered his guards on the prisons to release the friendly North Koreans. During the hours of darkness, 25,000 prisoners disappeared, absorbed into South Korean society. Though Eisenhower was outraged, he convinced Rhee not to undermine the armistice.

As the final details of the agreement were negotiated, the Communists sought one last military advantage. Their goal was to mount an offensive that would end at the same time that the truce agreement was signed, thus giving the illusion of a peaceful settlement following a communist victory. They sought to straighten the line in front of the ROK II Corps. Terrain objectives were limited to outpost hills in adjacent American sectors. The attacks began against the ROK II Corps on June 10, and by June 16 the U.N. line had been pushed 4,000 meters south. Eighth Army reinforced the ROK II Corps sector for a counterattack, but it was too late. Although some ground was recovered, fighting slackened as commanders of the contending armies prepared to sign the truce.

On July 27, 1953, Mark Clark signed the armistice documents to end the fighting in the Korean War.

✳   ✳   ✳   ✳

For a war intended to be limited, the Korean War exacted a staggering human toll. Although CCF and North Korean casualties are unknown, estimates of total losses range between 1.5 and 2 million, plus perhaps 1 million civilians. The U.N. Command suffered a total of 88,000 killed, of whom 23,300 were American. Total casualties for the U.N. (killed, wounded, missing) were 459,360; of these 300,000 were South Korean. For decades after the war, the two armies continued watching each other over the demilitarized zone and waiting for the day when fighting might begin again.

Until the outbreak of the Korean War, the Cold War had been waged mainly with economic, political, and psychological weapons. War in Korea, however, redefined the conflict between the United States and the Soviet Union as a much more dangerous contest in the nuclear age. Virtually all international incidents thereafter became crises that had the potential for global consequences. No inhabited region of the world was exempt. The antagonists and their allies in NATO and the Warsaw Pact armed themselves and enlisted other states to take sides.

Not surprisingly, after five years of minimal spending for defense, the Korean War also changed the military policy of the United States. Out went austerity as big defense budgets permanently rearmed American as well as allied forces. The war increased the number of U.S. military forces stationed overseas, particularly in Europe. It fostered a peacetime selective service system, the largest standing military force in the nation's history, and the growth of an unprecedented military-scientific-industrial alliance that greatly influenced the world economy thereafter. And it created effective military readiness aimed at going to war with little or no warning.

Perhaps most important in the history of warfare, Korea became a model for limited war and demonstrated alternative ways of gaining national objectives without resorting to atomic war. For the United States, it had been a war limited in scope and violence and fought for alliance objectives. For the communist forces, it had been a war that relied on prolonged armistice negotiations to gain what could not be gained on the battlefield. Thus the significance of the Korean War is less about changes in the technical methods of waging war than about the difficulties and complexities of attaining political goals through the use of military force.

SUGGESTED READINGS

Appleman, Roy E. *South to the Naktong, North to the Yalu, June-November 1950* (Washington, D. C.: Government Printing Office, 1961).

Clark, Mark W. *From the Danube to the Yalu* (New York: Harper, 1954).

Collins, J. Lawton. *War in Peacetime: The History and Lessons of Korea* (Boston: Houghton Mifflin, 1969).

Foot, Rosemary. *A Substitute for Victory: The Politics of Peacemaking at the Korean Armistice Talks* (Ithaca, N.Y.: Cornell University Press, 1990).

Futrell, Robert F. *The United States Air Force in Korea, 1950-1953* (Washington, D.C.: Government Printing Office, 1983).

Goodrich, Leland M. *Korea: A Study of U.S. Policy in the United Nations* (New York: Council on Foreign Relations, 1956).

Goulden, Joseph C. *Korea: The Untold Story of the War* (New York: Times Books, 1982).

Hermes, Walter G. *Truce Tent and Fighting Front* (Washington, D.C.: Government Printing Office, 1966).

Kaufman, Burton I. *The Korean War: Challenges in Crisis, Credibility, and Command* (New York: Knopf, 1986).

Marshall, S. L. A. *The River and the Gauntlet* (New York: Morrow, 1953).

Mossman, Billy C. *Ebb and Flow, November 1950–July 1951* (Washington, D.C.: Government Printing Office, 1990).

Rees, David. *Korea: The Limited War* (New York: St. Martin's Press, 1964).

Ridgway, Matthew B. *The Korean War* (Garden City, N.Y.: Doubleday, 1967).

Schnabel, James F. *Policy and Direction, The First Year* (Washington, D.C.: Government Printing Office, 1972).

21

THE VIETNAM WAR, 1961–1975: REVOLUTIONARY AND CONVENTIONAL WARFARE IN AN ERA OF LIMITED WAR

Vietnam and "People's War"

The United States:
Counterinsurgency
and Limited War

Escalation and Stalemate,
1965–1968

The Tet Offensive, 1968

Fighting While Negotiating,
1968–1975

$\mathbb{T}$he war in Vietnam represented a clash between two very different types of warfare. Fought on the Indochinese peninsula during the years 1961–1975, a direct offshoot of the Cold War, it matched the "revolutionary war" techniques of North Vietnam and the National Liberation Front of South Vietnam (NLF) insurgents against the limited war doctrines and modern, high-technology conventional forces of the United States and its South Vietnamese ally. Militarily, the two sides fought to a prolonged and bloody stalemate. As a consequence, the political dimensions of the war ultimately proved decisive. As long as the North Vietnamese and NLF did not lose, they won, and they successfully employed a protracted war strategy to take advantage of American impatience. Unwilling to expand the war to win in the traditional sense, the United States could do no better than a stalemate, and the war's increasing unpopularity at home eventually forced a U.S. military withdrawal. The United States' military power had never been able to compensate for the political weakness of its client government, and when the United States withdrew, the Saigon regime

633

collapsed in the face of a full-scale North Vietnamese invasion. Whether the war validated North Vietnam's revolutionary war doctrines remains very much in doubt in light of the end of the Cold War. It did prove the difficulty of fighting a limited war in the Cold War setting, and it provoked a major reconsideration of U.S. military doctrine, the outcome of which also remains quite uncertain.

Vietnam and "People's War"

During their thirty-year war against France and the United States the Vietnamese applied a concept variously labeled "People's War" or "Revolutionary War." The Vietnamese approach to warfare was multifaceted, combining military, political, and diplomatic measures in a tightly integrated manner. Even in the military realm, it involved guerrilla warfare as well as more conventional methods. The Vietnamese relied especially on a mobilized citizenry and the application of a protracted war strategy, and in both their wars with France and the United States, they counted on wearing down less patient enemies fighting unpopular wars far from their shores.

A Martial Tradition

The Vietnamese drew on a rich military tradition that was an essential part of their heritage. For roughly one thousand years, the land of Nam Viet (later Vietnam) was the southernmost province of China. During much of that time, the Vietnamese had fiercely resisted the domination of their larger northern neighbor. Perhaps the most famous of Vietnamese heroes, the Trung sisters, mounted elephants to lead the first major rebellion against a much superior Chinese force and, when defeated, drowned themselves in a lake in Hanoi. Another woman, Trieu Au, led yet another unsuccessful revolt in 248 A.D. In the tenth century the Vietnamese won their independence by luring an attacking Chinese fleet into a river bed in which they had planted iron-tipped spikes, impaling the ships of the invaders.

In the thirteenth century, the Vietnamese repulsed the legendary Mongol warrior Kublai Khan three times. Using the inhospitable climate and terrain to advantage, their leader, Tran Hung Dao, pioneered methods of guerrilla warfare later used against the French and Americans, avoiding head-on engagements and employing hit-and-run tactics to exhaust a stronger enemy. In his *Essential Summary of Military Arts*, Dao observed that "The enemy must fight his battles far from his home base for a long time. . . . We must further weaken him by drawing him into protracted campaigns. Once his initial dash is broken, it will be easier to destroy him." In the climactic battle against the Mongols in the Red River Valley in 1287, the Vietnamese defeated three hundred thousand enemy troops. Finally, in 1426, another legendary figure, Le Loi, defeated the Chinese and secured independence for Vietnam.

The years of resistance to China and the victories over the Mongols comprise an essential part of Vietnamese folklore. "Through the millennia of their history the Vietnamese people have struggled incessantly against foreign invaders . . . in great battles that took place one century after another," a contemporary history observes. In their own mythology, the Vietnamese repeatedly win against stronger enemies through cleverness, ingenuity, and virtue, and because of their ability to mobilize all the people, to make every citizen a soldier. "We fight and win . . . because we are . . . moral, loyal, patient, strong, indomitable, filled with compassion," Communist party chief Le Duan told soldiers during the American war. "We have been fighting for our independence for four thousand years," Premier Pham Van Dong warned the Americans through two French emissaries in 1967. "We have defeated the Mongols three times. The United States Army, strong as it is, is not as terrifying as Genghis [sic] Khan."

Although it is less celebrated by the Vietnamese, expansion to the south forms as important a part of their military heritage as resistance to northern invaders. After defeating the Mongols, they moved southward to conquer the kingdom of Champa and after nearly two centuries of fighting destroyed its capital of Indrapura and killed 40,000 people. National unity was always a fragile matter, however, and civil war continued until the French imposed peace on Vietnam through colonization.

Ironically in view of their long history of conflict, the Vietnamese approach to warfare also drew heavily on Chinese models, especially the ideas developed by Mao Zedong during the Chinese civil war. Maoist doctrine emphasized the formation of a broad united front comprised of all elements of the population with the goal of national liberation, recognized the equal importance of political and military struggle, and relied on protracted war to exhaust stronger enemies.

Mao's classic *On Protracted War* set forth three stages of revolutionary warfare. In the first, essentially defensive stage, the revolutionary force was to withdraw, hide from the enemy, and mount sporadic hit-and-run attacks, the main goal being survival. During this phase, the focus was on revolutionary activity among the people to establish a secure base for future operations. Terrain was to be exchanged for time. Second came a stage of equilibrium, when caution began to give way to boldness and the defensive to the offensive. The guerrillas in this stage would extend their hold across the countryside and force the enemy to retreat into shrinking urban enclaves. Battles were larger, more frequent, and more conventional. The third and final stage of Maoist protracted warfare was the counteroffensive, when politics gave way to military operations and guerrilla warfare to full-scale conventional war.

The First Indochina War, 1946–1954

The three-decade struggle for Indochina began September 2, 1945, when the charismatic nationalist leader Ho Chi Minh declared the independence of Vietnam. The Vietnamese revolution was in many ways the personal

During World War II, Nguyen Ai Quoc changed his name to Ho Chi Minh ("he who enlightens") to conceal his communist background from his Chinese sponsors in the war against the Japanese. Beginning in spring 1945, Americans from the Office of Strategic Services served at Ho's headquarters in an effort to hasten the defeat of the Japanese.

creation of Ho Chi Minh. Born in the province of Nghe An, the cradle of Vietnamese revolutionaries, Ho settled in France and after World War I joined the French Communist Party. During the 1920s and 1930s, he served as a party functionary and revolutionary organizer in the Soviet Union, China, and Thailand. He returned to Vietnam in 1940 to found the Vietminh (League for the Independence of Vietnam) and organize yet another Vietnamese revolution against outside control. For a brief period after World War II, Ho attempted to negotiate a settlement with the colonial power, France, but the two sides could not agree on the most basic issues. In November 1946 mounting tensions sparked a war that in its various phases would last for nearly thirty years.

In their revolutionary war against France, the Vietnamese adapted Maoist doctrine to their own needs and conditions. Space was at a premium in Vietnam, and instead of trading terrain for time, as Mao had proposed, the Communist-led Vietminh rebels emphasized in the first stage organization and clandestine activity. From small cells of three to five people, they constructed "liberated areas." Avoiding pitched battles, they cultivated support among the people and where feasible ambushed exposed enemy forces. The Vietnamese also placed greater emphasis than Mao on external forces, increasingly relying on moral and material support from the Soviet Union and after 1949 from Mao's China. Perhaps even more important, public opinion in France was deemed crucial in influencing French policy, and the Vietnamese calculated that the longer the war lasted the more support would be generated for their cause. Given these factors, party theoretician Truong Chinh reasoned, absolute military superiority might not be necessary to launch the third and climactic phase of revolutionary war. To the Vietminh also, the third stage, although predominantly military, remained a civil war in which political struggle continued to be vital.

The Vietminh applied these ideas with some modification in the conflict against France. After the outbreak of war in late 1946, they melted into the countryside, concentrating on avoiding pitched battles, mobilizing the population into a united anti-French front, and harassing French forces. In January 1948, the Vietminh leadership announced the second stage of equilibrium warfare where they sought to regain the initiative, wear down enemy forces, and expand the territory under their control. The emphasis was still on guerrilla warfare, but larger units were created to mount mobile operations over large areas. The communist victory in China in 1949 significantly altered the character of the war in Vietnam, making available to the Vietminh material aid and protected sanctuaries. Thus buoyed, they prematurely shifted to the third phase in 1951, launching an offensive that proved disastrous. After three more years, in which they combined vigorous political activity in the countryside, guerrilla warfare, and conventional operations, the Vietminh mounted the climactic battle. General Vo Nguyen Giap pulled off a logistical miracle by moving vast numbers of men and quantities of supplies through mountainous terrain into a position to attack. Surrounding isolated French forces at the remote outpost of Dien Bien Phu in the northwestern corner of Vietnam, they gradually closed the ring and, while the world watched, decisively defeated a major European power.

The war won by the Vietminh at Dien Bien Phu was lost at the conference table in Geneva. Largely at the insistence of its allies, the Soviet Union and China, the Vietminh was compelled to accept a temporary partition of its country with national elections to be held in 1956. It took control of the area above the seventeenth parallel. In the south, however, a government headed by Ngo Dinh Diem and backed by the United States used the two-year interval to establish a separate South Vietnam, undermining the spirit if not the precise letter of the Geneva Accords. The Diem government ignored the call for elections in 1956. It also launched a ruthless and highly effective campaign to root out former Vietminh operatives who remained in the south.

Origins of the Second Indochina War

On the verge of extinction by 1957, the southern Vietminh launched a rebellion that would eventually grow into the Second Indochina War. Seeking merely to salvage what remained of the revolution of 1945, they mounted an armed struggle against the government, reactivating the intelligence and propaganda networks that had fallen into disuse after Geneva and initiating a vigorous campaign of political agitation in the villages. Largely as a result of Diem's oppressive policies, they found a receptive audience in the countryside—the peasants were like a "mound of straw ready to be ignited." The Vietminh attracted thousands of adherents and established a presence in numerous villages. The level of violence increased dramatically. In 1958, an estimated 700 government officials were assassinated; in 1960, 2,500. In

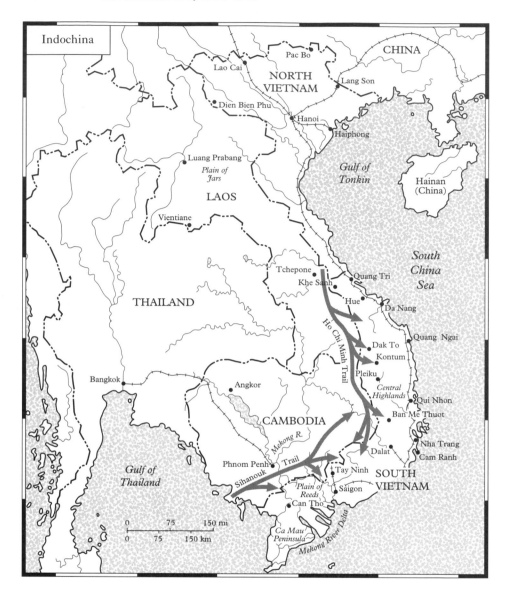

December 1960 the insurgents formed the National Liberation Front (NLF), a broad-based organization led by Communists but designed to rally all those disaffected with Diem by promising sweeping reforms and genuine independence.

North Vietnam gradually committed itself to the southern insurgency. In March 1957, Hanoi approved plans to modernize its own armed forces. Two years later, it formally authorized the resumption of armed struggle in the south and took measures to back it. The North Vietnamese established a special force to construct a supply route into the south—what would become the famed Ho Chi Minh Trail. They gradually increased the flow of men and matériel into the south and in September 1960 formally approved the shift to armed struggle.

From 1960 to 1965, the insurgency grew dramatically. Following the overthrow and assassination of Diem in a coup backed by the United States, South Vietnam degenerated into chaos, government succeeding government as through a revolving door. In December 1963, Hanoi instructed the NLF to step up its political agitation and military operations against the embattled South Vietnamese government. More important, it expanded infiltration into the south and even began to commit units of its own regular army. Over the next two years, the NLF extended its political control over the countryside, and its military units mounted increasingly bold attacks against South Vietnamese forces. The People's Army of North Vietnam (PAVN) was prepared for battle in the south. United States officials concluded by early 1965 that if they did not take drastic measures, South Vietnam would soon fall to the insurgents.

The NLF, PAVN, and Revolutionary War

To gain the upper hand in South Vietnam, NLF forces skillfully combined political and military "struggle." Their aims were to undermine the enemy's military and political positions and rally the people to their cause. In the political realm, NLF cadres created special organizations to give status to groups such as farmers, women, and youth. They used agitation and propaganda—"agitprop"—to arouse the people to the government's oppressiveness and lack of responsibility. They played to local grievances and used songs, skits, and speeches to explain their own program in terms the people could understand. Creating a mass organization where none had existed, they established a tightly knit political-military movement operating with often deadly efficiency from the village level to the central committee. By 1963, NLF strength in the rural areas of South Vietnam had grown to an estimated 300,000 people.

The NLF also assembled a highly disciplined and potent military organization. NLF main forces comprised some forty-seven battalions organized into five regiments and numbering by 1965 an estimated 80,000 of the "toughest, most experienced guerrilla fighters to be found anywhere in the world." Lightly equipped, usually clothed in the traditional black pajamas rather than uniforms, they relied on speed, surprise, and deception. Targets were chosen for maximum psychological significance, the NLF attacking villages and killing people who were deemed the greatest threats to their cause. They used violence selectively and judiciously to attain specified political ends—in general, to coerce or win over the population and undermine the legitimacy of the Saigon government. NLF units ambushed the forces of the South Vietnamese army (ARVN), attacked government-controlled hamlets, and sabotaged government communication links such as bridges, roads, and telephone or telegraph installations. They sought to provoke government officials to take oppressive measures that could be exploited politically. They assassinated and kidnapped village leaders who might cause problems for them, singling out those good officials whose removal could weaken the government and bad ones whose elimination could gain support for their cause.

The Main Forces were backed up by a popular army that operated at the village and hamlet level, a poorly equipped part-time guerrilla force of some 85,000 that worked the fields by day and ambushed and sabotaged by night.

By 1965, NLF forces were supported and in some areas supplanted by North Vietnamese regulars. Trained, organized, and equipped along Chinese lines, the People's Army of Vietnam numbered as many as 500,000 men and was supplemented by a ready reserve also of close to a half-million. Its divisions each possessed an authorized strength of 10,000 men, lightly armed and equipped for maximum mobility. Infantrymen generally carried Chinese-made pistols, 7.62-mm rifles, and three to five "potato-masher" grenades. Infantry divisions consisted of three infantry regiments when in the south, backed by weapons companies armed with 60-mm and 82-mm mortars, 57-mm and 75-mm recoilless rifles, and heavy machine guns. Training emphasized camouflage, the use of explosives, and small-unit tactics; field exercises were often conducted at night and under the most adverse conditions. The North Vietnamese made a virtue of the necessity of their light armament by constantly emphasizing that men, not weapons, constituted the decisive element in war. "People's war, not modern weapons and techniques, decides victory because war is the most acute form of struggle between man and man," party theorist Truong Chinh proclaimed in 1965.

The PAVN attempted to compensate for its weakness in firepower with rigorous discipline, tactical superiority, and careful preparation. As much as 50 percent of the training time of the PAVN soldier was spent in political education, and political commissars accompanied every unit above the company level. In battle, the North Vietnamese attempted to use the terrain to their best advantage, digging in even during rest periods and developing camouflage into a fine art. They tried to avoid battle except under favorable conditions and attacked the enemy at weak points rather than strong ones. They did not attempt to hold ground but rather sought to attack and withdraw before the enemy could react, hoping to inflict maximum casualties with rifles and automatic weapons in the opening moments of the fight. They were masters of the ambush. Actions of all sorts were planned and rehearsed with painstaking care. North Vietnamese units might take as much as a month to prepare the battlefield, massing ammunition and supplies, digging intricate systems of underground trenches, and stocking food and ammunition at attack points, ambush sites, and along withdrawal routes.

Mobility and small-unit maneuver were the hallmarks of North Vietnamese tactics. To minimize the impact of enemy firepower, PAVN forces attempted to close with the enemy as quickly as possible and to maintain close contact, even to the point of "hugging" and hand-to-hand combat. They preferred to overwhelm enemy forces by massing strength at a single point, and they excelled at encircling maneuvers with fifty to seventy-five men. Survival on the battlefield often depended on the ability to disengage, and North Vietnamese tactical doctrine held that the withdrawal was as important as the advance. At times, PAVN forces counterattacked to permit disengagement. If escape routes were blocked, they might attack a weak spot and slip away through the hole. Delaying forces were usually assigned the task of ambushing and harassing pursuers. Despite the lightness of its arma-

A detachment from the People's Army of Vietnam marches down a road as North Vietnamese civilians watch.

ments and a tendency to be repetitive and mechanistic in its tactical moves, the North Vietnamese army was a formidable fighting force. The French-born combat historian Bernard Fall did not exaggerate when he described it in September 1965 as "one of the best infantry combat forces in the world, capable of incredible feats of endurance and raw courage even against vastly superior firepower and under the worst physical conditions."

The United States: Counterinsurgency and Limited War

By the mid-1960s, Vietnam had become a focal point of United States' foreign policy. Perceiving the Soviet Union as a mortal threat, the Truman administration, in the aftermath of World War II, had committed itself to the containment of communist expansion. From the outbreak of revolution in Vietnam, U.S. policy makers had viewed Ho Chi Minh's Vietminh as an instrument of Moscow's larger global designs. Thus in early 1950, the United States began to provide military and economic aid to the French to assist in the suppression of the Vietminh insurgency. By 1954, Washington was paying nearly 80 percent of the cost of the war. When the French were defeated, the United States filled the vacuum, assisting the Diem government to solidify its position and providing lavish aid to sustain in South

Vietnam an independent, non-communist government that could stand as a bulwark against further communist expansion in Southeast Asia.

In the 1960s, Vietnam became a test case for new U.S. counterinsurgency doctrines. The Eisenhower administration had responded to the outbreak of war in Vietnam by providing the Diem government additional aid and U.S. military advisers. The Kennedy administration went further. Kennedy and his advisers were persuaded that so-called "brush-fire" wars such as the one taking place in Vietnam represented the new Soviet strategy for world domination. By fighting at a low level in peripheral areas, the communist adversary could avoid a nuclear confrontation and chip away at free-world strength. Kennedy and his advisers therefore scrapped Eisenhower's New Look defense policy, which had emphasized nuclear weapons and Massive Retaliation, and adopted a strategy of "Flexible Response" that permitted different types of military moves at different levels. They launched in 1961 a massive buildup of conventional forces to balance America's nuclear arsenal and implement Flexible Response.

The Kennedy administration also placed great emphasis on counterinsurgency. The president himself took a keen interest in the subject, and the works of Mao Zedong became required reading for top U.S. officials. Kennedy gave his blessings to the U.S. Army's elite Green Berets and required all the military services to develop counterinsurgency doctrine.

The administration first applied its new ideas and methods in Vietnam. As a senator, Kennedy had once referred to Vietnam as the "cornerstone of the free world in Southeast Asia." He and his advisers increasingly viewed it as a test case of America's determination to uphold its commitments and its capacity to meet the challenges of guerrilla warfare in the emerging nations. Between 1961 and 1963, the president thus launched a full-scale counterinsurgency program in Vietnam, approving a massive increase in U.S. military and economic aid and enlarging the number of U.S. advisers to more than 16,000.

The Kennedy program attacked the NLF insurgency on several fronts. Militarily, the United States provided the South Vietnamese army the latest hardware including armored personnel carriers, helicopters, and aircraft. Buoyed by American aid and advisers, the South Vietnamese armed forces took the offensive against the guerrillas. U.S. advisers performed ever-widening tasks. Special Forces units conducted civic action programs among the primitive peoples of the Central Highlands. Helicopter pilots dropped detachments of South Vietnamese troops into battle zones deep in the swamps and picked up the dead and wounded. Americans went with Vietnamese trainees on bombing and strafing missions and, when the Vietnamese ran short of pilots, flew the planes themselves. Army officers and enlisted men conducted expanded training programs for the South Vietnamese army, and advisers down to the battalion level accompanied its units on combat missions.

U.S. military and civilian advisers also assisted the South Vietnamese government in implementing the so-called Strategic Hamlet program. Developed by the British counterinsurgency expert Sir Robert Thompson on the basis of experiences in Malaya, the program was designed to isolate the

NLF from the people of South Vietnam. Peasants from scattered villages were brought together into hamlets surrounded by moats and bamboo stake fences and defended by military forces. The hamlets were intended to protect the people against the guerrillas and also to serve as an instrument for a social and economic revolution to draw the people to the government. Village elections, land reform, and the establishment of schools and medical services were to persuade the people that life under the South Vietnamese government offered more than the NLF. The objective, U.S. counterinsurgency expert Roger Hilsman observed, was to reduce the guerrillas to "hungry, marauding bands of outlaws devoting all their energies to remaining alive," forcing them out into the open where they would have to fight the South Vietnamese army on its terms.

The Kennedy counterinsurgency program failed. The Strategic Hamlet program was flawed both in conception and execution. It had worked well in Malaya, where Malay villages were fortified against Chinese insurgents, but in Vietnam the hamlets were to be erected against Vietnamese, many of whom had lived among the villagers for years, and they were easily infiltrated. In some regions, the hamlets could not be established without massive uprooting of the peasantry, and the displacement of people from ancestral lands added to the discontent that already pervaded the countryside. In many cases, the government moved too far too fast in implementing the program, establishing hamlets in areas where no real security existed. The vulnerable settlements were thus quickly overrun or infiltrated by the insurgents. Many of the hamlets lacked adequate defenses. Some were spread over such a large area that it would have required a full division to defend them. In the hands of Diem and his sinister brother-in-law, Ngo Dinh Nhu, moreover, the program alienated the people rather than attracted them to the government.

Militarily, the Kennedy program also failed. Despite relentless pressure from the White House, the armed services refused to embrace counterinsurgency and insisted on fighting the war the way they knew how. Even with modern aircraft, it proved impossible to locate the guerrillas amidst the dense forests and swampy paddy lands. The very nature of U.S.–South Vietnamese operations, an air strike followed by the landing of troops, gave the insurgents warning and permitted them to slip away. ARVN forces would often bomb and strafe large areas and land sizable detachments of troops with little result, and when they withdrew the guerrillas simply reoccupied the region. The insurgents learned how to bring down slow, clumsy helicopters with small arms. Sometimes they would lie in hiding until the helicopters had departed and then ambush the landing force. As operations became more costly, ARVN commanders, apparently under orders from Diem, relied more and more on air power and refused to risk their troops in battle.

The Battle of Ap Bac, 1963

The shift in the fortunes of war was dramatically revealed in January 1963. An American adviser, the legendary Colonel John Paul Vann, pressed his

South Vietnamese division commander to attack three guerrilla companies near the village of Ap Bac. The South Vietnamese commander delayed for a day, giving the NLF time to learn of the operation and prepare deadly defenses. Outnumbering the enemy ten to one—the classic ratio for success against guerrillas—the South Vietnamese planned a three-pronged assault. At the first signs of resistance, however, the attacking forces balked. One prong simply refused to attack. Other units failed to block enemy escape routes. The battle ended ingloriously with the South Vietnamese firing on each other while the enemy slipped away. The vastly superior ARVN forces suffered sixty-one dead and one hundred wounded, while the NLF left only three bodies behind. Continuing to think in conventional warfare terms, the U.S. command in Saigon claimed victory because the enemy had abandoned its territory. Those in the field and the American reporters who covered the action knew better.

By 1965, the United States faced a major turning point in Vietnam. Following the overthrow and assassination of Diem and the instability that followed, the NLF insurgency had gained momentum. Supported by a steadily growing flow of men and supplies from North Vietnam, the insurgents took advantage of the near anarchy in the south. By early 1965, the NLF had secured uncontested control of the vital Mekong Delta region south of Saigon and appeared capable of splitting the country in half. The corruption-ridden South Vietnamese army, even with sharply increased U.S. aid, could not slow, much less stop, the enemy onslaught.

The administration of Lyndon Baines Johnson saw little choice but to escalate the U.S. commitment. Responding to the urgent warnings of his advisers that South Vietnam was on the verge of collapse, the president in February 1965 mounted regular, sustained bombing raids against North Vietnam. The bombing had only a marginal impact on the war, however, and by late spring General William Westmoreland, head of the U.S. military assistance program in Vietnam, requested a massive increase in American military forces and the commitment of U.S. combat units to reverse a rapidly deteriorating situation. After several weeks of intensive deliberations, the president in late July made what amounted to a decision for full-scale war in Vietnam, committing himself to provide U.S. combat support as needed.

Limited War in Theory and Practice

Responding to the challenge in Vietnam, Johnson and his advisers were deeply influenced by the limited war theory so much in vogue in the United States during the 1950s and 1960s. When the Soviet Union developed effective delivery systems for nuclear weapons, it was obvious to many military theorists that the Eisenhower administration's emphasis on Massive Retaliation could not work. With nothing but nuclear weapons as a deterrent, the United States in responding to communist challenges in peripheral areas would face the unthinkable choice of starting a nuclear war or doing nothing.

To escape that dilemma and find the means to contain communist expansion without risking a nuclear holocaust, civilian and military theorists advocated the alternative of limited war. Such a strategy would harness the nation's military power more closely to the attainment of its political objectives. Through Flexible Response, a variety of military instruments would be readied to respond to different types of threats at different levels. The amount of force to be employed in any situation would be limited to that necessary to achieve the political aim. The objective was not to destroy an opponent but to persuade him to break off the conflict short of achieving his goals and without resorting to nuclear war.

The limited-war theorists provided a set of broad guidelines for the conduct of that sort of conflict. Statesmen must "scrupulously limit" the political objectives and clearly communicate them to the enemy. They must make every effort to keep open diplomatic channels to terminate the war through negotiations on the basis of limited objectives. They must keep the war precisely limited in terms of geography and must restrict the force used to that amount necessary to attain the political objectives. Limited war must be directed by the civilian leadership. The special needs of the military should not affect its conduct, and indeed the military must be a controllable instrument of national policy.

Limited-war theory also set forth methods for using military power to persuade an adversary to act in the desired way. Military action was less important for the damage it did, according to this reasoning, than for the message it sent. War became a sort of bargaining process through which force was employed to persuade an enemy that persisting in what he was doing would be too expensive to continue. "The object," political scientist Thomas Schelling observed, "is to exact good behavior or to oblige discontinuance of mischief, not to destroy the subject altogether." The implicit assumption was that the use of force could be orchestrated in such a way as to communicate precise and specific signals and that an opponent would back down in the face of such threats or pressure.

Limited-war theory had numerous flaws. It was primarily an academic, rather than a military concept, and it drastically misunderstood the dynamics of war. Its authors seemed to say that since limited war was mainly about bargaining and diplomacy, it required no knowledge of military matters and indeed military considerations should not affect its conduct. Despite the popular frustrations caused by fighting a limited war in Korea, the theorists seemed grandly indifferent to the domestic political problems it posed. Political scientist Robert Osgood conceded that this type of conflict ran counter to the American way of war and that Americans might not easily accept the "galling but indispensable restraints" required by it. But he neatly dodged the problem with platitudes, calling for candor and courage on the part of leaders and surmising that if Americans were treated as adults they would respond accordingly. Limited-war theorists also devoted more effort to explaining why this type of war should be fought rather than how it was to be fought. In terms of bargaining theory, moreover, they assumed a greater capacity than was warranted on the part of a gigantic bureaucracy like the United States government to send clear, precise signals, and they reduced the behavior of potential enemies to that of laboratory rats. These problems, however, are more obvious in retrospect than they were at the time.

The Johnson administration's strategy in Vietnam was deeply influenced by limited-war theory. Fearful that the actions they were taking to prevent a third world war might themselves provoke a dangerous confrontation with the Soviet Union and China, the president and his top civilian advisers put precise geographical limits on the war. They kept their military commanders on a tight rein, rejecting proposals to invade enemy sanctuaries in Laos, Cambodia, and North Vietnam, mine Haiphong Harbor, and bomb near the Chinese border. Vividly recalling the Korean War and the bitter controversy between President Harry S Truman and General Douglas MacArthur, Johnson and his civilian advisers fretted about military recklessness and a MacArthur-like challenge to civilian authority. "General, I have a lot riding on you," the president told Westmoreland in February 1966. "I hope you don't pull a MacArthur on me."

The administration fought the war according to the political dictates of limited-war theory. The theory of gradual escalation presumed that a steady increase in the level of military pressure would coerce an adversary into compliance. Thus the United States slowly increased the bombing and steadily expanded the number of U.S. troops and the intensity of ground operations. At no point did the president accede to the full requests of his military commanders. Yet once underway, the process of escalation achieved a momentum of its own, the failure of one level of force providing justification for the next level. By 1967, the United States had concentrated in Vietnam close to 500,000 men, roughly one-half its tactical airpower, and 30 percent of its naval strength. It was spending more than 2 billion dollars per month on the war.

A Modern, High-Tech Military Machine

The forces the United States sent to Vietnam were the best that money and modern technology could provide. During the Kennedy years, Secretary of Defense Robert S. McNamara had presided over a dramatic expansion and reorganization of the U.S. military to meet the perceived threats of a direct Soviet attack on Western Europe, limited conventional wars like Korea, and "brush-fire" wars in the Third World.

Although Vietnam was primarily a land war, air and sea power played an important role. Refitted World War II battleships pounded North Vietnamese bases from offshore. Conventional and nuclear-powered aircraft carriers were deployed in the Gulf of Tonkin, and their aircraft conducted Operation "Rolling Thunder" against North Vietnam from March 1965 until October 1968. Air force F-105 Thunderchiefs (known as "Thuds" by their pilots) carrying 7,500 pounds of bombs were also workhorses in the air war against North Vietnam. Air force and navy aircraft bombed enemy supply lines and staging areas in North and South Vietnam and flew close air-support missions for American and South Vietnamese forces in the field. The most formidable weapon—and most feared by the enemy—was the giant B-52 bomber that flew at 30,000 feet, carried a payload of 58,000 pounds, and left enormous craters in its path of destruction.

In what Westmoreland described as "the most sophisticated war in history," the United States attempted to exploit its technological superiority to cope with the peculiar problems posed by a guerrilla war. To locate an ever-elusive enemy, the military used small portable radar units and "people sniffers," which picked up the odor of human urine. IBM 1430 computers were programmed to predict likely times and places of enemy attacks. Herbicides were used on a wide scale and with devastating ecological and human consequences to deprive the NLF of natural cover. C-47 transports were converted into awesome gunships called "Puff the Magic Dragon" that could fire 18,000 rounds per minute.

The army that fought in Vietnam was one of the best clothed, best equipped, and best prepared the nation had ever sent to war. McNamara had increased the strength of the army to nearly one million men, raised the number of combat-ready divisions from eleven to sixteen, vastly expanded airlift capacity, and stockpiled huge quantities of equipment. The army was reorganized to create a flexible, adaptable organization capable of meeting its varied missions.

Innovations in equipment drastically increased its mobility and firepower. The advent of armored personnel carriers and troop-carrying helicopters significantly altered the nature of infantry operations. Helmets, pistols, and mortars were similar to those used in Korea, and machine guns and artillery were improved versions of weapons long in use, but two new

U.S. soldiers dismounting from a helicopter in a search and destroy operation. Airborne insertions often occurred when intelligence reported the presence of enemy soldiers. If the landing unit made contact with enemy forces, additional units "piled on" in an attempt to surround and destroy the enemy.

weapons vastly increased the firepower of the individual infantryman. The M-79 grenade launcher permitted the use of grenades at ranges up to 350 meters with far greater accuracy and were particularly useful in ambushes and against machine-gun nests. Claymore mines, which weighed only 3.5 pounds, were easy to place, had a destructive area of up to fifty meters, and were valuable in ambushes.

A major innovation of the 1960s was the creation of an air-cavalry division by the U.S. Army. Helicopters had been used effectively in restricted roles in Korea, and as their technology improved their potential began to seem almost limitless. They were widely employed during the advisory years in Vietnam and seemed increasingly to provide the solution to the difficult problem of locating and engaging elusive guerrillas in difficult terrain. After a period of tests, McNamara activated the 1st Cavalry Division (Airmobile) in June 1965. The new division made large-scale airmobile operations possible. Although lightly armed, it compensated with its fast-strike capability; its helicopters could land as many as 10,000 troops in battle zones within hours. Its greatest assets were its ability to cover all types of terrain, maneuver over large areas, react quickly to enemy attacks and reinforce embattled units, and conduct raids behind enemy lines. Thus by July 1965, two nations with very different military traditions and two powerful and quite different military forces were set to engage each other in Vietnam.

Escalation and Stalemate, 1965–1968

By the time the United States escalated the war in 1965, North Vietnam and the NLF appeared on the verge of victory. Sensing in the growing chaos in South Vietnam a splendid opportunity to attain long-sought goals, Hanoi had sharply escalated the war. North Vietnamese leaders still thought in terms of Maoist doctrine, a protracted struggle with victory to be attained through a series of stages. Always flexible in their thinking, however, their new strategy called for a gradual shift from low-level action to the use of large-scale military forces to annihilate enemy main forces. The final stage would be a military offensive in the rural areas and a popular uprising in the cities that would leave the United States no choice but to pull out of South Vietnam. In 1964 and 1965, the North Vietnamese implemented their strategy with great success. PAVN and NLF main forces gradually extended their control over the strategic Central Highlands of South Vietnam while NLF guerrillas scored equally impressive gains in the Mekong Delta south of Saigon. By early 1965, the insurgents controlled half the population and more than half the territory of South Vietnam. The only secure areas were the major cities, and they were increasingly threatened by civil disturbances.

In escalating the war, the Johnson administration sought to head off what seemed a certain enemy victory and to preserve an independent, non-communist South Vietnam. The administration's strategy was based on the assumption that if the United States slowly increased the level of military pain, it would reach a point at which the North Vietnamese would decide that the costs were greater than the potential gain. The Rolling Thunder bombing program initiated in March 1965 and gradually expanded thereafter was designed to reduce the infiltration of men and supplies into South Vietnam and to pressure North Vietnam into stopping its support of the insurgency. With the increased ground forces provided him in July 1965, General Westmoreland sought first to stem the momentum of communist advances in the countryside and to provide security in the urban areas. This accomplished, he planned to launch a number of major search-and-destroy operations to cripple enemy main-force units and break the NLF hold on the countryside. Once the enemy's regular forces had been destroyed, he reasoned, the South Vietnamese government would be able to stabilize its position and "pacify" the countryside, and the enemy would have no choice but to negotiate on terms acceptable to the United States. The marines were given responsibility for operations in the northern provinces (I Corps), while the army was assigned the task in the Central Highlands, along the central coast, and in the region around Saigon. In the meantime, the ARVN, with the support of U.S. civilian and military advisers, was to launch a "pacification" program to break the NLF hold on the countryside and build support for South Vietnam's government.

Battle of the Ia Drang, 1965

The first major clash of opposing armies came in the Ia Drang valley in the Central Highlands in late 1965. As part of its winter-spring campaign of 1965–1966, Hanoi ordered a PAVN army corps to execute a series of operations around Pleiku in the Central Highlands with the object of striking a knockout blow. The first stage of the operation was an attack on a U.S. Special Forces camp near Plei Me near the Cambodian border. Using a classic lure-and-ambush tactic, the North Vietnamese followed with the real object of their plan, a major attack against the South Vietnamese relief column sent to save the base. Using ground forces, artillery, and especially tactical air support and relying—as they would throughout the war—on the superiority of their firepower, the United States and South Vietnam launched a furious counterattack on the forces besieging Plei Me and repulsed the North Vietnamese ambush of the relief column. Their plan frustrated, the PAVN forces slipped away to their base areas in Cambodia. According to U.S. estimates, in this first encounter, the North Vietnamese lost as many as 850 killed and 1,700 wounded.

Seeking to follow up this initial success, Westmoreland dispatched the 1st Cavalry Division on search-and-destroy operations against retreating enemy forces. From October 28 to November 14, U.S. forces conducted a series of air and ground searches in the Ia Drang valley punctuated by sporadic and violent clashes. The largest action occurred on November 14 when four American companies fell upon a North Vietnamese regiment at

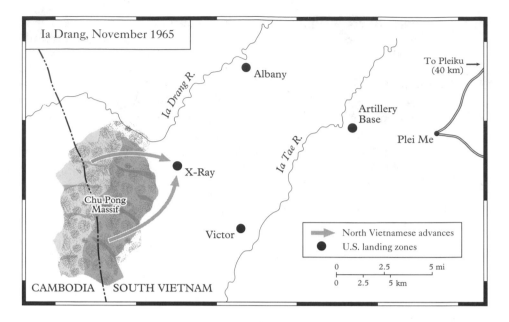

Ia Drang, November 1965

Albany

To Pleiku (40 km)

Ia Drang R.

Artillery Base

Ia Tae R.

Plei Me

X-Ray

Chu Pong Massif

Victor

North Vietnamese advances

U.S. landing zones

0   2.5   5 mi

0   2.5   5 km

CAMBODIA ¦ SOUTH VIETNAM

landing zone X-Ray. As at Plei Me, U.S. firepower eventually saved the day, artillery from nearby landing zones pouring more than 8,000 rounds against enemy positions, and air force fighter-bombers and even giant B-52s from Guam flying close air support. Pounded relentlessly for nearly two days, the battered North Vietnamese eventually withdrew to their sanctuaries. The following day, an American battalion stumbled into a disastrous ambush at nearby landing zone Albany, suffering huge casualties. In all, the North Vietnamese lost an estimated 3,000 killed in the Ia Drang fighting, the United States 300.

It remains difficult even today to assess this first (and one of the few) major battles of the Vietnam War. Thinking in entirely conventional terms, the U.S. military claimed victory because of the heavy losses it inflicted and because the enemy had been forced to withdraw from the battlefield. Some commentators also hailed as unusual if not indeed unique among America's first battles the outstanding performance of U.S. troops in this, their "blooding." North Vietnam indeed suffered staggering losses. In the aftermath of the Ia Drang, Giap reverted to guerrilla warfare and made major tactical adjustments to better cope with U.S. firepower. Still, U.S. officials were also stunned by the severity of their losses and abandoned any hope that success could be achieved at light cost. Americans failed to recognize, moreover, that in this kind of warfare if the enemy did not lose, it won. Finding in the Ia Drang confirmation of his belief that a search-and-destroy strategy would break the enemy's will to fight, Westmoreland made no major adjustments in his approach to the war. The Ia Drang battle thus set the tone for much of what lay ahead: more and larger search-and-destroy missions, numerous "victories"—and ultimately frustration.

Throughout 1966 and 1967, the United States continued to escalate the war. Rolling Thunder bombing sorties increased from 25,000 in 1965 to

U.S. Air Force F-5 Freedom Fighter engaged in close air support. Ground troops particularly valued missions against enemy bunkers and fortified positions. Air attacks proved less successful, however, in interdicting supplies from North Vietnam.

108,000 in 1967, and the tonnage of bombs dropped increased from 63,000 to 226,000. The number of ground troops grew from 184,300 at the end of 1965 to 485,600 at the end of 1967. Furnished with thousands of new ground troops and a massive arsenal of modern weaponry, Westmoreland took the war to the enemy. Throughout 1966 and 1967, intensive fighting raged across much of South Vietnam. Along the demilitarized zone, marines and North Vietnamese regulars were dug in like the armies of World War I, pounding each other relentlessly with artillery. In the jungle areas, small American units probed for a hidden enemy in a manner comparable to the Pacific island campaigns of World War II.

Increasingly, however, Westmoreland concentrated on large-scale search-and-destroy missions against enemy base areas. Operation Cedar Falls, a major campaign of early 1967, sent some 30,000 U.S. troops against the Iron Triangle, an NLF stronghold just north of Saigon. After B-52s saturated the area with bombs, U.S. troops surrounded it, and helicopters dropped large numbers of specially trained combat forces into the villages. Following removal of the population, giant Rome plows with huge spikes on the front leveled the area, destroying what remained of the vegetation and leaving the guerrillas no place to hide. The region was then burned and bombed again to destroy the miles of underground tunnels that formed the enemy military complex.

The most that could be achieved was a stalemate. North Vietnam was stunned by American intervention in 1965 and alarmed by the effectiveness of U.S. firepower in the Ia Drang. Hanoi thus abandoned any hope of an early victory and settled in for a protracted struggle against a greatly strengthened enemy. Learning from their war against France, the North Vietnamese leadership increasingly counted on the weakness of the South Vietnamese regime and antiwar opposition in the United States. The key to exploiting these advantages, they reasoned, was to keep maximum military pressure on the enemy without needlessly exposing their own forces to destruction. PAVN and NLF units thus retreated to their sanctuaries, seeking to avoid U.S. search-and-destroy operations. At the same time, they constantly harassed exposed U.S. and ARVN troops and launched attacks of up to regimental size at times and places of their own choosing. Hanoi's strategists concentrated against the South Vietnamese government and army to exploit their weaknesses and ultimately force their collapse. To keep the American casualty lists as high as possible and thereby keep the war on the front pages in the United States, they also attacked U.S. forces. They used tactics of "clinging to the G.I.s' belts" to minimize the effectiveness of U.S. artillery and air support. High priority was still given to political agitation, especially in the cities of South Vietnam that were swollen with increasing numbers of restless and disaffected refugees.

North Vietnam effectively countered the U.S. air war. By 1967, the tonnage of bombs dropped on North Vietnam exceeded that dropped on Germany, Italy, and Japan during World War II. America's heavy reliance on air power seriously underestimated the commitment of the North Vietnamese and overestimated the capabilities of strategic bombing. The gradual escalation of the bombing permitted the North Vietnamese to protect vital resources, and losses were more than made up by expanded aid from China and the Soviet Union. The North Vietnamese showed a remarkable capacity for coping with the bombing, repairing bridges and railroads within hours after destruction. The daily pounding from the air seemed to stiffen their will, and they showed no sign of bending under the pressure. The rate of infiltration into the south increased after the bombing was started and continued to increase as it expanded. By late 1967, North Vietnamese forces were four times greater than in 1965.

The North Vietnamese also blunted U.S. operations on the ground. Westmoreland's strategy of attrition assumed that the United States could inflict intolerable losses while keeping its own losses within acceptable bounds, an assumption that flew in the face of past experience with land wars on the Asian continent and the realities in Vietnam. An estimated 200,000 North Vietnamese came of draft age each year, and Hanoi was able to match each American escalation. Moreover, the conditions under which the war was fought permitted North Vietnam to control its losses. The North Vietnamese and NLF were generally able to avoid contact when it suited them. They fought at times and places of their own choosing and on ground favorable to them. If losses reached unacceptable proportions, they melted into the jungles or retreated into sanctuaries in North Vietnam, Laos, or Cambodia. North Vietnamese and NLF forces were hurt, sometimes badly, but their main forces could not be destroyed. They retained the strategic initiative and could strike sharply when and where they chose. Westmoreland did not have sufficient forces to wage war against enemy regulars and control the countryside. The NLF political structure thus remained intact, and even in areas such as the Iron Triangle, when American forces moved on to fight elsewhere, the NLF quietly slipped back in. It all added up to a "state of irresolution," journalist Robert Shaplen observed in 1967.

With the military situation a stalemate, the political aspect assumed greater importance, and the fundamental problem, the Saigon government, remained unresolved. A coalition of generals headed by Nguyen Cao Ky and Nguyen Van Thieu finally emerged from the long series of coups and countercoups from 1963 to 1965, but it represented none of the multiplicity of political factions in the south. Neither the government nor the United States was capable of broadening South Vietnam's narrow political base. The huge influx of Americans after 1965 and expansion of the war created problems that even the most responsible and effective government would have found difficult to handle. The massive bombing and artillery fire drove thousands of sullen refugees into already overcrowded cities. The South Vietnamese economy was geared around providing services to the Americans and quickly reached the point where it could not absorb the ever-expanding volume of money and goods. In the cities, corruption, profiteering, and vice ran rampant.

As the war dragged on inconclusively, moreover, popular support in the United States began to erode, and by the end of 1967 the American

In April 1967, General William C. Westmoreland briefed President Johnson and his top advisors on the need to send additional troops to Vietnam. By approving an increase of 50,000 instead of 200,000, the president refused to expand the war dramatically, but he also refused to accept Robert S. McNamara's advice about making basic changes in policy toward Vietnam.

people had become polarized over Vietnam as no other issue since their own Civil War a century earlier. Those labeled "hawks" protested the restraints imposed on the military and demanded that Johnson do what was necessary to win or get out of Vietnam. At the other extreme, growing numbers of so-called "doves" protested that the war was immoral or unnecessary or both and demanded that the United States get out of Vietnam. At this point in the war, the great majority of Americans rejected both extremes, but as the war dragged on and the debate became more divisive, disillusionment increased markedly. Public support for the war dropped sharply in 1967, and Johnson's approval rating fell even further, dipping to a low 28 percent in October.

The Tet Offensive, 1968

In the spring and summer of 1967, the North Vietnamese decided to attempt to break an increasingly costly deadlock. To lure American troops away from the major population centers and maintain high U.S. casualties, a series of large-scale diversionary attacks was to be launched in remote areas. These would be followed by coordinated NLF assaults against the major cities and towns of South Vietnam designed to weaken the government and ignite a "general uprising" among the people. At the same time efforts would be made to open negotiations with the United States. Hanoi probably hoped through these coordinated actions to get the bombing stopped, weaken the Saigon regime, exacerbate differences between the United States and its South Vietnamese ally, and intensify pressures for a change in U.S. policy. Its ultimate objective was to secure an acceptable settlement, the minimum ingredients of which would be a coalition government and U.S. withdrawal.

The first phase of the North Vietnamese plan worked to perfection. In October and November, PAVN forces attacked the Marine base at Con Thien across the Laotian border and the towns of Loc Ninh and Song Be near Saigon and Dak To in the Central Highlands. Shortly after, two PAVN divisions laid siege to the Marine garrison at Khe Sanh near the Laotian border. Westmoreland quickly dispatched reinforcements to these embattled areas, in each case driving back the enemy and inflicting heavy losses, but in the process dispersing his forces and leaving the cities vulnerable. By the end of the year, moreover, the attention of Westmoreland, President Johnson, and indeed much of the nation was riveted on Khe Sanh, which many Americans assumed was General Giap's play for a repetition of his smashing victory at Dien Bien Phu.

During the Tet holiday of early 1968, the North Vietnamese and NLF launched the second and major phase of their offensive. On January 30, 1968, the NLF carried out a series of attacks extending across the length of the country. In all, they struck thirty-six of forty-four provincial capitals, five of the six major cities, sixty-four district capitals, and fifty hamlets. In Saigon, they mounted a daring raid on the U.S. embassy, briefly penetrating

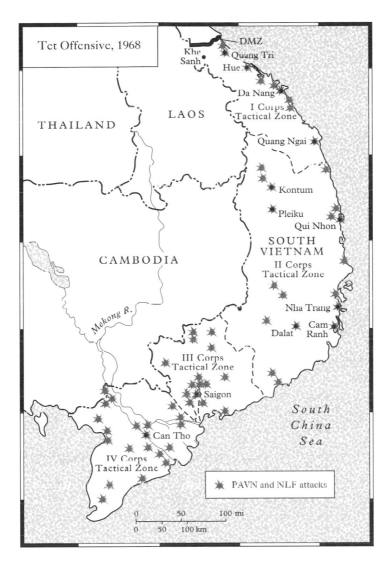

Tet Offensive, 1968

the compound, and assaulted Tan Son Nhut airport, the presidential palace, and the headquarters of South Vietnam's general staff. In Hue, 7,500 NLF and PAVN troops stormed and eventually took control of the ancient Citadel, the interior town that had been the seat of the emperors of the ancient kingdom of Vietnam.

Although taken by surprise, the United States and South Vietnam recovered quickly. The initial attacks were poorly coordinated, and premature assaults in some areas enabled Westmoreland to get reinforcements to vulnerable spots. In addition, the attackers were slow to capitalize on their early successes, giving the U.S. and South Vietnam time to mount strong defenses. In Saigon, U.S. and ARVN forces held off the initial attack and within several days had cleared the city, inflicting huge casualties, taking large numbers of prisoners, and forcing the remnants to melt into the countryside. Elsewhere, the result was much the same. ARVN fought better under pressure than anyone could have anticipated, and the United States and South Vietnam used their superior mobility and firepower to devastating advantage. The NLF launched a second round of attacks on February 18, but these were confined largely to rocket and mortar barrages against military installations and had little effect.

The Battle for Hue

Hue was the major exception. The battle to liberate that city pitted two PAVN regiments and two NLF battalions against eight U.S. and thirteen ARVN battalions, lasted from January 31 to March 2, and was one of the most savage and destructive battles of the entire war. For those ARVN forces and U.S. Marines who participated, the struggle for Hue involved some of the most brutal and deadly fighting since World War II.

Recognizing the value of holding even temporarily the cultural and religious center of the nation, North Vietnamese and NLF forces had infiltrated Hue before Tet, carefully stockpiling weapons and ammunition. They attained near-complete surprise, and as advance units took key points, reinforcements poured into the city. Undermanned because of holiday furloughs, ARVN responded ineffectually. Within hours of the opening of the battle, North Vietnamese and NLF units controlled all of the Citadel and much of the city south of the Perfume River, even threatening the headquarters of the U.S. military command.

Initial U.S. and South Vietnamese efforts to retake the city failed. ARVN units dispatched to liberate Hue were battered by carefully planned enemy ambushes. United States and ARVN forces staged a major attack on February 1, but met fierce resistance from well-emplaced enemy forces. They made painfully slow progress, only to be hurled back on February 6 by a PAVN/NLF counterattack.

Eventually, massive force and heavy fighting were needed to retake the city. At first reluctant to destroy Hue's architectural treasures, the United States and South Vietnam in time bowed to expediency. Ships from the U.S. Seventh Fleet, aircraft, and artillery pounded enemy positions, and tanks and flamethrowers cleared the way for attacking forces. Both sides used tear gas, and Hue was the only battle of the war where gas masks were regularly worn. Backed by massive firepower, South Vietnamese and U.S. forces launched a full-scale attack on February 9 against dug-in enemy forces and well-concealed snipers. The enemy responded the following day, counterattacking and decimating an entire ARVN battalion. Slowly, U.S. and South Vietnamese forces clawed their way, house by house, into the city, reaching the moat of the Citadel by February 21. After a night of bitter, hand-to-hand combat, advance ARVN units raised the South Vietnamese flag over the Citadel. That same day, another South Vietnamese unit retook the Imperial Palace. After more than a week of mopping up operations, Hue was finally liberated on March 2.

It remains difficult twenty-five years after the event to assess the impact of the battles of Tet. The North Vietnamese and NLF did not force the collapse of South Vietnam. They were unable to establish any firm positions in the urban areas, and the South Vietnamese people did not rise up to welcome them as "liberators." NLF and PAVN battle deaths have been estimated as high as 40,000, and although this figure may be inflated, the losses were huge. The NLF bore the brunt of the fighting throughout South Vietnam. Its main force units were decimated and would never completely recover, and its political infrastructure suffered crippling losses.

If in these terms Tet represented a defeat for North Vietnam and the NLF, it was still a costly and in some ways hollow victory for the United States and South Vietnam. ARVN forces had to be withdrawn from the countryside to defend the cities, and the pacification program incurred another major setback. The destruction visited upon the cities heaped formidable new problems on a government that had shown only limited capacity to deal with the routine. American and South Vietnamese losses did not approach those of the enemy, but they were still high: in the first two weeks of the Tet campaigns, the United States lost 1,100 killed in action and South Vietnam 2,300. An estimated 12,500 civilians were killed, and Tet created as many as one million new refugees. In Hue during the period of PAVN/NLF "liberation," 2,800 civilians were massacred and buried in mass graves. As with so much of the war, there was a great deal of destruction and suffering, but no clear-cut winner or loser.

Perhaps the major impact of Tet was in the United States. Westmoreland insisted that the attacks had been repulsed and that there was no need to fear a major setback, and administration officials publicly echoed his statements. Johnson and his advisers were shocked by the suddenness and magnitude of the offensive, however, and intelligence estimates were much more pessimistic than Westmoreland. Among the general public, Tet caused a mood of gloom. For those who had long opposed the conflict and some who had supported it, Tet seemed to provide compelling evidence of its folly. "The war in Vietnam is unwinnable," the columnist Joseph Kraft concluded, "and the longer it goes on the more the Americans . . . will be subjected to losses and humiliation." Approval of Johnson's handling of the war, which had risen significantly in late 1967, again plummeted sharply in 1968, hitting an all-time low of 26 percent during Tet. Senator Eugene McCarthy's strong showing against the president in the New Hampshire primary suggested the political damage done by the war. Johnson was further threatened by Senator Robert Kennedy's announcement that he too would run on an antiwar platform.

Tet eventually forced Johnson to approve important changes of policy. After nearly two months of soul-searching and intensive internal debate, the president rejected his military advisers' proposals for a major escalation of the war. In a dramatic speech on March 31, 1968, he went still further, cutting back the bombing to the area just north of the demilitarized zone, making clear his willingness to negotiate, and, to underscore his seriousness, withdrawing from the presidential race.

Johnson's speech is usually cited as a major turning point in the war, and in some ways it was. It brought an end to the policy of gradual escalation, yet it did not represent a change of goals. Apparent U.S. success in the battles of Tet reinforced the conviction of the president and some of his advisers that they could yet secure an independent, non-communist South Vietnam. By rejecting major troop reinforcements, reducing the bombing, shifting some of the fighting to the South Vietnamese, and withdrawing from the presidential race, Johnson hoped to salvage his policy at least to the end of his term. The president's March 31 speech did not represent a change of objective as much as a shift of tactics to sustain a policy that had come under bitter attack.

For the North Vietnamese and NLF as well, Tet produced disillusionment, even despair. The failure of the offensive to attain its major goals and the heavy losses suffered appear to have provoked heated internal debate. The Vietnamese recognized, as one document put it, that "Victory will come to us, not suddenly, but in a complicated and tortuous way." The North Vietnamese and NLF were no more prepared than Johnson to abandon their goals, however, and they recognized that unless they were able to maintain a high level of pressure on the United States and South Vietnam, victory would not come at all. Thus while the North Vietnamese accepted American proposals for negotiations, they determined to maintain maximum military pressure. Keeping their main force units out of battle, they sought to sustain small-scale attacks throughout South Vietnam, most of them conducted by paramilitary units.

As a consequence, while in many ways Tet represented a major turning point, it merely elevated the war to a new level of stalemate. During the last eight months of 1968, North Vietnamese and U.S. negotiators met in Paris. Neither was willing to make concessions that would jeopardize achievement of their goals, however, and the negotiations made little progress. When Johnson stopped the bombing of North Vietnam entirely on October 31, the South Vietnamese balked. Fearing that the United States might sell out South Vietnam, the government of Nguyen Van Thieu raised objections that blocked the opening of substantive negotiations until the end of Johnson's term of office.

In the meantime, military activity in South Vietnam grew to unprecedented levels. The air war in South Vietnam reached a new peak of intensity B-52s and fighter-bombers relentlessly attacked infiltration routes, lines of communication, and suspected enemy base camps in South Vietnam and Laos. The number of B-52 attacks tripled in 1968, and the bombs dropped on South Vietnam exceeded one million tons. In the spring and summer, the United States and South Vietnam conducted the largest search-and-destroy missions of the war. The year 1968 was thus the "bloodiest year" of the war, in the words of historian Ronald Spector, and both sides suffered heavy losses. Each could thus claim victory in the campaigns of Tet, but the position of each was also significantly weakened, and neither emerged with sufficient leverage to force a settlement. Tet merely hardened the deadlock, and it would take four more years of "fighting while negotiating" before it was finally broken.

Fighting While Negotiating, 1968–1975

In the aftermath of Tet, the United States and North Vietnam adjusted their strategies to the changed circumstances. After an unsuccessful attempt to win the war through intimidation, the new administration of Richard M. Nixon resorted to a "Vietnamization" strategy designed to hold the line in South Vietnam while easing antiwar pressures at home. In the meantime, Hanoi settled into a classic "fighting while negotiating" strategy, closely coordinating its military, political, and diplomatic moves to maximize pressures on the United States and exacerbate differences between Washington and Saigon.

Certain that they could succeed where their predecessors had failed, Nixon and his national security adviser, Henry A. Kissinger, at first attempted to end the war through threats and diplomacy. The Saigon government appeared stronger than ever in 1969 and with U.S. backing might hang on indefinitely. Nixon and Kissinger also hoped to use the prospect of trade and arms control agreements to secure the Soviet Union's assistance in forcing Hanoi to make major concessions. Comparing his situation to that of Dwight D. Eisenhower with the Korean War in 1953, Nixon concluded that the threat of "massive retaliation" might sway the North Vietnamese, as he believed it had the North Koreans a decade earlier, and he counted on his image as a hard-line anticommunist to make it credible.

In the summer and fall of 1969, Nixon and Kissinger put their plan into action. Through intermediaries, they conveyed to the North Vietnamese their desire for peace and proposed the mutual withdrawal of troops from South Vietnam and restoration of the demilitarized zone. To signal that he meant business, Nixon ordered intensive, secret bombing attacks against North Vietnamese sanctuaries in neutral Cambodia. Publicly, he unveiled what he described as a comprehensive peace plan, revealing proposals he had made privately and then announcing the withdrawal of 25,000 U.S. troops. Through French and Soviet intermediaries, he warned Hanoi that if a settlement were not attained soon he would be compelled to employ "measures of great consequence and force."

Nixon's secret diplomacy and military threats failed to wrench concessions from Hanoi. From the North Vietnamese standpoint, the president's proposals were no better than those of Johnson, and to accept them would be to abandon goals they had been pursuing for nearly a quarter century. Throughout 1968 and into 1969, North Vietnam had tried to sustain maximum military pressure on the United States and South Vietnam, but the results were disappointing. Still hurting from the horrendous losses suffered at Tet but stubbornly clinging to its goals, the leadership reevaluated its strategy. Militarily, it reverted to the defensive and to guerrilla warfare. At the same time, it sought to rebuild the political apparatus in the south so badly damaged by Tet and to drag out the negotiations in a way that would put pressure on the United States to make concessions. Still confident that public opinion would eventually force an American withdrawal from Vietnam, Hanoi ignored Nixon's threats and prepared to wait him out.

"Vietnamization"

His end-the-war strategy frustrated, Nixon fell back on the Vietnamization concept introduced by Johnson on a small scale after Tet. To quiet popular opposition to the war, he initiated a phased withdrawal of U.S. troops and a gradual transfer of primary military responsibility to the South Vietnamese. While U.S. combat forces sought to keep the enemy off balance by relentlessly attacking their supply lines and base areas, American advisers worked frantically to build up and modernize the South Vietnamese armed forces. The force level was increased to more than one million, and the United States turned over to South Vietnam vast quantities of the newest weapons. Nixon hoped that by mobilizing American opinion behind his policies and building up South Vietnam's military strength, he could persuade the North Vietnamese that it would be better to negotiate with him now than with South Vietnam later, and he could extract the concessions necessary to secure an honorable U.S. withdrawal.

In part as a means of supporting Vietnamization, in part to pressure the North Vietnamese, Nixon authorized in April 1970 an invasion of previously neutral Cambodia. The venture backfired. From a purely military standpoint, it achieved modest results, buying some time for Vietnamization. At home, however, the unexpected expansion of a war the president had promised to end enraged his critics, causing massive antiwar demonstrations across the country. The killing of six students during demonstrations at Kent State and Jackson State added to the furor. The Cambodian venture brought the most serious congressional challenge to presidential authority since the beginning of the war. And it merely hardened the diplomatic deadlock. North Vietnamese and NLF delegates boycotted the Paris peace talks until American troops had been withdrawn from Cambodia.

The result was more stalemate. A disastrous ARVN invasion of Laos in 1971 ended in a humiliating retreat back into South Vietnam and made clear that Vietnamization was a long-term undertaking if it could be accomplished at all. Despite continued troop withdrawals, opposition to the war in the United States rose to an all-time high in the summer of 1971. As the purpose of the war became more murky and protest mounted at home, rampant demoralization set in among U.S. troops in Vietnam. Enlisted men refused to obey orders, and "fragging" of officers reached unprecedented proportions. Problems with drugs and racial conflict among G.I.s further highlighted the breakdown of morale. Under these circumstances, Hanoi remained content to bide its time, more and more certain that domestic pressures would eventually force a U.S. withdrawal.

The Easter Offensive

In 1972, each side took measures to break the long-standing stalemate. Since 1969, North Vietnam had carefully built up its resources and manpower for a final military offensive to topple the South Vietnamese regime and force the United States from Vietnam. While attempting to keep Vietnam on the back burner, Nixon and Kissinger sought to negotiate major changes in U.S. relations with the Soviet Union and China, ensuring the president's reelection, isolating North Vietnam from its major allies and suppliers, and leaving it no choice but to come to terms. Neither side would achieve what it hoped with its dramatic moves of 1972, and each would pay a high price trying. But they did bring the war into a final, devastating phase that would ultimately lead to a compromise settlement.

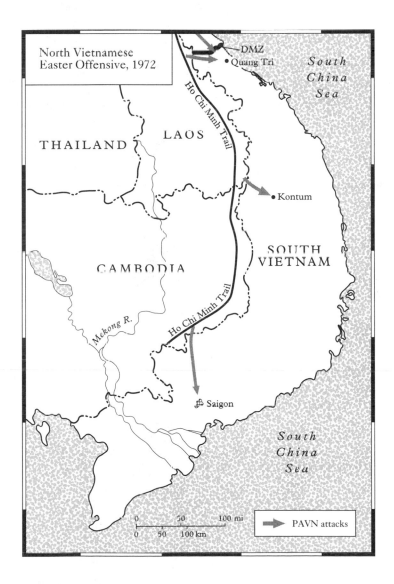

In March 1972, North Vietnam launched a massive, conventional invasion of the south. Hanoi correctly assumed that domestic pressures would prevent Nixon from putting U.S. forces back into Vietnam. The invasion, like that of 1968, was also probably timed to coincide with the presidential campaign in hopes that, as before, a major escalation would produce irresistible pressures for peace in the United States. The North Vietnamese aimed the offensive at the ARVN main force units, hoping to further discredit the Vietnamization policy and leave the countryside open for the NLF.

B-52 Stratofortress bombers played a key role in operations Linebacker and Linebacker II in 1972. A modified B-52D carried as many as 108 500-pound bombs; this bombload almost equaled that of a squadron of B-17s in World War II.

In its first stages, the offensive enjoyed great success. ARVN held off a major assault at An Loc, just sixty miles north of Saigon, but PAVN units forced abandonment of South Vietnamese strongholds at Quang Tri near the demilitarized zone and Kontum in the Central Highlands.

Although stunned by the swiftness and magnitude of the invasion, Nixon responded vigorously. Unwilling to send U.S. troops back to Vietnam, he nevertheless lashed out furiously. He quickly approved B-52 strikes across the demilitarized zone and followed with the most drastic escalation of the war since 1968, the mining of Haiphong harbor, a naval blockade of North Vietnam, and massive, sustained bombing attacks under the code name "Linebacker." The conventional military tactics employed by North Vietnam in the offensive required vast quantities of fuel and ammunition, and the bombing and blockade made resupply extremely difficult. Backed with devastating U.S. air power and fighting the conventional war for which they had been trained, the South Vietnamese stabilized lines in front of Saigon and Hue and even mounted a counteroffensive.

The military campaigns of 1972 raised the stalemate to a new level of violence. Both sides suffered heavily, the North Vietnamese losing an estimated 100,000 men and South Vietnam 25,000, but neither emerged appreciably stronger than before. North Vietnam had demonstrated ARVN's continued vulnerability and the NLF had scored some gains in the countryside, but the South Vietnamese government remained intact and Nixon had not given in. Despite heavy casualties and massive damage from U.S. bombing, the North Vietnamese retained sizable forces in the south, and intelligence reports indicated they could fight on for at least two more years.

Peace and More War, 1973–1975

Thus by the fall of 1972, each side found compelling reasons to compromise. Nixon recognized that an indefinite continuation of the air war might cause serious problems at home. He was eager to uphold earlier promises to end the war, and he wanted a settlement before the election if it could be achieved without embarrassment. North Vietnam had suffered terribly from the latest round of U.S. bombing and also wanted peace if it could be attained without abandonment of long-term goals. Battered, exhausted, and increasingly isolated from its allies, Hanoi apparently concluded that it might get better terms from Nixon before rather than after the election.

Each side thus moved cautiously toward a compromise. The United States had already made a major concession, agreeing to allow North Vietnamese troops to remain in the south after a cease-fire. It also retreated from its absolute commitment to the Thieu regime by agreeing to a tripartite electoral commission that would arrange a political settlement after the cease-fire. In the meantime, the North Vietnamese dropped their insistence on the ouster of Thieu, accepting the principle of a cease-fire that would leave him temporarily in control but would give the NLF status as a political entity in the south. After more than six months of tortuous, on-and-off negotiations, complicated by strenuous objections and obstructionism on the part of the Thieu regime and yet another round of massive bombing of North Vietnam—"Linebacker II," the so-called Christmas bombing—an agreement was signed in January 1973 providing for U.S. military extrication from Vietnam.

The Paris peace agreements did not bring an end to war. The Nixon administration still hoped to keep the Thieu government in power. The United States used various subterfuges to provide continued military assistance to the Saigon government, and civilian advisers assumed the role formerly played by military officials. Both the Thieu government and the North Vietnamese and NLF jockeyed for position in South Vietnam militarily and politically and refused to cooperate in furthering the peace process. Finally, in early 1975, North Vietnam launched another massive military offensive. Without U.S. support, South Vietnam could not withstand the onslaught. Nixon had been forced to resign the previous year because of the Watergate scandals, themselves in part a product of his efforts to control domestic opposition to the war in Vietnam. His successor, Gerald Ford, presiding over a nation traumatized by war-weariness and economic recession, could do nothing. To a large extent America's creation, and never able to stand without massive American support, South Vietnam fell on April 30, 1975, ending a war that in its various phases had lasted for nearly thirty years.

*   *   *   *

The legacy of Vietnam for warfare was as ambiguous as the war itself. At the tactical level, the utility of the helicopter was validated, and it seemed likely to assume an even greater role in the warfare of the future. The effectiveness of the so-called "smart" bombs first used by the United States in 1972, precisely guided to their targets by computers receiving signals from television cameras and laser beams, foreshadowed a new era in air warfare.

Such new technology failed to produce military success, however, and in the realm of strategy the significance of Vietnam was less certain. Flushed with victory, the Vietnamese hailed the triumph of people over technology, proclaimed the superiority of their revolutionary war doctrines, and heralded a new era in the unrelenting struggle against capitalism. The Vietnamese did wage war with skill and determination, to be sure, and they showed adaptability and even at times genius in conceiving and applying what turned out to be a successful strategy. As Martin van Creveld has observed, moreover, in all the low-intensity wars of the post–World War II era, the less-advanced nation has won, demonstrating the limits of sophisticated weaponry and conventional military forces.

In retrospect, however, the Vietnamese victory appears to owe as much to the unique circumstances of that war and the balance of forces prevailing in Vietnam as to ideology or abstract principles of warfare. Revolutionary war doctrine prevailed nowhere else, and the collapse of the Soviet Union and its eastern European empire less than fifteen years after the fall of Saigon left the Socialist Republic of Vietnam, along with China, North Korea, and Cuba, communist anachronisms in a world dominated by alien political and economic systems. The devastating display of high-technology military weaponry put on by the United States in the Persian Gulf War of 1991 at least called into question simplistic Vietnamese notions that people would always prevail over weapons.

Failure normally provokes more in the way of soul-searching than success, and in the aftermath of their first defeat in war, Americans engaged in an extended and at times agonizing reappraisal of their involvement in Vietnam. Some critics insisted that instead of attempting to wage a conventional war in the guerrilla-war setting of Vietnam, the United States should have recognized the sort of war it was in and employed counterinsurgency methods better designed for it. Others insisted that the United States had failed because timid civilian leaders, by imposing crippling restrictions, had prevented the military from using American power effectively to attain victory. The one thing on which most Americans could agree was that Vietnam had discredited the limited-war doctrines so much in vogue in the 1950s and 1960s. Politicians and military thinkers, liberals and conservatives, all generally concurred in the aftermath of America's failure in Vietnam that limited war was unworkable, even immoral. In going to war in the Persian Gulf in 1991, President George Bush made clear that he would not permit "another Vietnam" and gave his military commanders freedom to use American power swiftly and decisively.

The long-range implications of such conclusions nevertheless remained quite unclear. American success in the Persian Gulf War owed more to the circumstances peculiar to that war than to successful application of lessons from Vietnam. More important, the end of the Cold War eliminated the geopolitical setting in which limited-war doctrines had been conceived and the Vietnam War had been waged. The "lessons" of Vietnam thus remained as murky as the nature of warfare in the post–Cold War world.

SUGGESTED READINGS

Bergerud, Eric. *The Dynamics of Defeat: The Vietnam War in Hau Nghia Province* (Boulder, Col.: Westview Press, 1991).

Clodfelter, Mark. *The Limits of Air Power: The American Bombing of North Vietnam* (New York: Free Press, 1989).

Davidson, Phillip B. *Vietnam at War: The History, 1946–1975* (Novato, Calif.: Presidio Press, 1988).

DeBenedetti, Charles, and Charles Chatfield, assisting author. *An American Ordeal: The Antiwar Movement of the Vietnam Era* (Syracuse, N.Y.: Syracuse University Press, 1990).

Duiker, William. *The Communist Road to Power in Vietnam* (Boulder, Col.: Westview Press, 1981).

Giap, Vo Nguyen. *People's War; People's Army* (New York: Praeger, 1962).

Herring, George C. *America's Longest War: The United States and Vietnam, 1950–1975* (New York: McGraw-Hill, 1986).

Krepinevich, Andrew. *The Army and Vietnam* (Baltimore: Johns Hopkins University Press, 1986).

Pike, Douglas. *PAVN: People's Army of Vietnam* (Novato, Calif.: Presidio Press, 1986).

———. *Viet Cong* (Cambridge, Mass.: MIT Press, 1966).

Race, Jeffrey. *War Comes to Long An: Revolutionary Conflict in a Vietnamese Province* (Berkeley: University of California Press, 1972).

Sheehan, Neil. *A Bright Shining Lie: John Paul Vann and America in Vietnam* (New York: Random House, 1988).

Spector, Ronald H. *After Tet: The Bloodiest Year in Vietnam* (New York: Free Press, 1993).

Westmoreland, William C. *A Soldier Reports* (Garden City, N.Y.: Doubleday, 1976).

Young, Marilyn B. *The Vietnam Wars, 1945–1990* (New York: HarperCollins, 1990).

22

WAR IN THE MIDDLE EAST: VIOLENCE ACROSS THE SPECTRUM OF CONFLICT

The Arab-Israeli Wars
The Iran-Iraq War
The War in Afghanistan
The Cold War in Retrospect

During the Cold War from 1945 to 1990, wars tended to occur more frequently and to last longer than earlier in the century. By the late 1980s, some thirty-two major and seventy-five minor conflicts were being fought each year at widely varying scales of violence and for reasons often having little or nothing to do with the Cold War. Of the numerous conflicts during the post–World War II period, several of the most significant occurred in the Middle East and Southwest Asia, areas which had long been the scene of religious and ethnic wars. As colonial powers lost their control over this region after 1945, deep-rooted hostilities emerged among the diverse religious and ethnic groups, as well as the newly independent states. With the establishment of the state of Israel in 1948 and a refusal by neighboring Arab states to accept its existence, the region's instability increased. As tensions rose, international interest in the volatile area remained high because of its rich oil reserves and because three of the world's major religions (Islam, Judaism, and Christianity) had their roots in the area. Adding to the region's international importance were its position on the southern flank of the Soviet Union, the presence of Soviet and American client states, and the prominence of the Suez Canal as a vital link between the Red and Mediterranean seas. The strategic importance of the area increased the chances of superpower involvement, but that involvement usually remained indirect given the desire of the superpowers to avoid a direct confrontation and to prevent regional wars from getting out of hand.

The Middle East and Southwest Asia

The presence of advanced weapons and methods added to the significance of conflicts in the Middle East and Southwest Asia. In the post–World War II period, important advances in military technologies produced remarkably accurate and extremely lethal weapons, most notably, a new generation of precision-guided munitions. By the late 1980s, sophisticated electronics and computers promised even greater range, accuracy, and lethality in a wide range of lightweight and rugged weapons. Most of the economies in the Middle East and Southwest Asia had little or no capability to manufacture high-technology weapons and equipment, but foreign arms suppliers, especially the two superpowers, provided the latest arms to the belligerents, often as soon as those arms were fielded. When the superpowers refused to provide the most advanced weapons and equipment, regional powers were able to purchase them elsewhere with vast oil profits. With the employment of precision-guided munitions, medium-range missiles, and chemicals and with the use of constantly changing and improving methods, conflicts in the Middle East and Southwest Asia proved to be crucibles in which the most advanced ideas and technologies were tested and demonstrated.

Despite the numerous wars, continued violence, and active interest of the superpowers in these two regions, conflicts did not spill over into other areas and did not escalate to the point of direct superpower confrontation. Nuclear weapons remained unused, even though the threat of nuclear escalation by the superpowers remained constant. Nonetheless, the combatants often committed their entire populations and resources to the war effort and, in the case of Iraq in the Iran-Iraq War and Russia in the Afghanistan War, used chemical agents against their enemies. Thus, the various conflicts may have been "limited" in the eyes of the superpowers, but to the combatants there was little that was limited about them.

The Arab-Israeli Wars

Of the various conflicts in the Middle East, the Arab-Israeli wars came closest to causing a confrontation of the superpowers. Although the long-term roots of the Arab-Israeli conflict after World War II had little to do with the interests of the superpowers, and although neither superpower desired a confrontation, both provided much equipment and aid to their friends in the region. Many of the tensions stemmed from Jewish efforts to establish an independent state in Palestine and from the Arab rejection of such a state. For nearly two thousand years some Jewish people had yearned to return to the land of their origin and at the end of the nineteenth century began migrating to Palestine. European anti-Semitism in the 1930s and the Nazi Holocaust of World War II increased Jewish migration. The rise of Islam in the seventh century, however, had transformed the Middle East into a predominantly Islamic region, and Jerusalem had become one of Islam's holy cities. Though the Arabs tolerated the return of a small number of Jews to Palestine, they objected to large numbers of Jewish immigrants and rejected the idea of an independent Jewish state in what had become an Arab-Islamic region.

Following World War I and the dismantling of the Ottoman Empire, a League of Nations' mandate gave Great Britain control of Palestine. After World War II, the British reluctantly concluded that they could no longer contain the escalating violence between the Arabs and Jews and turned the problem over to the United Nations, which voted in November 1947 to partition Palestine. This partition intensified the war of guerrillas and terrorists, and savage attacks by both sides increased. When British forces withdrew, the Jews proclaimed on May 14, 1948, the establishment of the state of Israel. Minutes after the establishment of the new state, President Truman announced its recognition by the United States.

The next day Egyptian aircraft struck Tel Aviv, and soon thereafter forces from Egypt, Transjordan, Syria, Lebanon, Iraq, and Saudi Arabia attacked the new state. Most analysts expected the more numerous and better equipped Arabs to defeat the Jews easily. The Arabs, however, delivered a series of poorly coordinated attacks with only part of their forces, and the Israelis committed as many soldiers to battle as the attacking Arabs and fought with great courage and skill. The battles turned out to be a series of disorganized clashes between small units. After four weeks of fighting, both sides accepted a cease-fire sponsored by the United Nations.

Following 1948, tensions between Israelis and Arabs remained high but increased after 1954 when Gamal Abdel Nasser gained control of the Egyptian government. When Nasser's attempts to acquire weapons from the West failed, he turned to the Soviet Union for assistance in modernizing Egyptian forces. A September 1955 agreement between Egypt and Czechoslovakia enabled the Soviets to supply, indirectly, arms to Egypt for the next twenty years. Meanwhile, France objected to Egypt's providing arms to insurgents in Algeria and supplied arms to Israel. Seeking to end the British

presence in Egypt and the Suez Canal zone, Nasser unexpectedly nationalized the Suez Canal on July 27, 1956. The British and French decided to
intervene militarily, and the Israelis joined them in an attack against Egypt.

After calling up reserves on October 28, the Israelis began their
attack against Egypt with a daring airborne landing deep inside the Sinai east
of the Mitla Pass. Concurrent with the landing, a small Israeli force of
infantry and tanks crossed into the Sinai on the southern part of the Israeli
frontier, drove across the desert, and linked up with the paratroopers on
October 30. In the center of the Sinai front, the Israelis moved around the
strong Egyptian defenses at Abu Ageila and attacked them from the rear;
they then drove west toward Bir Gifgafa. In the south, they sent a small column toward Sharm el-Sheikh, the strategic point at the mouth of the Gulf of

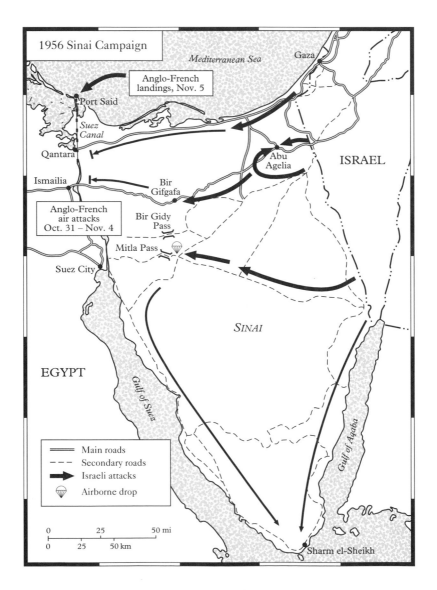

Aqaba. On October 31, French and British bombers began their attacks against Egyptian airfields and destroyed most of the Egyptian air force. Fearing that Egyptian forces in the Sinai would be cut off by the French and British seizure of the Suez Canal, Nasser ordered a withdrawal. Israeli forces eventually halted about fifteen kilometers east of the Suez Canal. As the Israelis expanded their control over the Sinai, the British and the French landed one-and-a-half divisions of infantry on November 6 near the northern mouth of the Suez Canal. After these forces started advancing down the canal, the French and British accepted a United Nations cease-fire.

Despite the decisiveness of the British, French, and Israeli victory, the United States—followed by the Soviet Union—demanded that they relinquish captured Egyptian territory. This was the first and only time the Americans sided with the Soviets against their closest allies. President Eisenhower believed that Western aggression would pressure Third World nations into the Communists' arms and opposed the reassertion by force of colonial control over less-developed nations. He warned the Russians, however, that if they placed troops in the Middle East, the United States would oppose them with force. Reflecting the explosiveness of the situation, a Soviet diplomat stated in a letter to Eisenhower, "If this war is not curbed, it . . . can develop into a third world war." The British, French, and Israelis had no choice but to accede to the American and Soviet demands. In the end, the Israelis withdrew from the territory they had seized, and the British and French lost much of their influence in the region.

Whatever the outcome of the war, the Israelis had developed an effective military force between 1948 and 1956. They organized a small, high-quality standing army always ready for action, and they used universal military conscription of men and women to form reserve units that could be ready for combat in seventy-two hours. With rigorous training and frequent active-duty tours by the reservists, the Israelis prepared their armed forces for extremely demanding operations. The 1956 campaign, however, had not been without difficulties. The Israelis had not forged a clear doctrine on the operations of armor and infantry in mobile warfare and had encountered problems with their loose system of command and control. The Israeli performance had been impressive, but it would be even more so in the future.

1967: The Six-Day War

A fragile peace existed in the Middle East until 1967. A United Nations force patrolled Israel's border on the Sinai and along the Gaza Strip, but along Israel's border with Syria and Jordan, ambushes, firings on civilians, and reprisal raids occurred frequently. The series of events that led to the 1967 war began in early May when Moscow informed Nasser that the Israelis were massing troops for a strike against Syria. Nasser responded to the report—which turned out to be false—by mobilizing his reserves and moving units into the Sinai. He also pressured the United Nations into withdrawing its troops from the Sinai and soon occupied Sharm el-Sheikh, the strategic point at the mouth of the Gulf of Aqaba. As soon as Egyptian units had control of Sharm El-Sheikh, Nasser cut off Israeli shipping through the Gulf of Aqaba, sparking the 1967 war.

The Arabs recognized that the defeat of Israel would require unity. Shortly before the outbreak of hostilities, they established a semblance of unity of command by having the Jordanian king accept an Egyptian general as commander of Arab forces on the Jordanian front. Iraq also permitted its troops to come under Egyptian command; contingents from Kuwait and Algeria joined the Arab forces encircling Israel. Prior to the war, the Arabs—according to an Israeli analyst—had some 250,000 troops, 2,000 tanks, and 700 aircraft available for use against Israel. Despite the nominal authority of the Egyptian general, no true unity of command ruled the diverse forces.

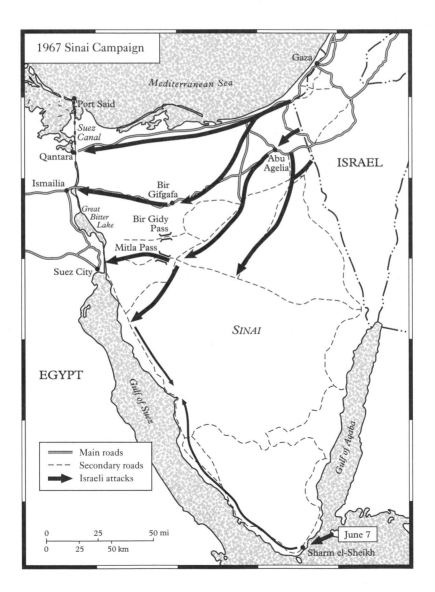

Facing an extremely unfavorable situation but with the advantages of central position, centralized command, and effective intelligence, the Israelis quietly mobilized their reserves to defend against the impending Arab attack and then launched a preemptive air strike. The attack began early on June 5, hit eleven Egyptian airfields, and caught the Arabs completely by surprise. In a matter of hours, the Israelis destroyed most of the Egyptian air force and then turned their attention to the other Arab air forces. By the evening of the second day the Israelis had destroyed more than 400 Arab aircraft, while losing only twenty-six. This remarkable performance provided the Israelis complete air superiority for the remainder of the campaign and was the key to their victory.

Relying on their central position, the Israelis intended to shift forces from one front to another and to defeat Egypt, Jordan, and Syria in turn. The Egyptians were first. In the northern part of the Sinai, an Israeli armored division attacked along the coast and then turned to secure Bir Gifgafa. In the central part of the Sinai, another armored division fought a desperate battle against Egyptian defenses around Abu Ageila and finally managed to capture the main enemy positions. After securing Abu Ageila, armored units raced southwest to secure the Bir Gidy and Mitla passes. By capturing Bir Gifgafa and the Mitla and Bir Gidy passes about fifty kilometers from the Suez Canal, the Israelis trapped most of the Egyptian forces. As the Egyptians attempted to flee, their columns became easy targets for the Israeli Air Force; Nasser later acknowledged that the Egyptian army lost about 80 percent of its equipment in the Sinai. On the fourth day of the war, June 8, some Israeli forces reached the Suez Canal and exchanged artillery and antitank fire with Egyptians across the canal.

On the central front, which included Jerusalem and the West Bank along the Jordan River, Jordan entered the battle around noon on June 5, the day the Israelis' preemptive strike destroyed most of the Arab air forces. Hesitant to cross the border with a sizable assault, the Jordanian army fired artillery and small arms into Israel and crossed the border with a small force south of Jerusalem. The Israelis responded by capturing Jerusalem and then isolating the high ground that runs north of Jerusalem, parallel to the Jordan River valley. After launching attacks on the north and south ends of the high ground, the Israelis gained control of all the bridges over the Jordan River. This cut off the Jordanians on the west bank of the river and ensured their complete defeat.

Having defeated Egypt and Jordan, the Israelis concentrated against the Syrians who had done little to aid their allies in the first days of the war. On the morning of June 9, the Israelis attacked, beginning their efforts with heavy air strikes. Despite strong Syrian fortifications, the Israelis seized the forward slope of the northern Golan Heights by the end of the first day's fighting. The next morning, they fought through the Syrian defenders. To the south of the Sea of Galilee, an Israeli armored division broke through the Syrians, and Israeli paratroopers, using helicopters, assaulted rear positions. As Syrian resistance crumbled, a United Nations cease-fire went into effect at 1830 hours on June 10.

Israeli tanks entered Jerusalem on June 7, 1967. The seizure of the Wailing Wall in the Old City of Jerusalem marked the emotional climax of the war for the Israelis.

Israel's decisive victory changed its strategic situation dramatically. For the first time, it controlled the Golan Heights, the West Bank, and the Sinai; it now had depth for its defense. It also had a very competent air force and army that functioned smoothly together in highly mobile operations. Additionally, the army had developed a strong armored force, improved its command and control system, and polished its methods for attacking fortified positions. Despite some progress, the Arabs still had not coordinated their efforts effectively and had not mastered armored operations. Their piecemeal and tentative attacks had given the Israelis time to mobilize and the opportunity to defeat each opponent in succession. Arab commanders had also displayed less confidence and initiative than their Israeli counterparts.

The 1967 war complicated the Arab-Israeli conflict and brought increased superpower involvement in the region. New controversy focused on the return of the Sinai and the Golan Heights and the status of the West Bank and the Gaza. The Arabs refused to accept the loss of additional territory to the Israelis and began a so-called "War of Attrition" that lasted for three years. This included numerous cross-border raids, artillery barrages, and air strikes. Washington supported Israel's demand for a negotiated peace settlement in exchange for the occupied territories and increased its shipment of arms to Israel. The Soviets also became more involved and agreed to rearm Egypt and Syria; no longer funneling their weapons through Czechoslovakia, they shipped them directly to the Arab states. The discontent of the Arabs uprooted by the establishment and expansion of Israel complicated the situation further. Known as Palestinians, they had formed the Palestine Liberation Organization. Most lived in neighboring Arab states and increasingly used terrorist tactics against the Israelis. Both the Arabs and Israelis soon became weary of the stalemate and casualties, and in August 1970, another cease-fire went into effect.

1973: The Yom Kippur War

After Nasser died in 1970, Anwar Sadat became the president of Egypt. More moderate than his predecessor, he nevertheless felt compelled in October 1973 to go to war against Israel, but he did not seek a decisive defeat of the Israelis. Instead, he sought to break down the aura of Israeli invulnerability. Recognizing that a limited military victory would provide significant political gains, Sadat coordinated his actions effectively with Syria and Jordan so that the Israelis would have to fight a debilitating war of attrition on two fronts.

Sadat also provided his forces with sophisticated weapons and energetically improved their readiness. When the Soviets refused to provide their most advanced weapons, he ordered Soviet advisors out of Egypt. Despite the shock of this expulsion, the Kremlin continued providing weapons, and oil money from other Arab states enabled the Egyptians to purchase arms from different sources. As Sadat worked to improve Egyptian forces, one of his most important steps was to draw officers and soldiers from the better-educated segments of Egyptian society. He recognized the importance of intelligent, well-trained soldiers capable of handling sophisticated weapons. He prepared his army to fight a set-piece battle in which superior numbers of personnel and weapons would wear down the Israelis and brunt the effectiveness of their mobile units.

In the Sinai, Israeli strategy played into the hands of Sadat, primarily because the Israelis had emerged overly confident from their 1967 victory. To defend the Sinai, the Israelis constructed the Bar-Lev line on the east bank of the Suez Canal. They first built huge ridges of sand with a few reaching as high as twenty-five meters. They then prepared small fortified positions every ten to twelve kilometers behind the ridges of sand. The small forces in these positions had the mission of delaying the Egyptians until the Israelis mobilized and deployed sufficient ground forces. Reflecting the prevailing overconfidence, one general officer remarked that the line would be "the Egyptian army's graveyard."

Though Israeli intelligence had performed well in 1967, it did not do so in 1973, and the Egyptian attack surprised the Israelis. As early as October 1, the Israelis had observed increased activity on the western edge of the canal, and on October 2 the commander of the Southern Command ordered a higher state of alert. The Israelis also brought their forces along the Golan Heights to a higher state of readiness. Intelligence officers, however, doubted that the Arab armies would attack during Ramadan, Islam's month of fasting which occurred in October. On the morning of the Arab attack,

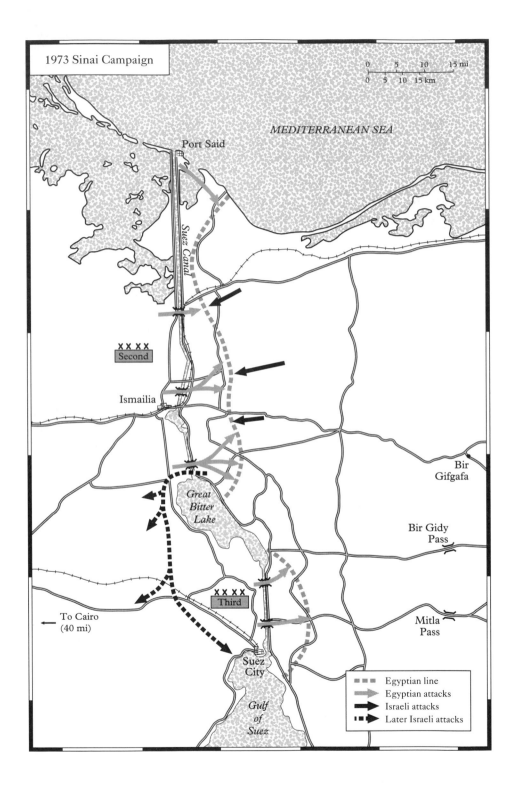

1973 Sinai Campaign

MEDITERRANEAN SEA

0   5   10   15 mi
0   5   10 15 km

Port Said

Suez Canal

X X X X
Second

Ismailia

Bir
Gifgafa

Great
Bitter
Lake

Bir Gidy
Pass

To Cairo
(40 mi)

X X X X
Third

Mitla
Pass

Suez
City

Gulf
of
Suez

▪▪▪▪ Egyptian line
➔   Egyptian attacks
➔   Israeli attacks
▪▪▪➤ Later Israeli attacks

Prime Minister Golda Meir approved a partial mobilization but ruled out a preemptive strike. In the approaching conflict, the Israelis would not have several of the key advantages they had had in 1967.

The Egyptians attacked along the entire front of the canal at 1405 hours on Saturday, October 6, the Jewish Sabbath as well as the Day of Atonement (Yom Kippur). Syria simultaneously struck in the Golan Heights. Preceded by air strikes throughout the Sinai and a huge artillery barrage, five infantry divisions, using about 1,000 rubber assault boats, crossed the Suez Canal. Engineers used high-pressure water hoses to wash away the ridges of sand and open crossing sites through which vehicles could pass; they also began constructing twenty bridges across the canal. After six hours of fighting, the Egyptians had established several bridgeheads with a depth of three to four kilometers. By October 9 the bridgeheads had a depth of about ten to twelve kilometers. Only after consolidating their position across the canal did the Egyptians expect to advance toward Bir Gifgafa and the Mitla and Bir Gidy passes. They intended to remain under the protection of their air defense and repel the expected Israeli armor and air attacks when they came.

The effectiveness of the Arab antiaircraft and antitank defenses shocked the Israelis. During the first week of fighting, the Israelis lost eighty aircraft, about one-quarter of all their front-line planes. With direct Russian participation and assistance, the Egyptians used a variety of surface-to-air missiles to establish an air barrier thirty kilometers wide and 140 kilometers long, along the canal. The Egyptians also beat back three Israeli armored brigades that launched several loosely coordinated attacks without infantry and artillery support. Following the victory of 1967, the Israelis had downplayed the need for infantry and artillery to support armor, and in the first days of the 1973 war, Sagger antitank missiles caused heavy damage to the Israeli tanks. Though awkward to fire, the Sagger had a range of about 3,000 meters and could be manually guided to a target with a hand-controlled stick. For the first time, the individual infantryman had a long-range, highly lethal antitank weapon, and the Israeli tanks found themselves in unfavorable circumstances without infantry and artillery support in a combined-arms team.

On Sunday, October 14, the Egyptians charged out of their bridgeheads in six major thrusts. In the subsequent battle, about 2,000 tanks on both sides fought the largest tank battle since Kursk in 1943. Though the Egyptians penetrated about fifteen to eighteen kilometers, they lost about 200 tanks. Instead of making one or two strong armored thrusts, they diluted the effect of their offensive by splitting their forces into six weaker efforts. Perhaps more important, the Egyptians moved outside the umbrella of their highly effective air defenses and suffered heavily from Israeli air strikes. They also encountered Israelis armed with newly arrived TOW (tube-launched, optically tracked, wire-guided) antitank missiles from the United States.

As soon as the opportunity appeared, the Israelis went on the offensive. At 1700 hours on October 15, the Israelis began a daring and bold operation to cross the Suez Canal north of the Great Bitter Lake. Brigadier

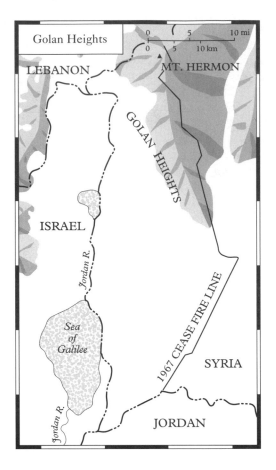

General Ariel Sharon's division cleared a corridor through the Egyptian forces on the east bank of the canal. Despite fierce fighting, the division crossed the canal and caused pandemonium among several Egyptian divisions that were surprised by its sudden appearance. As Sharon's division began expanding the bridgehead to the west of the canal, elements from two additional Israeli divisions crossed the canal. These forces destroyed air-defense sites on the west bank of the canal and thereby enabled the Israeli Air Force to operate more effectively. In addition to threatening the logistical support of the entire Egyptian army, the three divisions turned south and cut off the Egyptian Third Army, which was on the eastern bank of the canal.

Though huge forces participated in the Sinai action, some of the most critical fighting occurred on the Golan Heights, where the Israelis had very little space to trade for time. The Israelis initially had only two infantry battalions in the Golan Heights, reinforced by two tank battalions from the 188th (Barak) Brigade. In late September, the 7th Armored Brigade arrived, bringing the total number of tanks to about 175. On October 6 three Syrian mechanized divisions, reinforced by two armored divisions, attacked these small forces, which had to hold until reinforcements rushed to their assistance. With about 1,500 tanks, the Syrians greatly outnumbered the Israelis. During the desperate fighting, which lasted for three days and two nights without respite, the Israelis threw newly mobilized squads, platoons, and companies into the battle as soon as they arrived on the front. Israeli and Syrian units became intermingled, and artillery from both sides pounded the battlefield continuously. Despite the odds, the Israelis halted the Syrians, and by October 10 had driven them behind the 1967 truce line. The Syrians lost almost 900 tanks and hundreds of weapons and vehicles.

On October 11 the Israelis attacked Syria. Despite heavy losses, units from the 188th and 7th brigades led the attack. On the morning of October 13, the Israelis destroyed most of an Iraqi armored brigade that was attempting to reinforce the Syrians. That night, the Israelis punched through enemy defenses along the main Damascus road. Although a combination of Syrian, Jordanian, and Iraqi forces made several counterattacks, they failed to crack the Israeli positions. On October 22 the Israelis captured Mount Hermon on the northern end of the Golan Heights, but it was clear that any further advance into Syria would stretch Israeli logistical support beyond its limits and provoke an even stronger reaction from the Arabs.

As the Israeli victory became apparent, the United States and the Soviet Union called for an end to the fighting; even though Israel and Egypt agreed to a cease-fire, the fighting continued. Fearful of a complete destruction of Arab forces, the Soviet Union threatened to act "unilaterally" and to send in troops to enforce a cease-fire. This provoked a worldwide alert for U.S. armed forces; the crisis passed when Moscow agreed to an international peacekeeping force without American or Soviet participation. On October 24, the day prior to the alert of American forces, the Israelis reluctantly accepted a cease-fire. Despite overwhelmingly unfavorable odds, they had won a remarkable victory. As in the earlier Arab-Israeli wars, the key was their aggressive, highly mobile, hard-hitting style of fighting that placed a special premium on individual initiative.

Though the Israelis had won the war, Sadat had achieved his strategic objective of destroying the aura of Israeli invulnerability. As many as 12,000 soldiers from both sides lost their lives in the 1973 war, and Egypt and Syria lost about 2,000 tanks and 500 aircraft. Despite these losses, many Arabs believed they had won an important psychological victory. Their near-success demonstrated how some of them—particularly the Egyptians—had improved their loosely coordinated, oftentimes tentative style of fighting that had characterized earlier wars. Although the Israelis had gained territory on the Golan Heights and had halted only one hundred kilometers from Cairo, they had suffered a relatively large number of casualties (almost 3,000 killed), paid a high economic cost, and seen their regional and international position weakened at the expense of the Arabs. Their margin of victory would have been narrower if the United States had not rushed weapons and supplies to them.

Subsequent events also confirmed the reliance of the United States, Western Europe, and Japan on Middle Eastern oil and the utility of oil as a weapon to influence their behavior. To punish Israel's supporters, Arab members of the Organization of Petroleum Exporting Countries shut off the flow of oil in 1973 to the United States and the Netherlands (which had permitted the shipment of American military supplies to Israel across its territory). Though brief, the oil embargo demonstrated that whatever the outcome of future battles, the Arab countries had a powerful means to influence Western political priorities.

Following the 1973 war, the Camp David Accords of September 1978 provided for the establishment of normal relations between Egypt and Israel and resulted in the signing of a peace treaty between the two states in March 1979. The peace treaty caused great anguish among the other Arab states and did not solve the intractable problem of the Palestinians. The Palestine Liberation Organization (PLO) exercised considerable influence among the large numbers of Palestinian refugees in Lebanon. More a revolutionary military force than a classic military force, the PLO relied on subversion, kidnappings, and terrorism. With the presence of the PLO exacerbating relations in an already splintered society, a civil war erupted in Lebanon in early 1975. Responding to terrorist attacks, the Israelis launched air strikes and commando raids into Lebanon and in March 1978 and June 1982 invaded southern Lebanon. Thus even though Egypt and Israel established normal relations after the 1973 war, violence between the Arabs and Israelis did not end, and strife continued on Israel's northern border.

Between 1948 and 1973, the waging of war had changed dramatically in the Middle East. While the belligerents in 1948 engaged in numerous small, disorganized battles, the battles and campaigns of the 1956, 1967, and 1973 wars became larger, more complicated, and more sophisticated. For the extremely mobile campaigns of these wars, the Israelis were the first to recognize the need for high-quality leaders, capable of using their initiative and acting independently, but the Arab forces, particularly the Egyptians, slowly improved their forces. Nonetheless, the Arabs never displayed the flexibility and daring of the Israelis; they also never had unity of command. In each of the successive wars the combatants used increasingly complex and sophisticated weaponry. The 1967 campaign, in particular, demonstrated the remarkable ability of the Israelis to integrate air and ground operations and to wage mobile warfare reminiscent of the German *Blitzkrieg* of World War II. In 1973 about 2,000 tanks on both sides became engaged in the largest tank battle since Kursk in 1943. As is evident from Israeli successes in 1967 and 1973, they mastered armored operations before their opponents and employed their air and ground units in a more tightly coordinated and effective fashion; they also rapidly adapted to the requirement for combined-arms teams. The Egyptians, however, achieved great surprise with their use of precision-guided munitions and highly effective air-defense weapons in the 1973 war. Given the Middle East's strategic importance and the sophistication of the weapons employed, military leaders throughout the world carefully studied the Arab-Israeli wars for insights into how warfare was evolving and, particularly after the 1973 war, used that conflict as a benchmark to measure the readiness of their own forces.

The Iran-Iraq War

Another significant war in the Middle East and Southwest Asia during the Cold War was the Iran-Iraq War of 1980–1988. Though superpower involvement was limited, Iran and Iraq devoted their entire efforts to what was for them a total war without nuclear weapons. The fighting included a curious mixture of high-technology weapons and gruesomely bloody infantry assaults that seemed more appropriate for 1914 than for 1980. For the first time since World War I, chemicals were widely used, and for the first time since World War II, heavy aerial attacks hit population and economic centers. The Iraqis, having assembled a huge arsenal of modern weaponry, maintained an edge in the quality of their weapons, but the willingness of the Iranians to die for their nation and their religion enabled them to overcome significant disadvantages. The professionalism of the operations and the quality of generalship on both sides, however, were inferior to those of the Israelis in the Arab-Israeli wars.

The Iran-Iraq War stemmed from many centuries of religious (Sunni vs. Shi'ite) and ethnic (Persian vs. Arab) conflict, but President Saddam Hussein of Iraq attacked Iran for more immediate reasons. Concerned about Iran's efforts to undermine his regime, he hoped to curtail the spread of Islamic fundamentalism to which Iraq's Shi'ite population seemed particularly vulnerable. Seeking to increase his influence over the Persian Gulf area, he also wanted to seize key geographic areas that would enhance the political and economic power of Iraq.

Optimistic because of accounts of political, economic, and military turmoil in Iran, Saddam evidently expected a short, limited war. His confidence stemmed from the vast sums he had spent improving his armed forces and equipping them with more than 1,700 Soviet T-54, T-55, and T-62 tanks, 1,800 armored personnel carriers, and 340 combat aircraft. Saddam also knew that Iran had been weakened by the upheaval of its 1979 Islamic revolution and by the chaos engendered by Ayatollah Ruhollah Khomeini's efforts to subordinate Iranian political and military power to Islamic fundamentalists. As part of U.S. containment policy, the Americans had built up Iranian forces in the post–World War II period, but following the Islamic overthrow of the Shah of Iran, Khomeini had severely reduced the size of the Iranian armed forces, while dramatically increasing the number of militia and simultaneously replacing scores of officers with religious leaders who had little or no military experience. Despite Saddam's expectations of a quick and easy victory, the war would drag on for years and ultimately would cause somewhere between 600,000 and 970,000 deaths.

After a surprise air attack against ten Iranian air fields on September 22, 1980, the Iraqis launched ground attacks into Iran along four separate axes. Because many of Iran's most advanced planes were in protective hangars, the preemptive aerial attack failed to yield any real advantages. The ground attack also produced little, and about one week after the invasion began, Saddam called for a cease-fire. The Iraqis attempted several

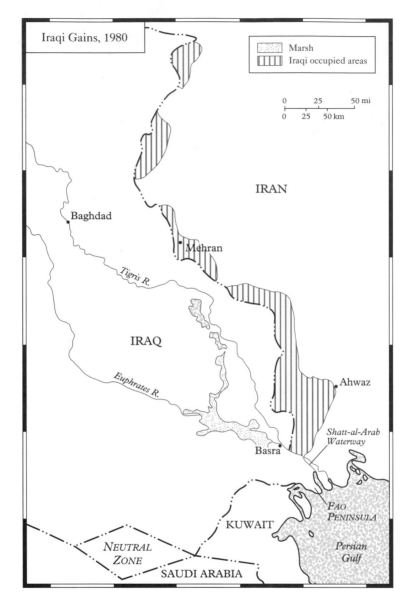

Iraqi Gains, 1980

Marsh
Iraqi occupied areas

0   25   50 mi
0   25   50 km

IRAN

Baghdad

Mehran

Tigris R.

IRAQ

Euphrates R.

Ahwaz

Shatt-al-Arab
Waterway

Basra

FAO
PENINSULA

KUWAIT

Persian
Gulf

NEUTRAL
ZONE

SAUDI ARABIA

subsequent attacks, but by March 1981 they had exhausted themselves. The attacks had gained little more than a narrow strip of Iranian territory along the 1,100-kilometer border. Instead of giving the Iraqis an important strategic advantage or a swift victory, the attacks provided the revolutionary regime in Teheran with a rallying cry for the mobilization of its people. A huge outpouring of patriotism and fury brought forth thousands of volunteers willing to die for their nation and the Islamic faith. Having failed to win a swift victory, the Iraqis struggled to avoid defeat and survive against Iran's far greater population and resources. Optimistic hopes for a short, limited war were replaced by the dreadful specter of a long war involving all of Iraq's population and resources.

As governments throughout the world watched the unfolding events, many feared the spread of Ayatollah Khomeini's influence in the Middle East more than Saddam's record of aggression and human rights abuses. Consequently, most members of the international community refused to sell Iran arms and equipment even though Saddam had initiated the war. The lack of international support caused the Iranians significant logistical problems for the remainder of the war. In particular, the inability to obtain repair parts quickly decreased the combat effectiveness of their air force.

From September 1981 through May 1982, Iran seized the initiative with a series of poorly coordinated and executed attacks. The inferior quality of its operations came from its inadequately trained commanders and staffs and its shortage of equipment. In some cases, the Iranians used human wave attacks. These attacks sometimes began with hundreds of children and old men, motivated by religious fervor, racing forward and using their bodies to detonate concealed mines. Then waves of poorly trained militia threw themselves on the barbed wire and attempted to cut the wire while under the fire of the Iraqis. Finally, better equipped and trained soldiers attacked over the mangled bodies of the initial waves of children, old men, and militia.

Iranian leaders hoped the religious zeal and nationalism of their people would enable them to expel the invaders, but such emotions did not overcome serious organizational and operational weaknesses. As Iranian commanders and staffs gained experience and became more effective, they used other methods such as the launching of night infantry assaults, supported by tanks and attack helicopters. Despite huge losses, the Iranians pushed the Iraqis back. At the end of June 1982 Saddam Hussein ordered the evacuation of most of the territory seized from Iran. This withdrawal, however, did not end hostilities, and Iran soon shifted from attempting to drive the invaders from its territory to defeating Iraq and deposing Saddam.

In July, the Iranians launched a huge offensive to capture Basra, Iraq's second largest city. After this attack failed, they began an offensive in October 1982 on the central front, seeking to drive toward Baghdad. Other attacks along the long front followed, but strong Iraqi defenses held the Iranians to relatively insignificant gains. By December 1982, the Iraqis were using limited amounts of mustard gas to repel night attacks and disrupt human wave assaults. They may also have used nerve gas. One Iraqi general officer compared the use of chemicals against the Iranians to the use of "pesticides" against "insects." Despite huge losses and no significant gains, the Iranians continued to press forward.

The war entered a new phase in 1984 when Saddam began using his superior air power to halt the shipment of Iranian oil through the Persian Gulf. In February, Iraq launched attacks on the Kharg oil terminal in the Gulf, and in subsequent weeks attacked several tankers with Exocet air-to-surface cruise missiles. Since the Iraqis shipped their oil by pipeline, mainly through Turkey, the Iranians could not attack Iraqi tankers, but they could attack the shipping of Iraq's allies, Kuwait and Saudi Arabia. Subsequent attacks against tankers were condemned by the United Nations' Security Council and began what came to be known as the "Tanker War." Throughout the remainder of 1984, attacks on commercial shipping and population centers continued. While Iran held the initiative on the ground, Iraq controlled the skies, and oil from Iraq and its allies continued to flow to the outside world.

From March to June 1985, the "War of the Cities" occurred. As early as 1980–1981, Iraq had used Frog 7A missiles against Iranian cities and in 1982 began using Scud missiles (a NATO code name for the Soviet-designed SS-1 missile). In 1985, however, Iraq intensified its attacks, including more than forty air strikes against Teheran. After Iran acquired its own Scud missiles from Libya, it too began firing missiles at Iraq's cities, mainly Baghdad. Both sides improved their tactics in 1984 and 1985, but no dramatic changes occurred. In early 1986 improvements in the quality of Iranian commanders and staffs enabled them to launch two major offensives simultaneously for the first time in the war. They made one attack north of Basra and the other in the Fao peninsula, to the west of the Shatt-al-Arab waterway. Despite strong Iraqi counterattacks, the Iranians clung to the Fao peninsula and severed Iraq's direct access to the Persian Gulf. The impression that things were going badly for Baghdad was heightened when an Iraqi offensive in May against Mehran in the central sector was driven back in July with heavy losses. Saddam had little choice but to intensify air attacks.

The key development in 1987 was the increasingly active role played by the United States. Washington reluctantly concluded that an Iranian victory was contrary to its interests and threatened the stability of the Middle East. After Kuwait transferred ownership of half its tankers to a U.S. shipping company, American warships began providing them security in the Persian Gulf. In May an Iraqi aircraft launched two Exocet cruise missiles—

The Exocet missile proved deadly against ships in the Falklands and in the Persian Gulf conflicts. The missile had a range of thirty-five to forty miles, and a pilot could launch a missile toward a target ship without making visual contact. After being launched, the missile traveled to its target only six to ten feet above the water at a speed of more than 600 miles an hour.

supposedly accidentally—against the USS *Stark*, killing thirty-seven crew-men and badly damaging the ship. When a tanker escorted by three U.S. warships hit a mine on July 22, a direct U.S.-Iran naval confrontation occurred. American forces made several attacks, including one against an Iranian gunboat laying mines and another against two offshore platforms being used as bases for Iranian gunboats. By the end of 1987, the United States had over thirty warships (but no aircraft carriers) in the Gulf, and Iran confronted the possibility of even greater American involvement.

In 1988 the strategic situation began to favor Iraq. The early part of that year brought a lull in the fighting, primarily because the Iranians could not mount their usual offensive. Increasing domestic discontent with the war hampered the mustering of sufficient forces. As the Iranians began to weaken, Iraq escalated its aerial attacks on Iranian cities. An important offensive occurred in the Fao peninsula on the night of April 16 when the Iraqis pushed the Iranians across the Shatt-al-Arab waterway. Iran's concerns were heightened by U.S. Navy attacks on April 18 that sank two of Iran's four frigates and one of its armed speedboats. These attacks forced Iran to confront the awful possibility of having to fight Iraq and a superpower at the same time.

Beginning in May, Saddam launched offensives in the north and central sectors, and then in the south. Perhaps more ominously for the Iranians, the Iraqis attacked at dawn in June against the southern part of the Haur-al-Hawizeh marshes. In addition to dropping airborne troops inside Iran, the Iraqis mounted an amphibious attack with Hovercraft. In about a day, they won one of their most important victories, but they soon withdrew from the captured territory. Saddam evidently sought to signal the Iranians his willingness to end the war.

Amidst the background of an increasingly bleak situation for the Iranians, the USS *Vincennes* mistakenly identified an Iranian airplane with 290 people aboard as a war plane and shot it down. The downing of the civilian aircraft sapped the morale of Iranian leaders, for it signaled the possibility of increased superpower involvement in the war. At the same time Iran experienced even more formidable problems in obtaining military supplies from other countries and adequately equipping its armed forces. Mismanagement and corruption magnified the effect of the international community's refusal to provide arms, spare parts, and supplies.

In late July, the Iraqis attacked in the northern, central, and southern sectors. In one case they penetrated more than sixty kilometers into Iran and came within twenty-five kilometers of a provincial capital, making it clear that they had the initiative on the ground and in the air. The Iranians managed to regain their lost territory by July 25, primarily through the use of human wave attacks. Unlike the initial outpouring of volunteers in 1980, however, the Iranians came forward less willingly. As Iran's situation became more desperate, cracks began to appear in Khomeini's tight control.

Having no real alternative, Iran finally accepted a truce. At 0300 hours on August 20, 1988, the long war ended. For years the war had provided Iranian leaders the opportunity to consolidate and expand the Islamic revolution, but the possibility of losing on the battlefield threatened the revolution's existence. In the end, neither country gained from the long and bitter war, and both plundered their economies and wasted thousands of lives. Some analysts, aware of the long enmity between the two countries and of the inconclusive ending of the war, wondered when it would resume.

The war itself witnessed few innovations, but the Iraqis used the latest chemicals, missiles, and high-technology weapons. They relied on their superior air power to attack Iranian cities and halt the shipment of Iranian oil through the Persian Gulf. They also integrated rudimentary airborne and amphibious operations into their campaigns, particularly in the latter part of the war. Nevertheless, neither Iraq nor Iran demonstrated a high level of operational proficiency during the war, though both did slowly improve their performance. When the United States became involved, the Americans' advanced naval weapons and methods dominated the Persian Gulf, but the damaging of the USS *Stark* by Iraqi Exocet missiles and the downing of the Iranian civilian airplane by a missile from the USS *Vincennes* demonstrated the complexities and dangers of employing such weapons in combat. In the broadest sense, however, the nature of the war and its place within the history of warfare is suggested more by the Iranians' human-wave attacks than by high-technology weapons or sophisticated operations.

The War in Afghanistan

A different type of war occurred in Afghanistan where Afghan guerrillas fought the Soviets from 1979–1988. For many reasons, the war bears a closer resemblance to the Vietnam War than to other conflicts in the Middle East and Southwest Asia. Strategically located between Russia, Persia (Iran), and India, Afghanistan had long been the scene of international conflict and intrigue, even though it was a backward, divided country with numerous quarrelsome tribes. A new conflict began in April 1978 with the overthrow of the government of Mahammed Daoud (who had overthrown the monarchy in 1973) and the seizure of power by the People's Democratic Party of Afghanistan. Armed resistance against the new Marxist government broke out quickly, and the situation deteriorated steadily, particularly when the ruling government split into factions openly contending for power. In December 1979, the Soviets, concerned about the key region on their southern border, supported a coup. While Soviet units already in Kabul seized control of key sites, two swiftly moving columns crossed the border, traveled along traditional invasion routes, reinforced the Soviet units already in Afghanistan, and seized important provincial cities. These actions neutralized the Afghan armed forces, established Soviet control over major urban centers, and enabled the Soviets to install Babrak Karmal as president of the Democratic Republic of Afghanistan (DRA). Some Afghan units resisted, but the Soviets disarmed them quickly.

Though hoping for a quick collapse of resistance similar to Czechoslovakia in 1968, the Soviets provoked a struggle that lasted until 1988 and

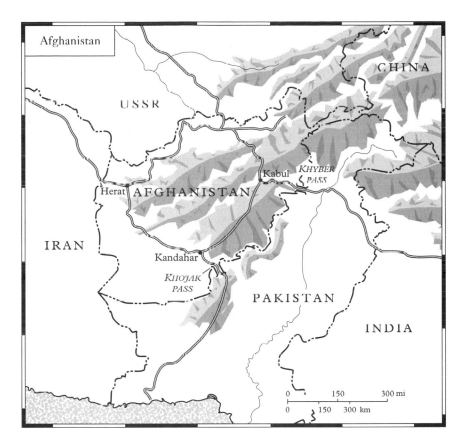

pitted regular troops and advanced technology against divided bands of guerrillas operating out of difficult mountainous terrain. Initially the Soviets were not overly concerned about Afghan resistance. The 15 million people living in Afghanistan seemed miniscule in comparison to the 265 million people in the Soviet Union and their vast industrial and military power. Soviet military leaders believed the various Afghan tribes had little unity and had only obsolete rifles and equipment left over from World War II. They did not anticipate the fierce resistance to Karmal's government from numerous factions of Afghan guerrillas, or Mujahideen. They also overlooked the Afghans' traditional hatred for foreign interference and the disastrous experience of the British in 1842 and 1879–1880.

During the first four years of the war, the Soviets and their Afghan allies held the major urban centers and launched attacks against the Mujahideen in remote and often mountainous areas. Opposition increased during this period as more than half of the 80,000 soldiers in the Afghan army deserted or joined the Mujahideen; many of the deserters brought their weapons with them. Relying on classic guerrilla tactics, the Mujahideen made numerous small-scale attacks and conducted ambushes of Soviet and DRA convoys along the major roads. Along with their indomitable fighting spirit, which was partially sustained by a wide wave of Islamic fundamentalism, the

Mujahideen possessed one other very important advantage—their ability to use sanctuaries in Pakistan and Iran as bases for support and training. Bands of guerrillas crossed the border with impunity and struck without warning throughout Afghanistan.

The initial Soviet and DRA tactics relied on standard techniques of mechanized warfare—a preliminary bombardment from artillery, helicopters, and airplanes, followed by a ground assault with tanks and armored personnel carriers. Especially in the first years of the war, Soviet and DRA forces often conducted division-sized offensives against Mujahideen sanctuaries. They also used large cordon and search operations in which they encircled an area and then combed it thoroughly for the elusive guerrillas. Particularly in the central and eastern portions of Afghanistan, however, the guerrillas found many hiding places among the rocks, crevices, and valleys of the rugged countryside. With their detailed knowledge of the area, they could operate easily in the mountainous areas and were not confined to the roads, but the Soviets usually had to move by helicopter or use road-bound vehicles.

Within months after arriving in Afghanistan, the Soviets slowly began modifying the structure of their units and changing their tactics. When they first intervened in Afghanistan, they employed an airborne division and four motorized rifle divisions, but they soon discovered that mechanized units and conventional attacks did not yield substantial success. They turned to decentralized, mobile operations with battalions and regiments reinforced by artillery, engineers, and helicopters. They also quickly increased their helicopters and trained their infantry for heliborne operations. Though still relying on mechanized infantry, they used air-transported infantry to strike swiftly at unsuspecting Afghan guerrillas. As time passed, their airmobile tactics resembled those employed by the Americans in Vietnam.

As the Soviets and DRA modified their organizations and tactics, the Mujahideen began receiving weapons from the west, including mines, recoilless rifles, and small antiaircraft guns. Though some unity of command would have ensured better coordination and perhaps greater effectiveness, most of the guerrilla factions operated independently. They moved back and forth across the border from Pakistan and Iran and launched operations with virtually no strategic or tactical purpose other than the killing of Soviet soldiers and their supporters. Rocket attacks against Kabul and other important cities became a standard practice. To starve and terrorize the guerrillas into submission, the Soviets used "scorched earth" tactics and destroyed villages and crops. They also used chemicals, particularly in the first three years of the war, but the Mujahideen stubbornly continued to resist and despite heavy losses controlled significant parts of Afghanistan.

By 1984 the Soviets had to choose between a massive increase in forces or a different strategy. Reluctant to accept higher casualties and to increase the size of their forces beyond 125–140,000, they adopted a different strategy. They shifted from destroying individual guerrillas to destroying the infrastructure needed by the guerrillas for survival and to disrupting their supply lines and bases in border provinces. To accomplish this, they attacked the supply lines along which men and equipment flowed from Pakistan; they also unleashed attacks against areas in the border provinces that previously had been sanctuaries for the guerrillas. Air and artillery strikes against hostile population centers became routine. Soviet troops attacked villages suspected of having sheltered guerrillas and destroyed their livestock and crops. For a time the Soviet and DRA forces seemed to have gained the upper hand. As attacks against villages increased in frequency and destruction, more and more Afghans fled Afghanistan. Analysts estimated that about 30–50 percent of the populace had departed by 1986. Nonetheless, the Soviets and DRA still had little control outside the urban centers.

In 1986, it became more and more apparent that battlefield victories and ruthless destruction of civilians and their property could not destroy the insurgents' will to fight. New air-defense weapons also began to have a significant effect. As early as February 1982, the Mujahideen had used the SAM-7 surface-to-air missile against Soviet aircraft, but in February 1986 the United States decided to send high-technology weapons to Afghanistan. By mid-1987 the Soviets were losing about one aircraft per day to shoulder-fired air-defense missiles, particularly the American-made Stinger. They quickly learned that aircraft had to take evasive measures and could not operate effectively near guerrilla units armed with the highly effective air-defense weapons.

The disruption of aerial operations reduced the Soviets' freedom to maneuver and forced them to launch ground attacks with less air support and fewer heliborne assaults. In 1987 and 1988, most operations reverted to reliance on mechanized infantry formations, supported by artillery. In

The first 340 Stinger missiles fired by Afghan rebels brought down 269 Soviet aircraft. These losses forced the Soviets to change their aviation tactics completely.

reality, the Soviets no longer had the mobility of the lightly equipped Afghan guerrillas. In November 1988, they began using Scud missiles—despite their inaccuracy—to provide fire support for units and to increase terror among the Afghan people. As the mobility of the Soviets decreased, they reluctantly withdrew from many remote areas and sought to secure urban areas, thereby permitting the Mujahideen slowly to gain the upper hand. The Mujahideen began using trucks rather than pack animals and main roads rather than trails. They also began using heavier weapons.

Karmal's presidency ended in November 1986. His replacement, Mohammed Najibullah, head of the secret police, adopted a more Islamic public image in November 1987 in an attempt to sway the Mujahideen. Though under Soviet control, he made another attempt at "national reconciliation" by dropping the word "democratic," which supposedly suggested Marxist leanings, and adopting the name, Republic of Afghanistan.

Continuing to search for alternatives, the Soviets and their Afghan allies launched air raids against Mujahideen bases in Pakistan. They stepped up attacks on villages controlled by guerillas and air-dropped thousands of mines along suspected supply routes. Despite these last-ditch efforts, the strategic initiative had shifted to the Mujahideen. The Soviet and Afghan forces still lacked popular support, and they had little control outside the major urban centers. In early 1988, the Mujahideen estimated that they controlled 80 percent of the countryside. Battlefield victories by the Soviets and heavy casualties among the Afghan people had neither ended the flow of troops and supplies across the border nor increased popular support for the new government. The deteriorating Soviet situation worsened as soldiers' morale dropped, discipline dwindled, and drug use became more prevalent.

Like the Americans after the Tet Offensive in Vietnam, the Soviets refused to increase the number of forces involved in the war. Facing overwhelming economic problems at home, they finally decided to withdraw. After signing an accord in Geneva in April 1988, they staged a farewell parade in Kabul in May and began to transfer equipment to the Kabul government and withdraw Soviet troops. The last Soviet soldiers departed Afghanistan on February 15, 1989. With the Cold War ending and the Soviet empire disintegrating, the government in Kabul remained faithful to the Soviets, and the war continued even though the Afghans were now fighting a civil war among themselves.

In April 1992, fourteen years after the Soviet-backed coup plunged Afghanistan into war, Najibullah gave up power, tried to flee, and ended up seeking refuge in a United Nations' building. As thousands of Mujahideen poured into Kabul, rival factions fought for control over the Afghan capital. An uneasy truce finally emerged, but factional strife—ethnic, tribal, and religious—continued. The outlook for Afghanistan remained bleak.

In the Afghanistan War, the Russians experienced numerous difficulties as they initially attempted to fight the Mujahideen with forces designed for combat in central Europe. Even after changing their methods and relying more on airmobile operations, the Russians failed to defeat the highly mobile Mujahideen and found themselves at a disadvantage when shoulder-fired air-defense weapons destroyed many of their aircraft and restricted the role of air support. Though facing defeat, the Russians refused to expand the war significantly in order to end the flow of weapons and supplies to the Mujahideen. In the end, the Russians limited their forces and objectives and by exercising self-restraint chose defeat rather than escalation.

The Cold War in Retrospect

The most unique aspect of the Cold War was the role played by nuclear weapons. From the dropping of the first atomic bomb in August 1945 to the formal dissolving of the Warsaw Pact in July 1991, atomic and then nuclear weapons exercised a dramatic influence over national security policy, military strategy, and the organizations and equipment of military forces. The influence of nuclear weapons over national security policy expanded as technological advances extended the range, improved the accuracy, and increased the payloads of nuclear delivery systems, vastly multiplying the destructive power of nuclear devices. Many changes in the nuclear era came from one of the superpowers reacting to actions or advances by the other. After the Soviet Union exploded an atomic and then a nuclear device, the Americans lost their monopoly over nuclear weapons, and deterrence became crucially important, particularly as Soviet nuclear forces approached parity with those of the Americans. Foremost among other factors influencing questions relating to nuclear weapons were concerns about the morality of destroying millions of people, military and civilian. To many critics, the acronym for Mutual Assured Destruction, MAD, aptly described the reasoning, or lack thereof, that underpinned theories relating to nuclear warfare. Nonetheless, changes in ideas and technologies pertaining to nuclear weapons greatly influenced the policies, strategies, and forces of both sides during the Cold War.

One of the most important consequences of the introduction of nuclear arms was the opening of an era of limited war. Throughout the Cold War, both the Americans and the Soviets feared the consequences of nuclear escalation and sometimes found themselves having to yield or compromise rather than raise the stakes in a crisis. Though both sides sought advantages in regional conflicts, neither wanted a crisis to draw the superpowers into a direct confrontation. Aware of the dangers of escalation and nuclear warfare, political and military leaders acknowledged the existence of various levels of conflict, ranging from low-intensity, to mid-intensity, to high-intensity, to general nuclear war. To avoid general nuclear war or high-intensity conflict (which presumably could escalate quickly), the superpowers limited their objectives or the size and nature of their military forces involved in a conflict. Nevertheless, both devoted considerable resources and efforts to the development of new weapons and methods, and both sold or shared these with friendly or client states. As a result, modern arms spread around the world at an unprecedented rate, and regular and irregular forces used them with terrifying effect in some 160 major conflicts and numerous minor ones between 1945 and 1990.

Though the superpowers avoided a direct confrontation, numerous revolutionary wars occurred in the post–World War II decades as European colonial empires dissolved and new successor states appeared. After Mao and the Communists successfully seized power in China in 1949, Mao's ideas wielded great influence. Along with other leaders such as Ho Chi Minh, he recognized the difficulty of achieving a quick victory against better-armed opponents, so he placed equal emphasis on political and military efforts and relied on a protracted struggle to exhaust his enemies and permit the seizure of power. In the ensuing decades of violence, dealing with guer-rillas became not only the most common but also one of the most complex aspects of the Cold War. Amidst increased concern about low-intensity con-flict in protracted wars, military forces developed special expertise and capa-bilities to deal with guerrillas. The Americans learned hard lessons about guerrilla warfare in Vietnam, while the Soviets learned similar lessons against the Mujahideen in Afghanistan.

Terrorism also became common. Though radicals had long used sustained, clandestine violence—murders, kidnappings, bombings, skyjack-ings—to achieve their political purposes, incidents of terrorism surged to his-torically high levels in the late 1960s and 1970s and became even more fre-quent in the 1980s. As acts of terrorism spilled outside the boundaries of ongoing conflicts, governments responded to the increased levels of violence by exchanging information about terrorist groups and accumulating intelli-gence about their membership and activities. Normal police procedures pre-vented some incidents. Israel, the United States, Great Britain, and Ger-many went a step farther and formed highly trained and specially equipped counterterrorist units to combat some of the gravest threats. In July 1976 an Israeli Army unit flew to Entebbe, Uganda, and freed a plane full of Jewish hostages. In October 1977, a West German counterterrorist group success-fully stormed a Lufthansa aircraft held by terrorists at Mogadishu in Soma-lia. And in May 1980 members of the British Special Air Service killed six terrorists who had seized twenty-six hostages in the Iranian Embassy in Lon-don. While efforts to eradicate terrorism did not yield complete success, the number of incidents seemed to ebb by 1990.

Along with the willingness to use violence against innocent civilians came an erosion of previous restraints on the use of chemicals. The Iraqis used chemicals against the Iranians and compared this use to the use of "pesticides" against "insects." The Soviets also used chemicals in Af-ghanistan, particularly in the first three years of the war. Additionally, the Egyptians used chemicals in Yemen, the Vietnamese in Kampuchea and Laos, the Libyans in Chad and Northern Uganda, the Cubans in Angola, and the Iraqis against the Kurds. The United States often used riot control gasses and hebicides in Indochina during the Vietnam War. In every case, the use of chemicals occurred in situations in which an opponent lacked ade-quate means of protection or retaliation. The apparent willingness to employ chemical weapons reflected in part some states' viewing chemical weapons as a "poor man's" nuclear weapon, but it also reflected a widespread willingness to use nearly any means available to achieve victory.

Most major conflicts during the Cold War proved to be protracted rather than brief. The United States hoped to end the Korean War quickly after the landing at Inchon and the breakout from the Pusan perimeter, but the entrance of the Chinese into the war and the complications of political questions and prisoner-of-war issues prevented an early termination of the war. In Vietnam, the Americans had even less success in ending the war early on favorable terms. At the beginning of the Iran-Iraq War, the Iraqi attack against Iran failed despite Iraq's possession of advanced weapons and despite the disorganized state of Iran's forces, and the war dragged on for years. Also, the Russians, despite their numerous advantages and initial success, failed in Afghanistan after years of fighting against a populace determined to pay any price to avoid defeat. Numerous other conflicts, many of which were civil wars stemming from the collapse of colonial empires, tended to last for years. Notable exceptions to long wars occurred with the Israeli victories in 1956, 1967, and 1973, but even these could be considered incidents in a much longer conflict extending over several decades.

In an age of astonishing progress in science and technology, the introduction of advanced weapons and equipment had a particularly significant effect on operations throughout the Cold War. In the Korean War, the combatants used weapons very similar to those of World War II, but in Vietnam the United States fielded a very different force that relied primarily on the helicopter for battlefield mobility. The United States also introduced some rudimentary precision-guided munitions in that war, but the potential of such weapons became most evident in the 1973 Arab-Israeli War. In the Afghanistan War, the Mujahideen used sophisticated and highly mobile air-defense weapons, which relied on advanced electronics, to transform the nature of the fighting. In the last two decades of the Cold War, electronic advances enhanced the ability of commanders to control their forces. With much-improved radios, commanders could maintain better contact with their subordinate units and often had a better grasp of the flow of events. Information about the enemy also increased as the introduction of remarkably capable cameras and high-flying, supersonic aircraft and then satellites permitted the gathering of critical intelligence by the most advanced armed forces. Similarly, advances in computers and information processing permitted improvements in logistical systems. By 1990, the capability of weapons and equipment, as well as intelligence and logistical systems, far exceeded those of 1945.

Despite some significant anomalies, as combat became more lethal, operations became more mobile and linked to air power. Reaching beyond the experience of World War II, battles truly became three-dimensional with the tightening of links between air and ground operations and the introduction of airmobile operations. The Israelis, particularly in the 1967 and 1973 wars, demonstrated their proficiency in conducting lightning-fast campaigns, relying on tightly integrated air and ground forces. Their successes in 1967 and 1973 stemmed more from their superior organizations, strategy, and doctrine than from their superior technology. Advantages in air power and in air mobility, however, did not enable the Americans to overcome the strategic advantages of the North Vietnamese or the tactical mobility of their lightly equipped infantry. Under similar circumstances the Russians failed to overcome the Mujahideen. Iraqi advantages in air power over the Iranians also did not inject mobility into the Iran-Iraq war.

In the final analysis, the conduct of war varied so greatly from conflict to conflict in the Cold War that no single example can serve adequately as a representation of all operations in the era. The key changes in warfare, nevertheless, were both conceptual and technological. Emphasis on limited war reflected the desire of the superpowers to avoid a direct confrontation and escalation to general nuclear war. And the notion of a spectrum of conflict—including low-, mid-, and high-intensity—reflected the various levels of conflict possible prior to all-out nuclear warfare. Within this spectrum, low-intensity conflict—including insurgency, counterinsurgency, and terrorism—received special attention as revolutionary groups often used violence to gain power or achieve their political aims. In an era of remarkable scientific and technological advances, new weapons and equipment frequently appeared, and numerous states fielded modern armed forces equipped with sophisticated arms. The Cold War was thus an era of innovation and change in which military leaders constantly confronted new ideas and weapons, as well as new challenges.

SUGGESTED READINGS

Amstutz, J. Bruce. *Afghanistan: The First Five Years of Soviet Occupation* (Washington, D.C.: National Defense University Press, 1986).

Badri, Hassan el, et al. *The Ramadan War, 1973* (Boulder, Col.: Westview Press, 1977).

Bradsher, Henry S. *Afghanistan and the Soviet Union* (Durham, N.C.: Duke University Press, 1985).

Carver, Michael. *War Since 1945* (London: Ashfield Press, 1990).

Chubin, Shahram, and Charles Tripp. *Iran and Iraq at War* (Boulder, Col.: Westview Press, 1988).

Collins, Joseph H. *The Soviet Invasion of Afghanistan: A Study of the Use of Force in Soviet Foreign Policy* (Lexington, Mass.: Lexington Books, 1986).

Department of National Defence, Canada, Operational Research and Analysis Establishment, ORAE Report No. R 95, G. D. Kaye, D. A. Grant, E. J. Emond. *Major Armed Conflict: A Compendium of Interstate and Intrastate Conflict, 1720 to 1985* (Ottawa, Canada: Orbita Consultants LTD, 1985).

Gawrych, George W. *Key to the Sinai: The Battles for Abu Ageila in the 1956 and 1967 Arab-Israeli Wars* (Fort Leavenworth, Kans.: Combat Studies Institute, 1990).

Hauner, Milan. *The Soviet War in Afghanistan: Patterns of Russian Imperialism* (Philadelphia: Foreign Policy Research Institute, 1991).

Herzog, Chaim. *The Arab-Israeli Wars: War and Peace in the Middle East* (New York: Random House, 1982).

_____. *The War of Atonement: October, 1973* (Boston: Little, Brown and Company, 1975).

Hiro, Dilip. *The Longest War: The Iran-Iraq Military Conflict* (New York: Routledge, 1991).

Kahalani, Avigdor. *The Heights of Courage: A Tank Leader's War on the Golan* (Westport, Conn.: Greenwood Press, 1984).

Klass, Rosanne, ed. *Afghanistan: The Great Game Revisited* (New York: Freedom House, 1987).

Laqueur, Walter. *The Age of Terrorism* (Boston: Little, Brown and Company, 1987).

Luttwak, Edward, and Dan Horowitz. *The Israeli Army* (Cambridge, Mass.: Abt Books, 1983).

O'Ballance, Edgar. *No Victor, No Vanquished: The Yom Kippur War* (San Rafael, Calif.: Presidio Press, 1978).

Small, Melvin, and J. David Singer. *Resort to Arms: International and Civil Wars, 1816–1980* (Beverly Hills, Calif.: Sage Publications, 1982).

Thompson, Robert. *War in Peace: Conventional and Guerrilla Warfare Since 1945* (New York: Harmony Books, 1985).

Zabih, Sepehr. *The Iranian Military in Revolution and War* (London: Routledge, 1988).

23

THE AGE OF INTERVENTIONS: PROJECTING POWER AND MAINTAINING PEACE

Interventions in the Cold War

Beyond the Cold War: The Persian Gulf

The United Nations: From Peacekeeping to Peace Enforcement

By the final decade of the Cold War, the major economic and military powers of the West had developed the capability to project force quickly over great distances. Improvements in air and sea transport had enhanced strategic mobility and enabled a few countries to move and support units across thousands of kilometers. In an age of science and technology, these same powers had built arsenals of high-technology weapons with remarkable accuracy and long range. Additionally, advances in electronics and communications permitted more effective command and control of units located at great distances from their homelands. In essence, rapid transport, advanced weapons, and modern communications provided a few countries the capability to project force almost anywhere on the globe. The states possessing this capability—primarily the United States, the Soviet Union, Great Britain, and France—often transported forces during the Cold War to distant regions to protect their own interests, limit the outbreak or spread of violence, or combat aggression. They consequently became embroiled in small conflicts in areas such as the Falklands, Grenada, and Panama.

When the Cold War ended in 1989–1990, the likelihood of interventions did not diminish. Although the confrontation between the two superpowers and their allies disappeared, a more complicated world, split by national, religious, ethnic, and regional differences, appeared. As the constraints of the Cold War dissolved, long-suppressed animosities and aspirations resurfaced, and violence broke out in several regions. Particularly in the Balkans and in the southern part of the former Soviet Union, civil strife, massacres, and pitched battles produced considerable turmoil. Fearing that the violence and turmoil would spread, almost like a cancer, to previously stable regions, some political and military leaders proposed interventions by national and multinational forces to end the violence and restore peace. To most observers' surprise, however, the first major conflict of the post–Cold War era began on August 2, 1990, when Iraq invaded and seized Kuwait. The international community responded to this aggression by transporting massive forces to Southwest Asia and then—in an astounding display of advanced weaponry—destroying much of the Iraqi armed forces with first an aerial attack and then a joint air and ground attack. The swift campaign revealed that not even a relatively wealthy and advanced country like Iraq could match the forces of the major military powers.

The ending of the Cold War also brought changes in the role of the United Nations and its use of intervening forces. No longer constrained by the likelihood of a veto in the U.N. Security Council or by the dangers of a superpower confrontation, U.N. leaders called for "peace-enforcement" operations in which multinational forces would intervene in conflicts, using appropriate levels of force, and restore peace. The reluctance of the United Nations to go beyond providing humanitarian aid in Bosnia-Herzegovina and the difficulties encountered with peace enforcement in Somalia demonstrated the complexities and problems of using international forces in interventions. These conflicts also reminded political and military leaders of the difficulties of employing force in regions riven by strong nationalistic, ethnic, or religious differences.

Interventions in the Cold War

During the Cold War, the major military powers often used their armed forces to support their foreign policy or to achieve specific political objectives. Many of these actions came from the effort to "contain" communism or to prevent a small crisis from erupting into a worldwide conflagration. Actions by the United States, for example, ranged from making a visit to a foreign port with a single warship, to reacting to the seizure of the USS *Pueblo* by the North Koreans in January 1968, to rushing supplies and equipment to Israel in October 1973 during the Arab-Israeli War. About forty crises reached the point where the United States had to confront the possibility of combat.

The U.S. Navy and Marines participated in most of the operations in which Americans were involved. The United States maintained fleets in most major oceans, and the Fleet Marine Force (which was established in

1933) provided battalions of marines that remained afloat with each fleet. In a crisis, marines could move quickly to an area as part of a fleet and could draw upon the fleet's firepower, aviation, and logistical support as they moved ashore. Such forces often proved ideal for dealing with small crises, and other countries such as Great Britain followed the American lead in increasing their fleet's capability to send units ashore.

Following World War II, airborne units and long-distance military air transport provided new means for interventions in distant regions. Much of the increased emphasis on airborne insertions came from the improved range and carrying capacity of military air transport. Particularly in the United States, each new aircraft (such as the Fairchild C-119 Flying Boxcar, the Lockheed C-130 Hercules, the Lockheed C-141B Starlifter, and the Lockheed C-5 Galaxy) provided greater range and carrying capacity than its predecessor. The transition from the C-119, widely used in the Korean War, to the C-5, widely used in the Persian Gulf War, included the change from a cruising speed of 325 kilometers per hour (200 miles per hour) and a range of 1,500 kilometers (900 miles) with a 20,000-pound cargo, to a cruising speed of 830 kilometers per hour (518 miles per hour) and a range of 5,600 kilometers (3,500 miles) with a 170,000-pound cargo. As the capability for air transport of large forces over long distances increased in the mid-to-late 1950s, military leaders recognized that improved transportation enabled light ground units to respond swiftly to an emergency, participate in a small war, or provide initial reinforcements in a much larger war.

An early example of the use of both air- and sea-transported forces occurred in April 1965. In the first American intervention in the Caribbean since U.S. Marines departed from Haiti in 1934, Washington dispatched troops to the Dominican Republic in April 1965. After a revolution broke out in the island nation, President Lyndon B. Johnson, fearing a communist takeover, decided to use military force to restore order. On April 28, 3rd Battalion, 6th Marines flew in helicopters from nearby American ships and landed in Santo Domingo. They assisted in the evacuation of Americans and reinforced the security guard at the U.S. Embassy. After being alerted on the night of April 26, elements of the U.S. Army's 82nd Airborne Division flew on C-130 aircraft from the United States to Puerto Rico and then landed at an airfield near Santo Domingo at 0216 hours on April 30. Members of 7th Special Forces Group and 5th Logistics Command followed. By May 4, more than 17,000 Americans were in Santo Domingo, and by May 17 more than 24,000.

The United States was not the only state to develop the capability for projecting power over great distances. In November 1956, after Gamal Abdel Nasser unexpectedly nationalized the Suez Canal, British and French forces seized the Canal. The operation included French and British airborne battalions jumping onto key targets while British marine battalions came ashore in amphibious landings and heliborne air assaults. Another multinational intervention occurred in November 1964, when U.S. Air Force C-130 aircraft flew 12,000 kilometers from Belgium to the Republic of the Congo and air-dropped a battalion from the Belgian Paracommando Regiment in an attempt to rescue 1,600 European and American hostages. Of those states intervening far outside their own frontiers, France demonstrated a special willingness to intervene in Africa, for it engaged in more than a dozen interventions from 1962 to 1994 in Dakar, Gabon, Chad, Zaire, the Central African Republic, Togo, and Rawanda.

The Falklands

Not all crises had direct ties to the Cold War. When Great Britain responded in 1982 to Argentina's seizure of the Falkland Islands, the roots of the conflict stretched back for more than a century. Known as Las Malvinas in Argentina, the Falklands are an archipelago of some 200 small and two large islands—East Falkland and West Falkland—located about 600 kilometers off the eastern shore of Argentina and 12,000 kilometers from the British Isles. The British claimed sovereignty over the islands, for they had occupied them for more than 150 years and most of the approximately 2,000 inhabitants were of British origin. Argentina denied London's claims and insisted that when Argentina became an independent republic in 1816, it had assumed title to those territories formerly ruled by Spain from Buenos Aires, including the Falklands. As early as 1965, the U.N. General Assembly recognized the dispute between the two states, and for almost two decades the two states discussed the islands' future. In December 1981, however, Argentina began preparing to seize the islands.

On April 2, 1982, the Argentines landed about 1,000 men at Port Stanley on the island of East Falkland and quickly overcame the small Royal Marine detachment. The next day the Argentines seized South Georgia, an island 1,300 kilometers east-southeast of the Falklands and a direct dependency of Britain. They then transported troops and supplies by air and sea until they had about 13,000 troops on the Falkland Islands. British leaders faced the uncomfortable choice of accepting the Argentine action or going to war nearly 12,000 kilometers from Britain with no force organized or prepared for such a contingency, no shore-based air, and little or no knowledge of their enemy.

The importance of sea power for the projection of power over great distances became particularly evident in subsequent British actions. Refusing to accept the Argentine action, the British quickly put together a "retrieval force," the lead elements of which departed Portsmouth on April 5. The task force eventually included a landing force of some 8,000 soldiers and marines and a naval force of more than one hundred ships, including two small aircraft carriers, eight destroyers, fifteen frigates, and six submarines. Fortunately for the British, they had not completed the previously arranged sale of the HMS *Hermes*, a small aircraft carrier, to the Australians. Much of the subsequent campaign would turn on control of the air provided for the British by Vertical/Short Take-off and Landing (VSTOL) aircraft from the HMS *Hermes* and the HMS *Invincible*.

British strategy first sought to isolate the Argentine forces on the Falklands. In early April, London announced that a "maritime" exclusion

The Falklands, April–June 1982

GREAT
BRITAIN

Portsmouth

6,000 km

ATLANTIC
OCEAN

ASCENSION
ISLAND

ATLANTIC
OCEAN

ARGENTINA

6,000 km

600 km

1,300 km

FALKLAND
ISLANDS

SOUTH
GEORGIA

SOUTH
SANDWICH
ISANDS

0   500   1000 mi
0   500   1000 km

zone with a 200–nautical mile (370 kilometer) radius would go into effect around the islands on April 12; on April 30 they expanded this into a "total" exclusion zone. Any Argentine aircraft or ship entering this zone would be treated as hostile and could be attacked. On May 1 the British began air and sea bombardment of Port Stanley and Goose Green. The following day, a British nuclear-powered submarine sank the Argentine cruiser, *General Belgrano*, well outside the exclusion zone; 323 members of the Belgrano's crew perished. For the next three weeks the British continued softening up the Argentine defenders on the Falklands.

Meanwhile, the British used Ascension Island, a small air and naval base in the Atlantic midway between Britain and the Falklands, as a staging base for the operation. After hastily assembling the requisite ships and personnel, the main task force, under Rear Admiral John Woodward, sailed from Ascension Island on April 18, even though additional personnel and ships continued to depart Britain for Ascension Island and the Falklands. As the main forces assembled in the South Atlantic, British special operating forces seized South Georgia on April 26, and on May 15 they struck a small Argentine airfield on Pebble Island, just off the north end of West Falkland, and destroyed eleven propeller-driven aircraft.

The Argentines did not remain passive. On May 1, when the British began their attacks on the Falklands, the Argentines launched fifty-six aerial sorties against the enemy's warships. Much to their dismay, they discovered that their best fighters, Mirages and Skyhawks, were no match for British Sea Harriers, which were armed with more advanced AIM-9G Sidewinder heat-seeking missiles. Part of the Argentines' problem came from their keeping their most advanced aircraft at airbases on the continent as many as one thousand kilometers from the Falklands, thus limiting these aircraft to only a few minutes in which they could loiter over a target or engage in a dogfight. In essence, the Argentines could not gain air superiority and could do little more than damage British naval forces and disrupt an amphibious landing. On May 4, from a range of about thirty-five kilometers, however, two Super Etendard aircraft fired two Exocet missiles at British ships; one missed the HMS *Hermes*, but the other struck the HMS *Sheffield*, a destroyer. The

Argentine air force personnel load antipersonnel rockets onto a propeller-driven aircraft. Despite the lethality of such weapons, attacks against British ships came closest to turning the war in Argentina's favor.

British had to abandon the burning *Sheffield*, which had twenty of its crew members killed. Despite the short loiter time, the Argentines continued launching strikes against British warships. On May 25, the Argentines sank the HMS *Coventry* and the *Atlantic Conveyor*, the first with 1,000-pound bombs and the second with an Exocet missile. Throughout the campaign, courageous Argentine pilots would sink six British ships and damage eighteen others. Had they possessed more than five of the French-manufactured Exocet missiles, they might have inflicted even greater damage.

By mid-May, the British had advanced into the South Atlantic, isolated Argentine forces on the Falklands, recaptured South Georgia, and launched commando raids and aerial reconnaissance in preparation for an amphibious landing. At dawn on May 21, after a diversionary operation farther south, British forces began landing at Port San Carlos and San Carlos on the northwest corner of East Falkland. The landing of the 3rd Commando Brigade (a marine unit commanded by Brigadier Julian Thompson) and two parachute battalions went smoothly and met almost no opposition, but Argentine pilots braved heavy antiaircraft fire to strike British ships. The British intended to consolidate their beachhead, unload supplies, and advance only a short distance until the 5th Infantry Brigade arrived. Although under heavy aerial attack, the British unloaded 12,000 tons of cargo in the first five days.

Concerned about British losses and desiring to show greater progress, London ordered the capture of Darwin and Goose Green, twenty kilometers south of the beachhead. Advancing on the night of May 27, the

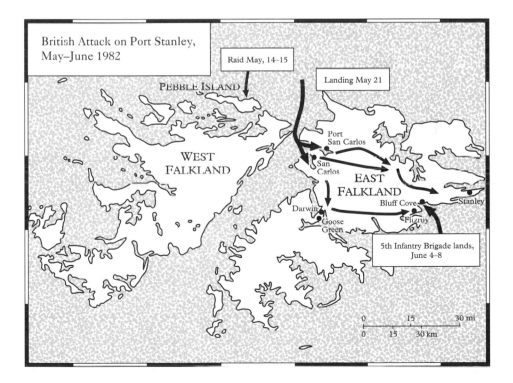

British Attack on Port Stanley, May–June 1982

Raid May, 14–15

Landing May 21

PEBBLE ISLAND

Port San Carlos

WEST FALKLAND

San Carlos

EAST FALKLAND

Darwin

Goose Green

Bluff Cove

Fitzroy

Stanley

5th Infantry Brigade lands, June 4–8

0   15   30 mi

0   15   30 km

2nd Battalion of the Parachute Regiment attacked early on May 28 and encountered strong opposition. Though their battalion commander was killed, the British continued pressing the Argentine defenders until they offered to surrender. Much to the paratroopers' surprise, more than 1,200 Argentines, some of whom were from the air force, surrendered their weapons and marched into captivity. With little support, a single British battalion had defeated a force triple its own strength.

The battle, however, produced considerable strain between the British military and the news media. Shortly before the attack on Goose Green, the BBC World News Service announced the location and mission of the 2nd Battalion. Other difficulties stemmed from few of the reporters having a sophisticated understanding of military affairs, and fewer still being prepared for the rigors of marching across the Falklands. Some reporters in the South Atlantic became particularly angry when they realized that their reports were being heavily censored and that some of the information removed by censors in the South Atlantic was being released by the Ministry of Defence in London.

After Goose Green, the British turned their attention to the capture of Port Stanley on the opposite side of East Falkland. Located at the tip of a twenty-five kilometer peninsula, Port Stanley had three chains of mountains between it and the approaching enemy. The Argentine commander, Brigadier General Mario B. Menéndez, had about 9,000 troops and placed them in well-organized and strong defensive positions in these mountains. Though apprehensive about an amphibious landing near Port Stanley, he evidently thought these mountainous positions were impregnable, and he expected his defenses and the approaching winter to force the British to seek a diplomatic end to the war. His lack of confidence in his soldiers, mostly conscripts, and the absence of air and sea support convinced him to wage a passive campaign and to keep his forces in static defenses. The morale of the defenders was very low. Few had proper cold-weather clothing, and many suffered from inadequate rations. Most apparently felt abandoned.

For the assault on Port Stanley, the British had intended to transport their troops by helicopter, but the sinking of the *Atlantic Conveyor*, a container ship, had resulted in the loss of critical helicopter support. Consequently many soldiers and marines had to trudge across some eighty kilometers of cold, wet, difficult terrain. The British advanced on two routes, one along the northern coast of East Falkland and the other along the southern coast. On June 1 they used helicopters to land troops on two mountains in the most westward chain, and other forces arrived by foot a few days later. On June 5 a battalion from the 5th Infantry Brigade landed on the coast to the south of the 3rd Commando Brigade, and two later days, another battalion landed but suffered heavily from an Argentine air strike.

The British land-force commander, Major General Jeremy Moore, eventually had two brigades in place for the final assault on Port Stanley. After doing everything possible to convince the Argentines to surrender, he decided to make a night attack on a broad front. On the night of June 11–12, the 3rd Commando Brigade, reinforced by the 3rd Parachute Battalion, attacked with three battalions abreast and seized, after some difficult

British troops rappelling from a helicopter. The superb training and highly competent performance of British troops enabled them easily to defeat the poorly trained and unmotivated Argentines.

fighting, the second chain of mountains. Two nights later the 5th Brigade passed through the marines and attacked the third chain. The British battalion in the north encountered strong opposition, but the two battalions in the south met little resistance. The Argentine defenders struck the northern battalion in two minor counterattacks, but heavy fire broke them. The failure of these counterattacks left the British in command of high ground from which they could dominate all the open ground to the west of Stanley. Within minutes, Argentine defenses collapsed. As the defenders fled in panic toward Port Stanley, white flags appeared throughout the Argentine positions. At 2100 hours on June 14, Menéndez signed an "instrument of surrender" given him by Moore.

In a stormy, mountainous, freezing environment, the British had won a difficult campaign. They had defeated a numerically superior force and had overcome the significant logistical problem of transporting and supporting large forces 12,000 kilometers from their home base. The war demonstrated the strengths of a well-trained, prepared force. British soldiers and marines, all of whom were volunteers, performed much better than the Argentines, most of whom were conscripts. Only the Argentine pilots performed on a par with the British. The war also demonstrated the importance of joint operations. Unlike the Argentines, who encountered problems in getting their services to cooperate, the British military achieved excellent cooperation among air, land, and sea elements as they waged a relatively short-warning, intense operation against an unexpected adversary. Another significant feature of the war was the demonstrated effect of the high-technology weapons entering the world's arsenals in the 1980s. The lethality and effectiveness of the Exocet over great distances cost the British dearly, just as the technical advantages of the more advanced Sidewinder missile cost the Argentines dearly. In the final analysis, however, the British won because of their ability to project power over great distances and their mastery of basic military skills.

Operation "Urgent Fury" in Grenada

Another significant intervention during the Cold War occurred in October 1983 when the United States relied on air and sea transport to intervene on extremely short notice in Grenada, a small island in the Caribbean. With marine units relying on naval transport, and army units relying on air transport, the brief conflict turned out to be unexpectedly difficult because of limited planning time, the great distances involved, the variety of forces participating, and the lack of adequate intelligence. Around noon on Saturday, October 22, President Reagan ordered the intervention in Grenada. Because of the breakdown of order on the island, he was initially concerned with the safety of Americans, but he soon expanded the operation's objectives to include restoring democratic government in Grenada and eliminating current and future Cuban intervention on the island. The Cubans were building a major air base in Grenada, and he feared the spread of Cuban and communist influence in the Caribbean.

A military policeman guards prisoners in Grenada. Planning for Urgent Fury included preparation not only for transport and combat but also for logistical support, medical care, civil affairs, and a host of other requirements.

The Joint Chiefs of Staff issued the formal order around 1700 hours on Saturday for Operation "Urgent Fury." Anticipating a mission to ensure the safety of Americans, the Commander-in-Chief of the Atlantic Command (CINCLANT) had already organized a joint force (designated Joint Task Force 120, under the command of Vice Admiral Joseph Metcalf, III) and sent it toward Grenada. Subsequent intelligence estimates of enemy forces in Grenada, however, identified about 700 Cubans (of whom 25 percent were military), 1,200–1,500 members of the People's Revolutionary Army (PRA), and 2,000–5,000 members of the People's Revolutionary Militia (PRM). Though the figures turned out to be inflated, the opposition appeared to consist of about ten combat battalions, plus supporting units. Responding to broader goals and facing what they thought was a large enemy force, planners increased the size of the American force by adding army units, flown in by the air force, to the operation. What had initially been envisaged as a relatively small and simple navy-marine rescue of American students became a much larger and more complicated operation.

Located about 200 kilometers off the coast of Venezuela, the island of Grenada is shaped like an oval, about thirty kilometers long and twelve kilometers wide, with a broad peninsula jutting out from the southwest corner. Much of the island consists of mountainous jungle, surrounded by a narrow coastal plain on which most of the island's towns are located. The Point Salines airfield with a 3,000-meter runway is on the peninsula in the southwest corner, and the capital city of St. George's is about seven kilometers north on the west coast of the island. Farther to the north and near the

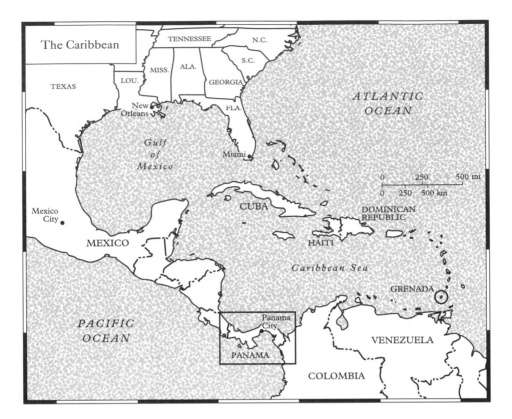

east coast is Pearls Airport. The airfields at Point Salines and Pearls and the city of St. George's became the focal points of American efforts. As planning proceeded, marine units received responsibility for the northern part of the island and army units for the southern part. Except for two small areas north and south of St. George's, the beaches were rocky, blocked by reefs, and unsuitable for amphibious landings.

The first force to move toward Grenada was an amphibious task force that—as a precaution—had been ordered around midnight on October 20 by CINCLANT to sail toward Grenada. The task force included the navy's Amphibious Squadron Four, consisting of five ships, and the 22nd Marine Amphibious Unit, consisting of an infantry battalion and a medium helicopter squadron. When the intervention began, however, Special Operations Forces led the Americans into Grenada. Among those participating were Delta Force, Seal Team 6, and C Company, 1st Battalion, 75th Rangers. The first attempt to use Special Operations Forces miscarried on Sunday night, October 23–24, when a joint Seal–air force combat-control team failed to land on Grenada and set up a sophisticated navigational aid for incoming aircraft. Early on Tuesday, October 25, other forces failed to seize the radio transmitting station north of St. George's and to release political prisoners from Richmond Hill Prison. A Seal team managed to seize the transmitting tower, but a counterattack by PRA soldiers forced them to withdraw. Nonetheless, the Seals destroyed the tower and prevented the PRA from transmitting any warning to the militia. In the one notable success of Special Operations Forces, a Seal team landed in helicopters at the Government House just outside St. George's and secured the safety of the British Governor General, Sir Paul Scoon. Despite strong counterattacks from PRA soldiers using Soviet armored personnel carriers, the Seals retained control over the Government House until rescued by marines the following morning.

Marine and army landings followed the actions of the Special Operations forces. Around 0730 hours on Tuesday, after receiving only a few small bursts of automatic weapons fire, heliborne marines secured Pearls Airport in the northeast corner of Grenada. Shortly thereafter, helicopters landed a company on a soccer field in the center of the town of Grenville about two kilometers to the south of Pearls Airport. The marines encountered no opposition and quickly secured the town and its port without taking any casualties. Farther to the south, U.S. Army units encountered much stronger opposition against well-prepared defenders. The first soldiers to arrive were from 1st Battalion, 75th Rangers; they had the mission of securing the Point Salines airfield before the arrival of 82nd Airborne Division. Not knowing whether they would land on the airfield or make an airborne drop, they flew about 3,000 kilometers from Savannah, Georgia, on C-130 aircraft. After the lead aircraft encountered strong antiaircraft fire, the ranger battalion commander ordered his soldiers to jump from 500 feet, thereby limiting their exposure to enemy fire. When the rangers landed around the airfield at 0530 hours on Tuesday, they received heavy automatic weapons and mortar fire from defenders on the high ground to the north of the airfield, but they quickly secured the airfield's periphery and cleared the runway of construction equipment, wire barriers, and metal stakes. Around 0900 hours, the rangers rescued 138 medical students at the True Blue campus just off the eastern end of the airfield.

While the rangers fought to expand the area under their control around the Point Salines airfield, the first elements of 82nd Airborne Division departed Fort Bragg, North Carolina, shortly after 1000 hours and landed at Point Salines around 1400 hours. Like the rangers, they had traveled more than 3,000 kilometers. When the first battalion from the 82nd landed, accompanied by the division commander, Major General Edward Trobaugh, sniper and automatic weapons fire continued sporadically from the high ground around the airfield. Despite the importance of pushing on to St. George's, Trobaugh focused on protecting the airfield and awaiting the arrival of another battalion before moving into the steep, heavily forested terrain along the route to Grenada's capital. Troop strength at Point Salines increased slowly because the unfinished runway had insufficient ramp space for parking landed aircraft, and a huge backlog of incoming forces and equipment quickly developed. The second battalion did not arrive until around 0300 hours on Wednesday.

On Tuesday afternoon, Admiral Metcalf decided to bypass the Cuban and PRA defenders around Point Salines and land marines at St.

George's. Around 1830 hours, without encountering any opposition, thirteen amphibian tracks landed about two kilometers north of St. George's. Using utility landing craft, a platoon of M-60 tanks and jeeps with heavy machine guns and antitank weapons followed. The next morning, around 0730 hours, one of the marine companies and the tank platoon reached the house where PRA soldiers besieged the Seals and Sir Paul Scoon. The appearance of the tanks and amphibian vehicles dispersed the PRA forces. On that day and the next, against little more than sniper fire, the marines secured the harbor works and the hilltops around St. George's.

At 0630 hours on Wednesday, two battalions of infantry from the 82nd Division attacked northeast out of the Point Salines airfield into the Calliste barracks, killing sixteen and capturing eighty-six Cubans. They then climbed a steep hill north of Calliste and captured a large ammunition depot about one and a half kilometers to the northeast. Six huge warehouses contained weapons, ammunition, uniforms, spare parts, and vehicles. As the paratroopers advanced, the rangers used marine CH-46s and CH-53s to travel to Grande Anse (about two kilometers to the north of the Point Salines airfield) and rescue additional students there. Despite the objections of one marine commander, who initially refused to transport army troops on marine helicopters, the rangers landed at about 1615 hours and quickly evacuated 224 students.

On Thursday, October 27, the 82nd, with six battalions on the ground plus its divisional artillery, pushed north toward St. George's. The operation went smoothly except for a navy A-7 aircraft accidentally strafing the headquarters of the 2nd Brigade and wounding sixteen soldiers, one of whom later died. At 1630 hours, the rangers launched an air assault into Calivigny Barracks, about five kilometers east of the Salines airfield. Though the rangers encountered no enemy, two helicopters collided, killing and injuring about two dozen men. The securing of the barracks around 2100 hours marked the end of significant military activity in Grenada.

Despite overwhelming superiority, the Americans had encountered many difficulties. Some problems stemmed from the operation's being cobbled together hastily without the participants having the time or opportunity for coordination. Other difficulties, particularly for the army and air force, revolved around the long distance—about 3,000 kilometers—between the units' home stations and Grenada. The complexities of launching an operation over such a long distance were accentuated by confusion over questions of command and control and by the lack of direct radio communications between the 82d Airborne, the marines, and Admiral Metcalf. As with many combat operations, intelligence could have been more accurate and timely. Urgent Fury became a controversial operation with criticisms surfacing for most aspects of the operation but focusing on the inability of the services to work together smoothly.

The October 1983 intervention in Grenada also marked a low point in relations between the U.S. armed forces and the news media. Heeding Department of Defense requests, President Reagan placed a total ban on press coverage during the first two days of the invasion and maintained tight restrictions on reporting in the following week. The Department of Defense provided several reasons for maintaining tight control over news reporting, including the necessity for secrecy and the inability to provide security for reporters. Some critics charged, however, that the American military leaders were suspicious of reporters and wanted to avoid negative media coverage. In the final analysis, strained relations between the military and the news media heightened criticism of the operation.

Operation "Just Cause" in Panama

Over the next few years the United States made some improvements in its conduct of joint operations and rapid interventions, and the effect of these changes was obvious in December 1989 when U.S. forces seized control of Panama. For several years tension had increased between Washington and Panama, and on Friday, December 15, the Panamanian National Assembly gave sweeping powers to General Manuel A. Noriega and declared Panama in a "state of war" against the United States as long as American "aggression" continued. On Sunday, December 17, President George Bush ordered U.S. military forces to intervene in Panama. In an address from the White House on the day of the operation, he explained that the objectives of "Just Cause" were "to safeguard the lives of Americans, to defend democracy in Panama, to combat drug trafficking, and to protect the integrity of the Panama Canal Treaty."

Unlike Urgent Fury in Grenada, Just Cause was smoothly and almost flawlessly executed. Those planning the operation relied on existing command relationships; they also had the crucial advantage of having sufficient time for planning and preparation and having 13,000 troops and a U.S.-controlled airbase immediately available. These advantages enabled most of the participating units to be well rehearsed for their combat mission and thoroughly familiar with the terrain. Even those units that parachuted onto key targets after being flown from the United States in transport planes had detailed information about their objectives. By striking twenty-seven targets almost simultaneously in the night, the Americans quickly gained control of Panama. Within seven hours after the assault began, the Panamanian Defense Forces no longer existed as a cohesive military organization and offered no organized resistance against U.S. forces.

Thus in the final decade of the Cold War, improvements in the ability to project force from fleets and increases in the cruising range and payloads of military air transport enhanced the capabilities of a few countries to intervene quickly in distant regions. Because of the need for rapid action over long distances, accomplishing critical planning and establishing effective command arrangements remained difficult. Problems with intelligence, logistics, communications, and coordination also appeared frequently. Interventions, nevertheless, continued to rely on offensive action and sought to overwhelm more poorly equipped and trained opponents swiftly.

Beyond the Cold War:
The Persian Gulf

As the Cold War ended, political and military leaders recognized the dangers of aggression from rogue states seeking territory, influence, or advantages. Common sense underlined the need to react swiftly with relatively large forces to counter such aggression. Hardly anyone, however, expected a major conflict immediately after the end of the Cold War. In many ways, the Persian Gulf War was as much a surprise as the Korean War, but unlike that experience, the United States, whose forces carried most of the weight of the war, proved to be far better prepared. Unfortunately for the Iraqis, the United States had developed the capability to reinforce Europe by transporting forces over great distances rapidly, and the campaign in Southwest Asia proved to be ideal for forces and doctrine designed to fight the Soviets in central Europe.

The war began when the military forces of President Saddam Hussein of Iraq invaded the tiny desert sheikdom of Kuwait on August 2, 1990. In a bold operation, Iraqi forces seized control of Kuwait's capital city and its rich oil fields and drove the emir of Kuwait into exile. With only 20,000 troops, thirty-six combat aircraft, and 275 tanks, Kuwait was no match for the Iraqis. Iraq's aggression and quick success convinced the international community that it threatened the traditional balance of power in the Middle East and Southwest Asia. Led by Egypt, Arab governments in the region sought an "Arab solution" to ease Iraq out of Kuwait, but Iraq announced on August 8 the annexation of Kuwait, dashing any hopes for peaceful resolution of the crisis. At a meeting of the Arab League shortly after the invasion, twelve of the twenty-one members expressed support for a United Nations embargo against Iraq and endorsed Saudi Arabia's invitation to the United States to send troops to deter Iraqi aggression. They also agreed to send Arab forces to defend Saudi Arabia. Many Arabs recognized that Saddam's ambitious desire to establish Iraq as the dominant power in the Middle East threatened their own way of life.

The seizure of Kuwait also captured the attention of much of the world. With the Soviet Union in disarray, with the Warsaw Pact crumbling, and with the two Germanys about to be reunited, the world seemed to be entering a period of peace. In what many hoped would be a new world order, aggression by one state against another could not be tolerated. For many, Saddam seemed to be nothing more than a "terrorist with an army." Moreover, Saddam's belligerence jeopardized much of the world's oil supplies. By seizing Kuwait and declaring it the nineteenth province of Iraq, Saddam doubled Iraq's oil reserves and gained control over 20 percent of the world's proven reserves. Even worse, his position in the Gulf, if unchallenged, could eventually allow him to dominate Saudi Arabia and increase his control to 40 percent of the world's oil reserves. The oil-dependent nations of the world could tolerate neither Iraq's aggression nor the threat of its controlling the world's oil supplies.

King Fahd of Saudi Arabia and General H. Norman Schwarzkopf. Keeping the diverse coalition together proved to be one of the most complex challenges of the war.

Much of the world united against Saddam. In a very important change closely associated with the ending of the Cold War and the willingness of Russia to oppose the Iraqi action, the United Nations Security Council adopted a resolution condemning the Iraqi invasion of Kuwait and soon imposed mandatory sanctions and an embargo against Iraq. After the United Nations adopted a resolution authorizing the use of force, thirty-six countries—not including Kuwait—dispatched forces to the Gulf.

Particularly during the period when the coalition was rushing ground forces to Saudi Arabia, the Iraqi ground forces, which had recently emerged from an eight-year war against Iran, seemed large and capable. Iraq's army dwarfed not only the other armies in the area—except for Iran's—but also many of those in Europe. As the fourth largest army in the world, it was bigger than those of Britain and France combined. It also possessed huge quantities of modern equipment and seemed to have a formidable tank force. U.S. intelligence agencies estimated that the Iraqis had some 4,550 main battle tanks and 2,880 armored personnel carriers in and around Kuwait. Though the great majority of the Iraqi tanks were older Soviet T-54 and T-62 models, about 500 of the main battle tanks were Soviet T-72 tanks, which weighed about 45 tons and were considered among the best tanks in the world. As for artillery, the Iraqis had 3,257 pieces in or near Kuwait; some analysts credited the Iraqis with a 7-to-1 advantage in artillery. The Iraqi air force had about 950 combat aircraft, and with more than 4,000 air defense guns and 300 long-range, Soviet-made SA-2 and SA-4 ground-to-air missiles, Iraqi air defenses seemed formidable.

Moreover, Saddam possessed a substantial store of chemical weapons and during the Iran-Iraq War had demonstrated his willingness to use them. The only thing lacking in Saddam's arsenal was nuclear weapons, but evidence strongly suggested that he was making a concerted effort to develop such weapons. On August 21, Pentagon officials acknowledged that the Iraqis had moved medium-range ballistic missiles into Kuwait. The missiles were Scud missiles which could carry conventional high-explosive warheads or chemical warheads with mustard or nerve gas. The possibility of Scud missiles spewing chemical or biological agents against coalition soldiers or against unprotected civilians caused considerable concern.

American Forces in the Gulf

The coalition facing Iraq established a centralized command system for Arab and Western air forces, but no single commander controlled all the coalition's ground forces. The coalition had two parallel commands for ground forces, one Arab and the other Western. A Saudi Arabian general officer maintained relatively loose command over the various Arab ground units. The Commander-in-Chief of U.S. Central Command, General H. Norman Schwarzkopf, commanded all American forces in the region of the Persian Gulf and Southwest Asia; the French and British governments also gave him control of their ground forces. As for air forces, U.S. Lieutenant General Charles A. Horner acted as the coalition's air commander and worked directly under Schwarzkopf.

Of those nations sending forces, the largest number by far came from the United States. With lead elements arriving on August 8, the 82nd Airborne Division was the first large American ground unit to arrive, followed by U.S. Marines. Virtually all of the first 35,000 American troops in Saudi Arabia were flown there by about sixty commercial aircraft chartered by the U.S. military, but the bulk of their equipment came by sea and arrived weeks later. When it became apparent that the U.N. embargo would not force the Iraqis to withdraw, the Americans increased their offensive capability. In November, President George Bush announced that the United States would substantially increase the size of its ground forces in Saudi Arabia by mobilizing additional reserve forces and by moving U.S. Army units from Europe. Shortly thereafter, armored units from the U.S. Army began to arrive.

The move of VII Corps from Germany was particularly challenging. After the public announcement on November 8 of VII Corps' deployment to Southwest Asia, the Americans moved 122,000 soldiers and 40,000 major pieces of equipment to the air- and seaports of embarkation, using 465 trains, 312 barges, and 119 convoys. From these ports, the corps used 578 aircraft and 140 ships to travel to Saudi Arabia. After arriving at ports in Saudi Arabia, some VII Corps units traveled as far as 500 kilometers in convoys along Saudi highways. Though the entire move took about twelve weeks, most tactical units arrived in sufficient time to conduct training in the desert in chemical protection, weapons firing, land navigation, breaching procedures, and tactical operations.

The Americans brought with them the technological weapons that they had created during the 1970s and 1980s. The air force's F-117A Stealth bomber was invisible to Iraqi defenses throughout the war. Precision-guided munitions from the F-117A and other aircraft allowed them to attack targets with unheard-of accuracy. Air-launched and sea-launched cruise missiles could strike targets from extreme distances and with accuracy similar to precision-guided munitions. Electronic warfare aircraft could jam and distort enemy radars, while air-launched missiles sought and destroyed active radars. The army also possessed weapons that allowed its troops to seek out and kill its opponents at great distances. Infrared and other devices allowed U.S. ground forces to "see" at night, while their opponents remained blinded by the darkness. Additionally, the Americans' training, doctrine, and operational conceptions provided them significant advantages. The competence, initiative, and flexibility of U.S. air and ground forces rendered irrelevant all considerations of Iraqi numbers, quality equipment, and battle experience.

From the beginning, it was clear that women would play a larger role in this war than any in history. Of the more than half-million American personnel in the Persian Gulf region at the height of the war, 35,000 were women. They operated air-defense systems, made intelligence assessments, drove trucks, sorted mail, operated water purification units, repaired equipment, acted as military police, and performed a host of other functions. Women helicopter pilots flew in combat zones, but not on direct combat missions; they moved supplies and soldiers around the battlefield and evacuated wounded soldiers. When the fighting began, five women were killed in hostile action; two others were captured by the Iraqis, one when her truck became lost and the other when her helicopter crashed.

Planning the Coalition's Defense and Attack

The outbreak of the war caught American military and diplomatic planners by surprise. Much of the prewar planning had viewed the Persian Gulf region as secondary to the European theater. Intelligence assessments in the region had focused mainly on the possibility of a Soviet advance, not on an Iraqi attack through Kuwait into Saudi Arabia. For most of August, as the

U.S. military deployed forces over enormous distances, the possibility of Iraq's moving south caused grave concern, but the situation was not as serious as it appeared at the time. While the Iraqis threatened Saudi Arabia, they possessed neither the training nor the logistical capabilities that such an operation would have required. By the end of August the Iraqis had settled into defensive positions in Kuwait to wait out the gathering coalition. Because of the solid performance of Iraqi defenses during the eight-year Iran-Iraq War, coalition commanders expected these positions to be strong.

The rapid buildup of U.S. combat aircraft initially focused General Schwarzkopf's attention on the use of air power. Six days after Iraq invaded Kuwait, he asked the air staff in Washington to prepare plans for aerial attacks against the Iraqis. Within a few days, a planning cell in the Pentagon produced a plan called "Instant Thunder" which envisaged a massive strategic air campaign against Iraq. Air planners believed that such a campaign would prevent a costly ground war and in six to nine days could achieve American national objectives, including "the immediate, complete, and unconditional withdrawal of all Iraqi forces from Kuwait." Schwarzkopf accepted the plan on August 10, apparently viewing it as a retaliatory plan. After briefing General Colin Powell, Chairman of the Joint Chiefs of Staff, planners added another phase to Instant Thunder, entitled "An Operational Air Campaign Against Iraqi Forces in Kuwait," which focused on destroying the Iraqi army. The air planners believed that Schwarzkopf intended to use only air power to force the Iraqis from Kuwait.

As events unfolded, however, Schwarzkopf conceived of the campaign against Iraq in four phases. In phase I, air attacks would strike Iraq. In phase II, coalition aircraft would gain air superiority over Kuwait. In phase III, air attacks would reduce Iraqi ground forces and destroy their ability to use chemicals. And in phase IV, ground forces with support from air forces would eject Iraqi forces from Kuwait. Schwarzkopf also made the crucial decision that Horner would run the air war and that the other air forces (marine and navy, but not army), as well as the other coalition air forces, would come under Horner's command. That decision allowed air planners to develop an integrated approach to air attacks against Iraq. To blend Instant Thunder into overall aerial planning, Horner established a special planning group in Saudi Arabia. The name Instant Thunder was dropped, and the air attack against Iraq—in essence a strategic campaign—became "Offensive Campaign Phase I." Before the first air attacks began, however, the idea of the air war being divided into distinct phases had almost disappeared, and target lists for phases I, II, and III had merged. Planners expected the focus of the aerial attacks to shift gradually from the strategic to the tactical arena and from Iraq to Kuwait.

Initial plans for the ground forces emphasized the defense, but early in September, Schwarzkopf's staff began planning for an offensive. On October 6, planners presented several alternatives to Schwarzkopf who selected an option calling for a two-week air attack followed by a ground attack that would penetrate Iraqi forces and advance into southern Kuwait. With the coalition's ground forces clearly outnumbered, planners ruled out a bold envelopment of the Iraqi forces. Concerned about the possibility of heavy casualties in such an attack, Schwarzkopf directed his staff on October 15 to begin planning for an attack with larger ground forces. His staff immediately began developing plans for an attack through the great Iraqi desert and around the flank of the Iraqis in Kuwait. In late October, Schwarzkopf approved the concept for an envelopment of Iraqi forces, and in mid-November, with President Bush having announced the commitment of VII Corps, he set mid-January as the time for the offensive.

The Coalition's Aerial Attack

Almost from the beginning of the crisis, the coalition had a distinct advantage in air power, concentrating 2,614 aircraft in the Persian Gulf area, 1,990 of which were American. Shortly before 0300 hours (local time) on January 17, 1991, the coalition's air plan unfolded when army AH-64 Apache helicopters attacked several frontier early-warning radar sites. The destruction of those sites created a corridor through which F-15Es were able to strike at Scud missile bases in western Iraq. A few minutes later, F-117A Stealth aircraft, undetected by Iraqi radar, arrived over Baghdad and other targets and began dropping precision-guided munitions. Minutes later, a wave of "Tomahawk" cruise missiles from naval vessels in the Gulf slammed into targets throughout Baghdad and elsewhere. At the same time, air-launched cruise missiles from B-52G bombers, which had flown from air bases as distant as Louisiana, hit their targets. The strikes caught the Iraqis completely by surprise, because they possessed no means of detecting the inward-bound missiles or Stealth aircraft.

The coalition made the destruction of the Iraqis' air defenses a high priority. From carriers in the Red Sea, the U.S. Navy sent F/A-18 Hornets and EA-6B Prowlers to strike Baghdad from the west; at the same time U.S. Air Force F-4G Wild Weasels approached the capital from the south. Decoys and drones gave the impression of even larger attacking groups, and chaff created additional confusion. As the Iraqi radar sites tracked the incoming aircraft, antiradar missiles homed in on their radar signals. Following this attack, many Iraqi air-defense units turned off their radar and fired their weapons aimlessly into the sky. Within hours, the Iraqi air-defense system ceased to operate as a coherent, functioning military system. Few Iraqi aircraft rose to meet the tide of aircraft sweeping over Saddam's lands; the few that did soon disappeared in explosions of air-to-air missiles.

When dawn came, amazed coalition air commanders discovered that they had lost only one aircraft during the night—far less than their prewar expectations of twenty-five to fifty aircraft. Most important, coalition air forces had achieved air supremacy over Iraq. Since coalition aircraft at heights above 10,000 feet could operate beyond the effective range of enemy antiaircraft guns, subsequent attacks suffered only minimal casualties. The coalition now had the luxury of continuing air attacks almost indefinitely.

The first night, coalition aircraft and missiles also hit a large number of special sites, particularly the nuclear, chemical, and biological special weapons programs on which the Iraqi regime was hard at work. Other strikes destroyed command-and-control centers, communications networks, and enemy airfields. Planners targeted Iraq's electrical network particularly heavily; they believed its destruction would lead to the collapse of communications, make it more difficult for the Iraqi military to function, and perhaps even lead to a collapse of national morale. By dawn on the morning of January 17, Iraq was well on its way to defeat.

Continuing the Air Attacks

From the allied perspective, the first few days of the air attack went like clockwork. Not only were losses well below expectations, but electrical power systems were down throughout much of Iraq. On day three weather began to interfere with air operations. Throughout the rest of the war, weather conditions created numerous difficulties for those planning and conducting air operations. Whatever the difficulties, the volume and accuracy of air attacks wore down the Iraqi military. At the end of the first week of air attacks, F-111Fs and the F-117As went after hardened shelters on Iraqi airbases. These attacks destroyed a substantial number of shelters on enemy airfields, as well as the aircraft parked inside. In a desperate move, Saddam

A Patriot missile leaps from its launcher. Initially designed to engage aircraft, the Patriot became the first successful antimissile system after modifications were made to the missile and its computers. Before the war its antimissile capability had undergone only limited testing.

ordered many of his remaining aircraft to fly to Iran. This action eliminated the Iraqi air force as a military factor in the war.

Despite the intensity of the coalition's air strikes, the Iraqis managed, beginning on January 18, to launch ninety-three Scud missiles, most of which were aimed at population centers in Saudi Arabia and Israel. Though lacking accuracy, the Scuds posed a strategic threat, for Saddam expected Scud attacks on Israel to bring Israeli forces into the war and thereby shatter the coalition. The U.S. Army's Patriot air-defense system intercepted 70 percent of the Scud missiles fired at Saudi Arabia and 40 percent of those fired at Israel. These were the first missiles ever intercepted in combat by an antimissile system, and the civilians and soldiers who had been the targets of Scud missiles loudly applauded the success of the Patriot. Nonetheless, the performance of the Patriot missiles was not flawless. Since the Patriot had been designed to explode near an incoming missile, not necessarily to destroy the warhead, some of the Scuds intercepted by the Patriots still caused damage on the ground. Due to a problem with computer software, a Patriot battery north of Dhahran failed to detect an incoming Scud missile on February 25, and the missile hit a barracks, killing twenty-eight American soldiers and wounding ninety-seven others.

On January 29, the Iraqis launched a raid with the 5th Mechanized Division, plus elements of two other divisions. They recognized that air attacks would continue for the foreseeable future. Moreover, air attacks had entirely shut down the Iraqi capacity to acquire intelligence. Consequently, they hoped the raid could gain valuable intelligence and perhaps force the coalition to begin the ground attack. Although the Iraqis got some troops into the Saudi frontier town of Khafji, most of the raiding force did not achieve even a brief success. One of the armored brigades got stuck in a minefield where coalition aircraft massacred vehicles and troops alike. Aircraft also hit units that were supposed to support the attack on Khafji and prevented them from reaching the front lines. By the end of the Khafji battle, the Iraqis had suffered several thousand casualties and lost several hundred armored vehicles. Khafji made clear that the Iraqis could not concentrate their armored and mechanized forces under a sky—night or day—dominated by coalition aircraft.

Air attacks thoroughly disrupted Iraq's command-and-control systems, political as well as military. Over the night of February 12–13, F117As executed a series of particularly heavy raids against Iraqi headquarters and bunker targets in the Baghdad area. One of those targets was the al-Firdos bunker; intelligence indicated that the Iraqis had just activated the bunker. Unfortunately, no one in either intelligence or in the planning cycle knew that the bunker also served as a shelter for families of the governmental elite (Saddam's regime constructed no bunkers for the general population of Baghdad). The result was a tragic loss of civilian lives that television immediately broadcast to the world. In response, political authorities in the United States forbade further attacks on Baghdad without Washington's approval; attacks on Iraq's political infrastructure virtually halted. Late in the war, F-117As did strike a few targets in Baghdad, but none that carried the risk of further civilian casualties.

As the time for the ground attack approached, coalition aircraft struck operational-level targets such as Iraq's military supply lines to Kuwait and the Republican Guard divisions in northern Kuwait. Among their targets, they destroyed thirty-one railway and highway bridges and thirty-two pontoon bridges. They also destroyed important fuel- and lubricant-distribution centers. At the end of the first week in February, the focus of the air campaign moved to preparing the battlefield for the ground attack.

Early in February, F-111F pilots discovered that their infrared sensors could accurately spot armored and other vehicles in the desert because of the heat differential between sand and metal. On February 5, F-111Fs attempted an experiment using their laser-guided bombs against enemy vehicles dispersed in the desert; these attacks were so successful that Horner, at Schwarzkopf's urgings, transferred the F-111Fs entirely into attacks in Kuwait. Dropping precision-guided bombs each night, the F-111Fs destroyed or damaged hundreds of Iraqi vehicles.

Aerial attacks significantly weakened the will to fight of Iraqi ground forces. Waves of B-52s pounded Iraqi positions, particularly the formidable Republican Guard units and the best Iraqi armored divisions. Meanwhile, psychological warfare efforts worked to weaken their morale further. Special radio programs broadcast antigovernment propaganda into Iraq, and aircraft dropped 30 million leaflets onto Iraqi positions. The constant bombardment severely demoralized the Iraqis, and a few deserters made their way across minefields into coalition hands in Kuwait. Larger numbers of deserters managed to flee into Turkey.

The Iraqis had entered Kuwait with a relatively well-equipped force manned by many combat-experienced soldiers and officers. At the end of the aerial operation, which lasted thirty-eight days and included more than 90,000 sorties, the coalition claimed to have destroyed 39 percent of the Iraqi tanks, 32 percent of the armored personnel carriers, and 48 percent of the artillery in Kuwait and southern Iraq. They also claimed to have destroyed more than one-third of the Iraqi aircraft, including thirty-five shot down in aerial combat. In addition to destroying much of the equipment and weakening the morale of the Iraqi army and air force, air strikes had destroyed key bridges across the Euphrates River, partially isolating the battlefield in preparation for the ground war. The final phase of the air attack, which gave priority to the support of ground operations, did not begin until after the launching of the ground attack.

The Hundred-Hour Ground Battle

Shortly before the ground assault, the Americans had about 527,000 troops in the Persian Gulf region, including those aboard ships. Among the U.S troops were seven U.S. Army divisions, three brigades from other divisions, two U.S. Marine divisions, and elements from a third marine division. Other large ground forces came from Great Britain, France, Egypt, and Syria, as well as Saudi Arabia and Kuwait. The coalition initially credited the Iraqis with having about 545,000 troops in southern Iraq and Kuwait, but by the time the ground assault began, the Iraqis may have had no more than 350,000 troops, including twelve armored divisions and thirty infantry divisions stationed in Kuwait and southern Iraq. Schwarzkopf later estimated that because of desertions and casualties, some Iraqi frontline divisions had less than 50 percent strength, and those in the second line had somewhere between 50–75 percent of their authorized strength.

To defend Kuwait, the Iraqis organized their defenses into three zones, similar to what they had done in the Iran-Iraq War. The first zone consisted of fortified defenses along the Saudi border and included two lines of infantry in bunkers and trenches behind huge sand berms, ditches filled with flammable oil, row after row of concertina wire, and minefields. The Iraqis expected these defenses to entangle the attacking coalition forces and expose them to massive artillery barrages, including chemicals. If the coalition's forces managed to penetrate this zone, they would then encounter the second defensive zone, which consisted of three Iraqi armored divisions poised to blunt any penetration. To the rear of these divisions, Republican Guard divisions occupied positions in a huge crescent pattern in southern Iraq. The Republican Guards functioned as a theater reserve, prepared to strike the coalition's forces with a massive counterattack if they managed to push through the forward two zones. Expecting an amphibious assault, the Iraqis also placed infantry divisions in strong defensive positions along the shores of the Persian Gulf. For reasons only Saddam understands, the western flank of the Iraqi forces had almost no defenses, providing the coalition an opening for a decisive blow.

To keep the Iraqis focused on the east, Schwarzkopf concocted an elaborate deception plan that convinced the Iraqis that the coalition's main attack would hit their main defenses in eastern Kuwait and that an amphibious assault near Kuwait City would also occur. Coalition forces remained in positions along the Kuwaiti border and conducted artillery raids and probes to create the impression that their attack would strike into the teeth of the Iraqi defenses in eastern Kuwait. At the same time, U.S. naval forces practiced for an amphibious landing along the Kuwaiti shoreline. These efforts convinced the Iraqis that major ground and amphibious assaults would advance directly into Iraq's strongest defenses and led them to hold six divisions in place along the coast of Kuwait.

Some observers described Schwarzkopf's campaign strategy as a "one-two punch" consisting of a "right jab" followed by a knockout blow from a "left hook." In the simplest terms, he concentrated his strength against the Iraqis' weakest point. With the Iraqis focused toward the east, Schwarzkopf intended to move west, sweep around front-line fortifications in Kuwait, and drive deep into Iraq in a gigantic envelopment. In preparation for the "left hook," Schwarzkopf began shifting forces far to the west of the Kuwaiti border with Iraq on January 17, three weeks prior to the launching of the ground attack. About 270,000 troops, complete with sixty days of ammunition and supplies, shifted west. The fact that the coalition had air supremacy made Schwarzkopf confident that the Iraqis would not detect this move, or if they did detect it, that they would not be able to shift most of their forces without exposing them to devastating air attacks.

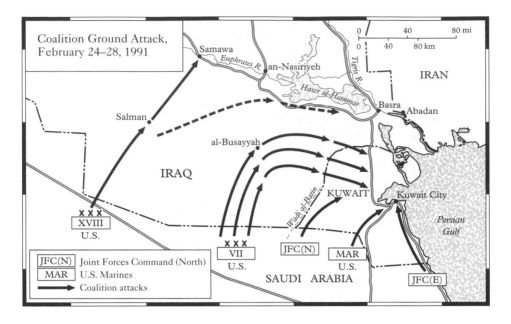

The Attack Begins

The ground attack was scheduled to begin on G-day, which was initially set for February 21, but a Russian peace initiative pushed G-day back. The coalition's ground attack officially began at 0400 hours on February 24. As part of the "right jab," Joint Forces Command East, consisting of five Saudi, Kuwaiti, Omani, and United Arab Emirate brigades, advanced between the coast and the main road leading to Kuwait City. To their left were the 1st and 2nd U.S. Marine divisions, reinforced by a U.S. Army armored brigade. The Joint Forces Command North, consisting of a combined Egyptian-Syrian force, advanced to the left of the marines but began moving later than the other forces to avoid having the Syrians' Soviet tanks accidentally engaged by the coalition's other forces.

As marines and other coalition forces advanced into eastern Kuwait, they passed through paths cleared through minefields and initially met only sporadic and uneven resistance. Nevertheless, two Iraqi mechanized brigades launched a counterattack and managed to come within 300 meters of the command post of 1st Marine Division. In the advance into Kuwait, the marines captured thousands of prisoners, as did other coalition forces. The numbers were so large that they slowed the advance of the attacking units.

As for the "left hook," VII Corps had the mission of advancing about one hundred kilometers into Iraq and then turning east into the rear and flank of the Iraqis. XVIII Airborne Corps was on VII Corps' left and had the mission of protecting the flank of the coalition's forces as they moved into Iraq. XVIII Airborne Corps was supposed to begin its move on G-day and VII Corps on G+1.

From an initial position about 300 kilometers west of the Kuwaiti border, XVIII Airborne Corps raced north toward the Euphrates River when the ground attack began on G-day, February 24. The corps consisted of 101st Airborne Division (Air Assault), 24th Infantry Division (Mechanized), a brigade of the 82nd Airborne Division, 3rd Armored Cavalry Regiment, and the French 6th Light Armored Division. In the largest air assault operation since Operation "Junction City" in the Vietnam War, 101st Airborne Division flew about 275 kilometers through driving rain to cut off the main highway between Baghdad and Kuwait. As the 101st moved forward rapidly, the French 6th Light Armored Division and a brigade from 82nd Airborne Division established a screen farther west to cover the flank and rear of the corps. Once the screen was established, 24th Infantry Division, with 3rd Armored Cavalry Regiment on its right, raced across the desert to link up with the 101st and block a crossing site over the Euphrates River just west of an-Nasiriyah. As soon as the Americans reached the Euphrates, Iraqi units could no longer move along the highway south of the Euphrates. Because of the water barrier formed by the Euphrates, the Hawr al-Hammar Lake, and extensive swamps, the Iraqis could escape only by crossing over hastily erected pontoon bridges across the Euphrates or withdrawing to the northeast toward Basra.

VII Corps had responsibility for delivering the knockout blow to the Republican Guard. Though the plan called for VII Corps to begin moving on G+1, the rapid advance of XVIII Corps and light opposition encountered by the "right jab" led Schwarzkopf to order VII Corps to begin moving on G-day. VII Corps included 1st Armored, 3rd Armored, 1st Infantry (Mechanized), and the British 1st Armored divisions, as well as 2nd Armored Cavalry Regiment. The Corps was reinforced by a brigade from 3rd Infantry Division (Mechanized), four field artillery brigades, and an aviation brigade. It numbered more than 145,000 soldiers and had more than 48,000 vehicles and aircraft. The magnitude of the logistical effort can be seen in the corps' expecting to consume more than 5.6 million gallons of fuel, 3.3 million gallons of water, and 6,075 tons of ammunition each day. When VII Corps moved into Iraq, hundreds of trucks followed closely behind; they carried tons of fuel, ammunition, and water to keep the huge force moving.

Ground Combat

VII Corps' attack passed through Iraqi defenses along the border easily. As 1st Cavalry Division created a diversion to the right of VII Corps by advancing up the Wadi al-Batin corridor, 2nd Armored Cavalry Regiment breached the border defenses and protected the rest of VII Corps' units as they moved into Iraq. 1st Armored Division, after crossing the border, moved to the left of 2nd Cavalry, and the two units led VII Corps' advance.

As 1st Armored Division raced forward, its initial objective was the town of al-Busayyah, about 110 kilometers inside Iraq. The town was an Iraqi logistics center on a main supply route and served as the headquarters for an Iraqi division. 1st Armored moved in a "compressed division wedge" formation twenty kilometers wide and fifty kilometers deep. With its cavalry squadron screening to the front, the division had its 1st Brigade as an advanced guard, its 2nd Brigade on its left, its 3rd Brigade on its right, its artillery between the two flank brigades, and its support elements (totaling nearly 1,000 vehicles) following closely.

On February 25, the VII Corps commander, Lieutenant General Frederick M. Franks, Jr., began turning his units to the east and inserting 3rd Armored Division between 1st Armored Division and 2nd Cavalry Regiment. By the time 1st Armored Division began turning, it had already moved about 150 kilometers in forty-one hours. Using the analogy of a hand closing into a fist, General Franks sought to concentrate his divisions and to destroy the Republican Guard. He soon had four divisions on line, including the 1st Armored, 3rd Armored, 1st Infantry, and British 1st Armored, and pressed the attack against the Republic Guard units and the north-south Basra–Kuwait City highway.

Before General Franks concentrated his divisions into a fist, 2nd Armored Cavalry Regiment took part in some of the heaviest combat of the war. When the Iraqi 12th Armored and Republican Guards Tawakalna divisions, as well as other units, attempted to pull out of Kuwait, they ran directly into 2nd Armored Cavalry. Much of the fighting occurred in a blinding sandstorm on February 26 with sporadic concentrations of Iraqi artillery falling on the Americans' position. Though visibility in the sandstorm was sometimes less than 200 meters, the M1A1 tanks' thermal sights could see almost one kilometer, and the Americans extracted a terrible toll from the waves of tanks that came charging toward them. Despite desperate

Iraqi tank crews had little chance of success since they were out-gunned by American tanks and not prepared to fight large armored formations. Not one American M1A1 tank was lost to Iraqi tank fire.

charges and the sacrifice of many lives, the Iraqis never managed to break out of the deadly trap that had closed behind them.

Though pounded by coalition air forces for weeks, the Republican Guard managed to shift some units from a southeast to a southwest orientation and awaited the arrival of VII Corps. The Republican Guards sometimes occupied strong defensive positions, but the superiority of the M1A1 tank proved decisive. The M1A1 could fire at and hit armored vehicles three kilometers away, well beyond the effective range of the Iraqi T-72s. Aerial attacks increased the effect of the ground attack. While American ground forces engaged tanks and armored personnel carriers, coalition air forces destroyed numerous enemy vehicles as they attempted to maneuver or escape. By the end of the campaign, only 700 of Iraq's tanks survived.

As the final thrust of the "left hook" continued forward, elements from 24th Infantry Division and 3rd Armored Cavalry Regiment attempted to close up on VII Corps' left flank. As the coalition's forces moved forward on February 27, the fourth day of the attack, they met alternating pockets of Iraqi soldiers ready to fight or to surrender. Around 1800 hours on the 27th the cavalry squadron of 1st Infantry Division reached the Basra–Kuwait City highway; the bulk of the division was about ten kilometers to its rear. Throughout the night of February 27–28, elements in the corps wiped out pockets of resistance left in their rear until the "cessation of offensive operations," proposed by Washington and accepted by Schwarzkopf, occurred at 0800 hours on the 28th.

Assessing the Victory

Although elements of the "left hook" had moved a great distance (the 24th Division traveled about 370 kilometers) in an attempt to close the "trap" completely, a sizable number of Iraqi units escaped on the nights of February 26 and 27 by fleeing to the northeast toward Basra. This opened Schwarzkopf and Franks to criticism for having failed to close that escape route and for having failed to destroy even more of Iraq's forces. The magnitude of the coalition's victory after forty-two days, however, can be seen in the estimates of damage done to the Iraqis. About one month after the cease-fire, U.S. intelligence agencies estimated that 85 percent of the Iraqi tanks, 50 percent of the armored personnel carriers, and 90 percent of the artillery in southern Iraq or Kuwait were damaged or destroyed. More than 10,000 Iraqi prisoners were taken in the first twenty-four hours of the ground battle, and more than 70,000 by its end. Although no final figure could be obtained, the Defense Intelligence Agency (DIA) estimated several months after the end of the war that the Iraqis suffered 100,000 soldiers killed and 300,000 wounded, and that 150,000 Iraqis had deserted. Acknowledging the difficulty of making estimates of enemy casualties, the DIA stated that its estimate had an "error factor" of 50 percent or higher. In sharp contrast to the Iraqi losses, the coalition suffered few. A total of eighty-nine Americans died in the war, including thirty-eight in the four-day ground battle, and 324 were wounded, including seventy eight in the ground battle.

Though exact Iraqi losses may never be known, the coalition had destroyed most of Saddam's armed forces and thereby significantly reduced his abili ty to threaten Kuwait. An advance on Baghdad, as some critics suggested, might have resulted in the overthrow of Saddam, but the coalition's goal had been to repel the Iraqi invaders from Kuwait, not to destroy Saddam's government.

Throughout the war, relations between the military and the news media were strained. Before the ground attack began, news reporters had only limited access to military personnel and were usually accompanied by escorts. In an attempt to fool the Iraqis into thinking that the coalition's main attack would hit the coast and would include an amphibious assault against Kuwait, however, Schwarzkopf permitted news reporters to broadcast live pictures of U.S. Marines conducting practice landings. Only after the ground battle began did news reporters gain greater access to other units participating in the operation. Another controversial aspect of war came from the broadcasting of reports from Baghdad. News reporters from the West provided live pictures of the aerial attack on Iraq and on bomb damage. Critics accused them of being used by the Iraqis to influence public opinion in the West; this led one news reporter to respond, "We're using them, they're using us." In the final analysis, the ability to transmit live television coverage from throughout the battle area intensified the desire of the military to control the access of reporters, while simultaneously increasing the desire of the news media for greater access.

In retrospect, Schwarzkopf's campaign strategy and the superiority of his forces were the keys to his victory. Weakened by thirty-eight days of air attack and surprised by the swiftness and the depth of the American move, the Iraqis simply could not respond adequately to the coalition's "left hook." The relentless aerial attack had severely weakened the Iraqi forces, and the ground attack defeated them completely. Though some of the Iraqi forces escaped, Saddam had foolishly placed his forces in a vulnerable position, had played to the strength of the coalition, particularly the Americans, and had offered a challenge the international community could not ignore.

The United Nations: From Peacekeeping to Peace Enforcement

During the Cold War, the United Nations often conducted peace-keeping operations where some semblance of peace existed and where the former combatants asked for U.N. assistance. Following the sending of officers into the Balkans and Indonesia in 1947, the U.N. began its first official peace-keeping operation in May 1948 with the establishment of the United Nations Truce Supervision Organization. U.N. forces subsequently participated in more than twenty-five peace-keeping missions in such diverse areas as Lebanon, the Congo, Yemen, Cyprus, the Dominican Republic, India-Pakistan, Angola, El Salvador, and Cambodia. Over half a million people served in U.N. peace-keeping forces after 1948, of which more than 800 from forty-three countries lost their lives. Always invited by both sides and always attempting to show impartiality, the U.N. forces sought to maintain peace by establishing a cease-fire between belligerents, serving as buffers between opposing forces, overseeing the implementation of peace plans, and providing humanitarian relief. Other missions included disarming guerrillas, preserving law and order, and monitoring elections.

After the Cold War ended in 1989–1990, the number of U.N. peace-keeping operations increased from an average of three or four in a year (several lasting for decades) to thirteen in December 1992. As the number of operations increased, and as violence and turmoil expanded in the aftermath of the Cold War, the United Nations asserted its right to intervene—without invitation—in the internal affairs of sovereign states. The U.N. Secretary General, Boutros Boutros-Ghali, emphasized the principle of "universal sovereignty" and the "legitimate involvement" of the United Nations "in issues affecting the world as a whole." Using the term "peace enforcement" to describe a military intervention by the United Nations, he called for multinational operations to end hostilities and enable diplomats to negotiate a final peace. He defined such diplomatic efforts as "peacemaking."

One of the first post–Cold War international interventions occurred at the end of the Persian Gulf War, when the Kurds in northern Iraq revolted against the authority of Saddam Hussein. The United Nations authorized humanitarian relief to the Kurds and forbade the Iraqis to interfere with relief efforts. The United States and other member nations soon conducted relief operations in Operation "Provide Comfort." A year later in Operation "Southern Watch," American and other nations' aircraft prevented the Iraqis from using air power against Shi'ites in southern Iraq. In essence, the U.N. enforced the peace over the objections of Saddam's government and went beyond providing observers for a cease-fire.

Somalia

Another crisis involving intervention by the U.N. occurred in Somalia. Despite the optimism of the international community, the complexities and difficulties of intervening with multinational forces quickly became apparent. The roots of the crisis came from prolonged drought, overpopulation, and decades of war—clan, ethnic, and religious—which turned Somalia into a scene of terrible human suffering. Although most Somalis speak the same language and are Sunni Muslims, the area has a long history of conflict between clan and tribal groups. Violence increased through the 1980s when the powers of the central government waned. As banditry and fighting between clans disrupted commerce and agriculture, many Somalis fled from their rural homes to cities or towns where they found some safety but little or no food. The situation worsened in 1991 when the central government

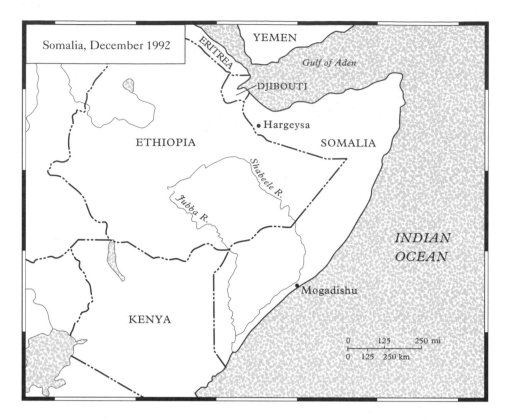

collapsed. By October 1992, hundreds of Somalis were dying daily from starvation. To alleviate the suffering, international relief agencies attempted to transport food to the starving Somalis, but bandits and clan members looted most of the supplies. A small U.N. force provided some security but had little effect. The United States dispatched large amounts of food to Somalia and saved numerous lives, but the violence and banditry continued.

As the situation in Somalia became more desperate and famine worsened, the United Nations decided to intervene. Though it had long refused to intervene in a sovereign country without an invitation, the U.N. Security Council decided that the magnitude of the "human tragedy" in Somalia had become a "threat to international peace and security" and thereby a legitimate object of U.N. action. Following the approval of a U.N. Security Council Resolution, President George Bush announced to the American people on December 4, 1992, that as part of the United Nations' effort he had ordered a "substantial force" to Somalia. The U.S. forces had the mission of creating "a secure environment in the hardest-hit parts of Somalia" and then passing the security mission to a U.N. peace-keeping force and withdrawing. Other states agreeing to send forces were France, Pakistan, Morocco, Malaysia, Italy, Belgium, Canada, Australia, and Egypt, but the largest number came from the United States.

As part of Operation "Restore Hope," the first Americans, U.S. Marines, landed at Mogadishu before dawn on December 9. The plan called for about 16,000 marines and 10,000 soldiers to land in Somalia. Americans established some control over Mogadishu and in subsequent days fanned out across the southern half of Somalia. By the end of December, the U.S. had 12,500 troops in Somalia, and seventeen other countries had 6,000. Planners envisaged a U.N. force of about 28,000 peacekeepers (3,000–5,000 Americans) eventually taking over the operation. In the middle of January 1993, the first Americans departed as military personnel from other countries began replacing them. By May most of the American personnel came from the U.S. Army's 10th Mountain Division.

Throughout this period, U.S. leaders resisted expanding their mission from providing humanitarian aid to disarming feuding clans. U.N. officials believed that if the Somalis were not disarmed, clashes between the clans would occur and starvation would return when international forces departed. Despite reservations about expanding their mission, American forces began seizing weapons, particularly in Mogadishu, after several incidents, but their focus remained on providing humanitarian aid.

In early May, the United Nations took control of the multinational effort, and Lieutenant General Cevik Bir of Turkey became its commander. Almost simultaneously, efforts to disarm the Somalis escalated, and low-level urban guerrilla warfare began. U.N. casualties also rose rapidly. In June, fighting erupted in and around Mogadishu between U.N. peace-keeping forces and Somalis loyal to General Mohammed Farah Aidid, one of the region's most powerful warlords. As U.N. forces operated in the Mogadishu area, they received sniper fire and became engaged in firefights. While returning on June 5 from an inspection, a Pakistani unit was caught in a three-sided ambush. By the end of the day, twenty-three Pakistani soldiers had died, and sixty-three other U.N. soldiers had been wounded.

The following day, the U.N. Security Council condemned the attacks and called for the "arrest and detention" of those responsible. In subsequent weeks, U.N. troops attempted to capture Aidid and had several skirmishes with his forces. Differences emerged among the coalition with the Italians' being particularly critical of the abandonment of neutrality and the shift away from humanitarian efforts. In mid-July, U.N. officials relieved the commander of the Italian contingent in the multinational force after he refused to engage his 2,500 troops in action against Aidid.

In late August, soldiers from the U.S. Army's Delta Force and 75th Ranger Regiment arrived and launched raids in search of Aidid and his top aides. On October 3, however, they suffered heavy losses in Mogadishu when a "snatch operation" went badly wrong. The raid went well at first, for the Americans captured several of Aidid's aides. But as they withdrew, the Somalis, using a rocket-propelled grenade, shot down a helicopter from 160th Special Operations Regiment. When the Americans moved to secure the helicopter, the Somalis shot down another helicopter. Then several hundred fighters loyal to Aidid rushed to the area and began pouring fire into the surrounded Americans. A rapid reaction force consisting of a company from the 10th Mountain Division attempted to rescue the surrounded rangers, but Somalis ambushed the truck-borne troops as they moved through the city's narrow streets. A relief column of American infantry, four Pakistani tanks, and Malaysian armored personnel carriers finally reached the Americans, but by the time the fighting stopped, eighteen American and one Malaysian peacekeeper had died and more than one hundred were wounded. During the battle, the Somalis may have captured and executed several Americans; they kept one pilot as a prisoner but finally released him. Estimates of the number of Somalis killed in the fighting on October 3 ranged from 200 to 300, including women and children.

Shortly after the battle, President Bill Clinton spelled out a more limited mission for American forces. This included keeping key roads and lines of communication open for relief workers and food supplies, maintaining pressure on those who had originally cut off the flow of relief supplies, and helping the Somali people "solve their own problems." In essence, the Americans had halted their efforts to capture Aidid and disarm the factions. Clinton also announced that American forces would withdraw prior to March 31, 1994. Other states eventually joined the exodus from Somalia. Despite the magnitude of the continuing human tragedy, members of the United Nations no longer perceived Somalia as a "threat to international peace and security."

Bosnia-Herzegovina

The United Nations also experienced difficulties in Yugoslavia where it found itself torn between—on the one hand—providing humanitarian relief and local security or—on the other hand—intervening and using force to halt a wave of slaughter, rape, and destruction. The crisis began in February 1991 when the northern republics of Slovenia and Croatia adopted measures that pushed them toward independence from Yugoslavia. After Slovenia and Croatia formally declared their independence in June, Yugoslavian federal troops intervened to halt the breakup of their state, but on December 19, Germany recognized the two breakaway republics. Two weeks later, after the United Nations promised to deploy peace-keeping forces in Croatia, the Yugoslav government accepted the breakup and agreed to a peace plan and a cease-fire.

The disintegration of Yugoslavia accelerated in early 1992 when citizens of the republic of Bosnia-Herzegovina held a referendum and overwhelmingly supported independence. With a population of about 4.4 million, 44 percent of the Bosnians were Muslim Slavs, 31 percent Serbs, and 17 percent Croats. Most of the Serbs belonged to the Eastern Orthodox Church, and most of the Croats to the Roman Catholic Church. Large-scale violence began in early April when Serbian militia and guerrillas seized control of much of Bosnia. In May, the president of Serbia (previously Yugoslavia) transferred substantial arms and ammunition and about 50,000 Yugoslav troops to the control of Bosnian Serbs. Widespread atrocities occurred as the Serbs tightened their control over most of Bosnia, occupied about 70 percent of the countryside, and forced about one million Muslims and Croats to become refugees. The fighting quickly degenerated into a three-sided civil war.

In May the United Nations imposed economic sanctions on Yugoslavia and established an embargo against the shipment of weapons to

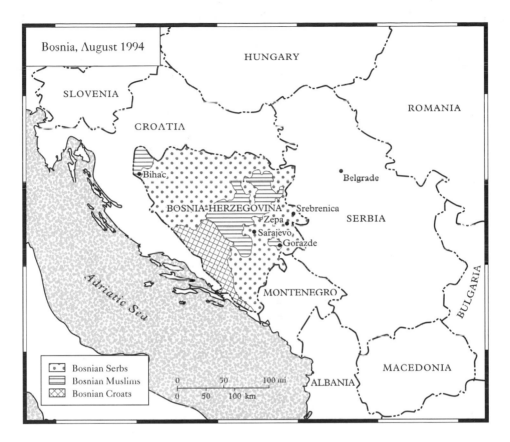

Bosnia, August 1994

HUNGARY

SLOVENIA

ROMANIA

CROATIA

Bihać

Belgrade

BOSNIA-HERZEGOVINA   Srebrenica

Žepa

SERBIA

Sarajevo

Goražde

Adriatic Sea

MONTENEGRO

BULGARIA

Bosnian Serbs
Bosnian Muslims
Bosnian Croats

0   50   100 mi
0   50   100 km

MACEDONIA

ALBANIA

Bosnia, but it stopped short of using force. While the Serbs received weapons from the Yugoslavian army and the Croats from Croatia, the Muslims had few weapons, and the U.N. embargo hampered their acquiring additional weapons. As the carnage continued, the United Nations issued an ultimatum in late June for the Serbs to stop shelling Sarajevo. When the bombardment slowed, the United Nations began airlifting food and medicine to Sarajevo. Meanwhile, Serbs continued terrorizing other Bosnian towns. The United Nations responded by banning military flights over Bosnia but initially did little to enforce the ban.

As the crisis intensified, evidence mounted of Serbian atrocities against civilians. Bosnian refugees reported that Serbian forces had massacred Muslims and Croats and established concentration camps in which they tortured and killed thousands. At the end of December the Bosnian government estimated that 150,000 Bosnians had been killed and 1.6 million made homeless. In early January 1993, a team of European Community investigators reported that approximately 20,000 Muslim women had been raped by Serbian soldiers. Many of the victims claimed that the Serbs had used rape as a "weapon of war." The investigators concluded that thousands of rapes had served the "strategic purpose" of "ethnic cleansing" by "demoralizing and terrorizing communities" and driving the Bosnians from their homes.

Despite evidence of slaughter, mass rapes, and "ethnic cleansing," the United Nations refused to use force or risk losing its neutrality. Believing the Bosnian problem could best be handled through negotiations, Boutros-Ghali insisted that U.N. military intervention could only make the situation worse and could draw the international organization into a long and costly war. Nonetheless, he placed U.N. forces in Bosnia but restricted their role; he made them responsible primarily for escorting relief supplies into Sarajevo and other besieged areas. Once on the ground, U.N. military commanders argued against the aerial bombing of Serbian positions around Sarajevo because of their fears of retaliation against U.N. ground forces. In late February 1993, with U.N. approval, U.S. Air Force planes began parachuting food and medical supplies to Muslim towns besieged by the Serbs. In March, French and German planes also began dropping relief supplies and in April, NATO aircraft began enforcing a "no-fly zone" over Bosnia's airspace. Beginning in June, talks in Geneva between the warring Serbian, Croatian, and Muslim factions of Bosnia-Herzegovina focused on dividing Bosnia into three ethnic states. With the talks yielding little, the U.N. Security Council declared Sarajevo and five other Muslim strongholds in Bosnia "safe areas" and agreed to send U.N. troops to guard them. Nevertheless, Serbian and Croatian forces prevented U.N. ground forces from entering Muslim enclaves, and the wanton killing continued.

As the horror of the international community increased, the U.N. began using limited force against the Serbs. After a mortar round killed 68 civilians in a public market in Sarajevo in February 1994, the United Nations, threatening air strikes, ordered the Serbs to withdraw heavy weapons from around Sarajevo or hand them over to U.N. forces; the Serbs reluctantly complied. In late February, NATO observers identified six Serbian planes blatantly violating the U.N. ban on flights over Bosnian airspace, and two American planes shot four of them down. Technically, it was the first combat operation by NATO forces. In April, with U.N. authorization, NATO planes bombed Serbian forces around Gorazde, a safe area, after they refused U.N. demands to stop shelling and withdraw. After some delays and negotiations, the Serbs finally agreed to withdraw their heavy weapons beyond twenty kilometers from Gorazde; nearly 400 U.N. troops deployed to monitor the Serbian withdrawal. In August and September, NATO planes hit Serbian heavy weapons when they entered a zone around Sarajevo from which heavy weapons had been excluded.

The conflict took an unexpected turn in November after Muslim forces attacked out of the safe area around Bihac and drove the Serbs back. The Serbs counterattacked and soon placed great pressure—including aerial attacks—on Bihac. In late November, NATO planes launched limited strikes against a Serbian-controlled airbase in Croatia, hitting the airfield and avoiding planes and fuel dumps; they also struck Serb missile sites on the outskirts of Bihac. The Serbs, however, continued attacking Bihac and detained more than 450 U.N. personnel as hostages. Air strikes against the Serbs quickly ended. The American secretary of defense, William J. Perry, stated publicly that Serbian gains could not be reversed, and some Western political leaders called for new peace proposals acceptable to the Serbs. In

Many of the combatants in the Balkans had little or no military training and had no reservations about destroying civilian lives and property and committing atrocities.

May 1995 the Serbs began bombarding Bosnian safe areas and forcibly taking back the heavy weapons they had previously yielded to U.N. custody. When the United Nations responded with NATO air strikes, the Serbs again seized U.N. troops as hostages and human shields. As the crisis worsened, the Serbs shot down a U.S. Air Force F-16 fighter.

Fifteen NATO and European defense ministers met to discuss the crisis and decided to increase the combat strength of U.N. forces in Bosnia by sending two rapid reaction brigades to Bosnia. While the British 24th Airmobile Brigade could respond rapidly to an attack on U.N. troops in a remote area, Task Force Alpha (a brigade consisting of French, British, and Dutch troops and light armored vehicles) could provide rapid reinforcement and armored protection. Some critics believed that by adding the two brigades U.N. forces risked crossing the "Mogadishu line" and forfeiting their neutrality. European leaders, however, insisted that the U.N. troops would remain peacekeepers and not become combatants.

Despite the United Nations' reluctance to use force, its role gradually had expanded from humanitarian relief to peace enforcement. It simultaneously had tried to use carefully calibrated air attacks to compel the Serbs to comply with its ultimatums and small ground forces to provide humanitarian aid and local security, particularly around the so-called safe areas. The unwillingness of U.N. members to be drawn into a wider war and the vulnerability of peace-keeping forces on the ground, however, restricted the peace enforcement efforts of the United Nations. The limited power of international forces became even more apparent in July when the Serbs captured the safe area at Srebrenica and expelled thousands of terrified Muslim refugess.

In both Bosnia and Somalia, military officials criticized the ad hoc nature and inefficiency of U.N. military operations. In their eyes, the conflicting interests and objectives of participating states made it difficult to identify clear missions for multinational military forces and precise conditions for their withdrawal. Moreover, the diversity of forces involved in U.N. operations made detailed coordination difficult; and a weak and diffuse chain of command, unreliable intelligence, incompatible communications equipment, and the absence of a common logistical system added further complexities. Not until operations were fully under way in Somalia and Bosnia, for example, did the U.N. establish a twenty-four-hour operations center in its headquarters. To some, deficiencies in the U.N. system ruled out swift, decisive interventions unless one or two states dominated the entire operation. Some analysts called for the establishment of a standing U.N. "rapid deployment force" or "peace-enforcement unit" which could deter or repel aggression by being transported to distant regions on short notice. Member states, however, remained opposed to a standing U.N. army. Despite the apparent limitations of multinational forces, U.N. Secretary General Boutros-Ghali remained convinced of their utility and did not abandon his call for international peace-enforcement operations with personnel from as many as "forty states."

☆   ☆   ☆   ☆

Throughout the post–World War II period, major military powers often sent expeditions to distant regions to conduct combat operations. Relying on air and sea transport, most expeditions deployed rapidly on short notice to unfamiliar locations such as the Dominican Republic, the Falkland Islands, or Grenada. The expeditions usually sought to overwhelm a poorly armed or less capable opponent quickly. Despite the relative brevity of the campaigns, the expeditions faced complex challenges; intervening forces frequently had to transport troops and equipment hastily over long distances and rely on combinations of air, sea, and land forces to gain victory swiftly. Since the operations typically took place in unexpected and unfamiliar locations, the intervening forces often encountered significant difficulties in obtaining adequate intelligence, securing sufficient logistical support, establishing effective communications, and accomplishing proper coordination. Advances in strategic transport and communications, nevertheless, provided a few states a true "global reach." As the Cold War faded from the scene, interventions by national or multinational forces in regional conflicts appeared likely in a world plagued by national, religious, ethnic, and regional antagonisms.

Iraq's aggression against Kuwait, however, provoked the first major conflict of the post–Cold War era, the Persian Gulf War. Those opposing the Iraqis brought with them forces and methods designed for high-intensity conflict in central Europe, and in the subsequent fighting, they provided an impressive display of advanced methods and weapons. After witnessing the swift defeat of Iraq and the remarkable performance of the coalition's forces in the Persian Gulf War, some analysts suggested that weapons based on the electronic microchip would replace the low-cost, mass-production weapons of the industrial age that had dominated warfare through much of the nineteenth and twentieth centuries. Highly lethal and accurate weapons would supposedly enable leaders to wage intense battles of short duration, rather than grinding battles of attrition. Increases in tactical, operational, and strategic mobility also suggested new possibilities for using maneuver against an opponent. Other advances in intelligence-gathering systems and in communications systems suggested new means of commanding and controlling military units, and the wide use of computers facilitated the processing of massive amounts of information. Those believing a new age of warfare had begun saw the need for new strategies, new tactics, and new relationships between military organizations and societies.

Despite such expectations, the initial challenges of the new post–Cold War era found little use for new strategies and tactics and only limited use for high-technology weapons. Amidst the spread of violence and turmoil, armed forces found themselves acting as peacekeepers and having to deal not with disciplined, well-equipped opponents but with paramilitary forces, militias, and gangster-like elements. In this environment, the United Nations expanded its role from peacekeeping to peace enforcement. In Bosnia the United Nations initially provided relief supplies to people besieged by forces attempting to starve them into submission, but the U.N. secretary general gradually permitted U.N. forces to use limited force. In Somalia, the United Nations intervened without a formal invitation, and the role of the intervening forces also expanded from providing humanitarian aid to peace enforcement. The reluctance of the United Nations to act more forcefully in Bosnia and Somalia and the difficulties encountered in both areas, however, demonstrated the complexities of interventions—whether launched by a single state or by a multinational force.

SUGGESTED READINGS

Adkin, Mark. *Urgent Fury: The Battle for Grenada* (Lexington, Mass.: D.C. Heath, 1989).

Atkinson, Rick. *Crusade: The Untold Story of the Persian Gulf War* (Boston: Houghton Mifflin, 1993).

Blechman, Barry M., and Stephen S. Kaplain. *Force Without War: U.S. Armed Forces as a Political Instrument* (Washington, D.C.: The Brookings Institute, 1978).

Bolger, Daniel P. *Americans at War: 1975–1986, An Era of Violent Peace* (Novato, Calif.: Presidio Press, 1988).

Callwell, C. E. *Small Wars: Their Principles and Practice* (London: Her Majesty's Stationery Office, 1899).

Dunn, Peter M., and Bruce W. Watson, eds. *American Intervention in Grenada: The Implications of Operation "Urgent Fury"* (Boulder, Col.: Westview Press, 1985).

Friedman, Norman. *Desert Victory: The War for Kuwait* (Annapolis: Naval Institute Press, 1991).

Hallion, Richard P. *Storm over Iraq: Air Power and the Gulf War* (Washington, D.C.: Smithsonian Institution Press, 1992).

Hastings, Max, and Simon Jenkins. *The Battle for the Falklands* (New York: W. W. Norton and Company, 1983).

Koburger, Charles W., Jr. *Sea Power in the Falklands* (New York: Praeger, 1983).

Middlebrook, Martin. *The Fight for the "Malvinas": The Argentine Forces in the Falklands War* (New York: Viking, 1989).

Musicant, Ivan. *The Banana Wars: A History of United States Military Intervention in Latin America from the Spanish–American War to the Invasion of Panama* (New York: Macmillan, 1990).

Odom, Thomas P. *Dragon Operations: Hostage Rescues in the Congo, 1964–1965* (Fort Leavenworth, Kans.: Combat Studies Institute, 1988).

Scales, Robert H., Jr. *Certain Victory: United States Army in the Gulf War* (Washington, D.C.: Government Printing Office, 1993).

Shaughnessy, Hugh. *Grenada: An Eyewitness Account of the U.S. Invasion and the Caribbean History that Provoked It* (New York: Dodd, Mead and Company, 1984).

Spector, Ronald H. *U.S. Marines in Grenada, 1983* (Washington, D.C.: Government Printing Office, 1987).

Spiller, Roger J. *"Not War But Like War": The American Intervention in Lebanon* (Fort Leavenworth, Kans.: Combat Studies Institute, 1981).

Summers, Harry G., Jr. *On Strategy II: A Critical Appraisal of the Gulf War* (New York: Dell Publishing, 1992).

United Nations. *The Blue Helmets: A Review of United Nations Peace-keeping* (New York: United Nations Department of Public Information, 1990).

Watson, Bruce W., and Peter G. Tsouras, eds. *Operation Just Cause: The U.S. Intervention in Panama* (Boulder, Col.: Westview Press, 1991).

Yates, Lawrence A. *Power Pack: U.S. Intervention in the Dominican Republic, 1964–1966* (Fort Leavenworth, Kans.: Combat Studies Institute, 1988).

PHOTOGRAPH CREDITS

Chapter 1: p. 16, National Gallery of Canada, Ottawa; p. 17, McCord Museum of Canadian History; p. 20, National Archives of Canada. **Chapter 2:** p. 34, Pennsylvania Academy of the Fine Arts. Gift of Maria McKean Allen and Phoebe Warren Downes through the bequest of their mother, Elizabeth Wharton McKean; p. 61, Courtesy, Independence National Historic Park. **Chapter 3:** p. 73, New York Historical Society; p. 76, Indiana Historical Society; p. 78, Courtesy of the Historic New Orleans Collection, Museum Research Center, Acc. No. 1958.98.6; p. 80, Anne S. K. Brown Military Collection, Brown University Library; p. 83, Library of Congress; p. 85, Library of Congress; p. 87, Library of Congress; p. 93, Beverly R. Robinson Collection, U.S. Naval Academy Museum; p. 95, Courtesy of the West Point Museum, United States Military Academy, West Point, NY. **Chapter 4:** p. 105, Library of Congress; p. 107, Library of Congress; p. 109, National Archives; p. 118, Library of Congress; p. 121, Beverly R. Robinson Collection, U.S. Naval Academy Museum; p. 126, Library of Congress. **Chapter 5:** p. 131, Library of Congress; p. 136, Valentine Museum; p. 140, Library of Congress; p. 143, Library of Congress; p. 144, Library of Congress; p. 149, American Heritage Picture Collection; p. 150, M. and M. Karolik Collection, Museum of Fine Arts; p. 152, Print Collection. Miriam and Ira D. Wallach Division of Art, Prints and Photographs. The New York Public Library. Astor, Lenox and Tilden Foundations. **Chapter 6:** p. 167, Valentine Museum; p. 169, National Archives; p. 171, Library of Congress; p. 178, U.S. Naval Historical Center; p. 179, Library of Congress; p. 185, Library of Congress; p. 186, National Archives; p. 193, William Gladstone Collection. **Chapter 7:** p. 199, National Archives; p. 202, Library of Congress; p. 211, Library of Congress; p. 212, National Archives; p. 218, National Gallery of Art, Washington, D.C. gift of Edgar William and Bernice Chrysler Garbisch; p. 220, Courtesy, Peabody & Essex Museum, Salem, MA; p. 224, Copyright by White House Historical Association; Photograph by National Geographic Society. **Chapter 8:** p. 235, National Archives; p. 247, National Archives; p. 248, Theodore Roosevelt Collection, Harvard College Library; p. 250, Wide World; p. 254, The Bettmann Archive; p. 256, National Archives. **Chapter 9:** p. 260, The Bettmann Archive; p. 268, Hulton Deutsch Collection Limited; p. 272, The Bettmann Archive; p. 282, Library of Congress; p. 285, The Bettmann Archive. **Chapter 10:** p. 292, Hulton Deutsch Collection Limited; p. 297, Australian War Museum; p. 306, National Archives; p. 310, Imperial War Museum; p. 315, The Bettmann Archive; p. 316, Hulton Deutsch Collection Limited; p. 318, Tank Museum Collection. **Chapter 11:** p. 324, National Archives; p. 330, National Archives; p. 332, National Archives; p. 334, Library of Congress. **Chapter 12:** p. 349, National Archives; p. 354, National Archives; p. 357, National Archives; p. 364, The Bettmann Archive;

p. 368, Bayerisches, Hauptstaatsarchiv, Munich. **Chapter 13:** p. 373, UPI/Bettmann; p. 379, Wide World; p. 386, UPI/Bettmann; p. 394, Bundesarchiv, Koblenz; p. 398, Imperial War Museum. **Chapter 14:** p. 404, Imperial War Museum; p. 407, Hulton Deutsch Collection Limited; p. 413, Imperial War Museum; p. 414, UPI/Bettmann; p. 420, UPI/Bettmann; p. 425, National Archives; p. 430, UPI/Bettmann. **Chapter 15:** p. 438, National Archives; p. 447, Coast Guard; p. 452, UPI/Bettmann; p. 464, Hulton Deutsch Collection Limited; p. 467, Hulton Deutsch Collection Limited. **Chapter 16:** p. 478, National Archives; p. 485, Wide World; p. 491, National Archives; p. 493, Library of Congress; p. 499, UPI/Bettmann. **Chapter 17:** p. 510, The Bettmann Archive; p. 513, Library of Congress; p. 517, National Archives; p. 521, National Archives; p. 522, National Archives; p. 538, UPI/Bettmann. **Chapter 18:** p. 545, National Archives; p. 553, Library of Congress; p. 557, National Archives; p. 565, National Archives; p. 566, National Archives; p. 573, National Archives. **Chapter 19:** p. 579, Los Alamos National Laboratories; p. 585, National Archives; p. 588, National Archives; p. 593, The Bettmann Archive; p. 597, National Archives; p. 601, National Archives. **Chapter 20:** p. 608, National Archives; p. 617, Wide World; p. 618, National Archives; p. 621, National Archives; p. 628, Wide World; p. 629, UPI/Bettmann. **Chapter 21:** p. 636, Wide World; p. 641, UPI/Bettmann; p. 647, UPI/Bettmann; p. 651, UPI/Bettmann; p. 653, Frank Wolfe/LBJ Library Collection; p. 662, UPI/Bettmann. **Chapter 22:** p. 674, UPI/Bettmann; p. 684, Wide World; p. 689, Gamma Liaison. **Chapter 23:** p. 702, UPI/Bettmann; p. 705, UPI/Bettmann; p. 707, © 1995 Abbas/Magnum Photos, Inc.; p. 713, Wide World; p. 718, Courtesy of Raytheon; p. 724, Wide World; p. 733, Reuters/Bettmann.